INTELLECTUAL
PROPERTY FUTURES

INTELLECTUAL PROPERTY FUTURES

Exploring the Global Landscape of IP Law and Policy

Edited by Graham J. Reynolds,
Alexandra Mogyoros,
and Teshager W. Dagne

University of Ottawa Press

2025

Les **Presses** de l'Université d'Ottawa
University of Ottawa **Press**

Les Presses de l'Université d'Ottawa / University of Ottawa Press (PUO-UOP) is North America's flagship bilingual university press, affiliated to one of Canada's top research universities. PUO-UOP enriches the intellectual and cultural discourse of our increasingly knowledge-based and globalized world with peer-reviewed, award-winning books.

www.Press.uOttawa.ca

Library and Archives Canada Cataloguing in Publication

Title: Intellectual property futures : exploring the global landscape of IP law and policy / edited by Graham J. Reynolds, Alexandra Mogyoros, Teshager Dagne.
Names: Reynolds, Graham, 1981- editor | Mogyoros, Alexandra, editor. | Dagne, Teshager W., editor
Description: Includes bibliographical references.
Identifiers: Canadiana (print) 2025014123X | Canadiana (ebook) 20250141302 | ISBN 9780776645469 (hardcover) | ISBN 9780776645360 (softcover) | ISBN 9780776645476 (EPUB) | ISBN 9780776645483 (PDF)
Subjects: LCSH: Intellectual property (International law)
Classification: LCC K1401 .I54 2025 | DDC 346.04/8-dc23

Legal Deposit: Fourth Quarter 2025
Library and Archives Canada

Production Team

Copy-editing	Valentina D'Aliesio
Proofreading	Lauren McClellan and Justine Hart
Typesetting	Will Brown
Cover design	Benoit Deneault
Cover image	MNI, Bad or no satellite signal on screen TV, Shutterstock, image no. 537395827.

 uOttawa

PUO-UOP gratefully acknowledges the funding support of the University of Ottawa, the Government of Canada, the Canada Council for the Arts, the Ontario Arts Council and the Government of Ontario.

    Ontario

Table of Contents

Part II
Canadian Intellectual Property Law

CHAPTER 4

CHAPTER 5

CHAPTER 6

CHAPTER 7

CHAPTER 8

Part III
Traditional Cultural Expression and Indigenous Legal Traditions

CHAPTER 9

Part V
Intellectual Property, Inequality, and Human Rights

List of Figures

Foreword

Mapping the future is always a perilous task and particularly so in a field as vast and as dynamic as international and comparative intellectual property. This volume brings together research that analyzes current issues, across many topics of intellectual property law and policy, and situates those issues both in their pasts and their possible futures. While some future pathways are partially predictable from experience, other intellectual property futures, particularly when affronted with global disruptions, are much more challenging to map. These challenges can become even more complex when the impacts and expectations of intellectual property shift with global events such as the COVID-19 pandemic, economic downturns, and geopolitical turbulence. Even in prosperous times, international intellectual property is a large and ever-evolving field both in terms of its subject matter and scope. The variety of connected topics in this volume discuss the future of intellectual property and reflect an ambitious and successful undertaking of the three editors whose work is impacting international discourse in this field.

When the *Agreement on Trade-Related Aspects of Intellectual Property Rights (TRIPS) Agreement* was negotiated, over thirty years ago, it included minimum standards of protection and enforcement covering patents, trademarks, copyright, and a few other categories of subject matter, such as geographical indications and some confidentiality requirements. Since that time there have been various attempts to expand protection across these areas. During the 30-year life of TRIPS a number of bilateral and plurilateral trade agreements have included increases in intellectual property. At the multilateral level, changes to increase the baseline norms have been less successful, but some changes are found in interpretations of the *TRIPS Agreement*, and there are additional multilateral instruments which have emerged. The *TRIPS Agreement* has been extensively debated and was amended to enable those making pharmaceuticals under compulsory license to make them for other countries without manufacturing capacity and expertise where an appropriate need arose. A limited waiver of patent rights relating to COVID-19 vaccines was reached. Both of these incremental developments leave many aspects of the fraught area of intellectual property and its relationship with access to medicines unresolved. At the multilateral level, the World Intellectual Property Organization (WIPO) has led negotiations concerning the Marrakesh Treaty to facilitate access to copyright works for the visually impaired, the Riyadh Design Law Treaty, and a treaty created to address aspects of disclosure of the origin of genetic resources and traditional knowledge. All these multilateral developments have been hard fought and come with significant compromises that reflect the competing viewpoints over the scope and role of intellectual property protection.

Intellectual Property Futures, in a unique and engaging way, gathers chapters that illuminate different aspects of the global challenges which intellectual property faces, including how to develop appropriate limitations and exceptions in copyright and enabling farmers to prosper through reusing their own seeds, to interactions between intellectual property and technologies new and old and related human rights implications. This volume also brings together several Canadian perspectives on both Canada's own laws and international issues.

Several new voices and perspectives in the field are featured in this collection and the diverse chapters have been carefully edited by three outstanding Canadian scholars whose own voices have contributed to shaping the international debate. Researchers and those seeking to impact policy developments, whether locally or internationally, should read and enjoy this volume. Congratulations to the authors and editors.

Professor Susy Frankel, FRSNZ

Chair in Intellectual Property and International Trade,
Te Herenga Waka, Victoria University of Wellington

March 2025

Acknowledgements

Thank you to Alex and Tesh for your partnership; to the team at the University of Ottawa Press for your help in bringing this collection to print; to the many peer reviewers for your time and feedback; to the Allard School of Law for its financial support of the workshop from which this book originated; and to Meg, Mal, and Ollie—thanks always for your love and support.

Graham J. Reynolds

For Graham, Tesh, and the greater intellectual property community— who have been as welcoming as you are inspiring. Thank you.

Alexandra Mogyoros

Thank you to Graham and Alex for wonderful collaboration and the Office of the Vice-President Research & Innovation at York University for financial support to organize the workshop leading to the book.

Teshager W. Dagne

Introduction

Graham J. Reynolds, Alexandra Mogyoros, and *Teshager W. Dagne*

The past few decades have been witness to a number of important developments with respect to the global intellectual property (IP) system, which, defined broadly, encompasses the network of international and regional treaties, constitutional documents, national laws, court decisions, and local practices that make up the substantive and procedural body of IP law worldwide. These developments include the movement away from multilateralism towards bilateralism/ regionalism; growing recognition of the various ways in which IP intersects with and impacts areas including human rights, development, trade, and social justice; broad acknowledgement of the economic worth of many IP rights; and important theoretical interventions that have challenged the principles and values underlying the global IP system, including through critical IP theory and the theory of new constitutionalism.

These developments have occurred alongside a number of other events, changes, and crises that have altered the landscape of our global communities. Chief among them are: climate change; armed conflicts; the COVID-19 pandemic; economic changes to work; and technological shifts, including those relating to the internet and artificial intelligence, and their role in society. These economic, environmental, and technological changes have occurred alongside a growing recognition of the inequities that exist within and between societies as well as the ways in which these inequities are reinforced and maintained through systemic discrimination and ongoing colonialism.

Given these developments, events, changes, and crises, what is the future of the global IP system? To what extent will the enactment of new treaties (or the reform or implementation of existing treaties) shape IP law over the coming years? What role, if any, will constitutional documents (including bills of rights) play in the context of the global IP system? Will today's transformations lead to substantive reform of areas of IP law including copyright, trademark, and patents, and if so, which reforms will be given priority? What principles and values will animate the global IP system moving forward?

This book is grounded in the belief that there are many possible futures for the global IP system. Countless pathways lie ahead of us that can be followed or pursued, leading to a multiplicity of outcomes. These futures can materialize in many different ways. Social movements can reach into and through IP to effect change and to embed new values and perspectives. An idea can emerge (sometimes in multiple places at the same time) and, through the hard work of individuals and collectives, both change the way in which individuals perceive a body of law and reshape the law itself. Technological change can create a set of futures that otherwise might not have been available or even imagined.

The belief that there are many different possible futures for the global IP system and that these futures can be realized is rooted in part in the authors' experiences during the early stages of the COVID-19 pandemic, during which many initiatives that had previously been dismissed as impractical or impossible were suddenly brought into existence. These initiatives include the widespread adoption of online teaching, a significant expansion in virtual court hearings, broad implementation of remote work for many employees, and the creation of additional financial supports for individuals and businesses. Although these initiatives have a myriad of complex effects (some of which are desirable and others problematic), change indeed occurred. While certain reforms in the IP context may be difficult to achieve, the rapid implementation of the initiatives noted above suggests that the possibility of achieving the IP reforms outlined in the following pages should not be dismissed. Change, and rapid change, is always a possibility.

This book offers the reader insight into aspects of 18 possible futures for elements of the global IP system, crafted by 23 authors. While many of these authors are senior or mid-career scholars who are thought leaders in their respective areas of research, this book also features the contributions of a number of early-career scholars. As used here, this term includes graduate students, research fellows, and assistant professors. The inclusion of these emerging voices is by design: one of the goals of this work has been to provide a platform for early-career scholars in the field of intellectual property law, both within Canada and abroad. These individuals are future leaders in the field of intellectual property law. They are IP law's futures.

As well, while the majority of the authors who participated in this text are based at Canadian institutions, a significant percentage of contributing authors — approximately 40 percent — are based outside of Canada. Their contributions have enriched the text in many ways, such as by providing different jurisdictional perspectives and by referencing authors, works, or primary sources that may not be as well known to scholars based at Canadian institutions. The vision of IP reflected in this book as well as the workshop from which it emerged — of colleagues representing different career stages and different jurisdictions supporting each other, learning from each other, and working together towards the achievement of common goals — is how we see its future.

Substantively, this book is divided into five parts. Part I focuses on the future of international agreements. It begins with Faith Majekolagbe's call for an international treaty on copyright limitations and exceptions for education and research. It continues with Mauro Barelli, Enrico Bonadio, and Cheryl Dine's co-written work which highlights the normative tension between the 1991 version of the International Convention for the Protection of New Varieties of Plants (UPOV) and the 2018 United Nations Declaration on the Rights of Peasants and Other People Working in Rural Areas (UNDROP). It concludes with Peter Yu's intervention on the future of the *Agreement on Trade-Related Aspects of Intellectual Property Rights*.

Part II considers the future of IP law in Canada. It begins with a chapter co-written by Myra Tawfik and Sara Bannerman in which they use Canada's copyright history as the lens through which to examine Canada's copyright present and future. It continues with Cody Rei-Anderson's intervention in which he considers whether the originality requirement in Canadian law could be met by an AI-generated work. It proceeds with Bassem Awad's exploration of the legal implications of AI systems in patent law, and whether and how patent law should protect inventions autonomously created by AI systems. It concludes with a chapter by Gregory Hagen which critically evaluates the present and future of Canada's patented medicine price regime.

Part III examines the future of protections for traditional cultural expression and Indigenous legal traditions in the context of IP. It begins with Anmol Patel's chapter which considers the possibility of a soft legal instrument for the governance of traditional cultural expressions. It continues with Richard Overstall's intervention which applies Robin Chapman Stacey's concept of performance as legal process to the issue of reconciling Indigenous IP concepts with those of the colonial Canadian state. It concludes with a chapter co-written by Johnny Mack and Graham Reynolds that highlights the risks to Indigenous peoples of relying on rights as the primary mechanism for achieving just outcomes in the context of Canadian copyright law, and which argues that what is needed is instead the creation of spaces of autonomy for Indigenous peoples in the context of copyright.

Part IV looks at the future of IP in the context of technological change. It begins with Anthony Rosborough's exploration of international source code security and his characterization of IP as national security. It continues with Naama Daniel's intervention on the future of IP in light of private international law and the continued development of the digital, global environment. It proceeds with Luciano Póvoa and Andrea Cabello's examination of the impact of AI on inventive activity and the patent system. It wraps up with Andelka Phillips' exploration of the acquisition by private companies of rights in sensitive consumer data in the contexts of the direct-to-consumer genetic testing, wearable technology, and online dating industries.

Part V—the concluding section—examines the future of IP as it intersects with inequality and human rights. It begins with David Watson's examination of the future of geographical indication protection in developing countries. It continues with Lisa Macklem's chapter which explores whether focusing on human rights in the context of copyright may lead to greater protection for the public interest. It concludes with Teshager Dagne's piece that sheds light on how copyright enables the exploitation of digital workers and their contributions to AI training or outputs.

These 18 chapters, collectively, re-envision international agreements; rethink Canadian IP law; argue for the creation of space for Indigenous legal traditions; highlight the possibilities and perils of technology as it relates to IP; and expose inequities and injustices, as well as provide pathways to correct them. They push the boundaries of what IP is and what it can accomplish. This set of interventions, many of which have been crafted by early-career scholars who are themselves the future of IP, provides a compelling set of possibilities for the future of the global IP system—possibilities that, if embraced and adopted, would help to make this system more just, inclusive, and compassionate. It is now up to us to do what we can to help realize these possibilities.

Part 1
INTERNATIONAL TREATIES

Towards an International Treaty on Copyright Limitations and Exceptions for Education and Research

Faith O. Majekolagbe

Abstract

This chapter delves into the demand for an international treaty that establishes and imposes minimum mandatory obligations to create, expand, or protect the policy space for user rights to access and use copyrighted works for educational and research purposes. It argues that this is the future the international copyright system must continue to pursue to ensure that copyright systems worldwide promote and protect, rather than neglect, the equally valid user rights in copyright law. The chapter also contends that such a treaty would offer a more secure legal foundation than the ambiguous three-step test that developing countries currently rely on to design their copyright systems in alignment with their development goals to promote education and research. Furthermore, having a set of uniform user rights is even more essential for cross-border uses of copyrighted works for research and education, which are inevitable in the digital and internet age. This will allow users to rely, with a greater degree of certainty, on a minimum uniform level of protection for their activities across different countries.

Copyright limitations and exceptions (L&Es) are legal provisions that balance the rights of copyright owners with the public's need for access to copyrighted works for essential activities like education and research.[1] These provisions allow certain uses of copyrighted works without the need for permission from the copyright owner, ensuring that copyright law does not stifle access to and use of knowledge.[2] Copyright L&Es are recognized within the international copyright system but not protected or guaranteed in the same way that the exclusive rights of copyright owners are. The international copyright system has played a significant role in guaranteeing rights-holders a minimum set of exclusive rights globally, through the use of treaties.[3] Until June 2013, when the *Marrakesh Treaty to Facilitate Access to Published Works for Persons Who Are Blind, Visually Impaired, or Otherwise Print Disabled* was adopted, the system was not utilized in the same manner to guarantee the interests of users of copyrighted materials by prescribing a minimum set of copyright L&Es in a treaty instrument.[4] The *marrakesh treaty* prescribes a set of L&Es that must be guaranteed in national legislation to ensure access to copyrighted materials in accessible formats for visually impaired persons (VIPs) and persons with other print disabilities.[5] Despite the real significance and benefits of the *marrakesh treaty*, the treaty does not completely satisfy the need for mandatory L&Es at the international level because it caters to the

1   See Faith O Majekolagbe, "Copyright and Quality Education for All (SGD4)" (2024) 46 EIPR 6 (2024); Ruth L Okediji, "Reframing International Copyright Limitations and Exceptions as Development Policy" in Ruth L Okediji, ed, *Copyright in an Age of Limitations and Exceptions* (Cambridge: Cambridge University Press, 2017) at 429; Pamela Samuelson, Justifications for Copyright Limitations and Exceptions in Copyright in an Age of Limitations and Exceptions (Ruth L. Okediji ed., 2017) at 1. The following article is informed by and builds on the discussions raised in this chapter: Faith O Majekolagbe, "The Case for a New International Instrument on Copyright Limitations and Exceptions" (2025) 43:1 *Cardozo Arts & Entertainment Law Journal* 73.

2   Andrew Rens, "Implementing WIPO's Development Agenda: Treaty Provisions on Minimum Exceptions and Limitations for Education" in Jeremy de Beer ed, *Implementing the World Intellectual Property Organization's Developing Agenda* (Wilfrid Laurier University Press, 2009) at 158–160.

3   See the *Berne Convention for the Protection of Literary and Artistic Works* of September 9, 1886 (as amended on September 28, 1979), opened for signature 28 September 1979 (entered into force November 19, 1984) ("Berne Convention"); *Marrakesh Agreement Establishing the World Trade Organization*, opened for signature 15 April 1994, 1867 UNTS 3 (entered into force 1 January 1995) Annex 1C *Agreement on Trade-Related Aspects of Intellectual Property Rights* (as amended on 23 January 2017) (TRIPS Agreement); WIPO Copyright Treaty, opened for signature 20 December 1996, 2186 UNTS 121 (entered into force 6 March 2002) ('WCT').

4   *Marrakesh Treaty to Facilitate Access to Published Works for Persons Who Are Blind, Visually Impaired, or Otherwise Print Disabled*, June 27, 2013 (hereinafter Marrakesh Treaty).

5   *Ibid*, art 4–6.

needs of a particular group of users in society and thus cannot be relied on to satisfy the access and use needs of other users of copyrighted works. As such, there remains a need for more mandatory L&Es at the international level, in particular, those that support education, research, educational and research institutions, libraries, and archives, and that can be implemented flexibly in national copyright laws.

The absence of a prescribed set of L&Es of this nature at the international level has led to variations in the scope of L&Es in national legislation. Consequently, copyright users globally (including institutional users of copyrighted works such as schools, libraries, and archives) cannot rely on a harmonized list of L&Es for domestic and cross-border access and use of copyrighted works. The lack of a list of minimum mandatory L&Es has also led to a situation where countries have obligations to grant exclusive rights and other protections to copyright owners, but have no concomitant obligations to balance their copyright systems and advance the dissemination, access, and use of protected works. Except for the quotation exception in the Berne Convention and the L&Es for VIPs in the Marrakesh Treaty, countries within the global copyright system will not run afoul of international copyright law by not permitting certain unlicensed copying and uses to be made of copyrighted works for educational and research purposes. Instead, countries might actually violate their obligations under international copyright law if they do not comply with the limitations (the three-step test) on the design and adoption of copyright L&Es that are imposed under various international treaties.

The absence of a set of L&Es that must be included in national copyright legislation to advance education and research threatens education and research in many ways. Given the robust protections and monopolies that copyright owners have, without copyright L&Es, many acts connected to education and research cannot be done in connection with protected works without securing copyright licenses. For instance, without L&Es, a library would not be able to digitize its print collections and make the digitized copies available to users who cannot otherwise access a physical library for legitimate reasons. Educators would not be able to make copies of copyrighted works available to learners for classroom use. Researchers would not be able to create cross-border databases of research materials that can be studied or mined collaboratively by researchers from multiple jurisdictions.

Many Member States of the World Intellectual Property Organization (WIPO) recognize the absence of a treaty instrument on minimum mandatory L&Es on education and research as problematic and harmful to the larger public interest in education and research. At the same time, some countries do not necessarily appreciate the need for international obligations of this nature. There are continuing debates at the Standing Committee on Copyright and Related Rights (SCCR) of WIPO as to whether an international treaty on copyright L&Es is necessary for facilitating and advancing education and research globally.[6] This chapter argues in favour of the adoption of an international treaty on copyright L&Es, emphasizing its critical role in supporting education and research across the world. Such a treaty would empower educational, research, and cultural institutions to engage in digital and non-digital activities that are integral to education and research. In part I, the chapter provides a background to the current SCCR debates on an L&Es treaty for education and research. It then presents a case for an international L&Es treaty for education and research in part II by examining five reasons why an international treaty is most desirable. Part III concludes the chapter.

The Push for International Treaties on Limitations and Exceptions

Following the conclusion of the *WIPO Copyright Treaty (WCT)* in 1996, which added layers of protection to copyrighted works beyond those contained in the Berne Convention,[7] developing countries at WIPO became concerned about how their obligations to expand copyright protection could affect access, use, and dissemination of copyrighted works for development objectives such as education.[8] In 2004, Argentina and Brazil presented a proposal for the establishment of a development agenda within WIPO, noting this concern[9] and highlighting that the existing copyright norms ought to be balanced with the mechanism of copyright limitations and exceptions (L&Es).[10] When a WIPO Development Agenda was eventually adopted in 2007, it contained a recommendation that the WIPO Secretariat should include considerations of issues such as L&Es for Member States in its working documents.[11] After the adoption of the Development Agenda, the subject of

---

6   See Standing Committee on Copyright and Related Rights: Meetings, Documents and Agenda, World Intellectual Property Organization, online: WIPO

7   WCT, *supra* note 3, arts 6–8, 11–12.

8   See World Intellectual Property Organization, *Proposal by Argentina and Brazil for the Establishment of a Development Agenda for WIPO*, WIPO Doc WO/GA/31/11 (2004) 3.

9   *Ibid*.

10   *Ibid*.

11   World Intellectual Property Organization, *Development Agenda of the General Assembly*, 34th Sess, WIPO Doc WO/GA/34/16 (12 November, 2007), recommendation 22, online:

L&Es became a standalone agenda item for the SCCR.[12] Brazil, Chile, Nicaragua, and Uruguay submitted a proposal for consideration at the 16th session of the SCCR in 2008.[13] They proposed a work plan for reaching an agreement on minimum mandatory L&Es, especially those concerning educational activities, people with disabilities, libraries, and archives.[14] They further requested that the Committee adopt a formal recognition and commitment to create mandatory minimum L&Es by any necessary means, including in the form of a recommendation to be adopted by the WIPO General Assembly.[15] This commitment to create mandatory minimum L&Es was made by the SCCR and was approved and adopted by the WIPO General Assembly in 2012, thus becoming a guiding mandate for the SCCR on the issue of L&Es.[16]

Meanwhile, in 2009, Brazil, Ecuador, and Paraguay submitted a draft treaty proposal for copyright L&Es for the benefit of visually impaired persons.[17] The African group submitted a proposed *Draft WIPO Treaty on Exceptions and Limitations for the Disabled, Educational and Research Institutions, Libraries and Archive Centers* in 2010.[18] The SCCR then agreed to "work towards an appropriate international legal instrument or instruments (whether model law, joint recommendation, treaty and/or other forms), taking into account the proposals already tabled or any additional submissions."[19] The SCCR developed a two-year work program for L&Es to engage in text-based work with the aim of reaching a consensus on L&Es for persons with print disabilities and other reading disabilities in the two years.[20] The Committee also agreed to engage in text-based work for L&Es for libraries, archives, educational, teaching and research institutions, and persons with other

---

https://www.wipo.int/ip-development/en/agenda/recommendations.html.

12   See World Intellectual Property Organization, *Agenda Item 7 of Draft Agenda*, WIPO Doc SCCR/16/1 (2007).

13   World Intellectual Property Organization, *Proposal by Brazil, Chile, Nicaragua and Uruguay for Work Related to Exceptions and Limitations*, WIPO Doc SCCR/16/2 (2008).

14   *Ibid* 2.

15   *Ibid* 3.

16   World Intellectual Property Organization, *Report of the Work of the Standing Committee on Copyright and Related Rights*, WIPO Doc WO/GA/41/14 (2012); World Intellectual Property Organization, *Report of the WIPO General Assembly*, WIPO Doc WO/GA/41/18 (2012) at 42–43.

17   *Proposal by Brazil, Ecuador and Paraguay, Relating to Limitations and Exceptions: Treaty Proposed by the World Blind Union (WBU)*, WIPO Doc SCCR/18/5 (25 March 2009).

18   *Draft WIPO Treaty on Exceptions and Limitations for the Disabled, Educational and Research Institutions, Libraries and Archive Centers*, WIPO Doc SCCR/20/11 (18 June 2010).

19   *Conclusions*, WIPO Doc SCCR/21 (8 November, 2010) 2.

20   *Ibid* 2.

disabilities, but without an objective to reach an agreement on L&Es in these areas in the two years.

By the end of the two years in 2012, significant progress had been made on the substantive provisions of a draft treaty on L&Es for persons with visual impairments and print disabilities.[21] The draft treaty was presented before the WIPO General Assembly in December 2012 and the Assembly decided to convene a Diplomatic Conference, to be held in June 2013, with the mandate to negotiate and adopt the treaty.[22] At the WIPO Diplomatic Conference in Marrakesh, Morocco, in June 2013, the treaty was successfully negotiated and concluded and became known as the *Marrakesh Treaty to Facilitate Access to Published Works for Persons Who Are Blind, Visually Impaired, or Otherwise Print Disabled (marrakesh treaty)*.[23] The *marrakesh treaty* became the first and only treaty in the international copyright system devoted entirely to establishing minimum mandatory standards for the benefit of copyright users. It specifically creates a set of minimum mandatory copyright L&Es to improve access to copyrighted materials for persons with print disabilities.[24]

In the period between 2011 and 2013 when the SCCR turned its attention mainly towards what eventually became the *marrakesh treaty*, developing countries submitted multiple treaty proposals for L&Es for education, research, educational and research institutions, libraries, and archives.[25] No developed country in the membership of WIPO submitted a treaty proposal. Instead, the United States submitted a non-treaty proposal document on *Objectives and Principles for Exceptions and Limitations*

---

21   WIPO, "SCCR 25 Update: Negotiators Advance Towards an International Treaty for the Visually Impaired," online: https://www.wipo.int/copyright/en/sccr/sccr_25_update.html.

22   WIPO, "WIPO Advances Toward Treaty to Facilitate Access to Published Works by Persons with Print Disabilities, Morocco Offers to Host Diplomatic Conference" (Press Release, 18 December, 2012), online: https://www.wipo.int/pressroom/en/articles/2012/article_0026.html.

23   Marrakesh Treaty, *supra* note 4.

24   See Marrakesh Treaty, *supra* note 4, arts 4–6.

25   *Draft WIPO Treaty on Exceptions and Limitations for the Persons with Disabilities, Educational and Research Institutions, Libraries and Archives*, WIPO Doc SCCR/22/12 (3 June, 2011); *The Case for a Treaty on Exceptions and Limitations for Libraries and Archives: Background Paper by IFLA, ICA, EIFL and Innovarte*, WIPO Doc SCCR/23/3 (18 November, 2011); *Proposal on Limitations and Exceptions for Libraries and Archives*, WIPO Doc SCCR/23/5 (22 November, 2011); *Limitations and Exceptions Regarding Education*, WIPO Doc SCCR/24/6 (16 July, 2012); *Draft Articles and Thematic Clusters on Limitations and Exceptions to Copyright for the Benefit of Educational, Teaching and Research Institutions*, WIPO Doc SCCR/24/7 (16 July, 2012).

for Libraries and Archives.[26] Based on these and other submissions received, in April 2013, the SCCR prepared working documents on an appropriate legal instrument on L&Es for libraries and archives as well as educational, teaching, and research institutions.[27] In 2014, the United States updated its document on *Objectives and Principles for Exceptions and Limitations for Libraries and Archives*[28] and submitted a document on *Objectives and Principles for Exceptions and Limitations for Educational, Teaching and Research Institutions*.[29]

Thus, during and after the period of negotiations for the *marrakesh treaty*, developing countries continued to reiterate the need for other mandatory minimum L&Es to be incorporated into the international copyright system for purposes of education and research. The continued push for further norm-setting activities in the area of L&Es led the SCCR in 2018 to adopt action plans for L&Es for (i) libraries and archives, and (ii) education, research, and persons with other disabilities for the period between SCCR sessions 36 and 39 (2018–2019).[30] The activities under the action plans were aimed at providing the "Committee with suggestions and possible areas for international cooperation."[31] The action plan featured an international conference on L&Es and three regional seminars where SCCR members and stakeholders would "analyze the situation of libraries, archives and museums as well as educational and research institutions, and areas for action, with respect to the limitations and exceptions regime."[32] The regional seminars and international conference were held in 2019 and WIPO presented a report of the discussions and suggestions that arose at these events at the 40th SCCR session in

---

26   *Objectives and Principles for Exceptions and Limitations for Libraries and Archives*, WIPO Doc SCCR/23/4 (22 November, 2011).

27   See *Working Document Containing Comments on and Textual Suggestions Towards an Appropriate International Legal Instrument (In Whatever Form) on Exceptions and Limitations for Libraries And Archives*, WIPO Doc SCCR/26/3 (15 April, 2013); *Provisional Working Document Towards an Appropriate International Legal Instrument (In Whatever Form) on Limitations and Exceptions for Educational, Teaching and Research Institutions and Persons With Other Disabilities Containing Comments and Textual Suggestions*, WIPO Doc SCCR/26/4 (15 April, 2013).

28   *Objectives and Principles for Exceptions and Limitations for Libraries and Archives*, WIPO Doc SCCR/26/8 (10 January, 2014).

29   *Objectives and Principles for Exceptions and Limitations for Educational, Teaching and Research Institutions*, WIPO Doc SCCR/27/8 (26 May, 2014).

30   *Action Plans on Limitations and Exceptions Through SCCR/39 (2nd Meeting in 2019)*, WIPO Doc SCCR/36/7 (1 June, 2018).

31   *Ibid* 2.

32   *Ibid*.

2020.[33] The report showed that most national copyright laws have no legal provisions on L&Es relating to digital preservation, access, and uses of copyrighted works by libraries, educational institutions, and research institutions, including cross-border exchange and uses of works.[34] The need for a new international framework to address legal uncertainties in the application of L&Es and through which existing provisions on L&Es could be extended or adapted to the digital environment was emphasized.[35]

In response to the report, the African Group, an informal group of WIPO Member States in Africa, submitted a proposal for a draft work program on L&Es at the 42nd session of the SCCR in 2022.[36] The African Group's "proposed Work Program sets out concrete and practical steps that the Committee can take both in order to provide guidance and support to Member States in the short term, while also allowing it to work towards the adoption of an appropriate international legal instrument or instruments on exceptions and limitations."[37] The Group noted that the SCCR should "continue to work towards an appropriate international legal instrument or instruments on L&Es for libraries, archives, museums, education, research and uses for person with other disabilities."[38] The African Group proposed that this begins with a consideration of previously proposed texts of various WIPO Member States on minimum L&Es that support the use of copyrighted materials for education, research, and the educational and cultural institutions involved.[39] The proposal was, however, opposed mainly by developed countries due to the emphasis on working towards an international legal instrument on L&Es. A watered-down version of the proposal was adopted by the SCCR, following concessions made by the African Group to enable the committee to reach a unanimous consensus.[40] Notably, the adopted version of the African Group's proposed work program did not require the SCCR to continue working towards an

---

33   *Report on Regional Seminars and International Conference on Limitations and Exceptions,* WIPO Doc SCCR/40/2 (15 September, 2020).

34   *Ibid,* 7–19.

35   *Ibid,* 44, 48–49, 52, 55–58.

36   *Proposal by the African Group for a Draft Work Program on Exceptions and Limitations,* WIPO Doc SCCR/42/4REV (12 March, 2022).

37   *Ibid* 2.

38   *Ibid.*

39   *Proposal by the African Group for a Draft Work Program on Exceptions and Limitations, supra* note 36, 3.

40   *Proposal by African Group for a Draft Work Program on Exceptions and Limitations,* WIPO Doc SCCR/43/8 (17 March, 2023).

international legal (that is, binding) instrument on L&Es. Instead, it asks that the activities proposed under the work program be done "without prejudging the final outcome." [41] Also, the SCCR was no longer asked to discuss the previously proposed legal texts on L&Es for education, research, and the educational and cultural institutions involved. The Committee is only asked to discuss these priority issues, invite expert presentations on them, and convene information sessions. [42] Drawing on the work completed by the committee up until the adoption of the work program, the WIPO secretariat is required to develop "tool kits to guide targeted technical assistance programs which help Member States exchange best practices and craft laws and policies which support education, research and preservation of cultural heritage." [43]

Notwithstanding the opposition of dominating minority countries in the membership of WIPO to an international legal instrument or treaty on copyright L&Es for education, research, and the educational, research, and cultural institutions involved, there is a strong case for another international treaty on L&Es in these areas.

The Significance of An International Treaty on Copyright Limitations and Exceptions for Education and Research

This section advances arguments for an international treaty of binding obligations regarding L&Es that are designed to support education and research globally and empower educational and research institutions, libraries, and archives.

A. Certainty Regarding the Scope of Permitted L&Es under the Three-Step Test

The Berne Convention contains one permitted use of copyrighted works for an expressly education-related purpose. Article 10(1) of the Convention permits the use of literary and artistic works by way of illustration for teaching purposes, provided the use is compatible with fair practice. The *TRIPS Agreement* and *WCT* contain no specific copyright exceptions regarding the work of educational institutions, libraries, and archives. However, these treaties establish a framework for determining L&Es that are permitted under international copyright

41   *Ibid* at 2, para 1.
42   *Ibid* at 3, para 5.
43   *Ibid* at 4, para 7.

law, including for education and research—the three-step test.[44] The three-step test outlines the conditions that countries must adhere to in incorporating L&Es into their national legislation. Expanding on Article 9(2) of the *Berne Convention*, which introduced the test into international copyright law, Article 13 of the *TRIPS Agreement* provides that "Members shall confine limitations or exceptions to exclusive rights to certain special cases which do not conflict with a normal exploitation of the work and do not unreasonably prejudice the legitimate interests of the right holder."[45]

The three-step test is designed to regulate the legislative freedom of states in drafting L&Es to copyright protection.[46] It serves as a safeguard against overly broad copyright exceptions in national laws.[47] Senftleben opines that the three-step test can be "both a limiting and enabling clause alike," noting that "it is a proportionality test which enables the weighing of the different interests involved at the national level so as to strike a proper balance between rights and limitations."[48] However, the test has mostly been construed as a restriction on copyright L&Es, discouraging the adoption of L&Es for education and research in national copyright laws.[49] Yet, without a robust set of L&Es for education and research in national laws, individual and institutional users of copyrighted works would have to seek and obtain permission for all uses of copyrighted works. Obtaining permission to use essential copyrighted works can be a huge burden for individuals and institutions, and this can discourage educators, learners, and researchers from utilizing them even in the absence of any substitutes.

---

44   See Berne Convention, *supra* note 3 at art 9(2); *TRIPS Agreement*, *supra* note 3 at art 13; WCT, *supra* note 3 at art 10.

45   *TRIPS Agreement*, *supra* note 3 at art 13.

46   Christophe Geiger et al, "Declaration on a Balanced Interpretation of the "Three-step Test" in Copyright Law" (2008) 39 IIC Int'l. Rev. of IP. and Comp. Law 707 at 710.

47   Laurence R Helfer et al, *The World Blind Union Guide to the Marrakesh Treaty: Facilitating Access to Books for Print-Disabled Individuals* (The World Blind Union, 2016) at 159.

48   Martin Senftleben, in Thomas Dreier & P Bernt Hugenholtz, eds, *Concise European Copyright Law* (Kluwer Law International, 2006) as cited in P Bernt Hugenholtz & Ruth L Okediji, *Conceiving an International Instrument on Limitations and Exceptions to Copyright*, Open Society Institute Final Report (2008) at 25.

49   Klaus Beiter, "Extraterritorial Human Rights Obligations to "Civilize" Intellectual Property Law: Access to Textbooks in Africa, Copyright, and the Right to Education"(2020) 23 J of World IP 232 at 237. See also Hugenholtz & Okediji, *supra* note 48 at 25.

For many countries, the challenge with the three-step test is the uncertainty it creates regarding the scope of L&Es that would be compliant with the test. [50] This legal uncertainty has created a disparate system of copyright L&Es globally. Some countries understand the three-step test as requiring that they impose a quantitative benchmark on the copying of works for educational and research purposes. Some others understand it as requiring a payment mechanism to be attached to every system of L&Es that allows copying beyond quotations and short extracts, and as such have adopted compulsory licensing systems. Certain countries permit the reproduction and adaptation of copyrighted materials that are in obsolete media and formats into newer media and formats to preserve those materials for educational and research purposes. Some do not. Copyright users, at the end of the day, pay for the uncertainties regarding the flexibility countries have to adopt L&Es that would clearly further educational and research uses of copyrighted works.

The only international decision on the interpretation of the three-step test is the 2002 WTO Dispute Settlement Panel's decision in *United States – Section 110(5) of US Copyright Act* ('*IMRO Decision*'). [51] The decision was based on the three-step test in the *TRIPS Agreement*. [52] In the *IMRO Decision*, the WTO Panel noted concerning the TRIPS' three-step test that "Its tenor [...] discloses that it was *not* intended to provide for exceptions or limitations *except for those of a limited nature*." [53] The Panel did not however suggest those specific L&Es of a limited nature that the *TRIPS Agreement* permits or intends for countries to have. Instead, the Panel interpreted the wording of the TRIPS' three-step test and applied it to the facts before it. [54] Okediji rightly surmised that the way

---

50   Hugenholtz and Okediji, *supra* note 48 at 7.

51   Panel Report, *United States – Section 110(5) of US Copyright Act*, WT/DS160/R (15 May, 2000) [*IMRO Decision*].

52   See *TRIPS Agreement, supra* note 3 at art 13; WCT, *supra* note 3 at art 10; *WIPO Performances and Phonograms Treaty*, 19 December 1996 (entered into force 19 May 2002) at art 16.

53   *IMRO Decision, supra* note 51 at para 6.97 (emphasis added).

54   The main issue was whether the two exemptions provided in section 110(5) are compatible with the three-step test in Article 13 of the *TRIPS Agreement*. The first exemption, "homestyle exemption," in section 110(5)(A) allows transmission of dramatic musical works on a single receiving device commonly used in private homes. The second exemption, "business exemption," in section 110(5)(B) permits the playing of music in retail shops, bars, and restaurants, under certain conditions, without the payment of royalties. The WTO Panel found that the homestyle exemption met the requirements of Article 13 of the *TRIPS Agreement* while the business exemption did not. In coming to this conclusion, the WTO Panel considered the exemptions against each step of the three-step test.

the three-step test was interpreted in the *IMRO Decision* confirms that the test is really "a limit on the discretion and means by which member States can constrain the exercise of exclusive rights." [55]

The three-step test indicates that countries have limited discretion regarding L&Es, but the lack of specific L&Es in the *TRIPS Agreement* and WCT, along with the very limited L&Es in the Berne Convention and Rome Convention, makes it challenging to determine which L&Es fall within this discretion. Since there has been only one international case on the three-step test, which dealt with a very specific exception in national legislation, there is not enough jurisprudence for countries to rely on when formulating national L&Es. While many scholars have discussed the interpretation of the three-step test and what exceptions could be deemed compliant with the test, [56] there remains a general legal uncertainty on which specific L&Es will in fact pass the test. The lack of certainty regarding what L&Es are permitted constrains national legislators and gives rights lobbyist groups a strong footing to challenge the expansion of L&Es within countries. Sovereign countries cannot simply exercise their own discretion when enacting L&Es in their laws, even if justifiable in the context of their development priorities. Recourse must be made to the "vague" yet constraining three-step test. This raises significant concerns and should compel a reconsideration of the lowly place of L&Es within the international copyright framework. The fact that countries are handicapped by the three-step test to formulate L&Es that support education and research justifies incorporating a set of mandatory minimum L&Es within the international framework that presumptively complies with the three-step test.

B. Further Integration of L&Es into the International Copyright System

An international treaty on L&Es for education and research would elevate the importance of L&Es within the international copyright system, thereby

55   Ruth L Okediji, "Public Welfare and the Role of the WTO: Reconsidering the TRIPS Agreement" (2003) 17 Emroy Int'l Law Rev 819.

56   Geiger et al suggest that the fair use and fair dealing exceptions will pass the test. See Christophe Geiger et al, "The Three-Step Test Revisited: How to Use the Test's Flexibility in National Copyright Law" (2014) 29 American Uni Int'l Law Rev 581. Hugenholtz & Okediji, *supra* note 48 at 25, suggest that "limitations and exceptions that (1) are not overly broad, (2) do not rob right holders of a real or potential source of income that is substantive, and (3) do not do disproportional harm to the right holders, will pass the test."

promoting a more balanced copyright system. Before the *marrakesh treaty*, the international copyright system operated mainly to promote exclusive rights for copyright owners. The *marrakesh treaty* disrupted that structure in part, by mandating the protection of the interests of a category of copyright users through copyright L&Es. However, there is a need to further integrate more L&Es within the international copyright system to achieve a necessary balance between exclusive rights and rights of access and use. The conclusion of an international treaty on copyright L&Es for education and research that mandates specific L&Es to be incorporated in national copyright legislation for the benefit of a broad category of copyright users is necessary to advance the balancing of the international copyright system. Such a treaty of wider application (in terms of beneficiaries) than the *marrakesh treaty* could help achieve the ideal equilibrium in the structure and operation of the international copyright system. A treaty on minimum mandatory L&Es, of broader application, would require countries to uphold the policy space for L&Es and safeguard it against undue encroachment during any copyright norm-setting activities.

C. Global Harmonization of Minimum L&Es for Education and Research

An international treaty on minimum mandatory copyright L&Es for education and research will create a corpus of harmonized L&Es globally, while leaving room for nations to adopt more L&Es as they deem necessary. Harmonization of L&Es would enhance digital education and research as it would provide for a set of permitted uses across national borders, which is important for uses of copyrighted works to continue seamlessly for educational and research purposes in the borderless world of the digital environment. The convergence of the internet and computing technologies has created a digital environment that supports remote learning, mass education and training, and international research collaborations. Many of these activities depend on the ability of students, educators, researchers, and their institutions to rely on copyright L&Es, including L&Es that operate in multiple countries.[57] Without a minimum uniformity of L&Es at a level required to support these activities, the transactional costs of supporting education and research that are being undertaken across geographical borders through

---

57   Okediji, *Reframing International Copyright Limitations and Exceptions as Development Policy, supra* note 1 at 493.

the aid of digital technologies would be burdensome.

The work of libraries and archives has also been hugely transformed by digital information and communication technologies. [58] The collaborative nature of research as well as cross-border education are driving cross-border demand for the collections of libraries and archives. [59] Libraries rely on copyright L&Es to provide access to educational and research materials. However, significant differences across national legislations in how libraries and archives can use or share copyrighted works threaten the ability of libraries to support cross-border education and research, and there are even countries that do not have L&Es for libraries. [60] For example, a library often cannot provide materials in its collections to another library outside its country if the receiving country does not have similar L&Es that permit such distribution, even if requests are made following the law of the source country and the materials are not available from any other source. [61] The absence of harmonized L&Es for libraries and archives thus hampers their ability to perform their roles efficiently and adequately in the digital environment. [62] Restricting the services of a library to a physical territory because of disparate national copyright L&Es, when the library can support the access needs of many users outside of its physical territory, undermines the gains of digital technologies and the internet. There is no reason why a library or archive in country A should not be able to serve people in country B. For instance, if controlled digital lending is allowed in the country where an archive operates, that archive should not have to geo-lock its services to prevent access to its digitized contents by users in countries where controlled digital lending is not expressly exempted from copyright control.

In this digital age, there must be harmonized minimum L&Es that facilitate education and research and support the work of educational institutions, libraries, and archives as enablers of educational and research endeavours. Where certain acts done with respect to copyrighted works for purposes of education and research by individuals

---

58   See Wendy Pradt Lougee, *Diffuse Libraries: Emergent Roles for the Research Library in the Digital Age* (Council on Library and Information Resources, 2002).

59   Okediji, *Reframing International Copyright Limitations and Exceptions as Development Policy, supra* note 1 at 492.

60   Teresa Hackett, "Time for a Single Global Copyright Framework for Libraries and Archives" (December 2015), WIPO Magazine, online: WIPO https://www.wipo.int/wipo_magazine/en/2015/06/article_0002.html.

61   Okediji, *Reframing International Copyright Limitations and Exceptions as Development Policy, supra* note 1 at 492.

62   *Ibid* 491.

and institutions are uniformly permissible in all countries under international copyright law, the tension between cross-border activities and the territorial nature of copyright could be resolved significantly. After the three regional seminars and international conference on copyright L&Es that were organized by WIPO in 2019, L&Es that relate to the use of copyrighted materials within and across borders emerged as one of the priority issues.[63] The harmonization of minimum L&Es could take away or minimize the legal complexities, administrative burden, and transactional costs of ascertaining what L&Es are applied in different jurisdictions for people and institutions engaging in cross-border educational and research activities. A set of uniform L&Es could provide a viable pathway for educators, students, researchers, and the institutions that support them to fully leverage the potential of digital technologies and the internet for education and research.

The required harmonization can hardly take place without prescribing a set of mandatory minimum L&Es that all countries must incorporate in their national copyright legislation. This further justifies the need for an international treaty on copyright L&Es for education and research. In the same way that an international treaty was used to harmonize the protection offered by countries to copyright owners in the digital environment,[64] a treaty is significant for harmonizing the permitted uses of copyrighted works for education and research in the digital environment.

D. International Legal Obligations Regarding L&Es for Education and Research

There is currently no obligation within the international copyright system to adopt copyright L&Es that support education and research. Even the optional teaching limitation in Article 10(2) of the Berne Convention, if taken by countries in an obligatory sense, is not enough to cater to the access and use needs in the areas of education and research. It is restricted to the utilization of copyrighted works "by way of illustration in publications, broadcasts or sound or visual recordings for teaching." Yet, even within the teaching context alone, there are several utilizations needed to support instructional activities in digital, non-digital, and hybrid educational settings. For example, copies of an entire

---

63   See *Report on Regional Seminars and International Conference on Limitations and Exceptions, supra* note 33.
64   See WCT, *supra* note 3, preamble.

journal article might be needed for instructional purposes, and this could involve emailing students the article or making it available on a closed digital course platform. There is no international obligation to have copyright L&Es that support research activities, and the mandatory quotation exception in Article 10(1) is of limited utility, especially for large-scale research activities that involve the digital mining of large and diverse volumes of copyrighted works in their entirety. Furthermore, there are no L&Es obligations regarding the works of libraries, archives, and museums. There is no obligation in international copyright law for countries to permit inter-library loans, large-scale translation activities by libraries and archives, or the copying and adaptation of works for preservation purposes and providing preserved copies of works to users for education or research purposes. These important access activities could thus be prevented by the exclusive rights of copyright owners to the detriment of educational and research advancements, and countries would not be obligated under international copyright law to remedy this through the adoption of L&Es.

While there are no international copyright obligations specifically focused on access and use of copyrighted works for educational and research purposes, there is a plethora of international obligations to strengthen copyright protection. Having obligations to protect rights-holders under international treaties without obligations to limit the scope of the protection in favour of education and research would lead to a situation where countries continually extend copyright protection without any ceiling point while no concomitant protections are advanced for users. Copyright users, the educational and cultural institutions that support them, and pro-access civil society organizations face an uphill battle when advocating for legislative changes in favour of L&Es. The advocacy for L&Es in national copyright legislation can be strengthened and empowered by the presence of international obligations in that regard. It is arguably easier to mount pressure on a country to join an international copyright L&Es treaty on education and research and/or implement obligations thereunder than to ask a country to devise and enact L&Es of its own.

Adopting more international instruments or tools that reinforce discretion is highly unlikely to be effective in guaranteeing global users a set of uniform minimum L&Es for education and research. An internationally binding treaty instrument is the most feasible mechanism to provide such guarantees and protections. The fact that all the main international instruments on copyright protection[65] have mandatory minimum provisions that must be implemented in national legislation lends support to this. Without binding obligations on minimum L&Es, it is unlikely that a global system of uniform effective protection for copyright users would emerge. International legal obligations regarding minimum L&Es for education, research, and access to information would entrench those L&Es when enacted into national legislation. Users would be assured that those L&Es cannot be removed from national legislation, or otherwise watered down, without violating international copyright law. International legal obligations would act as a safeguard for L&Es in national legislations that are currently unguarded. For example, in Canada, educational fair dealing—the main copyright exception on education—is under threat.[66] The fact that Canada has no international copyright obligations to maintain L&Es for education makes threats to remove the educational fair dealing exception in Canada's copyright law more likely to materialize.

E. Global Enjoyment of the Right to Education

An international treaty on copyright L&Es for education and research could lead to a greater enjoyment of the right to education globally, especially for the most marginalized and excluded from the education system.[67] The right to education has been globally recognized since the

---

65   Berne Convention, Rome Convention, *TRIPS Agreement*, WCT, WPPT, and Marrakesh Treaty.

66   See Kate Taylor, "Copyright Loophole for Education Should be Plugged," *The Globe and Mail* (20 May 2023), online: https://www.theglobeandmail.com/arts/article-copyright-loophole-for-education-should-be-plugged/ (arguing against the fair dealing exception for education in Canadian copyright law); Howard Knopf, "A Fair Deal for Canada on Fair Dealing, Excess Copyright, Excess Copyright," (26 May 2023), online: https://excesscopyright.blogspot.com/2023/05/a-fair-deal-for-canada-on-fair-dealing.html (responding to Kate Taylor's piece and highlighting some of the threats against the fair dealing exception).

67   See Mary W S Wong, "Toward an Alternative Normative Framework for Copyright: From Private Property to Human Rights," (2009) 26 Cardozo Arts & Ent LJ 775; Graeme W Austin & Amy G Zavidow, "Copyright Law Reform Through a Human Rights Lens ," in Paul L C Torremans, ed, *Intellectual Property and Human Rights* (Cheltenham: Edward Elgar, 2015) 301; Lawrence R Helfer, "Toward a Human Rights Framework for Intellectual Property" (2007) 40 UC Davis Law Rev 97; Peter K Yu, "Reconceptualizing Intellectual Property Interests in a Human Rights Framework" (2005) 40 UC Davis Law Rev 1039; Lawrence R Helfer, "Regime Shifting: the TRIPS Agreement and New Dynamics of International Intellectual Property Lawmaking" (2004) 29 Yale J of Int'l Law 1, 49–50.

adoption of the *Universal Declaration on Human Rights* (*UDHR*) in 1948. Article 26 of the *UDHR* provides that "Everyone has the right to education" and that education should be "directed to the full development of the human personality." [68] The right to education is also recognized in Article 13 of the *International Covenant on Economic, Social and Cultural Rights* (ICESCR). [69] Article 13 states that "primary education shall be compulsory and available free to all" and that other secondary and higher education should be made equally accessible to all. [70] It also recognizes a connection between the right to education and the "full development of the human personality." [71] According to the Committee on Economic, Social and Cultural Rights (CESCR), education is not just a human right, but also an empowerment right. [72] It provides individuals with the means to be participants in their own flourishing and well-being. [73]

For the right to education to be realized, education must at a minimum be available and accessible. [74] For education to be available, teaching and learning materials must be available insufficient quantities, just as there must be libraries. [75] The availability of books, including through educational institutions and libraries, is a "fundamental prerequisite of education" [76] and integral to the realization of the right to education for everyone. [77] Copyright L&Es can be leveraged by educational institutions and libraries to make teaching and learning materials available to students. For instance, if libraries globally are allowed to engage

---

68   *Universal Declaration of Human Rights*, GA Res 217 (III) A, UN GAOR, UN Doc A/810 (10 December, 1948) art 26(1); (2).

69   *International Covenant on Economic, Social and Cultural Rights*, 16 December, 1966, 993 UNTS 3 (entered into force 3 January 1976) art 13(1). The right is also protected in the *Convention on the Elimination of All Forms of Discrimination against Women*, GA Res 34/180, 18 December, 1979 (entered into force 3 September 1981) art 14(d); *Convention on the Rights of the Child*, GA Res 44/25, 20 November, 1989 (entered into force 2 September 1990) art 28; and *Convention on the Rights of Persons with Disabilities*, GA Res 61/106, 30 March, 2007, 2515 UNTS 3 (entered into force 3 May 2008) art 24.

70   *International Covenant on Economic, Social and Cultural Rights* art 13(1).

71   *Ibid.*

72   Committee on Economic Social and Cultural Rights, *General Comment No. 13: The Right to Education (Art. 13)*, 21st Sess, UN Doc E/C.12/1999/10 (8 December, 1999) at para 1.

73   *Ibid.*

74   *Ibid* at para 6.

75   *Ibid.*

76   United Nations Children's Fund, A Human Rights-based Approach to Education for All, (UNICEF, 2007).

77   *Ibid.* See also Beiter, *supra* note 49 at 240; Laurence R Helfer & Graeme W Austin, *Human Rights and Intellectual Property: Mapping the Global Interface* (Cambridge: Cambridge University Press, 2011) at 320.

in preservation activities, inter-library loans, and controlled digital lending without the permission of copyright owners, they can make more materials available to students. An international L&Es treaty can empower libraries and educational institutions globally to engage in activities that make education more available to people.

Accessibility of education has three overlapping dimensions: non-discrimination, physical accessibility, and economic accessibility.[78] Non-discrimination means that "education must be accessible to all, especially the most vulnerable groups, in law and fact" and economic accessibility involves the affordability of education for all.[79] Access to education includes access to educational materials. There are significant correlations between copyright protection and affordable access to educational materials, as well as between copyright and access to materials in local languages.[80] The adoption of a set of minimum mandatory L&Es for education could make it easier and less costly for educational institutions and libraries as well as non-profit organizations to provide substitute access to educational materials for those who cannot afford to purchase their copies of those materials. An international treaty on copyright L&Es for education could also permit translation of works into local languages for educational purposes, especially where the market for those languages is too small to encourage direct production of original works in those languages.

Physical access to education is also crucial to the enjoyment of the right to education. To be physically accessible, "education has to be within safe physical reach, either by attendance at some reasonably convenient geographic location (e.g. a neighbourhood school) or via modern technology (e.g. access to a 'distance learning' programme)".[81] The delivery of education, including educational materials, through modern technology in times when it is unsafe or otherwise impossible for education and educational materials to be accessed by physical means could be impeded by copyright rules in the absence of globally recognized L&Es, thereby impeding access to education. During the global COVID-19 pandemic, attending educational institutions and visiting libraries in person became unsafe. Consequently, most of these institutions were physically inaccessible, leading to an uptake in the use

---

78   *General Comment No. 13: The Right to Education (Art. 13), supra* note 72 at para 6.
79   *Ibid.*
80   See Lea Shaver, "Copyright and Inequality" (2014) 92 Washington Univ Law Rev 117 at 135–145.
81   *General Comment No. 13: The Right to Education (Art. 13), supra* note 82 at para 6.

of the internet and digital technologies to facilitate the delivery of and access to education and educational materials. [82] However, this shift to remote learning was fraught with challenges, including those associated with copyright rules and practices. [83] For example, the digitization of in-print library collections as an emergency measure to support the mission of libraries in providing access to their users was, in many ways, constrained by the reproduction right and other rights related to making works available in copyright law. [84] These rights, coupled with the absence of globally recognized L&Es for educational institutions and libraries in the digital environment, made it difficult for educators and libraries to ascertain the extent to which they could make digital uses of copyrighted materials without the need to first negotiate and obtain copyright licenses. In fact, organizations and individuals representing researchers, educators, students, and the institutions that support them sent a joint letter to the Director General of WIPO "to encourage WIPO to take a clear stand in favour of ensuring that intellectual property regimes are a support, and not a hindrance, to efforts to tackle both the Coronavirus outbreak and its consequences." [85] They wanted WIPO to encourage countries to take advantage of flexibilities in the international system that permit the use of copyrighted works for online education and research. [86] However, there were no mandatory L&Es for education and research within the international copyright system, nor was there any clear guidance on the scope of L&Es that are permitted for online education and research.

Copyright constraints on the use of copyrighted works for remote education and research can be mitigated by an international framework of minimum mandatory L&Es for education and research and

---

82   Matt Johnston, "Online Mass Exodus: How Australian Unis Are Coping with COVID-19," ITNews (20 March, 2020), online: https://www.itnews.com.au/news/online-mass-exodus-how-australian-unis-are-coping-with-the-COVID-19-pandemic-539630; John Ross, "Australian Universities Opt for Online," Insider Higher Ed (19 March, 2020), online: https://www.insidehighered.com/news/2020/03/19/australian-universities-go-online.

83   See Caroline Ncube, "The Musings of a Copyright Scholar Working in South Africa: Is Copyright Law Supportive of Emergency Remote Teaching?" Afronomics Law (13 May, 2020), online: https://www.afronomicslaw.org/2020/05/13/the-musings-of-a-copyright-scholar-working-in-south-africa-is-copyright-law-supportive-of-emergency-remote-teaching/#.

84   *Ibid.*

85   Joint Letter to Dr. Francis Gurry, Director General, World Intellectual Property Organization (3 April, 2020), online: https://www.communia-association.org/wp-content/uploads/2020/04/200403-Joint-Letter-to-Dr-Francis-Gurry.pdf

86   *Ibid.*

the institutions that support these activities. Mitigating such access constraints could help secure the right to education for everyone in both ideal and difficult circumstances. There is precedent for using copyright L&Es to realize human rights within the international copyright system. The *marrakesh treaty* aims to promote the human rights of persons with visual impairments or other print disabilities, as recognized in the *UDHR*[87] and the *United Nations Convention on the Rights of Persons with Disabilities,*[88] through copyright L&Es.[89] In the same vein, an international treaty on copyright L&Es for education and research could seek to facilitate the enjoyment of the right to education as recognized in international human rights instruments.

Conclusion

An international treaty on L&Es for education, research, educational and research institutions, libraries, and archives is the future of copyright that we must aim for. Having a set of uniform L&Es is even more important for cross-border uses of copyrighted works that are inevitable to support education and research in the digital and internet age. In the past, mandatory minimum rules that broaden the scope of copyright protection have dominated international norm-setting activities. There must be a shift towards making copyright L&Es an integral part of the structure and operation of the international copyright system for there to be a balanced international copyright system in the foreseeable future. Furthermore, the international copyright system cannot continue to be used to set obstacles to access, use, and dissemination of copyright works without using the same system to mitigate the impact of these obstacles in the interest of the public. International treaty-making cannot be ideal for protecting the rights of authors and publishers, but be undesirable to impose some limitations on those rights in the larger public interest in education, research, and access to information when rights and L&Es are supposed to be two sides of the same coin—the coin being the copyright system. To truly achieve a balanced copyright system both nationally and internationally, exclusive rights and copyright L&Es must both be negotiated in specific details, recognized through the same binding instruments and negotiated at the same table—the international copyright table. There should be

---

87   *Universal Declaration on Human Rights, supra* note 68.
88   *Convention on the Rights of Persons with Disabilities, supra* note 69.
89   Marrakesh Treaty, *supra* note 4, preamble.

internationally recognized obligations to promote the recognition and enjoyment of L&Es globally; L&Es should not, as they currently are in the international copyright system, be afterthoughts to be acted upon purely on discretion.

Chapter 2

Breeders' and Farmers' Rights: Navigating the Tension Between UPOV and UNDROP

Mauro Barelli, Enrico Bonadio, and Cheryl Dine

Abstract

Laws which protect plant breeders without properly acknowledging farmers' interests not only affect the human rights of the latter but also have broader societal consequences in terms of food security and biodiversity. Recognizing the multidimensional character of the conflict between breeders' and farmers' rights, this article highlights the normative tension that exists between the legal instrument sitting at the centre of the commodity seed systems—that is, the 1991 version of the International Convention for the Protection of New Varieties of Plants—and the instrument that best epitomizes a human rights approach to the question of seeds, namely, the 2018 United Nations Declaration on the Rights of Peasants and Other People Working in Rural Areas. Through an analysis of the legal value and effects of the UN peasants' declaration, the article argues that this instrument has significantly strengthened the human rights dimension of the conflict between breeders' and farmers' rights, reinvigorating calls for reconciliation and offering an important basis for legislative and judicial initiatives aimed at balancing these two opposing interests.

There are nowadays two main models of seed systems. On the one hand, there are farmers' seed systems, which are based on the principle of free distribution and promote the continuous regeneration of biodiversity.

On the other, there are commodity seed regimes, which aim at maximizing food production and making profits through property systems and contract law.[1] The clash between the two regimes is particularly acute given that farmers' seed systems work on the premise that farmers should be legally entitled to freely save, use, exchange, and sell seeds. Several consequences follow from this inherent tension in terms of environmental protection, food production, and enjoyment of basic human rights.

This article addresses the legal dimension of this clash of systems, focusing on the tension between the legal instrument sitting at the centre of the commodity seed systems—that is, the 1991 version of the International Convention for the Protection of New Varieties of Plants (UPOV)[2]—and the recently adopted United Nations Declaration on the Rights of Peasants and Other People Working in Rural Areas (UNDROP).[3] While UPOV seeks to provide and promote an effective proprietary system for the protection of new plant varieties, UNDROP is devoted to the protection and promotion of the rights of one of the most marginalized groups—that is, peasants.[4] Of special interest in this regard is Article 19 of UNDROP, which, in recognizing the right of peasants to seeds, requires States to "support peasant seed systems" and to ensure that seed policies and any intellectual property (IP) laws or certification schemes concerning seeds respect and take into due account the rights, needs, and realities of peasants.

The discussions developed in this article are particularly valuable for developing countries, which, often "encouraged" to ratify UPOV[5]

1   Seeds, Right to Life and Farmers' Rights: *Report of the UN Special Rapporteur on the right to food*, Michael Fakhri, UN Doc A/HRC/49/43 (30 December 2021).

2   *International Convention for the Protection of New Varieties of Plants*, DC/91/130 (18 March 1991).

3   *United Nations Declaration on the Rights of Peasants and Other People Working in Rural Areas* (UNDROP), UNGA Res 73/165, UN Doc A/RES/73/165 (21 January 2019).

4   For the purpose of this article, the terms "farmer" and "peasant" are used interchangeably to refer to "any person who engages or who seeks to engage alone, or in association with others or as a community, in small-scale agricultural production for subsistence and/or for the market, and who relies significantly, though not necessarily exclusively, on family or household labour and other non-monetized ways of organizing labour, and who has a special dependency on and attachment to the land." UNDROP, supra note 3, art 1.

5   On the negative impact of UPOV on developing countries' agricultural system, see Srividhya Ragavan & Jamie Mayer, "Has India Addressed Its Farmers' Woes? A Story of Plant Protection Issues" (2007) 20 *Georgetown International Environmental Law Review* 97; Mrinalini Kochupillai, "Is UPOV 1991 Good Fit for Developing Countries?" in Joseph Drexl & Sanders Kamperman Anselm, eds, *The Innovation*

as part of trade and economic partnership agreements,[6] may struggle to strike the right balance between providing some degree of protection to the breeders of plant varieties, on the one hand, and safeguarding the interests of farmers and promoting important public goods such as food security and biodiversity conservation, on the other.

Two countries that have sought to reconcile breeders' and farmers' rights outside of the UPOV framework are noteworthy and will be accordingly discussed in this article. The first is India, whose 2001 Protection of Plant Varieties and Farmers' Rights Act (PPVFRA) is often hailed as a unique legislation dealing with plant varieties in that it is capable of balancing breeders' and farmers' rights.[7] India's PPVFRA represents an extremely valuable example of best practice that could be followed by those countries that today seek to align their IP laws concerning breeders' rights with the key principles of UNDROP related to the right of peasants to seeds. The second country is Honduras, where a 2021 decision of the Supreme Court declared a local plant variety law, conforming with UPOV principles, both unconstitutional and against various internationally protected rights. The case of Honduras is of special relevance because it shows that, by strengthening the human rights dimension attached to this question, the adoption of UNDROP can boost countries' endeavours to resist implementing the UPOV regime, opting instead for alternative *sui generis* systems that better protect farmers' rights and their national agricultural systems more generally.

Following on from the introduction, this article proceeds to provide, in Section 2, a brief overview of the UPOV system, highlighting the challenges that the latter poses in terms of farmers' rights, food security, and biodiversity conservation. Section 3 focuses on the normative content of UNDROP, which, despite being a soft law instrument, has legal value and is simultaneously capable of producing important legal

Society and Intellectual Property (Cheltenham: Edward Elgar Publishing, 2019); Enrico Bonadio, "Crop Breeding and Intellectual Property in the Global Village" (2007) 29:5 *European Intellectual Property Review*; Tilahun Hindeya, "TRIPS, Plant Varieties and the Right to Food: A Case Study of Ethiopia's Legal Regime on Protection of Plant Varieties," in Markus Krajewski & Fikremarkos Markos, eds, *Acceding to the WTO from a Least Developed Country Perspective: The Case of Ethiopia* (Baden-Baden: Nomos, 2011).

6   Thaddeus Manu, "Self-defeating reasons for signing the African Growth and Opportunity Act: Analysing the pressure on African countries to enact UPOV Convention Plant Breeders' Rights as opposed to effective *sui generis* regimes under TRIPS" (2015) 44:1 *Common Law World Review*, at 3–27.

7   Sophy K Joseph, *Customary Rights of Farmers in Neoliberal India: A Legal and Policy Analysis* (Oxford: Oxford University Press, 2020) ch 5.

effects. Before the final remarks, Section 4 looks at successful examples of reconciliation of breeders' and farmers' rights by, first, *sui generis* legislation and, second, judicial intervention.

The UPOV Convention: Breeders' v. Farmers' Rights

The UPOV Convention is an international treaty that establishes minimum standards for the protection of plant varieties. It was first adopted in 1961 and revised in both 1978 and 1991. Plant variety protection (PVP) is a form of IP rights that grants breeders exclusive rights over the new plant varieties. The mantra is that this system is intended to encourage investments in the breeding of new plant varieties to increase agricultural diversity, food security, and sustainable farming. Specifically, the UPOV Convention offers protection in the form of exclusive rights of exploitation to those who come up with newly bred plant varieties that satisfy certain requirements, namely, distinctness, uniformity, stability, and novelty (the development of these new plants may also, and often does, occur via genetic engineering techniques). The principal reason why breeders are granted monopolistic rights is that they invest time and resources to develop their new varieties of plants—and these innovation processes often require large investments that can only be recouped by relying on IP exclusivity.

Most major jurisdictions, including the United States (US) and the European Union (EU), have a registration system of new plant varieties. There is an office that manages the procedure after an application for PVP is filed and then grants or refuses the registration of the new plant variety (for example, that of the EU is based in Angers, France). What are registered and protected are the external and visible features of the new plant, that is, the "phenotype." The genetic traits of the plant—the "genotype"—are not relevant here; they may be protected by a patent instead. PVP rights thus constitute a category of IP rights specifically aimed at protecting the external characteristics of the plant. Breeders usually license their exclusive rights to farmers. For example, a cooperative of farmers may be interested in cultivating and then commercializing a new variety of potatoes developed by a biotech company and registered with the local plant variety office. The reasons why these farmers may seek a licence could vary from the willingness to merely pursue a profit to the decision to make available an essential food product to the public. Farmers who use the registered seed but do not acquire the appropriate licences may be sued by breeders for PVP infringement and condemned to pay damages.

The 1991 version of UPOV is particularly protective of breeders' rights as opposed to the 1978 version, having brought important changes in PVP. Such an evolution has been curiously labelled as a case of "legislative Darwinism."[8] More specifically, unlike the 1978 version, the 1991 treaty expressly states that PVP must be extended to plant varieties which are, first, merely discovered and then developed by the breeder (and not only created),[9] and, second, essentially derived from protected varieties.[10] In addition, as will be discussed below, the 1991 version strongly limits the "farmers' exception."[11]

Thus, UPOV 1991 protects activities merely consisting of discovering and further developing varieties already existing in nature. The risk is that this provision (especially the use of term "developing") might be interpreted by plant variety offices which grant the registration as meaning that the relevant protection is granted without requiring breeders who discover new varieties to carry out a particularly "creative" action, such as hybridization or selective propagation.[12] This interpretation would not be consistent with the basic principle governing IP regimes, including PVP, namely, that exclusive rights are offered to provide an incentive for coming up with creative endeavours. Embracing this interpretation clearly increases the risk of progressive monopolization of plants already existing in nature. An empirical study, for example, has documented a pattern of breeders seeking PVP in one state for the "discovery" of a landrace or other traditional variety that is generally known and cultivated in another state. For example, in Australia 37 percent of the 188 claims offered no evidence of actual plant breeding, lending weight to the criticism that breeders were just "discovering" already known varieties from overseas.[13]

Second, UPOV 1991 extends the breeder's ownership rights to essentially derived varieties, which, as mentioned above, was not provided in

---

8   Marco Ricolfi, "La brevettazione delle invenzioni relative agli organismi geneticamente modificati" (2003) 1 *Rivista di Diritto Industriale* 16.

9   *International Convention for the Protection of New Varieties of Plants*, 2 December 1961, as revised 19 March 1991, art 1(4) (1991 Act of the UPOV Convention).

10   *Ibid*, art 14(5).

11   *Ibid*, art 15(2).

12   Selective propagation is established where the population of the new variety is different from the population from which the discovered plant originated. See, e.g., the Clarifications of Plant Breeding Issues under the Australian Plant Breeder's Rights Act 1994 of (December 2002), online: www.anbg.gov.au last accessed 26 February 2024.

13   RAFI Report, *Plant Breeders' Wrongs Righted in Australia?* (November 1998), online: www.etcgroup.org last accessed 26 February 2024.

the 1961 and 1978 versions. The introduction of this provision was justified on the grounds that it was necessary to prevent a second generation of breeders from making merely "cosmetic" changes to existing varieties to claim protection for a new variety. But some commentators have pointed out that by preventing a second generation of breeders from developing new plant varieties that are essentially derived from protected ones, the UPOV system would stifle research activities in the agricultural sector. This concern is amplified by the fact that ongoing progress in crop breeding often depends on the possibility of accessing existing genetic resources and further developing the same: as has been pointed out, "a new plant variety cannot be created from scratch."[14]

The main exceptions to breeders' rights under UPOV 1991 come under Article 15. The latter provides two set of exceptions to these rights: compulsory exceptions and optional exceptions. The compulsory exceptions entail that breeders' rights shall not extend to acts done privately and for non-commercial purposes, for experimental purposes, or for the purpose of breeding other varieties. The optional exception is more relevant here because it specifically considers farmers' interests. In particular, it provides States with the possibility, if they so choose, to restrict breeders' rights, albeit within reasonable limits, in relation to any variety to permit farmers to use, for propagating purposes on their own holdings, the product of the harvest which they have obtained by planting the registered variety. This is also known as the "farmers' privilege," which is aimed at guaranteeing the ability of farmers who have purchased a seed of a protected variety to save seeds from the resulting harvest for planting in the subsequent season.

Yet, the farmers' privilege under the 1991 version of the UPOV Convention is rather limited. Indeed, the 1991 version does not authorize farmers to save and exchange seeds with other farmers for propagating purposes. Crucially, that practice was allowed by UPOV 1978, which, despite not explicitly providing for the farmers' exception, did not ban it either, with the result that saving and exchanging seeds were commonly practiced in many countries. Such limitation has been criticized as inconsistent with traditional, age-old practices of farmers in many developing and least developed countries, where seeds are regularly exchanged for purposes of crop and variety rotation.[15] This is often

---

14   Carlos Correa, *Intellectual Property Rights, the WTO and Developing Countries. The TRIPS Agreement and Policy Options* (London, ZED-TWN: 2000) at 176.
15   Laurence Helfer, "Intellectual Property Rights in Plant Varieties: International Legal Regimes and Policy Options for National Governments", FAO Paper, 2004,

referred to as brown-bagging—that is, an agricultural practice which is believed to be beneficial to biodiversity conservation. Crop rotation is considered a wise practice for many reasons, disease avoidance being a major one, as it is believed that food security of many local communities in most developing countries depends largely on their saving, sharing, and replanting seeds from the previous harvest—which, as we have seen, UPOV 1991 significantly limits. Moreover, these practices often take place within the same community, are co-operative rather than profit-oriented, appear to be essential to preserve the vitality of the crops across their different generations, and contribute to genetic diversity.[16]

The fact that UPOV 1991 does not give due consideration to farmers' interests and, more broadly, the need to protect important public goods like food security and environmental protection, has made the treaty an easy target for criticism. Agribiotech multinationals, which conduct expensive research and development in the agribiotech field and often seek PVP and other IP rights, have often been criticized for their practice. Indeed, they frequently pursue aggressive IP enforcement strategies which have proved controversial, especially in developing countries where there has been for decades a polarized debate over how multinational corporations own and manage monopolies over genetically modified seeds and varieties to the detriment of local agriculture-based economies.[17]

UNDROP and the Right to Seeds

The previous section has discussed some of the problems deriving from the limitations on farmers' rights that were introduced by the 1991 version of UPOV. In addition to what was said before, these limitations are now also in tension with the normative framework of an important human rights instrument recently adopted under the auspices of the United Nations, namely, UNDROP. After six years of negotiations at the UN Human Rights Council, UNDROP was finally adopted by the UN

---

19 *www.fao.org* last accessed 26 February 2024.

16   Enrico Bonadio, "Crop Breeding and Intellectual Property in the Global Village" (2007) 29:5 *European Intellectual Property Review* 167–171.

17   Heidi Mustonen-Park, "Biotechnology Companies' Monopoly: Potentially Harming the Diversity and the Sustainability of Agriculture" (Thesis, 28 April 2018, Helsinki Metropolia University of Applied Sciences, Bachelor in Business Administration, International Business and Logistics), online: https://www.theseus.fi/bitstream/handle/10024/147224/Mustonen-Park_Heidi.pdf?sequence=1 last accessed 26 February 2024.

General Assembly (GA) on December 17, 2018 by a vote of 121 States in favour, 8 against, and 54 abstentions.[18] Among its provisions, special attention must be paid to Article 19, which provides that peasants have the right to seeds, including:

> (a) The right to the protection of traditional knowledge relevant to plant genetic resources for food and agriculture;

> (b) The right to equitably participate in sharing the benefits arising from the utilization of plant genetic resources for food and agriculture;

> (c) The right to participate in the making of decisions on matters relating to the conservation and sustainable use of plant genetic resources for food and agriculture;

> (d) The right to save, use, exchange and sell their farm-saved seed or propagating material.[19]

In essence, Article 19 recognizes the right of peasants "to choose seeds and crops they want to grow," allowing them to rely on local peasant markets for their seed security and guaranteeing access to seeds at an affordable price.[20] Moreover, seed rights not only protect the rights, and lives, of peasants but also contribute to preserving local plant varieties and biodiversity. As of today, Article 19 represents the most explicit endorsement of the right of peasants to seeds.[21] It is, therefore, not surprising that it was one of the most debated provisions during the drafting of the document. A minority of States opposed Article 19, noting that existing human rights provisions offer sufficient protection to peasants' interests, or warning that its content would clash

---

18   Christophe Golay et al, "Implementing the International Treaty on Plant Genetic Resources for Food and Agriculture in light of the United Nations Declaration on the Rights of Peasants and Other People Working in Rural Areas" (2022), online: https://www.twn.my/announcement/Apbrebes_BriefingPaper_9-22_final.pdf last accessed 26 February 2024.
19   UNDROP, supra note 3, art 19.1.
20   Sandrine Le Teno, Christine Frison & Samuel Cogolati, "The Right to Seeds: Using the commons as a sustainable governance scheme to implement peasants' rights?" in Mariagrazia Alabrese et al, eds, *The United Nations' Declaration on Peasants' Rights* (London: Taylor & Francis, 2022), at 122.
21   *Ibid*, 119–133.

with national and international IP regimes.[22] The main driver behind these objections is the fact that the full realization of farmers' right to seeds would require a recalibration of breeders' rights, especially if one accepts the premise that the right to seeds is a human right and as such should take precedence over other legal norms.[23] As such, the right to seeds challenges agribusiness at its heart. In this regard, it suffices to say that only four agrochemical companies control 60 percent of the global seed market.[24] Crucially, however, the opposition of a number of developed countries did not prevent this article, and UNDROP more generally, from being adopted and becoming embedded in the fabric of international law.

By reinforcing the legal basis of peasants' rights to seeds, Article 19 of UNDROP not only stands in stark conflict with the principles and provisions of UPOV but also offers States an additional asset in resisting the implementation of that regime.[25] Figures 2.1 and 2.2 visualize the geographical dimension of this normative clash.

As one would expect, given the economic interests at stake, UPOV is particularly popular in the Northern hemisphere, whereas UNDROP finds widespread support in the Global South. Taking a closer look, several countries which ratified UPOV maintained a coherent position by voting against UNDROP. At the same time, the vast majority of countries that voted for UNDROP are not parties to UPOV. Crucially, however, there are also discrepancies in the ways in which some nations have positioned themselves towards these two instruments. Some countries that were parties to UPOV, such as Austria and Singapore, remained neutral about UNDROP. More importantly, some states, including, for example, Peru, Costa Rica, and Ghana, actually voted in favour of UNDROP while being a parties to UPOV. Similarly, several States, for

---

22   Christophe Golay & Adriana Bessa, "The Right to Seeds in Europe: the UN Declaration on the Rights of Peasants and Other People Working in Rural Areas and the protection of the right to seeds in Europe" (2019), at 28.

23   Christophe Golay et al, "Implementing the International Treaty on Plant Genetic Resources for Food and Agriculture (ITPGRFA) in light of the United Nations Declaration on the Rights of Peasants and Other People Working in Rural Areas (UNDROP)" (2022) 1, online: https://www.twn.my/announcement/Apbrebes_BriefingPaper_9-22_final.pdf last accessed 26 February 2024.

24   Report of the Special Rapporteur on the right to food, Michael Fakhri, 'Seeds, right to life and farmers' rights', para. 18.

25   For a practical manifestation of this dynamic, see "Indonesia must resist EU's trade talk demands that undermine farmers' rights" The Jakarta Post (15 June 2023), online: https://www.thejakartapost.com/opinion/2023/06/15/indonesia-must-resist-eus-trade-talk-demands-that-undermine-farmers-rights.html, last accessed 26 February 2024.

Figure 2.1 Map of the United Nations General Assembly voting data based on Resolution A/RES/73/165.

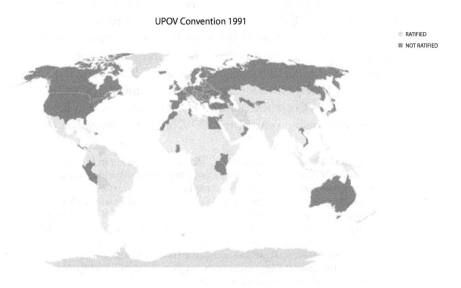

Figure 2.2 Map of UPOV ratifications based on WIPO data.

example, Afghanistan, Nigeria, and the Philippines, voted in favour of UNDROP despite having initiated accession procedures to join UPOV.[26]

These incongruences are not only significant in political terms; they can have legal consequences too. In 2007, in the context of a case dealing with Indigenous peoples' land rights, the Supreme Court of Belize attached significant weight to the fact that Belize had voted in favour of the UN Declaration on the Rights of Indigenous Peoples, demanding the government to live up to this solemn pledge.[27] In fact, as will be discussed below, a proactive judiciary could even demand that a State which abstained on a UN declaration align its national laws with the key principles contained therein. In other words, the adoption of UNDROP not only reinforces the human rights dimension of the normative clash between breeders' and farmers' rights but also affects the way in which countries are expected to respond to that clash. Since these considerations imply that, legally speaking, UPOV and UNDROP can be placed on an equal footing, the following section addresses a potential complication associated with this assumption.

The Legal Value and Effects of UNDROP

As an international treaty, UPOV is legally binding on those States that choose to ratify it. By contrast, being adopted by means of a UN General Assembly Resolution, UNDROP belongs to what is normally referred to in international law as soft law.[28] The key feature of a soft law instrument is that it is not legally binding. It is for this reason that soft law is not included among the formal sources of international law.[29] Under these circumstances, it is not surprising that States not supportive of UNDROP tried to accentuate its lack of binding force in an attempt to downplay its legal significance.[30]

---

26   Among the other States which have initiated accession procedures, Guatemala voted against UNDROP while Armenia and Honduras—as discussed in section 4—abstained.

27   *Manuel Coy et al* v *The Attorney General of Belize et al*, Supreme Court of Belize, Claims No 171 and 172 (10 October 2007).

28   On soft law generally, see Alan Boyle, "Soft Law in International Law-Making" in Malcolm Evans, ed, *International Law*, 2nd ed (Oxford: Oxford University Press, 2006) at 141–158; CM Chinkin, "The Challenge of Soft Law: Development and Change in International Law" (1989) 38 *International and Comparative Law Quarterly* 850–866.

29   Statute of the International Court of Justice (18 April 1946) art 38, online: https://www.refworld.org/docid/3deb4b9c0.html last accessed 26 February 2024.

30   See, e.g., United States Mission to the United Nations, "Explanation of Vote on a Third Committee Resolution on Rights of Peasants" (19 November 2018), online:

Yet, to say that UNDROP is not hard law is one thing; to say that it lacks legal value and capacity to produce legal effects is quite another. The first thing to note here is that, under the complexity and dynamism of contemporary international law making, international legal standards often emerge as a result of the interplay of different legal instruments, regardless of their nature.[31] Furthermore, the category of soft law includes, among others, inter-State conference declarations, UN General Assembly resolutions, codes of conduct, guidelines, and the recommendations of international organizations. It follows that not all soft law instruments are the same and that, consequently, the legal authority of each soft law instrument must be determined on the basis of the specific circumstances of each case. What matters, in particular, are the contexts within which a soft law instrument is established, its normative content, and the institutional setting within which it is to operate.[32] As the following analysis will show, there are important reasons for regarding UNDROP as an important legal instrument that contributes to define the international legal standards regarding access to and management of seeds.

As to the circumstances leading to the adoption of UNDROP, it is important to note that, despite the non-negligible number of abstentions (54), the majority of States (121) voted in favour of this instrument. These numbers are not indicative of an overwhelming endorsement and yet signal the existence of a broad, albeit geographically defined, consensus around the instrument. Further international support for UNDROP has come also from UN specialized agencies such as the Food and Agricultural Organization[33] and UN human rights experts such as the UN Special Rapporteur on the Right to Food.[34] Another important

https://usun.usmission.gov/explanation-of-vote-on-a-third-committee-resolution-on-rights-of-peasants/, last accessed 26 February 2024.

31   Dinah Shelton, "Law, Non-Law and the Problem of 'Soft Law'" in Dinah Shelton, ed, *Commitment and Compliance: The Role of Non-Binding Norms in the International Legal System* (Oxford: Oxford University Press, 2000) at 10.

32   Mauro Barelli, "The Role of Soft Law in the International Legal System: The Case of the United Nations Declaration on the Rights of Indigenous Peoples" (2019) 58:4 *International and Comparative Law Quarterly* 957–983.

33   See, e.g., "UN declaration on rights of peasants and rural people is a landmark, says FAO," online: https://www.fao.org/new-york/news/news-detail/UN-declaration-on-rights-of-peasants-and-rural-people-is-a-landmark-says-FAO/en, last accessed 26 February 2024.

34   See, for example, the position of the former UN Special Rapporteur on the right to food, Olivier de Schutter, *Final Study of the Human Rights Council Advisory Committee on the Advancement of the Rights of Peasants and Other People Working in Rural Areas*, UN doc A/HRC/19/75 (24 February 2012) at para. 70.

element to consider is the active participation of peasants' representatives in the drafting of UNDROP.[35] This is in line with modern calls to enhance "popular participation" in law-making processes in order to enhance the legitimacy and value of the concerned provisions.[36] The fact that this participation involved peasants is even more remarkable since they constitute an "invisible class" normally excluded from the negotiating tables.[37]

As to the normative content of UNDROP, Article 19 has a solid legal background in international human rights law. Of special importance in this regard is the relationship between the right to seeds and the fundamental human right to food, which is recognized in Article 11 of the International Covenant on Economic, Social and Cultural Rights (ICESCR). Authors like Haugen have underlined that Article 19 of UNDROP complements Article 11 of ICESCR by providing farmers with a legal avenue to access and control seeds in order to exercise their right to food,[38] which, it should not be forgotten, is vital for the realization of the right to life. This view is shared, among others, by the current UN Special Rapporteur on the Right to Food, who, reflecting on the broader societal implications of farmers' access to seeds, affirmed that the more a seed system supports farmers' rights, the more likely this system will fulfill the right to food.[39] It should also be highlighted that, in the view of the UN Committee on the Elimination of Discrimination against Women, rural women's rights to seeds are "fundamental human rights."[40] Accordingly, the committee has called on states to "respect and protect rural women's traditional and eco-friendly agricultural knowledge, in particular the right of women to preserve, use and exchange

---

35   Paul Nicholson & Saturnino M Borras Jr, "It wasn't an intellectual construction: the founding of La Via Campesina, achievements and challenges – a conversation" (2023) 50:2 *The Journal of Peasant Studies* 610–626.

36   Richard Falk, *Human Rights Horizons: the Pursuit of Justice in a Globalizing World* (New York: Routledge, 2000) at 62–63.

37   Francesco Francioni, "The Peasants' Declaration: State obligations and justiciability" in Mariagrazia Alabreseet al, eds, *The United Nations' Declaration on Peasants' Rights* (Taylor & Francis, 2022) at 4.

38   Hans Morten Haugen, "The UN Declaration on Peasants' Rights (UNDROP): Is Article 19 on seed rights adequately balancing intellectual property rights and the right to food?" (2020) 23:3–4 *The Journal of World Intellectual Property* 288–309.

39   "Seeds, right to life and farmers' rights", Report of the Special Rapporteur on the right to food, Michael Fakhri, UN Doc. A/HRC/49/43 (30 December 2021) https://www.ohchr.org/en/documents/thematic-reports/ahrc4943-seeds-right-life-and-farmers-rights-report-special-rapporteur last accessed 26 February 2024.

40   *General recommendation No. 34 (2016) on the Rights of Rural Women*, CEDAW Committee, UN Doc CEDAW/C/GC/34 (7 March 2016) at para 56.

traditional and native seeds." [41] Finally, it should not be forgotten that farmers' rights to seed have already been recognized in an important treaty that aims to ensure the conservation and sustainable use of plant genetic resources, namely, the 2001 International Treaty on Plant Genetic Resources for Food and Agriculture. In particular, despite the inclusion of a clause which subjects it to national law, Article 9 safeguards the rights of farmers "to save, use, exchange and sell farm-saved seed/propagating material." [42]

The last factor in assessing the significance of UNDROP relates to the existence, and effectiveness, of follow-up mechanisms. Such mechanisms should be focused on two connected actions, namely, promotion and monitoring of State compliance. Bearing in mind that, due to the well-known shortcomings of the international legal system, effective and systematic implementation cannot be guaranteed even with regard to international human rights treaties, a number of encouraging developments can be identified. Firstly, Article 27 requires unambiguously that UN specialized agencies and other intergovernmental organizations contribute to the full realization of UNDROP. Secondly, an existing mechanism within the UN human rights architecture—that is, the UN Special Rapporteur on the Right to Food—will guarantee continued support for UNDROP, including through efforts to promote its implementation on the ground. On top of that, pressure is mounting within the UN human rights system to create a mechanism devoted specifically to the promotion of the rights of peasants. [43] This would be a crucial step because the latter would use UNDROP as normative basis for its activities. Thirdly, through their scrutiny of States' policies with regard to peasants, UN human rights treaty bodies can monitor and promote State compliance with UNDROP. In this regard, it is noteworthy that references to UNDROP have already appeared in a number of general comments [44] as well as in a growing number of concluding

41   *Ibid* at para 62.
42   International Treaty on Plant Genetic Resources for Food and Agriculture, 23 November 2001, 2400 UNTS 303 (entered into force 29 June 2004).
43   See, e.g., *The UN Human Rights Council Should Create a New Special Procedure on the Rights of Peasants and Other People Working in Rural Areas*, Joint Statement by UN Human Rights Experts (17 November 2019), online: https://www.ohchr.org/en/statements/2019/12/joint-statement-un-human-rights-experts-1st-anniversary-adoption-un-declaration last accessed 26 February 2024.
44   E.g., General comment No. 26 (2022) on Land and Economic, Social and Cultural Rights (24 January 2023) and General comment No. 25 (2020) on Science and Economic, Social and Cultural Rights (20 April 2020), UN Committee on Economic, Social and Cultural Rights.

observations on individual States' reports adopted by bodies such as the Committee on Economic, Social and Cultural Rights and the Committee on Elimination of Discrimination against Women.[45] Crucially, UNDROP has also informed the reasoning of the Human Rights Committee in a recent decision concerning a peasant family in Paraguay.[46]

Finally, regional and domestic bodies can exert significant pressure to ensure compliance with UNDROP. Regionally, it can be expected that UNDROP will become increasingly relevant in the Inter-American context, where the Inter-American Court of Human Rights (IACtHR) has traditionally taken a flexible approach to soft-law instruments,[47] including in relation to the UN Declaration on the Rights of Indigenous Peoples. In keeping with this tradition, the IACtHR has already used UNDROP as a "supplementary reference" in its jurisprudence.[48] Turning to the national dimension, UNDROP has informed legislative processes in countries such as Colombia,[49] while recent judicial decisions in Honduras, which will be further examined below, and Ecuador have relied, *inter alia*, on provisions of UNDROP to declare national laws unconstitutional.[50] In conclusion, institutional mechanisms for the promotion and monitoring of UNDROP are in place, thus moving the relevant international setting closer to that of a hard law instrument. Positive developments at the national level further consolidate the view of UNDROP as a legally authoritative text.

---

45   E.g., Concluding observations on the initial report of Guinea, CESCR, E/C.12/GIN/CO/1 (30 March 2020); and Concluding observations on the ninth periodic report of Colombia, CEDAW/C/COL/CO/9 (14 March 2019).

46   *Portillo Caceres and Others v Paraguay*, CCPR/C/126/D/2751/2016 (20 September 2019).

47   E.g, in *Comunidad Indigena Yakye Axa v Paraguay*, Inter-American Court of Human Rights, Series C 125 (2005), para 128; *Juridical Condition and Rights of the Undocumented Migrants*, Advisory Opinion OC-18/03, Inter-American Court of Human Rights, Series A 18(2003), para 120; *The Right to Information on Consular Assistance in the Framework of Guarantees for Due Legal Process*, Advisory Opinion OC-16/99, Inter American Court of Human Rights, Series A 16(1999), para 115.

48   *Case of the Indigenous Communities of the Lhaka Honhat (Our Land) Association v Argentina*, IACtHR, Judgment of 6 February 2020.

49   Proyecto de Acto Legislativo 077/2022C, online (pdf): https://www.camara.gov.co/sites/default/files/2022-12/P.A.L.077-2022C%20%28CAMPESINO%20SUJETO%20DE%20DERECHOS%29.pdf last accessed 26 February 2024.

50   *Sentencia No. 22-17-IN y acumulados/22*, Corte Constitucional del Ecuador, 12 January 2022.

Reconciling Breeders' and Farmers' Rights: *Sui Generis* Legislation and Judicial Intervention

The existence of a normative clash between UPOV and a human rights approach to seed systems, encapsulated in UNDROP, is obviously not irremediable. First of all, there are countries such as India that have implemented—even before UNDROP—national legislations seeking to strike the right balance between breeders' and farmers' rights without adhering to UPOV's more economic-focused demands. As the adoption of UNDROP has boosted calls for more balanced approaches to breeders' and farmers' rights, those countries that today seek to achieve a reconciliation of these competing interests can, therefore, look at these types of *sui generis* legislation as valuable precedents. In addition, a promising development has recently occurred in Honduras, where the Supreme Court was called to review the legality of a national law concerning breeders' rights. As will be discussed below, this judicial intervention is particularly significant because it has revealed the potential of UNDROP in contributing to define the legal standards applicable to farmers' rights.

India: Reconciliation by Sui Generis *Legislation*

The share of agriculture in India's economy has progressively declined to less than 15 percent. Yet, this indicator does not reflect the full significance of this sector in the country's economic and social fabric.[51] In fact, agriculture accounts for 80 percent of rural income and employs 46 percent of the total workforce.[52] In light of the important role that agriculture plays in the country, in 2001 India passed a PVP law which not only grants PVP rights to breeders but also takes into account and positively protects the rights of farmers, namely, the Protection of Plant Variety and Farmers' Right Act.[53] This law, which entered into force in 2005 with the creation of the Plant Varieties and Farmers' Rights

---

51   World Bank, "India: Issues and Priorities for Agriculture" (17 May 2012), online: https://www.worldbank.org/en/news/feature/2012/05/17/india-agriculture-issues-priorities last accessed 26 February 2024.

52   India GDP from Agriculture (September 2023), see Trading Economics webpage at https://tradingeconomics.com/india/gdp-from-agriculture last accessed 26 February 2024; and Pushan Sharma, "Agriculture Budget 2023: Agriculture sector needs fresh fodder to improve farmer incomes" (*Times of India*, 31 January 2023), online: https://timesofindia.indiatimes.com/business/budget/union-budget-2023-agriculture-sector-needs-fresh-fodder-to-improve-farmer-incomes/articleshow/97458359.cms?from=mdr last accessed 26 February 2024.

53   *Plant Variety and Farmers' Right Act*, Act No. 53 of 2001.

Authority,[54] was driven by the necessity to comply with the World Trade Organization's requirement to protect plant varieties via proprietary IP rights,[55] with such protection being aimed at encouraging agritech innovation.

Having incorporated the UPOV 1991 regime, countries such as the US, Canada, and Japan strongly protect the IP rights of breeders, while allowing farmers to use the registered seeds in a very limited way via mere exceptions. By contrast, India has adopted a unique *sui generis* system which not only grants breeders a monopoly over new varieties, but also vests farmers with the positive rights to save, replant, exchange, and even sell the protected seeds in some circumstances. This normative solution, therefore, allows and promotes agricultural practices based on traditional seeds exchange and sharing—practices which, as seen above, are environmentally sound and thus beneficial to biodiversity. An important aspect of the law is that it protects farmers against the so-called innocent infringement (for example, due to cross-pollination) and exempts from liability farmers who are not aware of the existence of breeders' rights when the infringement occurs.[56] Moreover, the PPVFRA allows not only breeders but also farmers themselves to register as breeders of new varieties and includes rules on benefit-sharing and the creation of a gene fund. It is also worth mentioning that the PPVFRA states that varieties involving any kind of technology considered harmful to the life or health of humans, plants, or animals cannot be protected.

The Indian government has recently reaffirmed its support for farmers' rights and the PPVFRA in the context of a litigation started by the US food giant PepsiCo. In 2019, PepsiCo sued several farmers from the State of Gujarat before the Court of Ahmedabad for allegedly growing and selling a variety of potato—the FC5—which the US company grows exclusively for its popular Lay's potato chips. PepsiCo sought and obtained a permanent injunction to prevent the infringement of their plant variety rights over the potato in question. A particularly interesting aspect of this

---

54   On this Act, and in general on the role of intellectual property rights in agriculture, see Krishna Ravi Srinivas, "Intellectual Property Rights and Politics of Food" in Ronald Herring, ed, *The Oxford Handbook of Food, Politics, and Society* (Oxford: Oxford University Press, 2015) at 381–406.

55   See Article 27(3)(b) TRIPS, which provides that: "Members shall provide for the protection of plant varieties either by patents or by an effective sui generis system or by any combination thereof."

56   Anushka Verma, *"Plant Breeders' Rights v Farmers' Rights*: a contradistinction between the Indian approach and international protection" (2021) 16:9 *Journal of Intellectual Property Law & Practice* at 965.

case is that, although the FC5 variety had been introduced by PepsiCo in India in 2011, it was only registered years later, with the result that it had already spread before the registration by the US company among farmers who had no contractual obligations with them.[57] As significant public pressure mounted against PepsiCo,[58] the Indian government firmly intervened, asking the US company to withdraw the lawsuits, which, it should be noted, affected farmers from Modi's home State ruled by his Bharatiya Janata Party.[59] Crucially, after PepsiCo agreed to withdraw the cases and find "a long term and an amicable resolution of all issues around seed protection,"[60] the Protection of Plant Varieties & Farmers' Rights Authority passed an order revoking PepsiCo's registration of the FC5 potato variety.[61] Subsequently, on July 5, 2023 the Delhi High Court dismissed PepsiCo's appeal against the authority's decision.[62]

All that said, it is important to note that the spirit and principles

---

57   Khurana & Khurana Law Firm, "PepsiCo v Farmers (A Case of Misplaced Priorities or Possibilities of Laying Down a News Precedent)?" (22 July 2019), online: https://www.khuranaandkhurana.com/2019/07/22/pepsico-vs-farmers-a-case-of-misplaced-priorities-or-possibility-of-laying-down-a-news-precedent/ last accessed 26 February 2024. On this case see also Kavitha Iyer, "India's Potato-Chip Tussle: How Gujarat Farmers Won A Battle—But Not The War—Against Pepsico" (Article 14, 3 January 2022), online: *Article 14* https://www.article-14.com/post/india-s-potato-chip-tussle-how-gujarat-farmers-won-a-battle-but-not-the-war-against-pepsico-61d26768dd419 last accessed 26 February 2024; Parna Mukherjee & Urmil Shah, "The PepsiCo Dispute: A Case of David Versus Goliath?" (11 March 2020), 20:2 *Australian Journal of Asian Law* 399, online: https://ssrn.com/abstract=3552452 last accessed 26 February 2024.

58   Kavitha Iyer, "India's Potato-Chip Tussle: How Gujarat Farmers Won A Battle—But Not The War—Against Pepsico" (3 January 2022), online: *Article 14* https://www.article-14.com/post/india-s-potato-chip-tussle-how-gujarat-farmers-won-a-battle-but-not-the-war-against-pepsico-61d26768dd419#:~:text=Bipin%20Patel%20and%20Chhabil%20Patel,selling%20Lays%20brand%20of%20chips last accessed 26 February 2024.

59   Reuters, "PepsiCo withdraws lawsuits against Indian potato farmers" (10 May 2023), online: https://www.reuters.com/article/us-india-pepsi-farmers-idUSKCN1S-G1KT last accessed 26 February 2024.

60   Mayank Bhardwaj, "Pepsi withdraws Indian potato farmer lawsuits after political pressure" (2 May 2019), online: *Reuters* https://www.reuters.com/article/india-pepsi-farmers-idCNL3N22E2N5 last accessed 26 February 2024.

61   Sumit Khanna & Mayank Bhardwaj, "India revokes patent for PepsiCo's Lay's potatoes" (3 December 2021), online: *Reuters* https://www.reuters.com/markets/commodities/india-revokes-patent-pepsicos-lays-potatoes-2021-12-03/ last accessed 26 February 2024.

62   Reuters, "Delhi High Court turns down PepsiCo's appeal against revocation of potato patent" (8 July 2023), online: *The Hindu* https://www.thehindu.com/news/national/indian-court-turns-down-pepsicos-appeal-against-revocation-of-potato-patent/article67057105.ece last accessed 26 February 2024.

contained in the PPVFRA have recently come under attack following attempts to pass legislation aimed at regulating marketing rights
over seeds. In particular, the most recent seeds bill, proposed by
Narendra Modi's government in 2019, was criticized for bearing "the
imprint of the seed industry"[63] and seeking to impose measures which
may have an impact similar to that of a UPOV 1991 regime.[64] Among
other things, this bill would make it compulsory for farmers to register their seeds and implement a "minimum limit of germination,
physical purity and genetic purity."[65] According to a parliamentary
standard committee, this rule would contravene farmers' rights to
produce and sell the seeds, facilitating, instead, the penetration of
the private sector into the seed market.[66] The draft has been firmly
resisted by farmers and, at the time of writing, has not become law
yet.[67] It is crucial that India preserves the core values and principles of
PPVFRA to be able to continue being regarded as a positive example
of reconciliation between breeders' and farmers' rights.

Honduras: Reconciliation by Judicial Intervention

In 2012, as part of the (yet uncompleted) process of accession to UPOV
1991,[68] Honduras passed the Plant Variety Protection Act (PVPA).[69]
In a country where the agricultural sector employs almost 40 percent
of the population,[70] and approximately 70 percent of these workers

---

63   Suman Sahai, "The draft seeds bill favours the industry over farmers" (4 December
      2019), online: *Hindustan Times* https://www.hindustantimes.com/analysis/the-draft-
      seeds-bill-favours-the-industry-over-farmers-opinion/story-T3xuLM0ApoL2Z7f-
      HInUT4H.html last accessed 26 February 2024.
64   Monika Mandal, "Why the draft Seed Bill 2019 is bad for Indian farmers" (5 October
      2020), online: *Mongabay* https://india.mongabay.com/2020/10/commentary-why-
      the-draft-seed-bill-2019-is-bad-for-indian-farmers/ last accessed 26 February 2024.
65   *Draft Seeds Bill 2019*, https://prsindia.org/files/bills_acts/bills_parliament/1970/
      Draft%20Seeds%20Bill,%202019.pdf last accessed 26 February 2024.
66   Shruti Jain, 'Explainer: Do Farmers Have Reason to Criticise the Draft Seed Bill?'
      (*The Wire*, 1 April 2021).
67   Sophy K Joseph, *Reflections on Indian Legislations on Farmers' Rights* (Oxford: Oxford
      University Press 2020), ch 5. See also Shruti Jain, "Explainer: Do Farmers Have
      Reason to Criticise the Draft Seed Bill?" *The Wire* (1 April 2021).
68   UPOV Status of Ratification, online: UPOV https://www.upov.int/export/sites/
      upov/members/en/pdf/status.pdf last accessed 26 February 2024.
69   Legislative Decree No. 21-2012 containing the Law for the Protection of New
      Varieties of Plants, issued by the National Congress of Honduras on 12 March
      2012.
70   International Fund for Agricultural Development (IFAD), Honduras, online:
      https://www.ifad.org/en/web/operations/w/country/honduras/ last accessed 26

are smallholder farmers who primarily farm low-profit crops,[71] it is not surprising that the PVPA, a piece of legislation aimed at promoting "an environment aimed to stimulate national and international investments,"[72] was quickly labelled as Monsanto Law by peasants' organizations.[73] An initial attempt to block this law was made in 2016 by the National Association for the Promotion of Organic Farming (ANAFAE). Subsequently, in 2018 the ANAFAE, together with other peasant organizations and independent farmers, filed another legal action which ultimately resulted in a historic ruling, in 2021, by the Supreme Court.[74] The main concern about this law was that it limited the right of peasants to use farm-saved propagation material and prohibited them from giving away, exchanging, or selling seeds from plant varieties protected by breeders' rights. In doing so, it was argued, the PVPA contradicted fundamental human rights and principles protected under both the national constitution and the several international treaties to which Honduras is a party.[75]

The Court shared the farmers' concerns, issuing an important verdict that, in affirming the primacy of human rights over third parties' economic interests, can set an example for other judiciaries to follow.[76]

February 2024.

71   Ryan C Berg, Henry Ziemer & Michael Estopinan, "Financing Small Scale Agriculture in Honduras: A Case Study" (7 December 2022), Center for Strategic International Studies (CSIS), online: https://www.csis.org/analysis/financing-small-scale-agriculture-honduras-case-study last accessed 26 February 2024.

72   "Considerando que el Gobierno de Honduras se ha propuesto como parte de su estrategia de desarrollo, la inserción del país en el mercado internacional, propiciando un ambiente adecuado para la inversión nacional y extranjera," Preambular Paragraph 1 of the preliminary draft text of the Law for the Protection of New Varieties of Plants, online: https://docs.wto.org/dol2fe/Pages/SS/directdoc.aspx?filename=Q:/IP/Q4/HND1.pdf&Open=True last accessed 26 February 2024.

73   Grain, "Semillas en manos campesinas: un fallo a favor de la soberanía alimentaria en Honduras" (2 March 2022), online: https://grain.org/es/article/6808-semillas-en-manos-campesinas-un-fallo-a-favor-de-la-soberania-alimentaria-en-honduras#:~:text=1)%20%22El%20Decreto%20Legislativo%20N,nuestras%20riquezas%20y%20recursos%20naturales%2 last accessed 26 February 2024.

74   Karine Peschard, "Honduras: Supreme Court uses UNDROP article 19 on the right to seeds to declare unconstitutional the Monsanto Law" (7 February 2023), *Defending Peasants Rights*, online: https://defendingpeasantsrights.org/en/honduras-supreme-court-uses-undrop-article-19-on-the-right-to-seeds-to-declare-unconstitutional-the-monsanto-law/ last accessed 26 February 2024.

75   See also Biodiversidad, "Seeds in the hands of peasant farmers: a judgment in favour of food sovereignty in Honduras" (2 March 2022), *Grain*, online: https://grain.org/en/article/6809-seeds-in-the-hands-of-peasant-farmers-a-judgment-in-favour-of-food-sovereignty-in-honduras last accessed 26 February 2024.

76   The text of the decision can be found at https://www.apbrebes.org/sites/default/

At the outset, the Court noted that, reflecting the centrality of the human person in the constitutional architecture, the Constitution of Honduras must be interpreted in accordance with the *pro homine* principle.[77] It then referred to Article 64 of the Constitution, which prohibits the enforcement of laws that diminish fundamental rights and guarantees recognized by the State.[78] According to the Court, these rights and guarantees derive not only from the Constitution itself but also, in line with Article 16 of the same instrument, from the interaction between the latter and international human rights treaties to which Honduras is a party. For the Court, several of these rights and guarantees were hindered by the PVPA, including the right to food and the right of Indigenous communities to the use, conservation, and management of natural resources found on their lands. The Court also referred to the right to equitably participate in the distribution of benefits derived from the use of plant genetic resources for food and agriculture, citing Article 328 of the Constitution, which guarantees that the economic system is based on principles of efficiency in production and social justice, and Article 347, which affirms that agricultural production should preferably be oriented towards satisfying the food needs of Hondurans in line with a policy of adequate supply and fair prices for the producer and the consumer. In emphasizing the State's obligation to protect and promote farmers' traditional knowledge of plant genetic resources for food and agriculture, the Court further highlighted that the PVPA hindered Honduras' efforts to achieve food security through the promotion of biological diversity and the sustainable use of resources.

What is particularly remarkable, for the purpose of this discussion, is that the Court did not simply base its decision on provisions of the Constitution and human rights treaties ratified by Honduras, such as the International Covenant on Economic, Social and Cultural Rights, the Convention on Biological Diversity, and the International Treaty

---

files/2022-03/INCONSTITUCIONALIDAD%20LEY%20PROTECCION%20DE%20 OBTENCIONES%20VEGETALES%20HONDURAS%20ENERO%202022.pdf last accessed 26 February 2024; An unofficial English translation is available at https:// www.apbrebes.org/sites/default/files/2022-12/Sentence_Honduras_Engl_fin.pdf last accessed 26 February 2024.

77   For a broader discussion, see Álvaro Villareal, "El Principio Pro Homine: Interpretación Extensiva vs. El Consentimiento del Estado" (2005) 5 *Revista Colombiana de Derecho Internacional* at 337.

78   Honduras Constitution, online: https://constitutionnet.org/sites/default/files/ Honduras%20Constitution.pdf last accessed 26 February 2024.

on Plant Genetic Resources for Food and Agriculture. Instead, it also acknowledged—expressly—that Article 19 of UNDROP, concerning the right of peasants to seeds, contributes to define the international human rights standards that Honduras must follow in order to adequately protect the human right to food, which, the Court held, is inseparable from the inherent dignity of the human person and is essential for the enjoyment of other human rights. Crucially, the Supreme Court referred to UNDROP despite the fact that Honduras chose to abstain on the occasion of the General Assembly's vote that led to the adoption of the instrument, thus recognizing UNDROP as an influential instrument to clarify, interpret, and expand the meaning and scope of international and domestic provisions.

While, of course, deferential attitudes towards the executive power and traditionally hostile approaches to international law sources may affect the stand taken by a particular court, this case reveals the potential for judicial intervention as a means to reconcile breeders' and farmers' rights through a human rights lens. When national legislative action fails to strike the right balance between breeders' and farmers' rights, the judiciary can intervene to protect the human rights dimension attached to the question under scrutiny, and, in doing so, should not refrain from using UNDROP as an authoritative instrument in defining the applicable international legal standards.

Conclusions

The conflict between breeders' and farmers' rights has a complex, multidimensional character that places it at the intersection of agricultural systems, IP, food security, and human rights. Breeders' rights protect IP and innovation in plant breeding, ensuring that those who invest time and resources into developing new crop varieties can benefit from their investments. Furthermore, by encouraging research and development in this area, they contribute to promoting agricultural progress, including the production of more resilient crops. This, however, is only half the story. Breeders' rights in fact may also have negative repercussions on food security, human rights, and traditional agricultural practices. For this reason, they must be balanced with another important set of rights, namely, farmers' rights. The latter are centred on the age-old practice of saving, replanting, and sharing seeds that continues to define the livelihoods of countless farmers worldwide. Laws which unduly protect breeders' rights end up limiting farmers' ability to access and control seeds, with important repercussions on their fundamental human rights, such as the rights to food, as well as broader negative societal consequences in terms of food security and biodiversity.

Against this background, this article has examined the relationship between the two legal instruments that best epitomize the IP and human rights approaches to seeds, namely, UPOV 1991 and UNDROP, arguing that the principles underpinning the former are no longer aligned with the human rights of farmers that have now been embedded in the fabric of international human rights law. This should provide an incentive for States which have not yet ratified UPOV to consider alternative methods of protecting breeders' rights that are capable of striking a better balance between breeders' and farmers' rights. India represents a good example of a country that has been able to achieve this goal by enacting the PPVFRA. In particular, India has been described in this chapter as a country that has sought to achieve reconciliation of breeders' and farmers' rights by *sui generis* legislation. Recent developments, however, have shown that the core principles of the PPVFRA concerning seed systems must be constantly defended as pressure mounts towards extending breeders' rights to the detriment of farmers' rights.

This chapter has highlighted that, when legislative initiatives risk undermining the rights of farmers, domestic tribunals can intervene to safeguard relevant human rights values that are embedded not only in national but also international legal instruments. In this respect, Honduras represents a positive example of a country that has sought to reconcile breeders' and farmers' rights by judicial intervention. In particular, the recent decision of the Supreme Court of Honduras has showed that, in promoting a human rights approach to the question of seed systems, domestic tribunals should not shy away from using UNDROP as an influential human rights instrument that contributes to define the international legal standards applicable to breeders' and farmers' rights.

Chapter 3

TRIPS and Its Futures

Peter K. Yu

Abstract

The *Agreement on Trade-Related Aspects of Intellectual Property Rights* (*TRIPS Agreement*) was adopted on 15 April 1994, along with the establishment of the World Trade Organization (WTO). With the WTO's recent celebration of its thirtieth anniversary, it is high time we explore what the future will hold for this agreement. This chapter begins by revisiting the past to examine whether the *TRIPS Agreement* would be adopted if it were negotiated today. The chapter then discusses whether WTO members will undertake a major overhaul of this agreement in the future. Taking note of the fast-evolving international norm-setting environment and the lack of breakthroughs in the Doha Development Round of Trade Negotiations in the past decade, this chapter concludes by advancing three recommendations on how the *TRIPS Agreement* could, and should, be updated if WTO members could not reach a consensus on a major overhaul.

Three decades ago, the *Agreement on Trade-Related Aspects of Intellectual Property Rights* (*TRIPS Agreement*) arrived with the establishment of the World Trade Organization (WTO). This agreement transformed the international intellectual property regime by marrying intellectual property with trade.[1] Despite having its standards drawn mostly from the Global North,[2] the agreement has provided catch-up opportunities to large emerging countries such as Brazil, China, and India.[3] One could certainly debate whether it was the *TRIPS Agreement* or the WTO that lifted these countries economically and technologically, yet the "single undertaking" approach embraced by negotiators in the Uruguay Round of Multilateral Trade Negotiations[4] (Uruguay Round) has made it very difficult, if not impossible, to separate these two causal factors.[5]

While the *TRIPS Agreement* has provided benefits to some WTO members, other members have struggled with the high international intellectual property standards that arguably ignored their local needs, national interests, technological capabilities, institutional capacities, and public health conditions.[6] Struggling the most were the world's poorest countries. Classified by the United Nations (UN) as "least developed," this group of countries has repeatedly asked the WTO to extend their TRIPS transition period.[7] Governments, intergovernmental bodies,

---

1   R Michael Gadbaw, "Intellectual Property and International Trade: Merger or Marriage of Convenience" (1989) 22 Vanderbilt Journal of Transnational Law 223; Joseph Straus, "A Marriage of Convenience: World Economy and Intellectual Property from 1990 to 2012" (2012) 40 AIPLA Quarterly Journal 633; Peter K Yu, "The Second Transformation of the International Intellectual Property Regime" in Jonathan Griffiths & Tuomas Mylly, eds, *Global Intellectual Property Protection and New Constitutionalism: Hedging Exclusive Rights* (Oxford: Oxford University Press, 2021) at 178–80.

2   Peter K Yu, "Are Developing Countries Playing a Better TRIPS Game?" (2011) 16 UCLA Journal of International Law and Foreign Affairs 311 at 315–16.

3   Peter K Yu, "Caught in the Middle: WIPO and Emerging Economies" in Sam Ricketson, ed, *Research Handbook on the World Intellectual Property Organization: The First 50 Years and Beyond* (Cheltenham: Edward Elgar Publishing, 2020) at 361–63 ["Caught in the Middle"]; Peter K Yu, "Three Megatrends in the International Intellectual Property Regime" (2023) 41 Cardozo Arts and Entertainment Law Journal 457 at 458–66 ["Three Megatrends"].

4   Launched in Punta del Este, Uruguay, in September 1986, the Uruguay Round was the last round of trade negotiations under the *General Agreement on Tariffs and Trade*. The conclusion of the Uruguay Round led to the establishment of the WTO and its *TRIPS Agreement*.

5   Peter K Yu, "When the Chinese Intellectual Property System Hits 35" (2018) 8 Queen Mary Journal of Intellectual Property 3 at 12. Under this approach, "[v]irtually every item of the negotiation is part of a whole and indivisible package and cannot be agreed separately." World Trade Organization, "How the Negotiations Are Organized," online: https://www.wto.org/english/tratop_e/dda_e/work_organi_e. htm, accessed 20 May 2024.

6   Peter K Yu, "The International Enclosure Movement" (2007) 82 Indiana Law Journal 827 at 828.

7   Peter K Yu, "TRIPS and Its Contents" (2020) 60 IDEA 149 at 151 n 6. Article 66 of the *TRIPS Agreement* provides least developed countries with a 10-year transition

nongovernmental organizations, and individual experts have also condemned the significant deleterious effects of the *TRIPS Agreement* and the subsequently negotiated TRIPS-plus bilateral, regional, and plurilateral trade agreements.[8]

With the WTO's recent celebration of its thirtieth anniversary, it is high time we explore what the future will hold for the *TRIPS Agreement*. Keeping in mind the volume's focus on the future of the intellectual property system, this chapter begins by revisiting the past to examine whether this agreement would be adopted if it were negotiated today.[9] The chapter then discusses whether WTO members will undertake a major overhaul of this agreement in the future. Taking note of the fast-evolving international norm-setting environment and the lack of breakthroughs in the Doha Development Round of Trade Negotiations (Doha Round) in the past decade,[10] this chapter concludes by advancing three recommendations on how the *TRIPS Agreement* could, and should, be updated if WTO members could not reach a consensus on a major overhaul.

Would the *TRIPS Agreement* Be Adopted If It Were Negotiated Today?

Compared with the mid- to late 1980s, the international norm-setting environment has changed dramatically. As a result, many commentators, including those involved in the TRIPS negotiations or related matters, question whether the agreement would be adopted if it were negotiated today. As Antony Taubman and Jayashree Watal remind

---

period, which allows them to delay compliance with TRIPS obligations. That period was extended for seven and a half years in November 2005, another eight years in June 2013, and yet another 13 years in June 2021.

8   E.g., United Nations High Commissioner for Human Rights, *The Impact of the Agreement on Trade-Related Aspects of Intellectual Property Rights on Human Rights: Report of the High Commissioner* UN Doc E/CN.4/Sub.2/2001/13 (27 June 2001) at paras 22–27; Keith E Maskus, *Private Rights and Public Problems: The Global Economics of Intellectual Property in the 21st Century* (Washington, DC: Peterson Institute for International Economics, 2012) at 227; World Bank, *Global Economic Prospects and the Developing Countries 2002: Making Trade Work for the World's Poor* (Washington, DC: World Bank, 2001) at xvii.

9   Antony Taubman raised this interesting counterfactual question during his keynote remarks at the "TRIPS Agreement at 25" Symposium at Texas A&M University School of Law in March 2019.

10   The Doha Round is the current round of trade negotiations at the WTO. It was launched at the Fourth WTO Ministerial Conference in Doha, Qatar, in November 2001, about seven years after the formation of the international trading body.

us in their introduction to the WTO publication commemorating the twentieth anniversary of the *TRIPS Agreement*: "today's world differs considerably from that in which the TRIPS Agreement was negotiated and concluded."[11]

Answering counterfactual questions is always difficult,[12] and many factors can impede the successful negotiation of an international intellectual property agreement as extensive as the *TRIPS Agreement*. Without this agreement, many of the developments in the international intellectual property regime in the past three decades might not even have occurred in the first place. Nevertheless, there are notable differences in the international norm-setting environment between today and more than 30 years ago. Three key contributing factors to the adoption of the *TRIPS Agreement* are conspicuously absent from the current environment.

During the TRIPS negotiations, there was considerable information asymmetry between developed and developing countries in their understanding of intellectual property rights. As I noted in an article published in 2006, shortly after the Sixth WTO Ministerial Conference in Hong Kong, the ignorance narrative has provided one of the four dominant state-driven accounts of the origins of the *TRIPS Agreement*.[13] Under this narrative, countries were ignorant about the strengths and weaknesses of strong intellectual property protection. As a result, they had great difficulty evaluating the benefits of the new TRIPS standards as well as their ultimate economic and technological impacts.[14]

To be sure, the ignorance narrative has presented too simple a TRIPS origin story, even for the developing world.[15] When the Uruguay Round negotiations began, several large developing countries, most notably Brazil and India, had already acquired a sophisticated understanding of intellectual property law and policy. In November 1961, Brazil introduced a draft UN resolution entitled *The Role of Patents in*

---

11   Antony Taubman & Jayashree Watal, "Revisiting the TRIPS Negotiations: Genesis and Structure of This Book" in Jayashree Watal & Antony Taubman, eds, *The Making of the TRIPS Agreement: Personal Insights from the Uruguay Round Negotiations* (Geneva: World Trade Organization, 2015) at 13.

12   Peter K Yu, "What Ifs and Other Alternative Intellectual Property and Cyberlaw Stories: Foreword" (2008) Michigan State Law Review 1 at 2–3.

13   Peter K Yu, "TRIPs and Its Discontents" (2006) 10 Marquette Intellectual Property Law Review 369 at 375–76.

14   *Ibid* at 375.

15   *Ibid* at 370.

the Transfer of Technology to Under-Developed Countries.[16] More than a decade later, India demanded the revision of the *Paris Convention for the Protection of Industrial Property (Paris Convention).*[17] Its demand built on those critical inquiries into the patent system it had conducted since acquiring independence in 1947.[18]

From the very beginning of the TRIPS negotiations, these two countries, along with a few key allies,[19] strongly opposed the incorporation of intellectual property standards into the international trade regime.[20] Notably, India insisted that "it was only the restrictive and anti-competitive practices of the owners of the [intellectual property rights] that could be considered to be trade-related because they alone distorted or impeded international trade."[21]

Despite their active and vocal pushbacks, these powerful opponents were the rare exceptions in the developing world.[22] During the TRIPS negotiations, many other developing countries saw intellectual property as a "new, new thing."[23] Their understanding in this area

---

16   Andrea Koury Menescal, "Changing WIPO's Ways? The 2004 Development Agenda in Historical Perspective" (2005) 8 Journal of World Intellectual Property 761 at 764–73; Peter K Yu, "A Tale of Two Development Agendas" (2009) 35 Ohio Northern University Law Review 465 at 505–06.

17   Susan K Sell, *Power and Ideas: North–South Politics of Intellectual Property and Antitrust* (Albany: State University of New York Press, 1998) at 113–14. As Professor Sell recounts: "In 1974, India sought improvements in the existing [Paris C]onvention before it would consider joining. India felt that developing countries lacked sufficient leverage in the [...] Convention and that developing countries needed special provisions to grant them effective bargaining power. The Indian delegation felt that the Paris Convention needed a stronger emphasis on states' rights vis-à-vis patentees." *Ibid* at 114.

18   The most notable inquiries were those conducted by the Tek Chand Committee and the Ayyangar Committee in the late 1940s and the late 1950s, respectively. Srividhya Ragavan, "Of the Inequals of the Uruguay Round" (2006) 10 Marquette Intellectual Property Law Review 273 at 278–89; Yu, *supra* note 16 at 506–07.

19   These countries, which are sometimes described as "hardliner," included Argentina, Cuba, Egypt, Nicaragua, Nigeria, Peru, Tanzania, and Yugoslavia. Jayashree Watal, *Intellectual Property Rights in the WTO and Developing Countries* (The Hague: Kluwer Law International, 2001) at 19.

20   Peter K Yu, "The Objectives and Principles of the TRIPS Agreement" (2009) 46 Houston Law Review 979 at 983–89.

21   TRIPS Negotiating Group, "Meeting of Negotiating Group of 12–14 July 1989: Note by the Secretariat" GATT Doc MTN.GNG/NG11/14 (12 September 1989) at 4–5; Yu, *supra* note 20 at 987–88.

22   Duncan Matthews, *Globalising Intellectual Property Rights: The TRIPS Agreement* (London: Routledge, 2002) at 44.

23   Peter K Yu, "Intellectual Property Negotiations, the BRICS Factor and the Changing North–South Debate" in Rostam J Neuwirth, Alexandr Svetlicinii & Denis De Castro Halis, eds, *The BRICS-Lawyers' Guide to Global Cooperation* (Cambridge:

therefore lagged significantly behind Brazil, India, and their key allies.[24] Many developing countries were also deeply attracted by intellectual property–unrelated trade concessions that they could secure from developed countries, such as those in agriculture and textiles.[25]

Looking back, commentators have rightly pointed out that the developed countries' ideational power has been a key contributing factor to the successful negotiation of the *TRIPS Agreement*. For instance, the late Susan Sell refers to those having a sophisticated understanding of intellectual property law and policy as "privileged purveyors of expertise" and compares them to the Latin-trained clergy in the Catholic Church when the Bible was in Latin.[26] As she explains in relation to those industries that have actively pushed for high international intellectual property standards with the support of their governments, "[i]t was not merely their relative economic power that led to their ultimate success, but their command of [intellectual property] expertise, their ideas, their information, and their framing skills (translating complex issues into political discourse)."[27] Carolyn Deere points out that the developed countries' superior knowledge about intellectual property rights has benefited them not only during the TRIPS negotiations but also afterwards. As she recounts, these *demandeur* countries "used the power of ideas to advance distinctive perspectives on the pros and cons of different approaches to TRIPS implementation, to dominate the political environment for [intellectual property] reforms, to influence the terms of debate in international negotiations, and to shape how developing countries behaved at the national level."[28]

Since the adoption of the *TRIPS Agreement*, many developing countries have greatly strengthened their understanding of intellectual property rights as well as their legal and norm-setting capacities at the WTO.[29] Developing and least developed countries have also received

---

Cambridge University Press, 2017) at 168.

24   Watal, *supra* note 19 at 19.

25   *Ibid* at 44; Peter K Yu, "Currents and Crosscurrents in the International Intellectual Property Regime" (2004) 38 Loyola of Los Angeles Law Review 323 at 385.

26   Susan K Sell, *Private Power, Public Law: The Globalization of Intellectual Property Rights* (Cambridge: Cambridge University Press, 2003) at 99.

27   *Ibid* at 8.

28   Carolyn Deere, *The Implementation Game: The TRIPS Agreement and the Global Politics of Intellectual Property Reform in Developing Countries* (Oxford: Oxford University Press, 2009) at 19.

29   Gregory C Shaffer, *Emerging Powers and the World Trading System: The Past and Future of International Economic Law* (Cambridge: Cambridge University Press, 2021); Gregory C Shaffer & Ricardo Meléndez-Ortiz, eds, *Dispute Settlement at the*

considerable support and assistance from intergovernmental bodies, nongovernmental organizations, and academic experts.[30] While the developing countries' intellectual property knowledge is still not as sophisticated as what developed countries have, the gap between these two groups has been rapidly closing.

The second notable difference in the international norm-setting environment between today and more than 30 years ago is the rise of emerging countries.[31] Widely cited examples are Brazil, China, and India—which, along with Russia and South Africa, have been grouped together as the "BRICS countries." In a book chapter published more than a decade ago, I identified the 10 largest economies outside the Organisation for Economic Co-operation and Development (OECD) that had a gross national income per capita of less than US$15,000 yet some of the world's highest volumes of high-technology exports.[32] In addition to the BRICS countries, these economies included Argentina, Indonesia, Malaysia, the Philippines, and Thailand.[33] I labelled all 10 countries collectively as the "middle intellectual property powers," hinting at their increasingly important roles in the international intellectual property regime.

When the Uruguay Round negotiations were launched in the mid-1980s, the intellectual property positions of the negotiating parties fell mostly along the North–South fault line. The parties did not turn to North–North issues until later in the negotiations.[34]

WTO: The Developing Country Experience (New York: Cambridge University Press, 2011).

30   Duncan Matthews, Intellectual Property, Human Rights and Development: The Role of NGOs and Social Movements (Cheltenham: Edward Elgar Publishing, 2011) at 6, 223; Peter K Yu, "Access to Medicines, BRICS Alliances, and Collective Action" (2008) 34 American Journal of Law and Medicine 345 at 377 ["Access to Medicines"]; Peter K Yu, "Virotech Patents, Viropiracy, and Viral Sovereignty" (2013) 45 Arizona State Law Journal 1563.

31   Yu, "Caught in the Middle," supra note 3 at 361–63; Yu, "Three Megatrends," supra note 3 at 458–66.

32   Peter K Yu, "The Middle Intellectual Property Powers" in Randall Peerenboom & Tom Ginsburg, eds, Law and Development of Middle-Income Countries: Avoiding the Middle-Income Trap (New York: Cambridge University Press, 2014) at 89.

33   Ibid at 92–93. Although the earlier study included only 10 countries, one could certainly add other countries based on their economic and technological development in the past decade.

34   AV Ganesan, "Negotiating for India" in Watal & Taubman, supra note 11 at 230; Ruth L Okediji, "Public Welfare and the Role of the WTO: Reconsidering the TRIPS Agreement" (2003) 17 Emory International Law Review 819 at 840; Piragibe dos Santos Tarragô, "Negotiating for Brazil" in Watal & Taubman, supra note 11 at 246; Thu-Lang Tran Wasescha, "Negotiating for Switzerland" in Watal & Taubman,

Today, by contrast, emerging countries have taken positions that do not neatly reflect the classic divide between the Global North and the Global South. The positions taken by these countries have therefore made the international negotiating landscape more complex and less predictable.

As we have seen in more recent international trade and intellectual property negotiations, emerging countries sometimes align their positions closely with those of developed countries.[35] At other times, however, emerging countries try to remain supportive of their usual allies in the developing world. Because of these policy shifts, the WTO's developing country members now struggle to maintain a united negotiating front to fight off the developed countries' aggressive demands.[36] The emerging countries' varied negotiating positions and their shifting alliances have also impeded the WTO members' ability to reach consensuses on new international intellectual property standards.

During the COVID-19 pandemic, for instance, India and South Africa submitted a pioneering proposal to the Council for Trade-Related Aspects of Intellectual Property Rights (TRIPS Council), calling for the temporary suspension of more than 30 provisions in the *TRIPS Agreement* to facilitate the "prevention, containment or treatment of COVID-19."[37] China was supportive of this proposed waiver, even though it stopped short of endorsing the instrument. As a Chinese delegate stated at the October 2020 TRIPS Council meeting:

---

supra note 11 at 178; Jayashree Watal, "Patents: An Indian Perspective" in Watal & Taubman, *supra* note 11 at 309.

35   Peter K Yu, "Five Oft-Repeated Questions about China's Recent Rise as a Patent Power" (2013) Cardozo Law Review De Novo 78 at 113; Yu, *supra* note 23 at 169.

36   Yu, *supra* note 23 at 169–70.

37   TRIPS Council, "Waiver from Certain Provisions of the TRIPS Agreement for the Prevention, Containment and Treatment of COVID-19: Communication from India and South Africa" WTO Doc IP/C/W/669 (2 October 2020); TRIPS Council, "Waiver from Certain Provisions of the TRIPS Agreement for the Prevention, Containment and Treatment of COVID-19: Revised Decision Text" WTO Doc IP/C/W/669/Rev.1 (25 May 2021). For my earlier discussions of this proposal and its aftermath, see Peter K Yu, "A Critical Appraisal of the COVID-19 TRIPS Waiver" in Taina Pihlajarinne, Jukka Mähönen & Pratyush Nath Upreti, eds, *Intellectual Property Rights in the Post Pandemic World: An Integrated Framework of Sustainability, Innovation and Global Justice* (Cheltenham: Edward Elgar Publishing, 2023); Peter K Yu, "The COVID-19 TRIPS Waiver and the WTO Ministerial Decision" in Jens Schovsbo, ed, *Intellectual Property Rights in Times of Crisis* (Cheltenham: Edward Elgar Publishing, 2024).

China is willing to discuss access to commodities in relation to the prevention and control of COVID-19, including medicines and vaccines under the framework of the TRIPS Agreement, and supports the discussions on possible waiver or other emergency measures to respond to the pandemic, which are "targeted, proportional, transparent and temporary", and which do not create unnecessary barriers to trade or disruption to global supply chains.[38]

Meanwhile, Brazil strongly opposed the waiver, joining its rare allies in the developed world. At the same meeting, its delegate declared: "At this point in time, we are not convinced that a waiver to the TRIPS Agreement would guarantee us meaningful improvement of access, while it might give the wrong signs to innovators and potentially hinder efforts to produce the solutions we need."[39]

The third notable difference in the international norm-setting environment between today and more than 30 years ago involves the unique timing surrounding the launch of the Uruguay Round negotiations. From the late 1960s to the mid-1980s, developing countries had engaged in a series of pro-development initiatives, including the establishment of the *Protocol Regarding Developing Countries* to the *Berne Convention for the Protection of Literary and Artistic Works (Berne Convention)*,[40] the creation of the New International Economic Order at the United Nations,[41] the drafting of the *International Code of Conduct on the Transfer of Technology* under the auspices of the United Nations Conference on Trade and Development (UNCTAD),[42] and the demands for renegotiating the

---

38   TRIPS Council, "Minutes of Meeting: Held in the Centre William Rappard on 15–16 October and 10 December 2020" WTO Doc IP/C/M/96/Add.1 (16 February 2021) at para 977. On China's global pandemic diplomacy in relation to the COVID-19 TRIPS waiver, see Peter K Yu, "China, the TRIPS Waiver, and the Global Pandemic Response" in Sun Haochen & Madhavi Sunder, eds, *Intellectual Property, COVID-19, and the Next Pandemic: Diagnosing Problems, Developing Cures* (Cambridge: Cambridge University Press, 2024); Peter K Yu, "Vaccine Development, the China Dilemma, and International Regulatory Challenges" (2023) 55 New York University Journal of International Law and Politics 739 ["Vaccine Development"].

39   TRIPS Council, *supra* note 38 at para 1099.

40   Protocol Regarding Developing Countries to the Berne Convention for the Protection of Literary and Artistic Works, 14 July 1967, 828 UNTS 221 at 281; Yu, *supra* note 16 at 471–84.

41   Declaration on the Establishment of a New International Economic Order, GA Res 3201 (S-VI), UNGAOR, 6th Supp, UN Doc A/RES/S-6/3201 (1 May 1974).

42   Draft International Code of Conduct on the Transfer of Technology UN Doc TD/CODE TOT/33 (12 May 1981); Surendra J Patel, Pedro Roffe & Abdulqawi Yusuf, eds, *International Technology Transfer: The Origins and Aftermath of the United Nations*

Paris Convention.[43] Although all these initiatives were highly ambitious, they did not produce the results developing countries had hoped for.

By the time these countries entered the TRIPS negotiations in the mid-1980s, they were disillusioned with the developed countries' lack of support for the adjustments needed to address their economic and technological plight. They also experienced fatigue from the repeated efforts to transform the international trading and norm-setting environments, which had attained only limited success. Worse still, just before the launch of the Uruguay Round negotiations, some developing countries, such as those in Latin America, were confronted with major economic crises that had greatly weakened their ability to oppose the developed countries' demands for new international trade and intellectual property standards. As Professor Sell observes: "[T]he economic slump of the late 1970s and early 1980s […] was the strongest shock to the optimism of the Group of 77's member states. Not only did it take the wind out [of] their sails, but it led them to abandon the whole ship."[44]

In assessing the developing countries' negotiating positions in the Uruguay Round, one also needs to keep in mind what a key TRIPS negotiator recounted as the "background music of the peaceful revolutions in Eastern Europe and elsewhere and the impression that we were entering a new era of international cooperation."[45] The years 1989 and 1990, during which major breakthroughs occurred in the TRIPS negotiations, were historically significant.

Meanwhile, the developed countries' experiences were the direct opposite of those of developing countries. The former encountered highly favourable negotiating conditions both in international fora and on domestic soil. With the election of President Ronald Reagan in the United States and Prime Minister Margaret Thatcher in the United

Negotiations on a Draft Code of Conduct (The Hague: Kluwer Law International, 2001); Sell, *supra* note 17 at 79–106; Peter K Yu, "International Technology Contracts, Restrictive Covenants and the UNCTAD Code" in Christopher Heath & Anselm Kamperman Sanders, eds, *Employees, Trade Secrets and Restrictive Covenants* (Alphen aan den Rijn: Kluwer Law International, 2017).

43   Pedro Roffe & Gina Vea, "The WIPO Development Agenda in an Historical and Political Context" in Neil Weinstock Netanel, ed, *The Development Agenda: Global Intellectual Property and Developing Countries* (Oxford: Oxford University Press, 2009); Yu, *supra* note 16 at 505–11.

44   Sell, *supra* note 17 at 106.

45   Mogens Peter Carl, "Evaluating the TRIPS Negotiations: A Plea for a Substantial Review of the Agreement" in Watal & Taubman, *supra* note 11 at 105; Antonio Gustavo Trombetta, "Negotiating for Argentina" in Watal & Taubman, *supra* note 11 at 261.

Kingdom, these countries became more aggressive in pushing for a neoliberal international economic order. At that time, developed country governments also paid renewed attention to the protection of intellectual property rights.

Consider the United States, for example. The US Court of Appeals for the Federal Circuit was established in 1982. [46] Congress also actively enacted laws to support the development of the computer industry, including most notably the *Semiconductor Chip Protection Act of 1984*. In addition, in 1988, Congress enacted the *Omnibus Trade and Competitiveness Act*, which added the Special 301 process to the *Trade Act of 1974*, thereby enabling trade lobbies to have a louder voice in US intellectual property policy. [47]

Around that time, politicians and academic commentators began to use the changing US economy to justify greater protection of intellectual property rights. For instance, in the mid-1980s, Gerald Mossinghoff, then US Commissioner of Patents and Trademarks, "delivered a strong statement outlining the relationship between patents, trademarks, and international trade." [48] As the *TRIPS Agreement* was about to take effect, Thomas McCarthy, the author of the leading treatise on US trademark law, also labelled intellectual property as "America's overlooked export." [49] As he declared: "The rest of the world does not want to buy American cars or steel in the quantities purchased in years past. The world does want, however, to buy our computer programs, our movie and television entertainment and our high-tech information." [50]

Taken together, these three notable differences in the international norm-setting environment have revealed how dramatically the negotiating landscape at the WTO has changed since the adoption of the *TRIPS Agreement*. To the extent that the favourable conditions surrounding the international norm-setting environment have contributed to the successful negotiation of the *TRIPS Agreement*, the absence of those conditions may cast doubt on whether that same agreement would be adopted if it were negotiated today.

---

46   For comparison, the UK Patents Court was also established around that time—in 1980.

47   Michael P Ryan, *Playing by the Rules: American Trade Power and Diplomacy in the Pacific* (Washington, DC: Georgetown University Press, 1995); Peter K Yu, "From Pirates to Partners: Protecting Intellectual Property in China in the Twenty-First Century" (2000) 50 American University Law Review 131 at 139–40.

48   Sell, *supra* note 26 at 83.

49   J Thomas McCarthy, "Intellectual Property—America's Overlooked Export" (1995) 20 University of Dayton Law Review 809 at 809.

50   *Ibid* at 811.

Will the *TRIPS Agreement* Undergo a Major Overhaul in the Future?

A follow-up question that sheds light on the future of the *TRIPS Agreement* concerns whether WTO members will undertake a major overhaul in the future. The lack of negotiation breakthroughs in the Doha Round in the past decade and the developed countries' refusal to support the developing countries' proposal to waive a substantial portion of TRIPS obligations to combat the COVID-19 pandemic hints at a negative answer. The three notable changes in the international norm-setting environment discussed in the previous section also suggest a more limited momentum for setting new international intellectual property norms at the WTO. Nevertheless, there are at least four reasons why WTO members may still be willing to extensively revise the *TRIPS Agreement* in the future — perhaps not immediately but possibly down the road.

To begin with, the development of new international intellectual property standards has not slowed down — whether at the World Intellectual Property Organization (WIPO) or at the bilateral, regional, or plurilateral level. Two years after the completion of the *TRIPS Agreement* in 1994, WIPO quickly adopted the *WIPO Copyright Treaty* and the *WIPO Performances and Phonograms Treaty*. Although international norm-setting efforts at this intergovernmental body stalled for years when developing countries were actively pushing for the establishment of the WIPO Development Agenda, WIPO members adopted the *Beijing Treaty on Audiovisual Performances* in June 2012, the *Marrakesh Treaty to Facilitate Access to Published Works for Persons Who Are Blind, Visually Impaired or Otherwise Print Disabled* in June 2013, and the *Geneva Act* of the *Lisbon Agreement for the Protection of Appellations of Origin and Their International Registration* in May 2015. More recently, WIPO members adopted the *WIPO Treaty on Intellectual Property, Genetic Resources and Associated Traditional Knowledge* in May 2024.[51] Six months later, they also established the *Riyadh Design Law Treaty* in Saudi Arabia.

At the non-multilateral level, the past two decades have seen countries actively negotiating bilateral and regional trade agreements. Contained in these agreements are intellectual property chapters filled with a wide array of provisions governing the protection and enforcement of intellectual property rights, including those that do not exist

---

51   Peter K Yu, "WIPO Negotiations on Intellectual Property, Genetic Resources and Associated Traditional Knowledge" (2024) 57 Akron Law Review 277.

in the *TRIPS Agreement* or are not covered by the agreement.[52] Many countries—whether developed or emerging—have also worked closely with likeminded partners to establish plurilateral agreements, such as the *Anti-Counterfeiting Trade Agreement*, the *Trans-Pacific Partnership (TPP) Agreement*, and the *Regional Comprehensive Economic Partnership (RCEP) Agreement*.

With all these new standards being developed at both the multi-lateral and non-multilateral levels, it is not far-fetched to assume that countries will eventually become eager to bring some of these non-TRIPS commitments into the WTO through an extensive revision of the *TRIPS Agreement*. After all, the *TRIPS Agreement* remains the only major mul-tilateral intellectual property instrument whose provisions are subject to a mandatory dispute settlement process, which many policymakers and commentators have considered one of the WTO's crowning achieve-ments.[53] The history of international intellectual property agreements has also seen repeated efforts to consolidate international standards following decades of independent developments.[54] The *Paris Convention*, the *Berne Convention*, and the *TRIPS Agreement* are all textbook examples of these consolidation efforts.

The second reason concerns the WTO's past track record. Thus far, this international trading body has less success in amending its found-ing agreements (including the *TRIPS Agreement*) than developing new plurilateral trade agreements, such as the *Agreement on Trade in Civil Aircraft* and the *Agreement on Government Procurement*.[55] Notwithstanding this limited success, the *TRIPS Agreement* remains one of the few WTO agreements that has ever been amended. In fact, this agreement is the first to be amended and also the only to have been amended

---

52   Yu, *supra* note 6 at 866–70.

53   Rachel Brewster, "Shadow Unilateralism: Enforcing International Trade Law at the WTO" (2009) 30 University of Pennsylvania Journal of International Law 1133 at 1134; William J Davey, "The WTO Dispute Settlement System: The First Ten Years" (2005) 8 Journal of International Economic Law 17 at 32; Rochelle C Dreyfuss & Andreas F Lowenfeld, "Two Achievements of the Uruguay Round: Putting TRIPS and Dispute Settlement Together" (1997) 37 Virginia Journal of International Law 275 at 275; Ruth Okediji, "Toward an International Fair Use Doctrine" (2000) 39 Columbia Journal of Transnational Law 75 at 149–50.

54   Sungjoon Cho, "A Bridge Too Far: The Fall of the Fifth WTO Ministerial Conference in Cancun and the Future of Trade Constitution" (2004) 7 Journal of International Economic Law 219 at 238; Ruth L Okediji, "Back to Bilateralism? Pendulum Swings in International Intellectual Property Protection" (2004) 1 University of Ottawa Law and Technology Journal 125 at 143.

55   World Trade Organization, *Status of WTO Legal Instruments: 2021 Edition* (Geneva: World Trade Organization, 2021) at 11–12.

substantively, as opposed to procedurally. [56] As the WTO recounted in the 2021 edition of *Status of WTO Legal Instruments*:

> As of the cut-off date of this publication, three multilateral amendments have been adopted pursuant to this Article: the 2005 Protocol Amending the TRIPS Agreement, which entered into force on 23 January 2017; the 2014 Protocol Amending the WTO Agreement to insert the Agreement on Trade Facilitation into Annex 1A of the WTO Agreement, which entered into force on 22 February 2017; and the General Council decision amending the review periods set forth in paragraph C(ii) of the Trade Policy Review Mechanism as of 1 January 2019. [57]

In December 2005, WTO members adopted a protocol to amend the *TRIPS Agreement* to allow members with insufficient or no manufacturing capacity to import generic versions of patented pharmaceuticals. This amendment, which eventually became the new Article 31*bis* of the *TRIPS Agreement*, implemented the consensus reached at the beginning of the Doha Round. Although the ratification process took more than a decade, the amendment finally entered into effect in January 2017, after two-thirds of the WTO membership had ratified the instrument.

During the COVID-19 pandemic, WTO members also managed to reach the *Ministerial Decision on the TRIPS Agreement*, which called for a pandemic-related waiver of Article 31(f) of the *TRIPS Agreement*. [58] Although this decision was temporary and very narrow in scope—and its provisions were very far away from the waiver proposed by India and South Africa—the ministerial decision still indicates the WTO members' willingness to revise TRIPS standards. It remains to be seen, however, whether these members are open to a more extensive revision of the *TRIPS Agreement*, including a major overhaul.

The third reason pertains to the rise of emerging countries discussed above. The previous section has already explored how their rise, changing policy positions, and shifting alliances have upset the coalition dynamics within the WTO, WIPO, and other intergovernmental bodies. The rise of emerging countries has therefore undermined the developing countries' collective resistance to high international intellectual

---

56   *Ibid* at 11.

57   *Ibid*.

58   World Trade Organization, "Ministerial Decision on the TRIPS Agreement" WTO Doc WT/MIN(22)/30 (22 June 2022).

property standards while making international norm-setting efforts more complex and less predictable.[59]

Interestingly, the emerging countries' willingness to align their negotiating positions with those of developed countries suggests the growing possibility for these two groups of countries to use their shared interests to form common negotiating positions. Such cooperation will be instrumental in shaping the next generation of international intellectual property standards.

To be sure, the consensuses reached by these two groups of countries may ignore the needs of the remaining WTO members, especially small developing and least developed countries. What works well for China, the European Union, and the United States is unlikely to work well for Ethiopia, Madagascar, and Rwanda. Nevertheless, considering the developed countries' tendency to be more concerned about competition and trade diversion from emerging countries than from other less economically developed WTO members, the remaining developing countries might be able to revive special and differential treatment as part of a compromise. Although developed countries, most notably the United States, have been pushing hard to curtail the extension of such treatment to developing countries,[60] the former might be more willing to do so if the revived treatment would not benefit emerging countries and were merely adopted as a package deal to facilitate the adoption of new TRIPS standards.[61]

A good analogy is the developed countries' limited resistance to the least developed countries' requests for extending the TRIPS transition period. Past negotiations surrounding these requests have focused primarily on issues relating to the duration and permanency of the extension and the rollback of domestic laws that have already been enacted to implement higher TRIPS standards.[62] By comparison, there was very little debate about whether the extension should be

---

59   Yu, "Access to Medicines," *supra* note 30 at 371–72; Yu, "Caught in the Middle," *supra* note 3 at 368.

60   Sangeeta Shashikant, "Intense IP Negotiations Are Underway, Resolution on Eligibility Criteria Outstanding" (*TWN Info Service on Health Issues*, 16 June 2022), online: https://www.twn.my/title2/health.info/2022/hi220609.htm.

61   Henry Gao, "WTO Reform and China: Defining or Defiling the Multilateral Trading System?" (2021) 62 Harvard International Law Journal (Special Issue) 1 at 23.

62   Yu, *supra* note 7 at 151 n 6; Arno Hold & Bryan Christopher Mercurio, "After the Second Extension of the Transition Period for LDCs: How Can the WTO Gradually Integrate the Poorest Countries into TRIPS?" (2013) NCCR Trade Regulation, World Trade Institute, Working Paper No 2013/42.

granted in the first place. Most WTO members seemed to have been convinced—whether with open acknowledgement or not—that TRIPS standards were too high for the world's poorest countries. Many developed and emerging countries also recognize that their nationals and firms had not actively sought markets or intellectual property rights in least developed countries.[63] The choice of developed and emerging countries to support the least developed countries' extension requests was therefore low-cost, if not cost-free.

Finally, a range of new issues have now garnered the attention of WTO members. These issues include internet platforms, cybersecurity, digital trade, transborder data flows, and artificial intelligence.[64] Instead of falling neatly on either side of the North–South divide, virtually all these issues are global and therefore important to all WTO members. As Antony Taubman, the former director of the WTO Intellectual Property, Government Procurement and Competition Division, declares in his book on trade in knowledge, the changing technological environment is now "forcing a rethink of what constitutes the 'trade-related' aspects of [intellectual property]."[65] That exact question was also intensely debated at the beginning of the TRIPS negotiations more than three decades ago.[66]

Rethinking what constitutes the "trade-related" aspects of intellectual property is particularly important today considering that the *TRIPS Agreement* was already outdated in select areas at the time of its adoption.[67] In April 1994, the internet was about to enter the mainstream. Yet this agreement did not include provisions targeting online activities.[68] The lack of such provisions paved the way for the negotiation of two internet-related treaties at WIPO two short years after the adoption of the *TRIPS Agreement*.

---

63   Yu, *supra* note 6 at 841.
64   Antony Taubman & Jayashree Watal, eds, *Trade in Knowledge: Intellectual Property, Trade and Development in a Transformed Global Economy* (Cambridge: Cambridge University Press, 2022).
65   Antony Taubman, "The Shifting Contours of Trade in Knowledge: The New 'Trade-Related Aspects' of Intellectual Property" in Taubman & Watal, *supra* note 64 at 28.
66   Yu, *supra* note 20 at 984–89.
67   Yu, *supra* note 7 at 165–73.
68   David Fitzpatrick, "Negotiating for Hong Kong" in Watal & Taubman, *supra* note 11 at 287; Marci A Hamilton, "The TRIPS Agreement: Imperialistic, Outdated, and Overprotective" (1996) 29 Vanderbilt Journal of Transnational Law 613 at 614–15; Jagdish Sagar, "Copyright: An Indian Perspective" in Watal & Taubman, *supra* note 11 at 347; Antony Taubman, "Thematic Review: Negotiating 'Trade-Related Aspects' of Intellectual Property Rights" in Watal & Taubman, *supra* note 11 at 19–20.

The *TRIPS Agreement* has also given short shrift to breakthroughs in biotechnology while overestimating the future importance of intellectual property norms relating to layout designs of integrated circuits. [69] As far as I know, the latter form of protection has not been the subject of any negotiation at the bilateral, regional, or plurilateral level in the past two decades. By contrast, the standards for protecting undisclosed test or other data submitted for the regulatory approval of biological products were heavily debated during the negotiations for both the *TPP Agreement* and the *Canada–United States–Mexico Agreement*. [70]

Moreover, with the painful lessons drawn from the COVID-19 pandemic, there are now growing concerns about whether the existing international intellectual property system, including the *TRIPS Agreement*, is ready for the next pandemic. [71] Many medical and public health experts have already predicted that another global pandemic will happen in the next decade or two. [72] Because in a global health crisis no one is safe until everyone is safe, WTO members may become more eager to explore whether, and how, the *TRIPS Agreement* could be pre-emptively adjusted to prepare for the next pandemic. [73]

In sum, several reasons exist to suggest that WTO members might still be open to an extensive revision of the *TRIPS Agreement* when the time is right. The difficult question is not whether these members will undertake such a revision, but how soon they will do so and how extensively they will be willing to revise this agreement.

---

69   Trombetta, *supra* note 45 at 260; Yu, *supra* note 7 at 168.

70   Frederick M Abbott, "The Evolution of Public Health Provisions in Preferential Trade and Investment Agreements of the United States" in Pedro Roffe & Xavier Seuba, eds, *Current Alliances in International Intellectual Property Lawmaking: The Emergence and Impact of Mega-Regionals* (Geneva and Strasbourg: International Centre for Trade and Sustainable Development and Centre for International Intellectual Property Studies, 2017) at 55; Peter K Yu, "China's Innovative Turn and the Changing Pharmaceutical Landscape" (2020) 51 University of the Pacific Law Review 593 at 606–07.

71   Sun & Sunder, *supra* note 38; Peter K Yu, "Deferring Intellectual Property Rights in Pandemic Times" (2023) 74 Hastings Law Journal 489.

72   Stefan Elbe, *Pandemics, Pills, and Politics: Governing Global Health Security* (Baltimore: Johns Hopkins University Press, 2018) at 34; Sonia Shah, *Pandemic: Tracking Contagions, from Cholera to Ebola and Beyond* (New York: Farrar, Straus and Giroux, 2016) at 8.

73   To improve the *TRIPS Agreement*'s pandemic preparedness, I have advanced a proposal for deferring intellectual property rights in times of global crises. Yu, *supra* note 71 at 533–39.

Possible Options for Updating the *TRIPS Agreement* without a Major Overhaul

Under WTO rules, any proposed amendment, or amendments, to the *TRIPS Agreement* will not be adopted until it has been ratified by two-thirds of the membership. To make the amendment process even more difficult, decisions in the WTO are reached by consensus. Thus, to the extent that WTO members, especially the powerful ones, are not ready to undertake a major overhaul of the *TRIPS Agreement* in the immediate future, it will be constructive to explore what WTO members could, or should, do in the meantime.

This chapter advances three recommendations: (1) the institution of a periodic review mechanism; (2) the broadening of the focus of the *TRIPS Agreement* to cover other areas of innovation; and (3) greater regulatory coordination with other instruments relating to intellectual property protection and with the relevant intergovernmental bodies. These recommendations seek to update the *TRIPS Agreement* even when WTO members could not agree on a major overhaul. Because this agreement can benefit from reforms targeting different aspects of the agreement and the larger international trading body, this chapter anticipates that the proposed recommendations will complement many proposals that policymakers and other commentators have advanced to improve this agreement.

Article 68 of the *TRIPS Agreement* mandates the establishment of the TRIPS Council to "monitor the operation of this Agreement and, in particular, Members' compliance with their obligations hereunder, and [to] afford Members the opportunity of consulting on matters relating to the trade-related aspects of intellectual property rights." Although the TRIPS Council has met periodically and has handled issues such as treaty compliance, intellectual property enforcement, and the global pandemic response,[74] its structure was not designed to facilitate the periodic review and revision of the *TRIPS Agreement*.[75] Indeed, during the Uruguay Round negotiations, the amendment process has been made intentionally difficult, due in part to the WTO members' reluctance to reopen completed negotiations.

Without prejudice to the important work being done by the TRIPS Council, this chapter calls for instituting a periodic review mechanism

---

74   Yu, *supra* note 2 at 329–32; Yu, *supra* note 71 at 512–21; Peter K Yu, "TRIPS and Its Achilles' Heel" (2011) 18 Journal of Intellectual Property Law 479 at 505–08, 514–15, 518–21.

75   Matthews, *supra* note 22 at 79–83.

by convening a committee, or committees, of experts to be nominated by WTO members, similar to the committees of experts that used to be established at WIPO and its predecessor, the United International Bureau for the Protection of Intellectual Property (BIRPI).[76] The periodic convening of a committee, or committees, of experts will help evaluate the need and urgency for updating the *TRIPS Agreement*. Until the late 1960s and the early 1970s, the *Paris* and *Berne Conventions* were amended about every decade or two. The *Paris Convention* was revised in 1900, 1911, 1925, 1934, 1958, and 1967, while the *Berne Convention* was revised in 1908, 1928, 1948, 1967, and 1971. These successful revisions suggest the feasibility and advisability of reviewing the *TRIPS Agreement* every two decades or so.

To the extent that WTO members want to follow WIPO's lead in establishing standing committees that are tailored to specific forms of intellectual property rights, or a combination thereof, this proposed periodic review mechanism can be slightly modified to accommodate similar organizational structures. At the moment, WIPO has the Standing Committee on Copyright and Related Rights, the Standing Committee on the Law of Patents, the Standing Committee on the Law of Trademarks, Industrial Designs and Geographical Indications, the Intergovernmental Committee on Intellectual Property and Genetic Resources, Traditional Knowledge and Folklore, the Advisory Committee on Enforcement, and the Committee on Development and Intellectual Property, among others. With at least eight forms of intellectual property rights enshrined in the *TRIPS Agreement*,[77] similar committees could easily be set up at the WTO to help address issues relating to these rights as well as intellectual property enforcement and dispute settlement.

The second recommendation concerns the need for WTO members to broaden the focus of the *TRIPS Agreement* to cover innovation in general, as opposed to only intellectual property protection and enforcement. The need for such broadened coverage should be proactively instilled in the mind of not only the WTO membership but also the bodies

---

76   Carolyn Deere Birkbeck, *The World Intellectual Property Organization (WIPO): A Reference Guide* (Cheltenham: Edward Elgar Publishing, 2016) at 76–80.

77   Peter K Yu, "Teaching International Intellectual Property Law" (2008) 52 Saint Louis University Law Journal 923 at 930–31. These eight forms of intellectual property rights are copyrights, patents, trade marks, geographical indications, industrial designs, plant variety protection, layout designs of integrated circuits, and the protection of undisclosed information (which includes both trade secrets and other forms of undisclosed information).

administering and interpreting the *TRIPS Agreement*—namely, the TRIPS Council and the WTO Dispute Settlement Body. If the coverage cannot be significantly broadened, this agreement should at least engage with issues lying at the intersection of intellectual property rights and other areas of innovation. Even better, the broadened coverage could be achieved without revising the *TRIPS Agreement*. In lieu of a revision, this agreement could be broadly interpreted through the TRIPS Council and WTO panels—and, if revived, also the WTO Appellate Body.

There are several justifications for a broadened TRIPS coverage. Many areas of innovation now require protections beyond the eight forms of intellectual property rights explicitly covered in the *TRIPS Agreement*. Although WTO members have been engaging in norm-setting efforts outside the TRIPS context within the international trading body, such as those in the areas of electronic commerce and digital trade, [78] the mismatch between the *TRIPS Agreement* and the technological environment has grown significantly since the mid-1990s. As Daniel Gervais recalls, "TRIPS adjusted the level of intellectual property protection to what was the highest common denominator among major industrialized countries as of 1991," [79] not to mention the earlier discussion of how the agreement has overlooked the important changes brought about by the internet and biotechnology. Even worse, in the WTO's close to 30 years of existence, members have only slightly revised the *TRIPS Agreement* once—in the area of compulsory licensing for pharmaceutical products. This agreement is therefore in desperate need of a technological update.

A greater exploration of innovation in the trade-related context is also timely and urgent because policymakers and commentators have now actively embraced the use and development of alternative incentive frameworks. Examples of these frameworks include "grants, subsidies, prizes, advance market commitments, reputation gains, [and] open source drug discovery." [80] In addition, many developing

---

78   Mira Burri, *Should There Be New Multilateral Rules for Digital Trade?* (Geneva: International Centre for Trade and Sustainable Development and World Economic Forum, 2013); Anupam Chander & Paul Schwartz, "Privacy and/or Trade" (2023) 90 University of Chicago Law Review 49; Peter K Yu, "Fitting Machine-Generated Data into Trade Regulatory Holes" in Taubman & Watal, *supra* note 64 at 741; Peter K Yu, "The RCEP and Trans-Pacific Intellectual Property Norms" (2017) 50 Vanderbilt Journal of Transnational Law 706 ["RCEP and Trans-Pacific Norms"].

79   Daniel J Gervais, "The TRIPS Agreement and the Doha Round: History and Impact on Economic Development" in Peter K Yu, ed, *Intellectual Property and Information Wealth: Issues and Practices in the Digital Age*, vol 4 (Westport: Praeger Publishers, 2007) at 43.

80   Peter K Yu, "The Anatomy of the Human Rights Framework for Intellectual Property" (2016) 69 SMU Law Review 37 at 63.

countries and commentators have pioneered new forms of innovation, such as "frugal," "reverse," or "trickle-up" innovation.[81] Thus, if the *TRIPS Agreement* is to stay relevant to ongoing creative and innovative activities, it will need to adopt a much broader focus. The TRIPS Council and the WTO Dispute Settlement Body should therefore pay greater attention to developments in other areas of innovation and to their impacts on the operation, effectiveness, and continued vitality of the *TRIPS Agreement*.

One interesting question concerns whether the WTO Dispute Settlement Body's narrow interpretation of the *TRIPS Agreement* can be attributed to the *Vienna Convention on the Law of Treaties* (*Vienna Convention*)—and, if so, whether this convention should be amended and whether WTO panels and the Appellate Body should modify its current application in the TRIPS context.[82] While the amendment of the *Vienna Convention* is admittedly outside the scope of this chapter and will require consideration of its impacts on other areas of international law, nothing in the Convention would prevent the WTO Dispute Settlement Body from recognizing that the *TRIPS Agreement* cannot be "read in clinical isolation from public international law," a position taken by the Appellate Body in *United States—Standards for Reformulated and Conventional Gasoline* a year after the formation of the WTO.[83] This position is shared by academic commentators.[84] As Joost Pauwelyn declares, "a defendant should be allowed to invoke non-WTO rules as a justification for breach of WTO rules, even if the WTO treaty itself does not offer such justification (say, with respect to human rights)."[85]

81   World Intellectual Property Organization, *2011 World Intellectual Property Report* (Geneva: World Intellectual Property Organization, 2011) at 40.

82   Thanks to Rochelle Dreyfuss for encouraging the Author to consider this question. On the use of the *Vienna Convention* in TRIPS disputes, see Susy Frankel, "WTO Application of 'the Customary Rules of Interpretation of Public International Law' to Intellectual Property" (2006) 46 Virginia Journal of International Law 365 at 384–90; Daya Shanker, "The Vienna Convention on the Law of Treaties, the Dispute Settlement System of the WTO and the Doha Declaration on the TRIPs Agreement" (2002) 36 Journal of World Trade 721 at 723–36.

83   World Trade Organization, "United States—Standards for Reformulated and Conventional Gasoline: Report of the Appellate Body" WTO Doc WT/DS2/AB/R (29 April 1996) pt III.B.

84   Daniel Gervais & Peter K Yu, "TRIPS and the Tradification of Intellectual Property" in David Collins & Valentina Vadi, eds, *Routledge Handbook on International Economic Law* (Abingdon: Routledge, 2025); Joost Pauwelyn, "The Role of Public International Law in the WTO: How Far Can We Go?" (2001) 95 American Journal of International Law 535 at 577.

85   Pauwelyn, *supra* note 84 at 577.

The final recommendation pertains to the need for the *TRIPS Agreement* to undertake greater regulatory coordination with instruments relating to intellectual property protection and with the relevant intergovernmental bodies. The previous section has already listed many new agreements developed at WIPO following the adoption of the *TRIPS Agreement*. There are also many related agreements outside both the WTO and WIPO, such as the *Convention on Biological Diversity* and its *Nagoya Protocol on Access to Genetic Resources and the Fair and Equitable Sharing of Benefits Arising from Their Utilization*,[86] the *International Treaty on Plant Genetic Resources for Food and Agriculture* of the UN Food and Agriculture Organization, the *Pandemic Influenza Preparedness Framework* of the World Health Organization (WHO), and the newly adopted *WHO Pandemic Agreement*.

In addition, the past two decades have seen the emergence of many bilateral, regional, and plurilateral trade agreements.[87] Immediately coming to mind are the *TPP* and *RCEP Agreements* mentioned above. Following the United States' withdrawal, the former evolved into the *Comprehensive and Progressive Agreement for Trans-Pacific Partnership* (CPTPP), which entered into force in December 2018. Covering the 10-country Association of Southeast Asian Nations (ASEAN) and its five trading neighbours (Australia, China, Japan, New Zealand, and South Korea), the *RCEP Agreement* also entered into effect in January 2021.[88] While these two agreements do not directly conflict with the *TRIPS Agreement*,[89] due to the fact that they aimed to raise international intellectual property standards beyond TRIPS requirements, it could be quite helpful to foster greater regulatory

---

86   The *Convention on Biological Diversity* was adopted in June 1992, about two years before the conclusion of the *TRIPS Agreement*. Nevertheless, at the time of writing, the latter "has yet to develop an explicit relationship with the [former], other than to mention plants, plant varieties, and biological and microbiological processes in article 27(3)(b). Yu, *supra* note 16 at 531. Paragraph 19 of the *Doha Ministerial Declaration* did instruct the TRIPS Council "to examine [...] the relationship between the TRIPS Agreement and the Convention on Biological Diversity [and] the protection of traditional knowledge and folklore."

87   Peter K Yu, "The Non-Multilateral Approach to International Intellectual Property Normsetting" in Daniel J Gervais, ed, *International Intellectual Property: A Handbook of Contemporary Research* (Cheltenham: Edward Elgar Publishing, 2015).

88   India was originally part of the RCEP negotiations. It withdrew in November 2019, a year before the agreement's completion.

89   Yu, "RCEP and Trans-Pacific Norms," *supra* note 78 at 691; Peter K Yu, "TPP, RCEP and the Future of Copyright Norm-setting in the Asian Pacific" in Susan Corbett & Jessica C Lai, eds, *Making Copyright Work for the Asian Pacific: Juxtaposing Harmonisation with Flexibility* (Canberra: ANU Press, 2018) at 42–45.

coordination between the *TRIPS Agreement* and the intellectual property chapters in these agreements as well as in other bilateral, regional, and plurilateral trade agreements.

To the extent that countries are eager to maintain the vitality of the multilateral trading system, greater regulatory coordination could also help ensure the active and expanded use of this system. The need to strengthen multilateralism has never been more important considering that WTO members have now been deeply affected by the economic fallout caused by the COVID-19 pandemic, the US–China trade war, and other disruptions to the global supply chain, such as the ongoing Russo–Ukrainian war.[90] In the past few years, policymakers and commentators have begun actively exploring whether countries, in the near future, should refocus their norm-setting efforts on regional arrangements, as opposed to multilateral agreements.[91]

As if these justifications were not strong enough, the WTO has actively and effectively collaborated with other intergovernmental bodies during the COVID-19 pandemic, thereby suggesting the feasibility of greater regulatory coordination between these bodies. For instance, the WTO collaborated with WIPO and the WHO to release a revised trilateral study on access to medical technologies and innovation.[92] In December 2022, these three intergovernmental bodies also held a joint technical symposium to "examine the challenges of the COVID-19 pandemic and discuss possible ways forward within the health, [intellectual property] and trade frameworks."[93] In addition, the WTO worked together with the International Monetary Fund (IMF) to develop the WTO–IMF COVID-19 Vaccine Trade Tracker,[94] which provided a

90   Peter K Yu, "War and IP" (2024) 49 BYU Law Review 823.

91   Yu, "Vaccine Development," *supra* note 38 at 780; "Council of Councils Thirteenth Regional Conference: Insights from a Council of Councils Conference" (*Council on Foreign Relations*, 5 January 2023), online: https://www.cfr.org/report/council-councils-thirteenth-regional-conference, accessed 20 May 2024.

92   World Health Organization, World Intellectual Property Organization & World Trade Organization, *Promoting Access to Medical Technologies and Innovation: Intersections between Public Health, Intellectual Property and Trade*, 2nd ed (Geneva: World Health Organization, World Intellectual Property Organization & World Trade Organization, 2020).

93   World Health Organization, World Intellectual Property Organization & World Trade Organization, "WHO, WIPO, WTO Joint Technical Symposium on the COVID-19 Pandemic: Response, Preparedness, Resilience," online: https://www.wipo.int/meetings/en/2022/wipo-wto-who-technical-symposium.html, accessed 20 May 2024.

94   International Monetary Fund & World Health Organization, "IMF-WHO COVID-19 Vaccine Tracker," online: https://www.imf.org/en/Topics/imf-and-covid19/IMF-WHO-COVID-19-Vaccine-Tracker, accessed 20 May 2024.

helpful tool for determining whether developing countries were eligible to take advantage of the special arrangements developed through the *Ministerial Decision on the TRIPS Agreement*.[95] In short, there are strong precedents for the WTO to undertake greater regulatory coordination with other instruments relating to intellectual property protection and with the relevant intergovernmental bodies.

Conclusion

Counterfactuals and future predictions present inherent challenges, yet they also provide useful insights. Exploring the first question of whether the *TRIPS Agreement* would be adopted if it were negotiated today helps shed light on the second question concerning whether WTO members would be willing to undertake a major overhaul of the agreement in the future. Answering the second question, in turn, reveals the answers to the third question concerning what options WTO members would have for updating this agreement if they could not reach a consensus on a major overhaul.

The current version of the *TRIPS Agreement* is badly outdated in the age of Big Data and generative artificial intelligence. The past century of international intellectual property norm-setting has also shown that the current version is unlikely to be permanent if the agreement is to have the longevity of the *Paris Convention*, the *Berne Convention*, or other longstanding international intellectual property agreements. Nevertheless, because of the different—and, at times, conflicting—positions taken by WTO members, it may be a while before these members could agree to a major overhaul of the *TRIPS Agreement*.

To help update this agreement, this chapter advances three recommendations that WTO members could implement without an extensive revision: (1) the institution of a periodic review mechanism; (2) the broadening of the focus of the *TRIPS Agreement* to cover other areas of innovation; and (3) greater regulatory coordination with other instruments relating to intellectual property protection and with the relevant intergovernmental bodies. It is my hope that these recommendations will help update TRIPS standards while ensuring that the updated standards will better meet the current economic and technological needs of WTO members, regardless of their level of development.

---

95   World Trade Organization, *supra* note 58 at para 1 n1.

Part II
CANADIAN INTELLECTUAL PROPERTY LAW

Putting Copyright in Its Place: How Copyright History Can Help Chart the Future of the Global IP System

Myra Tawfik and Sara Bannerman

Abstract

In this chapter, the authors rely on the lessons from Canada's copyright history to examine some of the assumptions underlying the international copyright system today. More specifically, they draw from Canada's past to question whether copyright has ever fulfilled its stated policy goals at both domestic and international levels. They suggest that the international copyright system has largely been shaped by privilege and power and interrogate the role Canada has played in influencing outcomes. Finally, they suggest that copyright should be studied through a variety of multidisciplinary lenses to highlight the power disparities that exclude certain creators and creative communities from full participation.[1]

W e are at a crucial period of change in copyright law brought about, in large part, because of new technologies like generative artificial intelligence (AI).[2] In our view, addressing the challenges of the

---

1   This chapter is based on a presentation given by the authors in the form of a conversation on copyright history at the hybrid Conference *The Future of the Global IP System*, June 28–30, 2023, University of British Columbia. The authors would like to thank Charnjot Shokar for his research support in this chapter.

2   See, e.g., the Government of Canada's current consultation on the copyright implications of generative AI: https://www.canada.ca/en/innovation-science-economic-development/news/2023/10/government-of-canada-launches-consultation-on-the-

future of copyright requires revisiting the past, but a past retold from multiple vantage points. In this chapter, we offer some lessons from Canada's copyright history to inform discussions about copyright's present and its future.

The history of Canadian copyright law has only recently begun to be studied. For a long time, the assumption was that Canada's copyright history was effectively British or Imperial history — that Canada had no copyright history of its own. However, recent scholarship that focuses specifically on the Canadian experience tells a very different story.[3] This chapter does not propose to revisit Canada's copyright history in its entirety. Instead, it will focus on Canada's experience as it relates to specific issues of importance today. Indeed, Canada's copyright history can not only serve as a prism through which to interrogate this country's current domestic and international policy — it also offers sobering lessons about whether copyright, as currently constructed, can meet the challenges of new disruptive technologies or the demands of equity and inclusion.

We first examine Canada's pre-Confederation and pre-copyright systems, illustrating that there were significant changes in how creative and educational materials were governed in the nineteenth century. We caution that the introduction of copyright legislation in the first decades of the nineteenth century should not be viewed as obvious "progress" or a step forward from the previous system of individual petitions to the legislature. The lesson here is that copyright policy may not match copyright in practice.

We then examine the period following 1842, when Imperial copyright law, and then international copyright law, began to be imposed on Canada. We discuss the lost opportunities for innovative change in copyright as Canada's ambitions were thwarted by its colonial status. The lesson here is that the most powerful countries control the copyright

---

implications-of-generative-artificial-intelligence-for-copyright.html

3   Myra Tawfik, *For the Encouragement of Learning: The Origins of Canadian Copyright Law* (Toronto: University of Toronto Press, 2023); Sara Bannerman, *The Struggle for Canadian Copyright: Imperialism to Internationalism, 1842-1971* (Vancouver: UBC Press, 2013); Eli MacLaren, *Dominion and Agency* (Toronto: University of Toronto Press, 2011); Meera Nair, "The Geopolitics of Nineteenth-Century Canadian Copyright, as seen by some British Authors" (2017) 55:2 Pap Bibliogr Soc Can 245–270; Meera Nair, "The Copyright Act of 1889: A Canadian Declaration of Independence" (2009) 90:1 Can Hist Rev 1–28; Pierre-Emmanuel Moyse, "Canadian Colonial Copyright: The Colony Strikes Back" in Ysolde Gendreau, ed, *An Emerging Intellectual Property Paradigm: Perspectives from Canada* (Cheltenham: Edward Elgar Publishing, 2008) at 107–138.

agenda. Different and dissenting voices have little to no influence on policy outcomes.

Third, we ask whether change is possible from within the international copyright system. Here, we examine moments when Canada, as a member of the Berne Convention, was the most influential. However, there were also many instances when Canada fell short in its aspirations. The lesson here is that less powerful countries, on their own, cannot displace the dominant policy. However, allied individuals, networks, and collaborations can make a difference.

Finally, we ask what research methods and theoretical approaches can best advance a more inclusive and fair global copyright system. Rather than relying on traditional methods of interrogating the law, we suggest that alternative ways of examining copyright's history and development could provide a more robust approach to setting current domestic and international copyright policy, policies that fully integrate the interests of middle powers, emerging economies, and equity-seeking groups and communities. The lesson here is that copyright must be studied in a multitude of ways and from different perspectives, not only to highlight its successes but to expose its fault lines as well.

Paradigm Shifts: From the Petition System to the Copyright System[4]

Prior to the introduction of copyright statutes in British North America there existed an alternative to copyright—a moment in history when copyright was not the main way of encouraging or rewarding the production of books in Canada.[5] In the early nineteenth century, petitions to Parliament were the main way of funding the cost of printing books, especially educational materials. In this way, then, the prehistory of copyright in Canada is a history of petitions and petitioners.

4   The historical details about the petition system and the introduction of copyright legislation in British North America are from Tawfik, *supra* note 3, in particular pp 14–29, 33, 77–79, 100–108, 113–134, and 135–179. On the pre-history of copyright more generally, see John Willinsky, *The Intellectual Properties of Learning: A Pre-History from Saint Jerome to John Locke* (Chicago: University of Chicago Press, 2017).

5   The first copyright act in the British North American colonies was passed in Lower Canada (Quebec) in 1832. Nova Scotia enacted its own statute in 1839. In 1840, the British government united Lower Canada and Upper Canada into the province of Canada. In 1841, the province of Canada passed its own Copyright Act, which was a copy of the 1832 Lower Canadian Act. These were the only provinces with existing copyright legislation prior to Confederation in 1867.

Petitions are common in parliamentary systems; even today, individuals can appeal to the legislature to ask for grants or concessions. In the early period leading up to the first Copyright Act in British North America, the Lower Canadian statute of 1832, numerous petitioners came before the legislature seeking funds to support their printing and publishing endeavours. Most of these petitioners were teachers who had written their own schoolbooks. They declared that it was impossible for them to teach their students with only one manuscript copy of their books, and they could not afford the cost of printing copies for the entire class. They appealed to the legislature for grants or subsidies to help defray the printing costs.

The legislature would often grant the petitions and offer schoolbook printing subsidies because the advancement of education and learning was so fundamental to the development of the province. Schools needed to be able to provide books for students, especially domestically authored books that reflected the lived experience of Lower Canadians. At the same time, the petition system was awkward, cumbersome, time consuming, and inefficient because it was subjective and required case-by-case consideration. Copyright seemed like an appropriate alternative. It would encourage provincial teachers to write more schoolbooks and provincial publishers to publish and disseminate them at affordable prices. In addition, copyright would alleviate the need for individual petitions to the legislature. But did copyright actually succeed in meeting the legislature's expectations?

It is not obvious that the new system of copyright was better than the old petition system in achieving the policy goals of increasing the variety of schoolbooks and other useful material on the one hand and ensuring affordability on the other. It is true that the petition system was unreliable and only applied to a very small number of manuscripts. However, it is also the case that all the books that were granted printing subsidies were published and the legislature often required that these books be affordably priced. In some ways, the petition system was a better mechanism to ensure that manuscripts would be reproduced and circulated in multiple copies.

Turning to the impact of the 1832 Lower Canadian Copyright Act, a review of the copyright registration data offers no evidence that the advent of copyright led to a larger variety of affordable books, whether schoolbooks or otherwise. What the legislature thought copyright was doing was not necessarily what was happening in practice. In this period, the publishing industry was in its infancy and often in a precarious state. Copyright did not change this fact. On its own, the law could not provide sufficient incentive to enable printers and publishers to take risks on new books. They basically registered the bestsellers that they already had in their catalogues. In addition, even though publishers argued that copyright would enable them to reduce book prices for the benefit of readers, there is no evidence that this occurred. Authors did not benefit either. At the time, authors were the ones who usually had to assume the risks of printing and publishing their works. Copyright did nothing to ameliorate this circumstance, even though, in theory, copyright ought to have shifted the publishing costs from authors to publishers. The only party to clearly benefit from copyright legislation was the government, as the law was a cost-saving measure. After 1832, the legislature of Lower Canada refused to entertain any more printing petitions, declaring that authors and publishers could now avail themselves of copyright. The legislature of Nova Scotia similarly refused to grant printing petitions after it passed its copyright statute in 1839.

This raises questions about the assumptions we make today about copyright. Policymakers, scholars, and lawmakers never really look closely at whether current copyright laws, domestic or international, actually achieve their policy objectives (assuming that there is a consensus on what those policy goals are or ought to be, which is an entirely separate but no less fraught question.)

In moving from the petition system to the copyright system, early policymakers assumed that replacing an older system with a newer one was necessarily better. We need to develop better ways of testing our assumptions about how copyright behaves in relation to creators, industry, users, and the larger public interest in the circulation of knowledge. Evidence-based assessments of copyright's strengths and its failings should be an integral part of the policy agenda at national and international levels. When we looks closely at the history of copyright, we see the contingent nature of different approaches to the governance of knowledge: how changes arise and replace older systems, whether for better or for worse.

This history of copyright should liberate us from our attachment to a body of law that may not have been fit for purpose even for the technology that gave rise to it. At the very least, it suggests that the global community could consider different models or approaches for new technologies that do not involve the same considerations as print technology, or that are not as intimately tied to the human motivations and imperatives of the publishing era. We should not assume that copyright is immutable, especially as we confront major challenges to the current legal paradigm from multiple fronts, including the rise of AI.

The international debate over whether AI can be an author for copyright purposes is a case in point.[6] Copyright law is an incentive-based system that is rooted in human imperatives like creativity, industry, and education. How to justify such a long copyright term or the recognition of moral rights when dealing with machine-made works? AI may well require its own protective regime outside of copyright.[7] What the history teaches us is that there is nothing sacred about copyright that should compel the international community to focus on copyright to the exclusion of other regulatory possibilities.

Adversity Often Leads to Innovative Ideas but Politics and Power Tend to Carry the Day

In 1842, the United Kingdom Parliament enacted the Copyright Act 1842 to curb the flow of unauthorized American reprints of British copyright works into the UK and the colonies, especially British North America.[8] The idea was that British North Americans would now have to get their books directly from the United Kingdom, but this was entirely unrealistic as imported books were prohibitively expensive. The net result of this Imperial measure was that, in many cases, British North Americans lost all access to British copyright works. These readers couldn't afford to buy them directly, nor could they afford to import unauthorized reprints. The Act also prohibited British North American printers and publishers from reprinting their own cheaper Canadian versions of British copyright works. This devastating situation led to heated appeals to the United Kingdom for relief. In response to the outcry, the British compromised by passing the Foreign Reprints Act in 1847, which basically stipulated that if the colonies enacted statutes that addressed the interests of British

---

6   See generally Ryan Abbott, ed, *Research Handbook on Intellectual Property and Artificial Intelligence* (Cheltenham: Edward Elgar Publishing, 2023); Aviv Gaon, *The Future of Copyright in the Age of Artificial Intelligence* (Cheltenham: Edward Elgar Publishing, 2021).
7   See for example Xiang Yu, Runzhe Zhang, Ben Zhang & Hua Wang, "Challenges of Artificial Intelligence to Patent Law and Copyright Law and Countermeasures" in Daniel Gervais, ed, *The Future of Intellectual Property* (Cheltenham: Edward Elgar Publishing, 2021).
8   In addition to Tawfik (pp 210–247), and Bannerman (pp 14–18), *supra* note 3, see also Catherine Seville, *Literary Copyright Reform in Early Victorian England: The Framing of the 1842 Copyright Act* (Cambridge: Cambridge University Press, 1999).

authors, the British would allow unauthorized American reprints to re-enter the British North American border. The British thought that the best option was for the colonies to pass a law that would impose an importation duty on foreign reprints. The money levied would then be passed on to British copyright holders. Most of the British North American provinces adopted this approach but the Province of Canada tried something entirely different.

The province of Canada came into being in 1841, when the United Kingdom united the former provinces of Lower Canada (Quebec) and Upper Canada (Ontario), making it the largest, most populated, and most economically developed jurisdiction in British North America.[9] For provincial policymakers, the idea of imposing a duty on foreign reprints effectively meant that the Americans would continue to supply the provincial market. However, provincial printers and publishers were just as capable of reprinting British copyright works as their American counterparts. In light of this, the province took a different approach to the foreign reprints problem.

In 1847, the province of Canada amended its 1841 Copyright Act to extend domestic protection to British authors resident in the United Kingdom on the condition that they printed and published their works in the province. Until that time, provincial law only applied to authors resident in the province. If British authors secured a provincial copyright, they could stop foreign reprints from entering the jurisdiction, since provincial law forbade the importation of unauthorized reprints of copyright works. The provincial legislature believed this to be a legitimate way of meeting the concerns of the British authorities, basically saying: "let us supply our own market; we can provide cheap reprints, and we can give the British author a copyright interest so they can negotiate with our printers and publishers for the right to print, and they can get the royalties." This approach supported the interests of British authors, but it was also in keeping with provincial socio-economic interests. The United Kingdom disagreed. Spurred by the strong lobby of London printers and publishers, the British Crown never sanctioned the provincial measure. In 1850, the province of Canada had to toe the line and imposed a duty on foreign reprints to enable American reprints to re-enter the jurisdiction.

---

9   The province was established by virtue of *An Act to Reunite the Provinces of Upper and Lower Canada, and for the Government of Canada*, 1840, 3 & 4 Vict., c 35 (UK). Proclaimed into force 10 February 1841.

That 1847 moment was pivotal. It was a lost opportunity for innovative and collaborative copyright policy. If the British had agreed to the province of Canada's solution to the foreign reprints problem, Canada's copyright history would have been entirely different. Instead, the province's solution was unfairly criticized and misunderstood at the time, by the British Board of Trade, whose members were flabbergasted that the province could consider this measure a viable solution, and by the British Crown, which ultimately rejected the approach. The negative view of the province's solution became part of the British copyright narrative. Later scholarship referred to the initiative as "a marvel of subterfuge." [10]

That rejection in 1847 led to a lot of bitterness. Canadian politicians carried that burden of the past for decades, well into Confederation, as the Parliament of the Dominion of Canada again took up the cause of domestic publishing. Instead of the voluntary mechanism initiated by the province of Canada in 1847, the Canadian legislature introduced compulsory license provisions in its copyright legislation to force foreign authors and copyright holders to print and publish their works in Canada. All its attempts—in 1872, in 1889, and in 1895—were either denied Royal Assent or were not proclaimed into law. [11]

Compulsory licenses for copyright works were not unknown at the time. In fact, the UK Copyright Act 1842 had a compulsory license provision to address situations in which publishers wanted to publish the works of deceased authors. Although not a new copyright mechanism, Canada sought to use compulsory licensing in an innovative way. However, the British authorities took the position that such a measure was incompatible with British law and refused to allow it. As a compromise, Canada tried something different, and again it was an innovative approach to supporting the domestic publishing industry. The Copyright Act 1875 introduced an "interim copyright" to encourage foreign authors and publishers to print and publish their works in Canada. An interim copyright was granted to foreign authors who declared that they intended to print and publish a Canadian edition of their works within one month of filing their application for interim protection. When the work was actually printed and published, the copyright would retroact to the date of the filing of the interim copyright. However, this incentive was insufficient to meet Canada's policy objective of supporting its domestic publishing industry. Take-up was

10   James J Barnes, *Authors, publishers and politicians: The quest for an Anglo-American copyright agreement, 1815–1854* (Columbus: Ohio State University Press, 1974).

11   For details surrounding the 1889 Copyright Act, see Meera Nair, *supra* note 3.

low, partly due to the fact that the statute limited the availability of copyright to those domiciled in Canada, or in the British possessions or from countries that had bilateral treaties with the United Kingdom.

What does this experience teach us about the global and transnational copyright environment? As the province of Canada, and later the Dominion of Canada, struggled to establish itself economically and culturally, it sought creative ways of supporting domestic industry within the confines of its colonial circumstances. Imperial power, however, carried the day. We need to recognize that concentrations of power and politics in copyright policy-setting often prevail, especially at the international level. Innovative, effective, and equitable solutions to seemingly intractable copyright problems can only emerge if different voices are recognized and respected. Powerful copyright countries must cede some measure of control over copyright to other groups, such as middle powers, emerging economies, and traditionally underrepresented groups or communities who can offer more nuanced and contextual understanding of the law and its impacts. Without a more inclusive approach to copyright, we repeat the same power imbalances over and over.

For example, there is, currently, a large market for unauthorized reprints in India.[12] The arguments the reprinters give is that the authorized channels for books cannot meet the needs of rural readers. Aggrieved publishers and copyright holders argue that these reprinters undercut their ability to meet these reading needs themselves. However, they do not actually offer any realistic solutions to supplying rural communities with affordable material. These are exactly the same issues, and the same arguments, that were at the forefront in nineteenth-century Canada and the United States, and in respect of which copyright provided only limited redress. It was this same reprinting problem that led to the UK Foreign Reprints Act and the rejection of the province of Canada's policy solution. This contemporary example indicates that copyright has never matured over time to alleviate the concerns of affordable access to knowledge. The continued failure of copyright to provide universal and affordable access to books is evident. The burden has just shifted from the Global North to the Global South.

---

12   See for example, Iblina Begum & HK Sharma, "Piracy: A threat to Academicians and Publishers" (2018) 23 Journal of Intellectual Property Rights 264–265. See also Arul Scaria, *Piracy in the Indian Film Industry: Copyright and Cultural Consonance* (Cambridge: Cambridge University Press, 2014) at 23–46. See also doctoral work of Pritha Mukherjee at the University of Reading on English language trade book piracy in contemporary India.

Is Change Possible: Canada's Influence in the International Copyright System—A Middle Power with Middling Influence?[13]

While it never achieved full autonomy over its copyright law, Canada did exercise some influence in the early twentieth century in the context of the Berne Convention. Canada's copyright struggles had garnered significant international publicity and domestic political support. The country's advocacy and its important place within the British Empire caused the United Kingdom to negotiate on Canada's behalf within the Berne Convention lest Canada become a model for other British colonies to opt out of the new international copyright system.

For example, in 1914, Canada was able to force the United Kingdom to compel all the member states of the Berne Convention to sign on to an additional protocol that was introduced entirely for Canada's benefit. Essentially, this protocol allowed Berne Convention countries to impose compulsory licensing provisions on non-Berne Convention members such as the United States. The United Kingdom was so concerned to have Canada follow Imperial copyright in lock-step and join the international copyright system that it threatened to denounce the Berne Convention itself if the other member states did not sign on to this additional protocol. With that path paved, Canada eventually passed a new Copyright Act in 1921. However, this Act placed Canada in conflict with the Berne Convention once again. Often viewed as a reproduction of the British Copyright Act 1911, the Canadian version was quite different, especially in one material respect. The statute contained a compulsory licensing provision meant to foster the domestic printing and publishing industry for works that were not printed in Canada. This provision was considered to conflict with Berne Convention obligations. The Canadian Act did not come into force until 1924, when the compulsory licensing provision was narrowed to apply exclusively to authors from non-Berne Convention countries, especially the United States, and to Canadian authors who printed and published their works outside of Canada.

By 1967, another crisis in international copyright was afoot. Newly independent countries and other former colonies threatened to leave the Berne Convention in favour of greater rights of access under the alternative international copyright treaty, the Universal Copyright Convention, or to leave international copyright conventions entirely

---

13   The historical details about Canada and the Berne Convention are from Bannerman, *supra* note 3, chs 7 and 11.

and have bilateral arrangements. The crisis was eventually resolved in 1971 through a revision of the Berne Convention, but during the period of uncertainty, the Canadian delegation attempted to stand in solidarity with "developing countries" by seeking lower levels of protection for net copyright importers. The Canadian delegation explored the idea of creating a multilevel copyright treaty that would apply differently to different countries based on their circumstances and of establishing a coalition of intermediate countries as a buffer between the major exporters and importers. At that time, the Canadian delegation declared that "we are all developing countries."[14] These ideas did not come to fruition. This was the last time that Canada actively stood with middle powers and emerging economies to challenge the dominant power dynamics.

Since then, Canada has generally supported the powerful group of copyright-exporting countries. It has also sometimes played things differently at home than it has at the trade negotiating table. For example, as a matter of domestic policy, Canada held firm on not extending the duration of copyright from life of the author plus 50 years *post mortem* to life plus 70, but then turned around and granted the extension in trade negotiations, specifically under the *Canada–United States–Mexico Agreement* (CUSMA) in 2020.[15] Middle powers like Canada need to develop copyright policies that align with both their domestic and international interests and not try to play it both ways. These countries need to negotiate from positions of strength borne of certainty, transparency, and a consistent policy message that is demonstrably tied to the country's own best interests, whatever these may be.

History does demonstrate that it was possible for a country like Canada to have influence on the international copyright system when it was in a position of eliciting the United Kingdom to act on its behalf. In that one specific case, Canada negotiated from a position of strength. It had a legitimate argument in favour of compulsory licensing and it exercised some power and influence over the other British colonies such that the United Kingdom supported its position on a new protocol to the Berne Convention. However, outside of this one example,

---

14   Bannerman, *supra* note 3, p 185.
15   See in this regard Carys Craig et al, *Joint Submission of Canadian IP Scholars, Re: Consultation on How to Implement Canada's CUSMA Commitment to Extend the General Term of Copyright Protection.* https://ised-isde.canada.ca/site/strategic-policy-sector/en/marketplace-framework-policy/copyright-policy/submissions-consultation-how-implement-canadas-cusma-commitment-extend-general-term-copyright/joint-submission-canadian-ip-scholars.

a long-term lens shows that Canada was able to exert only minimal influence on its own.

International networks are important. Canada has always been in the position of being part of British and American networks, rather than forming networks with net copyright-importing countries. When Canada gained independence, it formed coalitions primarily with powerful countries rather than among, for example, former colonies. It would have taken considerable effort to form a coalition of intermediate countries, but the returns may well have been more in line with Canadian interests. However, Canadian delegations to international copyright negotiations did not prove to be up to the task.

Key individuals and networks have also played a large role in the history of Canadian and international copyright. For example, Myra Tawfik's book shows that the first copyright acts in British North America were the result of concerted efforts by like-minded individuals seeking to establish systems of public education. These education reformers and politicians banded together to push for copyright. Lobbyists—particularly lobbyists for British publishers—have also been very influential on Canadian copyright history. Sara Bannerman, Catherine Seville, Isabelle Alexander, Meera Nair, and others highlight the role of lobbyists such as London publisher Frederick Daldy and British novelist Hall Caine.[16] These British copyright lobbyists or publishing industry advocates managed to change the minds of many key government officials with their representations.

The history of copyright, whether domestic or international, is not only about powerful countries staking their claims. It is also a history of individuals, networks, and lobbyists—people who found common cause in copyright, even if their larger interests were not necessarily always aligned. Change often occurred because of the concerted efforts of committed alliances. Today, middle powers and others must develop stronger networks and greater collaborations in order to effectively resist the hegemonic influence of the most powerful copyright lobbies.

---

16   In addition to Bannerman (pp 24, 26, 28, 33–36, 52, 57–58, and 69), and Nair, *supra* note 3, see Catherine Seville, *The Internationalisation of Copyright Law: Books, Buccaneers and the Black Flag in the Nineteenth Century* (Cambridge: Cambridge University Press, 2006); Isabella Alexander, *Copyright Law and the Public Interest in the Nineteenth Century* (Oxford: Hart, 2010).

Multidisciplinary Research Methods: Colonial History, Equity, and Inclusion

Copyright law and policy tend to be studied in disciplinary siloes. This is not helpful. It is important to study copyright through a variety of lenses, including historical, comparative, and multidisciplinary ones, in order to provide as complete a picture as possible of the ways in which copyright interacts with both its stated objectives (whatever those might be) and its more opaque consequences.

Canadian copyright law does not reflect Canadian interests alone; it is the product of an imperial and international system built by the powerful centres of copyright ownership.[17] It is important to recognize and challenge these power dynamics. One way of doing this is to map the copyright histories of not only the strong powers like the United States or the United Kingdom, but also the middle powers, former colonies, the Global South, and so on.[18] Understanding copyright's history from their vantage points offers a more comprehensive and critical understanding of the way domestic copyright operates, how it engages with international forces and in international copyright contexts. Copyright history provides an important way of interrogating the power dynamics between powerful and less-powerful nations to help us understand that similar forces are at play in our contemporary copyright discourse. Copyright history also provides a meaningful way of examining the impact of these power dynamics on unrepresented, underrepresented, and marginalized groups and communities.

Studying the law in its multiple contexts and over the course of its history permits more granular explorations of not only what the law achieved, but also what it failed to achieve. It also affords greater opportunity for critical inquiries into who was included within the law and who was excluded from its scope. For example, the works of

17   Myra J Tawfik, "What Is Canada's International Copyright Policy?" (13 July 2015), online: *Centre for International Governance Innovation* https://www.cigionline.org/publications/what-canadas-international-copyright-policy/; Andrew A Keyes, "What Is Canada's International Copyright Policy?" (1993) 7 Intellectual Property Journal 209–319.

18   See for example, Isabella Alexander & H Tomas Gomez-Arostegui, eds, *Research Handbook on the History of Copyright Law* (Cheltenham: Edward Elgar Publishing, 2016); Michael D Birnhack, *Colonial Copyright: Intellectual Property in Mandate Palestine,* (Oxford: Oxford University Press, 2012); Kimberlee Gai Weatherall, "The Emergence and Development of Intellectual Property Law in Australia and New Zealand" in Rochelle Dreyfuss, Justine Pila, eds *The Oxford Handbook of Intellectual Property* (Oxford: Oxford University Press, 2018).

Indigenous creators, and the ways in which Indigenous communities were affected by copyright, are almost invisible in existing histories of copyright. Dominant research methods involve using the institutional and government archives, and the history of Indigenous legal traditions and culture is almost completely absent from these sources.[19] The historical record does show, however, that in the twentieth century Canada advocated at the international level *against* the recognition of copyright in folklore, which would include Indigenous knowledge, arguing that folklore was considered to be, and should remain, in the public domain.[20] Little is known about the background of the Canadian delegation's position at that moment, but Eva Hemmungs-Wirtén and Brad Sherman have both noted that such positioning of folklore and Indigenous knowledge in the public domain facilitated imperialistic plunder and appropriation.[21] Far more remains to be studied here.

Similarly, there is a huge opportunity for critical race IP in examining the history of international copyright in the context of international racial capitalism.[22] Indeed, questions of IP, race, and gender require greater attention from the international copyright community, and history can offer some preliminary avenues of inquiry. For example, even though Canada's copyright story remains the tale of white men, primarily English Protestant or French Catholic, there is a hidden history even within that. It is a history that sought to accommodate differences and allowed for some measure of linguistic, religious, and gender equity.

In 1840, the British united Upper Canada (Ontario) and Lower Canada (Quebec) into the Province of Canada as a means of assimilating

19   Adele Perry, "The Colonial Archive on Trial – Possession, Dispossession and History in Delgamuuk v. British Columbia" in Antoinette Burton, ed, *Archive Stories, Facts, Fictions and The Writing of History* (Durham: Duke University Press, 2005) at 325-350.

20   Bannerman, *supra* note 3.

21   Eva Hemmungs Wirtén, *Terms of of Use: Negotiating the Jungle of the Intellectual Commons* (University of Toronto Press, 2008); Brad Sherman, "From the Non-original to the Ab-original: A History" in Brad Sherman & Alain Strowel, eds, *Of Authors and Origins: Essays on Copyright Law* (Oxford: Clarendon Press, 1994) at 111–131. Sara Bannerman, "The Ins and Outs of the Public Domain" (2009) 2:1 Global Media Journal 167.

22   Anjali Vats & Deidre A Keller, "Critical Race IP" (2018) 36:3 Cardozo Arts Entertain Law J 735–795; Cedric J Robinson & Robin D G Kelley, *Black Marxism: The Making of the Black Radical Tradition*, revised and updated 3rd edition ed (Chapel Hill: The University of North Carolina Press, 2020). See also Anjali Vats, *Color of Creatorship: Intellectual Property, Race, and the Making of Americans* (Stanford: Stanford University Press, 2020).

the French-Canadian minority. Under the United Kingdom's Union Act, statutes and government texts were to be issued in English only. Prior to this, in Lower Canada, all legislative material and parliamentary records were in both French and English. Almost immediately, in 1841, the legislature of the province of Canada passed a law to provide for French translations of the laws of the province. In 1845, the legislature reinstated both English and French as the official languages of the legislature. Similarly, in an effort to compel the Imperial government to remove the tariff on imported French books, the legislature of the province of Canada appealed to the Imperial authorities, arguing:

> That without calling into Question the wisdom of [the UK Copyright Act 1842] it cannot in our opinion, be wise or consistent with sound policy to discourage the importation of Works promoting useful information originally written and published in Foreign Countries.
>
> That in consequence of the peculiar situation and peculiar circumstances of this Country, a large portion of the Inhabitants speak the French language; and that for this reason, the Standard Works required by them in the three great Departments of Religion, Literature, and Law, are French, and must be obtained from France. [23]

In this early history, English Canadians were allied with the more vulnerable minority French Canadians in challenging Imperial power. Even though the British refused the request, one sees in this example an attempt to accommodate the interests of an important linguistic and religious minority group within the province. Supporting the "three great Departments" of religion, literature, and law was an act of inclusion because it meant recognizing, respecting, and preserving the distinctiveness of French-Canadian identity.

Copyright registration data provide an important lens through which to view the law and its impact. Although copyright registrations cannot tell the whole story since only a small percentage of published material was registered at the time, they can, nevertheless, allow us a glimpse into early colonial society and its book and print culture. In her book, Myra Tawfik studied the copyright registration records of Lower

---

23   Journals of the Legislative Assembly of the Province of Canada, 1843, 7 Vict., 112 (9 November 1843). See Tawfik, *supra* note 3 at 238–239.

Canada from 1832–1841 and the province of Canada from 1841–1867. These records revealed that 12 women authors registered their copyright in the province of Canada between 1845 and 1868, despite the fact that the legislation at the time implicitly assumed that authors were men. The statute provided for a renewal of copyright to be exercised by the author's "widow and children"; under this formulation, women were the widows of authors, they were not authors themselves. Nevertheless, the provincial copyright registrar accepted to register their rights despite the language of the statute. Five of the registrants were married at the time they secured their copyright. Because of matrimonial property laws, married women were constrained in their ability to own property or to act in relation to their property.[24] And yet, these married authors sought the benefits of copyright. There is more to investigate here about what copyright might have meant to these women — whether married, unmarried, or widowed — and how early colonial societies viewed the creative contributions and intellectual labour of women.

Applying critical race, gender, and decolonial analysis to the early copyright period would yield important insights into the systemic biases within the copyright system at its very formation — whether in terms of the text of the law itself or the way it was practiced and interpreted. The vantage point of history could also provide a way of understanding copyright inclusion and exclusion within contemporary domestic and international law, policy, and practice. This historical mapping can inform the way in which to advocate for a fairer, more inclusive, and more equitable global copyright system.

Conclusion

Copyright as we know it is not inevitable. It may not even be the best vehicle to achieve its traditional objectives, let alone the new frontier of AI. It may be time for the international copyright community to let go of its deep attachment to copyright as the only policy vehicle for encouraging creativity, industry, and education. Although one should continue to celebrate the law's remarkable longevity and recognize what it does well, one should also acknowledge its very real limitations. A body of law developed out of print technology at a time of colonialism and empire-building, created mainly by men of privilege

---

24   In the context of early US copyright law and married women authors see Melissa J Homestead, *American Women Authors and Literary Property, 1822–1869* (Cambridge University Press, 2005).

and power, copyright continues to serve the interests of privilege and power. Recognizing these historical realities and putting copyright in its place might well provide a more auspicious environment for greater collaborative, innovative, inclusive, fair, and ethical approaches.

Chapter 5

Protection of AI-Generated Images in Canadian Copyright Law: Charting a Narrow Path to Originality

Cody Rei-Anderson

Abstract

The introduction of AI models capable of producing plausibly human-authored text, images, audio, and video has led to a veritable flood of AI-generated content. The question of whether AI-generated works are eligible for copyright protection will therefore have a significant impact on the landscape of intellectual property. If these works are broadly treated as copyrightable, generative AI applications could effectively fabricate new copyrights with minimal human input; if they are not, works produced by generative AI could constitute a major addition to the public domain.

This chapter will consider how AI-generated images fare under copyright's originality requirement, which in Canadian law demands a sufficient exercise of skill and judgment. While other scholarship has focused on the question of AI authorship, the related originality inquiry is important where human users of AI models seek copyright protection as authors, as in the US *Opéra Spatial* case. This chapter proposes that such a work may satisfy the originality requirement given two conditions: a sufficiently well-defined input and the faithful execution of the human user's instructions by the AI model.

However, the limitations of currently available AI text-to-image models raise serious doubts about whether they could ever produce outputs which satisfy both of these criteria. This chapter will argue that these criteria are nevertheless consistent with copyright law's goals of protecting authors. Explicitly adopting them would not hamper innovation in generative AI applications, but rather direct it towards the use of these technologies as assistive tools rather than replacements for human creativity.

In 2025, no issue looms as large for the future of copyright law as generative artificial intelligence (AI). Generative AI applications which can produce plausible simulacra of human-authored text and images are now widely available to consumers. They can be found built into products like Microsoft's Copilot chatbot (powered by OpenAI's DALL-E), Google's integration of AI image generation into its Android operating system, and Meta's AI chatbots and stickers.[1] A flood of AI-generated content is already being produced, and while it may not grab the same headlines as other pressing issues around AI safety, the question of whether AI-generated works are copyrightable will have a significant impact on the landscape of intellectual property.[2] If these works do turn out to be broadly copyrightable, generative AI applications could be machines for fabricating new copyright works with minimal human input; if they are not, works produced by generative AI could constitute a major addition to the public domain.[3]

This chapter will look at the case of AI-generated images, and in particular analyze their treatment under copyright's originality requirement. Copyright scholars have convincingly argued elsewhere that AI image generators cannot qualify as authors.[4] If these arguments are

---

1   See Nick Huber, "Software companies line up for share of generative AI spoils" (6 November 2023) *Financial Times*, online https://www.ft.com/content/d32ae3c2-b30e-46cb-b1ab-ccdf39107b2c.

2   See Madhumita Murgia, "Getty users gain access to AI image generator with legal protection" (25 September 2023) *Financial Times*, online: https://www.ft.com/content/b29f9f01-96cb-446e-a460-2817ee933e18; Getty Images, "Getty images launches commercially safe generative AI offering" (25 September 2023), online: newsroom.gettyimages.com/en/getty-images/getty-images-launches-commercially-safe-generative-ai-offering (noting that customers using Getty's generative AI tool "will receive Getty Images' standard royalty-free license, which includes representations and warranties, uncapped indemnification, and the right to perpetual, worldwide, nonexclusive use in all media").

3   See Carys Craig, "AI and Copyright" in Florian Martin-Bariteau & Teresa Scassa, eds, *Artificial Intelligence and the Law in Canada* (Toronto: LexisNexis, 2021) at 17.

4   For arguments against AI authorship, see Jane C Ginsburg & Luke Ali Budiardjo, "Authors and Machines" (2020) 34 Berkeley Technology Law Journal 343; James Grimmelmann, "There's No Such Thing as a Computer-Authored Work - And It's a Good Thing, Too" (2016) 39 Columbia Journal of Law & the Arts 403. While the current state of the law in Canada requires a human author, a recent Government of Canada consultation document contemplates two possible alternative approaches

borne out in further judicial decisions, one major path to copyright-ability for AI-generated artistic works will be blocked. But humans have made authorship claims to AI works too—including in the *Opéra Spatial* decision from the Review Board of the United States Copyright Office.[5] This chapter argues that going beyond authorship to look at the originality requirement for copyright with respect to AI-generated images is important both for resolving copyright claims in those works and for thinking about the role that copyright law ought to play in the age of generative AI.

This chapter suggests that the originality requirement of copyright subsistence in Canadian law could be met by an AI-generated work with the human user who operates the AI application as the author, but only if the process by which this work was made satisfies two conditions:[6]

1. a sufficiently well-defined input consisting of a text prompt and possibly other generation parameters, and
2. the faithful execution of the human user's instructions by the AI model.

---

to the authorship of AI-generated works. Legislation could fix the author of an AI-generated work as the person who arranged for the work to be created (the approach taken in the United Kingdom, Ireland, and New Zealand), or provide *sui generis* protection to AI-generated works analogous to the "neighbouring rights" protection of sound recordings: Innovation, Science and Economic Development Canada, "Consultation on Copyright in the Age of Generative Artificial Intelligence" (Government of Canada, 2023), online: https://ised-isde.canada.ca/site/strategic-policy-sector/en/marketplace-framework-policy/consultation-paper-consultation-copyright-age-generative-artificial-intelligence at 2.2.3. It is unclear whether an originality requirement would be imposed in either case; the consultation document primarily discusses the authorship question with respect to copyright subsistence in AI-generated works. However, it makes a glancing reference to the originality standard in laying out the consequences of determining that copyright protection applied only to works created by humans: "when a human author uses an AI to generate a work and in the process contributes skill and judgment to the work, that human would be the author and first owner": *Ibid*. This chapter is concerned with how skill and judgment could be exercised in creating an AI-assisted work in a way that would resolve both the authorship and originality questions.

5   *Re: Second Request for Reconsideration for Refusal to Register Théâtre D'opéra Spatial* (SR # 1-11743923581) [*Opéra Spatial*]. See also Anna Maria Stein, "US Copyright Office and AI: Notice of Inquiry and the Théâtre D'opéra Spatial case" (27 September 2023) *IPKitten*, online: ipkitten.blogspot.com/2023/09/us-copyright-office-and-ai-notice-of.html (providing a summary of the case).

6   These criteria are informed by the idea of an AI model acting as "amanuensis," as put forward by Ginsburg and Budiardjo: *supra* note 4.

If both these conditions are satisfied, the human user of the generative AI model may be able to claim ownership of the work created by the model if other requirements for copyright subsistence are satisfied. However, it is not clear that any currently existing generative AI model can satisfy condition 2 for an input which is sufficiently well-defined and complex to satisfy condition 1. Indeed, there may be inherent limitations in the current generation of text-to-image AI applications which would make them unable to satisfy both of these conditions, evidence for which will be considered below. While it would be premature to conclude that this generation of AI models is incapable of producing original works, it is reasonable to assume that these technologies will continue to have limitations—limitations which will ultimately only become known through their further development.

This chapter's focus on artistic works allows for a more concrete analysis than if the entire field of copyrightable works were under consideration. With respect to artistic works, some parameters which could be considered for condition 1, above, include the subjects of an image, its composition (such as the positioning, perspective, and proportion of elements in the image), colour, lighting, and other aspects of a visual image captured under the broad category of "style." With currently available image-generating models, these parameters can be influenced by the human user based on the text they use as inputs. In particular, models like DALL-E and Midjourney are adept at rendering subjects in specific styles, including photorealism.[7] But the ability to exercise precise control over the composition, lighting, and subjects of the AI-generated image is not in evidence with respect to current models.[8]

This may be because the "imagination" of trained AI models is strictly limited by what humans have already imagined and executed. An example raised by Bloomberg journalist Joe Weisenthal is illustrative: AI image generators (circa summer 2023) fail to generate an image

---

7   Such as the AI-generated image of Pope Francis in a Balenciaga puffer jacket which was widely circulated in early 2023: see Kalley Huang, "Why Pope Francis Is the Star of A.I.-Generated Photos" (8 April 2023) *The New York Times*, online: www.nytimes.com/2023/04/08/technology/ai-photos-pope-francis.html.

8   As with all the claims about the capabilities of AI image generation made in this chapter, this could very easily change. Already some AI image model implementations allow the user to control their output indirectly by providing image input along with a text prompt: see e.g., "LCM painter," online: https://huggingface.co/spaces/ilumine-AI/LCM-Painter. Tools like this are precisely why it is important to consider the originality analysis with respect to the use of AI tools: as I will argue below, the right course is to focus on what the user puts into the model, and its relationship to what comes out.

from the inside of an acoustic guitar looking out, even when provided with specific instructions.[9] These models work by recombining prior expression in novel ways based on human input; they struggle with unusual composition because they are ultimately dependent on the existing, human-authored images in their training corpus to create their outputs. Further, and relevant to the copyright analysis, a hypothetical AI image model which could "imagine" the inside of a guitar from a simple prompt (such as by composing and rendering it as a 3D representation) would be doing the work which a human author would have to do in order to render the same image—the exercise of skill and judgment which produces the originality protected by copyright. This raises the question: would this AI model then be exercising skill and judgment for the purposes of originality? If we accept that AI models cannot be authors, the answer must be no.

But this is not the end of the analysis. A dedicated human user of an AI image model might well expend significant labour in producing the text prompt to generate an image. They may over time develop their skill at crafting prompts and tweaking the AI model's other generation parameters—and may even succeed at generating a difficult image like in the guitar example above. They likely will also exercise judgment in selecting outputs which best approximate the image they wish to produce. However, what this chapter contends is that none of this counts towards originality except to the extent that there is a sufficiently direct relationship between the user and the creation of the output—that is, to the extent that we can say the human user's skill and judgment actually produces the output rather than merely initiating an independent "creative" process which is essentially machine-driven. Only then can we say that the human author has imparted originality into the resulting work.

This is where we can draw a line between use of an AI tool (or what might be called "AI-assisted creativity") and AI authorship. Yet even under this analysis, though AI-generated images could be considered original under copyright law, the vast bulk of them would not be. Casual users of AI image-generating models simply do not put in the necessary work to claim originality. We should not be duped by the apparent sophistication of the images that AI models can produce; if the human user only provides an idea, they cannot claim copyright in the AI model's expression of that idea.

---

9   Joe Weisenthal, X (29 June 2023), online: twitter.com/TheStalwart/status/ 1674489443556663312.

Finally, it is important to consider the broader context in which these copyright law questions are raised, and in particular the possibility of replacement of human creative work by use of AI applications. The prospects of the recent AI boom affecting employment in creative occupations, as in other industries, have been much speculated upon but remain uncertain. [10] This chapter will close by considering the implications of denying originality to AI-generated works, and how this may impact copyright law and creative industries.

What Is Generative AI?

Generative AI applications are technologies which produce works from user input in the form of text "prompts" and other parameters. [11] Recent technological advances in generative AI capabilities and their widespread availability have meant the question of how precisely generative AI will be integrated into creative industries is being worked out in real time. For example, the use of text-generating AI for film scripts and the AI-driven re use of actors' likenesses were significant issues in the 2023 Writers' Guild of America and Screen Actors' Guild strikes. [12] Several copyright infringement actions have been launched against developers of AI image generators, alleging that the "scraping" of works owned by the plaintiffs for use in AI training data violates their copyrights in those works, as well as the inclusion, or alleged reproduction, of elements of copyrighted works in AI-generated outputs. [13]

---

10   See Benjamin L W Sobel, "Artificial Intelligence's Fair Use Crisis" (2017) 41 Columbia Journal of Law & the Arts 45 at 80–81, 72–74 (speculating on the potential productivity and economic benefits of AI).

11   In the context of creative or artistic production, generative AI can be contrasted with other AI-driven art projects in which the artist is more directly involved in the construction of the model: see Joanna Zylinska, *AI Art: Machine Visions and Warped Dreams (Open Humanities Press, 2020)* at 75–85.

12   See Writers' Guild of America, "WGA Contract 2023: What We Won," online: www.wgacontract2023.org/the-campaign/what-we-won; Charles Pulliam-Moore, "SAG-AFTRA won't budge as studios push to own actors' likenesses in perpetuity" (7 November 2023), *The Verge*, online: www.theverge.com/2023/11/7/23950491/sag-aftra-amptp-ai-negotiations-strike-actor-likeness.

13   See Madhumita Murgia & Ian Johnston, "Art and artificial intelligence collide in landmark legal dispute" (21 January 2023), *Financial Times*, online: www.ft.com/content/d691d599-3cdb-48d8-9824-9b2784a17d90.

What is an AI-Generated Artistic Work?

The starting point for any consideration of AI-generated works is that they owe their existence to human-authored works. These form the raw material on which AI models are "trained." [14] Models must then be further tuned, a process which often involves human feedback. [15] The model can then be used to "infer" an output based on a text prompt, generating an image or set of images.

All "AI-generated" works involve human input in production: there is no real question of autonomously authored AI works here because these generative AI applications do not have independent agency; they only respond to human input. The question of authorship goes to whether generative AI can legally act as author within these constraints.

In addition to image generators, AI-powered tools are increasingly being integrated into consumer products, such as Adobe's Photoshop application, widely used by visual artists and photographers. [16] An exercise of human skill and judgment which uses AI tools arguably does not raise issues for originality or authorship any more than the use of digital filters which modify an existing image. But this means that to resolve the question of copyright subsistence in a given work, analyzing the process by which it was created ends up being unavoidable.

Copyright Law and Works Produced by Generative AI

The development and release of new image- and text-generating models since 2022 has reinvigorated interest in intellectual property issues stemming from artificial intelligence. In the context of image-generating AI models, we should soon have input from the courts: copyright suits have been launched against the creators of image generation models

---

14   See Gowthami Somepalli et al, "Diffusion Art or Digital Forgery? Investigating Data Replication in Diffusion Models" (2023) *Proceedings of the IEEE/CVF Conference on Computer Vision and Pattern Recognition*, online: http://arxiv.org/abs/2212.03860 at 2–3.

15   See Billy Perrigo, "Exclusive: OpenAI Used Kenyan Workers on Less Than $2 Per Hour to Make ChatGPT Less Toxic" (18 January 2023) *Time*, online: time.com/6247678/openai-chatgpt-kenya-workers/.

16   See Adobe, "Experience the Future of Photoshop with Generative Fill," online: helpx.adobe.com/ca/photoshop/using/generative-fill.html. Adobe's products are subscription-based, requiring users to pay a monthly or annual fee to continue using them—a natural fit for the significant and ongoing cloud computing costs incurred by most AI applications.

Stable Diffusion and Midjourney.[17] Terms of service for some consumer AI applications already contemplate the copyright subsistence question.[18] The following sections will briefly summarize the main issues around copyright infringement and generative AI before moving on to the question of copyright subsistence in generative AI works. While the subsistence and infringement questions continue to work their way through the courts, development on AI models continues at a fast pace. What we can do is attempt to think through how copyright law would apply given reasonable factual assumptions and the rules and principles of copyright law.

Infringement

Output issues concern the status and impacts of the works produced by (or with the assistance of) generative AI. A major output issue is whether, and in what circumstances, AI works can infringe copyright in existing, human-authored works. While AI image-generating models store only "mathematical representations of patterns collected from [training] images," a 2022 study found that they are capable of generating very close duplicates of training model images in some instances.[19] Artists have also objected to the use of image-generating models to mimic their distinctive styles.[20] In contrast to input issues, output issues with AI image models arise from user operation. In this sense, the output question poses similar issues to earlier disputes over technologies which can be used to infringe copyright but also have legitimate uses, such as VCRs, DVD decryption software, and the BitTorrent protocol.[21]

Copyright infringement liability arising from outputs may be relatively easier for AI firms to mitigate. For example, they may disallow

---

17   See Murgia & Johnston, *supra* note 13; James Vincent, "AI Art Tools Stable Diffusion and Midjourney Targeted with Copyright Lawsuit" *The Verge* (16 January 2023), online: https://www.theverge.com/2023/1/16/23557098/generative-ai-art-copyright-legal-lawsuit-stable-diffusion-midjourney-deviantart; Kyle Wiggers, "The Current Legal Cases against Generative AI are Just the Beginning" *TechCrunch* (27 January 2023), online: techcrunch.com/2023/01/27/the-current-legal-cases-against-generative-ai-are-just-the-beginning/.

18   See Getty Images, *supra* note 2.

19   See Somepalli et al, *supra* note 14.

20   See Vincent, "Stable Diffusion and Midjourney Copyright Lawsuit," *supra* note 17; Wiggers, *supra* note 17.

21   See Rebecca Giblin, *Code Wars: 10 Years of P2P Software Litigation* (Cheltenham: Edward Elgar Publishing, 2011) at 1–2.

prompts including specific artists' names whose works remain under copyright. Several of the prominent companies which provide AI image generators have made assurances that they will indemnify users in copyright infringement claims arising from the use of their tools. [22] This suggests a degree of confidence that the risks associated with input infringement are manageable, or that the burden of output infringement liability can be shifted to users. [23]

This may support the proposition that output issues are less threatening to AI image generators and the firms that offer them than input issues are. Broadly, input infringement issues address whether the use of works to train generative AI constitutes copyright infringement. [24] Image-generating models require a large corpus of images to train on, and requiring AI firms to license works for training would create a significant barrier to model development. [25] Whether the US fair use exception covers use of works for training is an open question under consideration in ongoing actions, and as of December 2024 the UK government is consulting on a proposal to create an "opt-out" copyright regime for AI training. [26] While the resolution of the training question will undoubtedly impact on model development, efforts to build models only on licensed images are already underway. [27]

---

22   These companies include Microsoft, Getty, Google, and Amazon: see Cristina Criddle, "Microsoft pledges legal protection for AI-generated copyright breaches" (7 September 2023) *Financial Times*, online: www.ft.com/content/cd7f5391-bba5-4af1-8309-346eb2eafa02; Murgia, *supra* note 2 (noting Getty's pledge to "assume full legal and financial responsibility on behalf of its business customers for any potential copyright disputes" arising from its AI image generator product); Emilia David, "Google promises to take the legal heat in users' AI copyright lawsuits" (12 October 2023) *The Verge*, online: www.theverge.com/2023/10/12/23914998/google-copyright-indemnification-generative-ai; Emilia David, "Amazon joins AI image creation fray with new model" (29 November 2023) *The Verge,* online: www.theverge.com/2023/11/29/23980697/amazon-ai-image-model-watermark-copyright.

23   For example, Google has been quoted as saying that its indemnification promise "only applies if [the user] didn't try to intentionally create or use generated output to infringe the rights of others": David, "Google AI indemnification," *Ibid.*

24   See Sobel, *supra* note 10 at 61–65.

25   See Wiggers, *supra* n 304.

26   See Murgia & Johnston, *supra* note 13; Intellectual Property Office, "Open Consultation: Copyright and Artificial Intelligence" (17 December 2024), online: www.gov.uk/government/consultations/copyright-and-artificial-intelligence.

27   See Getty Images, *supra* note 2; "Adobe Firefly – Free generative AI for creatives", online: www.adobe.com/products/firefly.html (noting that "[a]s part of Adobe's effort to design Firefly to be commercially safe, we are training our initial commercial Firefly model on licensed content, such as Adobe Stock, and public domain content where copyright has expired").

Subsistence

Whether works created through generative AI will receive the benefit of copyright protection is an open question which has concerned copyright scholars for some time. Generative AI models are already being used on a large scale to produce works which could pass for human-authored, and the copyright status of these works will need to be resolved at some point. Further, the technology companies deploying generative AI in consumer applications are already addressing copyright in those applications' terms of service.[28] Whether infringing or not, most AI-generated works will not be "mere copies" of existing works, and so the question of their originality and authorship will need to be resolved in order to determine whether they can indeed be protected by copyright.[29]

With respect to the authorship question, Carys Craig writes of AI-generated works that "unlike conventional works-made-for-hire [...] there is no human author-in-fact."[30] Similarly, Ginsburg and Budiardjo write that "today's generative machines do not earn the mantle of authorship because they are, at best, 'faithful agents' of the humans who interact with them."[31] The flip side to authorship, however, is originality. Human (putative) authors will try to claim originality (and copyrightability) of AI-generated works made at their behest—the next section looks to the originality analysis to consider how Canadian copyright law may respond.

---

28   See Getty Images, *supra* note 2. Whereas Getty asserts that content created through its tool is covered by its license (implying copyright subsistence in the outputs), other technology companies are more circumspect: "Microsoft doesn't claim ownership of any content" received from its Copilot AI, and advises users that they will "need to make [their] own determination regarding the intellectual property rights [they] have in output content," while Adobe notes that generative AI outputs "might not be protectable by Intellectual Property Rights": see Microsoft, "Copilot in Windows (Preview) Supplemental Terms," online: learn.microsoft.com/en-us/windows/privacy/copilot-supplemental-terms, cl 6; Adobe, "Adobe Creative Cloud Generative AI Beta Additional Terms" (8 May 2023), online: www.adobe.com/legal/licenses-terms/adobe-cc-beta-gen-ai-additional-terms.html, cl 3.2.

29   *CCH Canadian Ltd v Law Society of Upper Canada*, [2004] 1 SCR 339 at para 16.

30   Craig, *supra* note 3 at 24.

31   Ginsburg & Budiardjo, *supra* note 4 at 392. As I will discuss below, the AI image generating models being considered in this chapter seem to be incapable of acting as "faithful agents."

Originality Determination for AI-Generated Artistic Works

Phrased in the language of copyright law, can a work generated by an AI image model be "original"? In Canadian law, copyright in the expression of an idea requires "an exercise of skill and judgment," where skill means "the use of one's knowledge, developed aptitude or practised ability in producing the work" and judgment means "the use of one's capacity for discernment or ability to form an opinion or evaluation by comparing different possible options in producing the work." [32]

Authorship and originality are inextricably linked: the author of a copyright work is the source of the originality in the work. [33] However, the originality analysis emphasizes the substance and process by which the author creates the work rather than identifying the creating "agent" of the work. While Craig suggests that ultimately the originality analysis is "an attempt to establish whether the intellectual process involved was an *authorial* one," she also notes that "the originality threshold may be met by the software user who employs the program as a technical tool to assist in the production of works that nonetheless ultimately reflect his or her own authorial skill and judgment." [34]

This is where we ought to dig deeper: generative AI applications are not truly autonomous and require human input or intervention to produce anything. If it is "human input or intervention in the production of a work" that is required, how much will suffice? [35] Put another way, excluding the generative AI model itself as a source of originality does not exhaust the possible scope of originality in AI-generated images. This is an important distinction to make clear. In order to exclude originality for AI-generated works as a whole, one must establish that what the users of the models are doing is not a source of originality (or at least sufficient originality) for the analysis.

Analyzing originality in this way requires us to examine the process by which a work is produced. For the originality analysis, "[i]t is not sufficient that a work *looks like* something a person could have done"; we need to examine the process by which the work was created. [36] If we accept that generative AI cannot act as an author, then if

---

32   *CCH Canadian, supra* note 29 at para 16.
33   Craig, *supra* note 3.
34   *Ibid.* at 26.
35   *Ibid.*
36   *Ibid.* This contrasts with a line of argument against treating AI creations differently from human ones: that all human creativity reinterprets and recombines elements

there is to be originality in the work it must be the purported human author who exercises the labour (in the operation of the model) or judgment (in changing the generation parameters and selecting outputs). Nevertheless, it is worth examining the originality analysis as applied to AI models in the event that the authorship argument advanced by several other legal scholars is not ultimately adopted by courts. The first subsection below will therefore ask whether what generative AI does in producing an artistic work can be construed as skill or judgment under Canadian law.

Can An AI Model Produce Originality?

Setting aside the question of authorship/agency, which has been dealt with in other literature, we should look instead to the process by which images are created by generative AI models (which can be explained in the abstract) to evaluate whether it can be said that skill and judgment are exercised by the model.

One way we might approach this is to ask: Is what AI models do analogous to what human brains do? While we should be careful not to overrate the "intelligence" of AI, it is important to recognize that the neural network research which underlies modern AI applications does have its roots in research on human cognition and neuroscience. [37] Further, these models are "black boxes" which do not admit of direct explanation of how a given output was produced. [38] But we should also note that brains are not the only thing humans have or use in the process of creating a work: a painting, for example, does not come solely from the conscious efforts of the painter, but also from their physical exertions in painting it. While this may seem abstract, the fixation requirement for copyright protection also goes to the actual physical process of producing a work. [39]

In evaluating whether an AI model is capable of exercising originality as an author, the question is whether an (admittedly sophisticated) mechanical process to create new works by recombining aspects of pre-existing works can be said to be exercising skill or judgment. [40] The next

---

from already existing works. To which we may respond: yes—but is that all it does?

37   Zylinska, *supra* note 11 at 24.
38   *Ibid.* at 90.
39   Note also the "production" language in the *CCH Canadian* originality test: *supra* note 29.
40   Sobel, *supra* note 10 at 51 (writing in the US context that "[m]achinery must be used

two sections will briefly go over the steps to this determination, which will inform how we evaluate the human user's input into the process.

Does the Model Exercise Skill?

Is there "knowledge, developed aptitude, or practised ability" in an AI model? Can we say that "knowledge" exists in an artificial system rather than an individual person?[41] Or do the processes of AI model training and tuning result in a system with "developed aptitude" or "practised ability"? One way of thinking about AI image generation models is that they have a sort of embedded "knowledge" about form, lighting, proportion, and so on—things a visual artist learns (although not exhaustive of what visual artists do). This "knowledge" is not accessible directly (because it is impossible for a human to perceive in the data which makes up the models) but can be seen in their outputs. The artistic skill that a human author would exercise is being executed instead by an AI model—but when it is executed by an AI model, can it be called an exercise of skill?

Recall that AI models require a corpus of works to train on. While human artists can and do learn by imitation, that is not a constitutive requirement of human creativity in the same way.[42] It is not the imitative aspect of the act which is disqualifying for originality but rather that there is *nothing else there*. Human artists imitate, but this is not all they do. They perceive and reflect, they have a relationship to the world, and to themselves, which generative AI models lack. To put it another way: when AI models mimic artistic technique, it is not an exercise of skill. They do not use knowledge, developed aptitude, or practised ability because they lack *subjectivity*.

---

by or under the direction of an author who has 'original intellectual conceptions' if it is to produce copyrightable subject matter"); Ginsburg & Budiardjo, *supra* note 4 at 358 (distinguishing the *amanuensis* who carries out a plan to execute a creative work from the authorial "mastermind" whose "detailed conception so controls its subsequent execution that the individuals carrying out the embodiment exercise no creative autonomy"); Sarit K Mizrahi, "Faux-riginality in an Age of Mass Production: Why Copyright Should Not Protect Machine-Generated Content" 33 Intellectual Property Journal 59 at 73 (describing algorithms' "incapacity to manifest [...] intent" as rendering them incapable of being authors).

41   Thank you to Graham Reynolds for raising the point about databases.

42   If human artistic expression required imitation, it could never have been invented.

Does the Model Exercise Judgment?

Even if AI models can be seen as storing knowledge of artistic technique "learned" from the corpus of works they are trained on, the actual process of inference does not involve executing those techniques; rather, it imitates their expression. The inference process might look more like "judgment" since it ostensibly involves choosing between multiple options; however, this is still ultimately a mechanical process rather than one reflecting volition on the part of the model. As discussed further below, directing the application of artistic technique is not possible with these models as they currently are. The artistic "judgment" to, for example, put one part of a picture in shadow to emphasize the light in another part is not made by the AI model on any rational or intuitive basis, but rather based on how the model has been trained and tuned.

An advocate for AI creativity might suggest that "rationality" and "intuition" are poorly defined and that these in the human case also boil down to effectively statistical probability—but this is a strikingly reductive view of human cognition which should be approached with caution by the courts. Even if what we call "rationality" and "intuition" are merely emergent properties of statistical processes, there is no evidence that they are emergent from the statistical processes executed in AI models, and no compelling reason to give machine "intelligence" the benefit of the doubt.

Can the Human User of the Model Impart Sufficient Originality into an AI-Generated Work?

Continuing with our scrutiny of the process of creating an AI-generated work, we should next look to what the human user is doing, and whether it is enough to constitute sufficient skill and judgment for the purposes of originality. Manipulating the parameters of the model and changing the "prompt" is unlikely to be enough in most cases.

One such example is the *Opéra Spatial* case, in which the Midjourney AI model was used to generate images from "about 624 text prompts and revisions of text prompts," which were then altered by the claimant.[43] The US Copyright Office ruled that only the human-authored alterations could be copyrighted.[44] The Review Board affirmed

---

43   See Stein, *supra* note 5.
44   *Ibid*.

that "human authorship is a bedrock of copyright"; while they suggest that the "prompting process may involve creativity," it is not clear that it "actually forms the generated images." [45] The expression—the exercise of skill and judgment—consists in the execution of a piece, the actually doing it.

Originality from Using the Model to Produce a Work

What does a generative AI model do when called upon to generate an image? It constructs a graphical representation from the prompt and the various weightings in the model, all of which are set by having been trained on already existing works. As discussed above, the AI model itself cannot be said to be exercising skill or judgment; therefore, the only source of originality can be the human user. The only way that originality gets into the output work is through the inputs the user provides. If these are limited to merely words and settings provided to the AI model as parameters, how much skill and judgment is being exercised? The answer depends both on the specificity of the instructions and on how faithfully they are executed.

In their discussion of machine authorship, Ginsburg and Budiardjo argue that"[i]f the user of the machine supplies her creative contribution without influencing how the machine translates that contribution into a final work, then the user does not execute the final work and thus cannot claim authorship." [46] They do not take up the thread with respect to originality, however, writing that authorless outputs still "appear to possess sufficient 'originality' to fall within the domain of copyright." [47] They also raise another possible route to originality, introducing the idea of the machine acting as an "amanuensis": carrying out a plan to execute a creative work from the authorial "mastermind" whose "detailed conception so controls its subsequent execution that the individuals carrying out the embodiment exercise no creative autonomy." [48] In this case, the author "can outsource acts of execution to agents (machines or human helpers); as long as those agents act within the scope of the author's intended delegation of authority, and as long as the principal constrains how the agent carries out her task,

---

45   Ibid.
46   Ginsburg & Budiardjo, supra note 4 at 433.
47   Ibid. at 436.
48   Ibid. at 358.

the principal remains the author." [49] As proposed in the introduction to this chapter, this "amanuensis" analysis suggests two criteria: [50]

1. a sufficiently well-defined input instruction (i.e., one which reflects the human user's sufficient exercise of skill and judgment to satisfy originality), and
2. the faithful execution of the human user's instructions by the AI model.

Can generative AI models, as they currently exist, satisfy both these criteria? While this would have to be evaluated on a case-by-case basis, the guitar example cited in the introduction gives little reason for optimism. As the difficulty with the "view from the inside of an acoustic guitar" illustrates, AI image generation models struggle with complex prompts or ones which request subjects or perspectives not in the training set; attempting to elicit a particular result often requires trial and error, feeding a number of prompts to the model and hoping that the result reflects them. Crucially, it is not clear that, even when the user successfully generates a complex image using the model, they have effectively "constrain[ed] how the agent carries out her task" or that the model "act[ed] within the scope of the author's intended delegation of authority," except as a matter of random chance. [51] Image generation models are constantly being improved, and this may not hold true for long—but it may just as easily reflect a real limitation of these models.

On the other hand, tools which operate "image to image"—using the AI model to refine a generated image based on textual or other input, or to generate an image based on a user-provided image—may amount to an exercise of originality but could still face trouble with "faithful execution" depending on how tightly the user can control the output. The principle might be stated as "what you get out of it depends on what you put into it." [52] If the human user of such an AI image generator has exercised sufficient skill and judgment in conceiving and executing an image, and that exercise is actually reflected in the image which is produced, they would be entitled to protection for the work they put in. An example could be a sketch provided as an image input to which

49   Ibid.
50   Ginsburg and Budiardjo's analysis of authorship as consisting of "conception" and "execution" inform these two criteria: Ibid.
51   Ibid. at 361.
52   With apologies to Tom Lehrer.

the AI model colourizes and adds detail; the underlying sketch would be protected by copyright, and this protection would extend to the AI-enhanced work if not to the enhancements themselves.

Originality from Curating the Model's Outputs

Can a human user get copyright in individual works from curating outputs of an AI model? [53] The mere act of curating this creation process and selecting works which are visually pleasing or otherwise meet the user's requirements and discarding others should not be enough to grant originality in otherwise unoriginal works. Originality in Canadian copyright law means that the author uses their "capacity for discernment or ability to form an opinion or evaluation by comparing different possible options *in producing the work*." [54] This rules out selecting images after they have been created by an AI model, which might seem to satisfy judgment but for the clause "in producing the work." As Ginsburg and Budiardjo note in the context of other creative production, discarded drafts and photographs receive protection because copyright attaches with fixation in a material form. [55] If no originality has been exercised to that point, however, copyright cannot attach.

Some Implications of Denying Originality to AI-Generated Images

Whether AI outputs should be considered original in themselves is a separate question from whether AI models can play a legitimate role in what might be called "AI-assisted creativity." There should be a distinction made between a creative process which merely takes the outputs of AI models and one which uses those outputs in an independent exercise of skill, labour, and judgment. What copyright law may be able to accomplish is to help shape the role for AI in creative work, but in order to do that effectively it is necessary to understand what these technologies will actually be used for. The following sections will consider how AI image generation technologies may integrate into existing creative economies, and survey arguments for and against copyright protection for AI-generated works and their value to society.

---

53   The user could undoubtedly benefit from copyright protection in a selection of AI-generated images as a compilation of artistic works: see *Copyright Act*, s 2 "compilation." However, this protection would not extend to the individual works.

54   *CCH Canadian, supra* note 29 at para 16 [emphasis added].

55   Ginsburg & Budiardjo, *supra* note 4 at 411.

Generative AI and Commodification

The products of AI image generators would not be devoid of any relevance to copyright law simply because copyright does not extend to them. The role of copyright law is fundamentally tied up with the commodification of creative labour.[56] This commodification extends beyond the metes and bounds of copyright protection. Simply because the products of a creative labour process are not copyrightable does not mean that those products are not subsequently commodified.[57] What generative AI does, then, is make the vast corpus of training data used to create these models (and, it could be added, the extensive labour which fine-tunes these models) into an input for commodification processes which ultimately aim to produce marketable works. One could suggest that, given the labour requirements in tuning generative AI models, their implementation in the production of creative commodities represents not a replacement of labour, but rather a displacement—from creative work done by artists to work done tagging the training materials and tuning the AI models.[58]

The works which comprise the corpus of training data are scraped *as works* in a process which requires no additional labour from the works' originators: this is another instance where a new zero-marginal-cost use raises the question of how benefits from the new technology will be distributed among actors in the copyright system.[59] Whether or not the scope of copyright in works is extended to prevent unlicensed use as training data, the integration of these works into the commodification process as training data is likely to proceed. The question is whether rightsholders will be compensated; that is, who will share in the benefits from the new productive technology of generative AI.

What role will AI image generators play in creative economies? To take one example, consider the use of AI-generated images for headers in email newsletters. For an independent newsletter author, AI-generated

---

56   See Cody Rei-Anderson, *Copyright, Commodification and the Structure of Digital Media Economies: Independent Podcasting in Context* (PhD thesis, Victoria University of Wellington, 2023), online: doi.org/10.26686/wgtn.22961156, chs 2, 5.

57   For example, digital advertising on user-generated content is an important part of digital platform businesses. Such content may or may not be copyrightable—its copyright status is indifferent to its ability to make money for the platform because the real object of commodification is user attention.

58   For an example of poorly paid labour used by OpenAI to tune its ChatGPT product, see Perrigo, *supra* note 15.

59   See Ronald V Bettig, *Copyrighting Culture: The Political Economy of Intellectual Property*, (Boulder, Colo: Westview Press, 1996).

images have the advantages of being cheap and time-saving: in one example from the technology newsletter *Platformer*, a post focusing on US antitrust scrutiny of Google is accompanied by an image of "a leg kicking the google logo like a soccer ball, digital art." [60] The caption also functions as a kind of disclosure, both of the prompt used and the use of a particular AI image generator (DALL-E). While in this particular case a human artist might have been paid to create a similar image, the cost and time associated suggest that an independent newsletter, publishing timely analysis of an ongoing story, would likely not have commissioned a new image had the AI image generator not been available. In this case, there is a more plausible case for economic harm to a stock image company like Getty Images, whose ready photo and art libraries may have provided a more realistic alternative, than to a hypothetical independent artist. [61] Time will tell, however, whether AI image generation will come to be employed in other cases (such as replacing artists at magazine publications).

This points to AI image generators and the AI art debate as another platform/publisher or owner/innovator conflict in the making. In the first two decades of the twenty-first century, the proliferation of digital technologies for producing, reproducing, and consuming creative works opened new areas for contestation in the copyright system over different zero-marginal-cost uses. [62] These conflicts often took the form of a rightsholder (or a representative, such as an industry association or collecting society) objecting to some "innovative" new use of a copyrighted work by a technology company or individual end-user or users. While these were not always battles fought between internet platforms and content publishers directly, the alignment of interests in individual cases was difficult to miss. [63] In the case of the incipient conflicts over AI, OpenAI (the organization behind ChatGPT) is backed by the technology platform provider Microsoft, and Google and other major technology companies have their own internal AI teams and

---

60   Casey Newton, "Google's Most Serious Antitrust Challenge to Date" *Platformer* (24 January 2023), online: www.platformer.news/p/googles-most-serious-antitrust-challenge.

61   And, indeed, a *Platformer* newsletter put out a few weeks later uses a Getty Images header: see Zoë Schiffer & Casey Newton, "Yes, Elon Musk Created a Special System for Showing You All His Tweets First" *Platformer* (14 February 2023), online: www.platformer.news/p/yes-elon-musk-created-a-special-system.

62   See Bettig, *supra* note 59.

63   See Rei-Anderson, *supra* note 56, ch 3.

connections with AI firms.[64] On the other side, Getty Images and the copyright-holding independent artists in the image generation cases clearly line up with the rightsholder camp.

While the economic value of AI image and text generation technologies remains speculative, powerful actors in the political economy of technology clearly see an opportunity to dominate an emerging space. Once again, copyright law is a vital structural piece in the determination of how new communications technologies will develop and be controlled and how their economic benefits will be distributed.[65]

The Value of Creative Work

Whereas production of (new, original) works has historically meant (been coeval with) authorial labour, generative AI threatens to sever this connection. This means we have to ask: Is what copyright is concerned with — with respect to the public interest — merely the production of new works or supporting creative work itself? Even if they do not attract copyright, AI-generated works could still be made and distributed, so long as they do not otherwise infringe copyright.

Copyright law also has an important economic aspect, which is concerned primarily with providing a means for artists to support themselves through their work.[66] The threat to human artists arises from "[t]he sheer volume and rapidity with which AI can produce its outputs, and the increasingly elusive distinction between AI-generated and human-authored works."[67] There is a symmetry here with the doctrinal argument advanced above — one which focuses on the process (creative labour), not the outcomes (creative works). Creative work is already largely precarious — and "good work" in that it is seen as a good use of human faculties. A good policy reason to withhold originality from AI-generated images would be to preserve copyright's incentive function: if you want copyright, pay a human artist!

Other normative reasons towards AI-generated works not being considered original include that the goals of copyright law demand

---

64   See Huber, *supra* note 1.
65   See Bettig, *supra* note 59 at 121.
66   See Robert P Merges, *Justifying Intellectual Property* (Harvard University Press, 2011). Which is not to claim that it has been entirely successful in achieving this goal: see Rebecca Giblin "A New Copyright Bargain? Reclaiming Lost Culture and Getting Authors Paid" (2018) 41 Col J Law & Arts 369.
67   Craig, *supra* note 3 at 37.

limiting the kind of skill and judgment involved in creation of works to authorial labour—which is to say the actual work of creating. If it is a machine that is doing that work—as in, something without subjectivity, something that cannot be said to have a creative "mind"—the work cannot be said to be original. This raises the question of what importance copyright law places on human subjectivity. Even if we dispense with the notion of a romantic author whose creative efforts bring a work into existence out of nothing, subjectivity is important to originality because originality is achieved through (and measured by) "skill and judgment" which is exercised by an author or authors. [68]

There is also a "floodgates" concern: because these models can produce superficially original images quickly with minimal human input, awarding copyright to AI-generated works would be an invitation to copyright trolls. [69] Craig warns that if AI-generated works are given copyright protection "the cultural landscape would become cluttered with 'copyright landmines' and ever more difficult for human creators to navigate without legal risk." [70] Anything which requires very little of the human author has this issue—it is just the place for the originality standard to step in.

Absence of copyright protection for AI-generated works would distinguish them from human-created works and give human creators a potential competitive advantage in certain contexts. If copyright law is concerned with creators' economic well-being, granting a competitive advantage to human creators would promote this goal without meaningfully restricting potentially productive uses of generative AI. A lack of copyright protection for AI-generated images would not prevent their use in communication, or prevent their use in functional/ demonstrative applications—only entities which value retaining IP rights in their commissioned works would be affected, and perhaps it is exactly these entities who ought to be incentivized to hire artists.

An argument against finding no originality for AI-generated works is that it would stymie innovation. But where excluding AI training from fair use or fair dealing could hamper their development or raise barriers to firms without the resources to license works, denying copyright protection to the outputs of these models poses no such threat. At most, it would decrease the economic incentive to continue developing these models inasmuch as excluding AI-generated images from copyright

68   See Mizrahi, *supra* note 40.
69   See Craig, *supra* note 3.
70   *Ibid* at 29.

protection would cut against (some) marketable uses of these models. In terms of copyright's much-vaunted balancing act between authors' rights and users' rights, this response would be more moderate than failing to find an applicable fair use or fair dealing exception with respect to AI model inputs.

Indeed, perhaps artistic innovation would be better served by denying originality to AI-generated works. The mere recombination of pre-existing works in itself does not advance the practice of art. It has long been recognized that drawing inspiration from past works is a vital part of creative practice. However, the notion that this is the sole content of artistic labour is a startlingly nihilistic view of human creativity. New schools of art emerge not simply in imitation of previous work, but also in reaction to prevailing styles—had this "art machine" been invented in 1850 rather than 2022, would it have developed modernism, postmodernism, and other artistic movements? This is not to advance the hyperbolic claim that the dawn of AI-generated images sounds the death knell of human creativity. Rather, it is a suggestion that the normative goals of copyright law are not served by granting protection to AI-generated works, and so that protection should be denied.[71]

Does generative AI mean that anyone can be an artist? One can make the analogy to having a phone camera in everyone's pocket making everyone a photographer. But there is a crucial difference in that there remains a recognizable craft to photography. A digital camera sensor, like those in phones, operates analogously to what film cameras do: they make a record of incoming light and fix it to a medium. When a person takes a photograph, they capture a unique image at a specific point in space and time: their selection of when to click the shutter and the precise angle of the shot produces the image. (This is true whether the legal determination is that the photo is original—which some photos may well not be, for example, in jurisdictions with a higher originality standard.) Beyond technical operation of a camera (much of which can now be automated), what a photographer learns when they learn their craft is what to take pictures of and how to *express something* through that choice.

There is reason to doubt that the mere operation of a generative AI model is analogous to photography, drawing, or painting. As discussed above, the degree of control an AI model user has over the output is limited, casting doubt on whether they have a direct relationship to the

---

71   See also Mizrahi, *supra* note 40.

work created. While the user can make certain choices which direct the inference process, there is no direct control over, *inter alia*, composition of the resulting image, lighting, or forms. There is no direct interaction with the metaphorical "canvas." The user of an AI model may have some idea of what sort of image they wish to produce, but the image which results from the inference process has only a very tenuous connection to the user's original conception. While the accidental production of an image may still be creative or artistic, in the case of an AI model user, the accident is wholly due to the internal structure of the model rather than an individual's expressive act. It may be more appropriate to think of the resulting image as a discovery, rather than a creation.

With respect to generative AI devaluing creative work, the answer is unlikely to come from copyright law; rather, it requires looking to the broader structures of creative economies in which copyright plays a key role. One example of the rollout of generative AI coming up against these structures can be seen in the recent Writers' Guild of America contract negotiation, where one of the concessions made to the union was to forbid studios from requiring writers to rewrite AI-generated work—an important issue because, under the union's contract, rewrites demand lower royalties.[72] Needless to say, withholding copyright from the AI-generated works in question would not fix this conflict. More broadly, for those who are skeptical of generative AI, falling back on strong intellectual property rights risks benefitting the same parties who have always benefitted from strong copyright: publishers and other media companies who would be happy to embrace AI selectively where it benefits their bottom lines.

Technological Neutrality

Another objection to withholding copyright from AI-generated works based on what goes into creating them is that it would violate the principle of technological neutrality. An approach to technological neutrality, which is "naive" in the sense of not requiring information on how an image was created, would make it easy to determine if an image was copyrightable: the "looks like a duck" test. If an AI-generated image is something that conceivably could be created by a photographer or digital artist, such a naive technological neutrality position might say that this is no different from delivering music via

---

72   See Writers' Guild of America, *supra* note 12.

the internet instead of through a record store—and so should have the same copyright status.[73]

However, what in a photo or piece of visual art represents an investment of more or less skilled creative labour—skill and judgment—in an AI-generated image represents something quite different: a complex but ultimately mechanical process of "inference" of an image based on data represented in a model—and originating, in the first instance, with human-authored works. Without pre-existing works on which to train, AI image generation models would be unable to produce anything.[74] If denying originality to AI-generated works is a technologically specific result, it is only because the technological basis of present AI image generation models makes them dependent on human-authored works. These models may produce surprising or aesthetically pleasing results, but this on its own cannot be sufficient to achieve the standard of originality necessary for copyright protection.

Indeed, subjecting AI-generated works to the originality standard based on the amount of skill and judgment put into them by the user of the AI model ought to be seen as the more technologically neutral approach. Consider the lexical deficiencies of current AI image models. Inputting a prompt that specifies even a basic spatial relationship like "a cat on top of a table" will likely result in images of cats and images of tables, but not consistently cats on tables, because image-generating AI models do not have the capacity to lexically unpack that instruction. More complex prompts are, at present, even less likely to be interpreted correctly. This means they cannot perform the role of "amanuensis" suggested by Ginsburg and Budiardjo—that is, executing a creative plan devised by the putative artist. Where "a task-assigner who does no more than give a command does not intervene in the actual production of the output; he leaves it to another [...] to make all creative choices within the

---

73   See *Entertainment Software Association v Society of Composers, Authors and Music Publishers of Canada*, 2012 SCC 34 at para 9 (establishing technological neutrality as an interpretive principle requiring the court to "avoid[] imposing an additional layer of protections and fees based solely on the *method of delivery* of the work to the end user" absent Parliamentary intent to the contrary); *Canadian Broadcasting Corp v SODRAC 2003*, 2015 SCC 57 at para 152 (describing the principle of "functional equivalence" as part of technological neutrality which guides courts to interpret the *Copyright Act* in ways that "afford functionally equivalent technologies similar treatment, without getting caught up in the modalities through which the work is delivered"). It would be stretching the principle too far to suggest that AI image generation is functionally equivalent to photography or visual art applications because it can produce superficially similar results.

74   See Sobel, *supra* note 10 at 48; Somepalli et al, *supra* note 14.

broad contours of the command," the task-assigner is no author because they contribute neither conception nor execution.[75] This deficiency of AI models *may* change with time and further development, but we should not assume it will. At the same time, we should not prematurely discount the possibility of AI-assisted creativity. When AI image generation models arise which are able to respond to detailed instructions like this and truly *execute* the work of a human user, then copyright law should be ready to accept an argument for the originality of resultant works, on the same basis as other works created with digital tools. But we are not there yet, and it is helpful to clarify that the vast majority of images currently being produced by AI are not original.

Technological neutrality ought to be malleable enough to recognize that what looks like a duck is not necessarily a duck. What looks like "originality" in AI-generated images does not meet the doctrinal definition because of the way in which it is produced. That part of the "originality" in the image which does belong to the AI model's human user is unlikely to be sufficiently complex as to constitute "expression" rather than "idea", and, with current technologies, does not have the necessary direct relationship between originating mind and the artistic work produced. AI models exercise too much independent "creativity" between the user's instruction and the ultimate output. This contribution on the part of the AI model cannot be included in a putative human author's claim to copyright in the work.

A question of practical importance to artists is: What are the copyright implications of including AI in a creative process? As discussed above, generative AI is already being integrated into creative tools. Would denying originality have downstream consequences? In fact, this approach to AI would be effectively neutral here, neither providing rights over material which the artist did not produce nor denying them rights over the work which they did in fact do.[76] If the technology improves to the point of being able to act as "amanuensis," accurately carrying out detailed instructions, then it could be recognized conditional on sufficient originality (and authorship) exercised by author in the AI-assisted production of a work. But this may only be a "thin" originality since there will be no copyright in the unoriginal elements.[77]

---

75   Ginsburg & Budiardjo, *supra* note 4 at 444.
76   Notably, the Board in the *Opéra Spatial* case took this approach, finding that the claimant's modifications to the AI image were copyrightable: see Stein, *supra* note 5.
77   See *Cinar Corporation v Robinson*, 2013 SCC 73. See also the approach of the New

The proposed approach to the originality analysis leaves open the possibility that future refinements of AI image-generating models may be sufficiently complex or customizable to allow for significant expressive content in outputs. If this comes to pass, human users of AI models might be said to be operating in an art form and may well be granted copyright in their works. But it will remain one that is fundamentally distinct from photography or drawing, regardless of how much the works created might share a resemblance. This raises the question: If the result is a reduction in demand for these established, if perhaps less labour-efficient forms of creative labour, is this a development that should be welcomed?

Conclusion

Generative AI is part of a long history of "productive" improvements in creative industries, a history in which copyright law has played a major role from the printing press to the internet. Writing about the industrialization of creative work and the kind of art it produced, the cultural critic Clement Greenberg described what he termed *kitsch* in words that have an uncanny resonance with how generative AI operates, and what it produces:

> The precondition for kitsch, a condition without which kitsch would be impossible, is the availability close at hand of a fully matured cultural tradition, whose discoveries, acquisitions, and perfected self-consciousness kitsch can take advantage of for its own ends. It borrows from it devices, tricks, stratagems, rules of thumb, themes, converts them into a system, and discards the rest. It draws its life blood, so to speak, from this reservoir of accumulated experience.[78]

Likewise, in generative AI models we see machines poring over a vast field of works of human creative labour to churn out works which appear novel. When implemented as a tool, they distill from those authored works certain aspects and render them easy to hand: much of what is impressive about the outputs of AI image generators is their mimicry of technique. The pictures they make are able to convincingly

---

    Zealand Supreme Court to a composition of unoriginal elements in *Henkel v Holdfast New Zealand* [2006] NZSC 102 at para 41.

78   Clement Greenberg, "Avant-Garde and Kitsch" in Clement Greenberg, Art and Culture: Critical Essays (Norway: Beacon Press, 1961) 3.

portray lighting, texture, and forms, skills which take human artists thousands of hours of training to perfect.

The argument against these works' originality depends on seeing these images as essentially the product of a mechanical trick, and furthermore one which, at present, gives the human users of these machines a minimal range in which to express their own ideas. Whereas I as a photographer, even with the modern camera's assistance in focus, aperture, shutter speed, and so on, still choose the framing of a photo and the moment to click the shutter knowing more or less precisely how those choices will affect the image the machine will create, the user of an AI image generator—despite having a number of controls available to them—has no such relationship to the outputs of their machine. The process by which the image is produced is probabilistic and essentially unknowable; the settings available to the user merely change the variables in this process. There is no substantial connection between the image conceived in the user's mind and the one which is produced by the model.

What the originality analysis tells us is that what we purport to value in creative work is not the products *per se* but rather the process by which they are created. If generative AI automates away the exercise of skill and judgment which goes into a creative work, there is no justification for copyright to inhere in that work. Even if the work is commercially valuable, the work lacks what copyright law exists to protect: the exercise of human creative expression. When and where generative AI applications can act as a real extension of human creativity—that is to say, as a tool—copyright law should protect the human user's exercise of originality, to the extent that it has a direct relationship to the elements actually present in the work. But the vast majority of AI-generated artistic works will not satisfy this criterion. However sophisticated they may appear, works generated with minimal human input are merely a summary of works that have come before, assembled not by a discerning mind but by an automatic process. They are all appearance and no substance, and copyright law should treat them accordingly by withholding protection.

CHAPTER 6

Artificial Intelligence Generated Inventions and the Quest for a Normative Framework

Bassem Awad

Abstract

Artificial Intelligence (AI) is a rapidly developing area of study comprising many different techniques where machines are increasingly gaining human-like skills. AI's ability to quickly retrieve knowledge, interpret data, and produce new inventions makes it a major disruptor of innovation in today's economy.

Recent advancements in AI technologies are prompting scholars to reexamine the legal and regulatory implications of transformative technologies on traditional norms of law. This article critically examines the normative framework for AI-generated inventions and questions whether the patent system, designed to foster human ingenuity, is sufficiently flexible to accommodate non-human inventors.

The chapter examines the rationale for protecting AI-generated inventions and the potential normative frameworks that can be adopted to protect inventions autonomously created by AI systems. It then explores the role and function of soft law principles in the form of ethical standards or a code of ethics as a precursor to enforceable regulations. Next, it evaluates the characteristics and legitimacy of utility models or petty patents as a *sui generis* regime to respond to the fast-evolving nature of the AI industry while establishing appropriate safeguards for the public. Finally, the chapter presents a critical assessment of the current normative framework of AI-generated inventions, concluding that the patent system can function as a living tree capable of growth and expansion to encompass inventions autonomously created by AI systems within its natural limits. Such a living tree requires changes to existing norms, including those related to inventorship, the person skilled in the art, and patent examination practices, among others.

Technological innovation has always been a driving force for social progress and economic growth. In today's world, artificial intelligence (AI) technologies create significant new challenges for intellectual property law and public policy. The quest to define, refine, and regulate complex AI technologies is a necessity for driving innovation and accelerating development.

Despite its widespread use, there is no uniform or universally recognized definition of AI. AI refers in general to the capability of a machine to imitate intelligent human behaviour and varies in its levels of autonomy. The Organization for Economic Co-operation and Development (OECD) Council recently adopted an inclusive definition of "artificial intelligence system" as "a machine-based system that, for explicit or implicit objectives, infers, from the input it receives, how to generate outputs such as predictions, content, recommendations, or decisions that can influence physical or virtual environments."[1] The complexity of AI systems is compounded by its continuously evolving nature, necessitating periodic adjustments to its definition to capture the latest technological advancements.[2]

AI innovations present significant opportunities for economic growth. Canada's AI ecosystem is undeniably one of the world's leading players according to recent reports.[3] The Pan-Canadian Artificial

1   OECD, *Recommendation of the Council on Artificial Intelligence* (2023) OECD/LEGAL/0449, online: https://legalinstruments.oecd.org/en/instruments/oecd-legal-0449#supportDocuments. OECD, Explanatory memorandum on the updated OECD definition of an AI system (2024) OECD Artificial Intelligence Papers No 8, online: https://www.oecd-ilibrary.org/science-and-technology/explanatory-memorandum-on-the-updated-oecd-definition-of-an-ai-system_623da898-en.

2   Canadian Intellectual Property Office, "Process Artificial Intelligence: Highlighting the Canadian Patent Landscape" (2019) at 8, online: https://ised-isde.canada.ca/site/canadian-intellectual-property-office/sites/default/files/attachments/2022/AI_Report_ENG.pdf.

3   Impact and opportunities: Canada's AI ecosystem – 2023 report produced by Deloitte on behalf of CIFAR, Amii, Mila and the Vector Institute, online: https://www2.deloitte.com/ca/en/pages/press-releases/articles/impact-and-opportunities.html. Canada performs well when it comes to supplying AI expertise. Canada ranks highly on a number of international comparisons of AI talent, including fourth on the global AI index, fifth on Stanford's Global AI Vibrancy Tool, and second in the

Intelligence Strategy and Canada's Global Innovation Clusters program were established in 2017 to support AI innovation and Canadian researchers and developers to build a strong portfolio of patents on various generative AI applications. The number of AI patents filed by Canadian inventors rose by 57 percent in the 2022–2023 period compared to 23 percent in other G7 countries over the same period. There were 743 patent applications in machine learning filed by Canadian inventors in 2022, with the Canadian Intellectual Property Office (CIPO) experiencing an exponential growth in the number of AI applications since 2017. [4]

Canada also fares well in producing AI startups. The number of AI startups in Canada has doubled since 2018. [5] As of March 2023, Canada has more than 1,200 AI startups which raised $1.5 billion in venture capital (VC) funding in 2021 alone, bringing the total VC AI investment in the country to $8.64 billion. However, compared with global averages, Canadian inventors and businesses struggle to scale and commercialize their AI IP. Scale AI, the predominant AI innovation supercluster in Canada, reported that Canada's relative strength in AI research has not translated into a high level of Canadian AI IP ownership compared to global peers. [6] Only just over half of AI patents invented by Canadians are owned by Canadian companies. [7] The absence of a meaningful normative framework for AI systems is among other factors that diminish the commercialization of Canadian AI products and services compared to its international peers.

Some AI experts have predicted that "artificial intelligence singularity" (a system capable of human-level thinking with consciousness) is expected within the next seven years. [8] However, this may become a

---

world in AI hiring. Its cohort of AI talent rose an average of 38 percent annually outpacing the United States, United Kingdom, Germany, France, and Sweden. Canada established the Pan-Canadian Artificial Intelligence Strategy and Canada's Global Innovation Clusters program in 2017 to support the AI sector. See also Kathleen Sandusky, "Facts and Figures: Canada's AI Landscape," (20 March 2023), online: CIFAR https://cifar.ca/cifarnews/2023/03/20/facts-and-figures-canadas-ai-landscape/.

4   Sandusky, *supra* note 369.

5   *Ibid.*

6   *How Canada Can Build an AI-Powered Economy: Annual Report 2023*, by SCALE AI (SCALE AI, 2023) at 10.

7   *Ibid.*

8   On the idea of technological singularity, see Ray Kurzweil, *The Singularity is Near: When Humans Transcend Biology* (Penguin, 2006); Maria Odete Madeira & Carlos Pedro dos Santos Gonçalves, *A.I. Awakening – A Technological Singularity* (2017), online (pdf): SSRN https://ssrn.com/abstract=3022228; Darren Orf, "Humanity May Reach Singularity Within Just 7 Years, Trend Shows" (23 January 2023), online (blog): *Popular Mechanics* www.popularmechanics.com/technology/robots/

reality earlier that anticipated given the rapid emergence of generative AI models like DABUS (Device for the Autonomous Bootstrapping of Unified Sentience), Gemini, Microsoft Copilot, and ChatGPT, which marked the dawn of a new era in human–machine interaction.[9] Machine learning algorithms were primarily used in predictive models where they analyzed and categorized data patterns to forecast future outcomes. They can now generate new content using natural language processing, image, and speech recognition and produce intelligent works and inventions at high levels of accuracy. Generative AI applications are currently playing a critical role in our everyday lives and are increasingly being utilized to produce inventive outputs.[10] The speed of innovation in generative AI is being driven by improvements in cloud computing technology, software engineering, deep learning, and machine learning more broadly, which includes natural language processing (NLP) and large language models (LLMs).[11]

The collaborative intelligence model of innovation between human talents and machines has led to uncertainty in the field of patent law. Such uncertainty may lead to denying patent protection for generative AI inventions or delaying its regulation, which may have implications for the innovation ecosystem.[12] Legal certainty for inventions gener-

a42612745/singularity-when-will-it-happen/; Danny Sullivan, "Will we reach the singularity by 2035?" (19 January 2023), online (blog): *Longevity.Technology* https://longevity.technology/news/will-we-reach-the-singularity-by-2035/; James Felton, "Artificial Intelligence May Hit the Singularity Within 7 years, Researchers Claim" (25 January 2023), online (blog): *IFLScience* www.iflscience.com/artificial-intelligence-may-hit-the-singularity-within-7-years-researchers-claim-67242.

9   See Gaétan de Rassenfosse, Adam B Jaffe & Melissa F Wasserman, "AI-Generated Inventions: Implications for the Patent System" (14 September 2023) at 126, online (pdf): *SSRN* ssrn.com/abstract=4434054; Nitin Rane, "Roles and Challenges of ChatGPT and Similar Generative Artificial Intelligence for Achieving the Sustainable Development Goals (SDGs)" (4 August 2023) at 1, online (pdf): *SSRN* https://papers.ssrn.com/sol3/papers.cfm?abstract_id=4603244.

10   See Enrico Bonadio, Luke McDonagh & Plamen Dinev, "Artificial Intelligence as Inventor: Exploring the Consequences for Patent Law" (2021) 1 Intellectual Property Q 48 at 49, https://papers.ssrn.com/sol3/papers.cfm?abstract_id=3798767.

11   See Impact and Opportunities: Canada's AI Ecosystem (2023), Deloitte Report, online: https://www2.deloitte.com/ca/en/pages/press-releases/articles/impact-and-opportunities.html.

12   See Ryan Abbott, "I Think, Therefore I Invent: Creative Computers and the Future of Patent Law" (2016) 57:4 *Boston College Law Review* 1079 at 1106; W Michael Schuster, "Artificial Intelligence and Patent Ownership" (2018) 75:4 Wash & Lee L Rev 1946–52, online: https://scholarlycommons.law.wlu.edu/wlulr/vol75/iss4/5/ Marta Duque Lizarralde & Claudia Tapia, "Artificial Intelligence: IP Challenges and Proposed Way Forward" (2022) 16–21, online (pdf): *4iP Council* www.4ipcouncil.com/research/artificial-intelligence-ip-challenges-and-proposed-way-forward;

ated by AI systems is needed to stimulate innovation and ensure the dissemination of knowledge to the broader public.

This chapter explores the legal implications of AI systems in the realm of patent law and the role which soft law standards and a *sui generis* system can play to protect inventions that are autonomously created by AI systems. The chapter is composed of four parts. The first part examines the rationale for protecting AI-generated inventions and the potential normative frameworks that can be adopted. In the context of patent law, AI has been implemented in various ways in the inventive process based on the degree of human involvement. The term "AI-assisted inventions" refers to inventions created through the utilization of AI as a tool in the inventive process, while "AI-based inventions" involve AI integrated as a fundamental component of the inventive concept. In contrast, "AI-generated inventions," which are the focus of this chapter, are devoid of human input or direct intervention.[13] The second part explores the role of soft law standards in developing a set of rules that could be translated later to regulation; the following part examines the introduction of a *sui generis* system beyond the historical primary IP rights to protect a fast-evolving industry. A differentiated patent system using utility models or petty patents to protect AI-generated inventions is evaluated. The concluding section reviews the margins of the patent system and whether they can be responsive to the considerable changes in innovation patterns and effectively protect AI-generated inventions. The chapter concludes that the patent system can function as a living tree capable of growth and expansion to encompass the inventions autonomously created by AI systems within its natural limits.

The Quest for Regulating AI-Generated Inventions

Intellectual property by nature facilitates the commodification of knowledge by creating legal rights to protect and manage the fruits of the mind. The structural and fundamental principles of international intellectual property have set the minimum standards of protection in which

---

Liza Vertinsky, "Thinking machines and patent law" in Woodrow Barfield & Ugo Pagallo, eds, *Research Handbook on the Law of Artificial Intelligence* (Cheltenham, UK: Edward Elgar Publishing, 2018) at 489.

13   See WIPO, "WIPO Conversation: IP And Frontier Technologies, AI Inventions" (2023), online: https://www.wipo.int/export/sites/www/about-ip/en/frontier_technologies/pdf/wipo-ai-inventions-factsheet.pdf.

domestic intellectual property policies must adopt. While multilateral and preferential trade agreements have led to a number of developments in the global patent system, recent accelerated technological shifts with respect to AI systems and AI-generated inventions have raised new challenges and caused some scholars to wonder whether the margins of the patent system as a primary right can be responsive to such transformative technologies. [14]

The quest for regulating AI-generated inventions begins with identifying the rationale for seeking protection and the degree of human involvement required. It is also important to assess whether society will benefit from regulating generative AI inventions, or if such regulation would unduly restrict access to inventions that should otherwise be in the public domain.

Patent law was traditionally developed with human inventors in mind. Certain scholars have argued that generative AI systems, compared to human inventors, do not need financial incentives to innovate, which makes the economic monopoly afforded by the current system unnecessary. [15] Generative AI will continue to run code and produce inventions regardless of incentives. Providing a patent would over-reward the human creator of the AI system who has no meaningful input in creating the subsequent invention. [16] Generative AI produces unpredictable results, and therefore it cannot be said that its owner or creator has exerted an inventive effort to develop the new idea.

Gervais has raised a valid argument about incentivizing AI itself; however, it fails to deal with incentives for those who produce generative AIs. It is apparent that although patent protection will not motivate an AI system, it will motivate the people who are responsible for the development of the AI system. [17] AI developers may find their incentives

---

14   The term "primary rights" will be used to refer to rights in copyright, trademark, design, and patent law that have been part of both international treaties and many national laws for well over a century. For more details about international intellectual property principles and the primary rights, see Susy Frankel & Daniel Gervais, eds, *Advanced Introduction to International Intellectual Property* (Edward Elgar, 2016); Daniel J Gervais, ed, *The Future of Intellectual Property*, ATRIP Intellectual Property Series (Edward Elgar, 2018).

15   See Daniel J Gervais, "The Machine As Author" (2020) 105 Iowa L Rev 2053 at 2062, online: https://ilr.law.uiowa.edu/sites/ilr.law.uiowa.edu/files/2022-10/The%20 Machine%20as%20Author%20.pdf.

16   *Ibid* at 2070.

17   See Ryan Abbott, "The Artificial Inventor Project" (December 2019), online: *WIPO Magazine* www.wipo.int/wipo_magazine/en/2019/06/article_0002.html; de Rassenfosse, *supra* note 375 at 106; Adam B Jaffe & Melissa F Wasserman,

in social recognition and/or public acknowledgement of their work as the first to program and use the inventive system (the first-mover advantage theory).[18] Furthermore, the intellectual property system has been successfully able to maintain incentives for certain groups with an essential, but indirect role in generating intellectual property in the past. In the area of copyright and related rights, phonogram producers and broadcasting organizations were granted an exclusive neighbouring right to safeguard the considerable investments made for the production of phonograms and carrying signals.[19] Neither producers nor broadcasting organizations directly contributed to the creation of the works, however, without enabling the work to be produced and broadcast, it would not be available to the public.

Generative AIs require enormous amounts of money and time to create and continuous investments to improve. While the patent system may not be effective at incentivizing generative AIs themselves to innovate, it can still function to incentivize innovation from the creators or owners of generative AI. If the owner/creator of a generative AI can patent some of the inventions it produces, they can benefit from the economic returns produced by licensing or assigning it. Such returns should encourage the AI developer to innovate on their AI system and continue to improve it. However, limiting patent protection to the AI itself may not provide enough of an incentive. De Rassenfosse et al. argue that scarcity is needed to provide incentive to bring an invention to market.[20] If the inventions of a generative AI are in the public domain, no scarcity will exist to allow for the commercialization of those inventions. In the meantime, providing incentives to disclose the secret algorithms of AI-generated inventions can strive towards promoting welfare and sharing of information.

Failing to provide protection for AI-generated inventions could lead to unintended consequences. Abbott has argued that denying legal

---

AI-Generated Inventions: Implications for the Patent System (Rochester, NY, 2023) at 6.

18   See Ryan Abbott, "I Think, Therefore I Invent: Creative Computers and the Future of Patent Law" (2016) 57:4 *Boston College Law Review* 1079 at 1106; Enrico Bonadio, Luke McDonagh & Plamen Dinev, "Artificial Intelligence as Inventor: Exploring the Consequences for Patent Law" (2021) 1 Intellectual Property Q 48 at 49, online: ssrn.com/abstract=3798767.

19   The International Bureau of the World Intellectual Property Organisation (WIPO), "Protection of Neighbouring Rights (Rights of Performers, Producers of Phonograms and Broadcasting Organisations): International Conventions in the Field of Neighbouring Rights" (1986) 28:4 J Indian L Institute 450 at 450–469, online: www.jstor.org/stable/43951045.

20   See de Rassenfosse, *supra* note 375 at 107.

protection may encourage companies to file patent applications without disclosing that the invention was generated by an AI system. [21] This would violate the requirement for full disclosure of all relevant information related to the invention in patent applications, and could result in some patent applicants obtaining an unfair advantage over others who are not using AI systems to invent. Overall, the development and production of the inventive system itself necessitates a legal framework to effectively commercialize and protect the significant investments in developing such technology while enhancing social welfare.

The question that follows is: What normative framework should be adopted to protect AI-generated inventions? In recent years, soft law principles have been advanced as an effective way to regulate constantly evolving technology such as AI until it has matured. An alternative framework might include rights beyond the historical primary IP rights, called *sui generis* rights, to protect generative AI inventions. Another approach would be to continue relying on current primary rights such as patents to protect AI-generated inventions.

The Puzzle of Soft Law

New technologies often spur anxiety for regulators due to their fast pace of change and uncertain breadth of application. Many technology leaders believe that enacting new laws to regulate AI is premature and may negatively impact both the domestic AI industry and the public. Regulators in several countries have preferred the "wait-and-see approach" and are relying on soft law principles in the interim. [22] Soft law or self-regulation can take the form of AI guidelines, self-certifications, industry standards, codes of ethics, and data governance frameworks, among others. [23]

---

21   See Abbott, *supra* note 384.

22   See Céline Castets-Renard, "AI and the Law in the European Union and the United States" in Florian Martin-Bariteau & Teresa Scassa, eds, *Artificial Intelligence and the Law in Canada* (Toronto: LexisNexis, 2021) 397 at 402. A soft law instrument is any measure that imposes substantive expectations that are not directly enforceable by government. See also Gary Marchant & Carlos Ignacio Gutierrez, "Soft Law 2.0: An Agile and Effective Governance Approach for Artificial Intelligence" (2023) 24:2 Minn J L Sci & Tech 375 at 384, online: https://papers.ssrn.com/sol3/papers.cfm?abstract_id=4473812 Lorne Sossin & Chantelle van Wiltenburg, "The Puzzle of Soft Law" (2021) 58:3 Osgoode Hall Law Journal 623 at 624, online: https://digitalcommons.osgoode.yorku.ca/ohlj/vol58/iss3/3/.

23   In Canada, both governments and the private sector have recognized the need for normative frameworks for the development and deployment of AI. See Carlos

Soft law standards set out requirements, specifications, guidelines, or characteristics that, when applied consistently, ensure that products and services are safe and efficient.[24] Soft law instruments can provide useful guidelines to fill gaps in existing normative rules. They can also play a pivotal role in working towards domestic and international consensus, which may eventually lead to the creation of legally binding rules. The main advantage of soft law resides in the informality and speed by which it can be adopted and revised.[25]

The greatest limitation of soft law mechanisms is their unenforceability and lack of trustworthiness. These principles are voluntary and there is no assurance that AI developers and users will consent to or diligently comply with them. For example, there are no mandatory rules that draw the line between patentable subject matter and AI-generated inventions that should be in the public domain. Another critique of soft law standards is that they usually reflect the interests of a small group of players to the exclusion of a diverse set of voices.[26] Soft law is often viewed as merely performative, acting to deflect the criticisms of the industry. Soft law principles can also be created by different actors in any given technology field, which might create confusion for the broader public. The puzzle of soft law might create a "market of principles and values" as described by Castets-Renard.[27] Private and public actors shop for the ethical principles that are best retrofitted to

Ignacio Gutierrez, Gary E Marchant & Katina Michael, "Effective and Trustworthy Implementation of AI Soft Law Governance" (2021) 2:4 IEEE Transactions on Technology and Society 168 at 168, online: https://ieeexplore.ieee.org/document/9598168; "Voluntary Code of Conduct on the Responsible Development and Management of Advanced Generative AI Systems" (September 2023), online: *Innovation, Science and Economic Development Canada* https://ised-isde.canada.ca/site/ised/en/voluntary-code-conduct-responsible-development-and-management-advanced-generative-ai-systems.

24   See Michel Girard, "Canada Needs Standards to Support Big Data Analytics (CIGI Policy Brief No. 145)" (4 December 2018) at 2, online (pdf): *Centre for International Governance Innovation* www.cigionline.org/publications/canada-needs-standards-support-big-data-analytics/.

25   See Michael Geist, "AI and International Regulation" in Florian Martin-Bariteau & Teresa Scassa, eds, *Artificial Intelligence and the Law in Canada* (Toronto: LexisNexis, 2021) 367 (there are three notable approaches to regulate AI: the market-led approach in the United States, the government-led approach in the People's Republic of China, and the hybrid approach in the European Union).

26   See Luciano Floridi, "Translating Principles into Practices of Digital Ethics: Five Risks of Being Unethical" (2019) 32:2 Philosophy & Technology 185 at 186.

27   See Céline Castets-Renard, "AI and the Law in the European Union and the United States" in Florian Martin-Bariteau & Teresa Scassa, eds, *Artificial Intelligence and the Law in Canada* (Toronto: LexisNexis, 2021) 397 at 383.

justify their current behaviours, rather than revising them to ensure they are consistent with a socially accepted ethical framework.[28]

The governance of AI will soon require traditional regulations, or "hard law."[29] This may involve the creation of an independent hard law framework, or at the very least a hybrid model where both hard and soft law complement each other. There are two potential legal mechanisms to regulate AI-generated inventions in the realm of patent law. The first involves a tiered approach where AI-generated inventions are protected by a *sui generis* system. The second relies on the ability of the patent law to adapt and accommodate inventions emerging from the current collaborative intelligence innovation between humans and machines.[30]

Sui Generis Rights for AI-Generated Inventions

While soft law instruments such as ethical standards may be able to address some of the challenges created by AI-generated inventions, there is a need for a clear and robust legal framework to quickly protect and enforce rights related to these inventions. A *sui generis* system would bridge the gaps emerging from the inability of primary rights to fully respond to the rapid evolution of frontier technologies.[31]

In the fast-evolving field of AI, where inventions may have a short lifespan given the rate at which improvements can be made, a long examination period or a 20-year term of patent protection may not be the most appropriate or cost-effective option. A second tier of patent protection could grant rights more quickly for products with life cycles shorter than the average pendency of a regular patent application or in industry sectors where technology is rapidly changing.[32]

---

28   *Ibid.*
29   See Floridi Luciano, "The end of an era: from self-regulation to hard law for the digital industry" (2021), online: https://papers.ssrn.com/sol3/papers.cfm?abstract_id=3959766.
30   See H James Wilson & Paul R Daugherty, "Collaborative Intelligence: Humans and AI are Joining Forces" (2018), online: *Harvard Business Review* https://hbr.org/2018/07/collaborative-intelligence-humans-and-ai-are-joining-forces; Jerry Levine, "Combining Intelligence: How People and AI Can Collaborate" (26 April 2022), online: *Forbes* www.forbes.com/sites/forbesbusinesscouncil/2022/04/26/combining-intelligence-how-people-and-ai-can-collaborate/.
31   The rights against circumvention of Technological Protection Measures (TPMs) and the Rights Management Information (RMI) are examples of secondary right in the field of copyright. The *sui generis* right in databases is another example from Europe.
32   See Mark D Janis, "Second Tier Patent Protection" (1999) 40:1 Harvard Intl LJ 151 at 188.

Utility model regimes could be a potential mechanism for protecting AI-generated inventions. Utility models, also known as "petty patents" or "small patents," are short-term registered rights granted for inventions that lack the degree of inventiveness that patent law requires.[33] They are considered a type of "second-tier patent protection" and are part of the patent system in various jurisdictions. Utility models exist as "innovation patents" in Australia, "utility innovations" in Malaysia, and "utility certificates" in France.[34] This model of protection recognizes that minor improvements or adaptations of already existing products that do not fulfill the patentability requirements can have an important role to play in innovation. The requirements to obtain protection under utility models are less stringent than those for patents. The "inventive step" or "non-obviousness" requirement is either lower or not required, depending on the country.[35] The term of protection is shorter than regular patent protection, ranging between three and 10 years, and cannot be extended or renewed, making utility models ideal for products with an anticipated short commercial life.[36] In most countries, utility model applications are not substantially examined, making the registration process simpler and faster, taking between one and six months on average.

---

33   See Uma Suthersanan, "Utility Models: Do They Really Serve National Innovation Strategies?" in Josef Drexl & Anselm Kamperman Sanders, eds, *The Innovation Society and Intellectual Property* (Cheltenham, UK: Edward Elgar Publishing, 2019) 2 at 2, online: https://papers.ssrn.com/sol3/papers.cfm?abstract_id=3139963; Janis, *supra* note 398 at 189; "Utility models", online: *WIPO* www.wipo.int/patents/en/topics/utility_models.html [*WIPO Utility Models*].

34   Hans-Peter Brack, "Utility Models and Their Comparison with Patents and Implications for the US Intellectual Property Law System" (2009) Boston College Intellectual Property & Technology Forum 1–15 at 2, online: https://lira.bc.edu/work/ns/6bbfcd98-b1a1-4c07-8c52-6dd482965032 (accessed 30 November 2023) at 2.

35   Uma Suthersanan, "Utility Models: Do They Really Serve National Innovation Strategies?" in Josef Drexl & Anselm Kamperman Sanders, eds, *The Innovation Society and Intellectual Property* (Cheltenham: Edward Elgar Publishing, 2019), 2–24; Hans-Peter Brack, *supra* note 400; Mark D Janis, "Second Tier Patent Protection" (1999) 40:1 Harvard International Journal 151–219; WIPO, "utility models" (2022), online: *WIPO* https://www.wipo.int/en/web/patents/topics/utility_models.

36   Shohini Bagchee & Laura MacFarlane, "Canada: Utility Models, Petty Patents & Innovation Patents: Efficient IP Protection for SMEs" (8 March 2013), online: *Mondaq* www.mondaq.com/canada/patent/225794/utility-models-petty-patents-innovation-patents-efficient-ip-protection-for-smes.

Rationale of Utility Models as a Secondary Tier of Protection

Utility models were introduced primarily in the multilateral trading system to provide an easier route for inventors to obtain legal rights. Today, many countries have adopted this model to support the incremental nature of innovation and encourage "follow-on inventors" who contribute to cumulative improvements. When these innovations emanate from SMEs, having a faster and less expensive method of protection can prevent free riding by larger businesses. Smaller-scale inventors can also lean on the protection afforded by utility models to stay competitive in the face of rapid technological changes. [37]

The utility model first emerged in Germany in the nineteenth century to respond to the needs of local innovators for easier procedures to obtain protection. The fees for registration of a patent in Germany were high in comparison to those for industrial design registration and the process of registration was more complex due to the patentability requirements. This led to inventions being filed as industrial designs despite relating to functional innovations. [38] The Imperial Superior Trade Court forbade this practice in 1878, creating a gap wherein inventions which were innovative enough to require legal protection, but not innovative enough to be patentable, were without coverage. [39] Thus, the German Patent law of 1891 allowed for "supplementary patents" for incremental innovations. [40]

Japan was one of the first countries to follow Germany's lead and adopted its own utility model law in 1905. This law was heavily inspired by the system in Germany. [41] Initially, the term of protection was for six years total and substantive examination was required prior to granting (unlike in the German system). Utility models allowed Japanese innovators to protect incremental improvements over imported machinery and

---

37   See Uma Suthersanen, "Utility Models and Innovation in Developing Countries" (February 2006) at 1, online: (pdf): *United Nations Conference on Trade and Development* https://unctad.org/system/files/official-document/iteipc20066_en.pdf, at 7.

38   See Robert J Harrison, "Patents and Utility Models" (3 May 2011) at 1, online (pdf): *SSRN* papers.ssrn.com/sol3/papers.cfm?abstract_id=1828582.

39   *Ibid.*

40   See "Papers Relating to the Foreign Relations of the United States, Transmitted to Congress, With the Annual Message of the President, December 5, 1892," online: *Office of the Historian* history.state.gov/historicaldocuments/frus1892/d158.

41   See KS Kardam, "Utility Model - A Tool for Economic and Technological Development: A Case Study of Japan" (2007) at 41, online (pdf): *World Intellectual Property Office* www.wipo.int/export/sites/www/about-wipo/en/offices/japan/docs/research/india_2007.pdf.

equipment.[42] This encouraged the absorption and diffusion of foreign technology, which contributed significantly to the growth of Japan's economy during the second half of the twentieth century.[43]

A number of other East Asian countries have used utility models to their advantage. The general trend is that, as their economies developed during the twentieth century, utility models became the favoured method of patenting before being gradually replaced by standard patents as the technological gap closed.[44] Chinese utility models dominated the global scene in 2021, accounting for approximately 98 percent (2.9 million) of utility model applications, followed by those of Germany (10,576), the Russian Federation (9,079), Australia (7,844), and Japan (5,238).[45] Utility model regimes currently exist in some form or another worldwide in more than 75 countries, including countries with successful innovation strategies such as Japan, South Korea, China, and Germany.

At the multilateral level, utility models are recognized in the Paris Convention for the Protection of Industrial Property.[46] Article 1(2) states that the protection of industrial property has its object patents, utility models, industrial designs, trademarks, service marks, trade names, indications of source or appellations of origin, and the repression of unfair competition. While the Paris Convention includes utility models as a form of intellectual property, the text does not impose obligations on signatories in relation to the implementation of utility models.[47] The Patent Cooperation Treaty (PCT) of 1978 allows parties to file utility model applications through the national phase that applies to patents.[48]

---

42   See Nagesh Kumar, "Intellectual Property Rights, Technology and Economic Development: Experiences of Asian Countries" (2003) 38:3 Economic & Political Weekly 209 at 214, online: www.jstor.org/stable/4413100.

43   *Ibid.*

44   See Keith Maskus, "Strengthening Intellectual Property Rights in Asia: Implications for Australia" (1998) 37:3 Australian Economic Papers 346 at 351.

45   See "WIPO IP Facts and Figures 2022" (2022) at 14, online (pdf): *WIPO* www.wipo.int/publications/en/details.jsp?id=4642&plang=EN.

46   *Paris Convention for the Protection of Industrial Property*, 20 March 1883 (entered into force 7 July 1884), art 1(2), online: www.wipo.int/wipolex/en/text/287556.

47   See Uma Suthersanen, "Utility Models and Innovation in Developing Countries" (February 2006) at 1, online (pdf): *United Nations Conference on Trade and Development* unctad.org/system/files/officialdocument/iteipc20066_en.pdf; GHC Bodenhausen, "Guide to the Application of the Paris Convention for the Protection of Industrial Property as Revised at Stockholm in 1967" (1968) at 35, online (pdf): *WIPO* www.wipo.int/edocs/pubdocs/en/intproperty/611/wipo_pub_611.pdf.

48   *Patent Cooperation Treaty*, 19 June 1970, (entered into force 1 April 2002), online: *WIPO* www.wipo.int/wipolex/en/text/288637 (article 2(1) of the Patent Cooperation

The WTO *Agreement on Trade-Related Aspects of Intellectual Property Rights* (*TRIPS Agreement*) makes no specific reference to utility models, but does reference the sections of the Paris Convention which require signatories to abide by the principles of national treatment and the right of priority.[49] Under the *TRIPS Agreement*, WTO member states are free to adopt more extensive protection, leaving them free to formulate or reject second-tier regimes such as the utility model.[50]

Differences Between Utility Models and Patents

There are five main differences between the utility models and traditional patent protection, namely, (i) the requirements to obtain protection, (ii) the duration of protection, (iii) the registration process, (iv) the costs, and (v) the legal restrictions. First, the requirements for obtaining utility model protection are less stringent than for traditional patents. Utility model protection requires that the invention be "novel" but the level of "non-obviousness" required may be lower or absent altogether depending on the country.[51] Second, the term of protection for utility models is shorter than the 20-year term for patent protection in Canada. The term of protection varies from three to 10 years, depending on domestic laws and the role of utility models. Third, utility models and traditional patents differ in terms of their registration processes. In most countries, patent offices check compliance with formality requirements and register utility models without conducting a substantive examination.[52] This means that the registration process is often simpler and faster than that of traditional patents, sometimes taking six months or less, in contrast to

Treaty stipulates that "application" means an application for the protection of an invention; references to an "application" shall be construed as references to applications for patents for inventions, inventors' certificates, utility certificates, utility models, patents or certificates of addition, inventors' certificates of addition, and utility certificates of addition. Utility models are also mentioned in the International Patent Classification (IPC) which facilitates retrieval of patent documents in order to conduct effective novelty searches and determine the state of the art. Article 1 states that the IPC covers not just "patents for invention" but also "inventors' certificates, utility models and utility certificates").

49   *Agreement on Trade-Related Aspects of Intellectual Property Rights*, 15 April 1994, (entered into force 1 January 1995), online: www.wto.org/english/docs_e/legal_e/27-trips.pdf. See *WIPO Utility Models*, *supra* note 399.

50   See Mark D Janis, "Second Tier Patent Protection" (1999) 40:1 Harvard International Law Journal 151.

51   See *WIPO Utility Models*, *supra* note 399; "Utility Model," online: *European Commission* intellectual-property-helpdesk.ec.europa.eu/utility-model_en.

52   *Ibid.*

the average of three to five year examination process in Canada.[53] Fourth, fees for obtaining and maintaining utility models are less expensive.[54] For instance, in China, fees to file a utility model application start at 500 RMB ($98 CAD), compared to 950 RMB ($187 CAD) to file for traditional patent protection.[55] Lastly, unlike traditional patent protection, which allows for the protection of inventions that fall into the eligible subject matter, utility models generally protect innovations of incremental character that may not meet the standard patentability criteria. This includes new "technical inventions" that make small improvements to, and adaptations of, existing products or that have a shorter commercial life.[56]

Characteristics of Utility Models as a Secondary Right for Generative AI Inventions

The conceptualization of a *sui generis* regime as a gap filler to protect non-traditional subject matters has precedents in Europe with the *sui generis* database right and in the United States under the Semiconductor Chip Protection Act of 1984.[57] Utility model regimes may be used to respond to the AI industry needs to obtain a quick and effective protection for generative AI inventions while enabling the disclosure of AI-generated output.

The common features of utility models include a short term of protection, waiving the requirement of non-obviousness and an inventive step, and a simpler application procedure compared to patents. One of the advantages of adopting a utility model regime for AI-generated inventions is the limited term of protection. The shorter term of protection compared to regular patents can act as an advantage given that AI inventions may have a shorter lifespan due to their rate of advancements. Further, the limited term of protection balances the potential negative effects on competition and marketplace prices.

---

53   See "File a Canadian patent application: Request examination" (2023), online: *Canadian Intellectual Property Office* ised-isde.canada.ca/site/canadian-intellectual-property-office/en/patents/patent-application-and-examination/file-canadian-patent-application-request-examination [*CIPO, File a Canadian Patent Application*].

54   See *WIPO Utility Models, supra* note 399; "Utility Model," online: *European Commission* intellectual-property-helpdesk.ec.europa.eu/utility-model_en.

55   See Lindsay Gledhill, "Differences between utility models and patents: which should you choose?" (24 August 2021), online: *Harper James* harperjames.co.uk/article/utility-models-vs-patents-smarter-ip-strategy/#section-6.

56   See *WIPO Utility Models, supra* note 399.

57   17 USC §901–914, online: www.copyright.gov/title17/92chap9.html.

The adoption of a utility model system would also help to mitigate the traditional criteria of substantial examination. Since utility models do not require a certain level of inventiveness, AI-generated inventions can reach the market faster. The lack of full substantive examination results in a short acceptance and registration timeframe, often between three and six months from filing the application, compared to a minimum of two years for regular patent applications.[58] The quicker examination process allows the owners of AI-generated inventions to enforce their rights earlier than with standard patents. It is also less expensive to obtain and maintain a utility model compared to a traditional patent, which makes them more accessible for startups and small business-es.[59] The utility model mechanism will also facilitate a rapid source of knowledge that can be used to advance the AI innovation ecosystem and promote social benefits that justify the limited term of exclusivity.

Moreover, the comparative ease of obtaining utility models would allow AI developers to secure their exclusive rights and foster competi-tion in the AI industry. Meanwhile, the fast administrative process will reduce the current burden on both the patent offices and startups that cannot afford a lengthy process.[60]

The Legitimacy of the Two-Tier Approach for AI-Generated Inventions

Historically, the implementation of second-tier patent protection has been successful as a policy response to these perceived deficiencies in patent regimes. In some countries, utility model protection has been used to grant rights in certain technological fields, yet only for products, not processes.[61] For example, a second-tier system may allow for the shape or structure of products, such as mechanical devices and appara-tuses to be claimed, but not confer protection for technical, chemical, or

---

58   See John Richards, "Utility Model Protection Throughout the World" (2010), online (pdf): *Intellectual Property Owners Association* ipo.org/wp-content/uploads/2013/03/ Utility_Model_protection.pdf (innovation patents in Australia were usually granted within one month of filing the application, while standard patents could take six months to several years).

59   Robert Harrison, "Patents and Utility Model" (2011) at 3, online: SSRN https:// ssrn.com/abstract=1828582.

60   See Tim W Dornis, "Artificial Intelligence and Innovation: The End of Patent Law as We Know It" (2020) 23 Yale JL & Tech 97 at 151, online: yjolt.org/sites/default/ files/23_yale_j.l._tech._97_ai_patent_0.pdf; Tom Dent-Spargo, "Is it time for the "Petty Patent" model for AI?" (30 October 2019), online: *Robotics Law Journal* robot-icslawjournal.com/analysis/is-it-time-for-the-petty-patent-model-for-ai-98437194.

61   See Bagchee & MacFarlane, *supra* note 402.

biological processes. [62] Other countries allow utility models on processes, chemical compounds, pharmaceuticals, or software. [63]

While a *sui generis* regime for AI-generated inventions can provide legal certainty for the fast-growing AI industry, it could create several unintended consequences and a disproportionate burden for AI companies and regulators.

The first concern is related to the scope of a *sui generis* right. A differentiated system that awards AI-generated inventions shorter or weaker protection than other inventions would open the door to other sectors of industry being treated differently. Calls for a tiered approach could be advanced in the context of protecting clean technology inventions or business methods or other types of inventions.

Moreover, the creation of a *sui generis* right of reduced scope and duration could lead to a cumulation of rights of different kinds for inventions with the same subject matter and functionality. The evergreening practice of filing utility models for incremental innovations can create patent thickets which restrict access to the subject matter protected. The system may also be excessively used by large firms to limit access to certain technologies by the acquisition of defensive second-tier patent rights. A 2016 report commissioned by the Australian government found that low-value patents can lead to patent thickets in which a business creates a web of second-tier patents to surround their technology. This prevents legitimate competition in the marketplace. [64]

Another concern with utility models is the associated litigation costs for poor-quality patents or broad claims. Granting exclusive rights over weak and trifling patents would negatively affect the AI innovation ecosystem and its economic growth. Furthermore, startups and SMEs operating in a fast-evolving industry do not have the financial resources and time to deal with lengthy and costly litigation. Importantly, not

---

62   *Ibid.*
63   *Ibid.*
64   Australian Government, *Productivity Commission Inquiry Report* (Inquiry Report No 78) (Canberra, 2016) at 252, online: www.pc.gov.au/inquiries/completed/intellectual-property/report/intellectual-property.pdf. Thickets are "a dense web of overlapping intellectual property rights that a company must hack its way through in order to actually commercialise new technology" (Carl Sharpiro, "Navigating the Patent Thicket: Cross Licenses, Patent Pools, and Standard Setting" (2000) 1 Innovation Policy & Economy 119 at 120, online: www.journals.uchicago.edu/doi/epdf/10.1086/ipe.1.25056143). See also Bronwyn H Hall, Christian Helmers & Georg von Graevenitz, Technology Entry in the Presence of Patent Thickets (2015), National Bureau of Economic Research Working Paper No 21455, online: www.nber.org/system/files/working_papers/w21455/w21455.pdf.

all countries offer protection for and enforce utility models,[65] which may act as a barrier to widely enforcing rights related to AI-generated inventions.

While *sui generis* rights over AI-generated inventions may equip AI developers with the legal means to secure their inventions, the risks associated with creating a differentiated system in Canada prevail over potential cost and speed-related benefits.

Patent Law and the Living Tree Approach

Patents are legal instruments intended to encourage innovation by providing limited exclusive rights to the inventor in return for the disclosure of the invention. The main justification for the patent system is the incentive theory, which explains that innovation is encouraged because an inventor can obtain financial rewards for their invention in the marketplace. Patents enable inventors to recoup their research and development expenses by granting the time-limited ability to exclude others from making, selling, or importing their inventions. In exchange for the temporal monopoly, patentees must disclose the details of their inventions to the public to spread knowledge and innovation. In the absence of a patent system, inventors would likely keep new inventions secret, therefore impeding innovation.[66]

With the rapid emergence of transformative technologies, patent laws and regulations have been exposed to a new set of questions on whether AI-generated inventions can be protected under existing laws.[67]

65   Luigi Distefano & Clare Cornell, "UK: Utility Models" (16 May 2019), online: *Mondaq* www.mondaq.com/uk/patent/805960/utility-models.

66   Daniel J Gervais & Elizabeth F Judge, *Intellectual Property: The Law in Canada*, 2nd ed (Toronto: Carswell, 2011) at 644; Greg Hagen et al, *Canadian Intellectual Property Law: Cases and Materials*, 3rd ed (Toronto: Emond Montgomery, 2022) at 643; William Fisher, "Theories of Intellectual Property" in Stephen Munzer, ed, *New Essays in the Legal and Political Theory of Property* (Cambridge: Cambridge University Press, 2001), online: cyber.harvard.edu/people/tfisher/iptheory.pdf.

67   See Ryan Abbott, *The Reasonable Robot: Artificial Intelligence and the Law* (Cambridge: Cambridge University Press, 2020) at 27; Marta Duque Lizarralde & Claudia Tapia, "Artificial Intelligence: IP Challenges and Proposed Way Forward" (2022) at 16, online (pdf): *4iP Council* www.4ipcouncil.com/research/artificial-intelligence-ip-challenges-and-proposed-way-forward; Liza Vertinsky, "Thinking machines and patent law" in Woodrow Barfield & Ugo Pagallo, eds, *Research Handbook on the Law of Artificial Intelligence* (Cheltenham, UK: Edward Elgar Publishing, 2018) at 489; W Michael Schuster, "Artificial Intelligence and Patent Ownership" (2018) 75:4 Wash & Lee L Rev 1946 at 1953, online: scholarlycommons.law.wlu.edu/cgi/viewcontent.cgi?article=4627&context=wlulr; Shlomit Yanisky Ravid &

There are challenges in applying patent law to AI-generated inventions related to patentability standards, inventorship and ownership, the complexity of the examination process and the strain placed on patent offices, and the cost of granting patents and their duration. This leads to an important question as to whether Canadian courts can overcome some of these challenges by applying the constitutional law's "living tree" approach to the *Patent Act* provisions. [68] Can we consider the Canadian patent law as a living tree capable of growth and expansion to cover new conditions within its natural limits?

The unique nature of AI-generated inventions presents a challenge for IP offices and courts to apply the current patentability requirements, particularly, the requirement that an invention must not be considered "obvious" from the perspective of a "person skilled in the art" to be protected. [69] A generative AI invention might become obvious only when seen through the lens of a skilled person who can use a similar AI system to generate it. [70] Furthermore, the "inventive step" required to obtain the invention must be assessed from the

Xiaoqiong (Jackie) Liu, "When Artificial Intelligence Systems Produce Inventions: An Alternative Model for Patent Law at the 3A Era" (2018) 39 Cardozo L Rev 2215 at 2229, online: http://cardozolawreview.com/wp-content/uploads/2018/08/RAVID.LIU_.39.6.5-1.pdf; John Villasenor, "Reconceptualizing Conception: Making Room for Artificial Intelligence Inventions" (2023) 39:2 Santa Clara Comp & High Tech LJ 197 at 199–203, online: digitalcommons.law.scu.edu/chtlj/vol39/iss2/2/; Kemal Bengi & Christopher Heath, "Patents and Artificial Intelligence Inventions" in Christopher Heath, Anselm Kamperman Sanders & Anke Moerland, eds, *Intellectual Property Law and the Fourth Industrial Revolution* (The Netherlands: Kluwer Law International, 2020) 127 at 128.

68   For more details on the "living tree" approach to constitutional interpretation of federal legislation, See Peter Hogg & Wade Wright, *Constitutional Law of Canada*, 5th ed supp (Toronto: Thomson Reuters Canada, 2022) at 15:27; Andy Yu, "Constitutional Statutes are 'Always Speaking'" (Evolving Approaches to Constitutional Interpretation in Canada Conference, University of Ottawa Public Law Centre and University of Manitoba Faculty of Law address delivered at the University of Ottawa, November 2023) [unpublished]; Martin Kelly, *The Loquacious Legislature: Are Statutes 'Always Speaking'?* (PhD Thesis, University of Edinburgh, 2021).

69   Apotex Inc v Sanofi-Synthelabo Canada Inc, 2008 SCC 61 at para 67.

70   Ana Ramalho, "Patentability of AI-Generated Inventions: Is a Reform of the Patent System Needed?" (15 February 2018) at 1–2, online (pdf): *SSRN* papers. ssrn.com/sol3/papers.cfm?abstract_id=3168703 Erica Fraser, "Computers as Inventors – Legal and Policy Implications of Artificial Intelligence on Patent Law" (2016) 13:3 SCRIPTed 305 at 320, online (pdf): www.researchgate.net/profile/Erica-Fraser-3/publication/312237242_Computers_as_Inventors_-_Legal_and_Policy_Implications_of_Artificial_Intelligence_on_Patent_Law/links/5c8e44e5299bf14e7e81c5b7/Computers-as-Inventors-Legal-and-Policy-Implications-of-Artificial-Intelligence-on-Patent-Law.pdf.

viewpoint of an AI machine "skilled in the art" rather than human inventive activities. As such, modifications to the obviousness standard must be considered. It may be more appropriate to evaluate the obviousness of such inventions from the perspective of the person skilled in the art using an ordinary AI tool. It may also be necessary to determine that minor advancements to technology, such as upgrades from ChatGPT to ChatGPT-2, -3, and -4, will not be sufficient to meet the patentability standards as mere adaptations of existing products.[71]

Another challenge in applying the patent law regime is the long and expensive patent examination process, which is ill-suited to the stunning speed of AI innovation. The examination process for patent applications by the Canadian Intellectual Property Office (CIPO) is usually between four and seven years.[72] The cost of drafting and filing a patent in Canada can range between $5,000 and $25,000.[73] By the time a patent is granted, a new version of the invention may already be available. For example, OpenAI was able to upgrade ChatGPT-3.5 and launch ChatGPT-4, a more powerful technology responding to both text and images, within a few months.[74]

Furthermore, patent offices are too understaffed and overtaxed to deal with generative AI inventions.[75] They may be forced to resort to AI-assisted examination to keep up with the increase in patent applications. CIPO has already implemented a project using AI technology to assist with its existing trademark backlog.[76] However, it is unlikely that the examination process can be completely automated because of the need to ensure due process and the likelihood of legislative opposition. It is also unlikely that patent offices will have access to AI technology sophisticated enough to automate examination any time soon.[77]

Lastly, some scholars argue that the potential value of granting patent protection for AI-generated inventions is outweighed by

---

71   Bagchee & MacFarlane, *supra* note 402.
72   *CIPO, File a Canadian Patent Application, supra* note 419.
73   "Hiring an intellectual property professional" (20 October 2021), online: *Canadian Intellectual Property Office*, online: ised-isde.canada.ca/site/canadian-intellectual-property-office/en/hiring-intellectual-property-professional.
74   Will Douglas Heaven, "GPT-4 is bigger and better than ChatGPT – but OpenAI won't say why" (14 March 2023), online: *MIT Technology Review* www.technologyreview.com/2023/03/14/1069823/gpt-4-is-bigger-and-better-chatgpt-openai/.
75   Fraser, *supra* note 436 at 332.
76   Martha J Savoy & Paula Clancy, "CIPO using AI technology to assist with examination backlog" (27 April 2022), online: *Gowling WLG* gowlingwlg.com/en/insights-resources/articles/2022/cipo-using-ai-technology-for-examination-backlog.
77   de Rassenfosse, *supra* note 375 at 15.

its negative effect on competition in the marketplace. Technological advancements can allow AI-generated systems to generate a large number of low-quality patents at a low cost.[78] If all these inventions were to be protected for 20 years, it could lead to higher prices for consumers, along with patent thickets and patent trolls.[79]

Despite these challenges, the conceptual engineering of patent law has been successful over the years in protecting the rapid development of transformative innovation generally occurring outside of its traditional margins.[80] The history of the patent system demonstrates its ability to accommodate a wide range of complex technologies that display divergent characteristics such as software, biotechnology, organic chemistry, and business methods.[81] The current traditional norms of patent law could be sufficient to accommodate protection over generative AI inventions.

The substantial efforts conducted by AI professionals such as scientists, programmers, and data suppliers to build and train AI systems should be recognized by patent law. The granting of a patent privilege rewards human inventors for their skill and labor. The conclusion that an invention should be treated differently because it has been created by an AI also contradicts Canada's intellectual property obligation under multilateral agreements. The WTO's *Agreement on Trade-Related Aspects of Intellectual Property Rights* (TRIPS) prohibits any sort of discrimination based on an invention's field of technology.[82]

This article also argues for adopting a fast-track examination process for AI-generated inventions to secure the competitiveness of the Canadian AI sector. It is more reasonable to address the speed of issuance of patents than it is to create an entirely new *sui generis* system. An expedited examination process for patent applications related to

---

78   Fraser, *supra* note 436.
79   *Ibid*; Francesco Banterle, "Ownership of Inventions Created by Artificial Intelligence" (18 December 2018) at 23, online (pdf): *SSRN* ssrn.com/abstract=3276702.
80   Conceptual Engineering is both the name of a philosophical method and the name of an increasingly popular field of metaphilosophical research. It focuses on how to best assess and improve our conceptual schemes and repertoires. See Herman Cappelen & David Plunkett, "Introduction: A Guided Tour of Conceptual Engineering and Conceptual Ethics" in Alexis Burgess et al, eds, *Conceptual Engineering and Conceptual Ethics* (Oxford Academic, 2020), online: academic. oup.com/book/36673/chapter/321696749.
81   Dan L Burk, "AI Patents and the Self-Assembling Machine in the Future of Intellectual Property" (2021) 105 Minn L Rev Headnotes 301 at 304.
82   *Agreement on Trade-Related Aspects of Intellectual Property Rights*, 15 April 1994 (entered into force 1 January 1995) art 27(1).

AI-generated inventions can be introduced by CIPO and other patent offices around the world to facilitate the disclosure of otherwise-secret algorithms. The speed while maintaining the quality of the patent granting process would respond to the AI community needs where innovation cycles are short. The expedited process will allow the patent applicants of related to AI-generated inventions to obtain decisions on their patent applications in a more expeditious way compared to applications processed according to the conventional examination timeline.

Intellectual property offices have successfully implemented expedited patent examination programs to address global challenges such as technologies that help resolve or mitigate environmental impacts or conserve the natural environment or natural resources (green technologies) as well as COVID-19 diagnostics and therapeutics.[83] The eligible applications are examined as a matter of priority to facilitate the commercialization of patented products and the technology deployment. In addition to these programs, many countries (including Canada and the United States) currently participate in one or more examination cooperation programs between IP offices. The Patent Prosecution Highway (PPH) is a framework in which an application determined to be patentable in the Office of Earlier Examination (OEE) is eligible for accelerated examination in the Office of Later Examination (OLE) with a simple procedure upon an applicant's request.[84] In practice, when an applicant receives a final ruling from a first patent office stating that at least one claim is allowed, the applicant may request fast-track examination of corresponding claim(s) in a corresponding application that is pending in a second patent office.[85]

---

83   "Advanced examination for green technologies" (14 August 2023), online: *Canadian Intellectual Property Office* ised-isde.canada.ca/site/canadian-intellectual-property-office/en/patents/patent-application-and-examination/advanced-examination-green-technologies; Bassem Awad, "Patent Pledges in Green Technology" in Jorge L Contreras & Meredith Jacob, eds, *Patent Pledges: Global Perspectives on Patent Law's Private Ordering Frontier* (Cheltenham, UK: Edward Elgar Publishing, 2017) 82 at 95; "Accelerate examination for Canadian patent applications related to COVID-19 relief" (8 July 2020), online: *Canadian Intellectual Property Office* ised-isde.canada.ca/site/canadian-intellectual-property-office/en/accelerate-examination-canadian-patent-applications-related-COVID-19-relief.

84   "Expedited Examination: Patent Prosecution Highway" (6 April 2022), online: *Canadian Intellectual Property Office* ised-isde.canada.ca/site/canadian-intellectual-property-office/en/expedited-examination-patent-prosecution-highway.

85   The Canadian Intellectual Property Office (CIPO) has, as of January 2024, PPH partnerships with 27 intellectual property (IP) offices through a global PPH (GPPH) pilot program and with six IP offices through bilateral PPH pilot programs (European Patent Office, China, Taiwan, Mexico, France, and Brazil).

Canadian AI developers often do not have sufficient resources to submit a patent application in multiple jurisdictions to benefit from the PPH program. Thus, an expedited examination process for AI-generated inventions would enable them to effectively compete in the global markets while encouraging the disclosure of machine learning methods and generative AI outputs.

Conclusion

The creation of AI capable of generating inventions as brilliant as the human mind was considered, until recently, science fiction. Nowadays, AI systems are shaping the future of humanity across every industry and will continue to act as a technological innovator for the foreseeable future. Geoffrey Hinton, the godfather of AI, has recently expressed his concerns about the capabilities of AI technologies: "Artificial intelligence can be used as a force for good — but there are also big risks involved with the generative technology as it gets even smarter and more widespread."[86]

The quest to protect AI-generated inventions essential to accelerating innovation while providing appropriate safeguards to the disclosure of knowledge and social welfare. To harness the economic potential of AI, it is important to create legal certainty as a fundamental element of modern society.

Placing the AI-generated inventions in the public domain could have adverse implications for AI development. Allowing free riding — permitting anyone to use AI-generated inventions — would have negative impacts on the AI innovation spectrum. Companies investing in developing and training AI systems would find their inventions copied freely by human or AI competitors with no rewards. The use of soft law principles in the form of ethical standards or code of ethics sets effective social norms for AI-based technologies. However, these principles are not operationalized in the context of patent law. The wide variety of ethical standards and lack of enforceability do not make them the best option to regulate a fast-evolving industry.

A tiered approach to AI-generated inventions could be considered as an interim measure to protect a growing area of innovation. Protecting AI-generated inventions by utility models or petty patents with shorter

---

86   Geoffrey Hinton, "Risks of artificial intelligence must be considered as the technology evolves" (June 2023), online: https://www.utoronto.ca/news/risks-artificial-intelligence-must-be-considered-technology-evolves-geoffrey-hinton.

terms of protection and fast administrative processes might reflect the interests of the AI industry. However, it creates several unintended consequences and additional challenges for innovators and regulators. The creation of a *sui generis* right of reduced scope and duration could lead to a cumulation of rights of various kinds on the same subject matter and functionality.

Many scholars consider that the patent system can accommodate technical advancements generated autonomously by AI-powered systems. The need to incentivize technical innovation and the provision of an appropriate monopoly in return for making technical advances available to the public could be achieved by the patent system. However, the incorporation of AI-generated inventions in the current patent regime requires changes to existing concepts, including those related to inventorship and the person skilled in the art, among others. Additionally, these changes must be accompanied by revisiting the patent examination practices for AI inventions and the capacity of patent offices. Introducing an expedited patent examination program for AI-generated inventions is essential to safeguard the competitiveness of Canada's AI sector while ensuring the public gains timely access to these inventions.

Chapter 7

Tribulations of Open-Ended Concepts in Copyright Law

Mistrale Goudreau

Abstract

The Canadian *Copyright Act* contains several open-ended concepts, which leave space for different interpretations. This chapter discusses the legitimacy of those open-textured concepts. If they lead to legal uncertainty, are they compatible with the rule of law? Even if legal scholars approve of their use, do we know their advantages and disadvantages, especially in a field dominated by technological advances? The second part of this discussion looks at the open-ended concepts adopted in the Canadian Copyright Act in order to recognize the economic rights of the author. Our analysis first examines cases where the technological developments have eroded distinctions and have created ambiguities, leading to a nuanced landscape that is difficult to navigate. In this second part, we also survey some proposals made to reconstruct copyright, to make it more coherent and better align with the legislative purposes of copyright. Further, we emphasize how those pecuniary rights recognized in the Copyright Act are exercised in highly volatile market structures and may lose their economic significance, making it difficult for the statute to achieve its goal of providing a just financial reward to creators. We conclude with some observations which, we hope, could help the courts and Parliament establish the road map for a more coherent copyright regime in Canada.

Very early in the history of copyright in common law countries, it was decided that whatever protection of published works existed in common law, it was merged with or replaced by the Statute of Anne of 1709, passed in 1710.[1] The Canadian Copyright Act incorporated the same rule for all types of works, stating in section 89 that no one "is entitled to copyright otherwise than under and in accordance with this Act or any other Act of Parliament."[2] So, a careful reading of the statutory provisions is always the best way to establish the state of the law on a copyright issue. However, the Canadian legislation, like many foreign copyright legislations and international instruments, contains several open-ended concepts, which leave space for different interpretations. The Supreme Court of Canada has had to deal with such concepts in at least 14 cases in the last two decades, reversing in at least half of the cases the judgments of the courts of appeal.[3] Is the use of those wide concepts justified in the context of the Copyright Act, especially in matters of economic rights, often the subject of multiple litigations, as illustrated by the many decisions of Supreme Court of Canada over the last 20 years?[4]

---

1   *Donaldson v Becket* (1774) 98 Eng. Rep. 257; Sunny Handa, *Copyright Law in Canada*, (Markham: Butterworths 2002) at 40–41.

2   *Copyright Act*, RSC 1985, c. C-42.

3   *Théberge v. Galerie d'Art du Petit Champlain inc.*, [2002] 2 SCR 336, 2002 SCC 34; *CCH Canadian Ltd. v. Law Society of Upper Canada*, [2004] 1 SCR 339; *Society of Composers, Authors and Music Publishers of Canada v. Canadian Assn. of Internet Providers*, 2004 SCC 45, [2004] 2 SCR 427; *Robertson v. Thomson Corp.*, 2006 SCC 43, [2006] 2 SCR 363; *Euro-excellence Inc. v. Kraft Canada Inc*, 2007 SCC 37, [2007] 3 SCR 20; *Entertainment Software Association v. Society of Composers, Authors and Music Publishers of Canada* 2012 SCC 34, [2012] 2 SCR 231; *Society of Composers, Authors and Music Publishers of Canada c. Bell Canada*, 2012 SCC 36, [2012] 2 SCR 326; *Alberta (Education) c. Access Copyright*, 2012 SCC 37, [2012] 2 SCR 345; *Rogers Communications Inc. v. Society of Composers, Authors and Music Publishers of Canada*, 2012 SCC 35, [2012] 2 SCR 283; *Cinar Corporation v. Robinson*, 2013 SCC 73, [2013] 3 SCR 1168; *Canadian Broadcasting Corp. v. SODRAC 2003 Inc.*, 2015 SCC 57, [2015] 3 SCR 615; *Keatley Surveying Ltd. v. Teranet Inc.*, 2019 SCC 43, [2019] 3 SCR 418; *York University v. Canadian Copyright Licensing Agency (Access Copyright)*, 2021 SCC 32, [2021] 2 SCR 734; *Society of Composers, Authors and Music Publishers of Canada v. Entertainment Software Association*, 2022 SCC 30.

4   Seven cases dealt with some aspects of the economic rights of the author: *Théberge v. Galerie d'Art du Petit Champlain inc.*, [2002] 2 SCR 336, 2002 SCC 34; *Society of Composers, Authors and Music Publishers of Canada v. Canadian Assn. of Internet Providers*, 2004 SCC 45, [2004] 2 SCR 427; *Entertainment Software Association v. Society of Composers, Authors and Music Publishers of Canada*, 2012 SCC 34, [2012] 2 SCR 231; *Rogers Communications Inc. v. Society of Composers, Authors and Music Publishers of Canada*, 2012 SCC 35, [2012] 2 SCR 283; *Cinar Corporation v. Robinson*, 2013 SCC 73, [2013] 3 SCR 1168; *Société Radio-Canada c. SODRAC 2003 Inc.*, 2015

Focusing on copyright legislations, this chapter draws on theoretical frameworks dealing with legislative drafting, interpretation, and standards. The analysis seeks to identify the difficulties that have arisen when these open-textured concepts have been used in copyright law. In doing so, it will mainly use traditional legal methodology, looking for concrete cases where open concepts have led to uncertainties and controversies.

The text aims at discussing the legitimacy of those open-textured concepts. If they lead to legal uncertainty, are they compatible with the rule of law? Even if legal scholars approve of their use, do we know their advantages and disadvantages, especially in a field dominated by technological advances? In the second part of this chapter, we assess the open-ended concepts adopted in the Canadian Copyright Act to recognize the economic rights of the author. Our analysis will first examine cases where the technology developments have eroded distinctions and have created ambiguities, leading to nuances that are difficult to navigate. In this second part, we will also survey some proposals made to reconstruct copyright, to make it more coherent and better align with the legislative purposes of copyright. Further, we emphasize how those pecuniary rights recognized in the Copyright Act are exercised in highly volatile market structures and may lose their economic significance, making it difficult for the statute to achieve its goal of providing a just financial reward to creators. We conclude with some observations which, we hope, could help the courts and Parliament establish the road map for a more coherent copyright regime in Canada.

Our discussion begins with an overview of open-ended concepts from the perspectives of legal philosophers and legislative drafters.

The Open-Ended Concepts in Law

Open-ended means "having no predetermined limit or boundaries"[5] or "not rigorously fixed, [...] adaptable to the developing needs of a situation."[6] When an open-ended concept is used in a legal provision, it gives a large margin of discretion to the person in charge of ultimately

---

SCC 57, [2015] 3 SCR 615; Society of Composers, Authors and Music Publishers of Canada v. Entertainment Software Association, 2022 SCC 30.

5   Judy Pearsall, ed, *Oxford English Reference Dictionary* (Oxford: Oxford University Press, 2002), sub verbo "open."

6   Merriam-Webster Dictionary, "Open-ended," online: https://www.merriam-webster.com/dictionary/open-ended.

applying the rule. It may lead to some legal uncertainty, making legal outcome of some cases highly unpredictable. Is this unpredictability compatible with the rule of law?

The Open-Ended Concepts and the Rule of Law

It is a well-known truth that the use of open-ended concepts is frequent in modern legal systems and legal philosophers have stressed that their use is legitimate. For example, Hans Kelsen, while elaborating its *Pure Theory of Law*,[7] acknowledged that there are cases of "[i]ntentional [i]ndefiniteness" of norms[8] and hold that the judges applying general concepts are simply taking one of the steps in the normal hierarchical ordering of legal norms.[9] Herbert Hart in *The Concept of Law*[10] referred to general concepts as instances of the "open texture" of legal language[11] and argued this indeterminacy should be considered an advantage rather than a disadvantage.[12] But what are exactly the advantages and disadvantages of open-ended concepts? When is it appropriate to use them?

The Practical Advantages and Disadvantages of Open-Ended Concepts

Let us start with the disadvantages. Open-ended concepts are generally considered lacking in precision and imprecision in legal texts was traditionally frowned upon by common law legal drafters. For them, clarity was important because it helped to "eliminate ambiguity and vagueness."[13] The "older legal tradition was that the lawyer had to be precise to the last degree."[14] This was based on the assumption that the laws are drafted "for a potentially hostile audience"[15], which will try, focusing on the text vagueness, to limit their legal obligations.

---

7   Hans Kelsen, *Pure Theory of Law*, translated by Max Knight from the 2nd German ed (Berkeley: University of California Press, 1967).

8   Kelsen, *supra* note 7 at 349.

9   *Ibid.*

10   HLA Hart, *The Concept of Law*, (Oxford: Clarendon Press, 1961).

11   *Ibid* at 120–132.

12   *Ibid* at 125–126.

13   Victor Crabbe, *Legislative Drafting* (London: Routledge-Cavendish, 1993) at 43.

14   Robert C Dick, *Legal Drafting*, (Toronto: Carswell, 1972) at 15, speaking about the lawyer who drafts a contract for a client.

15   J Paul Salembier, *Legal and Legislative Drafting*, 2nd ed (Toronto: LexisNexis, 2018) at 3.

Nonetheless, commentators acknowledged that, at times, vagueness can be deliberately used [16]; it can even "be a friend of Parliamentary Council." [17] As Dick summarized, "[t]he draftsman should not be more general he has to be and yet he must not make a category too narrow." [18] Salembier lists four situations in which a drafter may deliberately choose vagueness:

- to effect an indirect delegation of power;
- to deliberately delegate policy decisions to the courts;
- to address what appear to be infinitely variable situations; and
- to reach negotiated agreements where precise language might
  pose an impediment. [19]

In the civil law countries, the tradition is different: the provisions are often framed as broad, general principles and there is a greater acceptance of general terms. For instance, civil law legislative drafters suggest that concepts should be as general as the reality they are intended to represent, as this will lead to a better understanding of the message to be communicated. First, the essential ideas or principles expressed by the text will be better highlighted. Second, the text will be more concise. [20]

Finally, in the legislative drafting world, a balancing act is recommended: the guidelines for legislative counsels suggest that a statute should be written "with the required degree of precision." [21]

In summary, both in civil law and common law, the use of general terms is acceptable and should be decided on a case-by-case basis. Choosing open-ended concepts may render the law more adaptable to widely variable situations and it may make it easier to get the necessary

---

16   Dick, *supra* note 14 at 17.
17   Crabbe, *supra* note 13 at 13.
18   Dick, *supra* note 14 at 18.
19   Salembier, *supra* note 15 at 111.
20   Here is the quote in French: "Les concepts devront être aussi généraux que le permet la réalité qu'ils servent à représenter, car il en résultera une meilleure compréhension du message à communiquer. D'une part, les idées essentielles ou principes exprimés par le texte seront mieux mis en évidence. D'autre part, le texte sera plus concis." Richard Tremblay et al, *Éléments de légistique: comment rédiger les lois et les règlements* (Montréal, Éditions Yvon Blais, 2010) at 320.
21   In the Drafting Conventions for Acts (2023), online: https://www.ulcc-chlc. ca/Civil-Section/Drafting/Drafting-Conventions, it is recommended that: (1) A legislative text should be drafted simply, clearly and concisely, with the required degree of precision, and as much as possible in ordinary language. (2) If the text is well-arranged, simplicity and conciseness can be achieved along with precision. It is important not to exaggerate the required degree of precision.

endorsement from the political decision-makers. However, it has the effect of delegating some policy decisions to the courts.

The cost of determining the precise scope of provisions is, when they are couched in general terms, transferred from the legal drafters to those being responsible for the application of the law. This can have many consequences. First, if the rule is to be followed by the members of the public, they will generally act in ignorance of the judicial interpretation of the norm or have to incur the expenses of legal advice to get it. The vagueness of the rule may also lead even well-intentioned citizens to break the rule, undermining the effectiveness of the law. It will also tend to disadvantage economically weaker parties who, because they fear or cannot bear the financial burden of litigation, will lean towards over-compliance. Also, in sectors where the stakeholders are known for their litigious attitudes, there is a risk of proliferation of litigations.[22]

In short, the choice between precise terms or open-textured concepts in statutes is not only a matter of words, it is also a matter of public policy. It is a balancing act between flexibility (with its inevitable unpredictability) and precision (which may lead to provisions becoming obsolete). It is determining how much can and must be resolved by Parliament and how much can and must be left to the judiciary.

Let us now examine the open-ended concepts used in the Canadian Copyright Act to set out the economic rights of the author.

Open-Ended Concepts in Economic Rights of the Author

This part illustrates how several concepts have seen their usefulness eroded by technological developments.

The Economic Rights Concepts Tested by Technological Developments

The Copyright Act grants to the copyright holders a list of exclusive rights to exercise specific acts in relation the work, this exclusivity precluding others from performing those acts without proper authorization.[23] Very early in the history of the copyright legislations, the exclusive rights of reproduction and public performance were recognized. In

---

22   Mistrale Goudreau, Légiférer par généralités ou en termes précis? Quelle question! (2019), Dernières nouvelles, en ligne: https://ciaj-icaj.ca/fr/author/mgoudreau/; Louis Kaplow, "Rules Versus Standards: An Economic Analysis," (1992) 42:3 Duke Law Journal 557.

23   The main rights are enumerated in section 3 of the *Copyright Act*.

England, the Statute of Anne of 1710 granted to authors exclusivity on book printing of their work[24] and the 1911 Act[25] expressly mentioned in the definition of copyright "the sole right to produce or reproduce the work or any substantial part thereof in any material form whatsoever, to perform [...] the work or any substantial part thereof in public; if the work is unpublished, to publish the work or any substantial part thereof." In France, the 1791 decree[26] recognized that a performance in a public theater could not be made without the written and formal consent of the authors[27], whereas the 1973 decree granted them the exclusive right to sell (or have sold) or to distribute their works in the territory of the Republic, implicitly recognizing the reproduction right.[28]

However, very early on, the technological developments created difficulties. In England, the Copyright Act 1842[29] replaced the Statute of Anne and included provisions granting exclusive rights on printing or multiplying copies of the sheets of music.[30] But would this right apply to perforated rolls for use in mechanical organs? Would it include the making and sale of records? The courts in England concluded that the rolls were not copies.[31] By the same token, the making and sale of records were not included in the copyright.[32] In the United States, in *White-Smith*

---

24   Section II of *An act for the encouragement of learning, by vesting the copies of printed books in the authors or purchasers of such copies, during the times therein mentioned,* 1710: 8 Anne c. 19 / c. 21.

25   *Copyright Act 1911,* 1 & 2 Geo. 5. c. 46, s. 1 (2) For the purposes of this Act, 'copyright' means the sole right to produce or reproduce the Copyright, work or any substantial part thereof in any material form whatsoever (...), to perform (...), or in the case of a lecture (a) to deliver (...), the work or any substantial part thereof in public ; if the work is unpublished (...), to publish the work or any substantial part thereof ;

26   *Loi du 13 janvier 1791, relative aux théâtres et au droit de représentation et d'exécution des œuvres dramatiques et musicales.*

27   Art. 3. Les ouvrages des auteurs vivants ne pourront être représentés sur aucun théâtre public, dans toute l'étendue de la France, sans le consentement formel et par écrit des auteurs, ...

28   *Loi du 19 juillet 1793, relative à la propriété littéraire et artistique,* article premier: Les auteurs d'écrits en tout genre, les compositeurs de musique, les peintres et dessinateurs qui feront graver des tableaux ou dessins, jouiront durant leur vie entière du droit exclusif de vendre, faire vendre, distribuer leurs ouvrages dans le territoire de la République, et d'en céder la propriété en tout ou en partie.

29   *Copyright Act 1842,* 5 & 6 Vict. c. 45.

30   Section II.

31   *Boosey v. Whight,* [1899] 1 Ch 836.

32   John S Mckeown, *Fox on Canadian Law of Copyright and Industrial Designs,* 4th ed (Toronto: Carswell), loose leaf § 14:6, citing *Monckton v. Gramophone Co.* (1912), 106 L.T. 84 (Eng. C.A.).

Music Publishing Company v. Apollo Company[33], the Supreme Court of the United States also ruled that music rolls for player pianos were not copies. Even the Closing Protocol of the Berne Convention, in its 1886 version, stated that the "manufacture and sale of instruments serving to reproduce mechanically the airs of music borrowed from the private domain are not considered as constituting musical infringement." In France, there was a similar provision.[34]

But some legislators intervened in favor of authors. In England and in Canada, the law was amended to specify that "copyright" means the right to produce or reproduce the work or any substantial part thereof *in any material form whatsoever* and that it includes "(d) in the case of a literary, dramatic or musical work, to make any record, perforated roll, cinematographic film, or other contrivance by means of which the work may be mechanically performed or delivered."[35] There was one caveat: where the owner of copyright in a work had allowed it to be recorded, any person could make recordings of it on giving notice and payment of a royalty of two cents per playing surface.[36] In the United States, the adaptation was similar: the Copyright Act of 1909[37] gave composers of music the rights to be compensated for mechanical reproductions of their works, through the creation of a compulsory license. The reason for establishing a compensation regime instead of a right was the fear of allowing the creation of monopolies. As the United States House Report 1 on the Copyright Act of 1909 explained:

> It became evident that there would be serious danger that if the grant
> of right was made too broad, the progress of science and useful arts
> would not be promoted, but rather hindered, and that powerful and
> dangerous monopolies might be fostered which would be prejudicial

33   *White-Smith Music Publishing Company v. Apollo Company*, 209 U.S. 1 (1907).

34   See the *Loi du 16 mai 1866, relative aux instruments de musique mécanique, article unique*. As Alexandre Portron recalls, the provision was soon abrogated when the use of phonographs emerged. However, no authorization from the composer was needed for the use of music boxes (See *Loi du 10 novembre 1917*, article 2); the exception was ultimately deleted in 1957 (see Loi n° 57-298, 11 mars 1957), article 77); Alexandre Portron, *Propriété intellectuelle, Chronique rédigée par Centre d'études et de coopération juridique interdisciplinaire* (UR 21665), *La Semaine Juridique Entreprise et Affaires* n° 31-35, 1er août 2022, 1280.

35   *Copyright Act 1911*, 1 & 2 Geo. 5. c. 46, s. 1; in Canada: *Copyright Act*, S.C. 1921, c.24, (11 and 12 Geo. V. Ch.24 (1924)), s. 3.

36   S 19 of the *Copyright Act 1911*, 1 & 2 Geo. 5. c. 46; s. 19 of *Copyright Act*, S.C. 1921, c.24, (11 and 12 Geo. V. Ch.24 (1924)).

37   Chap. 320, sec. 4952, § 1(e), 33 Stat. 1075, 1075-76 (1909).

to the public interests. This danger lies in the possibility that some one company might secure, by purchase or otherwise, a large number of copyrights of the most popular music, and by controlling these copyrights monopolize the business of manufacturing the selling music producing machines, otherwise free to the world.[38]

The legislative recognition of protection against a reproduction *in any material form*[39] in the UK and in Canada led to a broader understanding of the concept of reproduction. The courts concluded that a reproduction occurred even when the work (or its copy) was not in a humanly readable form.[40] The practical difficulties, if any, were thought to be better addressed through the creation of exceptions or compulsory licensing or compensatory schemes.[41]

But the technological advances continued to challenge the notion of reproduction. A reproduction involves normally a material fixation. But must it be a permanent fixation? The problem arises, for example, when a work is displayed on the screen (of a TV set, of a computer system). Is a copy made? An early case, *Canadian Admiral Corporation Ltd. v. Rediffusion Inc.*,[42] seemed to imply a negative answer. The court judged that "for copyright to subsist in a 'work' it must be expressed to some extent at least in some material form, capable of identification and having a more or less permanent endurance"[43] and that the live telecasts of a football game could not be considered protected works. The legislator overruled the decision, specifying in subsection 3(1.1) that a work communicated to public by telecommunication is "fixed" even if fixed simultaneously with communication.[44] However, does

---

38   H.R. REP. No. 60-2222, at 4 (1909), p 5.

39   *Apple Computer Inc. v. Mackintosh Computers Ltd.*, 1986 CanLII 6820 (FC), [1987] 1 FC 173; aff'd 1987 CanLII 9003 (FCA), [1988] 1 F.C. 673, aff'd 1990 CanLII 119 (SCC), [1990] 2 S.C.R. 209.

40   *Apple Computer Inc. v. Mackintosh Computers Ltd.*, 1986 CanLII 6820 (FC), [1987] 1 F.C. 173, aff'd 1987 CanLII 9003 (FCA), [1988] 1 F.C. 673, aff'd 1990 CanLII 119 (SCC), [1990] 2 S.C.R. 209.

41   One can even ask if a compensation scheme is equivalent to a copyright. David Vaver has raised the issue with the public book renting compensation scheme created in Canada: David Vaver, "Copyright in Foreign Works: Canada's International Obligations" (1987) 66:1 *Canadian Bar Review* 76 at 125; Graham J Reynolds, "An Essential Service: Public Libraries and their Role in Law and Society" (2020) 25:4 *Lex Electronica* 20, 2020 CanLIIDocs 3442, online: https://canlii.ca/t/t0k0.

42   1954 CanLII 712 (CA EXC), [1954] Ex CR 382.

43   *Ibid* at para 28.

44   Subsection 3 (1.1), introduced by *Canada-United States Free Trade Agreement Implementation Act*, S.C. 1988, c. 65, s. 62.

that solve the issue if no simultaneous "fixation," no recording at all, is made? Should we interpret the subsection *a contrario* and conclude that without simultaneous fixation, there is no work? Should this conclusion for the non-existence of work be extended to the non-existence of a copy during a live telecast? This issue — can a simple display on a screen be a copy? — continued to bother the specialists. It is worth noting that, during the elaboration of the WIPO Performances and Phonograms Treaty (WPPT) in 1996, the issue was debated and finally, in Article 7, no mention was made of transient or temporary embodiment of a work. [45]

But some in Canada were not in agreement with this restrictive view of the concept of reproduction. For example, the Copyright sub-committee of the Information Highway Advisory Council created in 1994 argued that the "act of browsing a work in a digital environment should be considered an act of reproduction." [46] In its 1995 report, the Council recognized the complexity of the issue, insisting on the need of further studies before reaching a conclusion. [47] However, in 2022, the Supreme Court, in its decision *Society of Composers, Authors and Music Publishers of Canada v. Entertainment Software Association* [48], seemed to have rejected this idea of temporary reproduction, stating that only when the "technology gives users durable copies of a work, the author's reproduction right is engaged." [49]

---

45   The words "whether permanent or temporary" do not appear in article 7. However, an Agreed Statement confirms that "It is understood that the storage of a protected work in digital form in an electronic medium constitutes a reproduction within the meaning of Article 9 of the Berne Convention." On the significance of this statement, see Mihaly Ficsor, *The Law of Copyright and the Internet*, Oxford, Oxford University Press, 2002, p 130–143; Mihály Ficsor, *The Law of Copyright and the Internet: The 1996 WIPO Treaties, their Interpretation and Implementation* (Oxford: Oxford University Press, 2002) at 130–43; Mihály Ficsor, "Copyright for the Digital Era: The WIPO Internet Treaties" (1997) 21:3–4 Colum-VLA JL & Arts 197 at 203–07.

46   Canada, *Connection, Community, Content: The Challenge of the Information Highway, Final Report of the Information Highway Advisory Council* (Ottawa: Ministry of Supply & Services, 1995) at 115.

47   *Ibid*, at 115 "The Council was cognizant of the need to strike a balance between the interest of creators and users. At end of the day, there was general agreement that copyright owners must be able to determine whether and when browsing should be permitted on the Information Highway. To assist both users and creators in the new digital environment, the council recommends that the Copyright Act be amended to provide clarification of what constitute "browsing" and what works are "publicly available." In formulating the following recommendation, the council members recognized that before further study and consultation with stakeholders will likely be required before the complex issues can be fully resolved."

48   2022 SCC 30.

49   *Ibid* at para 70. See also par 56, where the court stresses that a "reproduction, by

In Europe, the issue was clarified in the European Directive 2001–29[50]; Article 2 requires the member states to provide for the exclusive right to authorize or prohibit direct or indirect, *temporary or permanent reproduction by any means and in any form, in whole or in part.*[51]

But even then, some ambiguities persist: If the reproduction right applies to screen display (or user interface), does it raise the question of the "origin of the copy"? Is user interface a copy of the software that produces it? Or is it the result of a set of instructions[52], one that must be judged for originality?[53] Depending on the answers, there may be different or multiple copyright holders (designers of the page, designers of the computer program).

In fact, as noted by André Lucas, the idea that any communication by a medium implies a reproduction leads not only to ambiguities, it leads to a drastic conclusion: anything that carries a work even fleetingly, even as airwaves, and why not electric current, or even the

---

contrast, gives a user a durable copy of a work." The decision does not mention subsection 3(1.1) of the Copyright Act.

50   *Directive 2001/29/EC of the European Parliament and of the Council of 22 May 2001 on the Harmonisation Of Certain Aspects Of Copyright And Related Rights In The Information Society*, Official Journal L 167, 22/06/2001 P. 0010 – 0019.

51   Séverine Dusollier, "Chapter 6: Realigning Economic Rights With Exploitation of Works" in P Bernt Hugenholtz, ed, *Copyright Reconstructed: Rethinking Copyright's Economic Rights in a Time of Highly Dynamic Technological and Economic Change (Alphen aan den Rijn: Wolters Kluwer, 2018)* 163 at 167, 2018, 163 at p 167, concluding that the Court of Justice of the European Union has construed the notion of temporary reduction as covering any technical copy and citing Case C-360/13, *Public Relations Consultants Ass'n Ltd. v. Newspaper Licensing Agency Ltd.*, 2014 EUR-Lex CELEX 62013CJ0360 (Jun. 5, 2014); C-429/08, *Football Ass'n Premier League and Others v. QC Leisure and Others, Karen Murphy v. Media Protection Services*, EUR-Lex CELEX 62008CJ0403 (Oct. 4, 2011); C-5/08 *Infopaq International A/S v Danske Dagblades Forening*, CELEX number: 62008CJ0005 (16/07/2009); C-302/10 *Infopaq International A/S v Danske Dagblades Forening*, CELEX number: 62010CO0302 (17/01/2012).

52   In *Harmony Consulting Ltd. v. G.A. Foss Transport Ltd.*, 2012 CarswellNat 3341, 2012 CarswellNat 5994, 2012 CAF 226, 2012 FCA 226, [2012] F.C.J. No. 1131, 107 C.P.R. (4th) 1, 221 A.C.W.S. (3d) 976, 435 N.R. 200, the court wrote: 89 In my view, the screen display on a user monitor is the result of such a set of instructions rather than a reproduction of the set of instruction in another form. To use the analogy of the Supreme Court of Canada in Cuisenaire v. South West Imports Ltd. (1968), [1969] S.C.R. 208, 2 D.L.R. (3d) 430 (S.C.C.), the screen display is the rabbit pie rather than the recipe (the recipe being the set of instructions). See also *Fox on Canadian Law of Copyright and Industrial Designs*, 4th ed, *supra* note 32, § 3:17 (Browsing).

53   Cour de cassation, Chambre civile 1, 12 mai 2011, 09-12.536, Inédit, reversing in part Cour d'appel, Aix-en-Provence, Chambre 2, 11 Décembre 2008 - n° 2008/451

human voice, is a reproduction![54] There would no longer be any need
for the concept of representation or performance.

The concept of public performance has also faced significant challenges. An overview of the international law development gives an
illustration. Originally, as was reported by Ficsor, "public performance"
meant "performance of works in the public or, at least, at the place open
to the public" and the 1886 Berne Convention was drafted with this
concept in mind.[55] It was not covering the communication of work by
radio waves. Adjustments to the new technological reality was needed.

So, "communication to the public by radio-diffusion" was added
to the 1928 Rome text.[56] But the adjustment was too narrowly made; it
did not cover communication by coaxial cables or wire.[57] The distinction was also made in the interpretation[58] of the Canadian Act.[59] Could
such communication then be considered, in itself, a public performance?
In French law, the notion of performance "representation" consists of
communication of the work by any means.[60] In the common law juris-

---

54   André Lucas, *Traité de la propriété littéraire et artistique* (Paris: Litec, 1992) at 218, para 241.
55   See s 9 of the 1886 version and *Ficsor, The Law of Copyright, supra* note 45 at 155.
56   See art 11bis of the 1928 version; *Ficsor, The Law of Copyright, supra* note 45 at 156.
57   Sam Ricketson & Jane Ginsburg, *International Copyright and Neighbouring Rights*,
      (Oxford: Oxford University Press, 2022) at 708–709, although the wording origi-
      nally proposed covered "telegraphy or telephony whether by wire or not."
58   *Canadian Admiral Corporation Ltd. v. Rediffusion Inc.*, 1954 CanLII 712 (CA EXC),
      [1954] Ex CR 382, p 397.
59   The statute then recognized in s 3 the exclusive right "(f) In the case of any lit-
      erary, dramatic, musical or artistic work, to communicate such work by radio
      communication."
60   The notion of performance "representer" used in the Loi des 13-19 janvier
      1791 was interpreted extensively by the courts. Laurent Pfister recalls that the
      revolutionary laws and the Penal Code of 1810 applied only to performances in
      theater. Notably, section 428 of the Penal Code stated that "shall be punished
      … (e)very director or undertaker of a spectacle, every company of perform-
      ers, who shall cause to be represented at their theatre, of dramatic works" in
      violation of author's rights. Nonetheless, the provision was used to sentence the
      operator of a coffeehouse for infringement of musical works (See Cass. crim.,
      24 juin 1852 : D. 1852, 1, p. 221. – See also, Cass. crim., 16 déc. 1854 : D. 1855, 1,
      p. 45. – CA Orléans, 24 févr. 1872 : D. 1873, 1, p. 253, cited by Laurent Pfister).
      For the courts, the type of work or the place of the performance were irrelevant.
      As long as the performance was in front of an audience as opposed to a private
      group, it was an infringement, regardless of whether the performance was
      free or not, direct or through mechanical means (such as organ, records, films,
      radios, …). See Laurent Pfister, Fasc. 1110 : HISTOIRE DU DROIT D'AUTEUR,
      JCl. Propriété Littéraire et Artistique, no 72 and the cases cited therein. The 1957
      legislation adopted this large interpretation, stating:
      Loi 57-298 1957-03-11, JORF 14 mars 1957 rectificatif JORF 19 avril 1957 - Article 26
      Le droit d'exploitation appartenant à l'auteur comprend:

dictions, the answer varied [61], linked to another question: How do you evaluate if the communication by cable to households is public? Do you look at the audience at the receiving end [62] or to the people to which it was transmitted? [63] Finally, the Canadian legislator enacted a provision indicating that a communication of a work is not in itself a performance. [64]

The 1948 Brussels version of the Berne Convention finally extended the communication right by incorporating for dramatic, dramatico-musical, and musical works "any communication of the performance of the works." [65] In 1988, Canada also extended the right to communication by including the ones made by telecommunication and gave a wide definition of this new concept: it "means any transmission of signs, signals, writing, images or sounds or intelligence of any nature by wire, radio, visual, optical or other electromagnetic system." [66] It solved the issue of transmission by cable, but the technological developments kept changing the landscape.

Le droit de représentation ;
Le droit de reproduction.
Article 27 La représentation consiste dans la communication de l'oeuvre au public par un procédé quelconque, et notamment :
- par récitation publique, exécution lyrique, représentation dramatique, présentation publique, projection publique et transmission dans un lieu public de l'oeuvre télédiffusée;
- par télédiffusion.
La télédiffusion s'entend de la diffusion par tout procédé de télécommunication de sons, d'images, de documents, de données et de messages de toute nature. Est assimilée à une représentation l'émission d'une oeuvre vers un satellite.

61   *Fox on Canadian Law of Copyright and Industrial Designs*, 4th ed, *supra* note 32 at 400-402.
62   As the Court did in *Canadian Admiral Corporation Ltd. v. Rediffusion Inc.*, 1954 CanLII 712 (CA EXC), [1954] Ex CR 382, p 408.
63   *Canadian Cable Television Assn. v. Canada (Copyright Board)*, [1993] 2 F.C. 138.
64   The provision was added by *An Act to Amend the Copyright Act*, S.C. 1997, c. 24, s 2, and states: "2.3 A person who communicates a work or other subject-matter to the public by telecommunication does not by that act alone perform it in public, nor by that act alone is deemed to authorize its performance in public."
65   S 11. Not that all the issues were resolved. See, for a detailed analysis of a 11(1) (on communication) and a 11bis (on broadcasting), Ficsor, *The Law of Copyright, supra* note 45 at 156–158. For an overview of the ambiguities and gaps the Berne Convention left, see Jane C Ginsburg, "The (New?) Right of Making Available to the Public" in David Vaver & Lionel Bently, eds, *Intellectual Property in the New Millennium: Essays in Honour of William R. Cornish* (Cambridge: Cambridge University Press, 2004); Columbia Public Law Research Paper No. 04-78 (2004); Cheryl Foong, *The Making Available Right: Realizing the Potential of Copyright's Dissemination Function in the Digital Age* (Northampton, Mass: Edward Elgar Publishing, 2019) at 56–57
66   *Canada-United States Free Trade Agreement Implementation Act*, S.C. 1988, c. 65, s. 62.

The next challenge came from the information highway which provides the works on demand. This type of transmission is referred to as the *pull* transmissions, as opposed to "the *push* communications, such as cable transmissions and broadcasts (i.e., communications of preselected programming to a passive public)." [67] Was this covered by the communication to the public by telecommunication? Certainly, the words "any communication to the public right" [68] and "any other means" [69] can be understood to cover on-demand transmissions, [70] but as Jane Ginsburg observed, "given the historical context, it may be bold to assert that these articles *oblige* Member States to classify on-demand transmissions as communications to the public." [71] In Canada, the Supreme Court estimated that it matters little for the communication right that "the members of the public receive the communication in the same or in different places, at the same or at different times, or at their own or the sender's initiative." [72] Thus, according to the Supreme Court, streaming from an online music service triggered the communication right under section 3(1)(f) of the Act.

At the international level, to eliminate any ambiguity, the countries decided to reach a special agreement under the Berne Convention dealing with the authors rights in the digital environment. The WIPO Copyright Treaty (WCT) and the WIPO Performances and Phonograms Treaty (WPPT) were concluded in 1996 and entered into force in 2002. Those treaties give authors the exclusive right of "making available to the public of their works in such a way that members of the public may access these works from a place and at a time individually chosen by them." [73] The decision to create this new international norm of "making available" was reached because there was no agreement on which

---

67   Foong, *supra* note 65 at 56.

68   Used in art 11 of the 1948 version.

69   Used in art 11bis of the 1948 version.

70   Ricketson & Ginsburg, *supra* note 57 at 727.

71   Jane C Ginsburg, "The (New?) Right of Making Available to the Public" in David Vaver & Lionel Bently, eds, *Intellectual Property in the New Millennium: Essays in Honour of William R. Cornish* (Cambridge: Cambridge University Press, 2004), David Vaver & Lionel Bently, Eds., Cambridge University Press, 2004; Columbia Public Law Research Paper No. 04-78 (2004) at 8.

72   *Rogers Communications Inc. v. Society of Composers, Authors and Music Publishers of Canada*, 2012 SCC 35, [2012] 2 SCR 283, para 52.

73   Article 8 of the *WIPO Copyright Treaty*, 20 December 1996, S Treaty Doc No 105-17 (1997); 2186 U.N.T.S. 121; 36 I.L.M. 65 (1997) and Articles 10 and 14 of the *WIPO Performances and Phonograms Treaty*, 20 December 1996, S Treaty Doc No 105-17 (1997); 2186 UNTS 203; 36 ILM 76 (1997).

economic right was mainly concerned. For example, in the UK, some considered, for the liability of the internet content provider and host, the "reproduction" and "performing" rights[74] or the right of communication to the public.[75] In the United States, the rights of public distribution or public display could also be invoked.[76] During the preparatory work for the WIPO treaties, there were two main candidates: the right of communication to the public and the right of distribution. However, in the end, not a single right was selected and the "umbrella solution" was adopted.[77] The agreement would require a provision imposing an obligation to recognize an exclusive right or exclusive rights when works are used in an on-demand transmission, "described in such a neutral way, (that is, without involving any specific legal characterization) as possible," and "leaving the legal characterization to national legislation (whether it results in the combination—and possible extension—of existing rights, and/or in a new specific right)."[78] Thus the expression "umbrella" was used. Article 8 of the WIPO Copyright Treaty expresses this solution by stating:

> Without prejudice to the provisions of Articles 11(1)(ii), 11bis(1)(i) and (ii), 11ter(1)(ii), 14(1)(ii) and 14bis(1) of the Berne Convention, authors of literary and artistic works shall enjoy the exclusive right of authorizing any communication to the public of their works, by wire or wireless means, including the making available to the public of their works in such a way that members of the public may access these works from a place and at a time individually chosen by them.

In Canada, it led to the enactment of subsection 2.4(1.1) in the Copyright Act:

> (1.1) For the purposes of this Act, communication of a work or

---

74   William Rodolph Cornish, *Intellectual Property: Patents, Copyright, Trade Marks and Allied Rights*, 5th ed (London: Sweet & Maxwell, 2003) at 80.

75   Cornish *supra* note 74, citing *Shetland Times, Ltd. v. Dr. Jonathan Wills and Another* [1997] FSR 604

76   David L Hayes, "Advanced Copyright Issues on the Internet" (1998) 7:1 *Tex Intell Prop LJ* 1 at 31–39, citing *Playboy Enterprises, Inc. v. Frena*, 839 F.Supp. 1552 (M.D. Fla., 1993).

77   Mihály Ficsor, "Copyright for the Digital Era: The WIPO Internet Treaties" (1997) 21:3–4 *Colum-VLA JL & Arts* 197 at 207.

78   Ficsor, *The Law of Copyright, supra* note 45 at 206.

other subject-matter to the public by telecommunication includes
making it available to the public by telecommunication in a way
that allows a member of the public to have access to it from a place
and at a time individually chosen by that member of the public.

However, if the purpose of the legislative modification was to eliminate ambiguities, the objective was not reached.[79] The Supreme Court
revisited twice the issue of online transmission leading to streaming or
downloading of a protected work[80], leaving the commentators rather
critical of the Court's analysis.[81] In fact, in our view, the Copyright
Act left (and still leaves) unresolved very important issues. How do
you analyze an online transmission: as a single operation, or as a set of
separate acts, which, if covered by exclusive rights, should trigger each
a royalty? If an economic transaction grants a license for a specific use of
protected works, mainly corresponding to one exclusive right, should
all other rights be considered not granted? Or should it be considered
that, in order to permit the full enjoyment of the license, any ancillary
act or collateral rights are also authorized?

The answers vary from one legal system to another. In France, the
traditional view was that each right should be dealt with separately.
As André Françon explained, the general idea is that any transfer that
the author agrees to of his rights must be interpreted restrictively.[82]
The fact that the author authorizes reproduction does not imply that
he authorizes public representation, and vice versa.[83] The principle of
independence of the two rights means that an operator must sometimes

---

79   Even before the incorporation of subs. 2.4 (1.1), the Court had decided that point-
to-point transmission from a website to a member of the public for streaming is
a communication to the public covered by s. 3(1)(f) of the *Copyright Act*: *Rogers
Communications Inc. v. Society of Composers, Authors and Music Publishers of Canada*,
2012 SCC 35, [2012] 2 SCR 283.

80   In 2012: *Entertainment Software Association v. Society of Composers, Authors and Music
Publishers of Canada*, 2012 SCC 34, [2012] 2 SCR 231; *Rogers Communications Inc. v.
Society of Composers, Authors and Music Publishers of Canada*, 2012 SCC 35, [2012]
2 SCR 283; in 2022, *Society of Composers, Authors and Music Publishers of Canada v.
Entertainment Software Association*, 2022 SCC 30.

81   "Authorizing Two Royalties: A Comment on *Society of Composers, Authors and
Music Publishers of Canada v Entertainment Software Association*" (2023) 67 Can Bus
LJ 232; Mistrale Goudreau, "Interprétation du stare decisis découlant de la déci-
sion *SOCAN c Entertainment Software Association*" (2022) 35:1 *Cahiers de propriété
intellectuelle* 181.

82   André Françon, *La Propriété littéraire et artistique* (Paris: Presses Universitaires de
France, 1970) at 70.

83   *Ibid.*

deal with the author for each of the two rights, as will, for example, a producer of a musical. He will have to negotiate with the author to carry out the performance itself, and he must also obtain a separate license if he wants to reproduce the score and the libretto for the actors and the orchestra. [84]

This vision was reflected in the 1957 Act [85] and it is still in the current Code de la propriété intellectuelle. [86]

In the common law countries, as Jessica Litman reports, "[f]or much of copyright law's history, it was conventional to treat many incidental uses as impliedly licensed." [87] However, the same reasoning did not necessarily apply in the digital realm. Some commentators [88] refer to the United States decision *Country Road Music, Inc. v. MP3.com, Inc.*, [89] where the US district court decided that the holder of a license for streaming musical works did not have the right to create server copies of music on compact discs, stressing that "'performance' and 'reproduction' are clearly and unambiguously separate rights under the Copyright Act of 1976." [90]

---

84   *Ibid*.

85   Loi 57-298 1957-03-11 JORF 14 mars 1957 rectificatif JORF 19 avril 1957, art 30 et 31.

86   The relevant parts of sections 30 and 31 were reenacted in the Code.
Article 122-7 of de Code states:
…La cession du droit de représentation n'emporte pas celle du droit de reproduction. La cession du droit de reproduction n'emporte pas celle du droit de représentation. Lorsqu'un contrat comporte cession totale de l'un des deux droits visés au présent article, la portée en est limitée aux modes d'exploitation prévus au contrat.
Article L131-3 of the Code states:
La transmission des droits de l'auteur est subordonnée à la condition que chacun des droits cédés fasse l'objet d'une mention distincte dans l'acte de cession et que le domaine d'exploitation des droits cédés soit délimité quant à son étendue et à sa destination, quant au lieu et quant à la durée.
The Quebec legislator is going in the same direction, requesting that individual contracts in the fields of the visual arts, arts and crafts and literature clearly sets forth any transfer of right and any grant of licence: *Act respecting the professional status and conditions of engagement of performing, recording and film artists*, CQLR c S-32.1, s 47.

87   Jessica Litman, "Lawful Personal Use"(2007) 85 *Tex L Rev* 1871 at 1915.

88   Barry B Sookman, *Computer, Internet, and Electronic Commerce Law*, (Toronto: Carswell) at § 3:84. William F Patry, *Patry on Copyright* (St Paul, Minn: West Thomson Reuters, September 2023 update) at § 5:131; Litman, Lawful Personal Use, *supra* note 87 at 1915; David McGowan, "Things Are Bad Enough Already" (2010) 96 *Iowa Law Review Bulletin IALRB* 23 at 35; Henry H Perritt Jr, "Cut In Tiny Pieces: Ensuring That Fragmented Ownership Does Not Chill Creativity" (2011) 14 *Vand J Ent & Tech* L 1 at 12.

89   279 F. Supp. 2d 325, 333 (S.D.N.Y. 2003).

90   279 F. Supp. 2d 325, 333 (S.D.N.Y. 2003) at 327.

In Canada, the Supreme Court endorses the view that an act of communication to the public is separate from making synchronization and broadcast incidental copies of a work.[91] In fact, the Court stated that the "opening paragraph of s. 3(1) of the Copyright Act exhaustively sets out three copyright interests that authors have in their works: the right to (1) produce or reproduce a work in any material form; (2) perform a work in public; or (3) publish an unpublished work."[92] In its view, the "rights enumerated in s. 3(1) are distinct. A single activity can only engage one of the three copyright interests."[93] So, for online transmission of a work, the Court refused to see a reproduction in the act of uploading material on the internet and decided that the online transmission is a single operation, leading to only one royalty.[94]

All those distinctions, nuances, and complexities have led commentators to argue in favor of a reconstruction of copyright. One commentator summarized: "Economic rights have lost their meaning and their efficiency. Reduced to technical notions that are applied to uses that seem harmless, and whose interpretation is all but certain, they cannot ensure the legitimate control by authors of the exploitation of their works."[95] But what are the theories or concepts proposed by the legal community?

For a Different Copyright Regime

To guide themselves in their quest to better delineate the proper scope of protection for authors and leave appropriate room for the public domain, commentators have attempted to draw inspiration from existing theories and other legal fields. We would like to give as an example a collaborative research project entitled "Copyright Reconstructed: Rethinking Copyright's Economic Rights in a Time of Highly Dynamic Technological and Economic Change" which

---

91   *Bishop v. Stevens*, [1990] 2 SCR 467;
     Canadian Broadcasting Corp. v. SODRAC 2003 Inc., 2015 SCC 57, [2015] 3 SCR 615.
92   *Society of Composers, Authors and Music Publishers of Canada v. Entertainment Software Association*, 2022 SCC 30 at para 54.
93   *Ibid* at para 55.
94   *Society of Composers, Authors and Music Publishers of Canada v. Entertainment Software Association*, 2022 SCC 30, maintaining the distinction between a streaming and a transmission ending with a download.
95   Séverine Dusollier, "Chapter 6 : Realigning Economic Rights with Exploitation of Works," *supra* note 51 at 163.

was carried in Europe "with the aim of realigning these rights with economic and technological realities." [96]

Contributors to the book which resulted from the project all agreed that the economic rights are too formalistic: if an act is considered to be a reproduction or representation and not covered by an exception, it falls within the exclusive control of the copyright holder, without any consideration for the inefficiencies thus created or for the impact on the market. [97] To eliminate this overly formalistic application of copyright concepts, the commentators envisaged several possibilities. For example, one considered applying American antitrust concepts, such as the notion of "rule of reason," to the copyright scope issue. This concept was adopted by the Supreme Court of the United States [98] to determine if some agreements were in "restraint of trade" and thus illegal under the Sherman Antitrust Act of 1890. [99] Under this doctrine, the Court, instead of declaring the arrangements illegal *per se*, will assess its pro-competitive and anti-competitive effects in the relevant market. [100] Similarly, a use of copyrighted work would not be considered infringing if the "unauthorized use does not harm, but actually benefits the author." [101] Others suggested replacing the various economic rights with a "right to reasonable exploitation" [102] which would start with efficiency considerations but would also take into account other guiding principles, so as to be "in line with the interest of the public domain, in compliance with the principle of dignity in the wider sense, and apt

96   P Bernt Hugenholtz, ed, *Copyright Reconstructed: Rethinking Copyright's Economic Rights in a Time of Highly Dynamic Technological and Economic Change* (Alphen aan den Rijn: Wolters Kluwer, 2018)

97   P Bernt Hugenholtz, "Chapter 1: Reconstructing Rights: Project Synthesis and Recommendations" in P Bernt Hugenholtz, ed, *Copyright Reconstructed: Rethinking Copyright's Economic Rights in a Time of Highly Dynamic Technological and Economic Change* (Alphen aan den Rijn: Wolters Kluwer, 2018) 1 at 1–10.

98   *Standard Oil Co. of New Jersey v. United States*, 221 U.S. 1 (1911).

99   15 U.S.C. §§ 1.

100   *Bd. of Trade of Chi. v. United States*, 246 U.S. 231, 238 (1918).

101   Stefan Bechtold, "Chapter 3: Deconstructing Copyright" in P Bernt Hugenholtz, ed, *Copyright Reconstructed: Rethinking Copyright's Economic Rights in a Time of Highly Dynamic Technological and Economic Change* (Alphen aan den Rijn: Wolters Kluwer, 2018) 59 at 79.

102   Ole-Andreas Rognstad & Joost Poort, "Chapter 5: The Right to Reasonable Exploitation Concretized: An Incentive Based Approach" in *P Bernt Hugenholtz*, ed, *Copyright Reconstructed: Rethinking Copyright's Economic Rights in a Time of Highly Dynamic Technological and Economic Change* (Alphen aan den Rijn: Wolters Kluwer, 2018) 121–62.

to enhance freedom of expression and market integration." [103] Another commentator would limit the copyright infringements by requiring that the "use as a work" has occurred. [104] Then, for example, technical reproductions, being "non-communicative uses," would be outside the copyright protection. [105] Another author would tie the notions of exploitation and infringement to the fundamental copyright goal, which is to "provide creators with the rights to control the circulation of their works in the public sphere." [106] Thus copyright exploitation would not be a purely economic concept; instead it would be viewed as a "communicative act." [107] The copyright exploitation would require a public dimension with the consequence that "the personal uses are excluded from exploitation. Reading, viewing, receiving or enjoying a work are not exploitation activities as they lack any public dimension. The same is true of copies made for personal use." [108] However, since the social medias blur the private/public dimension, "[w]hat is posted or communicated on internet social networks, irrespective of the number of followers or friends, is an act of speech and public communication." [109]

Each of those proposals lead to diverging practical conclusions. [110] If we take the example of private copying, some argue that the market can be structured to provide compensation to copyright holders, without having to recognize it as a legal right; others classify unauthorized private copying as infringing acts while others would put them outside the copyright realm. [111]

---

103   *Ibid* at 132.

104   Alain Strowel, "Chapter 7: Reconstructing the Reproduction and Communication to the Public Rights: How to Align Copyright with Its Fundamentals" in P Bernt Hugenholtz, *Copyright Reconstructed: Rethinking Copyright's Economic Rights in a Time of Highly Dynamic Technological and Economic Change* (Alphen aan den Rijn: Wolters Kluwer, 2018) 203–240.

105   *Ibid*. p 225.

106   Séverine Dusollier, "Chapter 6: Realigning Economic Rights with Exploitation of Works: The Control of Authors over the Circulation of Works in the Public Sphere," *supra* note 51 at 173.

107   *Ibid* at 173.

108   *Ibid* at 186.

109   *Ibid*.

110   P Bernt Hugenholtz & Martin Kretschmer, "Chapter 1: Reconstructing Rights: Project Synthesis and Recommendations" in P Bernt Hugenholtz, ed, *Copyright Reconstructed: Rethinking Copyright's Economic Rights in a Time of Highly Dynamic Technological and Economic Change* (Alphen aan den Rijn: Wolters Kluwer, 2018) 1–10, detailing the differences between each proposal and the practical consequences in 5 areas : (a) digital resale, (b) private copying, (c) hyperlinking and embedding, (d) cable retransmission, and (e) text and data mining.

111   *Ibid* at 9.

All those proposals illustrate how the present copyright regimes are considered unsatisfactory by many in the academic community. We personally share this negative assessment, but we would like to emphasize another aspect that is essential to understanding the copyright economic rights regimes: the highly volatile market structure in which they operate. Above, in the section entitled *The Economic Rights Concepts Tested by Technological Developments,* we showed how technological developments led to a redefinition of the economic rights. But the technological developments also often changed the economic significance of those rights. There are two prominent examples: the rise in popularity, and later demise, of DVD sales and rentals (through specialized stores), and the newspaper business model.

Concerning the DVD phenomena, Stephen Prince, in his book *Digital Cinema,* explained how changes in the way audiences encounter films started to alter the well-established revenue sources of the movie business.[112] For nearly two decades, the DVD format was "the golden goose" for the industry. But, in 2016, it stopped being the major source of profits.[113] Subscription streaming and video-on-demand formed "a dark cloud over the future of ownership of packaged video content, both physical and digital."[114] According to the market research firm OMDIA, by the 2020s, DVD purchases amounted to only seven percent of the global home entertainment market.[115] So, in the film industry, the rights to reproduce and rent a copy went from being the most lucrative rights[116] to being not so important.[117]

---

112 Stephen Prince, *Digital Cinema* (New Brunswick, NJ: Rutgers University Press, 2019) at 140.

113 *Ibid.*

114 *Ibid* at 140-141, citing Andrew Wallenstein, "Home Entertainment 2016 Figures: Streaming Eclipses Disc Sales for the First Time," *Variety* (6 January 2017), online: https://variety.com/.

115 Chris Stokel-Walker, "Why Do DVDs Still Exist?" WIRED (27 November 2021), online: https://www.wired.com/story/why-do-dvds-exist/.

116 Interestingly, the Canadian *Copyright Act* did not recognize an exclusive rental right for cinematographic film, precisely because "the audiovisual industry has succeeded in establishing structures under which the video copy for rental is sold to the merchant at a price several times higher than that of the copy sold for retail resale" (Free translation: "l'industrie de l'audiovisuel a réussi à se doter de structures en vertu desquelles la copie vidéo pour la location est vendue au commerçant à un prix plusieurs fois supérieur à celui de la copie vendue pour la revente au détail"): C Brunet, "Le droit d'auteur au Canada de 1987 à 1977," (1997) 10 C.P.I. 79 at 85.

117 It was also the end of movie rental stores, which, except for few exceptions, disappeared: Nicole Williams, Ottawa

The newspaper market is another example of the impact of disruptive technological forces. Since the 1830s[118], newspapers, instead of
financing themselves by selling printed copies, have relied heavily on
advertisement revenues to make ends meet. However, this business
model has not thrived in the digital age.[119] When the internet opened to
commercial use, newspaper executives erroneously believed that that
their websites would generate digital advertising revenues.[120] In reality,
publicity occurred through portals, e-commerce sites, search engines,
and social networks.[121] For instance, a study found that by 2017 a major
part of the digital advertising revenues went to Google and Facebook.[122]

The market structure had changed so much that the previous
economic model could no longer guarantee financial stability for those
news outlets. In Canada, it led to the adoption of the *Online News Act*[123]
which "aims to ensure that dominant platforms compensate news
businesses"[124] when they make news content "available."[125]

Those two examples bring me to my conclusion. The Supreme
Court has recognized that one of the copyright goals is to provide

---

"The movie rental store lives — and it's not going anywhere", CBC News, Dec
31, 2022, reporting the existence of only 2 stores in Ottawa.

118   Faced with the cost of steam-powered presses and the necessity to find economy of scale, newspapers dropped the price of the copies they sold to the
public and "started charging businesses to advertise their goods and services
to their audience." Erinn Catherine Whitaker & Penelope Muse Abernathy
"Newspapers, history and economics of" in *The SAGE International Encyclopedia
of Mass Media and Society*, vol 5, 1243–1250 (SAGE Publications, 2020),
online: https://doi.org/10.4135/9781483375519 and https://www.cislm.org/
whathistory-teaches-us-how-newspapers-have-evolved-to-meet-market-demands/.

119   On the impact of digital technology on journalism, see Robert G Kaiser, The Bad
News About The News (The Brookings Essay, 16 October 2014), online: http://
csweb.brookings.edu/content/research/essays/2014/bad-news.html.

120   Whitaker & Abernathy, *supra* note 118.

121   *Ibid.*

122   *Ibid*, reporting that "A study by eMarketer estimated that by 2017, the duopoly of
Google and Facebook received about 60% of all digital advertising dollars in the
United States and were responsible for 99% of ad revenue growth in 2016."

123   S.C. 2023, c. 23.

124   Canadian Heritage, The Online News Act (3 January 2024), online: https://www.
canada.ca/en/canadian-heritage/services/online-news.html

125   The *Act* states at subs 2(2) that news content is made available "if (a) the news
content, or any portion of it, is reproduced; or (b) access to the news content, or
any portion of it, is facilitated by any means, including an index, aggregation
or ranking of news content." The bargaining for a compensation can only start
if the news business or group *owns* the copyright or is authorized to bargain for
that content (s 23). The law seems to introduce a new copyright regime for news
content, based on the rights to reproduce or to *facilitate access* to content.

copyright creators with rewards, those "necessary incentives," "ensuring that there is a steady flow of creative works injected into the public sphere." [126] But in many circumstances, because of the disruptive technological forces, copyright holders operate in precarious markets, making the "rewards" uncertain or unpredictable. [127] The technological changes have also forced the legal community to redefine the basic concepts, and have obscured the boundaries between reproduction and performance. The digital world is also blurring the distinction between private and public communicative acts. [128]

Could the legislators intervene by providing more detailed definitions and trying to clearly distinguish each economic right, even if it means introducing new separates rights? We personally think that, in a world where more and more people access their "copy" in a "cloud," the notions of reproduction and communication are merging. [129] Furthermore, the task of anticipating and keeping pace with the rapid evolution in technology will always make this course of legislative action a very hazardous one. [130] Certainly, adopting an open-ended concept, like "use of the work," "exploitation," or "reasonable exploitation," would bring flexibility and should be an option to consider. But undertaking such substantial reform requires

---

126 *York University v. Canadian Copyright Licensing Agency (Access Copyright)*, 2021 SCC 32 at para 92.

127 Hence the importance of strong cultural policies, with government funding and arts promotion activities.

128 Séverine Dusollier, "Chapter 6: Realigning Economic Rights with Exploitation of Works: The Control of Authors over the Circulation of Works in the Public Sphere," *supra* note 51 at 186.

129 André Lucas, *Traité, supra* note 54 at 213 para 235. So is accessing a work online in American law: see "Copyright Category Confusion and Its Consequences: Online Transmissions and the Right of Exclusive Use under Copyright" (1998) 16-SPG *Entertainment & Sports Law* 11 at 11. "A user can 'experience' a work by merely 'calling it into the RAM of [a] computer and accessing it.' This activity may constitute reproduction, performance, and display."

130 André Lucas, "Summary of the Proceedings of the Symposium," *WIPO Worldwide Symposium on the Future of Copyright and Neighboring Rights* (WIPO, 1994) at 278–279: "Whenever new technology has caused uncertainty as to the scope of an existing right, those involved have demanded the introduction of a separate right. This is understandable, but it is dangerous, because this 'fragmentation' of rights is liable to have an adverse effect on the cohesiveness of the system as a whole. It is not a question of neatness but rather of legal security. Such an accumulation of prerogatives results in overlaps that adversely affect the transparency of the law, which in turn leads to a logic of restrictive interpretation that backfires on the very people that one intended to protect better. To this it should be added that there is a risk of being very rapidly overtaken by technological evolution." See also *Ficsor, The Law of Copyright, supra* note 45 at 203.

a strong political will. There is no clear indication, at present, of such strong political will.

In the absence of the legislator's interventions, it is up to the courts to try to adapt copyright laws to this modern age (with the coming waves of social networking and artificial intelligence). In our view, the courts should, in their decision-making process—possibly by drawing inspiration from scholarly proposals—focus on the legislative purpose behind the economic rights of copyright, which is to grant some financial "reward" to creators while acknowledging the relevant public interest aspects of copyright. Importantly, in our opinion, the courts should at least refrain from adopting formalistic approaches to concepts or per-petuating outdated views of copyright. For instance, we argue that the Court should distance itself from the school of thought that presents copyright as a set of three separate and distinct rights: reproduction, performance, and publication.[131] Judges should recognize that they are ill-equipped to determine the exact economic impact of their decisions and that technological changes may rapidly undermine the rational and precedential value of their decisions. A wise course of action would be to decide the case before them without making broad legal propositions going well beyond the relevant facts. That is because, as Professors Hugenholtz and Kretschmer have brilliantly concluded: "[i]n sum, reconstructing copyright is not for the impatient or the faint-hearted; there remains much work to be done."[132]

---

131   In our opinion, the Court should reverse the statement it made in para 54 of the decision *Société canadienne des auteurs, compositeurs et éditeurs de musique c. Entertainment Software Association*, 2022 CSC 30.

132   Hugenholtz & Kretschmer, Chapter 1, *supra* note 110 at 9.

The Uncertain Future of Patented Medicine Price Regulation

Gregory R. Hagen

Abstract

Canada recently failed in its attempt to amend the *Patented Medicine Regulations* so as to require the Patented Medicine Price Review Board to consider economic affordability and value for money in its excessive pricing determinations under the *Patent Act*. The failure highlighted an asymmetry: patent rights in medicines are enforced by private actions of patentees, while upholding the public interest in access to patented medicines is done by the Board applying the excessive pricing provisions of the *Patent Act*. This chapter discusses several difficulties that the Board has faced in administering these provisions. It also chronicles the difficulties faced by the federal government in its reform attempt, including having to deal with a decision of the Court of Appeal of Québec that the requirement for the Board to apply economic factors is an unconstitutional form of price regulation. It is uncertain, going forward, therefore, whether the Board will use its discretion to apply relevant economic factors to its excessive price determinations, even given that its discretionary powers under the *Patent Act* were held by the Federal Court of Appeal to be constitutional. Ultimately, even if abusive pricing of patented medicines could be prevented, the inability to prevent undue delay of the sale of those medicines might itself result in patent abuse. Ensuring the timely availability of patented medicines at prices that are not excessive would likely require the daunting task of reforming international patent law.

When the federal government amended the *Patent Act*[1] in 1987 to permit patent rights in medicines, it created the Patented Medicine Price Review Board ("Board"), an independent quasi-judicial body, to review the first sale prices of patented medicines to ensure that they are not excessive as a result of the patent.[2] The power of the Board to review the prices of patented medicines reflects the fundamental principle that intellectual property rights are limited by the public interest in using the protected subject matter.[3] In its *Strategic Plan for 2015–18*, however, the Board recognized that patented medicine list prices were high and research and development investment by pharmaceutical companies in Canada was low relative to sales.[4] Indeed, the increasing sales of higher-cost medicines, such as biologics, oncology medication, and treatments for hepatitis C continue to be of concern.[5] By 2016, the Board had decided to "rethink" how to further the public interest in avoiding excessive patented medicine prices,[6] and by 2019 the federal government decided that amending the *Patented Medicine Regulations*[7] would provide the Board "a stronger basis from which to modernize its Guidelines."[8] This initiative resulted in the *Regulations Amending the Patented Medicines Regulations*, which added economic regulatory factors related to affordability and value for money that the Board was required to consider when determining whether the price of a patented medicine was excessive.[9]

---

1   *Patent Act*, RSC 1985, c. P-4 [*Patent Act*].

2   See *Merck Canada inc. c. Procureur général du Canada*, 2022 QCCA 240 at paras 29–35 [*Merck*]. (Unofficial English Translation of the Judgment of the Court.)

3   See *Théberge v. Galerie d'Art du Petit Champlain inc.*, 2002 SCC 34 at para 32 [*Théberge*].

4   Canada, Patented Medicine Price Review Board, *Strategic Plan 2015–2018*, (Ottawa: PMPRB, 2015) at 5, online: https://www.canada.ca/content/dam/pmprb-cepmb/documents/reports-and-studies/annual-report/2021/2021-Annual-Report-en.pdf.

5   See Canada, Patented Medicine Prices Review Board, *Annual Report* (18 November 2022), online: https://www.canada.ca/en/patented-medicine-prices-review/services/annual-reports/annual-report-2021.html. According to the report, as of 2021, Canadians paid the third highest prices for medicines among OECD countries.

6   Canada, Patented Medicine Price Review Board, *PMPRB Guidelines Modernization – Discussion Paper* at 3 (Ottawa: PMPRB, 2016), online: http://www.pmprb-cepmb.gc.ca/CMFiles/Consultations/DiscussionPaper/PMPRB_DiscussionPaper_June2016_E.pdf.

7   *Patented Medicine Regulations*, SOR/94-688.

8   *Regulatory Impact Analysis Statement*, SOR/2019-298 (2019) C Gaz II 5946 at 5962 [*RIAS*], online (pdf): https://canadagazette.gc.ca/rp-pr/p2/2019/2019-08-21/pdf/g2-15317.pdf.

9   *Regulations Amending the Patented Medicines Regulations (Additional Factors and Information Reporting Requirements)*, SOR/2019-298 s 4 (adding the mandatory economic regulatory factors) C Gaz II 5940 [*Regulatory Amendments*].

The addition of these mandatory economic regulatory factors was short lived, however, as the relevant provisions of the *Regulatory Amendments* were repealed[10] soon after the Court of Appeal of Québec declared in *Merck* that the new provisions were unconstitutional.[11] While the Court recognized that the "federal jurisdiction over patents of invention and discovery include[s] the right to control the effects of the monopoly granted by the patent on the price of patented medicines,"[12] it nevertheless found that the *purpose* of adding the new economic factors in the *Regulatory Amendments* was merely to lower patented drug prices to make them more affordable rather than protecting consumers from excessive prices.[13] The federal government decided not to seek leave to appeal *Merck* to the Supreme Court of Canada despite the fact that the Court of Appeal of Québec's view of the purpose of adding the economic regulatory factors differed from that of the Superior Court of Québec,[14] the Federal Court,[15] and the Federal Court of Appeal,[16] all of which understood the purpose to be updating the tools that the Board can use to prevent excessive patented medicine prices, just as it was described by the federal government in its *RIAS*.[17]

This chapter argues that the federal government's failed attempt to add the mandatory economic regulatory factors to the *Patented Medicine Regulations* revealed a deeply rooted asymmetry in the *Patent Act* between the protection of private patent rights in medicines and the protection of the public interest. On the one hand, patent rights are private rights that can be enforced in courts through private rights of action while, on the other hand, the public interest against "price abuse"[18] is upheld by

10   See *Regulations Amending the Regulations Amending the Patented Medicines Regulations (Additional Factors and Information Reporting Requirements), No. 5 under subsection 101(1)3 of the Patent Act*, SOR/2022-162, sections 2 & 3, repealing sections 3(4) and 4, respectively, of the *Regulatory Amendments* [*Repeal*].

11   See *Merck, supra* note 2. The Court declared sections 3(4) and 4 of the *Regulatory Amendments* unconstitutional.

12   *Ibid* at para 181, citing *Smith, Kline & French Laboratories v. Canada (Attorney General)*, 1985 CanLII 5509 (FC), [1986] 1 F.C. 274, 1985 CanLII 3151 (FC) at 294–295 and 296 [cited to F.C.].

13   See *ibid* at paras 152–176.

14   See *Merck Canada inc. c. Procureur général du Canada*, 2020 QCCS 4541 [*Merck QCCS*].

15   See *Innovative Medicines Canada v. Canada (Attorney General)*, 2020 FC 725 at para 104 [*Innovative Medicines FC*].

16   See *Innovative Medicines Canada v. Canada (Attorney General)*, 2022 FCA 210 at para 57 [*IMC FCA*]

17   See *RIAS, supra* note 8.

18   *Merck, supra* note 2 at 150, quoting *Manitoba Society of Seniors Inc. v. Canada (Attorney General) (1991)*, 77 D.L.R. (4th) 485, 1991 CanLII 8289 (Man. Q.B.) at para 23 [cited

the Board, in whose sole judgment the excessive price provisions of the *Patent Act* are administered and enforced.[19] The Board's work to further the public interest is vulnerable to a variety of difficulties not besetting the enforcement of private rights that will be identified and discussed in the context of the federal government's reform initiative. The continuing challenge to ensure public access to patented medicines at prices that are not excessive sets the agenda for future patent law reform.

The following sections briefly describe some of the difficulties involved in upholding the public interest in access to patented medicines that are not excessively priced. The second section describes the inherent trade-off in using patent law to both further the availability of patented medicines and to ensure that prices are not excessive. Section three introduces the difficulty of determining when the price of a medicine is excessive under the *Patent Act*. Section four describes the stated purpose of the federal government's addition of new economic factors into the *Patented Medicine Regulations*. Section five discusses the difficulty of consulting with industry to create or amend guidelines to administer the excessive price provisions of the *Patent Act* when there is no shared understanding of patent law. Section six critiques the Court of Appeal of Québec's *Merck* decision that ruled that adding the economic factors to the *Patented Medicine Regulations* was unconstitutional. Section seven discusses the lack of support for the Board by the Minister of Health and the federal Cabinet. Section eight discusses the difficulty of requiring the timely sales launch of patented medicines, suggesting that patent abuse through the undue delay of sales of patented medicines needs to be prohibited by international law. Section nine concludes.

Patent Rights in Medicines are Limited by the Public Interest

The twin objectives of the *Patent Act* are often described as being part of a bargain.[20] First, by granting a patent right for a limited period in an invention, society is providing an incentive to invent.[21] Patent rights exclude unauthorized persons from making, using, or selling the patented medicine for use within Canada.[22] Patents in medicines increase

---

to CanLII], aff'd (1992) 45 C.P.R. (3d) 194, 1992 CanLII 8541 (Man. C.A.) [*Manitoba*].

19   See *Patent Act, supra* note 1, ss 83–87.

20   See e.g. *Teva Canada Ltd. v. Pfizer Canada Inc.*, 2012 SCC 60 at para 32 [*Teva*].

21   See *ibid*. The term of the patent ends twenty years from the filing date. See *Patent Act, supra* note 1 at s 44.

22   See *Patent Act, supra* note 1 at s 42.

their prices, thereby rewarding or incentivizing the invention of useful medicines.[23] Second, in order to be granted patent rights, the applicant must disclose information that enables an expert to make the invention, thus benefitting society from the disclosure of such knowledge.[24] The Supreme Court has described the "inventive solutions to practical problems" as being "coaxed into the public domain by the promise of a limited monopoly for a limited time."[25] However, as will be discussed in section eight, of some importance is the fact that the grant of a patent in medicine does not require the disclosure of information that is needed to show that the medicine is sufficiently safe and efficacious to gain approval for sale.[26]

At the same time, the public has an interest in limiting the negative effects of intellectual property rights.[27] Thus, for example, there are statutory exceptions and limitations to patent rights contained in the *Patent Act*, such as experimentation related to the patented invention.[28] The Supreme Court of Canada considers statutory exceptions and limitations to be *rights* of users, not merely loopholes that need to be filled for the protection of intellectual property owners.[29] It has confirmed that "excessive control" of subject matter by intellectual property owners, including patentees, is against the public interest by, for example, creating impediments to its legitimate use.[30] However, while patent rights can be enforced by way of private action for infringement, user rights can typically only be "enforced" by obtaining a declaration of non-infringement or engaging in an allegedly infringing act and defending it in an infringement action if necessary.[31] Moreover, the *Patent Act* has been characterized as a "complete code" that precludes remedies outside of it for violations by the patentee of the *Patent Act*.[32]

---

23   See Gaelle Groux & Jeremy de Beer, "Access to Medicines in High Income Countries" in Srividhya Ragavan & Amaka Vanni, eds, *Intellectual Property Law and Access to Medicines* (London: Routledge, 2021) at 190 [*Groux*].
24   See *Teva, supra* note 20 at paras 32–33.
25   See *Apotex Inc. v. Wellcome Foundation Ltd.*, 2002 SCC 77 at para 37.
26   See *Patent Act, supra* note 1 at s 27.
27   See, e.g., the discussions of patent abuse in Stephen J Perry and T Andrew Currier, *Canadian Patent Law* (Toronto: LexisNexis) at s 20.1 [*Perry*]; David Vaver, *Intellectual Property Law* (Toronto: Irwin Law, 2011) [*Vaver*] at 415-417.
28   See *Patent Act, supra* note 1 at s 55.3(1).
29   See *CCH Canadian Ltd. v. Law Society of Upper Canada*, 2004 SCC 13 at para 48; *Vaver, supra* note 27 at 397.
30   *Théberge, supra* note 3 at para 32, referring to copyright "and other forms of intellectual property."
31   See *Perry, supra* note 27 at ch 19 for a discussion of defences to infringement.
32   See *Low v. Pfizer Canada Inc.*, 2015 BCCA 506 at para 91.

In the pharmaceutical context, "the monopoly granted by the patent allows innovative pharmaceutical companies to generate significant revenue to promote pharmaceutical research and development."[33] Additional incentives can include up to two years of patent-like supplementary protection[34] and up to eight years of data protection.[35] A patent "can also have the effect of increasing the price of a patented medicine in relation to what the pharmaceutical company could otherwise charge for the medicine in a competitive market free of any monopoly."[36] Drug prices typically drop to approximately 15 to 25 percent of the original patented product price after the patent expires.[37] Nevertheless, many patients may not be in a position to defer treatment until expiry, as they might do for a luxury item.[38] For some, elevated drug prices may reduce "economic accessibility (affordability)"[39] and result in negative impacts on individual health.[40] Differential impacts of patents on access to medicine among Canadian subpopulations based upon province, gender, and ethnicity have been observed.[41] These pricing effects may not be "socially acceptable" for medicines.[42] The *Patent Act*, thus,

33   *Merck, supra* note 2 at para 209.
34   These certificates of supplementary protection are patent-like rights that may be granted by the Minister of Health for up to two years under s 113 of the *Patent Act, supra* note 1.
35   See *Food and Drug Regulations*, CRC, c 870, s C.08.004.1. There is also a six-month extension available for clinical trials for pediatric populations (see Canada, Health Canada, "Guidance Document: Data Protection under C.08.004.1 of the Food and Drug Regulations"(Ottawa: 2021), online: https://www.canada.ca/content/dam/hc-sc/documents/services/drugs-health-products/drug-products/applications-submissions/guidance-documents/data_donnees_protection-eng.pdf).
36   *Merck, supra* note 2 at paras 208–213.
37   See Neil Palmer, "The Patented Medicines Prices Review Board has Lost its Way Again," (Ottawa: McDonald Laurier Institute, 2022) at 5 [*Palmer*], online: https://macdonaldlaurier.ca/wp-content/uploads/2022/11/20221031_PMPRB_fails_again_Palmer_COMMENTARY_FWeb.pdf.
38   See Steven G Morgan, Hannah S Bathula & Suerie Moon, "Pricing of Pharmaceuticals is Becoming a Major Challenge for Health Systems" (2020) 368:14627 BMJ [*Morgan*].
39   This concept is taken from *General Comment No. 14 (2000): The Right to the Highest Attainable Standard of Health (Art. 12 of the Covenant)*, UNCESCR, 22nd Sess, UN Doc E/C.12/2000/4 (2000).
40   See Canada, Advisory Council on the Implementation of National Health Care, *A Prescription for Canada: Achieving Pharmacare for All* (Ottawa, 2019) at 44–48 [*Prescription*], online: https://www.canada.ca/content/dam/hc-sc/images/corporate/about-health-canada/public-engagement/external-advisory-bodies/implementation-national-pharmacare/final-report/final-report.pdf.
41   See *Groux, supra* note 23.
42   See *Merck, supra* note 2 at para 208.

attempts to prevent rightsholders[43] from charging excessive prices for patented inventions pertaining to medicines.[44]

Thus, the first difficulty that the Board has in furthering the public interest is that it operates in a context where there is a difficult trade-off between granting patent rights that encourage the invention of medicines, which benefits the public, and ensuring that patent rights in medicines are not abused by charging excessive prices.

When is the Price of Medicine Excessive?

When is the price of a medicine so excessive that it amounts to patent abuse? In *Bristol-Myers Squibb Co. v. Canada (Attorney General)*, the Supreme Court of Canada characterized the public interest in the field of patented medicines as including "the desire to reduce health care costs while being fair to those whose ingenuity brought the drugs into existence in the first place."[45] Later, in *Celgene Corp. v. Canada (Attorney General)*, in writing a unanimous decision of the Supreme Court of Canada, Justice Abella characterized the Board as having a "consumer protection purpose."[46] She quoted with approval the Federal Court's statement in *ICN Pharmaceuticals, Inc. v. Patented Medicine Prices Review Board* that the intent of Parliament was to deal with the possibility that patent rights in medicines "might cause prices to rise to unacceptable levels."[47] In affirming the decision in *ICN*, the Federal Court of Appeal remarked that the objective of granting a patent "must not overtake the need to ensure that Canadians have access to patented medicines which are reasonably priced."[48] This remark is consistent with the more recent statement of the Court of Appeal of Québec in *Merck* that the "public interest aspect specific to patented medicines that permits the federal government to regulate them to mitigate the effects on prices of the monopoly granted by the patent" is designed

---

43   A rightsholder includes a patentee in respect of an invention pertaining to medicine and the holder of a certificate of supplementary protection. See *Patent Act, supra* note 1 at s 79(1).

44   *Ibid* at s 79–104. Section 79(2) of the *Patent Act* states that "an invention pertains to a medicine if the invention is intended or capable of being used for medicine or for the preparation or production of medicine."

45   *Bristol-Myers Squibb Co. v. Canada (Attorney General)*, 2005 SCC 26 at para 2.

46   *Celgene Corp. v. Canada (Attorney General)*, 2011 SCC 1 at paras 28–32 [*Celgene*].

47   *Ibid* at para 28, quoting *ICN Pharmaceuticals, Inc. v. Patented Medicine Prices Review Board*, 1996 CanLII 11903 (FC) [*ICN*].

48   *ICN Pharmaceuticals, Inc. v. Canada (Staff of the Patented Medicine Prices Review Board) (C.A.)*, 1996 CanLII 4089 (FCA), [1997] 1 FC 32 at 40–41.

"to prevent the patentee from unduly profiting at the expense of the public's access to the medicine." [49]

The Board is responsible "for ensuring that the monopoly that accompanies the granting of a patent is not abused to the financial detriment of Canadian patients and their insurers." [50] In *Canada (Attorney General) v. Galderma Canada Inc.*, the Federal Court of Appeal stated that the "[t]he Board's mandate is to ensure that the statutory monopoly granted to patentees of medicines is not abused by excessive pricing of those medicines." [51] If the Board is of the view that the first sale price of a patented medicine sold in Canada is excessive, it may order the rightsholder to reduce the ceiling price of the medicine in that market to a price that is not excessive in the opinion of the Board. [52]

A central difficulty in determining whether a price is excessive is that "excessive price" is not defined in the *Patent Act*. Rather, the *Patent Act* prescribes the factors that the Board *must* consider in determining whether the sales price of a patented medicine sold in Canada is excessive as follows: [53]

> 85 (1) In determining under section 83 whether a medicine is being or has been sold at an excessive price in any market in Canada, the Board shall take into consideration the following factors, to the extent that information on the factors is available to the Board:
>
> (a) the prices at which the medicine has been sold in the relevant market;
>
> (b) the prices at which other medicines in the same therapeutic class have been sold in the relevant market;
>
> (c) the prices at which the medicine and other medicines in the same therapeutic class have been sold in countries other than Canada;
>
> (d) changes in the Consumer Price Index; and
>
> (e) such other factors as may be specified in any regulations made for the purposes of this subsection.

49   *Supra* note 2 at para 210.
50   *Celgene, supra* note 46 at para 29.
51   *Canada (Attorney General) v. Galderma Canada Inc.*, 2019 FCA 196 at para 10.
52   See *Patent Act, supra* note 1 at ss 83(1).
53   *Ibid* at s 85(1).

The Governor in Council's addition (and subsequent deletion) of specified economic factors referred to in subsection 85(1)(e) will be discussed in section four.

Subsection 85(2)(a) of the *Patent Act* provides that, if the Board cannot determine whether the sales price of a medicine is excessive on the basis of factors in s. 85(1), it may consider both manufacturing and marketing costs.[54] In addition, where subsection 85(1) factors are not determinative, s. 85(2)(b) provides that the Board may consider, in addition to any regulatory factors made for subsection 85(2), "such other factors […] as are, in the opinion of the Board, relevant in the circumstances."[55]

Section 85 of the *Patent Act*, therefore, gives the Board "a very wide discretion" to determine when prices are excessive.[56] Because of its duty to apply the section 85(1) factors, the Board has broad discretionary power to adopt a *theory* of excessive prices that fits those factors and furthers the purpose of the patented medicine regime in sections 79–103 of the *Patent Act* as described in cases such as *Celgene*. A theory that explains *why* a price is excessive can help satisfy the Board's obligation to supply a "reasoned explanation of the proper meaning of section 85."[57] As the Federal Court of Appeal said in *Alexion FCA*, "[w]ithout an adequate explanation [of its order], it seems arbitrary."[58]

The Board's discretion is limited by the constitutional division of powers. According to the Federal Court of Appeal, "the excessive pricing provisions in the *Patent Act* are directed at controlling patent abuse, not reasonable pricing, price-regulation or consumer protection at large."[59] Regulating the prices of goods and services *per se* is the jurisdiction of the provinces.[60] The distinction is a subtle one, though, because the regulation of patented medicine prices can serve the goal of preventing patent abuse.[61] Thus, the Federal Court of Appeal appears to go too far in *Alexion FCA* when it states that the Board does *not* have a mandate

---

54   See *ibid* at s 85(2).

55   *Ibid.*

56   *Alexion Pharmaceuticals Inc. v. Canada (Attorney General)*, 2021 FCA 157 at para 40 [*Alexion FCA*].

57   *Ibid* at para 64.

58   *Ibid* at para 39.

59   *Ibid* at para 49. It appears that the Court of Appeal of Québec intended to distinguish between provincial and federal jurisdiction in a somewhat obscure statement in *Merck*, *supra* note 2 at para 216, where it said that "the federal jurisdiction over the price of patented medicines concerns the effects of the monopoly granted by the patent, not the effects on the market as a whole."

60   See *Manitoba*, *supra* note 18 at para 14.

61   See *Celgene*, *supra* note 46 at para 29.

to protect consumers or to ensure reasonable pricing. [62] Given that the Board has a "consumer protection purpose," [63] the prevention of excessive prices is a *limited* form of price-regulation that protects consumers from patent abuse. [64] In short, excessive price-regulation, reasonable pricing, and consumer protection are not mutually exclusive. [65]

Given the Board's discretionary authority to determine when the price of a patented medicine is excessive, it also has the authority to *change* its theory about what constitutes an excessive price given changes in circumstances, provided that it is consistent with the *Patent Act*. This power is confirmed by the fact that the Board is able to depart from its Guidelines [66] and has the ability to change them. [67] For example, if the Board's view is that patents in medicines have not resulted in sufficient research and development in Canada given their sales prices, then the prices of patented medicines in countries that do have a strong pharmaceutical research and manufacturing sector may be less relevant to an excessive price determination. [68]

More to the point, based upon subsection 85(2)(b) of the *Patent Act* alone, if the Board views economic factors, such as societal wealth, as relevant and necessary as to whether prices are excessive, it may consider those factors. [69] On such a view, while the notion of excessive—that is, too high—remains the same, judgments about whether and why prices *are* excessive and what factors are necessary to make that determination could change. Even in cases where the Board could resort to subsection 85(2), though, it would be easier for it to justify the relevance of economic factors in its determination if it were required to do so under subsection 85(1)(e), but this would require a regulatory amendment, such as described below.

---

62   See *Alexion FCA*, *supra* note 56 at para 51.

63   *Celgene*, *supra* note 46 at para 28.

64   This is in line with the Supreme Court of Canada decision in *Celgene*, *supra* note 46.

65   While the court's plea for linguistic precision is justified, its line of thought in paras 49–53 of *Alexion FCA*, *supra* note 56, that makes use of a distinction between "consumer protection" and preventing "patent abuse" appears to commit the fallacy of false dichotomy.

66   See *Alexion FCA*, *supra* note 56 at para 39.

67   See *Merck*, *supra* note 2 at para 172.

68   In *Celgene*, *supra* note 46, it was reported the innovative pharmaceutical industry agreed to spend 10% of its sales on research and development in Canada. By 2021, the percentage was 3.4%. See: Canada, Patented Medicine Prices Review Board, *Annual Report 2021* (18 November 2022), online: https://www.canada.ca/en/patented-medicine-prices-review/services/annual-reports/annual-report-2021.html. See also *Merck*, *supra* note 2 paras 219–221.

69   See *Patent Act*, *supra* note 1.

The Governor in Council Attempted to Incorporate Economic Factors into Subsection 85(1)(e) by Regulatory Amendment

The Government of Canada described the purpose of the *Regulatory Amendments* as providing "the [Board] with the regulatory tools and information reporting authorities it needs to effectively protect Canadian consumers from excessively priced patented medicines in today's regulatory environment."[70] To further this purpose, it introduced three amendments.[71] First, the schedule of comparator countries for which patentees report pricing information was amended, changing it from the PMPRB7 countries to the PMPRB11,[72] so as to include countries with similar wealth, medicines, and consumer protection policies.[73] Second, new reporting requirements were introduced, including a requirement to report sales price and revenue net of all price adjustments,[74] so that the reported information more accurately reflects the actual sales prices.[75] Third, and the focus of this chapter, is that the amendment added three mandatory economic factors to be considered under s. 85(1)(e) of the *Patent Act*.[76] The factors are (i) the medicine's "pharmacoeconomic value," (ii) the market size for the medicine in Canada, and (iii) the gross domestic product (GDP) and the GDP per capita in Canada.[77] These new economic regulatory factors were intended to enable the Board to assess the effect of a patent on purchasers of patented medicines in terms of cost-effectiveness and societal affordability.[78]

The *RIAS* explicitly stated that the new economic factors would be used to determine "a national ceiling price above which it would be unreasonable for any consumer in Canada to pay, as opposed to an ideal price for different types of consumers having regard to their individual ability and willingness to pay."[79] The federal government's two main con-

---

70 See *RIAS, supra* note 8 at 5954.
71 *Regulatory Amendments, supra* note 9.
72 See *ibid* at s 6. The PMPRB7 were France, Germany, Italy, Sweden, Switzerland, United Kingdom, and the United States. The PMPRB 11 drops Switzerland and the United States and adds Australia, Belgium, Japan, the Netherlands, Norway, and Spain.
73 See *RIAS, supra* note 8 at 5946–5947.
74 See *Regulatory Amendments, supra* note 9 at ss 3(4).
75 See *RIAS, supra* note 8 at 5947. Typically, self-styled innovative pharmaceutical companies provide rebates and discounts to purchasers of medicines from wholesalers, obscuring the net price. See *Morgan, supra* note 38.
76 See *Regulatory Amendments, supra* note 9 s 4.
77 See *ibid*.
78 See *RIAS, supra* note 8 at 5954.
79 *RIAS, supra* note 8 at 5954.

cerns identified in the *RIAS* were the insufficiency of the current statutory factors for determining when a price is excessive and the incompleteness of information that is required to be provided by patentees relating to the statutory factors.[80] The *RIAS* carefully distinguished the purpose of the amendments from the "desired result" that the prices would be "more reflective of their value" and "more informed by affordability constraints."[81]

Innovative Medicines Canada Objected to the Inclusion of Economic Factors in Excessive Price Determinations

The *Patent Act* authorizes the Board to issue non-binding administrative guidelines in relation to matters within its jurisdiction.[82] Prior to issuing such guidelines, however, it is required to consult with the Minister, provincial ministers of health, as well as representatives of consumer groups and the pharmaceutical industry that may be designated by the federal Minister of Health.[83] This section discusses how the differing views of patent law and excessive pricing held by Innovative Medicines Canada (IMC) and the Board made it difficult to engage in consultations about *how* Board staff should administer excessive price regulation under the proposed *Regulatory Amendments*. As an illustration, at the beginning of every guideline consultation meeting, IMC read out a disclaimer saying that their presence "is not intended and should not be interpreted as supporting the amendments to the Regulations."[84] IMC also raised several substantive objections to the use of the standard measure of pharmacoeconomic value, the quality-adjusted life year,[85] in exces-

---

80   See *RIAS, supra* note 8 at 5953.
81   *RIAS, supra* note 8 at 5594.
82   See *Patent Act, supra* note 1 at s 96(4). There are currently no guidelines in force. However, recent draft Guidelines included information to patentees about the process that Board staff would follow in their review of whether a medicine appears to have an excessive price in Canada. See: Canada, PMPRB, Guidelines (Ottawa: 2020), online: https://www.canada.ca/content/dam/pmprb-cepmb/documents/legislation/guidelines/PMPRB-Guidelines-en.pdf.
83   See *Patent Act, supra* note 1 at s 96(5).
84   Memorandum from Mélanie Bourassa Forcier to the Honourable Jean-Yves Duclos, Minister of Health (8 December 2021), in Correspondence Submitted by Douglas Clark Pursuant to the Motion Adopted by the Committee on Thursday, May 4, 2023, at tab 9 [*Clark Correspondence*], online: https://www.ourcommons.ca/content/Committee/441/HESA/WebDoc/WD12457330/12457330/ClarkDouglas-e.pdf.
85   The quality-adjusted-life-year, or QALY, equates to one year of perfect health (see Milton C Weinstein, George Torrance & Alistair McGuire, "QALYs: The Basics" (2009) 12:1 *Value in Health* S5 at S5).

sive pricing determinations, but these issues are outside the scope of this chapter. [86]

The Acting Chair of the Board described the pharmaceutical industry as "simply not amenable to any measure that would further constrain its ability to sell patented medicine in Canada at free market prices." [87] Similarly, in *Innovative Medicines FC*, one of the applicants' expert witnesses opined that patent rights permit rightsholders to offer their patented medicines for sale at the price of their choice. [88] According to that view, regulating excessive prices of patented medicines by incorporating affordability considerations, such as market size and GDP, would be "inconsistent with the patent bargain." [89] However, to the contrary, as Justice Manson pointed out in *Innovative Medicines FC*, a patent right does not grant the patentees "unfettered pricing discretion," [90] as the regulation of the prices of patented medicines has been validly enacted. [91]

Earlier, in 2016, IMC had contended that "[e]xcessive prices are formally defined as prices set significantly above competitive levels as a result of monopoly or market power." [92] It follows on this view

86   See Innovative Medicines Canada, "Submission – Canada Gazette, Part I – Regulations Amending the Patented Medicines Regulations," [*IMC 2018 Submission*], online (pdf): http://innovativemedicines.ca/wp-content/uploads/2018/02/20180212_IMC_CG1_Submission_Regulations_Amending_the_Patented_Medicines_Regulations_Final.pdf. For a useful defence of cost-effectiveness analysis, see Shepley Orr & Jonathan Wolff, "Reconciling cost-effectiveness with the rule of rescue: the institutional division of moral labour" (2015) 78 *Theory Decis* 525.

87   Memorandum from Mélanie Bourassa Forcier to the Honourable Jean-Yves Duclos, Minister of Health (8 December 2021), in *Clark Correspondence, supra* note 84 at tab 9.

88   *Innovative Medicines FC, supra* note 15 at paras 125 and 157.

89   *Ibid.* In *Alexion Pharmaceuticals Inc v. Canada (Attorney General)*, 2016 FC 716 at para 15 [*Alexion 2016*], an expert witness for Alexion Pharmaceuticals opined that the protection of consumers is "in effect, antithetical to the real purpose of the *Patent Act.*"

90   *Innovative Medicines FC, supra* note 15 at para 127.

91   *Ibid* at para 128.

92   Innovative Medicines Canada, "Submission to the Patented Medicine Prices Review Board" (Ottawa, 24 October, 2016) at 4, online: http://www.pmprb-cepmb.gc.ca/CMFiles/Consultations/Rethinking_the_Guidelines_2016/Submission_Innovative_Medicines_Canada_Oct_2016.pdf. This definition was taken by IMC from the Glossary of Industrial Organisation Economics and Competition Law of the OECD. At the same time, IMC has not always been consistent on this matter, as in a 2022 letter it defined "excessive prices" as "prices that exceed the PMPRB11 and other section 85 benchmarks." See Letter from Pamela C. Fralick to Melanie Bourassa Forcier (28 November, 2022) in Correspondence Submitted by Melanie Bourassa Forcier Pursuant to the Motion Adopted by the Committee on

that, since the "mere exercise of an IP right is not cause for concern under the general provisions of the [Competition] Act,"[93] medicinal price increases that are due to a patent are not *per se* excessive. Unsurprisingly, then, "it was evident that industry would not accept the Board scrutinizing any price below the highest international price of the new basket of comparator countries."[94] However, this "free market" definition of "excessive" is inconsistent with the fact the patented medicine regime in the *Patent Act* is not intended to merely duplicate general competition law nor the more general patent abuse section of the *Patent Act* but was instituted because of "the public interest specific to the pharmaceutical sector."[95]

IMC also maintained that pharmacoeconomic value, market size, and GDP factors are not legitimate concerns of a regulator, like the Board, because the regulator is not a payer.[96] In *Innovative Medicines FC*, IMC similarly contended that "inputs related to pharmacoeconomic value relate to policy decisions that have nothing to do with the patent grant."[97] However, as Justice Manson observed, the price regulation provisions of the *Patent Act* were validly enacted by Parliament,[98] and, therefore, the Board is the regulator of excessive prices *for the benefit of payers* under the *Patent Act*. What's more, Justice Manson found that IMC and the applicants in *Innovative Medicines FC* "misconstrue[d] the relevance of pharmacoeconomic value to a determination of excessive pricing," finding it increasingly relevant for high-cost medicines that have few or no alternatives because there are limited reference prices available.[99]

Thursday, May 4, 2023, at 2 [*Bourassa Forcier Correspondence*] online: https://www.ourcommons.ca/content/Committee/441/HESA/WebDoc/WD12457329/12457329/BourassaForcierMelanie-e.pdf.

93   Canada, Competition Bureau, *Intellectual Property Enforcement Guidelines*, (Ottawa: 2023) at para 36, online: https://ised-isde.canada.ca/site/competition-bureau-canada/en/how-we-foster-competition/education-and-outreach/intellectual-property-enforcement-guidelines.

94   Mathew Herder, "Letter of Resignation" [*Resignation Letter*], online: https://cdn.dal.ca/content/dam/dalhousie/pdf/sites/noveltechethics/nte-Herder%20-%20Letter%20of%20Resignation%20-%20final.pdf.

95   *Merck, supra* note 2 at para 48.

96   See *IMC 2018 Submission, supra* note 86 at 15–19.

97   *Innovative Medicines FC, supra* note 15 at para 115.

98   See *ibid* at para 128.

99   *Ibid* at 118.

The Court of Appeal of Québec Declared the New Economic Regulatory Factors Unconstitutional and Made Several Errors

In *Innovative Medicines FC*, IMC and several innovative pharmaceutical industry applicants challenged the provisions of the *Regulatory Amendments* relating to the new economic factors as being *ultra vires* the *Patent Act*.[100] Among other objections, the applicants claimed, citing a number of statements from the federal Minister of Health and Health Canada, that the purpose of the *Regulatory Amendments* is "to deliver health care savings and pave the way for national pharmacare."[101] After examining the regulations and the *RIAS*, however, Justice Manson of the Federal Court found that the purpose of the *Regulatory Amendments* was "to modernize the Board with new regulatory tools and information reporting authority, and to lower patented medicines prices to protect Canadian consumers from the abuse of excessively pricing."[102] He found that the applicants had "blurred the lines between" purpose and motive in contending otherwise.[103] The finding of the Federal Court in *Innovative Medicines FC* regarding the *vires* to use the economic factors was not appealed to the Federal Court of Appeal since the federal government had by then repealed the provision adding those factors as well as the new price reporting requirements.[104] On appeal of the changes to the list of comparator countries, the Federal Court of Appeal upheld the Federal Court's decision and agreed that "the purpose is the modernization of tools the Board uses to police the excessive pricing of patented medicines."[105] The intent was to protect Canadians "from the abuse of excessively priced patented medicines, such that the prices remain reasonable and affordable to Canadians."[106] It did not, however, include the power to set prices.[107]

The purpose of the *Regulatory Amendments* was also at issue in *Merck* at the Court of Appeal of Québec.[108] Merck Canada Inc. and several other appellants challenged the constitutionality of the *Regulatory Amendments*, the entire patented medicine regime of the *Patent Act*

---

100   *Innovative Medicines FC, supra* note 15 at para 1.
101   *Ibid* at para 93.
102   *Ibid* at para 104.
103   See *ibid* at para 102.
104   See *IMC FCA, supra* note 16 at para 3.
105   *Ibid* at para 57.
106   *Innovative Medicines FC, supra* note 15 at para 84.
107   See *ibid* at para 85.
108   See *Merck, supra* note 2.

and the *Patented Medicine Regulations*.[109] Earlier, the Superior Court of Québec had declared the single purpose of adding the new economic regulatory factors to be that of assisting the Board to determine whether patented medicine prices are excessive.[110] However, on appeal, the Court of Appeal of Québec found that there were *two* purposes to the *Regulatory Amendments*.[111] First, it said, by comparing the sales prices of medicines with specific domestic and international comparators, the purpose is "to determine a price in Canada that is not excessive for the medicine in question so as to mitigate the effect on prices of the monopoly granted by the patent."[112] Second, in contrast to the view of the Federal Court, the Federal Court of Appeal and the Superior Court of Québec, the Court of Appeal of Québec found that "the very purpose of the new factors—their pith and substance—is to impose significant arbitrary reductions in the price of patented medicines."[113] The new regulatory factors were found to be unconstitutional, said to have been introduced to regulate the price of medicines "under the guise of its jurisdiction over patents," and to "have little or nothing to do with the monopoly granted by patents."[114] Is the cynicism of the Court of Appeal of Québec justified?

In support of its analysis of the pith and substance of the provisions, the Court of Appeal of Québec relied upon several Supreme Court statements that the pith and substance of a statute or regulation depends on *both* its purpose and effects.[115] Unfortunately, the Court of Appeal of Québec did not expressly consider or cite the text in the *RIAS* that explicitly describes the purpose of the amendments that was quoted above.[116] Nor did it quote or consider the sentence in the *RIAS* explicitly describing the intent of the amendment.[117] Instead, it expressly

---

See *ibid* at *para* 85. The claim of unconstitutionality of the patented medicine regime had earlier been unsuccessfully made in *Alexion 2016*, *supra* note 89 at para 3.

110 See *Merck QCCS*, *supra* note 14 at para 395, translated in *Merck*, *supra* note 2 at para 103.

111 See *Merck*, *supra* note 2 at para 152–154.

112 *Ibid* at para 153.

113 *Merck, supra* note 2 at para 231. At *Merck*, para 163, the court added that the price reductions were "so that patented medicines are more affordable."

114 *Ibid* at para 239.

115 See *ibid* at paras 137–142, citing, e.g., *References re Greenhouse Gas Pollution Pricing Act*, 2021 SCC 11 at paras 51–56.

116 *RIAS, supra* note 8 at 5954.

117 See *ibid*. The sentence reads: "Given the PMPRB's mandate and status as a federal regulator, the intention is for the Board to use these tools in order to identify a national ceiling price above which it would be unreasonable for any consumer in Canada to pay, as opposed to an ideal price for different types of consumers

considered the text in the *RIAS* relating to effects and quoted it, saying that "[t]he desired result of these changes is for the gross and net ceiling prices of patented medicines in Canada to be more closely aligned with prices in like-minded countries, more reflective of their value to Canadian consumers and more informed by the affordability constraints of the Canadian economy."[118] As to purpose, it relied upon the Board's (non-binding) draft Guidelines to identify the "true purpose"[119] of the *Regulatory Amendments*.

A pivotal part of the Court of Appeal of Québec's argument about pith and substance turned on how it understood the application of s. 85 of the *Patent Act*. It relied upon the assumption that an excessive price can only be determined by comparing it to other international reference prices or "market factor[s]."[120] Indeed, it appeared to adopt the "free market" view of excessive prices criticized above that "the objective sought remains that of ensuring that prices in Canada are competitive in relation to those in other countries."[121] The Court noted that after the *Regulatory Amendments* are in force, the Board would continue to compare the sales price of patented medicines with appropriate international and domestic comparators.[122] It described the purpose of this comparative exercise as determining whether the price is "objectively excessive."[123] It reasoned that after this "objective" comparative assessment, the application of the economic regulatory factors could only result in an "arbitrary reduction" in drug prices because "its price has previously been found not to be excessive further to the application of the factors set out in the Act."[124]

There are numerous problems with the Court of Appeal of Québec's argument that was just described, and they can be briefly stated.[125] First,

---

having regard to their individual ability and willingness to pay."

118   *Merck, supra* note 2 at para 156, quoting *RIAS, supra* note 8, at 5954. In fact, in my view, the court mischaracterizes the quoted statement at para 156 as one "that adds that the purpose is to reorient the Board's role towards controlling the affordability of prices of patented medicines rather than controlling excessive prices." Contrast this statement with that of the Federal Court of Appeal in *IMC FCA, supra* note 16 at para 57: "But, as the Federal Court stated (at para. 103), an honest recognition that the amendments may cause overall cost savings as a natural consequence of the measure does not mean that that is the pith and substance of the amendments."

119   *Merck, supra* note 2 at para 170.

120   *Ibid* at para 226.

121   *Ibid* at para 222.

122   See *ibid* at para 153.

123   *Ibid.*

124   *Ibid at* para 154.

125   In the space of a chapter, this can only be a short summary of potential issues

a reference price, for example, an international drug price, cannot itself be the sole determinant of whether a price is excessive, as the reference price might itself be excessive. Second, and relatedly, it would be incorrect to look *only* at reference prices because that would ignore the legal *requirement* to consider the economic regulatory factors that would be incorporated by reference in s. 85(1)(e) of the *Patent Act*, as well as any other relevant and necessary factors referred to in s. 85(2). Third, the Court's characterization of the application of s. 85 wrongly assumes that price excessiveness is determined by looking solely at factors that are *explicitly expressed* in the legislation and not by consideration of the factors that are referentially incorporated into the legislation by the regulations referred to in s. 85(1)(e). Fourth, and relatedly, by stating that the new economic regulatory factors would be considered *after* a determination of excessiveness is made, the reasoning also wrongly assumes that the new regulatory factors cannot be considered at the *same time* as the other legislated factors in the *Patent Act*.[126] Fifth, there is the question as to whether the Court has incorrectly based its pith and substance analysis on a substitution of its own (distinct) theory of excessive pricing for that of the Board and done so illegitimately, ignoring the fact that the Board is the quasi-judicial body that has the sole legislated authority to exercise discretion about what constitutes an excessive price. Sixth, the Court's judgment appears not to recognize that the Board's theory of what constitutes an excessive price can change based upon different circumstances and the addition of regulatory factors.[127] Seventh, far from being *arbitrary* price reductions as the Court contends, when applied, the economic factors can function as (non-arbitrary) *reasons* for reducing prices. Eighth, the Court nowhere disputes that the price reductions it describes are within the scope of the price effects of the patent.

More generally, the Court of Appeal of Québec's constitutional analysis also appears deficient in a couple of respects. First, in coming to its conclusion, the Court of Appeal of Québec cited with approval the Federal Court of Appeal's decision that the previous excessive

---

which need to be addressed in more depth in subsequent research. This list of problems is enough, nevertheless, to cast sufficient doubt on the Court of Appeal of Québec judgment to have warranted seeking leave to appeal.

126   A similar point was made in *Innovative Medicines FC, supra* note 15 at paras 119–120, and which was not overruled by the Federal Court of Appeal in *IMC FCA, supra* note 16.

127   The failure exists despite indications to the contrary, as when the Court of Appeal of Québec notes at para 220 of *Merck, supra* note 2 at para 172, that the guidelines can "evolve" over time.

pricing provisions of the *Patent Act* (enacted in 1987 and amended in 1993) were constitutionally valid. [128] Yet, the constitutionally validity of s. 85 *implies* that the application of s. 85(2) factors (including economic factors when relevant and necessary) is also valid. Adding economic factors to s. 85(1) by regulatory amendment merely makes those factors mandatory to consider.

Second, the Court of Appeal of Québec is required to presume the constitutional validity of legislation. [129] Consequently, if there are "competing plausible interpretations" a court is required to choose the interpretation under which the law is valid. [130] The fact that the Federal Court, the Federal Court of Appeal, and the Superior Court of Québec had the same interpretation of the purpose of the *Regulatory Amendments,* one that differed from the interpretation held by the Court of Appeal of Québec, is evidence that the competing interpretation was plausible, and that the Court of Appeal of Québec was required to have chosen the competing interpretation under which the *Regulatory Amendments* were considered legally valid. Insofar as the Court of Appeal presumed that the Board would apply its non-binding Guidelines to make an unconstitutional decision, it violated the "presumption of constitutionally conforming administration," a doctrine that implies that the Board's determinations about whether prices are excessive or not are presumed to be in compliance with the Constitution. [131]

The Federal Government Did Not Seek Leave to Appeal the Court of Appeal of Québec's Decision and the Minister Asked the Board to Pause its Consultations

While the federal government's reform initiative was initially designed to assist the Board, it became obvious that the federal Cabinet and Health Minister no longer publicly supported the *Regulatory Amendments* relating to the new economic factors after the decision of the Court of Appeal

---

128 See *Canada (Attorney General) v. Sandoz Canada Inc. and Ratiopharm Inc. (now Teva Canada Limited),* 2015 FCA 249 at para 116, cited in *Merck, supra* note 2 at para 185. See also *Alexion FCA, supra* note 56.

129 See *Reference re Impact Assessment Act,* 2023 SCC 23 at paras 69–75 [*Reference*].

130 *Ibid* at para 72, citing Peter W Hogg & Wade K Wright, *Constitutional Law of Canada,* 5th ed Supp (Toronto: Thomson Reuters, 2021) (updated 2023, release 1).

131 *Ibid* at para 230 in dissent, citing Paul Daly, "Constitutionally Conforming Interpretation in Canada" in Matthias Klatt, ed, *Constitutionally Conforming Interpretation — Comparative Perspectives,* vol 1, National Reports (New York: Bloomsbury, 2023).

of Québec in *Merck*.[132] After the Court declared the addition of the new economic regulatory factors to be invalid, the Government of Canada failed to seek leave to appeal the Québec decision to the Supreme Court of Canada and the Cabinet ultimately repealed sections 3(4) and 4 of the *Regulatory Amendments*.[133] The repeal was done despite the fact that the Québec decision is not binding on courts in Canadian provinces or territories other than Québec,[134] that the *Regulatory Amendments* were designed to "protect Canadian consumers,"[135] that they were previously supported by many provincial ministries of health,[136] and that no provinces besides Québec had intervened to support the pharmaceutical companies' position in *Merck*.[137] The repeal of s. 4 of the *Regulatory Amendments* meant that the new economic factors would not be mandatory factors for the Board to consider in its excessive price determinations, suggesting that affordability and value for money are not necessarily relevant factors in every case.

The federal government's stated rationale for abandoning its support for adding the economic regulatory factors was twofold. First, it said that it was not in the public interest to have provisions of the *Patented Medicine Regulations* that would only apply in Canada outside of Québec.[138] Even granting that harmonized regulations would be preferable, however, it would still be in the public interest *outside* of Québec not to repeal the impugned provisions if those provisions furthered the objectives of patent law. The response that would have furthered the public interest was to appeal the Court of Appeal of Québec decision. Second, the government said it would rely upon the introduction

132   See *Merck, supra* note 2.

133   See *Repeal, supra* note 10. It also repealed s 3(4) of the *Regulatory Amendments* that added the new reporting requirements. See also Canada, "Statement from Minister of Health on the Coming-into-Force of the Regulations Amending the Patented Medicines Regulations" online: https://www.canada.ca/en/health-canada/news/2022/04/statement-from-minister-of-health-on-the-coming-into-force-of-the-regulations-amending-the-patented-medicines-regulations.html.

134   See *R. v. Sullivan*, 2022 SCC 19 at paras 50–59, for a discussion of *stare decisis*.

135   See *RIAS, supra* note 8 at 5594.

136   See *ibid* at 3375.

137   *Merck, supra* note 2.

138   See *Regulatory Impact Analysis Statement* SOR/2022-162, C Gaz II at 3372 [*RIAS, 2022*]. See also Canada, *Statement from Minister of Health on the Coming-into-Force of the Regulations Amending the Patented Medicines Regulations* (14 April 2022), online: https://www.canada.ca/en/health-canada/news/2022/04/statement-from-minister-of-health-on-the-coming-into-force-of-the-regulations-amending-the-patented-medicines-regulations.html.

of several initiatives to "[improve] access to quality medicines." [139] It stated that the creation of the Canadian Drug Agency to formulate a bulk purchasing plan (a national pharmacare program), the National Strategy for Rare Diseases, and the Biomanufacturing and Life Sciences Strategy would improve "access to quality medicines and [ensure] the sustainability of the health care system while supporting innovation and investment in the pharmaceutical sector." [140] Whatever the merits of these strategies, they don't directly support the Board's function of regulating excessive prices of patented medicines. Moreover, the repeal of the impugned provisions of the *Regulatory Amendments* runs counter to the *A Prescription for Canada* report on a national pharmacare that recommended that the new economic regulatory factors be implemented. [141]

Even before the *Merck* decision, though, there were signals that the Minister of Health no longer supported regulatory reform. On November 8, 2022, IMC sent a letter to the Minister asking him to "call upon the Board to suspend its consultation process." [142] IMC's December 5, 2022 submission to the Board called for it to "suspend" and "reset" the consultation process. [143] In the submission, IMC also called for "the Federal Government to intervene to provide more leadership and oversight of the PMPRB file." [144] Around the same time, the Minister met approximately 13 times with pharmaceutical industry members, [145] possibly to try to attract investment in domestic manufacturing capacity for vaccines. [146] According to the Executive Director of

---

139   *RIAS, 2022, ibid* at 3371.

140   *RIAS, 2022, ibid.*

141   See *Prescription, supra* note 40. The ground in favour of implementation was that where there is only a single drug available for treatment, such as in the case of most rare disease drugs, a single payer has limited bargaining power to negotiate an affordable price.

142   Letter from Innovative Medicines Canada to the Honourable Jean-Yves Duclos, (9 November 2022), online: https://innovativemedicines.ca/resources/all-resources/letter-to-the-honourable-jean-yves-duclos-p-c-m-p/ .

143   Innovative Medicines Canada, "The Suspension and Reformulation of the PMPRB Guidelines is Urgently Required: IMC Response to the PMPRB 2022 Guidelines Proposals" online: https://www.canada.ca/content/dam/pmprb-cepmb/documents/consultations/draft-guidelines-2022/submissions/Draft%20guidelines%202022%20submission_IMC_EN.pdf.

144   *Ibid.*

145   See Canada, Standing Committee on Health, "Evidence" (2 May 2023) at 1145 (p 9 in pdf) [*May Evidence*], online (pdf): https://www.ourcommons.ca/Content/Committee/441/HESA/Evidence/EV12390080/HESAEV65-E.PDF.

146   See *ibid* at 1140 (p 8 in pdf).

the Board, "the reforms are the fly in the ointment of those efforts." [147] The Minister did not respond to several requests by the Board (through the Minister's office) for meetings with it. [148] On November 28, 2022, the Health Minister requested by letter "that the Board consider pausing" its consultations. [149] Given that the Board had a duty to consult when developing guidelines, the Minister's claim that his request to *pause* the Board's consultations was done to satisfy his obligation *to* consult seemed inaccurate. [150] The letter from the Minister was characterized by one Board member as "divisive" and as a "demand" to suspend consultations. [151] The letter's content was said to be "largely indistinguishable in form and substance from industry talking points on the proposed guidelines." [152] and an "end-around" [153] the Board that "undermined the Board's independence and credibility." [154] The Ministerial intervention was disruptive to the Board's work, and two Board resignations [155] and that of the Executive Director followed. [156]

The Board Cannot Generally Prevent Undue Delays in Selling Patented Medicines

The final and perhaps most important difficulty is that the Board cannot order a pharmaceutical company to launch new patented medicines

---

147   *Ibid* at 1140 (p 8 in pdf).
148   See *ibid* at 1135 (p 8 in pdf).
149   Letter from Jean-Yves Duclos to Melanie Bourassa Forcier, in *Clark Correspondence*, *supra* note 84 at tab 3 [*Letter from Minister*]. The Minister's letter is undated, but it is said to have been received on November 28th in *Bourassa Forcier Correspondence*, *supra* note 92.
150   See Canada, Standing Committee on Health, "Evidence" (27 April 2023) at 1110 (p 2 in pdf), online: https://www.ourcommons.ca/Content/Committee/441/HESA/Evidence/EV12377024/HESAEV64-E.PDF, where the Minister also said at 1105 that the "pause" was a means for "stakeholders *to engage* meaningfully in the consultation process." (Emphasis added.)
151   *May Evidence*, *supra* note 145 at 1135 (p 7 in pdf).
152   *Resignation Letter*, *supra* note 94.
153   *May Evidence*, *supra* note 145, at 1115 (p 3 in pdf).
154   *Resignation Letter*, *supra* note 94.
155   One Board member resigned as a result of the Minister's letter. See *Resignation Letter*, *supra* note 94. The Acting Chair's written reasons for resigning included the fact that staying "silent" in the face of minister's request made her "extremely uncomfortable." See *Bourassa Forcier Correspondence*, *supra* note 92.
156   See Canada, Patented Medicine Price Review Board, "Douglas Clark stepping down as Executive Director of the PMPRB," online: https://www.canada.ca/en/patented-medicine-prices-review/news/2023/02/douglas-clark-stepping-down-as-executive-director-of-the-pmprb.html.

in a timely way. The Board remains "the David to the Goliath of a transnational trillion-dollar industry" [157] in which the "best practice" [158] of pharmaceutical companies is to launch new drugs sequentially, beginning with high drug price countries and ending with low drug price countries. [159] According to IMC, the Board's role under the proposed *Regulatory Amendments* would have had "serious and negative consequences for patients' access to medicines in Canada." [160] On its view, using economic factors to establish ceiling prices could result in delayed product sales launches or decisions not to launch at all. [161] Arguably, then, the prevention of excessive price abuse might merely result in a different form of patent abuse: unduly delaying access to patented medicines. [162]

The ability of pharmaceutical companies to control the timing of market entry is rooted in the fact that patent rights exclude third parties from manufacturing and selling patented medicines without the authorization of the patent owner, [163] leaving patent owners free to decide whether, where, and when to apply for marketing authorization and, if approved, to sell patented medicines. [164] At the same time, the scope and limits of domestic patent law is constrained by international patent law, which requires medicines to be statutory subject matter to which patent rights may attach but does not sufficiently prohibit patent abuse. In terms of patent rights, for instance, Article 27.1 of *Agreement on Trade-Related Aspects of Intellectual Property Rights* requires Canada to make patents available to applicants in all areas of technology, including medicine, provided the standard statutory requirements of novelty, utility, and non-obviousness are met. [165] Patent-like

---

157   *May Evidence, supra* note 145 at 1135 (p 8 in pdf).

158   See *Palmer, supra* note 37 at 5.

159   Nicolas Houy & Izabela Jelovac, "Drug Launch Timing and International Reference Pricing," (2015) 24:8 *Health Econ* at 978.

160   *IMC 2018 Submission, supra* note 86 at 2.

161   See *ibid* at 18. It should be noted that the *RIAS, supra* note 8 at 5991–5992, suggested that the amendments would not result in a delayed market entry. But see Oliver Spicer & Paul Grootendorst, "The Effect of Patented Drug Price on the Share of New Medicines Across OECD Countries," (2022) 126:8 *Health Policy* 795.

162   This form of abuse would result when there is "excessive control… [that] create[s] "practical obstacles to proper utilization." See *Théberge, supra* note 3.

163   See *Patent Act, supra* note 1 at s 42.

164   This also applies to rightsholders, although currently there is a domestic timely submission requirement for rightsholders under s 106(1)(f) of the *Patent Act* and s 6, *Certificate of Supplementary Protection Regulations* (SOR/2017-165).

165   See *Agreement on Trade-Related Aspects of Intellectual Property Rights*, 15 April 1994, Annex 1C of *Marrakesh Agreement Establishing the World Trade Organization*, 1867

supplementary protection or data protection rights that are required by the *Canada–United States–Mexico Agreement* [166] and other treaties [167] provide additional "constitutional hedges" [168] to protect rightsholders' interests in medicines.

To illustrate the ineffectiveness of international law to help prevent abusive delays in selling patented medicines, consider, *arguendo*, that the *Patent Act* unjustifiably infringes the right to life, liberty, and security of the person under the *Canadian Charter of Rights and Freedoms* [169] when patents on medicines result in delayed drug launches that unduly reduce access to medicines. [170] As a result, suppose that the *Patent Act* were amended to enact a domestic legal requirement for rightsholders to submit a satisfactory marketing authorization application (including the necessary clinical trial data to show that the medicine is safe and efficacious) and to launch domestic sales, all within a prescribed period, failing which patent rights would be revoked. [171] Some countries, such as the US, would consider such a patent revocation to be in conflict with the minimum requirement under Article 27.1 of *TRIPS* to grant patents in all areas of technology, including medicines, [172] and with the patent

---

UNTS 3 (entered into force 1 January 1995), art 27.1 [*TRIPS*].

166   *Canada-United States-Mexico Agreement as amended by Protocol of Amendment to the Agreement between Canada, the United States of America, and the United Mexican States*, 10 December 2019, CAN TS 2020 No 6 (entered into force 1 July 2020) [*CUSMA*].

167   See e.g. *Canada-European Union Comprehensive Economic and Trade Agreement, Can.-E.U., 30 October 2016, O.J. (L 11) 23* (provisional application as of 21 September 2017); *Comprehensive and Progressive Agreement for Trans-Pacific Partnership*, 8 March 2018, Can TS 2018 (entered into force 30 December 2018, for all countries except Vietnam).

168   Tuomas Mylly & Jonathan Griffiths, "The Transformation of Global Intellectual Property Protection: General Introduction" in Jonathan Griffiths & Tuomas Mylly, eds, *Global Intellectual Property Protection and New Constitutionalism: Hedging Exclusive Rights* (Oxford: Oxford University Press, 2021) [*Mylly*].

169   *Canadian Charter of Rights and Freedoms*, s 28, Part 1 of the *Constitution Act, 1982*, being Schedule B to the *Canada Act 1982 (UK)*, 1982, c 11 [*Charter*].

170   This is intended to be analogous to the finding of three members of the Supreme Court that the prohibition on private health insurance violated s 7 of the *Charter* in *Chaoulli v. Québec (Attorney General)*, 2005 SCC 35. For a discussion on the scope and limitations of using the *Charter* as a counterweight to international IP law, see Graham Reynolds, "Hedge or Counterweight? New Constitutionalism and the Role of the Canadian Charter of Rights and Freedoms in Intellectual Property Litigation" in *Mylly, supra* note 168 at 318.

171   As Vaver, *supra* note 27 at 415 notes, patents are not granted unconditionally.

172   See, e.g., Council for Trade-Related Aspects of Intellectual Property Rights, "Minutes of Meeting Held in the Centre William Rappard from 22 to 25 July 1996" (IP/C/M/8). The exception in Article 27.2 based upon *ordre public* is not available to exempt patents on medicines. See Holger Hestermeyer, *Human Rights and the*

revocation section in *CUSMA*. [173] Even if it did not so conflict, Article 5 of the *Paris Convention for the Protection of Industrial Property* provides that patent forfeiture shall only occur when the grant of a compulsory license would not have prevented the abuses. [174]

Suppose, then, that a compulsory license of the patent rights in a medicine is immediately made available to a third party if a pharmaceutical company does not make a timely application for marketing authorization or a sales launch. [175] Even assuming that there is a third party capable of manufacturing the licensed medicine in Canada, there would not necessarily be sufficient clinical data about its safety and efficacy to approve its sale. What's more, the rightsholder has a five-year period of data protection for any data that it submits relating to the safety and efficacy of the pharmaceutical under *CUSMA* that would, if submitted, prevent the patented medicine from being marketed by a third party during the protected period. [176] Apart from an amendment to, or waiver of, *TRIPS*, the public interest exception to data protection under *CUSMA* is limited to public health measures permitted under the *Declaration on the TRIPS Agreement and Public Health*, [177] a non-binding document that doesn't offer any means to limit data protection. [178]

Conclusion

Although the federal government's recent initiative to add new mandatory economic regulatory factors to the *Patented Medicines Regulations* failed, it was instructive. It highlighted an asymmetry between the enforcement of patent rights in medicines via private rights of action and the protection of the public interest by the Board through an application of the excessive pricing provisions of the *Patent Act*. This chapter

---

WTO (Oxford: Oxford University Press, 2007) at 56–57. Neither can Articles 7 & 8 be used to permit the revocation of patents on medicines (see Hestermeyer at 57–58).

173   See *CUSMA, supra* note 166.

174   *Paris Convention for the Protection of Industrial Property*, signed on 20 March 1883, arts 1 (2)–(3).

175   In fact, compulsory licensing of patented medicines is already available three years after the patent grant where there has been abuse of the patent. See *Patent Act, supra* note 1 at s 65.

176   *CUSMA, supra* note 166, art 20.48.

177   See *ibid*, art 20.48; WTO, *Declaration on the TRIPS Agreement and Public Health*, WTO Doc WT/MIN(01)/DEC/2 (2001).

178   Eric M Solovy, "The Doha Declaration at Twenty: Interpretation, Implementation, and Lessons Learned on the Relationship Between the *TRIPS Agreement* and Global Health" (2022) 42:2 Nw J Int'l L & Bus 253 at 255–256.

discussed several difficulties that the Board has faced as a result of that asymmetry. In light of *Merck*, it is uncertain as to whether the Board will use its constitutionally affirmed s. 85 discretion to consider economic regulatory factors in excessive price determinations. It also chronicled the difficulties faced by the federal government in trying to reform the *Patented Medicines Regulations*. If the Board does not use its discretion to apply economic factors in its excessive price determinations, then there may be future calls for the federal government to try again to legislatively mandate the Board to apply economic factors. Ultimately, however, even *if* abusive patented medicine pricing is prevented by the Board, ensuring that patent rights are not abused by unduly limiting timely access to patented medicines would likely require the daunting task of reforming international patent law.[179]

---

179   My sincere thanks to participants who provided feedback on an earlier presentation of this paper at the *Future of IP* conference at the University of British Columbia in June 2023, especially Mathew Herder. Thanks also to Maria Lavelle and an anonymous referee for helpful comments.

Part III
TRADITIONAL CULTURAL EXPRESSION AND INDIGENOUS LEGAL TRADITIONS

Bottom-up Law-Making: A Critical Legal Pluralist's View of a Soft Legal Instrument for the Governance of Traditional Cultural Expressions

Anmol Patel

Abstract

This chapter explores the intersection of traditional cultural expressions (TCEs) and intellectual property (IP) law, highlighting the inherent incompatibility between Western legal frameworks and non-Western normative orders, particularly those of Indigenous peoples and local communities (IPLC). It uses the framework of critical legal pluralism to analyze how TCE governance can challenge dominant legal structures. It examines the role of soft-law instruments as a means of resistance against the encroachment of Indigenous normative orders by external forces. The analysis uses Alaska's Alutiiq Museum's collections policy as a case study to illustrate how soft-law tools can facilitate a syncretic blend of Western and non-Western legal traditions without privileging one over the other. It does not, however, equate Indigenous normative orders with soft law. Instead, it examines how soft law functions as a distinct form of resistance against the encroachment of Indigenous normative orders by external norms. By analyzing the museum's policy, the chapter demonstrates how Indigenous communities can create their own norms while engaging with broader legal systems, thus empowering and emancipating themselves. The research is grounded in a critical legal pluralist framework, which challenges the traditional view of legal centralism and acknowledges the legitimacy of non-state law-making processes. The chapter underscores the importance of consultation and collaboration in developing governance mechanisms for TCEs. It intends to contribute to the discourse on legal pluralism and the governance of TCEs, advocating for a more inclusive approach that acknowledges the legitimacy of non-state law-making processes and the potential for bottom-up law-making by marginalized groups.

The incompatibility between traditional knowledge (including traditional knowledge, traditional cultural expression, and genetic resources and associated traditional knowledge as defined by the World Intellectual Property Organization) and intellectual property rights (IP) creates a dialectic between the Western legal systems on the one hand and non-Western normative orders on the other. The IP protection framework, based on international legal instruments grounded in Western legal values, allows for the appropriation and exploitation of traditional knowledge (TK) without the consent of the Indigenous peoples and local communities (IPLC) who are the source of that knowledge. When Indigenous peoples approach Western legal forums to legitimize their customary law, they must resort to methods suitable to the Western legal systems to make claims and defend their interests.[1] The preference for elements of Western legal tradition, for example, in the Dja Dja Wurrung artefacts dispute, reveals that Indigenous traditions occupy a space similar to the one occupied by non-legal systems of regulation in comparison with legal systems.[2] While there is autonomy, often Western legal systems will be seen as the superior form of normative ordering and the ultimate source of coercive power.[3] In postcolonial societies, appropriation may be in a different form, for example, through nationalization or commodification

---

1   See Sarah Holcombe, "Confidential Information and Anthropology: The Politics of the Digital Knowledge Economy" in Matthew Rimmer, ed, *Indigenous Intellectual Property: A Handbook of Contemporary Research* (Cheltenham: Edward Elgar Publishing, 2015) 417 at 418. See also Jane Anderson, "The Making of Indigenous Knowledge in Intellectual Property Law in Australia" (2005) 12:3 IJCP 347 at 364. She contends that law is an institution that has the power to redistribute interpretations of a problem once it enters legal frameworks. It constructs the legal subject and determines the way that claims are made. Intellectual property law has, in this sense, constructed the conundrum of TK that needs protection. Its unitary categorization of Indigenous knowledge ignores real-world complexities. Law tends to reduce cultural differences making them invisible and accommodates such differences only when they are presented within its own categories.

2   See *Museums Board of Victoria v Carter*, [2005] 146 FCR 213; Georgina Safe, "Artefact Stoush Risks Future Loans," *The Australian* (22 October 2004) at 19.

3   Sally Engle Merry, "Legal Pluralism" (1988) 22:5 Law & Soc'y Rev 869 at 874.

of TCE as art in its own right.[4] In both these kinds of cases, Western IP law interacts with non-Western normative orders.

IPLCs are developing their own IP protocols and consent agreements based on their customary law, and keeping in mind their rights and interests, to govern access and benefit-sharing arrangements.[5] There are also institutions, for example, the Museum of New Zealand Te Papa Tongarewa, that have themselves taken the initiative of developing and implementing such instruments in consultation with Indigenous communities.[6] There may be disputes and disagreements over rights and responsibilities of cultural institutions towards Indigenous peoples when consultations and negotiations take place.[7] The use of soft legal tools for the governance of TCEs shows resistance offered by Indigenous peoples and results in the blending of two different traditions. This chapter studies one such tool as a case study, namely, Alaska's Alutiiq Museum's collections policy[8] and its supplementary guidelines, as part of the analysis of this set of instruments to identify characteristics of normative ordering under a critical legal pluralist framework.[9] We argue that when soft legal instruments are employed for normative ordering in the dialectic between Western legal systems and non-Western normative orders, the result is a syncretic blend of the two that does not necessarily privilege one over the other. While the author is mindful of the fact that the political relationship between the state and IPLCs is a crucial factor that can affect the normative autonomy of IPLCs, this chapter does not delve into state–IPLC relationship politics. For example, it can be argued that IPLCs in Hawaii[10] may be worse off compared

---

4   See e.g. Rashmi Varma, "Primitive Accumulation" (2013) 27:6 Third Text 748.

5   World Intellectual Property Organization, "Codes, guidelines and practices relating to the recording, digitization and dissemination of TCEs," online: *World Intellectual Property Organization* https://www.wipo.int/tk/en/databases/creative_heritage/index.html.

6   Museum of New Zealand Te Papa Tongarewa, "Te Papa Resource Guides: Mātauranga Māori and Museum Practice" (2005), online (pdf): *World Intellectual Property Organization* https://www.wipo.int/export/sites/www/tk/en/databases/creative_heritage/docs/tepapa_matauranga_maori.pdf.

7   Jane Anderson & Molly Torsen, *Intellectual Property and the Safeguarding of Traditional Cultures: Legal Issues and Practical Options for Museums, Libraries and Archives* (World Intellectual Property Organization, 2010).

8   Alutiiq Museum and Archaeological Repository, *Alutiiq Museum Collections Policy* (2019).

9   Alutiiq Museum and Archaeological Repository, *The Alutiiq Museum's Guidelines for the Spiritual Care of Objects* (2022); Alutiiq Museum and Archaeological Repository, *Guidelines for Evaluating Contemporary Works of Alutiiq Art.*

10   "The US government has always given Native Hawaiians a raw deal. It still

to those in Alaska due to a difference in their respective relationships with the federal state. [11]

IPLCs can be understood as "semi-autonomous social fields" that "can generate rules and induce compliance to them" [12], using Sally Falk Moore's framework. In each instance where an element of a Western legal tradition has been upheld over an element of IPLC custom regarding TK, the semi-autonomous social field of IPLCs failed to prevent penetration by external norms. There are many ways in which "resistance" [13] has been offered by IPLCs. The use of soft law instruments is a more recent method of resisting the harm caused to TK by the Western IP framework.

The concept of soft-law instruments originated in international law. [14] Despite its origin, it can be used to refer to norm-setting instruments in other circumstances as well. Snyder defines it as "those rules of conduct which, in principle, have no legally binding force but which nevertheless may have practical effect." [15] Scholars have moved away from this oversimplified binary view that is based on the binding nature of legal instruments. There are ample examples of compliance with binding legal instruments as a result of factors like influence and socio-economic pressure, and, similarly, of compliance with non-binding and non-enforceable instruments. [16] A more nuanced notion of soft law in the era of globalization characterizes law as the product of multiple creators and the privatization of legal regimes. [17] It is this broader, more nuanced connotation of soft law that I rely on since it can acknowledge bottom-up law-making by marginalized groups. The instrument that I examine was identified from among codes, guidelines, and practices

does," *The Guardian* (4 March 2021), online: https://www.theguardian.com/commentisfree/2021/mar/04/us-government-native-hawaiians-raw-deal.

11   Sovereignty and the right to self-determination are correlated with the governance of TK and TCEs. See Danielle M Conway, "Safeguarding Hawaiian Traditional Knowledge and Cultural Heritage: Recognizing the Right to Self-Determination and Preventing the Commodification of Culture" (2005) 48 Howard Law Journal 737.

12   See Sally Falk Moore, "Law and Social Change: The Semi-Autonomous Social Field as an Appropriate Subject of Study" (1972) 7:4 Law & Soc'y Rev 719 at 722.

13   *Ibid.*

14   See generally Anna di Robilant, "Genealogies of Soft Law" (2006) 54:3 Am J Comp L 499.

15   Sally Engle Merry, "Global Legal Pluralism and the Temporality of Soft Law Special Issue: Dedicated to Franz von Benda-Beckmann" (2014) 46:1 J Legal Pluralism & Unofficial L 108.

16   *Ibid.*

17   di Robilant, *supra* note 14 at 500.

relating to recording, digitization, and dissemination of TCEs available in the World Intellectual Property Organization's (WIPO) database.[18]

This research attempts to address various interrelated questions raised from a critical legal pluralist perspective. What are the goals sought to be achieved by the identified soft law instrument pertaining to TCEs? What kinds of tools, mechanisms, or methods are used in the instrument to govern TCEs in order to achieve these goals (in other terms, in what ways is the instrument normative?)? Does the instrument governing TCEs reflect the characteristics of conventional state-made law? Does it refer to conventional IP instruments like national laws or treaties in order to frame its normative stance? How is the legal subject defined by this instrument? This study intends to initiate a discourse about perusing soft law instruments to address these questions.

This chapter's theoretical framework is based on the interface between law and society studies and critical legal studies. The view that only state-made law was law, as part of the ideology of legal centralism, was a key aspect of early legal pluralism scholarship.[19] Some of the earliest approaches to legal pluralism that were about the role of customary law in colonial and postcolonial contexts were premised on the ultimate goal of unification of customary law into colonial law.[20] This was an act of othering by initially accommodating customary law and then intending to turn the "other" into an image of the "self." Critical legal pluralism, while adopting a critical view of legal pluralism, avoids this tempting premise that supports legal centralism. This critical stance allows for a broader view of the role of law in the dialectic between Western IP law and non-Western normative orders. It addresses the failure of conventional social-scientific legal pluralism to discuss fundamental questions about how legal subjects understand themselves, that is, the *being* of these subjects, and the law.[21] Epistemologically, critical legal pluralism relies on the notion that it is knowledge that creates and maintains realities.[22] Therefore, rather than determining legal subjects, as liberal legalism conventionally does, critical legal pluralism accepts that legal subjects possess a "transformative capacity

---

18   WIPO, *supra* note 5.
19   John Griffiths, "What is Legal Pluralism?" (1986) 18:24 The Journal of Legal Pluralism and Unofficial Law 1.
20   *Ibid*.
21   Martha-Marie Kleinhans & Roderick A Macdonald, "What Is a Critical Legal Pluralism?" (1997) 12:2 Can JL & Soc 25 at 36.
22   *Ibid at* 38.

that enables them to produce legal knowledge" and to shape the law that shapes them.[23] A form of law where IPLCs can recognize and create their own legal subjectivity is soft law instruments, which is the subject of this chapter. Critical legal pluralism conceives legal subjects as participants in multiple social normative fields carrying multiple identities. In the case of IPLCs, while state-administered law and their own customary traditions may apply to them, they also work towards the creation of such soft legal instruments.

This chapter examines the text of the collections policy of Alaska's Alutiiq Museum, run by the Alutiiq Heritage Foundation. The examination looked at the text to draw interpretations from the document itself. The language of soft law instruments exposes the tension between "the universalising language of the state and the multiple legal dialects of intermediate social formations" by drawing an analogy between law and language.[24] While there is a broad range of instruments available in the aforesaid WIPO database[25], as this chapter views them as a form of resistance offered by IPLCs, the scope of this discussion is limited to an instrument that was made by an organization run by Indigenous peoples. The involvement of Indigenous peoples in the formulation of the instrument ensures that this discussion answers the research questions raised within the paradigm of critical legal pluralism. The policies of the Alutiiq Museum available in WIPO's database are dated and hence their most recent versions, at the time of writing, were included. The intention is to test the process and replicate it for other kinds of soft-law instruments governing TCEs to generate more useful insights about soft-law instruments as normative ordering tools.

The first section elucidates the TK-IP law incompatibility in the context of TCEs. This includes the various ways in which copyright, trademark and geographical indications, and industrial design are ill-fitted for TCE protection. The next section discusses existing literature about the utility and limitations of soft legal instruments and their relevance to the interests of IPLCs. The following section analyzes of a specific soft law instrument governing TCEs to attempt to answer the research questions itemized earlier.

---

23   *Ibid.*
24   di Robilant, *supra* note 14 at 530.
25   WIPO, *supra* note 5.

Traditional Cultural Expressions and Intellectual Property Law Incompatibility

At the outset, it is important to clarify certain terms used in this chapter since language is not value-neutral. The term "traditional cultural expressions" includes, but is not limited to, art, designs, music, dance, names, signs, symbols, performances, stories, and narratives that constitute a part of the identity and heritage of IPLCs.[26] This definition is that of the WIPO.[27] IPLCs may not find such abstract definitions as important as the relationships and dynamics surrounding the possession of such knowledge and skills.[28] While acknowledging that the term and classification may be narrow-sighted since it is difficult to separate it from IPLCs' worldview, it is being used to avoid confusion and maintain consistency with legal scholarship and international norm-setting activities in the area. The use of the word *traditional* may imply something that is not modern, but it could not be further from the truth to say that TCEs and their governing principles remain static over time.[29] The fact that TK is learned and shared through social processes unique to Indigenous cultures is what makes it "traditional."[30] The term "traditional cultural expressions" is distinct from "traditional knowledge" in its narrow sense. This distinction has been criticized on the grounds that it may erroneously imply that the two are mutually exclusive and independent of each other.[31] For the purpose of this chapter, this distinction is significant since the legal framework, municipal as well as international, that governs TCEs is different from the legal framework governing TK. The soft legal tool studied in this chapter governs only TCEs. Legal scholarship has largely focused on TK in

---

26   WIPO, "Traditional Cultural Expressions," online: *WIPO World Intellectual Property Organization* https://www.wipo.int/tk/en/folklore/.

27   *Ibid.*

28   Peter Drahos & Susy Frankel, "Indigenous Peoples' Innovation and Intellectual Property: The Issues" in Peter Drahos & Susy Frankel, eds, *Indigenous Peoples' Innovation Intellectual Property Pathways to Development* (Canberra: ANU Press, 2012) 1 at 9.

29   Jessica Christine Lai, "Best Practices to Protect Indigenous Knowledge?" in Irini Stamatoudi, ed, *Research Handbook on Intellectual Property and Cultural Heritage* (Cheltenham: Edward Elgar Publishing, 2021) 312 at 312.

30   Four Directions Council, *Forests, Indigenous Peoples and Biodiversity: Contribution of the Four Directions Council* (Lethbridge, Canada: Submission to the Secretariat for the Convention on Biological Diversity, 1996).

31   See Christoph Antons, *Traditional Knowledge, Traditional Cultural Expressions, and Intellectual Property Law in the Asia-Pacific Region* (The Hague: Kluwer Law International, 2009) at 4.

terms of studying soft legal tools as a method of governance.[32] This chapter focuses on TCEs as subject matter governed through soft-law.

The term IPLCs is not meant to overlook the differences and diversity both within Indigenous peoples and between them and local communities. Rather, it is primarily used to highlight commonalities and shared concerns among Indigenous peoples and local communities in preserving their traditional practices. It also serves to maintain consistency with more recent international instruments and legal scholarship.

Legal and anthropological scholarship tend to use the term "custom" or "customary law"[33] when referring to traditions, rules, and

---

32   See e.g. Allison Fish, "Monitoring Compliance with Nagoya: Lessons from India on Building a Techno-Legal Infrastructure to Track Bioprospecting Activities" in Charles Lawson, Michelle Rourke & Fran Humphries, eds, *Access and Benefit Sharing of Genetic Resources, Information and Traditional Knowledge* (New York: Routledge, 2022) 288; Elsa Tsioumani, Christine Frison & Louisa Parks, "Biocultural Community Protocols: Making Space for Indigenous and Local Cultures in Access and Benefit Sharing?" in Charles Lawson, Michelle Rourke & Fran Humphries, eds, *Access and Benefit Sharing of Genetic Resources, Information and Traditional Knowledge* (New York: Routledge, 2022) 177; Michael Halewood et al, "Enhancing Farmers' Agency in the Global Crop Commons Through Use Of Biocultural Community Protocols" (2021) 38:2 Agriculture and Human Values 579; Rachel Wynberg, "One Step Forward, Two Steps Back?: Implementing Access and Benefit-Sharing Legislation in South Africa" in Charles R McManis & Burton Ong, eds, *Routledge Handbook of Biodiversity and the Law*, 1st ed (London: Routledge, 2017) 198; Pamela Andanda, "Codes and Protocols: Protecting Transboundary Traditional Medical Knowledge in Southern Africa" in Patricia Covarrubia, ed, *Transboundary Heritage and Intellectual Property Law* (London: Routledge, 2022) 181; Margaret Raven & Daniel Robinson, "Access and Benefit Sharing and Biocultural Protocols in the Pacific" in Charles Lawson, Michelle Rourke & Fran Humphries, eds, *Access and Benefit Sharing of Genetic Resources, Information and Traditional Knowledge* (New York: Routledge, 2022) 191.

33   See e.g. Chris Cunneen & Melanie Schwartz, "Background Paper 11: Customary Law, Human Rights and International Law: Some Conceptual Issues" in *Aboriginal Customary Laws* Project 94 (Perth, Australia: Law Reform Commission of Western Australia, 2006) 429; Nopera Dennis-McCarthy, "Indigenous Customary Law and International Intellectual Property: Ascertaining an Effective Indigenous Definition for Misappropriation of Traditional Knowledge" (2020) 51:4 Victoria U Wellington L Rev 597; Terri Janke & Robynne Quiggin, "Background Paper 12: Indigenous cultural and intellectual property and customary law" in *Aboriginal Customary Laws* Project 94 (Perth, Australia: Law Reform Commission of Western Australia, 2006) 451; Brendan Tobin, "Traditional knowledge sovereignty: the fundamental role of customary law in the protection of traditional knowledge" in Matthew Rimmer, ed, *Indigenous Intellectual Property* (Cheltenham, UK: Edward Elgar Publishing, 2015) 565; Brendan Tobin, "Where custom is the law: State and user obligations to 'take into consideration' customary law governing traditional knowledge and genetic resources" in Charles R McManis & Burton Ong, eds, *Routledge Handbook of Biodiversity and the Law*, 1st ed (London: Routledge, 2017) 291; Jeremy Webber, "The Grammar of Customary Law" (2009) 54:4 McGill L J 579.

practices of IPLCs. Using the term, as a translation of law[34], is both a misrepresentation of traditional culture and limiting in scope. In order to highlight the differences, and how material they are to this analysis, between the Western legal system and normative frameworks of IPLCs, this chapter adopts an "abstract level analysis" since there is no exact equivalent of legal systems in non-Western cultures. The abstract level where this discussion can take place is at the level of "normative orders"[35] (Western legal system as a normative order and non-Western normative orders). Legal scholarship has been using the term "normative orders" to refer to both Western legal system as well as non-Western normative orders.[36] It is also a more inclusive term compared to "custom." Finally, it is important to clarify that this chapter does not equate Indigenous normative orders with soft law. Rather, it examines how soft law symbolizes a distinct tool of resistance against the encroachment of Indigenous normative orders by external legal and regulatory systems.

TCEs are a result of generations of handing down knowledge, skills, expressions, and stories, without a single known author, that manifest in the form of music, designs, performances, symbols, art and crafts. They are subject to IPLCs' customs and practices. They may not have been created as artistic and cultural expressions for monetary benefits. Over time, TCEs, like TK, evolve to reflect the social circumstances of their source community.[37] Studies, recordings, and dissemination of TCEs by researchers, museums, and other cultural institutions have not necessarily benefitted their source communities. IPLCs have raised objections about such "preservation" activities that do not serve their interests.[38] These activities have often created opportunities for appropriation of TCEs due to their free availability and absence of any legal protection.[39] Sacred or confidential material may also become freely available without any regard for traditions or customs. Legal protection is, however, afforded to works derived out of TCEs by IP law. On the other hand, cultural institutions like museums are contextualizers

---

34   Elizabeth Mertz, "A New Social Constructionism for Sociolegal Studies Conclusion" (1994) 28:5 Law & Soc'y Rev 1243 at 1253.

35   John Scott, "normative order" in *A Dictionary of Sociology* (Oxford University Press, 2015).

36   See e.g. Merry, *supra* note 3.

37   Rina Elster Pantalony, *Managing Intellectual Property for Museums*, (Geneva: World Intellectual Property Organization, 2013) at 15.

38   *Ibid.*

39   *Ibid* at 16.

of content[40] in a digital age where a lot of content is accessible, but not so much in its actual context. IPLCs are contesting for access to such material to reinterpret it and give new meanings.[41] Copyright law prevents them from doing so. Even aside from problems regarding access, TCEs raise issues that are different from other collections in cultural institutions. The ambiguity in IP law about their legal status makes matters worse.[42]

Copyright and TCEs

Although there are variations, there are two kinds of theoretical justifications for copyright protection. Under the Anglo-American system, copyright is an incentivizing property right tool to encourage creators to create for use by the public at large.[43] However, the continental European system is centred around the creator's relationship and control over their work as a personality right.[44] Many countries have created copyright law frameworks adopting a combination of these systems (for example, Canada). The Berne Convention for the Protection of Literary and Artistic Works is the primary agreement at the international level that sets the standards for copyright protection.[45] Although it does not explicitly mention TCE, it does give discretion to the states to make laws regarding "unpublished works where the identity of the author is unknown."[46] Therefore, it lays no standards regarding the treatment of TCEs, and in doing so it allows states to continue treating TCE like other works of authorship.[47] Although the Berne Convention does not mention folklore, WIPO, the body that administers the convention,

---

40   Anderson & Torsen, *supra* note 7.

41   Brigitte Vézina, "Traditional Cultures, Indigenous Peoples and Cultural Institutions" (2010) *WIPO Magazine* (2010) 23 at 24.

42   Anderson & Torsen, *supra* note 7.

43   Silke von Lewinksi, *International Copyright Law and Policy* (Oxford: Oxford University Press, 2008) at 38.

44   *Ibid.*

45   *Berne Convention for the Protection of Literary and Artistic Works*, 9 September 1886, 828 UNTS 221 (entered into force 5 December 1887).

46   *Ibid* art 14.

47   Similarly, *Convention on the Protection and Promotion of the Diversity of Cultural Expressions*, 20 October 2005, UNTS 2440 (entered into force 18 March 2007) mentions Indigenous groups as requiring protection while allowing states to decide the premises of protection. The *Convention for the Safeguarding of the Intangible Cultural Heritage*, 17 October 2003, UNTS 2368 (entered into force 20 April 2006) adds an additional responsibility to create inventories for the identification of intangible cultural heritage (with a view to safeguarding them).

considers folklore as a key element of the future well-being and sustainable development of IPLCs. [48] The WIPO Performances and Phonograms Treaty of 1996 requires Member States to provide copyright protection to performers of expressions of folklore. [49]

The prerequisites of copyright protection are similar on a fundamental level across the world to the extent that they require expression in material form. The person who first expresses the work in material form is credited as the author under copyright law. This is in direct contradiction with IPLCs who may want to prevent dissemination of a work derived [50] from cultural expression, for example, (instead of actual sculpture or performance) photographs of rock sculptures or paintings, or a video recording of a dance performance taken by an outsider. [51] Questions of originality are also likely to come up when TCEs are used to create works by living folk artists. This leaves, if any, a very narrow scope of copyright protection for the works they create and makes their work vulnerable to copying without permission, credit, or any kind of benefit-sharing. There are also instances of modes of expressions like face painting, body painting, and sand carvings which cannot meet the fixation requirements in and of themselves while outsiders record them in a tangible form to claim benefit out of the work. [52]

A similar issue is that of the public domain. The fact that copyright protection is for a limited duration (varying by country, usually life of the author plus a certain number of years) does not serve artists from IPLCs whose cultural knowledge is generations old. [53] Falling

48   S Rama Rao, "The Relationship between Intellectual Property and the Protection of Traditional Knowledge and Cultural Expressions" in Ulia Popova-Gosart, ed, *Traditional Knowledge and Indigenous Peoples* (World Intellectual Property Organization and L'auravetl'an Information & Education Network of Indigenous Peoples, 2009) 40 at 40.

49   *WIPO Performances and Phonograms Treaty*, 19 December 1996 (entered into force 19 May 2002).

50   "Derivative works" are defined under *Copyright Act*, 17 USC § 101 (1976) as "works that are produced based one or more existing works." The Canadian Copyright Act also makes a similar distinction between derivative works and original works under *Copyright Act*, RSC 1985, c C-42, s 3(1)(a)–(e).

51   Erin MacKay, "Indigenous Traditional Knowledge, Copyright and Art - Shortcomings in Protection and an Alternative Approach" (2009) 32:1 UNSWLJ 1 at 3.

52   WIPO, Intergovernmental Committee on Intellectual Property and Genetic Resources, Traditional Knowledge and Folklore, 38th Sess, WIPO/GRTKF/IC/38/7 (2018).

53   Terri Janke, "Minding Culture: Case Studies on Intellectual Property and Traditional Cultural Expression," (2003), online (pdf): *Geneva: World Intellectual Property*

in the public domain does not serve any public interest, as envisaged by theories of copyright law, to the IPLCs.[54] The public domain is a construct of IP law that does not respect the kind of protection of TCE that non-Western normative orders require to continue pursuing their cultural interests.[55]

Another technical issue surrounding authorization is ownership. Indigenous groups demand collective ownership of TCEs originating in their community. Copyright law envisages individual ownership. The question of collective ownership was raised in *John Bulun Bulun v R & T Textiles Pvt Ltd*[56] before the Federal Court of Australia. The applicants were Aboriginal artists and senior members of the Ganalbingu people.[57] Bulun Bulun created a bark painting with the permission of senior members of the Ganalbingu people since it was derived from ritual knowledge inherited by the Ganalbingu from their ancestors.[58] The respondent imported and sold fabric that infringed on Bulun Bulun's work. The court accepted that Bulun Bulun owed a fiduciary duty to the Ganalbingu people "not to exploit the artistic work in a way that is contrary to the laws and customs of the Ganalbingu people and, in the event of infringement by a third party, to take reasonable and appropriate action to restrain and remedy infringement of the copyright in the artistic work."[59] It also held that if a copyright owner of a work of authorship which uses ritual knowledge of an Aboriginal clan is being used inappropriately and the copyright owner fails to take action to enforce the copyright, the Aboriginal clan would have recourse to the courts for remedial action.[60] Therefore, although collective ownership could not be strictly established over the entire array

---

Organization https://www.wipo.int/edocs/pubdocs/en/tk/781/wipo_pub_781.pdf.

54   *Ibid.*

55   Susy Frankel & Megan Richardson, "Cultural Property and 'the Public Domain' Case Studies from New Zealand and Australia" in Christoph Antons, ed, *Traditional Knowledge, Traditional Cultural Expressions, and Intellectual Property Law in the Asia-Pacific Region* (The Netherlands: Kluwer Law International, 2009) 275; Ruth L Okediji, "Traditional Knowledge and the Public Domain in Intellectual Property" in Carlos Correa & Xavier Seuba, eds, *Intellectual Property and Development: Understanding the Interfaces: Liber amicorum Pedro Roffe* (Singapore: Springer, 2019) 249.

56   *John Bulun Bulun v R & T Textiles Pty Ltd*, [1998] 86 FCR 244 (FCA).

57   *Ibid.*

58   *Ibid.*

59   *Ibid.*

60   *Ibid.* The requirement of an existing and valid copyright was also discussed in the case of *Milpurrurru v Indofurn Pty Ltd*, [1994] 54 FCR 240 (FCA) where the respondents were importing carpets manufactured in Vietnam which had reproductions of paintings made by aboriginal artists and placed for display in the Australian National Gallery.

of traditional knowledge, a fiduciary relationship through equity was accepted to have existed between the Indigenous group and the artist belonging to the group. The case brings to the fore the questions regarding the creation of styles of work that are often a culmination of generations of contribution. They cannot be attributed to individual authors.

a. Trademark (and Geographical Indication) and TCEs

Trademarks are marks or signs that identify the goods or services of persons or organizations. Trademark law essentially protects the relationship created by the provider of goods or services between the good or service and its source. This relationship helps the consumer to distinguish between goods or services provided by one organization from those of another organization. In order to obtain trademark protection, use or intention to use the mark in relation to particular goods or services needs to be established. Unlike copyright, collective ownership is much easier in the case of trademarks. Indigenous organizations can seek trademark registration. [61] The life of a trademark is also not limited in terms of years but rather relies on usage. Protection is effective if there is use by the owner and upon meeting any other formal requirements. This means that Indigenous users would have to continue using the mark to not lose it. These features of trademark law also make it easier for anyone other than IPLCs to trademark their names, phrases, or any cultural expression without authorization.

The Canadian Trademarks Act has been useful for Indigenous groups in Canada to protect their cultural designs and words from misappropriation for commercial use. The legislation prohibits the use of "official marks" [62] as trademarks by others. Indigenous groups that are "public authorities" under the provision have successfully registered their designs and words under the act. [63]

An example of the misappropriation of Indigenous names is the

---

61   Despite registration, unauthorized uses of TCEs may continue. See e.g. Sophia O'Rourke & Leah McLennan, "Kimberley artists contemplate legal action over misappropriation of sacred Wandjina figure," (15 February 2019), online: *ABC News* https://www.abc.net.au/news/2019-02-16/kimberley-artists-legal-action-over-wandjina-misappropriation/10813488.

62   *Trade-marks Act*, RSC 1985, c T-13, s 9(1)(n)(iii).

63   For some examples, see Simon Brascoupé & Karin Endemann, "Intellectual Property and Aboriginal People: A Working Paper", Intellectual Property Policy Directorate, Industry Canada (1999), online: https://www.wipo.int/export/sites/www/tk/en/databases/creative_heritage/docs/ip_aboriginal_people.pdf at 21.

use of "Wandjina" in the names of three Australian companies.[64] Elders of the Ngarinyin community built a website to spread awareness about their culture and requested the owners of these companies to stop using the word "Wandjina."[65] Two of those companies agreed.[66]

In the United States, the Indian Arts and Crafts Act is a specific legislation to provide protection against deceptive marketing practices of Native American and Alaskan arts and crafts from non-Native American and Alaskan sources.[67] A producer managed to convince a village in the Philippines to change its name to Zuni in order to sell the goods they produced there as those made in the Zuni region of New Mexico by the Zuni tribe.[68] Another producer used the brand name "Indian Maid" to market jewellery under the false pretense that it was made by Native Americans.[69] In a similar matter where a non-Native American manufacturer tried to pass off jewellery under names of tribes such as Navajo, Crow, Southwest tribes, and Zuni bear, the United States Court of Appeals also ruled on the constitutional validity of the legislation.[70] The court drew an analogy with trademark law stating that the purpose of the legislation is the same except it is specifically meant for the marks denoting products made by Indians.[71] The purpose of the act seems to have been purely economic as it was explained in *Native American Arts, Inc v Contract Specialties, Inc.*[72]

The Indian Arts and Crafts Board, the body that administers this law, has a similar economic goal.[73] The information brochures regarding the legislation that are distributed are also aimed at encouraging Native American artists to use conventional IP protection, which has the same economic objective.[74] Therefore, the law does not attach any value to the cultural significance a form of art or style may have within

---

64   Janke, *supra* note 53.
65   *Ibid.*
66   *Ibid.*
67   *Indian Arts and Crafts Act*, Pub L No 101-644, 25 USC 305 (1990).
68   Jennie D Woltz, "The Economics of Cultural Misrepresentation: How Should the Indian Arts and Crafts Act of 1990 Be Marketed" (2007) 17:2 Fordham IP Media & Ent LJ 443 at 470
69   *Ibid* at 469.
70   *Native American Arts, Inc v Waldron Corp*, 399 F (3d) 871 (7th Cir 2005).
71   *Ibid.*
72   *Native American Arts, Inc v Contract Specialties, Inc*, 754 F Supp (2d) 386 (RI 2010).
73   Rebecca Tushnet, "The Indian Arts and Crafts Act: The Limits of Trademark Analogies" in Matthew Rimmer, ed, *Indigenous Intellectual Property: A Handbook of Contemporary Research* (Cheltenham, UK: Edward Elgar Publishing, 2015) 250 at 251.
74   *Ibid* at 253.

Indigenous communities. The branding orientation of the act turns tribes into brands.[75] One may say that at least it seems to be coherent with the benefit-sharing objectives of the United Nations Declaration on the Rights of Indigenous Peoples.[76] However, it does not fully satisfy this purpose either. The law prohibits goods that are marked falsely, but it permits goods that are marked correctly but emulate Native American styles.[77] This means that although action can be initiated by Native American groups, the legislation is beneficial only to the extent that consumers are able to identify and demand for authentic Native American-made goods.[78] It is also limited only to tangible goods ("arts and crafts") and does not cover other types of cultural expression such as music, dance, or literary works which can also be commercially exploited.[79]

There have also been uses of labels of authenticity and certification trademarks by Indigenous groups in Tonga, Panama, Fiji, and New Zealand to reduce the sale of fake traditional creative arts.[80] Some nations[81] and Indigenous groups[82] have resorted to geographical indications (GI) to protect tangible traditional cultural expressions since they allow collective ownership and management. GIs are indications which identify the origin of a good based on some characteristics like quality or reputation attributable to its geographical origin. Compared to trademark's individualistic and assignable nature, GI seems like a better option for the protection of TCEs due to its characteristics of collective ownership and relation to a geographical region.[83] However, GIs are

---

75   Naomi Mezey, "The Paradoxes of Cultural Property" (2007) 107:8 Colum L Rev 2004.

76   *United Nations Declaration on the Rights of Indigenous Peoples*, GA Res 61/295, UNGAOR, 61st Sess, Supp No 49, UN Doc A/61/295 (2007).

77   Tushnet, *supra* note 73 at 252.

78   Jennie D Woltz, "The Economics of Cultural Misrepresentation: How Should the Indian Arts and Crafts Act of 1990 Be Marketed?" (2007) 17:2 Fordham IP Medi a & Ent LJ 443 at 460.

79   Tushnet, *supra* note 73 at 252.

80   Rao, *supra* note 48 at 42.

81   Argentina, Brazil, Paraguay, and Uruguay through the 1995 Protocol for the Harmonization of Intellectual Property Norms in MERCOSUR with respect to Trademarks and Indications of Source or Denominations of Origin as part of the 1991 Southern Common Market agreement, see Emily Cox et al, "Module 8: Traditional Knowledge", online: *Berkman Klein Center for Internet and Society at Harvard University* <https://cyber.harvard.edu/copyrightforlibrarians/Module_8:_Traditional_Knowledge>.

82   For example, the Alaska Silver Hand program, see *Ibid*.

83   Cerkia Bramley & Estelle Bienabe, "Developments and considerations around geographical indications in the developing world" (2012) 2:1 Queen Mary Journal of Intellectual Property 14 at 24.

limited to "goods" and therefore cannot protect TCEs like music and dance.[84] Although the collective nature of GIs may seem suitable for TCEs, they are meant to support individual businesses and will fail to give due regard to the customs surrounding usage and development of TCEs for future generations.[85] The requirement of production within a specific geographical location can also become a limitation since artists who relocate to other geographical regions would no longer receive the same GI protection even if they produce the same good with the exact same characteristics.[86] Due to its TM-like commercial premise, GI also cannot prevent offensive usage that could harm the spiritual or sentimental significance of the TCE for its source community.[87] Since GIs are limited to the protection of names, they are inadequate to protect the knowledge behind the production of TCEs.[88]

b. Industrial Design and TCEs

Industrial design (ID) is meant to protect the visual or aesthetic aspects of wares. These aspects should not have a function or utility for the ware. TCEs in designs, motifs, emblems, patterns, and cultural objects could have different kinds of significance for IPLCs.[89] In terms of the essential elements required for protection, ID is like a combination of patent and copyright in that it needs both originality and novelty. While most countries use *sui generis* legislations, the US and China issue design patents. A limited term of protection, normally shorter than that for copyright, does not make it worth the trouble[90] for IPLCs. In Canada, TCEs were registered by Indigenous organizations like the West Baffin Eskimo Co-operative Ltd. for more than 50 fabric designs[91]

84   Shivani Singhal, "Geographical indications and traditional knowledge" (2008) 3:11 Journal of Intellectual Property Law & Practice 732 at 733.
85   Susy Frankel, "The Mismatch of Geographical Indications and Innovative Traditional Knowledge: Prometheus (Routledge)" (2011) 29:3 Prometheus (Routledge) 253 at 259.
86   Singhal, *supra* note 84 at 736.
87   *Ibid* at 735.
88   Frankel, *supra* note 85 at 258.
89   Janke, *supra* note 53.
90   Brascoupé & Endemann, *supra* note 63.
91   Canadian Intellectual Property Office, "National Application/Registration: 30510," online: *Innovation, Science and Economic Development Canada* https://www.ic.gc.ca/app/opic-cipo/id/dsgnDtls.do?appNm=30510&lang=eng&status=&ordNum=1 at 30510.

and the Conseil des Montagnais (du Lac St. Jean) for its toy doll,[92] both of which have expired and are not protected anymore. The elements of design which can be protected by ID may also be protected by copyright. Much like in the case of patents, the novelty requirement may be challenging to meet since the visual appeal of the Indigenous products derives heavily from existing Indigenous products. On the other hand, TCEs could be easily appropriated by others applying design elements on different wares and securing ID protection.[93] For example, Christian Louboutin obtained a design patent for a kind of handbag which was later sold with a Ghanian Kente pattern on it.[94] Although it is not known whether the Kente pattern was registered as design patent, the law would certainly permit it if it was to be registered.[95] The recently concluded WIPO Design Law Treaty in Riyadh, aimed at harmonizing design protection, finds mention of TCEs and TK but leaves it at the discretion of states to require any disclosure relevant to filing an application for ID registration.

Soft Law as an Instrument for the Protection of Traditional Knowledge

The concept of soft law in international law normally involves sovereign nations interacting with each other. Although in the case of soft legal instruments concerning TCEs we are not concerned with nation-states in the same way that they are referred to in scholarly discussions in international law, these discussions provide useful insights for the purpose of this chapter. The theoretical deliberations on the topic explore the role of soft legal tools as normative instruments which are relevant and, therefore, can be borrowed for the present context of governance of TCEs. As clarified earlier, the purpose of introducing the concept of soft law in this study is not to evoke a discussion equating Indigenous

---

92   Canadian Intellectual Property Office, "National Application/Registration: 31971," online: *Innovation, Science and Economic Development Canada* https://www.ic.gc.ca/app/opic-cipo/id/dsgnDtls.do?appNm=31971&lang=eng&status=&ordNum=1 at 31971.

93   Margo A Bagley, "Illegal Designs? Enhancing Cultural and Genetic Resource Protection Through Design Law" (2017) 155 Centre for International Governance Innovation 1.

94   Margo A Bagley, "'Ask Me No Questions': The Struggle for Disclosure of Cultural and Genetic Resource Utilization in Design" (2020) 20:4 Vanderbilt Journal of Entertainment and Technology Law 975 at 993.

95   *Ibid.*

normative orders with soft law. This section draws from the legal literature about soft law to identify some of its characteristics as legal tools that can inform the current discussion.

In more general terms, when this chapter mentions soft law or soft legal instruments, it refers to a broad range of quasi-legal instruments that have no binding legal force. [96] Although they may not have a binding legal force, they may have other characteristics of law or may be intended to have effects similar to law [97] which makes them relevant to the study of laws. Legal scholarship started discussing the concept of soft law in 1980s. [98] Legal positivists tend to prefer hard law over soft law as a normative instrument and at best may find soft law as a means to eventually establish hard law. [99] Since it cannot be enforced by courts, soft law is just a second-best alternative when attempts to formulate hard law fail. [100] This view fails to account for soft legal instruments that may not be created with the intention of ultimately transforming into hard law. Rationalist scholars view hard law and soft law as serving different purposes. According to them, soft law has lower contracting costs, making it easier to conclude bargains and giving greater flexibility in implementation of commitments. [101] While this view is attractive for the present deliberation about governance of TCEs, its conformity to the hard law/soft law binary may reduce the value of soft legal tools used for this purpose. Constructivists, on the other hand, contend that the dividing line between hard law and soft is not as clear as it is presumed to be. [102] Their focus is on the effectiveness of the legal instrument in practice rather than the formal binding nature of the law during its initial enactment. [103] The socializing role of soft law in arriving at a con-

---

96   Bryan H Druzin, "Why Does Soft Law Have Any Power Anyway?" (2017) 7:2 Asian Journal of International Law 361.

97   Linda Senden, *Soft Law in European Community Law*, 1st ed (London: Hart Publishing, 2004) at 112.

98   Hanna Mattila & Aleksi Heinilä, "Soft spaces, soft planning, soft law: Examining the institutionalisation of city-regional planning in Finland" (2022) 119 Land Use Policy, online: https://www.sciencedirect.com/science/article/pii/S0264837722001831.

99   Gregory C Shaffer & Mark A Pollack, "Hard vs. Soft Law: Alternatives, Complements, and Antagonists in International Governance" (2010) 94:3 Minn L Rev 706 at 723.

100   Jan Klabbers, "The Redundancy of Soft Law" (1996) 65:2 Nordic J Int'l L 167.

101   Kenneth W Abbott & Duncan Snidal, "Hard and Soft Law in International Governance" (2000) 54:3 Int Org 421.

102   David M Trubek, Patrick Cottrell & Mark Nance, "'Soft Law', 'Hard Law' and EU Integration" in Gráinne de Búrca & Joanne Scott, eds, *Law and New Governance in the EU and the US*, 1st ed (London: Hart Publishing, 2006) 65.

103   Shaffer & Pollack, *supra* note 99 at 713.

sensus and building shared norms is significant for them. All of them suggest that soft law can become binding hard law despite valuing soft law differently. It is the constructivist view that makes the use of soft legal tools for the governance of TCEs more meaningful since it values how soft law can "facilitate constitutive processes such as persuasion, learning, argumentation and socialisation" [104] and neither privileges hard law over soft law nor conforms to the binary of soft law/hard law. The arguments made in this chapter rely on the constructivist view. The following section illustrates how these values are imbibed within the soft law instrument examined in this chapter.

Analysis of a Soft Legal Instrument Governing TCEs

This section will analyze a specific soft law instrument in order to answer the research questions itemized in the introduction section earlier. While there is a wide range of soft legal instruments that have been identified by WIPO for the governance of TCEs, the one chosen for this work is Alaska's Kodiak community's Alutiiq Museum Collections Policy. [105] Since the policy is supplemented by the Alutiiq Museum's Guidelines for the Spiritual Care of Objects [106] and Guidelines for Evaluating Contemporary Works of Alutiiq Art [107], they have also been examined as a part of this study. This section is divided into five parts. The first one elucidates the goals sought to be achieved by the policy instrument. The second part identifies the tools, mechanisms, or methods used to govern TCEs in order to achieve the goals of the policy. The third one uncovers the meaning of TCEs inherent in the policy. The fourth part identifies how the legal subject is defined by the policy instrument and the final one consolidates the findings discussed in the preceding parts. The underlying framework for this analysis is the one informed by critical legal pluralism elucidated in the introduction section above. The Alutiiq (or Sugpiaq, as is the traditional self-designating term) people constitute one of the eight native communities of Alaska. [108] They have been living along the coast of Alaska for thousands of years, [109] relying

---

104   Trubek, Cottrell & Nance, *supra* note 102 at 75.
105   Alutiiq Museum and Archaeological Repository, *supra* note 8.
106   Alutiiq Museum and Archaeological Repository, *supra* note 9.
107   *Ibid.*
108   Alutiiq Museum and Archaeological Repository, "Alutiiq / Sugpiaq People," online: *Alutiiq Museum and Archaeological Repository* https://alutiiqmuseum.org/learn/the-alutiiq-sugpiaq-people.
109   *Ibid.*

on fishing as well as cultivation.[110] They also have a history of Russian colonization followed by the purchase of the territory by the United States. The Alutiiq Museum was established by a Kodiak organization promoting native arts and culture that secured funds from the Exxon-Valdez oil spill trustee council.[111]

Goals of the Alutiiq Museum Collections Policy

The mission set for the museum is to "preserve and share the living culture and heritage of the Alutiiq people".[112] This forms the underlying principle for the governance of TCEs within the museum framework. One of the most important sections of the policy, the one about access and use, proclaims that access is integral to achieving the mission of the museum.[113] The intention of the policy is to create a balance between the needs to encourage the use of collections to promote awareness about the cultural heritage of the Alutiiq people and to protect the collections from harm while treating them sensitively.[114] This is reflected in the concrete policy guidelines regarding use, access, and care of collections, which will be discussed later. It is pertinent to note that the policy goals avoid the temptation to create a simple binary between access and protection and instead choose to provide a more nuanced form of access that is mindful of the culturally sensitive care of artefacts.

Museums the world over are presented with artefacts that are stolen or illegally obtained.[115] Museums are also aware of the involvement of criminal elements in artefacts that end up being sold to them.[116] While most of them have formally added restrictions on purchasing or obtaining artefacts without provenance

---

110   Alutiiq Museum and Archaeological Repository, "Subsistence," online: https://alutiiqmuseum.org/learn/the-alutiiq-sugpiaq-people/subsistence.

111   Alutiiq Museum and Archaeological Repository, "Museum History," online: *Alutiiq Museum and Archaeological Repository* https://alutiiqmuseum.org/learn/history-of-the-alutiiq-museum. The archaeological resources of the region were affected by the oil spill per Kirsten Dobroth, "Alutiiq Museum to receive funding through CORaL Network collaboration," (29 June 2022), online: *KMXT 1001 FM* https://kmxt.org/2022/06/alutiiq-museum-to-receive-funding-through-coral-network-collaboration/.

112   Alutiiq Museum and Archaeological Repository, *supra* note 8 at 2.

113   *Ibid* at 15.

114   *Ibid*.

115   See Staffan Lunden, "Perspectives on Looting, the Illicit Antiquities Trade, Art and Heritage" (2012) 17:2 Art Antiquity & L 109.

116   See Blythe Bowman Proulx, "Organized Criminal Involvement in the Illicit Antiquities Trade" (2011) 14:1 Trends Org Crime 1.

information[117] and confirmation of ownership, the illicit trade in
cultural material continues and unprovenanced artefacts are found
in museums.[118] In terms of advocacy and awareness programs, they
tend to focus more on identification of fakes rather than the grave
issue of illicit trade of artefacts.[119] On the other hand, the Alutiiq
Museum Collections Policy is aimed to discourage the collection of
artefacts by amateurs.[120] However, because of its role as a preserver
of Alutiiq heritage, it may accept unprovenanced Alutiiq artefacts or
artefacts of neighbouring communities that may have ended up with
Kodiak people due to the history of interaction between the Kodiak
and their neighbours. The museum has signed memorandums of
understanding (MOU) with state entities and major landowners of
Kodiak regarding acceptance and care of such artefacts whose ownership cannot be determined.[121] The MOUs require the museum to
first make efforts to determine the origin of the artefacts and contact
the owners.[122] In case of a failure to find the owners, the artefacts
would be placed in their teaching collection, not accessible without
request, instead of their permanent collection.[123] It would not be possible to legally acquire unprovenanced artefacts due to the absence
of ownership information. However, as custodians of Alutiiq culture,
they can care for such artefacts while being culturally sensitive. This
decolonizes the process of care of artefacts, something that may not
be institutionally possible for museums with colonial legacies. The
process of dealing with unprovenanced artefacts is well-codified
within the ambit of state-made law while being equally deferential
to the Kodiak community's culture and customs. The museum has
also signified its intent pertaining to unprovenanced artefacts openly

---

117   See Charles C Kolb, "Provenance Studies in Archaeology" in Claire Smith, ed,
       Encyclopedia of Global Archaeology, 1st ed (New York: Springer, 2014) 6172 for an
       understanding of the relevance of provenance information for museums. The
       Alutiiq museum's collections policy uses the terms "provenance" and "prove-
       nience" interchangeably. The policy seems to have implied the connotation of
       the term that refers to determination of ownership of the artefact.
118   See Neil Brodie, Jennifer Doole & Peter Watson, *Stealing History: The Illicit Trade in
       Cultural Material* (Cambridge, UK: McDonald Institute for Archaeological Research,
       2000).
119   Vasiliki Kassianidou et al, "Museum Education and Archaeological Ethics: An
       Approach to the Illicit Trade of Antiquities" (2014) 12:1 Journal of Conservation
       and Museum Studies art 2.
120   Alutiiq Museum and Archaeological Repository, *supra* note 8 at 27.
121   *Ibid.*
122   *Ibid* at 8.
123   *Ibid* at 27.

and transparently by signing the MOUs.

Tools, Mechanisms, or Methods Used to Govern TCEs

The collections policy requires compliance with state laws within the US as well as international laws governing antiquities management, wildlife protection, and treatment of human remains. [124] Although IP law does not find mention in the inexhaustive list of laws itemized in the first section of the policy, copyrights, patents, and trademarks are cited later in the policy when it discusses acquisition, access, and purchase of artefacts. Collections can be acquired by the museum only if they are free from encumbrances by IP rights, literary rights, or property rights. [125] In case of acquiring collections through purchase, copyrights and literary rights may be conveyed for non-exclusive use by the museum, unless agreed to otherwise by the previous owner and the museum. [126] When it comes to providing access, the museum shall avoid sharing materials for which it does not hold copyright. [127] Access and usage is discussed in the fourth part of this section. Reference to IP laws is limited to the extent mentioned here. In terms of artefacts like human remains, funerary objects, and sacred items, the policy reminds the museum to comply with the federal Native American Graves Protection and Repatriation Act (NAGPRA) by refraining from accepting such collections and repatriating existing artefacts respectfully. [128] International law has been cited to restrict borrowing of material that the museum believes was acquired unethically. [129] Property law principles of clear title and transfer of ownership are followed to add artefacts to the museum's permanent collection. This kind of deference to Western legal knowledge in the policy reflects the aspect of soft legal instruments being shaped by conventional state-made laws. While the policy is not even remotely based on the same principles that justify IP laws, it ensures that these laws are complied with, thereby accepting the sovereignty of the state to that extent. Despite adhering to IP law, the institution focuses on the process of collecting, caring, and usage of artefacts as a community-run organization that serves the interests

---

124   *Ibid* at 3.
125   *Ibid* at 9.
126   *Ibid* at 11.
127   *Ibid* at 16.
128   *Ibid* at 12.
129   *Ibid* at 20.

of the Kodiak community. It prioritizes collective benefits over the economic goals of exclusive ownership typically associated with IP law.

The museum is governed by the Alutiiq Heritage Foundation board that serves as the final authority in the museum's collections operations.[130] The members of the board are expected to follow the policy in the fulfillment of their fiduciary responsibilities, including ensuring public confidence in the museum's acquisitions, care of collections, and deaccession practices. The museum collections policy goes beyond merely showing deference to Western legal knowledge by adopting other kinds of tools that are more aligned with the beliefs of the Kodiak people. The policy allows culturally sensitive information regarding collections to be kept private.[131] This may seem counterintuitive to some of the objectives of a museum but fulfills the community's needs of confidentiality regarding sensitive information.

The museum's Guidelines for the Spiritual Care of Objects is a tool that introduces the normative values of the Kodiak people to the governance of their TCEs in the museum. Although it is not entirely uncommon for museums to consider spiritual care of its collections[132] in consultation with source communities, this is a rare example of a formal codified set of rules to normalize the practice. The guidelines, unlike state-made law such as NAGPRA, attempt to concisely explain the significance that museum artefacts may have for Alutiiq people in order to justify the kind of care it requires.[133] They create a narrative by placing the objectives of the museum within the Alutiiq worldview. The guidelines accept that the history of colonization has affected the meaning of sacredness among different communities of the Kodiak people[134] rather than imposing a fixed definition like Western law often does. They are not claimed to be the ultimate authority on spiritual care. They must be considered as the "starting place for establishing

---

130   *Ibid* at 2.
131   *Ibid* at 13.
132   See "A new path: B.C. museums and historical attractions consulting with First Nations on how to honour Indigenous history" (30 May 2022), online: *Vancouver Sun* https://vancouversun.com/news/local-news/a-new-path-b-c-museums-and-historical-attractions-consulting-with-first-nations-on-how-to-honour-indigenous-history; Smithsonian Magazine, "How Shared Stewardship Is Bringing to Light One of the World's Most Significant Holdings of Mi'kmaw Cultural Items," online: http://www.smithsonianmag.com/blogs/national-museum-american-indian/2023/02/21/home-to-mikmaki-shared-stewardship-between-the-nmai-and-the-mdcc/.
133   Alutiiq Museum and Archaeological Repository, *supra* note 9 at 1.
134   *Ibid* at 3.

culturally meaningful collections care."[135] They "recognize and honour the multiplicity of views on cultural property"[136] within the Alutiiq community given the diverse religious practices that exist in the region since the colonial era. This makes the soft law instrument sensitive to the social reality of the people to whom it is intended to apply. It is something that Western liberal law has always strived to do but has more often than not failed to achieve. The guidelines attempt to classify artefacts that could be sacred. This classification is based on oral accounts, anthropological research, consultation with elders, and guidance from Kodiak Repatriation Commission, a regional body formed in 2007 to facilitate the return of Kodiak cultural items under NAGPRA.[137] Such sources lie outside the conventional sources of legal knowledge production and some may even represent an antithesis to legal knowledge. These guidelines are meant to be coherent with the goals set out in the repatriation commission's manual.[138] The museum and the repatriation commission coordinate their actions to meet their respective functions of collection and repatriation. In case of items that do not fall within the categories of sacred items listed in the guidelines, they lay down an elaborate process of research to identify their sacredness. This process, much like the one used to create the classifications discussed above, accepts a wide variety of knowledge sources. Therefore, the process is inherently collaborative in nature. It demonstrates how soft legal tools, within the constructivist view, can not only enable but also encourage constitutive processes such as persuasion, learning, argumentation, and socialization as a part of norm-setting. Sensitivity to the colonial past and current social reality ensures that the guidelines are living rules and not frozen in time. As is evident from the discussion so far, the spiritual care guidelines focus more on the process of decision-making or rulemaking. The collections policy is far more specific in its rules. The flexibility in the spiritual care guidelines is intentionally infused to promote a careful assessment of the spiritual needs of every single item received by the museum.[139]

---

135   *Ibid.*
136   *Ibid.*
137   *Ibid* at 4.
138   Alutiiq Museum and Archaeological Repository, "Repatriation" (28 May 2024), online: *Alutiiq Museum and Archaeological Repository* https://alutiiqmuseum.org/museum/repatriation/.
139   Alutiiq Museum and Archaeological Repository, *supra* note 9 at 4.

The Alutiiq tradition teaches that everything in the universe is alive and has a "sua," or a human-like consciousness. [140] This is reflected in the guideline about conservation of sacred objects. The museum must maintain sacred objects in the best possible condition to honour their "sua." [141] This makes the policy unique. The museum staff must consider traditional techniques for conservation and exhibition where possible and handle sacred items as little as possible to preserve their physical and spiritual integrity. [142] Staff members sign a pledge to respect the physical and spiritual nature of sacred objects and the views of their co-workers and museum patrons towards collections. [143] They have a choice to refuse to handle certain sacred items or human remains if they feel uncomfortable doing so. [144] It allows the staff members to work within their individual or native community's beliefs. Sacred objects may be lent to and borrowed from other organizations subject to the ability of the receiving organization to meet the physical and spiritual care requirements. [145]

The museum receives many offers to add contemporary Alutiiq works of art to its collection. The Guidelines for Evaluating Contemporary Works of Alutiiq Art see contemporary art as a way to connect the museum's historic and prehistoric collections to the present. [146] These guidelines help the museum select pieces to add to its collection, given limited funds for acquisition and resources for their care. Artists are encouraged to submit a written statement about themselves and their work followed by an assessment of their artistic expertise, craftsmanship, expression, and the museum's ability to care for their work. [147] The criteria for assessing expression includes the work's quality to represent the evolution and development of Alutiiq traditions, ability to tell a unique story, and educational value to help educate future generations about Alutiiq heritage. [148] These guidelines help to meet the objectives both as a conventional museum and as a cultural institution upholding Kodiak community's values.

---

140   *Ibid* at 1.
141   *Ibid* at 6.
142   *Ibid.*
143   *Ibid.*
144   *Ibid.*
145   *Ibid* at 7.
146   *Ibid* at 1.
147   *Ibid.*
148   *Ibid.*

Meaning of TCEs Inherent in the Policy

The Alutiiq museum arose from the Kodiak Area Native Association's Culture and Heritage division that had been working to encourage archaeological research, educate about Alutiiq culture, and promote Alutiiq language and arts since 1987.[149] As a museum, it recognizes the body of traditional Alutiiq knowledge that is preserved in the native community.[150] It has been accepting materials relating to the prehistoric, historic, and contemporary cultural history of the Alutiiq nation.[151] The policy requires the museum staff to work with Alutiiq people to obtain information about artefacts, their context, their source and ownership, and their appropriate treatment.[152] The documentation of this information is considered essential to maintain the identity, cultural value, and spiritual care of material.[153] Even conventional museums perform the standard functions of preservation, research, education, and institutionalization through their activities. Aside from these objectives, the Alutiiq Museum's purpose for discovering and recording of information regarding their collections is also directed towards safeguarding the artefacts' identity and cultural significance, and for ensuring its spiritual care.

Although the museum may accept collections from neighbouring communities and those with whom the Alutiiq people have historically been connected it would not proactively seek any material that relates to other native communities.[154] The rationale behind this is that cultural materials need to be cared for in the context of their source societies.[155] This will not only prevent the materials from being treated in culturally insensitive ways but also keep them tied to their source communities more meaningfully.[156] As a practical principle, it may appear contrary to the objectives of a museum—preserving artefacts and educating others about them. However, this policy ultimately supports those objectives by ensuring that TCEs remain within their source communities, where they hold the greatest value. Additionally, TCEs would continue to serve their own communities and stay culturally relevant.

149   Alutiiq Museum and Archaeological Repository, *supra* note 8 at 2.
150   *Ibid* at 13.
151   *Ibid* at 3.
152   *Ibid* at 13.
153   *Ibid* at 12.
154   *Ibid* at 3.
155   *Ibid*.
156   *Ibid*.

The policy does permit the use of destructive scientific analysis techniques like radio-carbon dating and chemical analysis on objects other than human remains. [157] However, this is only allowed for objects that the museum owns and if the technique has the potential to increase the understanding of Alutiiq history and culture. [158] Therefore, the policy permits the use of modern methods of knowledge exploration, but within the bounds of the beliefs of the community it serves.

Determination of the Legal Subject by the Policy Instrument

Ownership of the artefact is essential for the ability to transfer it to the museum. Acquisition and addition to the permanent collection of the museum requires clear title, a Western notion of property. It may be possible to provide proof of ownership for contemporary art but not in the case of older artefacts. Photographs of objects not cared for by the museum, copies of archived material [159], films, and audio recordings for which rights have not been transferred to the museum are added to the museum's library instead of the permanent collection. [160] Therefore, ownership and the ability to transfer it are essential characteristics of the legal subject that can interact with the museum. The exception to this was mentioned earlier in the discussion about the MOUs for the care of unprovenanced artefacts which the museum may accept since it is obligated to respectfully care for artefacts of Alutiiq ancestry.

The care and management of the museum is vested in the Collections Advisory Committee. It is composed of an Alutiiq Heritage Foundation (AHF) board representative, a curatorial staff representative, and eight volunteer members selected from the community by AHF board of directors based on their knowledge of Alutiiq culture, language, and history, native Alaskan art and natural history, education, collections care, and/or property law. [161] The involvement of community members in a key decision-making body of the organization reflects the inclusion of the community in its governance. This body prepares the collections plan outlining the priorities of the museum based on what it "feels a strong stewardship responsibility toward and would most like to acquire to enhance the spiritual, educational, scientific, and

---

157   *Ibid* at 14.
158   *Ibid*.
159   *Ibid* at 5.
160   *Ibid* at 6.
161   *Ibid* at 7.

historical value of its holdings." [162] In the interest of transparency, the plan is shared through the museum's website.

Access to the museum collection and its information is subject to the spiritual care guidelines and based on concerns of Alutiiq people determined on a case by case basis. [163] In case of certain items, the museum will be mindful of copyright and other permissions. The teaching collection of the museum has been specifically created for use by the Alutiiq community (for purposes like ceremonial practices), students, researchers, and for public outreach activities. [164] In case of a conflict between competing interests, the museum shall adopt Alutiiq First as a policy. [165] This is also specified in the spiritual care guidelines. Therefore, in terms of access, use, management (including decision-making), and care of TCEs, the Alutiiq subject is prioritized over others.

A Discussion of the Insights Generated from the Analysis

The Alutiiq Museum — as a museum — falls at the intersection of the Western way of governance of TCEs and an Indigenous method of governance of the same. As a Western tool it offers an opportunity for exercising control over preservation and promotion of Alutiiq cultural heritage [166] through Alutiiq ways that have evolved over time.

IP law directly affects, often causing harm to, the methods of sharing information and cultural expression. [167] However, the development of the Alutiiq Museum and the evolution of its governance policy by the community is an ongoing effort to encourage transmission of information and expression. This will not only preserve Alutiiq cultural heritage but also promote the production of TCEs within their own normative order. The guidelines for evaluating contemporary works of Alutiiq art

---

162   *Ibid.*

163   *Ibid.*

164   *Ibid* at 16.

165   *Ibid* at 16.

166   For a condensed discussion on the tensions in defining "cultural heritage" in legal scholarship, see generally Pinar Oruç & Uma Suthersanen, "Intellectual property and cultural heritage issues for museums of archaeological materials" in Irini Stamatoudi, ed, *Research Handbook on Intellectual Property and Cultural Heritage* (Cheltenham, UK: Edward Elgar Publishing, 2021) 392 at 393. Although the collections policy of Alutiiq museum does not define the word while using it, it is safe to presume that they know what they intend it to mean for the people implementing the policy. Defining it could be problematic in that it may be insufficient to account its significance within the Alutiiq worldview.

167   MacKay, *supra* note 51.

encourage artists to create works that reflect the community's current history.[168] This ensures the continuity of Alutiiq cultural heritage.[169] IP law also tends to affect the use and economic exploitation of TCEs.[170] Contemporary Alutiiq artists who choose to benefit from the economic exploitation of their work can exercise this choice by offering it to the museum which will also ensure culturally sensitive care of the work.

The analysis of the Alutiiq Museum's collections policy as a soft law instrument illustrates a practical approach for the governance of TCEs that respects and integrates the traditions and values of IPLCs. Instead of claiming to be an authority, as legal instruments ordinarily do, it is comfortable with both the known reality and the unknown. For example, it is grounded in reality since it accepts the truth about the colonization and at the same time understands that a vast amount of history of rich artefacts may not necessarily be uncovered. Development of guidelines for spiritual care of artefacts is therefore considered as an "ongoing process"[171] which does not require specifying a fixed defini-tion of sacred objects. A continuous practice of implementation of soft legal frameworks like this one increases their normative strength. While it is possible that the application of such soft legal tools can facilitate the framing of more hard law based on similar normative principles, there is ample, and indeed distinct, value in what it achieves in the soft form. Since it is a local community-based organization, it is also possible to review and update it through consultations regularly. This is another benefit of soft law implemented at the local level. Although the movement for cultural preservation may have received a jumpstart because of the funding received from the Exxon-Valdez oil spill trustee council, the desire for it and its development since inception has been profoundly organic[172] in character.

Riley has pointed out that the application of the Western legal framework of IP rights, which relies heavily on economic objectives and market dynamics, to IPLCs could adversely impact their culture and tradition.[173] Western legal traditions value individual property rights.[174] Common law principles of ownership, exploitation, and

---

168   Alutiiq Museum and Archaeological Repository, *supra* note 9.
169   *Ibid.*
170   MacKay, *supra* note 51.
171   Alutiiq Museum and Archaeological Repository, *supra* note 9 at 2.
172   di Robilant, *supra* note 14 at 533.
173   See Angela R Riley, "'Straight Stealing': Towards an Indigenous System of Cultural Property Protection" (2005) 80 Wash L Rev 69 at 88.
174   Johan Söderberg, "Copyleft vs. Copyright: A Marxist Critique"(2002) 7:3 First

alienation of property cannot be applied to TCEs. They allow a shifting of the authority over IP to those who can buy it.[175] Museums must obtain permissions for adding any items that may be protected by IP law. The Alutiiq Museum's collections policy adheres to this legal requirement while also focusing on what is important to the Alutiiq community. It holds these artefacts as an institution run by the community collectively. The social processes of collaboration and persuasion that constitute the "traditional"[176] in traditional cultural expressions are evidently institutionalized in the policy. A combination of sensitivity to the past and an acceptance of the present social reality makes the guidelines a living set of rules that defy the conventional meaning of the term traditional.

The policy demonstrates a new form of resistance offered to Western methods of governance of TCEs through the implementation of tools that incorporate non-Western values while staying within the bounds of the Western legal framework. The Alutiiq Museum as a functioning institution shows that the legal subject has a transformative capacity to produce legal knowledge and shape new norms within its semi-autonomous social field. The semi-autonomous social field of the Kodiak people creates its own norms through this policy while being subject to the norms of the larger social field as a member community of the US. The substance of the policy reflects the needs and lived experiences of the community, making it an instrument for empowerment and emancipation.[177] The policy shows that the in case of soft-law instruments created by IPLCs, there is no need to completely privilege any single form of normative ordering from among those based on Western legal systems and those based on non-Western normative orders. A workable balance can be achieved. Given the availability of resources, soft legal instruments can organically develop to meet the needs of the community while being fully compliant with hard law. There is also further scope for the study of soft legal tools for the governance of TK and TCEs, especially, though not exclusively, in terms of the potential it could have for IPLCs if the harmful effects of Western IP law on TCEs could be neutralized.

Monday online : https://firstmonday.org/ojs/index.php/fm/article/view/938.

175   See Peter Jaszi, *Traditional Culture: A Step Forward for Protection in Indonesia: A Research Report* (Institute for Press and Development Studies, 2009) 92–93.

176   Four Directions Council, *supra* note 30.

177   di Robilant, *supra* note 14.

Conclusion

This chapter is based on a textual survey of the Alutiiq Museum's policy documents available in the public domain. A constructivist approach within the critical legal pluralist framework has helped in understanding the case of the Alutiiq Museum. It offers a fresh perspective to look at the values and priorities of the Alutiiq community towards the governance of TCEs. More extensive studies involving a range of qualitative research methods can potentially generate more meaningful and comprehensive insights. The arguments made here should not be seen as normatively in support of the subordination of IPLCs' legal traditions. Positive law made in the interest of, and respecting the right of self-determination of IPLCs, is certainly valuable for the benefits it accrues to IPLCs. This is rather an opportunity to learn about other ways of governance of TCEs despite falling within the larger social fields that prioritize Western IP law.[178]

178   Email: anmol.patel795@gmail.com; apate262@uottawa.ca. Open African Innovation Research (Open AIR) is carried out with financial support from the International Development Research Centre, Canada, the Social Sciences and Humanities Research Council of Canada, and the Queen Elizabeth Scholars Program. More information about Open AIR's current and previous supporters can be found at www.openair.africa. The views expressed herein do not necessarily represent those of Open AIR's funders. The author sincerely thanks Chidi Oguamanam, Susy Frankel, Margaret Chon, Jeremy de Beer, the anonymous reviewer, and the participants of The Future of the Global IP System workshop (organized in June 2023 at the University of British Columbia) for their thoughtful feedback and suggestions on earlier drafts of this chapter.

CHAPTER 10

The Performance of Law

Richard Overstall

Abstract

In many indigenous societies, law is performed. Assertions of identity and relationships, contestations and settlements occur through the media of publicly performed and displayed art. Indeed, most dramatized, sung, spoken, and visual art has legal significance.

This chapter looks at the legal order of northern Northwest Coast societies as practiced in a 1945 series of Gitxsan pole-raisings in the Skeena River village of Gitsegukla, meticulously recorded by the Tsimshian ethnographer William Beynon. Each lineage holds a unique set of dramatis personae, songs, histories, and images. These holdings are subject to scrutiny and judicial review by other related and allied lineages. The drama, masks, and costumes of the *halayt* performances conjure up the moral standards—the norms—that the people were required to uphold. The images on the poles, and the speeches, ceremonies, regalia, and songs at the *yukw* feasts that followed, proclaimed each host lineage's identity, the closeness of its relationships and alliances with other lineages, and the natural resource territories it held. The immortal feast-names each participant held indicated their legal role in the society, while their seating position and order of speaking showed the connections and relative reputational rank of the lineages and families they embodied.

This embedded legal meaning, the shared nature and extended timeframe of most indigenous legal art confounds its reconciliation with commercial intellectual property. The chapter suggests that English and Canadian armorial law may be the cultural and legal analogue for multi-juridical intellectual property.

Performative events [...] have the potential to reshape a community from within far more dramatically than could a purely prescriptive pronouncement by an external authority. As a type of art, legal performance carries within itself the seeds of both stability and of fragmentation, of predictability and of risk.[1]

Performance as legal process, then, emerges from within a community. In her analysis of the indigenous law of early medieval Ireland, Robin Chapman Stacey attributes the transformative potency of the symbols used in legal performance to their resonance with everyday life: "A full understanding of what is taking place depends on the audience recognising that a performance is occurring and an act of interpretation is required." Participants are both "not themselves" in the sense that they are now claimants, defendants, and witnesses, but, at the same time, are "not not themselves" in the sense that they have not quite left their day-to-day identities behind them. Performed words and gestures thus take on the power given to them by the participants.[2]

This chapter takes Stacey's performative law and applies it to the issue of reconciling indigenous[3] intellectual property concepts with those of the colonial Canadian state without undermining the integrity of either. It will attempt to do this in three parts. First, it will look at a mid-twentieth century Northwest Coast feast or potlatch series.[4] Although some of the region's indigenous case law is recorded in the peoples' oral histories, detailed legal procedure generally is not. An exception is an account of a series of pole-raising feasts held in the Gitxsan village of Gitsegukla in 1945 recorded by the Tsimshian ethnographer William Beynon. Beynon held the name Gusgai'in and at the time was the Wolf Clan chief of the Gitlan, one of the nine Tsimshian tribes of the lower Skeena River and adjacent coast of British Columbia. He also studied

---

1   Robin Chapman Stacey, *Dark Speech: The Performance of Law in Early Ireland* (Philadelphia: University of Pennsylvania Press, 2007) [*Dark Speech*] at 89.
2   *Dark Speech* at 49 and 50.
3   It seems wrong to try to take away a people's lands, governance, and children and in return put capital letters on the collective nouns employed to classify them. I attempt to show my respect for indigenous peoples by using the same grammatical rules as I do with all other legal orders. Similarly, contrary to current provincial and federal government style guides, I also italicise all *Gitksanemx* terms as I find it makes the text easier to read—in much the same way as lawyers and judges italicise legal Latin words and phrases.
4   "Feast" is the general English translation for a group of legal performances in the Northwest Coast cultural region, each of which has its own indigenous language term. "Potlatch" is the generic Chinook trading creole term for a feast.

ethnography under Marius Barbeau of the then-National Museum of Canada. Beynon therefore attended the feasts both as a participating chief and as an ethnographer. His detailed notes, sketches, and photographs were subsequently archived at the National Museum and later edited and published in book form.[5] Here, his records are examined with attention to the role of performance and display to engage all feast participants as they reaffirmed their societal norms, as the host lineages announced their decisions, and as their guests legally reviewed and validated those decisions.

In its second part, the chapter will look at the case history of a dispute over the privilege of one of the 1945 Gitsegukla House groups[6] to display a certain image, called a *dzept* or crest, on the pole it was raising.[7] The case brings into sharper focus the role that crest images play in defining the identity of lineages that make up Gitxsan Houses and in describing their relationships and alliances with other lineages in other Houses living in villages throughout the northern Northwest Coast region. In doing so, the account also gives insights into the mediation roles played by non-disputing Houses and into the people's ethic of not mentioning the conflict again after it had been settled.

The third part starts by relating the history of another crest image. This one is carved into a Wolf Clan pole in the village of Kitwancool, now called Gitanyow.[8] In the 1920s, it became the subject of a painting by the prominent Canadian artist Emily Carr, which has subsequently been

---

5   Margaret Anderson & Marjorie Halpin, eds, *Potlatch at Gitsegukla: William Beynon's 1945 Field Notebooks* (Vancouver: UBC Press, 2000) [*Potlatch at Gitsegukla*]. For other analyses of this important record, see Richard Overstall, "Encountering the Spirit in the Land: 'Property' in a Kinship-Based Legal Order" in John McLaren, AR Buck & Nancy E Wright, eds, *Despotic Dominion: Property Rights in British Settler Societies* (Vancouver: UBC Press, 2005) 22 and Val Napoleon, "Living Together: Gitksan Legal Reasoning as a Foundation for Consent" in J Webber & CM Macleod, eds, *Between Consenting Peoples: Political Community and the Meaning of Consent* (Vancouver: UBC Press, 2010) 45.

6   A House or *wilp* (*huwilp* pl.) is a group of one or more closely related matrilineal lineages that historically was based in a single longhouse and which is the primary landholding and feast-hosting legal actor in Gitxsan society.

7   *Dzept* refers to the tangible object depicting the image; the Gitxsan term *ayuks* refers to the intangible specific powers or privileges a lineage holds and which may be displayed by a *dzept*. Both terms are often translated into English by the word "crest": *Potlatch at Gitsegukla, supra* note 5 at 16.

8   Within Northwest Coast societies, the broadest group of nominal relatives is the *pdeek* or clan, of which there are four within Gitxsan society: the Fireweed, Frog or Raven, Wolf, and Eagle. The clans largely serve as exogamous groups for the purposes of marriage alliances. Each House is thus a member of one of the four clans.

reproduced on T-shirts, coffee mugs, and other consumer objects. Finally, we step beyond the use of Indigenous images in the state-regulated commercial sphere—the current law of intellectual property—to examine how indigenous performances and images could be recognized within a Canadian multi-juridical order for the legal import they carry under each indigenous people's own law. Copyright, patent, and trademark law presently have difficulty accommodating indigenous ownership rights even within the narrow commercial context.[9] In this way, the chapter charts an imagined future whereby *intellectual property* can be mutually recognized by the laws of each Canadian indigenous society and by the federal and provincial Crowns.

Gitsegukla, 1945

The series of pole-raising feasts described by Beynon were hosted by four Fireweed Clan Houses and one Frog Clan House over two weeks. A House's main purpose in raising its pole was to complete a successor chief's obligations to his predecessor and thus maintain the House's powers, or *daxgyet*, and its standing in the society.[10] Usually, each House would have staged its pole-raising as a discrete event, but in 1945 the Houses were attempting to fulfill their legal obligations following a disastrous flood in 1936 that washed away a large number of poles from the banks of the Skeena River. Generally, a pole-raising feast will follow four steps: the decision by the host House to hold the feast and to set its date; the host's formal invitation to Houses of clans other than its own to witness the event; the *halayt* performances that invoke the spirit world; and the feast proper at which the host's announcement of its business—in this case, its claim to the crests displayed on the pole and their attendant privileges—is validated by the witnesses.

---

9   See chapters in this volume by Anmol Patel, and by Johnny Mack & Graham Reynolds.

10   *Daxgyet*, literally a "firmly bound person," is a concept not easily translated, although the English term "powers" is often used. Two of its many elements are crucial: a chief's initial marriage with the spirit of particular territories, and his successors' and his lineage's subsequent duty to respect both the human and supernatural partners of the marriage.

Li'ligit

The *li'ligit* is a planning feast. The chiefs and lineages within the host
House, as well as closely related Houses within the host's clan, decide
if they are able to collectively gather the resources needed to have the
pole carved and raised and to host the necessary feast that will validate
their rights to the crest images displayed on it. The responsibilities for
scouting and falling a suitable cedar tree, the removal of its bark, the
carving of the pole, and its transport to the site of its raising are the
responsibility of the host chief's father's clan and the planning would
necessarily have involved them. At each stage, a small ceremony would
have been performed to acknowledge the contributions being made.[11]
The *li'ligit* feast itself is the culmination of less formal negotiations to
ensure the necessary personnel and wealth will be available. At both
the informal and formal stages, the hard work of achieving consensus and coordination among House members and their allies falls to
the *simoogit*, the House Chief, this being his or her principal function
within the House.[12] Because of their political and personal nature,
the planning discussions remain within the host House and are not
formally recorded or open to outsiders. For this reason, Beynon does
not record the *li'ligit* feasts and the discussions that preceded the 1945
pole-raisings and feasts.

Tets

The *tets* is the formal inviting party sent out by the host House to the
guest witnesses from the host's and surrounding villages. The host chief
normally does not accompany them but usually designates a nephew[13] as
his or her representative.[14] The *tets* party was given careful instructions as

---

11   For a full description of the preparations and ceremonies prior to a pole-raising,
      see Richard Daly, *Our Box Was Full: An Ethnography for the* Delgamuukw *Plaintiffs*
      (Vancouver: UBC Press, 2005) [*Our Box Was Full*] at 70–74.
12   *Simoogit* (pl. *simgiget*) literally means "real person." They would have other impor-
      tant functions embodying the House in its external relations as described later in
      this chapter.
13   The representative is the chief's *galdim'algax*, literally a "box of words."
14   For the 1945 pole-raising feasts, the Fireweed Clan and Frog Clan host chiefs
      themselves were the messengers. This may have been in response to the unusual
      collective nature of the feast series and may have been why it was the highest-
      ranking Fireweed Clan chief (Wiigyet) and the highest-ranking Frog Clan chief
      (Mool'xan) in Gitsegukla who instructed that the *tets* party be sent, but who did
      not travel themselves: *Potlatch at Gitsegukla, supra* note 5 at 57.

to which chiefs to invite as the embodiments of their Houses. This would include the high-ranking Houses in the local area[15] as well as Houses from the host's village and other villages that have marriage alliances with the host House. In other words, the host must invite all parties with a substantive interest in the host House's asserted legal claims inhered in the crest images displayed on the pole being raised. These witnesses are the *gandit*, without whom the pole-raising could not take place.[16]

When a *tets* party first arrived in a village, they signalled their peaceful intentions by singing an *'alus* (greeting song)[17] in front of the house of the chief of the village's highest ranked House group.[18] After billeting their guests, the receiving House called the visitors to the hall and its chief danced his *naxnox*[19] before them. The visiting messengers responded by dancing their *naxnox*. Then the welcoming chief dressed in his regalia danced swansdown[20] over his visitors, accompanied by the singing of *halayt* songs. This dance was repeated three times, telling the messengers that the chief accepted their invitation with peace and goodwill. The highest ranked House's spokesperson then repeated their acceptance with a speech.[21] The *tets* party was then given food, publicly contributed by the invited clan members, as well as their spouses and those whose fathers were of the clan. The following day, the messengers proceeded to the house of the leading chief of the next ranked clan in the village, where the acceptance ceremony was repeated until the invited chiefs and Houses of all the clans in the village had indicated

---

15   Generally, Houses from the three western Gitxsan villages, Gitseguekla, Gitwangak, and Kiwancool (now Gitanyow) formed marriage alliances with each other and regularly participated in each other's feasts. As a result, residents of these villages spoke a western dialect of *Gitxsanemx* called *Gyeets*: BC Ministry of Education, Gitksan Wet'suwet'en Education Society & School District 88, "Ha'niimagooansxwhum Algaxhl" (1995).

16   *Potlatch at Gitsegukla, supra* note 5 at 152.

17   When visitors arrived by canoe, they would raise their paddles to further signal their intentions. The *'alus* is therefore sometimes called the "paddle song."

18   For example, Beynon records that when the Gitsegukla chiefs arrived at Gitwangak village, they were first greeted and billeted by T'awa'lesk of the Eagle Clan on behalf of the absent Sakxumhigookx, the highest ranked Eagle Clan chief and then the highest ranked chief in Gitwangak: *Potlatch at Gitsegukla, supra* note 5 at 57.

19   A *naxnox* is an acted, sung, and danced performance often with masks and costumes that demonstrates the spiritual facets of a chief's bundle of powers or *daxgyet*. When performing his or her *naxnox*, the chief is a *wiihalayt* or "great dancer."

20   *Mixk'aax*.

21   The language used here and at all Gitxsan feasts was an ancient, formal dialect, *Sm'algax*, literally "real speech," while the everyday form was *Gitksanemx*: *Potlatch at Gitsegukla, supra* note 5 at 13 and 51.

their intention to come to the pole-raising feasts in Gitsegukla.[22] After that, the messengers travelled on to the remaining villages whose chiefs would similarly be needed to witness the proceedings.

For the host House, the most critical group of guests would have been from the House with which it was most densely allied through marriage ties and which therefore would have the greatest interest in its ongoing legal standing and social vitality. This House would generally belong to the other clan in the predominantly two-clan village. At the feast, its chief was called the *'nidinsxwit* (plural, *'nidins*), who lead the judicial review and approval of the host's announced business.[23] For example, at the 1945 Gitsegukla feasts, the *'nidinsxwit* for the Fireweed hosts was the chief of the highest ranked Frog Clan House in the village, Mool'xan, and the *'nidinsxwit* for the single Frog host, Gaxsgabaxs, was a chief in the highest ranked Gitsegukla Fireweed Clan House, Wii Seeks.[24]

Halayt

Halayts are the spiritual face of a chief's powers. They are dramatized through *naxnox* performances with dance, songs, masks, and other costumes and special effects. The *naxnox* were acquired by the chief's ancestor from spirits that had transformed themselves into earthly forms to interact with humans. In the days preceding the 1945 pole-raising feasts, each host performed a charade of his *naxnox* name in the centre of the feast house. This was done without words and often fully costumed with a face-covering mask to hide the performer's everyday identity.[25] In Stacey's characterization, they were "not themselves." The charade was reciprocated by each visiting chief acting out their own *naxnox*.

Halayt performances sometimes depicted supernatural animals or other beings but most often dramatized one of three recurring aspects of Gitxsan law. One aspect was the immortality of the lineages, their feast names, and the spirit encounters that created them. These were captured by the host chief feigning death or a coma while each guest chief attempted to restore him using their own powers.[26] Eventually

---

22   *Ibid.* at 62.
23   *Ibid.* at 254, where the editors' 1997 interviews with Gwaans (Olive Mulwain) of the House of Hanamuxw and Gaxsgabaxs (Gertie Watson) confirm that *'nidins* means "the ones who approve."
24   *Ibid.* at 123, 139, 159, 174, and 188.
25   *Ibid.* at 96.
26   Each chief attempting to restore the comatose performer was called forward in order of their reputational rank: *Ibid.* at 85 and 259 n 62.

they were successful, and the fused human and spirit identities lived on. The participating guests were compensated by the host for their role in the improv. Of the 27 *halayt* performances recorded by Beynon in 1945, 13 were revivals of comatose persons. Another 12 depicted the second aspect of law, undesirable human traits—lying, indifference, tardiness, stealing, envy, and so on—until the actor was ushered out of the hall by his attendants. [27] Thus, the chiefs reinforced societal norms by parading and then vanquishing their opposites. The third aspect of law was often depicted by a mechanical *naxnox* mask that allowed the wearer to switch from being a blind person to someone who could see and, arguably, became aware of a world peopled by spirits and sentient animals as well as by humans. [28]

Baxmaga

The pole-raising ceremony, the *baxmaga*, began by the House chief's father's side bringing the pole into the village. At Wii Seeks' pole-raising, for example, the cedar tree was selected, felled, and hauled out of the forest by Axti Hiik, a Gitwangak Wolf Clan chief. Wii Seeks instructed the carver as to the crests to be displayed, which normally would have been carved by a Wolf Clan chief, but the work was done by a Fireweed chief, thus of the same clan as Wii Seeks. This anomaly may have occurred because of a dearth of Wolf Clan carvers at that time. The father's side dug the hole and built the A-frame used to raise the pole. [29] Before the pole was erected, a Fireweed chief's wife threw a valuable rifle into the hole. Beynon suggests this act was similar to the older convention of burying a copper shield, a *hayatsxw*, the most valuable symbol of a chief's and House's wealth, beneath a new pole. In this instance, the gun was retrieved and at the subsequent feast given as part of the compensation to those helping with the *baxmaga*. [30]

The pole was raised by "all of the people" grouped by clan from each village pulling on ropes looped over the A-frame, [31] while Wii

---

27   *Ibid.* at 26–27.

28   See Wilson Duff's insights on a set of paired, stone, unseeing/seeing Tsimshian masks in Wilson Duff, *Images Stone B.C.* (Saanichton: Hancock House Publishers, 1975) at 162–167.

29   *Potlatch at Gitsegukla, supra* note 5, at 110.

30   *Ibid.* at 37 and 261.

31   Beynon's sketches of the apparatus are reproduced from his notebooks in *Potlatch at Gitsegukla, supra* note 5 at 109 and 130.

Seeks and Haxpegwootxw sang a *limx' oo'y*, a song linked to a particular sorrowful incident in the House's *adaawk*.[32] When the pole had been raised, the pulling ropes were cut into "fathom lengths" and distributed to all who had helped pull.[33] Beynon more briefly describes similar mechanics and performances for raising the other four poles in 1945.[34]

Yukw

At the 1945 pole-raisings, a *yukw* feast followed in the evening of the day each pole was raised. The primary purpose of such an event was for the host House to announce its business, in this case, the raising of its pole and the House's crests displayed on it, and to invite the visiting *'nidins* and other chiefs to validate the legality of its announced action. The guests demonstrated their concurrence both by their speeches and by their acceptance of the host's food and payments. For this they have to be fed and compensated. The process of the *yukw* was for the host House to publicly draw in all the wealth it could muster and then to publicly distribute it to those judicially reviewing its actions.

From the *li'ligit* feast to the *yukw* feast, the role of the host chief changed from that of mediating a consensus decision among his House members to that of embodying the House in its interactions with other Houses. These societal relationships are mapped in the feast hall. The clans of the host's village not involved in hosting placed themselves at the back of the hall, facing the entrance. The host clan members themselves were not seated but stood by to announce and seat their guests, to serve food and to distribute payments. Guests were seated by village and then by clan around the remaining three sides of the room. The chief of each guest House sat in the second row behind his successor and with the next in line seated behind him. A person's seat in the feast hall was their *ant'aa* and reflected their place within the societal and legal structure.[35] The feast hall matrix thus distinguished the hosts from their guests, and identified each guest according to village, clan, and individual roles within their House.[36]

---

32   *Ibid.* at 20 and 111, photograph at 18.
33   *Ibid.* at 111 and 112.
34   *Ibid.* at 130 to 131 for Gaxsgabaxs, at 151 to 152 for Tsa'wals, at 166 for Hanamukw, and at 179 for Guxsan.
35   *Our Box Was Full, supra* note 11 at 82.
36   See Beynon's sketch of the *halayt* seating reproduced in *Potlatch at Gitsegukla, supra* note 5 at 71, and his description of the *yukw* seating at 113.

Food was then served by the younger members of the host House. While the meal proceeded, the contributors of the food were announced.[37] The host House then proceeded to gather its wealth. The host *simoogit* started the process by making his contribution, followed by his siblings and nephews—the pool of his likely successors. Next came his spouse and his children as well as his other clan members, spouses of his clan members, and those whose fathers were of his clan. Each contributor walked or danced to the front of the hall where they put their payments in a bowl—the chief in full regalia. In contrast to the *halayt* costumes and masks that hid the performer's identity, the chief's *yukw* headpiece, the *amhalayt*, allowed the wearer's face to be seen and both it and the blanket, the *gwishalayt*, show the wearer's principal House crests, thus evoking the lineage's history and identity in the minds of their guests. The chiefs were "not not themselves." In contrast, the spouses of the House entered with an ad hoc spirited dance in humorous costumes. The name of each contributor and the amount they contributed was clearly announced. Each contribution reflected the rank of the contributor within the House—the chief giving the most and each other House or family member successively putting in a lesser amount.[38] At the pole-raising feast, two sets of contributions were being managed. One was to distribute to the witnessing guests, the other was to pay the host's father's clan for bringing the cedar tree out from the forest and carving it, as well as to repay any other loans by the father's side.[39]

The distribution of wealth occurred in two stages. First, a small amount, the *xgwiikw* or groundhog,[40] was paid equally to all witnesses. Then, the guest House chiefs, lineage chiefs, and their potential successors[41] were paid additional amounts according to their reputational rank.

---

37   Food contributions came from the same categories of persons as the wealth contributions that follow.

38   For example, at Wii Seeks' pole-raising feast, the chief contributed $400, his successor, T'sibasaa, $200, and other House members followed with amounts ranging from $100 down to $20. Wii Seeks' wife and her relatives collectively gave over $100. Beynon does not record the amounts given by the host's clan members, other spouses of the host House, and those whose fathers were of the host House and clan. The total came to $1,157.00: *Potlatch at Gitsegukla, supra* note 5 at 114–115. The contributions at the other 1945 Gitsegukla pole-raising feasts were similar to those noted here for Wii Seeks' feast.

39   The repayment is termed the *xk'ayhl*.

40   Before the introduction of money, a groundhog skin symbolized a House's wealth. Long-hibernating groundhogs are rich in fat, an ample stored supply of which could help sustain House members through the northern winter: *Our Box Was Full, supra* note 11 at 112.

41   *Potlatch at Gitsegukla, supra* note 5 at 157, 169, and 184.

Ideally, dispersing these payments should exactly exhaust all the contributions, a process requiring some deft money management by the host. Beynon notes that the amount the host House gave to each guest witness indicated its assessment of their relative rank.[42] He gives complete lists of those payment amounts for two of the five Gitsegukla feasts. These data show that generally three ranks of chiefs were recognized—those that received $10 or more each, those that received $5 each, and those that received $2 or $3 each. Generally, the names that received the highest amounts were the *simgiget*, the House chiefs, while the lesser amounts were given to heads of lineages within a House and the House chiefs' intended successors.[43]

The guests' acceptance of the host House's food and payments signaled that they validated the announced business. This signal was confirmed by the chiefs' response speeches from those Houses most affected by the announcement. In each of the 1945 feasts, the first response speech was from the host's *'nidinsxwit*, the chief of the House most intermarried and thus most allied with the host House. That speech was followed by others from the leading House of each participating village.

Legal Analysis

While Beynon's record of the 1945 Gitsegukla pole-raising feasts provides only a glimpse into Gitxsan legal performance, it is enough to begin mapping the society's norms, its societal structure, and the legal dynamics within that structure. It enables a reader to identify the kinship groups that are its legal actors, and to identify the alliances made among them. The warp of kin connections and the weft of allied connections weave a network within which three principal dynamics can be seen at work: societal bonding, reciprocity, and reputation.

---

42   Beynon's editors in their headings indicate that the order of payments reflected the recipients' rank: *Potlatch at Gitsegukla, supra* note 5 at 117–119, 136, 157, and 169–172. Beynon's notes, however, say that only the amount of the gift reflected the recipient's rank. In the two Gitsegukla feasts where Beynon records both the payment order and the payment amounts—the Wii Seeks feast and the Hanamuxw feast—there are obvious discrepancies between the order and the amount, showing that only one of these measures of rank could be correct: *Potlatch at Gitsegukla, supra* note 5 at 117–119 and 170–172.

43   There were a few variations to this formula, which may have been the result of the host House attempting to balance the distributions with the contributions in its books.

Stagecraft, costume, and song predominate the *halayt*, recreating times when encounters with *naxnox* powers revealed to humans their norms and values. Theatrical recreation manifests those meetings, which descendants of each original human participant are now exclusively privileged to perform. These manifestations, however, required reciprocal dances from the chiefs of other lineages to evoke their power. A dominant theme of *halayts* was for actors to perform acts contrary to the society's norms, but who are then driven from the room. Paradoxically perhaps, some performances of spirit powers took the form of riddles and jokes, invoking laughter. Others so convincingly portrayed gruesome killings that spectators recoiled in terror. [44] Laughter, singing, dancing, feasting, ritual, and "emotionally charged storytelling" are all behaviours, particularly when synchronized, that have been found experimentally to activate endorphins in the brain. Experimental psychologist Robin Dunbar suggests that these induce social bonding and trust among performers by acting as a form of "virtual touch," which triggers the endorphin system remotely in the same way as soft touch does physically. He has proposed that endorphin-activating behaviours have enabled human group size to evolve to 150 persons without command-and-control governance, [45] which is about the size of a Gitxsan House group. [46] They also reinforce the legal norms and legal processes by allowing an audience to recognize, in Stacey's words, "that a performance is occurring and an act of interpretation is required." [47]

The *wilp*, the House group, is the main legal actor in Gitxsan society. Houses, embodied by their *smoogit* or House Chief, raise poles, host feasts, tell their *adaawk* histories, display their crests, and establish alliances. Houses that share historical events or that have a common ancestor are said to comprise a *wil'naat'ahl*, that is, be more closely related to each other than to other Houses. This is shown at a *yukw* feast where the *wil'naat'ahl* and its widest manifestation, the *pdeek* or clan, support the host House with food and wealth. Houses form alliances with other Houses not of the same clan by intermarriage. Although spouses also

---

44   *Potlatch at Gitsegukla, supra* note 5 at 28–29.

45   RIM Dunbar, "Virtual Touch and the Human Social World" (2021) 44 Curr Opin Behav Sci 14.

46   A Gitxsan House has been described as comprising "as many as thirty [nuclear] families" which, assuming a replacement family size of five persons, would make a maximum House size of 150 persons: Niislaganoos (Fred Good), House of Malii, Wolf Clan, Kitwancool in Wilson Duff, ed, *Histories, Territories and Laws of the Kitwancool* (Victoria: BC Provincial Museum, 1959) at 25.

47   *Dark Speech, supra* note 1 at 50.

support host chiefs at the feast, the most onerous duties are those of a father to his children and, at the end of each child's life, by the father's House and clan. An example is the obligation of the "father's side" to help a House chief find, carve, and raise the House's pole.

Beynon notes that performances at the *tets* invitations, at the *halayt* dramas, and at the host's *yukw* speeches are all reciprocated by other chiefs who occupy specific places relative to the host within the societal network. The reciprocity here is not an exchange of direct help between two entities, but rather by each making an indirect contribution to the collective good. This general reciprocity has been shown in experimental exchange games and modelling to foster cooperation within the society.[48]

As Manfred Milinski's experiments show, indirect reciprocity requires general knowledge of which individuals and groups within a society have a reputation to care for others. A positive reputation pays off in indirect reciprocity. In Gitxsan and other Northwest Coast societies, reputation is often termed rank or status by anthropologists. In the 1945 records, for example, the reputation of Houses in Gitwangak was publicly performed by the order in which the Houses received the Gitsegukla *tets* party. At the *yukw* feasts, reputation was shown by the amount paid to witnesses and by the selection of validating speakers and the order in which they spoke. Compared with the longevity of House lineages and individual feast-names, reputations are relatively fluid. For example, Beynon notes that the ranking of Gitwangak Houses in 1945 as shown by the order of the *tets* party's receptions was Sakxumhigookx (Eagle Clan), Hlengwax (Frog Clan) and Axti Hiix (Wolf Clan).[49] By the mid-1990s, the ranking had shifted. *Tets* parties went first to Hlengwax, then to Axti Hiix, and lastly to Sakxumhigookx.[50]

It could be said that a House's rank or reputation is asserted at a feast by its chiefs' knowledge of its histories, crests and songs, by its proper following of feast protocols and decorum, by the legal validity and splendor of its regalia and crest poles, and by the generosity of its food and wealth distribution. Furthermore, high rank is accorded to those demonstrating honesty, wisdom, charisma, modesty, hard work, and managerial competence—values illuminated in the *halayt* ceremonies. The higher a person's rank, the more likely they will be asked to speak first in any deliberation, perform first in any event,

---

48   Manfred Milinski, "Reputation, a Universal Currency for Human Social Relations" (2016) Philosophical Transactions of the Royal Society B 371.

49   *Potlatch at Gitsegukla, supra* note 5 at 57–65.

50   *Our Box Was Full, supra* note 11 at 75.

and be called upon to mediate disputes. They are thus able to set the tone and context for decisions and strongly influence the outcomes. [51] Being the first to speak, however, does not mean command of the deliberations. Later speakers can still respectfully differ from those who preceded them but generally do so by adding to, rather than contradicting, what previous speakers have said. [52] The society's acceptance of that assertion is shown at subsequent feasts by the House's rank in receiving *tets* parties, in the amounts paid to its chiefs as feast guests, and the selection of its chiefs and their order as response speakers.

Reputation is thus publicly negotiated through face-to-face performances. As such, it allows the society members to fairly govern themselves by avoiding both the tyranny of autocracy or majoritarianism and the paralysis of unamended political equality.

An Indigenous "Intellectual Property" Dispute

The crucial role that crest images displayed on poles played in a House's identity can be seen in the controversy surrounding one crest carved on the pole raised in 1945 by the Gitsegukla Frog Clan House of Gaxsgabaxs. The steps taken in the unfolding and eventual resolution of this controversy provide a detailed case history of the operation of Gitxsan law and legal process surrounding what might be called indigenous intellectual property. [53]

The crest image at issue, called the *Ganuget*, [54] was of one of the large logs used by the Frog Clan warrior chief Neek't for the defence of the Gitwangak fort, which was eventually abandoned around 1835. [55] The logs had been designed to roll down the steep sides of the hill-fort

---

51 For example, all four guest chiefs who spoke in validation of each host's pole-raising were of a rank that received $15 or $10 gifts, some with an additional present of moosehide or deerskin.

52 For example, when contributing to the feast guests' validation of Gaxsgabaxs' claim to display the *Ganuget* crest, Luutkudjiiwus began by saying, "What you have said and done my brother, is just as you state it to be. There is much more you have left out [...]" and went on to make a further relevant point: *Potlatch at Gitsegukla, supra* note 5 at 140.

53 For an argument that the legal term "property" does not accurately apply to Gitxsan and other indigenous hereditaments, see Overstall, *supra* note 5.

54 *Ganuget* means "logs for destroying people": Potlatch at Gitsegukla supra note 5 at 132.

55 The abandonment date was determined archeologically: George F MacDonald, *The Totem Poles and Monuments of Gitwangak Village* (Ottawa: Parks Canada, 1984) [*Totem Poles of Gitwangak*] at 9.

and crush attacking warriors. The image was of the log with the bodies of Neek't's Kitimat enemies wrapped around it.[56] By 1923, and likely earlier, the Neek't lineage in Gitwangak had been subsumed into the House of Hlengwax, the village's leading Frog House,[57] which then claimed the crest as its exclusive privilege and threatened to stay away from the feasts if Gaxsgabaxs used the crest on his pole. As Hlengwax had indicated that all the Gitwangak chiefs would then join his boycott of all the Gitsegukla feasts, their absence would have severely weakened the Gitsegukla Houses' *daxgyet* powers.

Hlengwax then appealed to the local federal Indian Agent to stop Gaxsgabaxs from using the crest. According to Beynon, the Department of Indian Affairs "referred the matter to other authorities" but subsequently informed Hlengwax "there was nothing in the Indian Act covering this particular phase of Indian life," so the agent could do nothing. At this point, the Gitsegukla chiefs told Hlengwax that the name of the pole would be changed and the offending *Ganuget* image chopped off. Nevertheless, Beynon reports that "the incident is causing some feeling among the people."[58]

This feeling apparently persisted as the matter was not resolved by the time the Gitwangak chiefs arrived in Gitsegukla. When Gaxsgabaxs gave his *halayt* prior to raising his pole, the Frog Clan Houses of Gitwangak vacated their usual seats and sat at the rear of the hall, not participating in the *halayt* performances. Hlengwax absented himself altogether. At this, the House of Gaxsgabaxs singers sang a taunting song about people "who use false myths and traditions to speak of themselves."[59] Later, Hlengwax sent word that he and his group would challenge Gaxsgabaxs' use of the *Ganuget* crest. He did this from his billet, the house of Wistis, a Gitsegukla Frog Clan chief in Gaxsgabaxs' House, who attempted to placate Hlengwax by saying that the "situation would be explained and properly adjusted" and that he should

---

56   Three generations of Gitwangak poles bearing the *Ganuget* crest are pictured in *Totem Poles of Gitwangak, supra* note 55 at 95–101 (Figs 107–117), 119–129 (Figs 142–156). The same Gitwangak poles are shown in Marius Barbeau, *Totem Poles of the Gitksan* (Ottawa: National Museum of Canada, 1929) at 223 (Plate VII, Figs 4–6), 225 (Plate VIII, Figs 1–3). Gaxsgabaxs' 1945 *Ganuget* pole is in *Potlatch at Gitsegukla, supra* note 5 at 131–132.

57   To the author's knowledge, the last holder of the Neek't name was Silas Brown, who was killed by a Kitwancool Wolf Clan chief in 1931 for reasons that could not be determined by the assize court that tried him: "Hearing [of] Indian Murder Case Proceeding at Assizes" *The [Prince Rupert] Daily News* (8 May 1931) 1.

58   *Potlatch at Gitsegukla, supra* note 5 at 65–66.

59   *Ibid.* at 77–78.

not be alarmed "as none of your rights will be invaded." An angry meeting ensued among the Gitwangak chiefs, some of whom were for immediately returning to their own village and thus boycotting all the pole-raising feasts. In the end, others advocating a wait-and-see position prevailed. It was decided that only Hlengwax would voice any feelings, but that the others would stand by him whatever he did.[60]

On the day Gaxsgabaxs was to raise his pole, Hlengwax sent his wife with a message to the Fireweed chief who was directing the pole-raising ceremonies reminding him that Gaxsgabaxs had not complied with the promised removal of the *Ganuget* crest. She returned with the information that while Gaxsgabaxs would not be naming the pole *Ganuget*, he would not be removing the disputed crest. Hlengwax retorted, "He is lying. No matter what he may call it, he has made it known that he is going to erect whatever he wants and is going to have no regard for my feelings." At this point, T'awa'lesk, an Eagle Clan chief from Gitwangak, counselled Hlengwax:

> Let these people do as they wish. If they do anything that will not be proper or correct and usurp the rights of anybody, it will become known at once. So, Chief Hlengwax, I ask of you not to interfere in any way. We will all know when they do anything wrong. If you but say the word we will immediately leave here and return to Gitwangak, but this will bring ridicule upon us. They will say we are jealous and afraid, but if you so wish we can all return to our homes at once. It is they who have broken their promise to you, but as I said, we will be called many names.

T'awa'lesk then advised that if Gaxsgabaxs is wrong, the chiefs from Kitwancool will know, "and they are wise people and will know what to say." Hlengwax agreed to a compromise. He would not leave Gitsegukla but would also not attend Gaxsgabaxs' feast that day "as something may be said that will anger me and cause me to say or do something which I may regret and I will bring shame and ridicule on you all."[61]

That evening, Gaxsgabaxs' feast got under way. After the food had been served and the money contributions gathered and properly distributed, Gaxsgabaxs rose to speak. He related his satisfaction

---

60   Beynon was present throughout this meeting: *Potlatch at Gitsegukla, supra* note 5 at 79–81.

61   *Ibid.* at 129–130. Note here that Tawa'lesk assumed mediator role as a chief in a clan not involved in the dispute but the highest ranked House and clan in his village.

with raising his House's pole, thus completing his responsibilities as a chief. He then told the story[62] that justified why he had erected a pole "which in every way resembles that of our dear brother Neek't's pole at Gitwangak." By way of explanation, he prefaced his story by noting that his House and its rights have connections with those of other Houses in other villages. The story starts with the warrior Neek't moving from the Gitwangak fort or *ta'oots'ip* to Gitsegukla, where his then-wife lived. In the course of exploring the new territories his father-in-law had given him, he came across the coastal Haisla village of Kitimat, which he and his nephews later attacked, taking many captives and acquiring a crest in the form of an eagle.[63] Neek't then returned to Gitwangak but one of his nephews, who had been on the Kitimat raid, returned to Gitsegukla, revived the House that his uncle had founded there, and assumed the privilege of all the Neek't crests. Neek't himself went on to found further Houses in Kispiox, in Gitlaxdamks among the Nisga'a, and in Hagwilget among the Wet'suwet'en. In all these places, Gaxsgabaxs told his listeners, those Houses were entitled to use all the Neek't crests.[64] He concluded his speech by placing the legal issue on which he had just related the relevant history firmly in the hands of his invited guests: "I do not have to go to court to determine my own rights and now you chiefs will know whether what I say is true or whether I am doing something that I have no right to do. I leave this to you."[65]

The leading chiefs in Gitsegukla, Gitanmaax, and Kitwancool all spoke to verify Gaxsgabaxs' history and his right to the crests. The Gitwangak chiefs, aside from Hlengwax, were present but did not speak. In an oblique reference to Hlengwax's earlier appeal to the Indian Agent, some of the speakers took up Gaxsgabaxs' point that Gitxsan chiefs should not try to resolve their disputes before a Canadian court or government official, who would be ignorant of the House histories and the relevant

---

62   The story was in the nature of what the Canadian legal system has come to know as an indigenous oral history, and in Gitxsan law as an *adaawk* — a history with the legal clout to define a lineage group and set out its relationships to other groups, to supernatural beings, and to its territories and fishing sites.

63   The Haisla called this crest an eagle. On its capture by Neek't, it lost its previous name and meanings and, therefore, its story in the Gitxsan Frog Clan *adaawk* began with its capture in Kitimat. As the eagle was already a clan crest of the Eagle Clan in Gitwangak, the eagle-like image was retained but was then called a *Moodziks* to avoid offending the Eagles: *Potlatch at Gitsegukla, supra* note 5 at 133, 138, and 144.

64   Gaxsgabaxs did not specifically mention the *Ganuget* crest in his speech, perhaps for diplomatic reasons.

65   *Potlatch at Gitsegukla, supra* note 5 at 136–139.

indigenous law.[66] Nothing further was done about the *Ganuget* crest dispute and nothing further was said.[67]

Case Commentary

The dispute over the display of the *Ganuget* crest provides more detail on how Gitxsan chiefs managed their House's identity, legal relationships, and reputation in the face of conflict. This is because conflict management always has the potential to change governance rules.

At first glance, the issue of which Houses and lineages held the privilege to show the crest may seem trivial. There is no evidence in Beynon's account that any use or holding of territories or fishing sites was at stake. A closer look at where the House of Gaxsgabaxs was situated in the societal network, however, reveals its imperative to maintain its identity in that place through the display and feasting of the crest. A successful pole-raising would assure Gaxsgabaxs that his House was recognized as one of a group of lineages within a common *wil'naat'ahl* that originated from Neek't and his nephews and which now included lineages among the Nisga'a, the Wet'suwet'en, and the Gitxsan villages of Kispiox and Gitwangak. Gaxsgabaxs could call on these other lineages for support; for example, if the House was in danger of becoming extinct because the vagaries of sex distribution among its members resulted in there being no women to keep its matriline viable.

In his speech confirming Gaxsgabaxs' right to use the *Ganuget* crest, the Gitanmaax Frog chief, Luutkudjiiwus, alluded to the proper practice in such circumstances when he advised how the Gitwangak branch of the Neek't *wil'naat'ahl* should have proceeded when it faced extinction and its rights and property were being absorbed into another Frog House. The depleted Gitwangak House should have adopted a member of Gaxsgabaxs' House[68] and reestablished the Neek't group at Gitwangak.[69] Adoptions from closely related Houses would thus have preserved the particular identity of the newly revived group, maintained its historical connections, and saved it from being the poor relation of a more distant branch of the Frog Clan.

If Gaxsgabaxs' goal was to preserve his House's identity, Hlengwax's objective in the end was to preserve his House's reputation.

---

66   *Ibid.* at 139–142.
67   *Ibid.* at 151.
68   Presumably a female member of child-bearing age.
69   *Potlatch at Gitsegukla, supra* note 5 at 140.

We have seen how reputation can be enhanced through the performance of honourable conduct but can also be degraded by dishonourable or shameful conduct. In this case, non-performance was being used in attempts to shame others. Recall that Hlengwax stayed away from Gaxsgabaxs' *halayt* and the other Gitwangak chiefs did not take their usual *ant'aa* seats. At Gaxsgabaxs' *yukw* feast, Hlengwax again absented himself and the other Gitwangak chiefs attended but did not speak to validate Gaxsgabaxs' display of the *Ganuget* crest. These non-actions and actions showed both Hlengwax's disagreement and the Gitwangak chiefs' compromise abstention from his decision. However, the support of Houses from all the other clans and all the other villages, including Gaxsgabaxs' *'nidinsxwit*, Wii Seeks, was sufficient to validate the display of the disputed crest. Prior to the feast, the Gitwangak chiefs considered, but rejected, the nuclear option of them all returning home and not attending any of the other Gitsesegukla feasts. This would have severely disrupted the planned pole-raisings but, as T'awa'lesk counselled and Hlengwax acknowledged, it would also have brought ridicule and shame on the Gitwangak chiefs. Non-performance could thus have legal implications as well as performance.

As Stacey found in medieval Ireland, there was, and continues to be, stability and predictability in Gitxsan society. But there were also elements of risk and fragmentation, as the crest dispute shows. This provided an opportunity for the society to evolve in response to changing external environmental conditions and to changing internal societal dynamics. This was shown in the first section of this chapter by the practice of reputational ranking, which allows those who best exemplify the society's norms and values to be more consistently consulted on important decisions. Other events such as the extinction of Houses or the removal of a chief's name from circulation are more disruptive, less frequent and take place over a longer timescale. The history of the House and name of Neek't is an example. The oral histories of his Frog Clan *wil'naat'ahl* [70] show him to be what the Gitxsan and Tsimshian would call in English a *tyrant* and what today might be called a *warlord* or *terrorist*. As already noted, the last holder of the Neek't name in Gitwangak was killed in 1931, and the Neek't name was no longer used in Kispiox by the mid-1920s. The feast-names of other tyrants,

---

70   *Totem Poles of the Gitksan, supra* note 56 at 40 and 52.

for example the Tsimshian tribal chiefs Ligeex[71] and Haymaas,[72] were also retired by the twentieth century as their successors feared reprisals and demands for compensation from their victims' successors.[73] Thus, while the slower evolution of Houses, lineages, and feast-names enables the society to adapt to long-term changes, the faster evolution of rank enables it to respond to short-term changes.

An Imagined Indigenous IP Future

In this section I suggest ways in which the art performed and displayed in Gitxsan legal processes might be reconciled with Canadian intellectual property law and with the nation-state more broadly. Two aspects of this reconciliation will be considered. First is the use of legally significant indigenous images in the commercial art and decorative spheres. Second, we look at the more politically fraught area of how the Canadian state could recognize a legal order where crests and their associated *adaawk* establish a House group's responsibility for particular land territories and fishing sites.

We start by looking at a Gitxsan crest image that has wended its way into the contemporary commercial world. In 1928, Emily Carr visited the village of Kitwancool on a painting expedition that included other Gitxsan and Nisga'a villages. She was following the advice of Marius Barbeau and shared his belief that the Indigenous peoples of British Columbia were losing their authenticity through assimilation and colonization. In 1927, Carr participated in an exhibition Barbeau had helped organize at Canada's National Gallery that featured artifacts collected during his 1923–1924 visit to Gitxsan villages, along with paintings of the villages, many by artists who had accompanied him. Carr subsequently took on his "idea of recording the native tragedy in art."[74]

---

71   Ligeek used violence, competitive feasting and property destruction, as well as an entrepreneurial exploitation of the nineteenth-century colonial fur trade: Susan Marsden & Robert Galois, "The Tsimshian, the Hudson's Bay Company and the Geopolitics of the Northwest Coast Fur Trade, 1787 to 1840" (1995) 39:2 The Canadian Geographer 169.

72   Haymaas, like Neek't, carried out raids and mass killings as head of an outlaw warrior band, as well as theft of his father's property and the murder of other Tsimshian chiefs he had invited to a feast: University of British Columbia, Museum of Anthropology Archives, Duff Tsimshian Files, Box 41, File 63. These files contain Wilson Duff's extensive notes compiled between 1960 and 1972 from the Barbeau/Beynon notebooks archived at what is now the Canadian Museum of History.

73   *Ibid.*

74   Marcia Crosby, "A Chronology of Love's Contingencies" in Charles C Hill, Johanne

Kitwancool was one of the Gitxsan villages whose member Houses had participated in the 1945 feasts, although the particular image discussed here had been carved on a pole a half-century previously.[75] Carr arrived there having hitched a wagon ride from the Gitwangak railhead with the family of the two leading Kitwancool House chiefs, Richard and Miriam Douse,[76] on whose veranda she eventually camped. One of the paintings from her week-long stay was of the base crest figure on a Wolf Clan pole of the House of 'Wixaa,[77] which she titled *Totem Mother*.[78] A decade later, she would describe it and similar crest figures:

> They were carved elaborately and with great sincerity. Several times the figure of a woman that held a child was represented. The babies had faces like wise little old men. The mothers expressed all womanhood – the big wooden hands holding the child were so full of tenderness they had to be distorted enormously in order to contain it all. Womanhood was strong in Kitwancool.[79]

Today, Carr's *Totem Mother* image can be purchased on beach bags, T-shirts, phone cases, and coffee mugs.[80] These reproductions followed the expiry of her estate's copyright 50 years after her death in 1945.[81]

By the time she painted the figure, it was missing a large, pointed nose, which had fallen off the pole.[82] The crest is known as *Git'weedzarat* (Large-nosed person or Huge-belly) or *Dzaraohlaw* (Glass-nose or Cutting nose) (See Figures 10.1 and 10.2). Barbeau outlines the associated *adaawk* or oral history:

Lamoureux & Ian M Thom, eds, *Emily Carr: New Perspectives on a Canadian Icon* (Ottawa & Vancouver: National Gallery of Canada & Vancouver Art Gallery, 2006) 156 [*Emily Carr*] at 162.

75   *Totem Poles of the Gitksan, supra* note 56 at 119.
76   Richard Douse was Gwashlaa'm of the Wolf Clan, Miriam Douse was Gamlaxyeltxw of the Frog Clan. Carr's portrait of Mrs. Douse is reproduced in *Emily Carr, supra* note 74 at 167.
77   This pole is pictured in *Totem Poles of the Gitksan, supra* note 56 at 259 (Plate XXV, Fig 1).
78   *Totem Mother* is reproduced in *Emily Carr, supra* note 74 at 174.
79   Emily Carr, "Klee Wyck" in *The Emily Carr Collection* (Ottawa: Prospero Books, 2002) 7 at 76–77.
80   See Fine Art America webpage at https://fineartamerica.com/featured/totem-mother-kitwancool-by-emily-carr-1928-emily-carr.html, accessed October 2, 2023.
81   *Copyright Act*, RSC 1985, c C-42, s 6. The Act was amended in 2022 to extend the copyright term to 70 years, but not retroactively.
82   *Totem Poles of the Gitksan, supra* note 56 at 117.

A young woman [...] Yaw'l, broke her seclusion taboos, to play with her brothers. Although it was summertime, a deluge of snow covered the ground at night. When the brothers and sister awoke, they found themselves in a strange country [...] Huge-belly, a monstrous being, appeared from time to time, calling the young taboo-breakers outside, one by one, to cut them open with his long, sharp, glass-like nose, and hang their bodies on the rafters of his lodge to smoke and dry like split salmon. One of them managed to slay him. The slayer took flight with his sister and remaining brothers. But to little avail. A female being of the same kind, Ksemkaigyet, who could draw her nose into a sharp knife pursued them. As they hid in a tree at the edge of a lake, she detected their shadows in the frosty waters, and dived several times to capture them, until she was quite frozen. Then they killed her [...][83]

As with Neek't's relatives' *Ganuget* crest, the Glass-nose is a Wolf crest that belongs to related Houses in a number of Skeena watershed and northwest coastal villages. Besides Kitwancool, it has been displayed on the poles of 'Wixaa's relatives in the Gitxsan villages of Kuldo and Kispiox,[84] the Nisga'a villages of Gitiks and Angidaa, and the Tsimshian village of Gitkxaahla.[85]

Even if Carr had been cognizant of the relevant indigenous law and had been willing to comply with it, the process of obtaining permission to sell the image in the commercial market would have been impossibly onerous. As we have seen, each House with an interest in the crest would have had to be involved in reaching a consensus through the feast system. One approach to this conundrum was more recently outlined by a Gitsegukla chief, Niis Noolh.[86] In the late 1970s, as an *Indian Act* band administrator, he applied for a government grant to make regalia for a village dance group. As he described later:

"[I]ntellectual property" was not a term that was used at the time. The intellectual property issue was therefore solely in the hands of the hereditary chiefs of the village. These chiefs gave permission

---

83   *Ibid* at 128. Another, extended version of the same *adaawk* is in Marius Barbeau, *Totem Poles* (Ottawa: National Museum of Canada, 1950) [*Totem Poles*] at 262–264. The "seclusion taboos" referred to the practice of isolating young women from the community during the time of their first period.

84   *Totem Poles of the Gitksan, supra* note 56 at 126–128.

85   *Totem Poles, supra* note 83 at 261, 265–268.

86   Niis Noolh (Ray Jones), House of Xsgogimlaxha, Fireweed Clan, Gitesgukla.

Figure 10.1: 'Wixaa pole at Kitwancool shows the basal figure of Dzaraohlaw (Glass-nose), a crest that identified 'Wixaa as a member of an ancient Wolf Clan lineage that killed a "monstrous being."

Source: University of Washington Libraries, Special Collections, NA 3480.

Figure 10.2: In 1928, Emily Carr made a painting of the Dzaraohlaw crest, which she called *Totem Mother*.

Source: Wikimedia Commons.

for the blanket makers to use generalised images representing
the three main clans in Gitsegukla: Wolf, Frog and Fireweed [...]

But, he emphasises, there was no specific image that belonged to a
House group because that would have been the House's property
[G]eneralised images on blankets would have had no role in the feast
system and, as such, had no [indigenous] law governing them. [87]

The story of the *Totem Mother* image is one where the operation of
Canadian copyright law resulted in Carr and one of the Gitxsan holders
of a crest image losing control of any original mutual understanding they
may have had. Carr and subsequent users' unwillingness or inability
to understand the oral history behind the image potentially tarnishes
both its use as fine art and as commercial product decoration, as well
as tarnishes its use in the performance of Gitxsan law. From a Gitxsan
perspective, the solution developed by the Gitsegukla chiefs in the 1970s
could be applied by the House groups to disallow the reproduction
of crest images for any purpose other than for each House to hold its
relevant oral histories, crests, identity, and territories under the laws
of the Gitxsan and their neighbours.

Can IP Law be Reconciled with Indigenous Legal Orders?

To date, the application of intellectual property law to indigenous
peoples has been primarily concerned with the protection and control of
so-called traditional knowledge, intangible heritage, and cultural expressions, either from or for commercial exploitation. [88] Intellectual property
regimes assume a discrete author in copyright laws, a discrete inventor
in patent laws, and a discrete trader in trademark laws, for such are
necessary to enable the smooth function of the marketplace. As the first
two parts of this chapter have shown, knowledge and responsibility for
the intangible symbols of legal identity, autonomy, and societal norms
are dispersed among individuals and lineages throughout northern
Northwest Coast societies.

---

87   Richard Overstall, "The Law is Opened: The Constitutional Role of Tangible and
     Intangible Property in Gitanyow" in Catherine Bell & Val Napoleon, eds, *First
     Nations Cultural Heritage and Law: Case Studies, Voices, and Perspectives* (Vancouver:
     UBC Press, 2008) 92 at 101–102.
88   A comprehensive overview of international developments in this area is Peter
     K Yu, "Cultural Relics, Intellectual Property, and Intangible Heritage" (2008) 81
     Temple Law Review 433 [*Cultural Relics*].

The individual-based, command-and-control nation-state has had a difficult interaction, let alone reconciliation, with kinship-based, bottom-up, dispersed, consensus-seeking indigenous legal orders. Constitutionalism and federalism between state and indigenous societies might therefore consider a pluralistic approach.[89] Legal pluralism has long been a necessity among indigenous peoples in what is now northern British Columbia. A multi-juridical approach to state reconciliation with indigenous legal orders requires the recognition of similarities as well as differences among them so that rules of external recognition can be applied. A Canadian constitutional framework can be imagined "in which distinct legal orders can mutually constitute each other without one dominating the other."[90] The singular commercial purpose of much existing state intellectual property law, including its focus on discrete and unencumbered property ownership, has proved to be a difficult legal basis even for a just commercialization of indigenous knowledge, let alone mutual legal recognition.[91]

One area of intellectual property law, however, may provide a bridge for the mutual recognition needed for legal pluralism. Armorial law governs the creation and display of heraldic art—that is, coats of arms and other symbols originally held solely by European aristocratic families and now also by states, municipalities, military units, and others. However, as it currently stands in Canada, the law is ambiguous and not obviously helpful in giving legal effect to the display and performance of indigenous law. Canadian armorial law is historically tied to that of England and Christopher Mackie argues that since Canadian colonists received grants of arms from an English herald, they must also have received the English law of arms.[92] If that is the case, a 1955 decision of the English Court of Chivalry may be relevant. A municipality, the Corporation of Manchester, claimed that a city theatre had usurped its arms by publicly displaying them in its auditorium and by using them as its common seal. The Court held that the display of arms for decoration was not a ground for intervention, but that "[a] deed sealed with an armorial device is thereby authenticated as the act

89   Val Napoleon, "Legal Pluralism and Reconciliation" (November 2019), Maori Law Review 3.
90   Kelty McKerracher, "Relational Legal Pluralism and Indigenous Legal Orders in Canada" (2023) 12:1 Global Constitutionalism 133 at 136.
91   *Cultural Relics, supra* note 88 at 484–499.
92   C.S.T. Mackie, "The Reception of England's Armorial Law into Canada" (2008) IV:216 The Coat of Arms 137 at 142.

and deed of the person entitled to bear the arms [...] For the defendant company to use the arms of the city as its seal looks very much like an attempt to identify the company with the Corporation."[93] The Court enjoined the theatre company from "any display of the corporation's arms."[94] Heraldic arms on English seals thus share with Gitxsan and their neighbours' crests on poles, house fronts, and regalia the purpose of legally identifying certain entities, including lineages.

Canadian legislation appears to protect commercial but not legal use of arms. The *Trademarks Act* prohibits the adoption of armorial bearings "in connection with a business"[95] but is silent in respect of their legal use. Since 1988, the royal prerogative to grant coats of arms in Canada has been exercised by the Canadian Heraldic Authority within the office of the Governor General. Its website "allows for the recording of First Nations emblems" but a search of the Authority's website shows no granting of arms comprised of crests and other images to indigenous groups constituted under their own laws.[96] While armorial law has strong parallels with indigenous law of crests and other performances, it remains to be seen if the equivalences would allow a prerogative recognition of them by the Authority and what legal effect that would have on indigenous societies' place in a multi-juridical Canada.

Canada's common law also has had difficulty recognizing and interpreting legal performance. During the trial of the Gitxsan and Wet'suwet'en peoples' *Delgamuukw* aboriginal title case, a plaintiffs' lawyer asked a Gitxsan witness[97] to sing a *limx' oo'y*, a lament often sung during a pole-raising, that recorded part of her House's history when it experienced great deprivation. The judge said he was legally embarrassed by the sung evidence. "Could it not be written out and the witness asked if this is the wording?" he enquired, "I have a tin ear, Mr. Grant, it's not going to do any good to sing it to me." Chief Justice McEachern also had "serious doubts about the reliability of

---

93   *Manchester Corporation v Manchester Palace of Varieties Ltd.*, [1955] 1 All ER 387 at 394. This finding is similar to the common law tort of passing off.

94   *Ibid.* at 395

95   *Trademarks Act*, RSC 1985, c T-13, s 9(1).

96   A search using the terms "First Nation," "aboriginal," and "indigenous" showed only arms with indigenous-appearing motifs granted to non-indigenous municipalities, military units, police units, and universities. Canadian Heraldic Authority, online: https://www.gg.ca/en/heraldry/canadian-heraldic-authority [accessed 12 October 2023].

97   Antgulilibix (Mary Johnson) House of Tsibasaa, Fireweed Clan, Kispiox.

the *adaawk* as evidence." [98] In his 1991 trial decision, he gave the plaintiffs' oral histories no independent weight. [99] The Supreme Court of
Canada overturned this error, but said a new trial would be needed
"as it would be impossible for the Court to do justice to the parties by
sifting through the record itself and making new factual findings." [100]

This chapter has shown that a multi-juridical Canada would
have to accommodate two distinct conceptions of law and two distinct
conceptions of the role of performance in law. The Gitxsan and their
neighbours' kinship-based legal order melds formal legal process with
performance. In doing so, it reminds participants of their norms and
values while its societal structures and dynamics foster collaboratively
determined cooperation. While Canadian courts will now more readily
admit and give some evidentiary weight to oral histories, songs, and
other performed law, [101] they remain unwilling to recognize and interpret
performance as a complete indigenous land-holding and governance
order in a multi-juridical Canada. Taking performed and displayed
indigenous law out of the ambit of copyright, patent, and trademark
law and considering it alongside ancient Crown armorial law may be
a small nudge towards such reconciliation.

---

98   Leslie Hall Pinder, "The Carriers of No" (1999) 4 Index on Censorship 65 at 67–69.
99   *Delgamuukw v. British Columbia*, 1997 CanLII 302 (SCC), [1997] 3 SCR 1010 at para
      96.
100   *Ibid* at para 108.
101   See, e.g., Hon A Lutfy & Emily McCarthy, "Rulemaking in a Mixed Jurisdiction:
      The Federal Court (Canada)" (2010) 49 SCLR (2d) 313 at 323–324.

CHAPTER 11

Thinking Differently: Creating Spaces of Autonomy for the Revitalization of Indigenous Legal Traditions in the Context of Copyright

Johnny Mack and Graham J. Reynolds

Abstract

There is an urgent need to think differently. Colonialism, in its settler variant, has developed new and particularly dangerous strategies to advance its dual imperatives of the dispossession of Indigenous peoples and the erasure of Indigeneity as a politicized identity construct with a legitimate claim to law. This goal is advanced today through rights frameworks, which have generated a worrisome platform to support the logic of elimination by drawing Indigenous calls for autonomy, self-determination, and sovereignty into a settler colonial framework of authority. In this chapter, we highlight how these strategies function in the context of Canadian copyright law. Canadian copyright law is deeply implicated in a number of issues that matter greatly to Indigenous peoples today. One possible response by Indigenous peoples to the role played by copyright in relation to these issues is to work within the copyright system: to either engage with the system as structured or to seek to reform the copyright system to make it more responsive to Indigenous concerns. While protections may be secured through either of these methods, this chapter highlights a few of the risks associated with these approaches, in particular how they draw Indigenous peoples into the settler colonial framework of authority potentially resulting in a diminishment of Indigenous sovereignty. This argument suggests that in seeking to protect Indigenous modes of expression, we should be wary of reliance on rights. Instead, we should seek to create spaces of autonomy for the revitalization of Indigenous legal traditions.

M y intention here, and with much of my scholarly work, is to convey a critique of law as it has become formalized within settler state institutions while at the same time inhabiting an ethical sensibility toward law as an interactive social phenomenon. My view is that most often, law gains meaning and becomes tangible as we engage with it. Through interaction, we position ourselves not just to identify a rule to follow but also to identify the logics, norms, and values that rationalize the need for the rule as well as what are understood as its authoritative interpretations. What I offer in the following is a critique of the formal sites of state law while trying to do so in a manner that does not further reify or naturalize this law on its own terms, in accordance with its own rules. What I would focus on instead is the field of lived experience, centering my tangible and observed encounters with a normative world, fashioned by the storied context and "jurisgenerative" agency I inherit as a Nuu-chah-nulth legal subject. [1] These encounters include the world of embodied experience, where the material enjoins with the ideational, and the spaces in between work together to enable a particular comprehension of social life and the co-creation of normativity. I write these words with a commitment to a normative world, a nomos if you will, that is distinctly Nuu-chah-nulth. I am guided here by the idea that so long as my engagement with the material and social facts, which is driving my argument, is ethically and rationally grounded and defensible on both fronts, then I am justified in carrying on.

These words are intended to open conversations. This is not a manifesto but an invitation to join in my attempt to think and act differently relative to the categories of law and normativity, particularly their relationship to land and tradition for Indigenous peoples in the Pacific Northwest of Turtle Island and elsewhere. This invitation is a general one extending to audiences and interlocutors known and not yet known. For the purposes of this chapter, this invitation is specific and has been taken up by Graham Reynolds as an interlocutor and friend to whom I have been talking about these problems for almost 15 years. We do not study in the same fields; he is an intellectual property specialist, and

---

1   Robert Cover, "The Supreme Court, 1982 Term – Foreword: Nomos and Narrative'" (1983) 2705 Faculty Scholarship Series, Paper 67–68. I am drawing on Cover's concept of jurisgenesis because of its relationship to a normative world that does not center a state's institutional framework when considering law. The object of study, for Cover as a law scholar, is a normative world or what he refers to as a nomos. His theory and general concept of law is inherently plural, and as such I find it helpful when considering Indigenous law and the normative worlds Indigenous peoples inhabited before and following the colonial encounter.

my focus is on Indigenous law and its theoretical underpinnings. But we share a view that settler state law in its current form has not done enough to account for the normative world that preceded the arrival and imposition of European legal traditions. We share an understanding that if state law remains in its current forms, it will continue to advance the colonial imperative. And we both believe that the aberrations and injustices of colonialism are things law can and should be working to uproot, rather than articulate and rationalize into Canada's common law, and therefore perpetuate. Graham has accepted my invitation to join in my attempt to think and act differently relative to the categories of law and normativity, in the context of Canadian copyright law. Through this piece, we invite you, reader, to join with us as well.

Accounting for Position and Voice

Before proceeding any further, it is important to set out who we are, why we seek to address this problem, and why we are well-positioned to intervene in this debate. We do so in part to ensure that the reader understands the voice and structure of the analysis developed in the chapter. Our approach to writing this chapter is experimental. Our voices, while certainly influenced by past conversations, will remain distinct through most of the chapter. The reasons for this are obvious, as we both come to the project of writing this chapter from distinct locations, as both subjects and scholars of law.

I approach law through a lens of legal pluralism and self-consciously ground myself in a Nuu-chah-nulth world when thinking carefully about matters of normativity and lawful conduct. I come to this position, in part, because both of my parents are Nuu-chah-nulth. I was raised by my father in my home territory on the West Coast of Vancouver Island. My father comes from a Hawiih family, his father was our Tyee Hawiih (head chief), and his mother was from a high-ranking Ucluelet family. He carried forward a sense of groundedness in our history on the land. In his younger years, he was a proud wolf dancer in our Potlatching tradition. He was born into a Nuu-chah-nulth world, and his first language was Nuu-chah-nulth. He also attended the Port Alberni Residential School for nine years, which he described as brutally violent. [2] I could tell many stories about life in my ancestral

---

2   The Port Alberni Residential School was notorious for its mistreatment of First Nations children.

homelands with my father, but for my purposes here, I will just say that there he planted seeds of doubt regarding the legitimacy of Canada's authority over our bodies and our homelands. As will become apparent later in this chapter, those seeds of doubt have been nourished in my legal studies and developed into an ethical commitment to articulating Indigenous legal traditions and defending the norms emerging from this space as legitimate sources of law.[3]

My time with my mother was brief, and my memory of life with her was in urban settings, in the greater Vancouver area. My parents separated shortly after I was born, and I spent my first five years with her. She was Tla-o-qui-aht but was not enrolled with the Nation. Her mother was a Tla-o-qui-aht residential school survivor, and her father was a Canadian of German/French descent. The state did not see her as Indigenous because at the time, Indian status was traced through the male line.[4] There were many Indigenous relatives and friends mixed into our circle, but I was too young to have developed a rationalized sense of Indigenous identity. In these years, I learned to distinguish between the rules my mother gave us, and the laws of the state. My mom's rules were to be followed without exception, and intentional breaches of these rules would be met with consequences. Think of solitary bedroom confinement and the wooden spoon. State laws relating to property were also to be observed, but here there were exceptions made, especially in times of scarcity.

She remarried for a few years, but the marriage turned toxic. They split up and my mother moved us, her kids, into a transition house and then into an apartment on our own. My mother was raising three boys under seven while in her early twenties, and when her husband left, she began to seriously struggle. Because she did not have status, she did not have an Indigenous home to return to and relied on social assistance available to state citizens. We moved to a transition house and then briefly into an apartment. The state would place us, her children,

---

3   When I began law school in 2003, Indigenous law was very much a peripheral area of study in law school curriculums across Canada and internationally as well. I was fortunate to be studying at the University of Victoria, where John Borrows was on faculty and where Val Napoleon was completing her doctoral studies. These two law scholars are field leaders who have pushed law schools and the legal profession to understand the complexities of Indigenous normative traditions and to be able to identify and work with Indigenous sources of law in parallel with the common and civil law traditions arriving from Europe.

4   The version of the *Indian Act* in force when my mother was born was *Indian Act*, RSC 1952, c 149, as amended.

into group homes and foster care for a short period before two of us moved in with our father. We lost touch with our youngest brother and our mother. I would learn that my mother struggled with addiction and turned to sex work for support. She lived a hard life, always adjacent to the streets when she was not in prison. She died in her early forties. My mother's story is a complicated one, marred by systemic forms of sexism, racism, and colonialism. What I carry forward from her is an understanding that state law and policy is experienced differently by different people. As an Indigenous woman born in 1955, who was part of what scholars call the Sixties Scoop, she would experience Canadian institutions as an invasive and hostile force. From her story, I inherit a dual imperative. On one side, I aim to refashion state law in ways that are less violent to Indigenous people, particularly women. On the other side, I aim to live my life in fidelity to our Indigenous legal traditions and find ways to work with Indigenous law to achieve justice for the most vulnerable of our people.

One last thing I will add here is the connection to Nuu-chah-nulth lands. From a Nuu-chah-nulth perspective, obligations and privileges with respect to land are best understood within a broad theory of kinship. We understand ourselves to be bonded to the same lands as our ancient elders, with whom we have a historic and ongoing intersubjective relationship. It is a relationship that goes back to times beyond our collective memory and perpetually forward, whether or not we acknowledge or recognize that the land has standing to speak into our consciousness and lives. In a way, the land is read as a foundational legal text that does not answer to the pacts we make among ourselves to coordinate exploitation and wealth accumulation. The ontological presence of land sits beyond our constitutional conundrums and our modern conceptualizations of space and time. The land's existence precedes our collective memory and exceeds what we see as our present time and our futurity. My understanding is that our objectives are certainly not to harness the immense power of the land through our understandings and rationalizations but rather to cultivate practices that open up new ways of listening and conversing, such that we know better how to conduct ourselves harmoniously, understanding ourselves as components of an extensive kinship network we broadly refer to as Nuu-chah-nulth territories. In this way, territory stands as the dynamic, intersubjective, and always agonistic *grundnorm* in Nuu-chah-nulth legal thought.[5]

---

5   Appending dynamism, intersubjectivity, and agonism as descriptors of a *grundnorm*

Like Johnny, I also approach law through a sense of legal pluralism. I have come to this position both because of the scholarship that I have engaged with as a law student and legal academic, and more importantly because of the relationships that I have formed over these many years (including my friendship with Johnny). With respect to matters of normativity and lawful conduct, my childhood was rooted in western legal traditions. I grew up in Winnipeg, in an upper-middle-class household in a suburban neighbourhood, with my mother, father, and sister. My parents were both teachers. Growing up, law was not a significant presence in our lives. For the most part, where law was discussed, it was as a potential profession for myself or for my sister. There were moments in my childhood where law became visible—speeding tickets or one incident in a hockey game in which a teammate's actions went so far beyond what could reasonably be expected from a contact sport that the game was stopped, the police were called, and charges laid. But for the most part, law for me was an invisible presence. I did not experience the violence or the cruelty of law as Johnny has described; or feel at a deep and personal level the conflict between legal traditions. It was not until law school that I began to more fully understand the ways in which laws are neither neutral nor objective; along with the full extent of the systemic and ongoing violence that settler laws cause to Indigenous peoples and Indigenous legal traditions.

It was also in law school that I began to learn about the ways through which law could be employed to achieve progressive reform. From the *Canadian Charter of Rights and Freedoms* to human rights codes to international human rights treaties, I came to see rights as a mechanism through which to address social injustice. At the same time, I began to embrace intellectual property law as the body of substantive law that I found most interesting and engaging. My research today continues to focus on the intersection of intellectual property, human rights, and social justice. Through my work, I seek to highlight ways through which the IP system (and in particular the copyright system) fails to provide adequate protection for human rights or to sufficiently advance social justice goals, and to suggest reforms that would help address these

---

here is meant to push the analysis toward a relational understanding of the texts we turn to when making sense of law. On the idea of land as a legal text, see John Borrows, *Drawing Out Law: A Spirit's Guide* (Toronto: University of Toronto Press, 2010), particularly p. 67–88. Also see John Borrows, *Canada's Indigenous Constitution* (Toronto: University of Toronto Press, 2010), and Borrows' discussion of natural law in Chapter 2 of this work (p. 28–35).

points of failure. One of the animating themes of my work has been the idea that rights, including those set out in constitutional bills of rights like Canada's *Charter of Rights and Freedoms* and in international human rights treaties, can be effective mechanisms to achieve protection for important social interests. This idea—which is challenged in important ways in this chapter—is my entry point into this topic, and the expertise that I bring to this collaboration. I am not an expert in Indigenous treaties, rights, or legal traditions. As well, as a non-Indigenous settler Canadian, I do not have any lived experience that is relevant for this chapter. I seek to intervene in this debate in partnership with Johnny, recognizing both what I can bring to the conversation as well as my limitations as a scholar.

Outline, Context, and Background Facts

There is an urgent need to think differently in our time. It appears to me that colonialism, in its settler variant, has developed new and particularly dangerous strategies that appear to be working more effectively than other settler colonial strategies including violence, paternalism, and forced isolation to advance its dual imperatives of the dispossession of Indigenous peoples and the erasure of Indigeneity as a politicized identity construct with a legitimate claim to law. In settler colonial states we observe an overarching structural goal of *replacing* Indigenous people with a new settler native.[6] This goal is advanced today through rights frameworks, which I argue has generated a worrisome platform to support the logic of elimination by drawing Indigenous calls for autonomy, self-determination, and sovereignty into a settler colonial framework of authority.

In "Turning Sideways" and "Hoquotist", I discussed how these strategies have operated in the context of the Aboriginal rights framework and the work of the BC Treaty Commission.[7] This chapter builds on

6   Wolfe writes, "[o]n the one hand, settler society required the practical elimination of the natives in order to establish itself on their territory. On the symbolic level, however, settler society subsequently sought to recuperate indigeneity in order to express its difference—and, accordingly, its independence—from the mother country." Patrick Wolfe, "Settler Colonialism and the Elimination of the Native" (2006) 8 Journal of Genocide Research 387–409 at 389.

7   Johnny Mack, "'Turning Sideways': Intimate Critique and the Regeneration of Tradition" [forthcoming in *Review of Constitutional Studies*]; Johnny Mack, "Hoquotist: Reorienting Through Storied Practice" in Hester Lessard, Rebecca Johnson, and Jeremy Webber, *Storied Communities: Narratives of Contact and Arrival*

these works. Together with Graham Reynolds, we highlight how these strategies function in the context of Canadian copyright law, including the role that copyright might play in the further dispossession of Indigenous peoples' lands and laws, and the elimination of Indigeneity as a politically grounding concept.

Canadian copyright law is deeply implicated in a number of issues that matter greatly to Indigenous peoples today. These include data sovereignty;[8] the question of who is able to engage with the Stories of Residential School Survivors that have been recorded by third parties (and in what ways); and the commercialization and sale of stories, images, and belongings that are connected to or grounded in Indigenous cultural or legal traditions.[9] In each of these areas, Canada's copyright laws help determine and allocate rights of ownership, access, and use.

One possible response by Indigenous peoples to the role played by copyright in relation to these issues is to work within the copyright system: to either engage with the system as structured or to seek to reform the copyright system to make it more responsive to Indigenous concerns. While protections may be secured through either of these methods, this chapter highlights a few of the risks associated with these approaches, in particular how they draw Indigenous peoples into the settler colonial framework of authority, potentially resulting in a diminishment of Indigenous sovereignty. This argument suggests that in seeking to protect Indigenous modes of expression (along with other interests in which copyright is implicated that hold particular significance for Indigenous peoples, for instance as noted above), we should be wary of reliance on rights. Instead, we should seek to create spaces of autonomy for the revitalization of Indigenous legal traditions. Our work here adds to the voices of scholars who have advocated for such an approach, including Gordon Christie, Val

---

in Constituting Political Community (Vancouver: UBC Press, 2011).

8   See, for instance, The First Nations Information Governance Centre, "A First Nations Data Governance Strategy" (2020), online: https://fnigc.ca/wp-content/uploads/2020/09/FNIGC_FNDGS_report_EN_FINAL.pdf; Rebecca Tsosie, "Tribal Data Governance and Informational Privacy: Constructing Indigenous Data Sovereignty" (2019) 80 Mont L Rev 229; Tahu Kukutai and John Taylor, ed, *Indigenous Data Sovereignty: Toward an Agenda* (Canberra: Australian National University Press, 2016).

9   See, for instance, Marie Battiste and James Youngblood (Sa'Ke'j) Henderson, *Protecting Indigenous Knowledge: A Global Challenge* (UBC Press, 2000); Andrea Bear Nicholas, "Who owns Indigenous cultural and intellectual property?" (2017) Policy Options, online: https://policyoptions.irpp.org/magazines/june-2017/who-owns-Indigenous-cultural-and-intellectual-property/.

Napoleon, Rebecca Johnson, Richard Overstall, Debra McKenzie, and Sa'Ke'j Youngblood Henderson. [10]

Our chapter is structured in five parts. I began by explaining my intention with respect to this chapter, and by extending an invitation to all readers to join in my attempt to think and act differently relative to the categories of law and normativity (an invitation that Graham has taken up). Second, both Graham and I situated ourselves in relation to this work. Third (in this section), I provide an outline of the chapter as well as some background points to help set up the chapter's core argument. Fourth, I will outline the chapter's core argument. Fifth, Graham and I will apply this argument in the context of Canadian copyright law.

I will proceed by offering a few basic background points for those less familiar with the situation in Canada. These background points are helpful in setting up my argument, which I outline in the following pages. As Canada transitioned from a colony with illegitimate claims over Indigenous territories and peoples to a Nation, it did so in a peculiar manner. Rather than returning colonialism's plunder to Indigenous peoples, those takings were passed on to those Europeans who were recently on native land. As a result, Indigenous peoples' storied history and place in the world has had to negotiate with these newly settled forms of colonial power before being allowed to "emerge" through institutional recognition as lawful, constitutionally significant entities. Lacking the comprehensive economic, political, or military might required to be taken seriously by imperial power, Indigenous pleas for justice have taken on, for the most part, a normative, moral dimension. Many of these pleas are taken up and channeled into a human rights discourse.

As Samuel Moyn suggests, in our post-1989 moment, human rights represent humanity's last utopia. [11] There is no discussion of regime change in Canada, as we understand that replacing a violent governance structure with a new more egalitarian one is not how we are allowed to imagine our utopias. Rather, we accede to the idea that

---

10   Gordon Christie, "Aboriginal Rights, Aboriginal Culture, and Protection" (1998) 36 Osgoode Hall LJ 447; Val Napoleon, Rebecca Johnson, Richard Overstall, Debra McKenzie, eds, *Indigenous Intellectual Property* (Toronto: University of Toronto Press, 2024); James [Sa'ke'j] Youngblood Henderson, "The Indigenous Domain and Intellectual Property Rights" (2021) 4 Lakehead Law Journal 93.

11   Samuel Moyn, *The Last Utopia* (Harvard University Press, 2012). Moyne argues that human rights emerged in the 1970s as a foundational ideology and political concept, in part because of broad disillusionment with revolutionary alternatives (chapter 4) and the parallel decline of other political ideologies such as socialism and anti-colonial nationalism (chapter 6).

a new regime will be subject to the same set of global conditions that contorted the old one toward violence. The old regime—created through violence—remains in place, its structure and institutions intact. The avenue through which we enliven our utopic ideals within the state's social, political, and legal institutions, is one of rights. Rights are the small compromise that the nation state makes to secure the legitimacy of its claims to sovereignty. But do they really represent our last utopia? We know that rights are the stuff of legal argumentation and doctrine. They are designed to test the validity of rights claims and balance them against the more entrenched interests of the state. The warriors in this new world are lawyers, legislators, judges—perhaps we can call them the "word warriors" Dale Turner spoke of some time ago.[12] My question here, the first question I invite you to ponder with me, is whether rights, in their Aboriginal variant and more generally when engaged by Indigenous peoples, are moving us toward a defensible liberal ideal? Do these rights represent an opportunity to unwind the asymmetrical relations associated with imperialism and colonial relations, leading to a more just set of relations? Or does this rights discourse and its associated doctrinal paraphernalia allow the story of dominance and subordination to continue with reduced friction, or worse, toward its conclusion? My view is the latter. As such, I think we face an urgent imperative to think beyond rights in seeking to improve the conditions of the world we share in common. So let me start with James Tully's seminal work on citizenship, *Public Philosophy in a New Key*.[13]

The Rights Framework as a Platform on which to Operationalize the Logic of Elimination

Let's begin with the observation that citizenship is plural. In citizens we find a diverse set of allegiances and commitments to separate, distinct forms of authority—perhaps we can think of them as sovereigns—with

---

12   Dale Turner, *This is Not a Peace Pipe* (University of Toronto Press, 2006).

13   James Tully, *Public Philosophy in a New Key Vol. 1 and 2* (Cambridge University Press, 2008). In Chapter 9 volume 2, "On local and Global Citizenship: An Apprenticeship Manual," at 243, Tully offers a unique way of understanding citizenship that is plural and accounts for diverse modes of citizenship on global and local registers. He refers to this mode of citizenship as "glocal," and he argues that "this mode of citizenship has the capacity to overcome Imperialism of the present age and bring a democratic world into being." In this chapter we are engaging the concept of citizenship in settler colonial contexts similarly, with the hope that these ideas may open up new and productive spaces to disrupt contemporary forms of empire.

local, national, and/or transnational dimensions and that source their legitimacy in distinct historical and normative locations.[14] These authorities come into being as a result of citizens' shared histories of belonging to one another and the normative commitments arising from those intersubjective spaces. It is these commitments that inform their collective aspirations and give shape to the dynamic contours of Indigenous sovereignty and collective obligation. This is where we find law on the grounded fields of lived experience.

The second proposition is to say that a critical first step of the settler colonial project was to eliminate the multiplicity of sovereigns that preceded European arrival. The basic argument has two parts. The first is to suggest that the settler state adopts a legal centralist view of law. Within the legal centralist framework, according to John Griffiths, "law is and should be the law of the state, uniform for all persons, exclusive of all other law, and administered by a single set of state institutions."[15] The second step of the argument is to say that, within the ideological frame of a legal centralist, the legitimate existence of the settler state as a nation state demands the elimination of competing Indigenous legal authorities. The point to highlight here is that it is Indigenous law that supports Indigenous peoples' territorial claims. Therefore, to the extent that it is understood as legitimate, Indigenous law would pre-empt the settler state's claim to Indigenous lands and people. Absent some form of agreement, or conquest, state law would have no force or effect on Indigenous peoples and their territories. The point here is that the strength of the settler state's sovereign and centralized assertions and the strength of Indigenous law are inversely related. The expansion of one requires the retraction of the other. Eliminating Indigenous law or at least thinning it out is a jurispathic precondition of the entire settler colonial project. As Audra Simpson and others working with settler colonial studies tell us, "[c]olonialism survives in a settler form" and it aims (although in Simpson's view ultimately fails) to "eliminate Indigenous people; take all their land; absorb them into a white, property-owning body politic".[16]

In Canada, as we all know, the diminishment of Indigenous law has been achieved with reference to a *terra nullius* logic that presumed Indigenous lands to be empty of an authority equivalent to those imagined in Europe. It is true that Indigenous authority was acknowledged

---

14   See, for instance, Joanne Barker, ed, *Sovereignty Matters* (University of Nebraska Press, 2006).

15   John Griffiths, "What is Legal Pluralism" (1986) 18 J Legal Plur 1 at 3.

16   Audra Simpson, *Mohawk Interruptus* (Duke University Press, 2014) at 7–8.

in the pre and early settlement period of colonization. We see clear acknowledgement of this in the early peace and friendship treaties, and the Treaty of Niagara, and it is embedded in the two-row wampum model of shared authority. But as the colonial project turned to settlement and the establishment of a robust Westphalian state, these sovereigns and the plurality they represented became less tolerable. The move at this point was to topple these competing sovereigns, first with a universal history narrative that placed Indigenous peoples on a lower rung of universalised human social development, and later to impose an abstract, contractual conception of law and justice within the state. In this updated model, all legislative power and formal decision-making authority would be exhaustively vested in the nation state.

To a large extent Indigenous sovereigns did fall. What remains of them is significantly diminished. [17] The contemporary existence of these "sovereigns" continues to interrupt and burden Canadian authority, but they do not present a realistic or viable alternative to it and have not done so for some time. Within this constitutional imaginary, Indigenous peoples are treated as subjects of the constitutional order — as a matter to be regulated rather than as a partner authority. The point I want to emphasize is that in this period, Indigenous peoples were not citizens with access to the set of democratic and human rights and freedoms associated with citizenship in the liberal state.

The third proposition highlights the failure of the settler state's elimination imperative. While this earlier period effectively subordinated the formalized sites of Indigenous sovereignty, the isolation and containment of Indigenous peoples in this period served to sustain an Indigenous civic imaginary and practice. While Indigenous institutions of governance and social order were significantly diminished by state policy, the state's resort to violence, paternalism, and forced isolation worked also to generate a counter imperative of Indigenous survivance [18] under which Indigenous peoples would embed the longstanding forms of relationality on the registers of culture and everyday practice. The paternalistic wardship model of Indian policy targeted Indigenous governing structures as means of clearing the land of competing sovereign

---

17   There is, of course, a scale where some groups have done better than others to hold onto and practice traditional forms of governance. Generally speaking, those nations who experience more independence are those that have successfully leaned into capitalist forms of economic development.

18   I am drawing on Gerald Vizenor's concept of survivance. See generally Gerald Vizenor, *Survivance* (University of Nebraska Press, 2008).

authority. But this policy did not do so well at addressing the authoritative source of those competing sovereigns—the shared normative commitments of Indigenous citizens to recall the land, the stories, and the histories that rationalized their now "intolerable" sovereignty. Without a functional institutional framework, this sovereignty would manifest in the fields of practiced engagement with the land, the stories of belonging and how to belong, the appropriate registers of authority, and the limits of that authority in everyday social life. Absent formalized institutional expression, this field would be characterized as cultural rather than political and legal. Culture, stripped of its political and legal dimensions, would be reduced to a topic of consideration thought to be firmly within the settler state's sovereign regulatory framework.

My fourth and final proposition—and this is where the argument turns bleak—is that the general rights framework within the liberal state has constructed a new and dangerously effective platform on which to operationalize the logic of elimination. I have spoken of this concern in the context of comprehensive Aboriginal Rights agreements in "Turning Sideways" and "Hoquotist" to make the point that Aboriginal rights are working much more effectively than other settler colonial strategies to draw us, our jurisgenerative imagination and practice, and our civic commitments, into the settler colonial framework of authority. In the next section of this chapter, Graham and I will build on this discussion to explore whether similar processes can be seen in the context of Canadian copyright law.

The (Copy)right Framework as a Platform on which to Operationalize the Logic of Elimination?

The first proposition as noted above is that citizenship is plural; that citizens have a diverse set of allegiances and commitments to separate, distinct forms of authority (sovereigns); and that these sovereigns come into being because of citizens' shared histories of belonging to one another, as well as the normative commitments informing collective aspirations and giving shape to collective obligation. The role played by, for example, stories, symbols, songs, images, dances, and belongings in bringing sovereigns into being cannot be understated. Shared histories are reflected, constructed, remembered, given life, and kept alive through these forms of expression, which often take on an intersubjective and sacred character and are understood to possess their own independent agency. Similarly, these complex forms of expression function to articulate and affirm citizens' collective aspirations and are the traditional material through which a sense of collective obligation is built, re-built, repaired, and maintained. The way in which these forms of expression are performed—who is permitted to tell stories, to wear masks, to display images and songs, to dance, and to hold and use belongings—is regulated by a multiplicity of laws, and under several independent but intertwined legal traditions, including Indigenous legal traditions and Canada's copyright laws. These background laws perform various functions, depending on the legal tradition. Canadian copyright law might direct us to consider who, under this law, is considered the owner of expression (along with the question of whether copyright subsists at all). It also provides for the rights of both owners and users to access or engage with the expression. Indigenous laws might guide interaction with an agentic object and assist us in our efforts to lawfully interpret the being/object/expression. Indigenous laws may also assist in the development of collective interpretations of the complex expression to which they relate, perhaps helping to fashion and refashion the histories, aspirations, and obligations that inform the foundations of Indigenous sovereignty. While these laws may support each other, they may also be in tension or in direct conflict.

Under the second proposition as outlined above, the settler state adopts a legal centralist view of law; this view of law casts Indigenous law as non-existent for the most part and centers its analytical gaze on the law of the state. Where Indigenous law might exist, it is seen as "hierarchically subordinate" and tolerated as a holdover from pre-colonial times. [19] The legal centralists' objective now is to fully integrate Indigenous law into the broader legal structures of the state and on terms cognizable to common law thinkers. The core idea is that society should be moving toward a place where all law is state law, unified within the state's institutions, and applied equally to all citizens. I have framed this process above as eliminatory and justified by a *terra nullius* logic that presumes Indigenous law as primitive, and therefore lacking the sophistication needed to deal with complex social issues arising in modern, contemporary times.

Canada's copyright regime can be understood as driven by legal centralist presumptions. In Canada, laws regulating expression that can be considered to be copyright matter are the laws of the state, expressed primarily through the vehicle of the *Copyright Act*. This is

---

19   John Griffiths, "What Is Legal Pluralism" (1986) 18 J Legal Plur 1 at 3.

reflected in s. 89 of the *Copyright Act*, which provides that "[n]o person is entitled to copyright otherwise than under and in accordance with this Act or any other Act of Parliament, but nothing in this section shall be construed as abrogating any right or jurisdiction in respect of a breach of trust or confidence." It is also reflected in statements by courts that "[i]n Canada, copyright is a creature of statute and the rights and remedies provided by the *Copyright Act* are exhaustive." [20] These statements, both legislative and judicial, are rooted in an attempt to clarify that there is no common law copyright that exists outside of the *Copyright Act*; all laws relating to copyright are those of the state expressed through legislation. However, these statements also serve to foreclose or severely constrain the application of other competing authorities, including Indigenous legal authorities. While this may not have been the intention of the state in relation to copyright, it is arguably an outcome of the process of centralization of copyright first as a matter of state law, and second under the authority of Parliament. [21]

Also consistent with legal centralist presumptions is the idea that the *Copyright Act* applies uniformly to all citizens of the state. This approach to copyright is increasingly being challenged by scholars who highlight the many ways in which copyright's benefits and burdens are distributed unequally. [22] These scholars also highlight how copyright legislation is not neutral but is in fact imbued with a specific set of values and perspectives rooted in western legal traditions and in liberal (and neo-liberal) ideas of possessive individualism and private property. [23]

Above it is noted how one mechanism through which Indigenous sovereignty, citizenship, and law has been diminished is through

---

20   See *Théberge v. Galerie d'Art du Petit Champlain inc.*, [2002] 2 S.C.R. 336, 2002 SCC 34, at para 5; *Bishop v. Stevens*, 1990 CanLII 75 (SCC), [1990] 2 S.C.R. 467, at 477; *Compo Co. v. Blue Crest Music Inc.*, 1979 CanLII 6 (SCC), [1980] 1 S.C.R. 357, at 373.

21   *Constitution Act, 1867*, s. 91(23).

22   See, for instance, Margaret Chon, "Intellectual Property and Critical Methods," in Irene Calboli and Maria Lillà Montagnani, eds, *Handbook of Intellectual Property Research* (Oxford University Press, 2021); Carys Craig, "Critical Copyright Law & the Politics of 'IP'," in Emilios Christodoulidis, Ruth Dukes, & Marco Goldoni, eds, *Research Handbook on Critical Legal Theory* (Edward Elgar Publishing, 2019) at 301; John Tehranian, "Towards a Critical IP Theory: Copyright, Consecration & Control" (2012) Brigham Young University Law Review 1233; Anjali Vats and Deirdré A. Keller, "Critical Race Theory as Intellectual Property Methodology," in Irene Calboli and Maria Lillà Montagnani, eds, *Handbook of Intellectual Property Research* (Oxford University Press, 2021); Laura A. Foster, *Situating Feminism, Patent Law, and the Public Domain*, 20 Columbia Journal Gender & Law 262 (2011).

23   See, for instance, Carys Craig, *Copyright, Communication, and Culture* (Northampton, Edward Elgar: 2011).

reference to a *terra nullius* logic. This logic is well known to have been applied in the context of Indigenous territorial claims.[24] It has also been applied in copyright contexts, under which for instance stories, symbols, images, dances, and belongings are presumed to be artful expressions, empty of authority equivalent to those imagined in Europe.[25] This presumption is false. Gregory Younging writes how Indigenous laws support Indigenous peoples' claims not just to territory but also to many stories, crests, songs, and teachings that animate or give meaning to those claims.[26] As such, Indigenous laws preempt the settler state's claim to be able to delineate the rights and obligations relating to these stories, crests, songs, and teachings. In the absence of a recognized Indigenous sovereign, however, power and authority in relation to these modes of expression are assumed by the Canadian state and regulated through the mechanism of the *Copyright Act* or other relevant pieces of legislation.

The incompatibility between Indigenous norms and western copyright regimes has been well established, leading to an additional layer of loss for Indigenous peoples and communities.[27] For various reasons including copyright's fixation requirement, term limits, and a privileging of ideas of individual authorship, many mediums of expression created or stewarded by Indigenous individuals or communities do not qualify for protection under the *Copyright Act.*[28] In the absence

---

24   See, for instance, John Borrows, "The Durability of Terra Nullius: Tsilhqot'in Nation v British Columbia" (2015) 48 UBC Law Review 701.

25   Gregory Younging, "Traditional Knowledge Exists; Intellectual Property Is Invented or Created" (2015) 36 Univ. Pennsylvania Journal of International Law 1077 at 1079.

26   Gregory Younging, "Traditional Knowledge Exists; Intellectual Property Is Invented or Created" (2015) 36 Univ. Pennsylvania Journal of International Law 1077 at 1079.

27   See, for instance, Chidi Oguamanam, "Rethinking copyright for Indigenous creative works" (2017) Policy Options, online: https://policyoptions.irpp.org/magazines/june-2017/rethinking-copyright-Indigenous-creative-works/; Innovation, Science and Economic Development Canada, "Introduction to Intellectual Property Rights and the Protection of Indigenous Knowledge and Cultural Expressions in Canada" (2020), online: https://ised-isde.canada.ca/site/intellectual-property-strategy/en/introduction-intellectual-property-rights-and-protection-Indigenous-knowledge-and-cultural.

28   See, for instance, Marie Battiste and James Youngblood (Sa'Ke'j) Henderson, *Protecting Indigenous Knowledge: A Global Challenge* (UBC Press, 2000); James (Sa'Ke'j) Youngblood Henderson, "The Indigenous Domain and Intellectual Property Rights" (2021) 4 Lakehead Law Journal 93; Ruth Okediji, "Traditional Knowledge and the Public Domain" (2018) Centre for International Governance Innovation Papers No. 176, online: https://www.cigionline.org/sites/default/files/documents/Paper%20no.176web.pdf.

of protection, copyright law permits this expression to be appropriated and used without the need to seek or receive permission from the appropriate sources of authority.[29] This further underscores the way in which Indigenous peoples have been denied access to the set of democratic and human rights and freedoms associated with citizenship in the liberal state. Indigenous norms were clearly not considered by the copyright drafters at the outset, when Indigenous people were subjects of the state, rather than citizens. Now, as Indigenous people are citizens of the state and experience the blunt application of copyright legislation, they have called for reform.[30]

Under the third proposition outlined above, the isolation and containment of Indigenous peoples served to sustain an Indigenous civic imaginary and practice and to generate a counter imperative of Indigenous survivance. In the absence of an Indigenous institutional framework, sovereignty has manifested in fields including practiced engagement with the land and stories of belonging and how to belong. The state views these fields as material governed under copyright law; as culture capable of being owned, licensed, or assigned. However, they are intimately connected to Indigenous ontologies, to structures of governance and belonging, and to land. As Younging has emphasized:

> In some Indigenous Nations the abstract subtlety of Indigenous customary law is indivisible from cultural expressions such as stories, designs, and songs. That is, a story may have an underlying principle of environmental law or natural resource planning. A song may explain the custodial relationship that a certain community has with a particular animal species. A design may be a symbol that expresses sovereignty over a territory or the social hierarchy of a Nation's clan system. A watchman's pole may be considered an assertion of Aboriginal title, tell a story of a historical figure, or have a sacred significance.[31]

29   See, for instance, Marie Battiste and James Youngblood (Sa'Ke'j) Henderson, *Protecting Indigenous Knowledge: A Global Challenge* (UBC Press, 2000); James Youngblood (Sa'Ke'j) Henderson, "The Indigenous Domain and Intellectual Property Rights" (2021) 4 Lakehead Law Journal 93; Ruth Okediji, "Traditional Knowledge and the Public Domain" (2018) Centre for International Governance Innovation Papers No. 176, online: https://www.cigionline.org/sites/default/files/documents/Paper%20no.176web.pdf.
30   See, for instance, Andrea Bear Nicholas, "Who Owns Indigenous Cultural and Intellectual Property" (2017) Policy Options, online: https://policyoptions.irpp.org/magazines/june-2017/who-owns-Indigenous-cultural-and-intellectual-property/.
31   Gregory Younging, "Traditional Knowledge Exists; Intellectual Property is Invented

Resurfacing and highlighting the structures of governance and belonging that are entwined with these works serves to further emphasize the inappropriateness of copyright law, which requires the identification of an owner and is grounded in economic concepts including a "dollars and cents" logic[32] as the governing regulatory framework.

The fourth proposition outlined above suggests that the general rights framework available to Indigenous peoples as state citizens has generated a new (and more effective) platform to support the logic of elimination, in that it serves to draw Indigenous peoples and communities into the settler colonial frameworks of authority. Under this approach, rights are seen as the only way to interpret the juridical self. These processes can be seen to apply in the context of Canadian copyright law. Indigenous peoples may choose to engage with the Canadian copyright regime for a host of reasons, including but not limited to the desire to use this regime as a mechanism through which to gain protections that can be asserted against corporate, institutional, or state interests.[33] While Indigenous peoples may benefit from engaging with the copyright regime in such a manner, there are also costs to doing so. For one, the dominant conception of copyright views expression as matter that can be owned and controlled by one party, within the limits of the relevant legislation. Viewing expression through this lens may impact the way in which Indigenous peoples relate to this expression and may complicate the relationship between land and its beings as manifested in the expression. Moreover, by relying on the *Copyright Act* as the primary mechanism through which to protect Indigenous modes of expression (or other interests), the power of Indigenous institutions and sources of authority that would otherwise be able to speak to and address these issues lies inactive and perhaps even dormant. This results in the capacity of Indigenous institutions to deal with such issues of day-to-day importance being diminished, ultimately leading to the undermining of Indigenous sovereignties and the forms of authority that operationalize them.

---

or Created" (2015) 36 Univ. Pennsylvania Journal of International Law 1077 at 1081.

32   *Théberge v. Galerie d'Art du Petit Champlain*, 2002 SCC 34 at para 15.

33   See, for instance, Innovation, Science and Economic Development Canada, "Introduction to Intellectual Property Rights and the Protection of Indigenous Knowledge and Cultural Expressions in Canada" (2020), online: https://ised-isde. canada.ca/site/intellectual-property-strategy/en/introduction-intellectual-property-rights-and-protection-Indigenous-knowledge-and-cultural.

A similar argument can be applied in response to efforts to modify the existing copyright regime to provide greater protection for Indigenous modes of expression. A significant body of work engages with the question of how the copyright regime can be modified so that Indigenous modes of expression are given protection under the existing rights structure.[34] Arguments based on international human rights law—including through reference to the United Nations Declaration on the Rights of Indigenous Peoples—can also be used to support claims to this effect. As described above, however, while such steps could result in greater copyright protections being available to Indigenous peoples in relation to mediums of expression that hold particular significance, proceeding in such a manner could support the logic of elimination by drawing Indigenous peoples and communities further into the settler colonial framework of authority, including its legal institutions and frameworks, and further away from Indigenous institutions and sources of authority.

To clarify, we are not advocating for the rights framework to be dispensed with—just for caution to be used when engaging with it. We seek a reorientation of thinking, under which the risks or potential harms of protecting Indigenous modes of protection through rights are made visible. Our argument is that any attempts at reform through rights should be advanced with caution. It follows from this fourth proposition that there is also a need to think beyond state-based rights, including the rights of copyright owners and users as well as international human rights, to the extent that these rights are relied upon to justify expanding the scope and coverage of the copyright regime. Instead, a just approach should be informed by an understanding of Indigenous sovereignty as robust and meaningful. Our policies—including in relation to copyright—might then aim to create spaces of autonomy and, alongside our Indigenous interlocutors, identify opportunities for Indigenous peoples to be treated as partner authorities within the regime.[35] A preliminary step moving toward this kind of partnership is to expand and strengthen Indigenous law, institutions, and authorities. This requires that we recast the legal centralist stories we tell ourselves about a unified state

---

34   See, for instance, Megan M. Carpenter, "Intellectual Property Law and Indigenous Peoples: Adapting Copyright Law to the Needs of a Global Community" (2004) 7 Yale Human Rights & Development Law Journal 51.

35   See, for instance, *Haida Nation Recognition Act*, SBC 2023, c. 24.; Jeremy Webber, "We Are Still in the Age of Encounter: Section 35 and a Canada Beyond Sovereignty," in Patrick Macklem and Douglas Sanderson, eds, *From Recognition to Reconciliation* (Toronto: University of Toronto Press, 2016).

sovereign and allow more honest, plural, and de-colonial conceptions of authority to take hold and provide the resources to move past the imperial structure of our present toward an authentic collaborative partnership. For several decades, scholars including Gordon Christie, Val Napoleon, and James [Sa'ke'j] Youngblood Henderson have advocated for such an approach.[36] Our work builds on their efforts. This needs to be a focus of discussion in the context of copyright law — and intellectual property law more broadly — both nationally and internationally.

Conclusion

Since the 1970s onward, the primary mechanism that has been relied upon to address inequities in society has been the vehicle of rights.[37] This chapter illustrates the risk to Indigenous sovereignty of relying solely on rights as the primary mechanism for achieving just outcomes in the context of issues in which copyright may be engaged. While benefits may flow to Indigenous people and communities from engaging with the *Copyright Act* either as structured or as it may be amended, the result is to draw Indigenous peoples and communities further into settler colonial frameworks of authority. While both individuals and communities may find relief as a result of their engagement with the *Copyright Act*, they may also find themselves working within a set of logics that make it easier to transition to forms of imposed citizenship that don't leave much space for themselves or for the legal world that preceded it. Ultimately, this risks diminishing the capacity of Indigenous institutions and sources of authority that might otherwise address these claims, leading to the undermining of Indigenous sovereignties and the forms of authority that operationalize them. This is not to say

---

36   Gordon Christie, "Aboriginal Rights, Aboriginal Culture, and Protection" (1998) 36 Osgoode Hall LJ 447; Val Napoleon, Rebecca Johnson, Richard Overstall, and Debra McKenzie, eds, *Indigenous Intellectual Property* (Toronto: University of Toronto Press, 2024); James (Sa'Ke'j) Youngblood Henderson, "The Indigenous Domain and Intellectual Property Rights" (2021) 4 Lakehead Law Journal 93.

37   Samuel Moyne identifies the 1970s as the time when the concept of rights ascended to hegemonic levels because of global geopolitical factors. Locally, in the Nuu-chah-nulth context, we can think of Canada's post-1969 White Paper policies that began to shift away from the exercise of unilateral federal discretion to address Indigenous peoples' place within the Canadian constitutional imaginary toward fixes based on defining a subset of Aboriginal rights within Canada's constitutional system (Canada, Department of Indian and Northern Affairs, "Statement of the Government of Canada on Indian Policy" (1969) [White Paper], online: http://epe. lac-bac.gc.ca/100/200/301/inac-ainc/indian_policy-e/cp1969_e.pdf).

that Indigenous peoples and communities should not engage with the *Copyright Act*; there are protections that can be secured through engagement with this regime. Rather, Indigenous peoples and communities should proceed with an awareness of the imperial pitfalls that pervade our theorizations of rights in this area. Furthermore, given the potential cost to Indigenous sovereignty of engaging solely with settler law, this chapter has highlighted the importance of seeking out ways through which to create spaces of autonomy for Indigenous peoples in the context of copyright, for instance by expanding and strengthening Indigenous law, institutions, and authorities in this area. In light of this analysis, we believe that the time has come to think differently.

Part IV
TECHNOLOGY AND
INTELLECTUAL PROPERTY

International Source Code Secrecy and the Characterization of Intellectual Property as National Security

Anthony D. Rosborough

Abstract

This chapter explores the emergence of source code secrecy rules in Free Trade Agreements (FTAs) and their implications for the future of intellectual property (IP). Rooted in geopolitical rivalry, these rules are framed as safeguards for national security and cybersecurity but carry significant potential social, economic, and environmental costs.

It traces the historical and geopolitical contexts that have shaped the rise of source code secrecy. Given that software-dependent technologies are now the dominant modality of innovation, the chapter highlights the impact of source code secrecy on domestic regulatory oversight, innovation, the right to repair, and equitable technology transfer to least-developed countries.

The larger theme addressed is the growing entanglement of intellectual property with national security, evidencing a shift from private economic rights to IP's appropriation for state control and geopolitical positioning. This securitization precludes the public interest dimensions of intellectual property. In turn, this undermines the TRIPS bargain and limits governmental discretion to pursue public interest objectives, such as fostering open innovation and knowledge dissemination.

Through an interdisciplinary analysis, the chapter critiques the opacity of source code governance and its negative impacts on democratic accountability, participatory innovation, the right to repair, and development-oriented global technology transfer. It argues that the gradual characterization of IP as national security risks exacerbating global inequities in access to technology and knowledge. The chapter concludes with a call for collective resistance and advocating for intellectual property norms that prioritize decentralized innovation, transparency, accountability, and the broader public interest.

N ot too long ago, computers were clunky boxes; distinct machines designed for specific tasks and applications. A "computer" was a collection of grey plastic-encased hardware that assisted with word processing, spreadsheets, and perhaps the occasional game of solitaire. The monitor, keyboard, mouse, and other peripherals made for a rigid and static user interface. This effectively limited access and use cases to stationary, indoor settings, and required the user to choose the manner and duration of use. And while the internet greatly expanded upon the functionality of personal computers, cyberspace took the shape of a separate and distinct realm for rulemaking, commerce, and other profit-maximizing pursuits. Transformative as this was, cyberspace was established as a parallel virtual environment that was functionally cordoned off from "real space," as Lessig put it.[1]

But today's computing paradigm is the result of an enormous technological shift from distinct and static systems to dynamic, dispersed, and interconnected devices and sensors where data and analytics provide users with predictions and insights. As the result of smaller and more energy-efficient hardware, computers are now embedded and integrated into seemingly everything that surrounds us. Ubiquitous and pervasive computing is now the paradigm that tethers[2] together our personal and wearable devices, appliances, homes, cars, public utilities, infrastructure, and larger physical environments.[3] As the result of an embodied virtuality, there is now far less distinction between cyberspace and real-world spaces than there once was.[4] As Mirielle Hildebrandt aptly proclaims, we now live in an "onlife world."[5]

---

1   Lawrence Lessig, *Code Version 2.0* (New York: Basic Books, 2006) at 6.

2   Chris Jay Hoofnagle, Aniket Kesari, & Aaron Perzanowski, "The Tethered Economy" (2019) 87:4 Geo Wash L Rev 783 at 788–792.

3   Adam Greenfield, *Everyware: The Dawning Age of Ubiquitous Computing* (Berkeley: Pearson Education, 2006) at 35–43.

4   Jerry Kang & Dana Cuff, "Pervasive Computing: Embedding the Public Sphere" (2005) 62:1 Wash & Lee L Rev 93–146 at 94–95.

5   Mireille Hildebrandt, *Smart Technologies and the End(s) of Law: Novel Entanglements of Law and Technology* (Northampton: Edward Elgar, 2015) at 41–64.

This chapter illustrates that an important consequence of these transformations in computing is a gradual recharacterization of the role and function of intellectual property rights, the values underpinning them, and the contexts in which they are asserted. Threats to exclusive rights in software and related intangibles no longer present merely economic risks or profit losses. Rather, in the tethered and ubiquitous computing context, exclusive rights in software serve to gatekeep who may access and control computing systems that form far-reaching networks—often including tangible objects and devices. Whether it is a facial recognition surveillance system used for border security or network-connected agricultural equipment that reports farm data to its manufacturer, intellectual property is increasingly invoked to leverage the exclusive economic rights in intangibles (namely, software) as absolute functional controls over embodied physical systems.[6]

Parallel to these new domains of intellectual property governance, this chapter points to the gradual transformation of intellectual property (insofar as it relates to computing and software) from a system of economic incentives and rights to a vehicle for ensuring opaqueness, secrecy, and security of technologies. It explores the shifting values that underly this transformation. To contextualize this shift, it looks at trade secrecy and technological protection measures (TPMs) in relation to software that have been increasingly invoked upon national security-related rationales. These invocations have often achieved ends entirely unrelated to the exercise of economic rights.[7] These instances follow copyright's gradual shift from a regime governing works, performers' performances, communication signals, and sound recordings, to one governing use and access to technologies.[8] In focusing on an

6   See, e.g., Maurizio Borghi & Benjamin White, "Data Extractivism and Public Access to Algorithms" in Maurizio Borghi & Roger Brownsword, eds., *Law, Regulation and Governance in the Information Society* (London: Routledge, 2022) at 122–125 where the authors note that "[t]he source of value is now a further layer of information which exceeds *both* the informational content as such, *and* the organization thereof: value is directly extracted from the *human interaction* with information and the vast amount of data that is generated by such relentless interaction."

7   The cybersecurity and public safety rationales for prohibiting a whole host of activities involving tangible devices has been asserted by manufacturers of agricultural equipment, medical equipment, and consumer electronics for justifying implementations of technological protection measures under copyright law that bear no relationship to infringement or exclusive rights of authors. For an example of this, see *infra* note 114.

8   For a detailed analysis of the gradual shift in copyright law from a regime protecting content to one managing *rights in content*, see Zohar Efroni, *Access-Right: The Future of Digital Copyright Law* (Oxford: OUP, 2011) at 125–154.

acute example of this phenomenon, this chapter looks to source code secrecy provisions as enshrined in recent bilateral and plurilateral free-trade agreements (FTA source code secrecy). These provisions prohibit states from requiring the transfer or access to software's source code or algorithms as a precondition for the import, sale, distribution, or use of software or "products containing software." They impose new restraints on the use and access to software that transcend the existing framework of intellectual property rights and in doing so invoke significant social costs.

The second part begins with a brief history of FTA source code secrecy, the geopolitical tensions acting as impetus for it, and some recent implementations found in "digital trade" chapters of FTAs. The following section then discusses these rules' deeper misalignment with intellectual property doctrine and the role of FTAs in creating *sui generis* rights in relation to software and algorithms. It surveys a selection of social costs imposed by source code secrecy, including the suppression of competition and innovative processes (including the right to repair), hand-tying states' ability to inspect and interrogate systems that may present public harms, and the potential to further weaken intellectual property's promised global development role through impairing technology transfer and the dissemination of knowledge. Finally, the last part argues that the misalignment between FTA source code secrecy and intellectual property doctrine can be understood as an extension of a longstanding, troubling, and growing value underpinning the global intellectual property system: national security.[9] "Intellectual property as security" views the primary role and function of intellectual property quite differently from the conventional utilitarian incentives, rewards for investment/labour, or protection of authorial personality. Instead, the security rationale for intellectual property views its primary purpose as a *regulatory tool for maximizing security of the state*.[10] In analyzing FTA source code secrecy, a prominent example, the chapter's overall contention is that national security may become a dominant characterization of intellectual property, shaping its development at the global

---

9   Peter Drahos, "Immoral Intangibles: Engaging with Ned Snow's *Intellectual Property and Immorality*" (2023) 28:1 Jerusalem Review of Legal Studies 124–143 at 140.

10   In making this argument, this chapter builds primarily upon David S Levine, "Bring in the Nerds: Secrecy, National Security, and the Creation of International Intellectual Property Law" (2012) 30 Cardozo Arts & Entertainment Law Journal 105–152; and Debora Halbert, "Intellectual Property Theft and National Security: Agendas and Assumptions" (2016) 32:4 The Information Society 256–268.

level. It warns that in the future, intellectual property's public interest and global development ideals may be further neglected in pursuit of national security objectives, undermining access to knowledge and participatory innovation.

International Source Code Secrecy

In recent years, free-trade agreements (FTAs) have commonly sought to address various aspects of the digital economy with so-called "digital trade" chapters. The provisions included in these chapters vary and are far reaching, but generally address subjects such as cross-border data flow, personal information protection, and consumer protection in relation to online platforms.[11] In a small but growing number of FTAs[12], digital trade chapters have begun to include "source code" provisions. These provisions prohibit states from requiring the transfer of, or access to, "source code of software" or to "an algorithm expressed in that source code" as a condition for the import, distribution, sale, or use of that software, or of "products containing that software."[13] For example, Article 19.16 of the Canada-United States-Mexico Agreement (CUSMA) stipulates that:

> No Party shall require the transfer of, or access to, a source code of software owned by a person of another Party, or to an algorithm expressed in that source code, as a condition for the import, distribution, sale or use of that software, or of products containing that software, in its territory.

---

11   "Cross-border data flow" refers to data collected from users in one jurisdiction to freely flow to another for aggregation and analytics, which digital trade chapters in FTAs ordinarily permit. See, e.g., Organization for Economic Co-Operation and Development (OECD), "Cross-Border Data Flows: Taking Stock of Key Policies and Initiatives" (2022) at 11–13, online: https://www.oecd-ilibrary.org/docserver/5031dd97-en.pdf?expires=1706718441&id=id&accname=guest&checksum=A34702477DC56214D6B6C27B130CE33C

12   See, e.g., The Japan-Mongolia Economic Partnership Agreement (2015), Art 9.11; The EU-Japan Economic Partnership Agreement (2018), Art 8.73; The EU-UK Trade and Cooperation Agreement (2020), Art 207; Comprehensive and Progressive Agreement for Trans-Pacific Partnership (2018) (CPTPP), Art 14.17; The Indonesia-Australia Comprehensive Economic Partnership Agreement (IA-CEPA) (2020), Art 13.13; and Agreement between the United States of America and Japan concerning Digital Trade (2019) (US-JAPAN), Art 17.

13   Protocol replacing the North American Free Trade Agreement with the Agreement between Canada, the United States of America, and the United Mexican States, 30 November 2018, Can TS 2020/5 (entered into force 1 July 2020), Art 19.16 [CUSMA].

Similar wording is found in the Comprehensive and Progressive Agreement for Trans-Pacific Partnership (CPTPP) and other agreements, albeit with minor differences. [14] For example, some agreements include exceptions where states may require access or transfer of source code for "software used in critical infrastructure," and others permit required disclosure of source code as part of a freely negotiated commercial contract. The more recent provisions are more of a blanket ban and omit these caveats altogether. [15] Overall, the effect of these provisions is to prohibit states from requiring disclosure or access to source code, effectively granting additional protections and safeguards to private owners in a manner that transcends existing intellectual property doctrine and legal frameworks. This can be understood as a shield protecting source code from expropriation. In some ways FTA source code secrecy operates similarly to TPMs, only instead of imposing *technological* means of supplementary protection, the means are derived from treaty obligations. Common to both, however, is that states are acting to provide an additional layer of protection for rightsholders.

The Importance of Source Code

To understand the broader significance of these source code secrecy provisions, it is worth briefly sketching a picture of what source code is and why it is given such prominence in FTAs. At a basic level, "source code" is a representation of a computer program in high, level human, readable language. [16] It is normally the version of software as originally written. [17] This can be distinguished from object code, [18] which is produced when source code is translated into a machine-readable language understandable by a computer such as a binary of ones and

---

14   For example, the CPTPP's source code provision is somewhat narrower than CUSMA's in that the secrecy obligations are limited to "mass-market software or products containing such software and do not include software used for critical infrastructure."

15   Jane Kelsey, "Digital Trade Rules and Big Tech: Surrendering Public Good to Private Power" (2020) *Public Services International* at 16, online: https://pop-umbrella. s3.amazonaws.com/uploads/f2bddc3d-c353-4846-a23b-82dec9a9e6d7_2020_-_ ASIA_DIG_REPORT_3__1_.pdf.

16   Reiffen v Microsoft Corp., 214 F.3d 1342, 1344 (Fed. Cir. 2000) (United States).

17   "Source Code Definition", *Linux Information Project* (14 February 2006), online: https://www.linfo.org/source_code.html#:~:text=Source%20code%20(also%20 referred%20to,human%20readable%20alphanumeric%20characters.

18   "Object code" may be treated as synonymous with "executable code" or "machine language" for the purposes of this chapter.

zeroes.[19] In addition to the human/machine readability distinction, a further difference is that source code is generally written at a high level of abstraction and therefore agnostic to the end computing platform or hardware that it will be executed on. Object code, however, must be custom tailored to a particular computer, system, virtual environment, or platform on which it is executed.[20]

By analogy, source code is like the architectural blueprints for a building—detailing the structure's design, materials, and functionality, while object code reflects the building's physical components assembled into a tangible whole. Access to source code therefore not only enables the creation of binaries (i.e., object code), but its generality and versatility enables a whole host of secondary activities and discoveries, including bug detection and error correction, as well as modification and enhancement. Access to source code also enables the ability to reverse engineer software for other uses, platforms, and hardware for interoperability purposes.[21]

In today's world of ubiquitous computing, these wide-ranging capabilities provide immense power to those with access to source code. This power transcends traditional computing contexts and reaches into domains such as manufacturing and industrial processes, logistics and supply chain management systems, healthcare delivery, and emergency response systems.[22] The extension of source code governance into these contexts rachets higher the importance of exclusivity and control in terms of who can access, inspect, or modify it. As the primary means of production for both private industry and public infrastructure, the securitization of research and innovation in computing has in recent years become a priority for the military-industrial complex within advanced economies.[23]

19   *Guest Tek Interactive Entertainment LTD v Nomadix Inc*, 2018 FC 818 at 8–10.
20   Daniel S. Lin, Matthew Sag, & Ronald S. Laurie, "Source Code versus Object Code: Patent Implications for the Open Source Community" (2002) 18:2 Santa Clara High Technology LJ 235–258 at 238.
21   Fernando Almeida, José Oliveira, and José Cruz, "Open Standards and Open Source: Enabling Interoperability" (2011) 2:1 IJSEA at 1–11.
22   Sonia K Katyal, "The Paradox of Source Code Secrecy" (2019) 104:5 Cornell L Rev 1183 at 1194–1195.
23   See, e.g., Government of Canada, "Policy on Sensitive Technology Research and Affiliations of Concern" (January 2024) at 4, "…[T]he illicit transfer of knowledge – especially in transformational research areas such as AI, quantum computing, and genetic engineering that could have dual-use applications for military and surveillance purposes – poses major challenges to Canada and its allies."; and Jinghan Zeng, "Securitization of Artificial Intelligence in China" (2021) 0:00 The

The Impetus for Source Code Secrecy in FTAs

Source code's protection as a trade secret is not a novel proposition or unprecedented legal phenomenon. In fact, it is commonplace in the software industry and the preferred route for protection over copyright or other forms of intellectual property. The reasons for this stem from the peculiar nature of source code. Though copyright technically extends to both the source code and object code of computer programs,[24] it provides less than absolute protection. This is because copyright only extends to the original expression contained in source code and not the underlying ideas or utilitarian concepts. Yet, the latter are what provide source code with much of its value. At the same time, the power afforded to holders of source code is not tied to its reproduction or distribution (the primary focus of copyright), but rather its private and exclusive nature. It is akin to a secret recipe or the proverbial "keys to the castle."[25] Therefore, copyright law's focus on maximizing the benefits of publication and dissemination runs counter to the goal of keeping source code from prying eyes. For these reasons, trade secrecy is a common avenue for protecting source code, while copyright is preferred for protecting object code commonly distributed to end-users.[26]

Why, then, have recent FTAs carved out source code–specific secrecy rules? The reasons largely stem from perceived inadequacies of conventional trade secrecy when it comes to source code that may implicate or pose risks for national security. Though conventional trade secrecy may provide legal remedies for unauthorized appropriation, those remedies are ill-suited for curtailing the perceived risks stemming from unauthorized disclosure of code with wide-ranging end-uses, powers, and capabilities. Once source code has been unveiled, trade secrecy offers no means to put the toothpaste back in the tube, as it were. It is

Chinese Journal of International Politics at 1–29.

24   The decision to extend copyright protection to both the source code and object code of computer programs was not without considerable debate and pushback, and the consequences of this decision live with us today and form part of prominent questions of copyright law and policy, including those raised in *Oracle America Inc v Google Inc*, 750 F.3d 1139 (Fed. Cir. 2014). For the crux of this debate, see, e.g., Stephen Breyer, "The Uneasy Case for Copyright: A Study of Copyright in Books, Photocopies, and Computer Programs" (1970) 84:2 Harv L Rev 281 at 340–350; and Pamela Samuelson, "CONTU Revisited: The Case Against Copyright Protection for Computer Programs in Machine-Readable Form" (1984) Duke L J at 663–769.

25   James Gibson, "Once and Future Copyright" (2005) 81:1 Notre Dame Law Review 167 at 177.

26   Ibid at 175.

put out in the daylight for all to see, use, and modify. Whereas patents grant owners the right to exclude and prevent remaking or ongoing unauthorized uses of an invention by others, source code remains vulnerable to reverse engineering, or discovery in a single instance.[27] In response to this perceived vulnerability, the source code secrecy rules in FTAs attempt to expand upon the role and function of trade secrecy by extending it to the international realm. This prevents governments from imposing regulatory requirements that would require disclosure in the first place. In an approach that some authors have labelled "secrecy by default," FTA source code secrecy rules transcend the *ex post* structure of conventional trade secrecy (namely, a prohibition on disclosure) and instead provide guarantees of non-disclosure to governments *ex ante*.[28]

But the source code secrecy rules in FTAs represent much more than an attempt to patch perceived inadequacies in trade secrecy law to benefit technology companies. They must also be understood in the broader geopolitical context, and notably the United States and China's rivalry as technology superpowers. Featuring strongly in these dynamics has been an increasing and reciprocal skepticism from a national security and cybersecurity perspective, often resulting in bilateral ratcheting up of intellectual property for strategic national security purposes.[29] In some cases, this context has been explicit; one example being a 2013 Obama-era paper putting forward a strategy to secure new trade secrecy provisions in trade agreements to address national security concerns.[30] Understanding the values that underpin these source code secrecy rules requires an exploration of this geopolitical tension.

The precise origins of today's US-China geopolitical spat are difficult to pin down with great accuracy. Gradually over the past decade, reciprocal fears of espionage and "back doors" in computer hardware and software have grown between the United States and China; whether wielded by the United States' National Security Agency (NSA) or Huawei, the Chinese technology giant.[31] Following NSA

---

27   Jonas Anderson, "Secret Inventions" (2011) 26 Berkeley Technology Law Journal 917 at 924-925.

28   Magdalena Słok-Wódkowska & Joanna Mazur, "Secrecy by Default: How Regional Trade Agreements Reshape Protection of Source Code" (2022) 25 Journal of International Economic Law 91 at 96–98.

29   Peter Drahos, "BITS and BIPS: Bilateralism in Intellectual Property" (2001) 4 The Journal of World Intellectual Property 791.

30   Administration Strategy on Mitigating the Theft of U.S. Trade Secrets (February 2013), online: https://www.justice.gov/criminal-ccips/file/938321/download.

31   Jeremy Hsu, "U.S. Suspicions of China's Huawei Based Partly on NSA's Own

contractor Edward Snowden's document leak in 2014 revealing that US officials had successfully infiltrated Huawei's servers,[32] the Chinese government announced that it would be implementing its controversial *Cybersecurity Law*.[33] Among other things, this legal framework targets purchases of foreign software and hardware by government agencies or critical information infrastructure operators,[34] requiring that any purchases undergo a "national security review." Importantly, this review process envisions scenarios where the Chinese government may insist on being given access to source code and other intangibles held by foreign firms.[35]

Unsurprisingly, the announcement of these rules resulted in pushback from technology companies, business groups, and trade associations in the United States and around the world. In a letter spearheaded by the United States Chamber of Commerce in early 2015, a coalition of global technology companies and industry stakeholders penned a letter to Chinese authorities, raising concerns about China's approach to national security. "Sovereign interest in a secure and development-friendly cyber economy is best served, in any country [...]," the letter reads, "by policies that encourage competition and customer choice, both of which necessitate openness...as well as close collaboration between industry and government [...]."[36] But when IBM agreed to allow Chinese authorities to review certain product source codes later that year,[37] the type of open collaboration between industry and

Spy Tricks" (26 March 2014) *IEEE Spectrum*, online: https://spectrum.ieee.org/us-suspicions-of-chinas-huawei-based-partly-on-nsas-own-spy-tricks.

32   Noah Rayman, "Report: NSA Spied on Chinese Telecoms Giant" (22 March 2014) *Time Magazine*, online: https://time.com/34517/report-nsa-spied-on-chinese-telecoms-giant/.

33   Cybersecurity Law of People's Republic of China, "National People's Congress of the People's Republic of China" (7 November 2016), online: http://www.npc.gov.cn/npc/xinwen/2016-11/07/content_2001605.htm.

34   Jeremy Hsu, "China's New Rules Ask Tech Firms to Hand Over Source Code" (2 February 2015) *IEEE Spectrum*, online: https://spectrum.ieee.org/chinas-new-rules-ask-tech-firms-to-hand-over-source-code.

35   Though it should be noted that there remains some debate as to whether China's *Cybersecurity Law* actually *requires* disclosure of source code in every case, or whether it is merely envisioned as a requirement that may be imposed as part of the national security review process. See, e.g., Max Parasol, "The Impact of China's 2016 Cyber Security Law on Foreign Technology Firms, and on China's Big Data and Smart City Dreams" (2018) 34 Computer Law & Security Review 67 at 93.

36   Bill Ide, "US Firms Concerned About China's New Cyber Regulations" (29 January 2015) *Voa News*, online: https://www.voanews.com/a/us-firms-concerned-about-chinas-new-cyber-regulations/2618229.html.

37   Eva Dou, "IBM Allows Chinese Government to Review Source Code" (16

government embodied in Beijing's approach was clearly much different than what industry had hoped for.

As China formalized the national security review process and implemented its *Cybersecurity Law* over the ensuing years, suspicion, fear, and tensions gradually increased on both sides of the Pacific. Various organs of the United States government and groups of American technology companies began to overtly complain of coercive tactics by China to "pry away American intellectual property" through "state-sponsored IP theft" and "coerced technology transfer." [38] These fears and concerns were also echoed in European circles. [39] In a June 2018 report authored by the White House Office of Trade and Manufacturing Policy, the US position began to explicitly recognize source code as particularly vulnerable to involuntary disclosure:

> China uses security reviews to force foreign enterprises to dis-
> close proprietary information. At risk are source codes, encryption
> algorithms, and other sensitive IP. [I]t is likely that 'companies
> will have to submit information on [product] design and source
> codes to government-affiliated review organisations.' Similarly, the
> USTR has warned: 'Companies may be forced to disclose critical
> technologies, including source code, complete design databases,
> behaviour models, logic models, and even floor plans and physical
> layouts of central processing units.' [40]

Reflecting the increasing importance of national security, both the United States and China have since engaged in a highly publicized tit-for-tat trade war, levying tariffs on each other's imports, and resorting to increasingly protectionist policies. [41] What has emerged from this

October 2015) *The Wall Street Journal,* online: https://www.wsj.com/articles/ibm-allows-chinese-government-to-review-source-code-1444989039.

38   Lingling Wei & Bob Davis, "How China Systematically Pries Technology From U.S. Companies" (27 September 2018) *The Wall Street Journal,* online: https://www.wsj.com/articles/how-china-systematically-pries-technology-from-u-s-companies-1537972066.

39   European Chamber, "China Manufacturing 2025: Putting Industrial Policy Ahead of Market Forces" Special Report (2017) at 24 online: http://docs.dpaq.de/12007-european_chamber_cm2025-en.pdf.

40   White House Office of Trade Manufacturing Policy, "How China's Economic Aggression Threatens the Technologies and Intellectual Property of the United States and the World" (June 2018) online: https://trumpwhitehouse.archives.gov/wp-content/uploads/2018/06/FINAL-China-Technology-Report-6.18.18-PDF.pdf.

41   Howard Schneider, "Trump, Biden Policies Shifted Trade from China at a Cost, Study Shows" (26 August 2023) *Reuters,* online: https://www.reuters.com/markets/

dispute has been growing global recognition and repeated references to China's practice of forced technology transfer (FTT) and intellectual property "theft" within various international trade forums. [42]

The FTA source code secrecy rules are intended to address FTT practices; at least insofar as they relate to source code. [43] But a more nuanced understanding of what constitutes FTT is helpful here. The concept admittedly suffers from a lack of precise definition, partly because the lines between "forced" and voluntary technology transfer are not always clear. [44] Nevertheless, the concept generally refers to situations where governments compel foreign companies to share proprietary information as a condition for conducting business in the country. [45] FTT of source code falls along two lines. The first is when foreign technology companies are required to disclose their source code as part of an administrative procedure (as is the case for China's national security review process). And the second is where a foreign entity is required, as a condition of market access, to enter into a joint venture or similar arrangement with a government entity or non–arm's length organization and in the process divulge its source code. [46]

The introduction of FTA source code secrecy rules to combat FTT can be traced back as far as the 2015 with the Japan-Mongolia Economic Partnership Agreement. [47] The first clear articulation of the object and purpose of these rules, however, was made during the early days of the Trans-Pacific Partnership (TPP). Then, the United States Trade Representative (USTR) released its "Digital 2 Dozen" document that lays out the 24 key tenets of the TPP. [48] In pointing to the TPP's source code secrecy provision (Article 14.17), the document explains:

---

us/trump-biden-policies-shifted-trade-china-cost-study-shows-2023-08-26/.

42   See, e.g., European Commission, *WTO-EU's Proposals on WTO Modernisation* (5 July 2018) online: https://borderlex.net/wp-content/uploads/2018/07/2018-07-17-EU-REFORM-PROPOSALS-WTO.pdf.

43   Słok-Wódkowska & Mazur, *supra* note 1107 at 96.

44   Andrea Andrenelli, Julien Gourdon, & Evdokia Moïsé, "International Technology Transfer Policies" (2019) *OECD Trade Policy Papers*, No 222 at 6, online: https://www.oecd-ilibrary.org/docserver/7103eabf-en.pdf?expires=1707189438&id=id&accname=guest&checksum=2EF808BC9B3AB1E5417316DBEB138777.

45   Julia Ya Qin, "Forced Technology Transfer and the US-China Trade War: Implications for International Economic Law" (2019) 22 J Int'l Econ L 743 at 744.

46   *Ibid* at 745.

47   CUSMA, *supra* note 1092.

48   United States Trade Representative, "The Digital 2 Dozen" (2017) online: https://ustr.gov/sites/default/files/Digital-2-Dozen-Final.pdf.

U.S. innovators should not have to hand over their source code or proprietary algorithms to their competitors or a regulator that will pass them along to a State-owned enterprise. TPP ensures that companies do not have to share source code, trade secrets, or substitute local technology into their products and services in order to access new markets [...]

The references to "regulators" and "State-owned enterprise" makes clear that FTA source code secrecy rules are intended to shield source code from foreign government disclosure rather than private competitors.

Perhaps unsurprisingly, the global support and opposition to FTT follows a loose developed/developing country dichotomy. Opposition to forced source code disclosure is mostly asserted by developed countries with large and innovative technology sectors, such as the United States.[49] Meanwhile, requiring disclosure or access to source is a trend that has grown among developing nations in recent years, with India, Russia, Nigeria, and South Africa reportedly adopting similar practices.[50] For these reasons, it should be made clear that FTT is neither new nor unique to China. What *has* shifted in recent years, however, is the relative geopolitical importance, interest, and value in software and source code along with the downstream consequences of its disclosure.[51]

Concurrent with the rise of FTA source code secrecy rules, a conglomerate of countries has been seeking to expand upon the World Trade Organization's (WTO) digital trade rules to make source code secrecy a truly global standard. This group of some 90 countries comprises the WTO Joint Statement Initiative on E-Commerce (JSI), and a portion of its members have been working toward an agreement on various e-commerce initiatives, including source code.[52] Since 2019, consensus and support within the JSI has been gradually building in secrecy's favour. But in a largely unanticipated move in late 2023, the USTR announced the United States' withdrawal of US support for source code secrecy rules at the WTO and as part of the Indo-Pacific Economic Framework. The rationale for the reversal stems from concerns that these rules could further empower tech companies and stifle

49   Andrenelli, *supra* note 1123 at 13.
50   Słok-Wódkowska & Mazur, *supra* note 1107 at 96.
51   Dan Prud'homme & Max von Zedtwitz, "Managing 'Forced' Technology Transfer in Emerging Markets: The Case of China" (2019) 25 Journal of International Management 100670.
52   World Trade Organization, "Joint Statement Initiative on E-commerce," https://www.wto.org/english/tratop_e/ecom_e/joint_statement_e.htm.

competition within the domestic US economy.[53] Opponents of source code secrecy rules in the United States point to existing WTO obligations that already address FTT, and the potential for these rules to tie the hands of western democratic countries when it comes to regulating emerging algorithmic technologies such as artificial intelligence (AI).[54]

Naturally, the reversal has caused consternation and pushback from the US tech industry and among some lawmakers, leaving the future of source code secrecy at the WTO uncertain.[55] This uncertainty persisted throughout 2024, with the United States also suspending digital trade talks as part of the Indo-Pacific Economic Framework for Prosperity (IPEF), citing the need for policy space to better understand the impacts on the American technology sector.[56] The USTR's reversal on digital trade has since spurred confusion and controversy in the US congress, with the House Committee on Oversight and Accountability conducting an investigation and releasing a report alleging that the Federal Trade Commission (FTC) and the Department of Justice (DOJ)'s Antitrust Division put pressure on the USTR to abandon digital trade provisions without congressional consultation.[57]

Viewed optimistically, this enduring period of uncertainty may offer the opportunity to consider more thoroughly the downstream consequences and social costs of FTA source code secrecy rules at the global level. But cloudiness and ambiguity in the meantime are not likely to produce positive results either. This leaves a credible risk of further fragmentation on intellectual property and digital trade issues

---

53   Gopal Ratnam, "Democrats Divided over Biden's Move on Digital Trade" (5 December 2023) *Roll Call,* online: https://rollcall.com/2023/12/05/democrats-divided-over-bidens-move-on-digital-trade/#:~:text=The%20Biden%20administration's%20decision%20to,opposite%20sides%20over%20the%20issue.

54   Rethink Trade, "Report: Undermining AI Regulation in the U.S. and Abroad: The 'Digital Trade' Secrecy Ploy" (27 July 2023), *American Economic Liberties Project,* online: https://rethinktrade.org/wp-content/uploads/2023/07/AELP_RethinkTrade_AIAccountability.pdf.

55   Gavin Bade, "Why Biden's Trade Agenda Is Dividing Democrats" (2 February 2024), *Politico,* online: https://www.politico.com/newsletters/politico-nightly/2024/02/02/why-bidens-trade-agenda-is-dividing-democrats-00139412.

56   Danielle M Trachtenberg, "Digital Trade and Data Policy: Key Issues Facing Congress" (6 January 2025), Congressional Research Service: In Focus, online: https://crsreports.congress.gov/product/pdf/IF/IF12347/9

57   House Committee on Oversight and Accountability, "The Federal Trade Commission Under Chair Lina Khan: Undue Biden-Harris White House Influence and Sweeping Destruction of Agency Norms" (Staff Report, 31 October 2024), online: https://oversight.house.gov/wp-content/uploads/2024/10/HCOA-Majority-Staff-Report-FTC-Investigation.pdf at 22–25.

that could sideline collective action toward positive reforms. If the trade policy of the second Trump administration will resemble anything of the first, it is likely that uncertainty and confusion will persist. This may result in a heterogeneous international landscape of source code regulation, with bespoke rules being invoked haphazardly to further the national security interests of various countries.[58]

The Social Costs of Source Code Secrecy

The source code secrecy rules in FTAs present formidable challenges to traditional conceptions of intellectual property and the public interest. In mandating secrecy as the starting point for source code, these new rules have the potential to circumvent exceptions and limitations relating to software and may impede public oversight of emerging technologies.[59] In the sections that follow, source code secrecy's (mis) alignment with intellectual property norms is analyzed along with a selection of social costs.

Intellectual Property Doctrine

Even in the absence of mandated source code secrecy found in FTAs, the invocation of conventional trade secrecy for source code is not without its own complications and difficulties from an intellectual property perspective. This is because of the concurrent protection software receives from both trade secrecy and copyright law. These two branches of intellectual property embody starkly different regulatory and public policy objectives. As discussed above, the conventional orientation of trade secrecy is in protecting industrial know-how and functional processes. In effect, trade secrets supplement patent law by offering limited protection to non-patentable but commercially valuable secrets.[60] This is perhaps an intuitive fit for source code, as it resembles

---

58   Patrick Leblond, "After USTR's Move, Global Governance of Digital Trade Is Fraught with Unknowns" (11 December 2023), *Centre for International Governance Innovation*, online: https://www.cigionline.org/articles/after-ustrs-move-global-governance-of-digital-trade-is-fraught-with-unknowns/.

59   For a discussion of how source code secrecy poses particular challenges for regulating tools that could be used as part of "algorithmic governance," including artificial intelligence systems, see (Słok-Wódkowska & Mazur, *supra* note 1107 at 106–108).

60   Maria Ptashkina and Dan Ciuriak, "Quantifying Trade Secret Theft: Policy Implications" CIGI Papers 253 (May 2021) online: https://www.cigionline.org/

in many ways a commercially valuable secret or process. On the other hand, copyright provides protections against unauthorized distribution, communication, and reproduction of works. This applies more appropriately to object code rather than source code.

While typically this dichotomy would present authors with a "one or the other" decision for protection, software's bifurcation between source code and object code grants authors a unique opportunity to double up on rights and extend copyright's practical scope. Copyright ends up being asserted only in the non-expressive and primarily utilitarian object code, while trade secrecy safeguards source code—arguably software's only expressive or original component. Rightsholders can therefore "have their cake and eat it too." [61] The effect of this paradoxical application of copyright and trade secrecy permits copyright to (in effect) protect purely facts, ideas, and utilitarian concepts. While the idea/expression dichotomy, a core tenet of copyright law, would ordinarily reject this result, trade secrecy's application to source code enables a convenient workaround to receive protection regardless.

FTA source code secrecy rules further expand upon conventional intellectual property doctrines in several ways. In applying to not only source code, but "algorithms expressed in source code," these rules provide protections to algorithms even where patent protection is explicitly excluded at the domestic level. For example, the European Patent Convention (EPC) specifically excludes "programs for computers" from patentability while allowing patents for "computer-implemented inventions" that provide a technical contribution. [62] The global landscape for algorithm patentability varies widely, with countries such as India, Germany, Japan, and the United Kingdom taking restrictive approaches, and countries such as Australia, Canada, the United States, and the Republic of Korea taking a more permissive approach. [63] By expanding trade secrecy protection to "algorithms expressed in source code" the effect is to provide secrecy guarantees that override domestic policy choices to exclude algorithms from exclusivity.

---

static/documents/documents/no.253.pdf.

61   Gibson, *supra* note 1104 at 178.

62   Convention on the Grant of European Patents (5 October 1973), Art 52(2)(c) [*European Patent Convention*].

63   For a discussion of these approaches, see Anton Matveev & Elizaveta Martyanova, "Patentability of Computer Program Algorithms in the G20 States" (2022) 4:3 Brics Law Journal 144–173.

It is not disputed that algorithms, particularly those developed by large technology companies, are often these companies' most valuable primary asset. Nor is it disputed that the disclosure of these algorithms, even in the absence of FTA source code secrecy rules, would be uncontroversial or without legitimate opposition. What is particularly remarkable about this aspect of FTA source code secrecy rules, however, is the loose and ambiguous concept of "algorithm" that reaches far beyond the obvious scenarios where disclosure would be unreasonable or undesirable.

Throughout FTAs which include these provisions, "source code" and "algorithm" are often treated as separate concepts. Chapter 19 of CUSMA, for example, defines an algorithm distinctly from source code as "a defined sequence of steps, taken to solve a problem or obtain a result." [64] It is not clear why these concepts are distinguished in FTAs, but one plausible interpretation is that it is intended to preclude transfer or access to information detailing the functioning of software when expressed in forms *other* than source code. [65] The most intuitive example of such an alternative is object code, but a loose definition of "algorithm" could be interpreted even more broadly. It could feasibly include any written explanation or representation of how a computer program works or what it does, irrespective of whether those representations or explanations are commercially valuable. The result is a potential expansion of trade secrecy's practical scope to encompass virtually any aspect of a computer program that could be inspected or analyzed to determine how it functions. Adopting such a loose and broad interpretation of "algorithm" may therefore do away with the formal conditions for trade secrecy under TRIPS, including that the information have commercial value and taking "reasonable steps" to keep algorithms (broadly defined) secret. [66] This creates potential for unprecedented expansion of secrecy in relation to software that finds only tangential support from conventional trade secrecy doctrine.

The above are just two of many potential social costs presented by FTA source code secrecy. The first is an overlap of copyright and trade secrecy in a way that effectively grants copyright protection in purely utilitarian works. In the long run, this undermines the public interest and

---

64   *CUSMA, supra* note 1092 "Definitions".
65   Borghi & White, *supra* note 1085 at 115.
66   *TRIPS: Agreement on Trade-Related Aspects of Intellectual Property Rights*, Apr. 15, 1994, Marrakesh Agreement Establishing the World Trade Organization, Annex 1C, 1869 U.N.T.S. 299, 33 I.L.M. 1197 (1994), Art 39(2)(a) [*TRIPS*].

enrichment of the public domain by granting exclusive economic rights in object code while preventing public access and understanding of the source code otherwise necessary for follow-on creativity and innovation. The second is the expansion of conventional trade secrecy law to apply to a poorly defined concept of "algorithm" in a way that expands the practical scope of patentable subject matter in many jurisdictions.

Effective Regulation of Software-Dependent Technologies

The second way that source code secrecy rules in FTAs expand upon existing intellectual property doctrine is by precluding states' "access" to source code and related information about how software applications work. Though motivation for source code secrecy originates in the context of FTT, the prohibition on "access" restricts states far beyond prohibiting source code *transfer.* In some cases, states may have good reason to enact regulatory processes that result in access (through dissecting, decompiling, or reverse engineering) to source code and technical information relating to software. For example, when IBM announced its controversial decision to allow Chinese authorities to inspect product source code, it issued statements clarifying that the process is carried out under "strict control." The company clarified that national security reviews are conducted through an IBM security application and that the code cannot be "taken out of the room." [67] Source code "transfer," on the other hand, implies the legal conveyance of the source code from one entity to another or joint ownership and control. This could take place, for example, through a regulatory requirement that a foreign technology company must enter a joint venture with a government agency or government-controlled company as a condition for market access.

Prohibiting access to source code may result in downstream social costs where source code relates to algorithmic governance tools that could impact public health and safety (for example, policing, law enforcement, and healthcare). [68] Indeed, algorithms increasingly form part of various governmental processes, including criminal proceedings. [69] Foreshadowing the future, Estonia's digital society approach

---

67   Joseph Menn, "IBM Says Some Governments Allowed to Review Its Source Code" (16 October 2015) *Reuters,* online: https://www.reuters.com/article/idUSKCN0SA1BZ/.

68   Wódkowska & Mazur, *supra* note 1107 at 107.

69   Francesa Palmiotto, "The Black Box on Trial: The Impact of Algorithmic Opacity

to digital public infrastructure suggests that these tools will become increasingly prevalent. [70] But with this prevalence comes the potential for significant potential harms where algorithms remain opaque or obscured from public inspection. Indeed, as reliance on these tools becomes more prevalent, the need for regulatory oversight is only likely to increase with time. Without the ability to require access to source code, governments may find limitations in the degree of oversight and public accountability that is required in procuring and implementing these technologies.

Beyond digital public infrastructure, restricted ability to require source code access may interfere with attempts to regulate artificial intelligence at a more general level. Countries around the world are currently devising ambitious regulations governing the use of AI, most of which envision transparency and accountability standards that presume source code access and inspection by public authorities. The United Kingdom, for example, has put guidelines and policies in place for public procurement of AI-related technologies used in specific sectors, [71] including healthcare. [72] Included in these guidelines are recommendations to "avoid black box algorithms and vendor lock in" through "using methods and techniques that allow the results to be understood." [73] Canada's Treasury Board has issued guiding principles that follow similar themes to the UK's guidelines. Among these principles is a commitment to "be as open as we can by sharing source code, training data, and other relevant information, all while protecting personal information, system integration, and national security defence." [74] The oversight and access to source code envisioned by

on Fair Trial Rights in Criminal Proceedings," in Martin Ebers & Marta Cantero Gamito, eds, *Algorithmic Governance and Governance of Algorithms* (Cham: Springer, 2021) 49 at 51–56.

70   Marten Kaevats, "How to Build Digital Public Infrastructure: 7 Lessons from Estonia" (4 October 2021) *World Economic Forum*, online: https://www.weforum.org/agenda/2021/10/how-to-build-digital-public-infrastructure-estonia/.

71   Cosmina Dorobantu, Florian Ostmann & Christina Hitrova, "Source Code Disclosure: A Primer for Trade Negotiators" in *Addressing Impediments to Digital Trade* (London: CEPR Press, 2021) 105 at 121.

72   NHS England, "A Buyer's Guide to AI in Health and Care" (8 September 2020), online: https://transform.england.nhs.uk/ai-lab/explore-all-resources/adopt-ai/a-buyers-guide-to-ai-in-health-and-care/.

73   UK Government, "Guidance: Guidelines for AI Procurement" (8 June 2020), online: https://www.gov.uk/government/publications/guidelines-for-ai-procurement/guidelines-for-ai-procurement.

74   Government of Canada, "Responsible Use of Artificial Intelligence (AI): Exploring the Future of Responsible AI in Government" (01 August 2024) online: https://

principles and guidelines of this sort are likely to be crucial regulatory tools in the years to come. And yet, source code secrecy rules may act as a significant impediment to effective regulation in this area.

Beyond algorithmic technologies, there are many other software-dependent technologies over which governments ought to retain the right to inspect or seek source code access. Computing and software used throughout the automotive industry is one of many pertinent examples. Beginning in the mid-2000s, Volkswagen began designing its "EA 189" diesel engine, but the company found difficulty in meeting increasingly strict emission standards in the United States and elsewhere.[75] Volkswagen's engineers solved this problem by devising a software-based solution, known as a "defeat device" that could detect when the vehicle was being tested for emissions and display misleading or fraudulent readings. These software controls allowed some car models to produce 40 times the maximum limit in the United States without being properly detected.[76] Following discovery of the defeat device, a torrent of government and civil actions were filed against Volkswagen, and by mid-2020 the scandal had cost the company $31.3 billion Euros in various settlements, fines, and buyback costs.[77]

The scandal shed light on how software can be used to evade regulatory measures, produce fraudulent results, and expose the public to risks. It also revealed the importance of regulatory oversight and inspection of source code embedded in physical devices and technologies. This may not always require "transfer" in a formal sense, but it may amount to access. For this reason, FTA source code secrecy rules may pose a real and credible challenge to effective regulation of emerging algorithmic technologies and embedded software used by companies to cheat or evade public accountability.

---

www.canada.ca/en/government/system/digital-government/digital-government-innovations/responsible-use-ai.html#toc1.

75   U.S. Department of Justice, "Volkswagen Engineer Sentenced for His Role in Conspiracy to Cheat U.S. Emissions Tests" (25 August 2017) online: https://www.justice.gov/archives/opa/pr/volkswagen-engineer-sentenced-his-role-conspiracy-cheat-us-emissions-tests.

76   Guilbert Gates, Jack Ewing, Karl Russell, and Derek Watkins, "How Volkswagen's 'Defeat Devices' Worked" (16 March 2017) The New York Times, online: https://www.nytimes.com/interactive/2015/business/international/vw-diesel-emissions-scandal-explained.html.

77   Reuters, "Volkswagen Says Diesel Scandal Has Cost It 31.3 Billion Euros" (17 March 2020), online: https://www.reuters.com/article/idUSKBN2141JA/.

Right to Repair, Interoperability, and Participatory Innovation

Access to source code is socially beneficial not only for public oversight of technologies, but also in allowing access to the inner workings of products and devices. As alluded to in this chapter's introduction, embedded computer systems and the Internet of Things (IoT) devices are conduits through which software and source code can govern the ownership and use of tangible things in new and unprecedented ways. Over the past decade or so, these developments have unveiled new technical, legal, and social challenges posed by restricted access source code and firmware. These include undermining traditional conceptions of personal property, [78] denying users from experimenting and engaging analytically with devices, [79] preventing third parties from developing interoperable and complimentary technologies, [80] and restricting access to repair, maintenance, and diagnosis. [81] For the latter, access to software and source code play various roles in these processes, whether for diagnosis, [82] reverse engineering, or as special codes and encryption keys necessary to unlock functionality and authentication. [83] The costs that stem from this phenomena range from decreased access and dissemination of technological knowledge [84], suppression of competition

---

78   Aaron Perzanowski & Jason Schultz, *The End of Ownership* (Cambridge: MIT Press, 2016) at 139–154.

79   Anthony D Rosborough & Aaron Perzanowski, "Repair as Research: How Copyright Impedes Learning About Devices" (2023) Joint PIJIP/TLS Research Paper Series, American University Washington College of Law, online: https://digitalcommons.wcl.american.edu/cgi/viewcontent.cgi?article=1103&context=research.

80   Anthony D Rosborough, "If a Machine Could Talk, We Would Not Understand It: Canadian Innovation and the Copyright Act's TPM Interoperability Framework" (2023) 19:1 CJLT 141–171.

81   See, e.g., Leah Chan Grinvald & Ofer Tur-Sinai, "Intellectual Property and the Right to Repair" (2019) 88 Fordham L Rev 63–128; Aaron Perzanowski, *The Right to Repair* (Cambridge: CUP, 2022); Anthony D Rosborough, "Toward a Canadian Right to Repair: Opportunities and Challenges" (2022) 37 BTLJ 1197–1226.

82   Kevin Purdy, "iFixit Tears Down a McDonald's Ice Cream Machine, Demands DMCA Exemption for It" (29 August 2023) *Ars Technica*, online: https://arstechnica.com/gadgets/2023/08/mcdonalds-ice-cream-machine-teardown-shows-error-codes-dmca-keep-it-broken/.

83   See, e.g., the analysis of "payload files" and part serialization used in certain John Deere tractors and combines in Rosborough & Perzanowski, *supra* note 1158.

84   United States–based security researchers have faced difficulty carrying out their research and sharing results under the United States *Digital Millennium Copyright Act* framework of anti-circumvention laws. Since 2016, the Electronic Frontier Foundation (EFF) has been seeking to overturn anti-circumvention laws on constitutional grounds in *Green v Department of Justice*.

and secondary markets,[85] shortened product lifespan,[86] and unsustainable consumption patterns that exacerbate climate change.[87]

On at least a few of these fronts, public interest movements in various countries have successfully motivated governments to initiate legal reforms permitting repair and interoperability of software-dependent devices. For example, the United States' Federal Trade Commission's 2021 report on the right to repair found "scant evidence to support manufacturers' justifications for repair restrictions."[88] Over the past several years, a quickly growing number of US states have proposed and enacted Right to Repair legislation that forces greater access to source code and prevents manufacturers from restricting repair of agricultural equipment, wheelchairs, mobile electronics, home appliances, and certain medical devices.[89]

Canada has taken meaningful action on this front as well. In late 2024, two private member's bills furthering the right to repair became law. They have successfully amended Canada's *Copyright Act* to permit circumvention of technological protection measures for the purposes of repair, maintenance, diagnosis,[90] and for interoperability purposes.[91] Both bills acknowledge the unique role of software and computerization in denying access to the inputs necessary for diagnosis, repair, innovation, and related competition issues. Canada has also amended its *Competition Act* to clarify that a manufacturer's refusal to provide the means of diagnosis or repair may constitute a refusal to deal.[92] This

---

85   Anthony Rosborough & Carlo Dade, "The Serious Hidden Problem Facing Canada's Agricultural Innovators" (25 February 2021) *Policy Options*, online: https://policyoptions.irpp.org/magazines/february-2021/the-serious-hidden-problem-facing-canadas-agricultural-innovators/.

86   Emma Fillman, "Comprehensive Right to Repair: The Fight Against Planned Obsolescence in Canada" (2023) 22 Dal J Leg Stud 123 at 126–131.

87   Graham J Reynolds, "Of Lock-Breaking and Stock Taking: IP, Climate Change, and the Right to Repair in Canada" (2023) 101:1 Can Bar Rev 31 at 41–44.

88   Federal Trade Commission, "Nixing the Fix: An FTC Report to Congress on Repair Restrictions" (May 2021) at 6 online: https://www.ftc.gov/system/files/documents/reports/nixing-fix-ftc-report-congress-repair-restrictions/nixing_the_fix_report_final_5521_630pm-508_002.pdf.

89   Nathan Proctor, "20 States File Right to Repair Bills as Momentum Grows" (7 February 2023) *PIRG*, online: https://pirg.org/articles/20-states-file-right-to-repair-bills-as-momentum-grows/.

90   Bill C-244, An Act to Amend the Copyright Act (diagnosis, maintenance and repair). As Passed by the House of Commons.

91   Bill C-294, An Act to Amend the Copyright Act (interoperability), Adopted by the House on June 14, 2023.

92   Bill C-59. Fall Economic Statement Implementation Act, 2023. An Act to Implement Certain Provisions of the Fall Economic Statement Tabled in Parliament on

would presumably extend to proprietary source code and software. These changes could result in device manufacturers being compelled by Canada's Competition Bureau to provide or disclose source code or software in certain circumstances, contrary to digital trade provisions in various FTAs.

The European Union has also taken bold steps in this direction. In 2019, it introduced its Ecodesign Directive's implementing regulations, which require that manufacturers provide access to parts, tools, and information for the repair of certain product categories. The EU policy debate on these issues has (until recently) largely ignored questions about software and source code, instead focusing on increasing access to repair through strengthening consumer laws and devising repairability rating systems.[93] But recently the European focus has centred more strongly on software-based restrictions,[94] with the European Parliament and Council reaching a preliminary agreement on a bill that will prohibit manufacturers "from using contractual clauses, software and hardware techniques that hinder repair."[95] This ban includes a prohibition on so-called "parts pairing," a system design technique where the physical components of devices are given unique signatures and authenticated by a central computing system. In the case of certain equipment, parts pairing can mean that the replacement of certain device components without authorization permitted by source code can result in feature loss or "bricking" where entire devices become inoperable.[96] In taking regulatory action that prevents software and computerization from imposing these types of restrictions, the European Union appears to be taking a greater interest in software and source code as key factors in its right to repair policy.

November 21, 2023.

93   European Commission, Internal Market, Industry, Entrepreneurship and SMEs, "Decree Relating to the Repairability Index of Electrical and Electronic Equipment" (30 October 2020).

94   Chloé Mikolajczak, "Part pairing: A major threat to independent repair" (6 August 2021) *Repair.eu*, online: https://repair.eu/news/part-pairing-a-major-threat-to-independent-repair/.

95   European Parliament, "Deal on Strengthening Consumers' Right to Repair" (2 February 2024) online: https://www.europarl.europa.eu/news/en/press-room/20240129IPR17216/deal-on-strengthening-consumers-right-to-repair.

96   In one alarming case, a Polish passenger train bricked itself after its manufacturer's parts pairing and authentication system detected the use of replacement parts that lacked manufacturer-approved serial numbers. See, Ashley Belanger, "Trains Were Designed to Break Down after Third-Party Repairs, Hackers Find" (13 December 2023) *Ars Technica*, online: https://arstechnica.com/tech-policy/2023/12/manufacturer-deliberately-bricked-trains-repaired-by-competitors-hackers-find/.

Cumulatively, these efforts point to a strengthening global recognition of the need to develop law and regulation that prevents software from being used to hinder open uses of technologies that further the public interest. The common denominator is an increased appetite for governments to intervene in software implementation to either force disclosure or impose restrictions on the types of restrictive software-based techniques that can be invoked. Though these trends show promise, source code secrecy risks jeopardizing it.[97] If governments are prohibited from mandating transfer or access to source code and technical information relating to software, this may undermine regulatory competence and domestic sovereignty over the right to repair, open innovation, and safeguarding market competition. For these reasons, source code secrecy could amount to a serious and significant setback for those advocating for a more coherent and principled treatment of intellectual property rights in these contexts.

Global Development and Technology Transfer

As demonstrated by the US-China trade war and intellectual property theft fears, geopolitical tensions create a mostly negative view of technology transfer. But theoretically at least, it plays an important role in the global intellectual property system. In principle, an important objective of the *TRIPS Agreement* is to facilitate the dissemination of technology to support global development.[98] This reflects the "bargain" underlying the TRIPS negotiations,[99] wherein developing and least developed countries made clear that a global intellectual property system that does not include binding commitments for technology transfer is both illegitimate and ineffective for development.[100] Indeed, if a multilateral trade system

---

97   Anthony Rosborough & Daniel Rangel, "The Right to Repair Needs to Extend to Software, Too – And Trade Deals Could Be in the Way" (23 November 2023) *The Globe and Mail,* online: https://www.theglobeandmail.com/business/commentary/article-right-to-repair-movement-digital-trade/.

98   TRIPS, Preamble, "*Recognising* the underling public policy objectives of national systems for the protection of intellectual property, including developmental and technological objectives"; and "*Recognising* also the special needs of the least-developed country Members in respect of maximum flexibility in the domestic application of laws and regulations in order to enable them to create a sound and viable technological base."

99   David M. Fox, "Technology Transfer and the *TRIPS Agreement:* Are Developed Countries Meeting Their End of the Bargain?" (2019) 10:1 Hastings Sci & Tech LJ 1 at 8.

100 Padmashree Gehl Sampath, "Intellectual Property and Technology Transfer:

incorporating western conceptions of intellectual property was *fait accompli*, developing and least developed countries (LDCs) were right to seek procedural and equitable guarantees from which they might benefit. [101]

Leaving much to be desired, the TRIPS text reflects these principles and objectives to some extent. Article 7, for example, notes that the agreement's objectives include contributing "[...] to the promotion of technological innovation *and to the transfer and dissemination of technology* [...] in a manner conducive to social and economic welfare [...]" Article 8(2) also envisions scenarios where states take measures to prevent the abuse of intellectual property that adversely affect the international transfer of technology.

The much sought-after binding obligation for technology transfer is lacking in many respects, however. Article 66(2) obligates developed country members to provide: "[...] incentives to enterprises and institutions in their territories for the purpose of promoting and encouraging technology transfer to least-developed country Members in order to enable them to create a sound and viable technological base."

The nature, scope, and extent of this obligation remains ambiguous and unclear despite the 30 years that have passed since TRIPS' signing. Over this period, developing countries and LDCs have repeatedly complained that WTO members have not shown enough interest in achieving Article 66(2)'s mandate. [102] History corroborates this view, showing inadequate enforcement and measurement of results. In the first four years of TRIPS' existence, not a single developed country member reported on their technology transfer fulfilment progress, prompting the TRIPS Council to implement a mandatory monitoring scheme during the 2003 Doha Ministerial Conference. [103] Though reporting has increased over the years, the actual substance of

---

Why We Need a New Agenda" in Carlos Correa & Xavier Seuba, eds, *Intellectual Property and Development: Understanding the Interfaces* (Singapore: Springer, 2019) at 41–42.

101   Ruth L Gana, "Prospects for Developing Countries Under the *TRIPS Agreement*" (1996) 29: 4 Vanderbilt Law Review 735 at 774.

102   Cameron J. Hutchinson, "Does TRIPS Facilitate or Impede Climate Change Technology Transfer into Developing Countries?" (2006) 3 U Ottawa L & Tech J 517 at 524.

103   Council for Trade-Related Aspects of Intellectual Property Rights, Implementation of Article 66.2 of the *TRIPS Agreement*, WTO Doc. IP/C/28 (Feb. 20, 2003) online: https://docs.wto.org/dol2fe/Pages/FE_Search/FE_S_S009-DP.aspx?language=E& CatalogueIdList=11737&CurrentCatalogueIdIndex=0&FullTextSearch=.

technology transfer has left much to be desired according to many experts.[104]

History shows that technological progress in LDCs is often inversely related to the steadfast assertion and protection of intellectual property rights. Japan and South Korea's industrial transformations over the past 70 years are cases in point.[105] In a digitized economy fuelled by software and algorithmic-driven innovation, open-source technologies are therefore key to (and perhaps the only tangible means of) technology transfer.

Though far from a comprehensive solution to TRIPS' deeper "legitimacy gap",[106] Article 66(2)'s efficacy could be strengthened by incentivizing and promoting the use of open-source software and hardware in developed countries.[107] This could also be implemented through laws and regulations that mandate the use of open-source technologies in certain industries or applications. When combined with training and education, greater proliferation of open-source technology such as medical devices, water sanitation systems, and logistics and supply systems, could result in meaningful technology transfer to LDCs. This potential extends to less critical technologies as well. Personal computers, smartphones, and myriad consumer ICT devices have the potential to serve as valuable learning and innovation platforms[108] that can spur a whole host of new discoveries and technologies when built using open-source software and hardware.[109]

---

104   World Trade Organization, Report of the Working Group on Trade and Transfer of Technology to the General Council, WTO Doc WT/WGTTT/19 (8 Nov 2017) at 2 online: https://docs.wto.org/dol2fe/Pages/SS/directdoc.aspx?filename=q:/WT/WGTTT/19.pdf&Open=True.

105   Keith E Maskus & Jerome H Reichman, "The Globalization of Private Knowledge Goods and the Privatization of Global Public Goods" in Keith Maskus & Jerome Reichman, eds, *International Public Goods & Transfer of Technology under a Globalized Intellectual Property Regime* (Cambridge: Cambridge University Press, 2004) at 290.

106   Hanns Ullrich, "The Political Foundations of TRIPS Revisited" in Hanns Ullrich et al, eds, *TRIPS Plus 20: From Trade Rules to Market Principles* (Berlin: Springer, 2016) at 98–102.

107   Jean-Michel Dalle, "Open-Source Technology Transfer" (Paper presented at EPIP2 Conference, Maastrict, The Netherlands, November 24–25, 2003).

108   Stan Kurkovsky & Chad Williams, "Raspberry Pi as a Platform for the Internet of Things Projects: Experiences and Lessons" (2017) ITiSCE '17: Proceedings of the 2017 ACM Conference on Innovation and Technology in Computer Science Education 64 at 64–65.

109   David Cassel, "The Open Source Lesson of the Linksys WRT54G Router" (24 January 2021) *The New Stack*, online: https://thenewstack.io/the-open-source-lesson-of-the-linksys-wrt54g-router/.

Despite this enormous potential for open source, FTA source code secrecy rules risk severely impairing it. Though developed countries' incentivization of open-source technology may result in trickle-down benefits for LDCs, the FTA source code secrecy rules prevent LDC governments from enforcing the terms of open-source licences. Software built on the GNU General Public License (GPL), for example, mandates disclosure and access to source code. Where GNU-derived software is incorporated into products or devices, manufacturers can be legally compelled to release both source and object code.[110] The success of US-based open-source NGOs and copyleft advocates in forcing manufacturers to provide access to source code in certain cases shows that this obligation has real teeth.[111]

FTA source code secrecy also prevents LDC governments (along with developing and wealthy countries) from requiring or mandating that imported technologies be built on open-source licensing. Requirements of this sort may perform an important global development function by spurring domestic research, capacity, and expertise in the implementation and development of foreign technologies. But requirements of this sort may effectively amount to requiring "access" or "transfer" of source code that is conditional for market access. Taken together, the lack of ability for LDC governments to require access to source code and related information about software risks further impairing TRIPS, confining the subject of technology transfer to twentieth-century modalities of innovation and technology.

The above sections reveal numerous social, economic, and environmental costs of FTA source code secrecy. These rules may prevent countries from effectively regulating software-based technologies that impact democratic deliberation, public health, and safety. It could reverse promising efforts toward recalibrating copyright laws to prevent their misuse in preventing the right to repair and innovation. And finally, it could undermine incentives to remedy the technology gap that promote global development. The following and final section of this chapter canvasses one explanation for how we might

---

110   For an explanation of "GPL Enforcement" investigations and legal actions taken by the US-based Free Software Foundation, and Software Freedom Conservancy, see Joshua Gay, "The Principles of Community-Oriented GPL Enforcement" (30 September 2015) *Free Software Foundation,* online: https://www.fsf.org/licensing/enforcement-principles.

111   Steven Vaughan-Nichols, "Software Freedom Conservancy Wins Big Step Forward For Open-Source Rights" (17 May 2022) *Zdnet,* online: https://www.zdnet.com/article/software-freedom-conservancy-wins-big-step-forward-for-open-source-rights/.

have arrived at this point and what this may tell us about the future of intellectual property.

The Trend Toward Intellectual Property as National Security

The push toward FTA source code secrecy evidences a larger and worrying shift in the global intellectual property system. Beyond the numerous social costs, these rules exemplify a transformation in the understanding of "intellectual property" from private economic rights to a tool used by governments to safeguard national security.[112] In relation to FTA source code secrecy, this recharacterization finds support on both sides of the US-China rivalry. After all, China's national security review process (which largely precipitated the West's moral panic over source code) was put forward under the auspices of state security and cybersecurity. FTA source code secrecy furthers this recharacterization of intellectual property as part and parcel of national security interests. Even as early as 2012, the United States Defence Security Service (DSS) identified these blurred lines in a report:

> The stakes are high in the battle against foreign collection efforts and espionage that target U.S. technology, intellectual property, trade secrets, and proprietary information. Our national security relies on our collective success at thwarting these persistent attacks [...] Our national security is also at risk in the potential loss of our technological edge, which is closely tied to [...] economic success [...] and the well-being of our economy.[113]

Regardless of the country perpetrating it, there are numerous downstream effects of entangling intellectual property with national security in this way. One of which is to challenge a core premise of the *TRIPS Agreement*, that "intellectual property rights are private rights." By imposing transfer and access restrictions on governments and regulators, FTA source code secrecy rules force software and trade secrecy to perform distinctly public and international trade functions. Ultimately trade secrecy in source code held by private actors is being used as impetus to restrict the actions of foreign governments within international trade

---

112   Debora Halbert, "Intellectual Property Theft and National Security: Agendas and Assumptions" (2016) 32:4 The Information Society 256 at 260.

113   United States Defense Security Service, "Targeting U.S. Technologies: A Trend Analysis of Reporting from Defense Industry" (2012).

frameworks. In theory these rules could be enforced by FTA panels, leading to the authorization of sanctions and other punitive measures with international economic and market impacts. FTA source code secrecy rules therefore permit states to mobilize private economic rights for core state and governmental objectives. On either account, this introduces a new approach to global intellectual property regulation. FTA source code secrecy rules evidence that states may expand the practical scope of intellectual property rights beyond doctrinal coherence in pursuit of national security. In this way, the objective and purpose of these expanded rights is no longer merely private but also imbues expanded intellectual property rights with public and governmental functions.

The national security rationale for FTA source code secrecy also reshapes the crucial balance of public and private interests at the core of intellectual property law. The most direct example is in practically limiting governmental discretion to find creative uses of exceptions and limitations that would otherwise further the public interest. But it also reshapes the values underpinning exceptions and limitations. In furthering national security, intellectual property protection acquires a maximalist agenda and leaves little room for compromise. Intellectual property is either protected in rather absolute fashion, or the subject of "theft." In effect, this reshapes our understanding of open knowledge and information as positive inputs for innovation, education, and health, to a series of risks that must be managed. Viewed within a national security lens, therefore, technique and know-how must be tightly controlled and owned by industry and state actors.[114] This lays the groundwork for (often monopolistic) private interests to convincingly argue for an expansionist approach to intellectual property[115] and characterize any type of openness in the system as a vulnerability and potential security threat.[116] In the end, the public interest pays the cost.

---

114   World Trade Organization, *supra* note 1183 at 260.
115   For example, Hewlett-Packard has defended a microchip authentication system in its printers that prevents the use of third-party ink, which it claims is necessary to prevent cyberattacks and to protect public safety and security. Critics claim that this is in fact a thinly veiled attempt to use pseudo-intellectual property rights for anti-competitive purposes. See, Scharon Harding, "HP CEO Evokes James Bond-Style Hack via Ink Cartridges" (22 January 2024) *Ars Technica*, online: https://arstechnica.com/gadgets/2024/01/hp-ceo-blocking-third-party-ink-from-printers-fights-viruses/.
116   For example, cybersecurity, industrial espionage, and public security were core reasons for the Intellectual Property Institute of Canada's opposition to Bill C-244, proposing an amendment to the *Copyright Act*'s anti-circumvention regime to permit the repair, maintenance, and diagnosis of computerised devices. See, e.g., Intellectual Property Institute of Canada (IPIC) Submission on Bill C-244 – An

Importantly, intellectual property's entanglement with national security is not a new phenomenon. Over the last two centuries, particularly during the two World Wars, there have been countless examples of states using intellectual property as a regulatory tool to maximize national security objectives. [117] But FTA source code secrecy rules present something new in this story. It is not just another recalibration of intellectual property rights to suit certain national security objectives. It is also evidence of intellectual property's expanding practical scope to assume relevance in new domains and encompass intangible interests that cannot otherwise be protected by private parties. Troublingly, this expansion may require dismissing doctrinal and moral critique, and may be left confined to the domain of trade negotiators and national security experts. Viewed as a larger global trend, the national security characterization of intellectual property should call for deep concern among experts and thinkers in this area. If the further "securitization" of intellectual property is indeed its future, we risk a further falling out of relevance with the actual processes of innovative and creative production. [118] By extension, we risk a global intellectual property system that is even further removed from public deliberation and accountability.

Conclusions

Today, software-dependent technologies are the primary tools of innovation, knowledge dissemination, democratic deliberation, and cultural and creative production. Intellectual property has long been the principal regulator of these technologies, but the expanding role of software-dependent technologies has increased the importance of balancing exclusive rights in software with public interest access. Digitization has conferred enormous power to those who hold and control access to source code, and the rules governing these processes therefore have profound social, economic, environmental, and moral consequences. By extension, these rules are also increasingly crucial for democratic accountability and legitimacy. Yet, FTA source code secrecy

---

Act to Amend the Copyright Act (6 December 2022), online: https://www.our-commons.ca/Content/Committee/441/INDU/Brief/BR12178536/br-external/IntellectualPropertyInstituteOfCanada-e.pdf.

117   For an overview of this history, see, e.g., Peter Drahos, "Immoral Intangibles: Engaging with Ned Snow's Intellectual Property and Immorality" (2023) 28:1 Jerusalem Review of Legal Studies 124 at 139–140.

118   World Trade Organization, *supra* note 1183 at 264.

rules evidence an ever-tightening grip on access to source code and software under the auspices of national security and in the absence of democratic oversight and deliberation. Black box technological design appears poised to become not just the industry norm, but indeed the international rule. Put bluntly, if we leave the rules of source code access to national security experts and international trade negotiators, we are not likely to be happy with what results.

The central theme of this chapter is the far-reaching impact of source code opaqueness, casting shadows on regulatory efficacy, participatory innovation, dissemination of knowledge, and development-oriented global technology transfer. Its asserts that FTA source code secrecy and the challenges it presents also evidence a larger trend toward intellectual property as national security. Mandating *ex ante* source code secrecy under the threat of intellectual property theft only further harms the prospects of a functional global intellectual property system. We ought to look to the future of these trends with caution and trepidation. The future will require collective resistance against the appropriation of intellectual property and distortion of its underlying values in service of national security frameworks.

CHAPTER 13

Location, Location, Location: The Future of Intellectual Property in Light of Private International Law

Naama Daniel

Abstract

When discussing the future of the global intellectual property (IP) system, referring only to developments in the IP field is not enough. Private international law (PIL) rules applied to IP may affect the future of the global IP system just as much as the development of IP laws themselves, yet this subject is rarely discussed. The lack of attention granted to the subject may result in the unintentional undermining of IP goals and principles. This chapter refers to a matter still not resolved by legal scholarship—the underlying reasons for the threats that PIL rules might pose to IP principles. This chapter uses the prism of legal transplants to analyze the intersection between IP and PIL both on the case-by-case, *ad hoc* level, and on the general level, demonstrating that although the "home environment," where the intersection is discussed, is perceived to be PIL, in fact, IP is the field being affected and undermined when the two intersect. The criticism pertaining to legal transplants assists in demonstrating that perceiving PIL as the home environment to discuss this intersection, dictates an outcome that inherently prioritizes PIL notions while undermining fundamental principles of IP. This chapter suggests a conceptual change in this perception, proposing that national and international discussions on the intersection between IP and PIL take place in the IP realm, focusing on IP goals and principles, rather than in the PIL realm, to shield IP principles, and to protect the future of the global IP system

What are we missing when we discuss the future of intellectual property (IP)? This chapter argues that in the digital, global world, any discussion on the future of IP is incomplete unless referring to another realm of law: private international law (PIL). As PIL is focused on the international sphere, seeking to bridge the gap between different jurisdictions, it may be pitted against IP, which is territorial in nature and is rooted in the national sphere, incorporating each nation's national economic, social, political, and cultural policies. Therefore, applying PIL rules to IP matters may undermine, and even nullify IP goals, principles, and the balances incorporated by national IP laws.[1] Nevertheless, PIL rules are applied to IP matters routinely.[2] Moreover, when discussing the future of IP, PIL matters are rarely discussed, as they are perceived to be external to the IP realm. However, this chapter argues that the application of PIL rules to IP issues is very much an internal matter of IP, in that it affects, and undermines, internal IP principles and the balances IP laws incorporate.[3]

This chapter fills a gap in current literature as it refers to questions still not resolved by legal scholarship—how did we get here? Why, after so much international debate, do PIL rules still threaten core IP policies and principles? Where does the international debate on PIL, a field that was designed to accommodate different principles and policies incorporated into other fields of law, fall short with regard to doing so for IP principles and policies, if at all? By examining the axioms and principles of both IP and PIL, and conceptualizing the actual effect of applying PIL rules to IP matters, this chapter attempts to answer these questions.

---

1   See, e.g., Rochelle C. Dreyfuss & Jane C. Ginsburg, "Draft Convention on Jurisdiction and Recognition of Judgments in Intellectual Property Matters" (2002) 77 Chi.-Kent L Rev 1065 at 1088; Marketa Trimble, "The Territorial Discrepancy Between Intellectual Property Rights Infringement Claims and Remedies" (2019) 23 Lewis & Clark L Rev 501 at 541; Pedro A. De Miguel Asensio, "Recognition and Enforcement of Judgments: Recent Developments" in Paul Torremans, ed, *Research Handbook on Cross-Border Enforcement of Intellectual Property* (Cheltenham: Edward Elgar Publishing, 2014) 469 at 490.

2   See, e.g., C-38/98, Renault v. Maxicar and Formento [2000] ECR I-2973; Google Inc. v. Equustek Solutions Inc., [2017] 1 S.C.R. 824; Google LLC v. Equustek Solutions, Inc., No. 5:17-cv-04207-EJD, 2017 WL 500834 (N.D. Cal. Nov. 2, 2017) (U.S. Google v. Equustek I); Google LLC. v, Equustek Solutions, Inc., No. 5:17-cv-04207-EJD, 2017 WL 11573727 (N.D. Cal. Dec. 14, 2017) (U.S. Google v. Equustek II); See, e.g., Lucasfilm Ltd. v. Ainsworth, [2011] UKSC 39, para. 50, 105 (appeal taken from Eng.) (U.K.); Performing Right Soc'y Ltd. v. Qatar Airways Grp. Q.C.S.C, [2020] EWHC (Ch) 1872, para. 11, 72 (U.K.). See also the discussions of the *2019 Convention, infra* notes 61–68 and accompanying text.

3   See sources cited in note 1.

To do so, this discussion looks at the intersection of the two fields of law—IP and PIL—to analyze which of the two is the home environment to the intersection and, as a result, which of the two fields is the appropriate one in which rules on the matter should be designed. Following that, the chapter uses the prism of legal transplants, and the criticism pertaining to it, to analyze the intersection between IP and PIL, on two levels. On the case-by-case, *ad hoc* level, the prism of legal transplants is applied directly, for example, in cases of enforcement of foreign IP judgments, that *de facto* import foreign IP laws into the enforcing country. On the general level, the prism of legal transplants is used by way of analogy to conceptualize the intersection between the two general fields of law, by assisting in detecting the "home environment" that is being affected at this intersection.

Aided by the prism of legal transplants, this chapter demonstrates that despite the international (and some national) tendencies to discuss the intersection between IP and PIL under national, regional, or international PIL instruments, the field of law that is actually being affected in this intersection is IP. The criticism pertaining to legal transplants, referring to the incompatibility of rules from one jurisdiction to be transplanted into another, further assists in this assessment. Following these findings, this chapter suggests a conceptual shift in the national and international perception of the intersection between IP and PIL, and proposes that further debate on the matter should take place in the IP realm, rather than that of PIL.

The first part demonstrates the basic principles, goals, and justifications of IP and of PIL, and analyzes the conflicts that arise when these two fields of law meet. Subsequently, the second part proposes to go back to the drawing board and examine where rules regarding the intersection of IP and PIL are being discussed and set, and uses the prism of legal transplants to analyze the effect of the location of debates on the substantive rule-making regarding this intersection. The following part looks to the future, demonstrating the problems that the digital, global age brings with it, and proposes solutions to resolve the problems indicated by this chapter. To that end, this chapter seeks to provide tools for legal professionals, judges, and policymakers, to better understand and resolve the problems arising at the intersection between IP and PIL.

Back to Basics

To understand the complexities of the intersection between IP and PIL, it is essential to examine the basics and assess the goals, principles, and main justifications of each of these fields of law. Doing so will provide the necessary backdrop to analyze the conflicts that arise when they intersect.

Intellectual Property

The main goal of IP rights is to incentivize new inventions and creations, and to disseminate them, to promote social welfare.[4] The main challenge of IP law, derived from this goal, is striking a balance between protecting novel subject matters, thereby incentivizing creation, while still leaving enough subject matter in the public domain to facilitate further developments, innovation, and creativity.[5] In the realm of IP, it is common to refer to current researchers, authors, and innovators as "standing on the shoulders of giants," the giants being their predecessors.[6]

The protection of IP rights is anchored in numerous international conventions.[7] However, IP rights remain territorial—they confer a

---

4   See, e.g., Jerome H. Reichman & Ruth L. Okediji, "When Copyright Law and Science Collide: Empowering Digitally Integrated Research Methods on a Global Scale" (2012) 96 Minn L Rev 1362 at 1377; W. Landes & R. Posner, "An Economic Analysis of Copyright Law" (1989) 18 J Legal Stud 325 at 325–363; Pierre N. Leval, "Toward a Fair Use Standard" (1990) 103 Harv L Rev 1105 at 1107–1110, 1132; Ruth Okediji, "Givers, Takers and Other Kinds of Users: A Fair Use Doctrine for Cyberspace" (2001) 53 Fla. L. Rev. 107 at 153–161; Martin Senftleben, "Bridging the Differences Between Copyright's Legal Traditions – The Emerging EC Fair Use Doctrine" (2010) 57 J Copyright Soc'y U.S.A. 521 at 526.

5   Regarding the public domain, see generally A. Samuel Oddi, *The Tragicomedy of the Public Domain in Intellectual Property Law*, 25 Hastings Comm. & Ent. L.J. 1 (2002).

6   See, e.g., Suzanne Scotchmer, "Standing on the Shoulders of Giants: Cumulative Research and the Patent Law" (1991) 5 J Econ Persps 29. Another goal of intellectual property rights is to protect the author, inventor, or creator. Historically, civil law regimes implemented natural law notions which emphasize authors' personality interests in their work, while common law regimes based the grant of IP protection on utilitarian notions of social welfare or "public good," perceiving IP as a prerogative granted to enhance the overall welfare of society by ensuring a sufficient supply of knowledge and information. See Reichman & Okediji, *supra* note 4 at 1375–1378; Senftleben, *supra* note 4 at 524.

7   See, e.g., *Agreement on Trade-Related Aspects of Intellectual Property Rights*, Apr. 15, 1994, *Marrakesh Agreement Establishing the World Trade Organization*, Annex 1C, 1869 U.N.T.S. 299 [hereinafter *TRIPS Agreement*]; *Paris Convention for the Protection of Industrial Property*, as last revised at the Stockholm Revision Conference, Mar. 20, 1883, 21 U.S.T. 1583; 828 U.N.T.S. 305; *Berne Convention for the Protection of Literary*

territorial protection upon the subject matters to which they apply,[8] allowing each country the sovereign power to design the IP laws in its territory as it sees fit,[9] considering, *inter alia*, national, economic, and cultural considerations.[10] The international instruments establishing—or strengthening—the protection of IP, allow for this leeway for their Member States, granting them freedom to design their national IP laws in a manner that complies with their national economic, social, political, and cultural policies.[11] The territoriality of IP rights is thus

---

     and Artistic Works, Sept. 9, 1886, as revised at Paris on July 24, 1971 and amended in 1979, S. Treaty Doc. No. 99-27 (as amended Sept. 28, 1979) [hereinafter *Berne Convention*]. These are mere examples.

8   See, e.g., Jane C. Ginsburg, "Global Use/Territorial Rights: Private International Law Questions of the Global Information Infrastructure" (1995) 42 J. Copyright Soc'y U.S.A. 318 at 319; Jane C. Ginsburg, "The Cyberian Captivity of Copyright: Territoriality and Authors' Rights in a Networked World" (1999) 15 Santa Clara Comput & High Tech LJ 347; Jacklyn Hoffman, Note, "Crossing Borders in the Digital Market: A Proposal to End Copyright Territoriality and Geo-Blocking in The European Union" (2016) 49 Geo Wash Int'l L Rev 143; Graeme B. Dinwoodie, "International Intellectual Property Litigation: A Vehicle for Resurgent Comparativist Thought" (2001) 49 Am J Compar L 429, 437–438; Trimble, *supra* note 1 at 510 ("Because IP rights are territorial-they arise from a particular country's laws and exist only within the scope of that country's prescriptive jurisdiction— they cannot be infringed in countries where a country's laws do not establish or recognize the rights.").

9   *Berne Convention, supra* note 7 at art. 5(2); Toshiyuki Kono et al, "Editorial," 12 J. Intell Prop, Info Tech, & Elec Com L 1 (2021); Alexander Peukert & Benedetta Ubertazzi, "International Law Association's Guidelines on Intellectual Property and Private International Law ("Kyoto Guidelines"): General Provisions" (2021) 12 J Intell Prop, Info Tech, & Elec Com L 4, 6; Marie-Elodie Ancel et al, "International Law Association's Guidelines on Intellectual Property and Private International Law ("Kyoto Guidelines"): Applicable Law" 12 (2021) J Intell Prop, Info Tech, & Elec Com L 44, 56–58; Maxence Rivoire, "An Alternative to Choice of Law in (First) Ownership of Copyright Cases: The Substantive Law Method" (2018) 65 J. Copyright Soc'y U.S.A. 203 at 211–212; Jane C. Ginsburg, "Copyright Without Borders—Choice of Forum and Choice of Law for Copyright Infringement in Cyberspace" (1997) 15 Cardozo Arts & Ent. L.J. 153, 154.

10   See, e.g., Christophe Geiger et al, "The Three Step Test Revisited: How to Use the Test's Flexibility in National Copyright Law" 29 (2013)Am. U. Int'l L. Rev. 581 at 582–583; Pamela Samuelson, "Justifications for Copyright Limitations and Exceptions" in Ruth L. Okediji, ed, Copyright Law in an Age of Limitations and Exceptions (New York: Cambridge University Press, 2017), at 52; Dreyfuss & Ginsburg, *supra* note 1 at 1066 ("The strong link between culture on the one hand, and intellectual production and utilization on the other, means that the territoriality of these rights is of crucial importance: individual nations must be able to retain some control over the local conditions under which these products are created, exploited, and accessed.").

11   For example, the *Berne Convention* and the *TRIPS Agreement* provide general guidelines on the national implementation of permitted uses through an Article often

one of the main principles around which IP laws are designed. [12] In this regard, IP limits and limitations are of specific interest. [13] Different countries adopt different rules regarding the limits and limitations of IP protection in their territories. [14]

First, different countries adopt different rules with regard to the *ab initio* scope of protection of IP (hereinafter IP limits). For example, the

referred to as "the three step test," which allows their Member States to implement a wide range of permitted uses in their national laws, thereby facilitating the use of works for various purposes considered to be beneficial for their respective publics. See *Berne Convention, supra* note 7 at art. 9; *TRIPS Agreement, supra* note 7 at arts. 13, 17, 26.2, 30; Reichman & Okediji, *supra* note 4 at 1378–1390. It should be noted that legal scholarship and inter-governmental organizations often discuss the "harmonization" of intellectual property rights, *inter alia*, by virtue of the intellectual property treaties that set a minimum standard of protection for intellectual property rights. See, e.g., Ruth L. Okediji, "New Treaty Development and Harmonization of Intellectual Property Law" in Christophe Bellmann & Ricardo Melendez-Ortiz, eds, *Trading in Knowledge: Development Perspectives on TRIPS, Trade and Sustainability* (New York: Routledge, 2003) 89 at 89–98; see Junji Nakagawa, *International Harmonization of Economic Regulation* (Oxford: Oxford University Press, 2011)137 at 137–168 (2011). But see Pamela Samuelson, "Implications of the Agreement on Trade Related Aspects of Intellectual Property Rights for Cultural Dimensions of National Copyright Laws" (1999) 23 J. Cultural Econ. 95 at 96–98 stating that intellectual property policies "are often intertwined with cultural values and policies that are deeply connected to national identity," and that "substantial harmonization of national intellectual property laws may be difficult to achieve"); Sarah R. Wasserman Rajec, "The Harmonization Myth in International Intellectual Property Law" (2020) 62 Ariz. L. Rev. 735 at 735–751 (noting, *inter alia*, that "the harmonization narrative is a myth"); See Dinwoodie, *supra* note 8 at 437–438, 440. *See* also the webpage titled "Patent Law Harmonization" on the WIPO website. *Patent Law Harmonization*, WIPO, https://www.wipo.int/patent-law/en/patent_law_harmonization.htm. See, e.g., Geiger et al, *supra* note 10 at 582; Samuelson, *supra* note 10 at 52; Jane C. Ginsburg, "International Copyright: From a Bundle of National Copyright Laws to a Supranational Code" (2000) 47 J. Copyright Soc'y U.S.A. 265, 267; Dinwoodie, *supra* note 8 at 436. In the words of Jerome Reichman, international intellectual property instruments allow countries "ample 'wiggle room' in which to implement national policies favoring the public interest." See Jerome. H. Reichman, "From Free Riders to Fair Followers: Global Competition Under the *TRIPS Agreement* (1996). 29 N.Y.U. J. Int'l L. & Pol. 11 at 28.
12   See Dinwoodie, *supra* note 8 at 437.
13   See, for example, *Berne Convention, supra* note 7 at art. 9, *TRIPS Agreement, supra* note 7 at arts. 13, 17, 26.2, 30; Trimble, *supra* note 1 at 541; see also De Miguel Asensio, *supra* note 1 at 490. Dinwoodie goes even further by noting that "[e]ven identical rules of law may lead to different results when applied in different social contexts by different tribunals. National laws—including harmonized national laws—are normally applied by reference to national market conditions. Factual differences in social practices, competitive conditions or consumer attitudes will lead to different legal conclusions (even under the same legal standard)." Dinwoodie *supra* note 8 at 436.
14   See Dinwoodie, *supra* note 8 at 436.

maximum duration of protection afforded to registered designs varies significantly between countries.[15] In the United States, the maximum term of protection for design patents is 15 years from the date of grant.[16] In the European Union and in Israel the maximum term of protection is 25 years from the date of filing of the application.[17] In Canada, the maximum term of protection is 10 years from registration or 15 years from the filing date, whichever is the later.[18] In Australia, the maximum term of protection is 10 years from the filing of the application.[19] After the term of protection expires, the design falls into the public domain and is free to use by designers in their new designs, as well as for the enjoyment of the public.

Second, different countries adopt different rules with regard to exceptions and limitations to IP rights (hereinafter IP limitations), also referred to as "permitted uses" or "user rights."[20] Permitted uses are "permissions" granted to users by law, to make certain uses of subject matters protected by IP rights in certain conditions for important social goals, even though the use itself is included within the scope of protection granted to the IP right owner.[21] For example, it is prohibited to

---

15   The international instruments only set a floor in this regard, maintaining that industrial designs shall be protected for at least 10 years. See *TRIPS Agreement, supra* note 7 at art. 26.3.

16   35 U.S.C. § 173; the maximum term is 14 years from the date of grant for applications filed before May 13, 2015.

17   Directive 98/71/EC of the European Parliament and of the Council of 13 October 1998 on the legal protection of designs, at art. 10, 1998 O.J. (L 289/28); *The Designs Act*, 5777-2017 (IL), at art. 39.

18   *Industrial Design Act*, R.S.C., 1985, c. I-9 (CA), at art. 10.

19   *Designs Act* 2003, at art. 46 (AUS).

20   The discussion on whether such permitted uses take the form or definition of "rights," "privileges," "interests," etc., is outside the scope of this article. In this regard, see, e.g., Niva Elkin-Koren, "Copyright in a Digital Ecosystem: A User Rights Approach" in Ruth L. Okediji, ed, *Copyright Law in an Age of Limitations and Exceptions* (New York: Cambridge University Press, 2017)132; Niva Elkin-Koren, "The New Frontiers of User Rights" (2016) 32 Am. U. Int'l L. Rev. 1; David Vaver, "Copyright Defenses as User Rights" (2013) 60 J. Copyright Soc'y U.S.A. 661; Abraham Drassinower, "Taking User Rights Seriously" in Michael Geist, ed, *In the Public Interest: The Future of Canadian Copyright Law* 462 (Toronto: Irwin Law, 2005); Jane C. Ginsburg, "Authors and Users in Copyright" (1997) 45 J. Copyright Soc'y U.S.A. 1; Haochen Sun, "Fair Use as a Collective User Right" (2011) 90 N.C. L. Rev. 125. Cf. Jane C. Ginsburg, "Fair Use for Free, or Permitted-but-Paid?" (2014) 29 Berkeley Tech. L.J. 1383.

21   See, e.g., 17 U.S.C. § 107; see Samuelson, *supra* note 10. This can be viewed as a "carve out" from copyright protection. See, e.g., Reichman & Okediji, *supra* note 4 at 1376–1377. The international instruments permit this leeway by the three step test. See *supra* note 11.

copy an academic article without the consent of the copyright owner, but the law of a certain country may allow such copying for research purposes even absent such consent.[22] A concrete example of different permitted uses adopted by different countries is the confined lists of exceptions to copyright typical to civil law countries, as opposed to the open-ended list of such exceptions, mostly adopted by the implementation of an open-ended fair use standard combined with a list of other specific exceptions, more prevalent in common law countries such as the United States.[23] These differences should come as no surprise. As Jane Ginsburg notes in the context of copyright protection: "[N]ational copyright laws are a component of local cultural and information policies. As such, they express each sovereign nation's twin aspirations for its citizens: exposure to works of authorship, and participation in their country's cultural patrimony."[24]

As IP is so deeply entwined with notions such as social benefits, fundamental rights including freedom of expression, and economic considerations, it is only natural that different countries incorporate into their IP laws their own national balances, resulting in the creation of different rules regarding both the scope of IP protection (IP limits) and permitted uses (IP limitations) in their respective national laws. It is important to assert here that the principle of territoriality is not a technical feature of IP, but rather a substantive one, as it allows countries to realize their sovereign power and national policies by striking important balances pertaining, *inter alia*, to fundamental rights such as freedom of expression and freedom of information, and to public interests such as the development of their economies. In this regard, the principle of territoriality is a manifestation of the sovereign power of countries to express and protect fundamental rights and their national policies.[25]

PIL, on the other hand, seeks to regulate the crossroads between different national laws in cases involving international elements. The very core of IP and that of PIL are therefore distinct: IP law is, by

---

22   See, e.g., Samuelson, *supra* note 10 at 28.
23   See Reichman & Okediji, *supra* note 4, at 1375–1378; Niva Elkin-Koren & Neil Weinstock Netanel, "Transplanting Fair Use Across the Globe: A Case Study Testing the Credibility of U.S. Opposition" (2021) 72 Hastings L.J. 1121 at 1129 at 1135–1136. For a general discussion on the differences between the approaches of continental (civil law) countries and common law countries in this context, see Reichman & Okediji, *supra* note 4 at 1375–1389; Senftleben, *supra* note 4 at 524–526.
24   See Ginsburg, *supra* note 11 at 267.
25   See Naama Daniel, "Transnational Competition: From Enforcement of Foreign Unfair Competition Judgments to Global Trademarks" (2023) 64 IDEA 31 at 60–61.

definition, rooted in the national sphere, whereas PIL is, by definition, focused on the inter-national sphere.

Private International Law

The general goal of PIL (also sometimes referred to as "choice of laws") is to set rules for cases in which more than one jurisdiction or law may be involved—i.e., to regulate cases involving a foreign element.[26] The three pillars of PIL are jurisdiction, applicable law, and enforcement of foreign judgments.[27] Jurisdiction regards rules that determine whether a court has jurisdiction to hear a claim where one or more of the parties are foreign, or where the case involves other foreign elements.[28] Applicable law concerns the rules a court would implement to determine which law to apply to a case that involves foreign elements: its own law, a foreign law, or a combination of laws.[29] Enforcement of foreign judgments sets rules to determine when a court would order to enforce a judgment granted by a court of a foreign country.[30] This usually happens when the judgment cannot be enforced within the borders of the country where the judgment was granted, for example, if the judgment granted an injunction that contains cross-border elements, or if a monetary judgment was granted but the defendant refuses to pay and has no assets in the issuing country. IP intersects with all three pillars of PIL—jurisdiction, applicable law, and enforcement of foreign judgments.[31] However, as will be demonstrated below, the most significant intersection is between IP and the pillar of enforcement of foreign judgments.

With regard to enforcement of foreign judgments in general, PIL goals are to facilitate mechanisms that minimize litigation and duplicative proceedings; reduce costs and time associated with cross-border disputes, increase judicial efficiency, and promote access to justice;

---

26   See David Hill, *Private International Law* (Edinburgh: Edinburgh University Press, 2014) 1.
27   Annabelle Bennett & Sam Granata, "When Private International Law Meets Intellectual Property Law—A Guide for Judges" (2019) 6 WIPO Magazine at 13.
28   Adrian Briggs, *The Conflict of Laws*, 4th ed (Oxford: Oxford University, 2020) at 4.
29   Id. note at 4–5.
30   See, e.g., *2019 Convention, infra* note 38 at art. 4.
31   See, regarding the pillars of private international law, Briggs, *supra* note 28 at 1–3; Ralf Michaels, "Recognition and Enforcement of Foreign Judgments" in Rüdiger Wolfrum, ed., *Max Planck Encyclopedia of Public International Law* (Oxford: Oxford University Press, 2009) at para 2; See also Kono et al, *supra* note 9 at 1.

increase predictability and legal certainty; and facilitate judicial cooperation.[32] It is based on a general public interest in having parties who
have had their day in court and received a judgment abide by it.[33] It
is further based on the public interest in discouraging and preventing
the reopening of disputes that have been heard and determined.[34]
These goals are added to the general goals or notions underlying PIL
as a whole, including comity, protecting territorial sovereignty, and
promoting private international commerce.[35] As will be demonstrated
below, at the intersection of IP and PIL, some of these general goals
are challenged.

Generally, the mechanisms incorporated by PIL rules and instruments apply similarly to any civil or commercial proceeding, from any
relevant field of law caught within the scope of national rules or international instruments on the matter.[36] PIL is thus intended to be flexible
enough to accommodate different fields of law that incorporate different
balances and are based on different rationales. But the fact that one of the
main features of IP is its territoriality, which allows countries to incorporate public policy considerations into their national IP laws, whereas PIL
seeks to bridge the gap between different jurisdictions, creates conflicts
between the two that, combined with the core differences between them,
may pose threats for IP laws and the balances they incorporate.

As mentioned, IP intersects with all three pillars of PIL. If the
parties to the IP case that is brought to court are not all domiciled in
that court's territory, the court would have to determine its jurisdiction to hear the case (the pillar of jurisdiction). Similarly, a case may

---

32   See, e.g., Francisco Garcimartín & Geneviève Saumier, *Convention of 2 July 2019 on
the Recognition and Enforcement of Foreign Judgments in Civil or Commercial Matters,
Explanatory Report* (2019), online https://assets.hcch.net/docs/a1b0b0fc-95b1-
4544-935b-b842534a120f.pdf para. 12–19 at 48; Ning Zhao, "Completing a Long-
Awaited Puzzle in the Landscape of Cross-Border Recognition and Enforcement
of Judgments: An Overview of the HCCH 2019 Judgments Convention" (2020)
30 Swiss. Rev. Int'l & Eur. L. 345 at 351.

33   Briggs, *supra* note 28 at 127.

34   Briggs, *supra* note 28.

35   Marco Basile, "Private International Law's Origins as a Branch of the Universal
Law of Nations" in Poomintr Sooksripaisarnkit & Dharmita Prasad, eds, *Blurry
Boundaries of Public and Private International Law* (Singapore: Springer Nature, 2022)
15 at 16.

36   See, e.g., *2019 Convention*, *infra* note 38 at art. 1.1 ("This Convention shall apply to
the recognition and enforcement of judgments in civil or commercial matters.").
The Convention thus applies to any judgment, on any civil or commercial matters,
unless the matter is explicitly excluded from the scope of the convention. See also
2019 Convention, *infra* note 38 at art. 2.

involve alleged IP infringements that cross borders, especially in the digital, global age. A person domiciled in a certain country may sell trademarked goods, for example, to buyers from all around the world, or upload a copyrighted work and make it accessible in numerous countries. In such cases, once the court assumes jurisdiction of the case, the court would then have to decide which of the laws of the involved countries should be applied to the case (the pillar of applicable law). Lastly, a court may be requested to enforce a foreign IP judgment in its territory and would have to decide whether to do so (the pillar of enforcement of foreign judgments).

While IP intersects with all three pillars of PIL, the most significant intersection for the purposes of this chapter is the pillar of enforcement of foreign judgments. Enforcement of foreign judgments differs from determining jurisdiction and applicable law in that the latter two are internal to the decision of the court discussing the case. That a court in country X assumes jurisdiction of a case involving a citizen of country Y, or decides to apply to that case the laws of country Z, bears no immediate effects on the laws of country Y nor Z. As opposed to that, enforcement of a foreign judgment in a country means that the court accepts a decision granted by a foreign court and gives it effect within its own jurisdiction. The enforcing court does not review the foreign case or judgment on its merits, but rather gives the foreign judgment, as is, an effect in the enforcing country, as if it were a judgment rendered by its own domestic court.[37] This act may interfere with the laws of the enforcing country itself, if the foreign judgment contradicts these laws. While specific rules on jurisdiction and applicable law may mitigate this difficulty to some extent (for example, a rule determining that for actions done in country X, country X's laws would apply even if a court in country Y assumes jurisdiction of the case), such internationally agreed-upon rules are nowhere to be found today. In addition, the most recent international instrument adopted by an intergovernmental organization that concerned the intersection between IP and PIL is the *2019 Convention on the Recognition and Enforcement of Foreign Judgments in Civil or Commercial Matters* (hereinafter *2019 Convention*), which focuses

---

37   See, e.g., De Miguel Asensio, *supra* note 1, at 485, 495; *2019 Convention, infra* note 38, at art. 4.2; Catherine Kessedjian, "Comment on the Hague Convention of 2 July 2019 on the Recognition and Enforcement of Foreign Judgments in Civil or Commercial Matters: Is the Hague Convention of 2 July 2019 a Useful Tool for Companies Who Are Conducting International Activities?" (2020) 1 Nederlands Internationaal Privaatrecht 19 at 27.

solely on enforcement of foreign judgments.[38] This chapter thus focuses on the pillar of enforcement of foreign judgments, and its intersection with IP.

The differences between IP and PIL goals and approaches and the conflicts arising in the intersection of the two fields of law are analyzed below.

When Intellectual Property and Private International Law Meet

Two types of conflicts should be considered when IP and PIL meet—the *ad hoc* conflict that arises on a case-by-case basis, and the systematic conflict that arises as a result of the differences between the goals of the two fields of law. This part demonstrates these conflicts. The next part offers a prism that can be used to conceptualize and understand these conflicts, and to successfully resolve them.

The *ad hoc*, case-by-case conflict arises when PIL rules are applied to a specific IP case, for example when considering requests for enforcement of foreign IP judgments. A foreign judgment requested to be enforced may originate in a country that implements different IP rules on a given matter than the enforcing country, thereby exposing the discrepancies between IP national regimes. These discrepancies may be derived from different limits or different limitations of the national IP systems. With regard to IP limits, some countries may grant protection to subject matters that are not protected by others. For example, in Renault v. Maxicar, the Court of Justice of the European Union (CJEU) discussed Italy's obligation to enforce a French judgment that granted protection to spare car parts, while Italian IP laws did not grant such protection (IP limit).[39] The CJEU ruled that a court is prohibited from

---

38   See *Convention of 2 July 2019 on the Recognition and Enforcement of Foreign Judgments in Civil or Commercial Matters*, July 2, 2019, 2019 O.J. (L 339) 3 [hereinafter *2019 Convention*], at art. 4.2. The Convention entered into force on September 1, 2023. See *2019 Convention*, art. 28(1); HCCH, *The EU and Ukraine join the 2019 Judgments Convention – Ukraine ratifies the 2007 Maintenance Obligations Protocol* (Aug. 29, 2022) online https://www.hcch.net/en/news-archive/details/?varevent=870.

39   C-38/98, Renault v. Maxicar and Formento [2000] ECR I-2973. In that case, the CJEU discussed the exception of public policy—one of the reasons to refuse enforcement of foreign judgments—in the context of European recognition and enforcement instruments. The question before the CJEU was whether a French judgment is to be considered contrary to public policy for recognizing intellectual property rights over spare parts for cars, which prevented third parties trading in another EU Member State (Italy) from manufacturing and selling such parts in Italy, even though spare parts are not protected in Italy. The question was raised by

refusing to enforce a judgment solely on the ground of discrepancies between its own legal rules and the legal rules applied by the court of the state of origin (that granted the judgment). Therefore, an EU Member State has no grounds to refuse the enforcement of a judgment recognizing the existence of IP rights in spare parts, which enables the rightsholder to prevent third parties trading in another EU State from manufacturing and selling such parts in that State.[40]

Another example concerns determining the jurisdiction and law applicable to a case, which in turn may result in problematic requests to enforce the foreign judgment. In the case of Trader Joe's Co. v. Hallatt, for instance, a Canadian defendant bought products of the famous American grocery store Trader Joe's in the United States, drove them over the border to Canada, and sold them in Canada.[41] While Trader Joe's owned several US registered and unregistered (common-law) trademarks, it did not own such marks in Canada, nor did it operate in Canada at the time.[42] Nevertheless, a US court ruled that the US trademark act—the *Lanham Act*—applied to the acts done by the defendant.[43] *De facto*, the Court broadened the scope of protection of

the Italian court due to its doubts that the French protection of spare parts (and therefore the French judgment) is compatible with principles of the free movement of goods and freedom of competition. See *id*; the *Convention of 27 September 1968 on Jurisdiction and the Enforcement of Judgments in Civil and Commercial Matters*, OJ 1978 L 304, p. 36 (1968), as amended [1998] OJ C27/1, later replaced by Council Regulation (EC) No 44/2001 on Jurisdiction and the Recognition and Enforcement of Judgments in Civil and Commercial Matters [2001] OJ L12/1, which was itself repealed by Council Regulation (EC) No. 1215/ 2012 of the European Parliament and of the Council of 12 December 2012 on Jurisdiction and the Recognition and Enforcement of Judgments in Civil and Commercial Matters (recast), OJ 2012 L 351/1, p. 1 (often referred to as "'Brussels I' Regulation").

40   The court ruled that this cannot be considered to be contrary to public policy. See Renault v. Maxicar and Formento, *ibid*.

41   Trader Joe's Co. v. Hallatt, 835 F.3d 960, 962–963 (9th Cir. 2016).

42   Trader Joe's Co. v. Hallatt, *ibid*. at 963.

43   Trader Joe's Co. v. Hallatt, *ibid*. The United States Court of Appeals for the Ninth Circuit found that a US trademark may essentially prevent the sale of products carrying the trademark in Canada, even though the mark was not registered there. Trader Joe's Co. v. Hallatt, *supra* note 41 at 975. The Ninth Circuit further remanded the case for further proceedings. However, before such proceedings took place, the defendant, Hallatt, decided to shut down said business in Canada due to the costs of legal proceedings and fighting the court battle, rather than because of the judgment itself. See Christopher Mele, "Pirate Joe's, Maverick Distributor of Trader Joe's Products, Shuts Down *New York Times* (Jun. 8, 2017) online https:// www.nytimes.com/2017/06/08/business/pirate-joes-trader-joes-vancouver.html; Benjamin Miljure, "Vancouver's Pirate Joe's Shuts Down, Ending Legal Battle with Trader Joe's" *CTV News* (Jun. 8, 2017) online: https://www.ctvnews.ca/

the territorial US trademark so as to apply it beyond the borders of the US, to encompass acts done in a country where the trademark was not registered and therefore (*prima facie*) not protected. If Canada was obligated to enforce any judgment resulting from the US Trader Joe's case, Canada may have been forced to prohibit acts that were argu-ably permitted according to Canadian IP law, thereby negating and undermining national Canadian IP and competition laws and policies. It follows that PIL rules can play a crucial role in preserving—or in undermining—the territoriality of IP rights.

With regard to IP limitations (permitted uses), an infringement of an IP right in one country may be considered to be a permitted use by the IP laws of another. In the context of video games, for instance, Let's Play videos, [44] livestreaming, [45] and E-sports come to mind. [46] A recently published study suggests that these may be permitted in certain territories, while constituting an infringement of IP rights in others. [47] For example, in the United States, such uses may be permitted under the fair use doctrine, whereas in a recent case in China, a plaintiff was successful in stopping unauthorized livestreaming and the broadcast-ing of E-sports tournaments. [48]

In case the plaintiff is granted a judgment in their favour, find-ing an IP infringement, and especially if they are granted monetary remedies or injunctions, they may request enforcement of the foreign judgment in another country, based on PIL rules. If the injunction granted has any extraterritorial elements, this incentive intensifies. As the examples above demonstrate, this may become problematic if the enforcement is requested in a country that does not grant IP protection to the subject matter at hand, sees it as a part of the public domain,

---

canada/vancouver-s-pirate-joe-s-shuts-down-ending-legal-battle-with-trader-joe-s-1.3448949

44   Let's Play videos document the play of a video game, usually whilst the player adds commentary. See Gaetano Dimita, Yin Harn Lee, and Michaela Macdonald, "Copyright infringement in the Video Game Industry" WIPO Doc. WIPO/ACE/15/4 (Aug. 30, 2022) online: WIPO https://www.wipo.int/edocs/mdocs/enforcement/en/wipo_ace_15/wipo_ace_15_4.pdf at 47–50.

45   In livestreaming, the player broadcasts themselves playing a video game to a live audience online, usually whilst adding commentary. Dimita et al, *Ibid.*

46   E-sports are professional or semi-professional competitive gaming tournaments, typically streamed live to an audience online. Dimita et al, *supra* note 44.

47   Dimita et al, *supra* note 44.

48   Although based on unfair competition claims. See Dimita et al, *supra* note 44 at 47–50. For a general discussion on the enforcement of foreign unfair competition judgments in this regard, see Daniel, *supra* note 25 at 108–111.

or considers the contested use to be permitted. From the perspective of national IP laws, which are based on national economic, social, political, and cultural policies,[49] the enforcement of the foreign judgment might entail the *de facto* importation of foreign IP laws contrary to the aforementioned policies, and negating them.[50] In addition, it should be noted that the accumulation of *ad hoc* cases may lead to a systematic effect creating a race to the bottom where rightsholders seek injunctions for IP infringement in the most restrictive jurisdictions, and then try to enforce these judgments in other countries that implement more lenient IP rules.[51]

Applying PIL rules to IP, and specifically enforcement of foreign IP judgments, may thus *de facto* import foreign IP laws into the enforcing country. Due to discrepancies between national rules concerning IP, countries may find themselves required to *de facto* prohibit uses that are *de jure* permitted in their respective territories, by virtue of foreign IP judgments enforcement.[52] Such enforcement undermines the principle of territoriality in IP—the core principle that allows countries the sovereign power to express and protect fundamental rights and their national policies through their IP laws.[53] As Marketa

---

49   See *supra* note 10 and 11 and accompanying text.
50   See Asensio, *supra* note 1 at 480; *cf.* Trimble, *supra* note 1 at 540–541 (noting that the use of extraterritorial cross-border remedies in intellectual property results in "the exportation of IP rights from the country of the underlying law to a target country [...] without any consideration of the laws of the target country, a shortcoming that is most apparent when the particular IP rights do not even exist in the target country, the same IP is owned there by another person or entity, or exceptions and limitations to the IP rights exist in the target country that would make the acts non-infringing or otherwise permissible in the target country").
51   This is especially the case since in most cases the rightsholder would be the party pursuing legal proceedings and seeking enforcement of the judgment granted in their favour, creating a bias which I called "the ICE bias." See Naama Daniel, "Lost in Transit: How Enforcement of Foreign Copyright Judgments Undermines the Right to Research" (2023) 38 Am. U. Int'l L. Rev., 87 at 118–128.
52   See, e.g., Ronald A. Brand, "Intellectual Property, Electronic Commerce and the Preliminary Draft Hague Jurisdiction and Judgments Convention" (2001) 62 U. Pitt. L. Rev. 581 at 602 [hereinafter Brand, *Intellectual Property*]. It may be argued that this is true to any field of law, and that a tension will always exist between the enforcement of foreign judgments and the national policies implemented by the enforcing country. I discuss this argument elsewhere and maintain that IP has features that make it distinctive to other fields of law, therefore reinforcing the problems raised by this article with regard to IP. See Daniel, *supra* note 25 at 122–124.
53   Trimble notes, regarding enforcement of foreign IP judgments prohibiting a use, by a country where the use is permitted, that "In this case the [user] is definitely not the only person affected negatively by the importation of the IP rights from another country; the importation diminishes the public domain and encroaches

Trimble describes in a similar context:

> One of the reasons that IP laws are not uniform around the world is
> that they are shaped by countries' differing public policies. Freedom
> of speech, the right to access information, the right to health and
> healthcare, the right to education, and other rights and freedoms
> affect the content of IP laws, and affect them differently by country;
> a combination of national public policies and international obli-
> gations form the mold from which individual country's IP laws
> are cast. By exporting IP rights and features from one country to
> another, extraterritorial remedies affect the mold—containing other
> rights and freedoms—that shapes IP rights.[54]

In other words, in these cases, PIL—that is conceived to be applied
between two private parties—ceases to be "private" and becomes a
national issue of the enforcing country.[55]

The second type of conflict that arises when IP and PIL meet
is the inherent, systematic conflict of goals between the two fields of
law. The goals of IP rights are to incentivize creativity and disseminate
creations to promote social welfare, and the field is deeply entwined
with fundamental right notions and protection of national policies.[56]
As IP is territorial, countries incorporate into their IP regimes their
own national public policy considerations—including economic, social,
political, and cultural policies, and protect human rights such as freedom of expression and freedom of information through their IP laws
as they find desirable.[57] The goals of PIL, and specifically enforcement
of foreign judgments, focus on efficiency, legal certainty, and international judicial cooperation.[58] The very cores of the two fields of law

---

onto the rights of the public in the target country." Trimble, *supra* note 1 at 541–542.

54   Trimble, *supra* note 1 at 541; see also Asensio, *supra* note 1 at 490 ("[I]ntellectual
      property disputes may affect significant public interests in sensitive areas in which
      basic values differ across different jurisdictions.").

55   *Cf.* Briggs, *supra* note 28 at 5 (stating that the heading "private international law"
      may suggest a relationship with public international law that regulates relations
      between countries, whereas very little public international law infiltrates PIL);
      Basile, *supra* note 35 at 15–16 ("Private international law governed relations among
      private persons"), although the author notes that in some instances developers
      of PIL sought "to place private international law on a firm basis within the law
      of nations, not to depart from it."); Bennett & Granata, *supra* note 27 at 13.

56   See *supra* note 4 and accompanying text.

57   See *supra* notes 10 and 11 and accompanying text.

58   See *supra* note 32 and accompanying text.

are therefore different. IP is an internal national system incorporating national balances (albeit subjected to international standards). In that respect, IP laws "look inside" into their own jurisdiction, to national policies and the balances that their national IP laws incorporate. PIL, by definition, focuses on the conflict between rules originating in two or more jurisdictions. In that respect, PIL "looks from the outside," at numerous jurisdictions, seeking the ultimate external means to regulate the intersection between various jurisdictions. While one of the main principles of IP is its territoriality, PIL, by definition, deals with extraterritorial aspects of laws and proceedings. Moreover, when IP is concerned, imposing foreign laws on a given country is wholly objectionable as such, whereas PIL aims to regulate the intersection between different national laws so they can coexist in harmony, and peacefully accepts the presumption that in the appropriate cases, foreign laws will be applied to a case.

This does not mean that PIL may never be applied in IP cases successfully, in a manner that maintains national IP regimes and the balances they incorporate. Since the general goal of PIL is to set rules for cases in which more than one jurisdiction may be involved, its core principles aspire to provide the flexibilities necessary to accommodate the intersection between different legal regimes, and between them to the rules of PIL themselves. However, this part demonstrates that the two fields of law — IP and PIL — inherently differ by both their main goals and notions. Therefore, applying PIL notions, which seek to promote global cooperation and efficiency, to IP, which is based on internal, national balances, could prove highly problematic, as will be demonstrated below.

This part examined the different goals of IP and PIL and identified the two types of conflicts caused at the intersection between the two fields — the *ad hoc*, case-by-case conflict, and the systematic, conceptual conflict. The next part offers to go back to the drawing board and explore these conflicts. Using the prism of legal transplants, the next part analyzes the reasons causing these conflicts and serves as a basis for their successful resolution.

Back to the Drawing Board

To better understand why conflicts arise at the intersection between IP and PIL, this part examines the location — or the drawing board — where this intersection is discussed and regulated nationally and internationally. Once identified, this part uses the prism of legal transplants to examine whether the location that was chosen to discuss these matters is indeed appropriate, and the implications of the choice of said location.

Identifying the Drawing Board

This chapter argues that the environment in which the intersection between IP and PIL is discussed and regulated, and in which rules on the matter are established or "drawn," greatly influences the outcomes of these discussions and of this rule-making. It further argues that discussing this intersection in PIL forums and hence from a PIL perspective leads to different results than discussing it in IP law forums, and therefore from an IP perspective. To understand what is considered to be the home environment, or the natural drawing board, to hold the discussions on the IP-PIL intersection, this chapter looks at the most recent international efforts to conclude an intergovernmental instrument on the matter. Interestingly, these efforts concern the pillar of PIL that this chapter identifies as the most problematic when intersecting with IP: enforcement of foreign judgments.

Between the years 2016 and 2019, the Hague Conference on Private International Law (HCCH) was home to the negotiations aiming to conclude an international instrument on the enforcement of foreign judgments.[59] The HCCH is an intergovernmental organization established in 1893, composed of approximately 90 Member States today.[60] The HCCH develops legal instruments in the field of PIL, and as such, it is not a forum specializing in IP law. On July 2, 2019, following the aforementioned negotiations, the HCCH adopted the *Convention on the Recognition and Enforcement of Foreign Judgments in Civil or Commercial Matters (2019 Convention)*.[61] In line with the goals of the HCCH, the *2019 Convention*, which entered into force on September 1, 2023, establishes a general international framework for enforcement of foreign judgments in civil and commercial matters, which applies between the Member States of the Convention, subject to its provisions.[62] Most

---

59   Garcimartín & Saumier, *supra* note 32 at 45–46.
60   See *About the HCCH*, HCCH , ONLINE: https://www.hcch.net/en/about.
61   *2019 Convention, supra* note 38.
62   See *ibid.*, arts. 1, 28–29; *The EU and Ukraine Join the 2019 Judgments Convention — Ukraine Ratifies the 2007 Maintenance Obligations Protocol*, HCCH (Aug. 29, 2022), online: https://www.hcch.net/en/news-archive/details/?varevent=870.

drafts of the *2019 Convention* discussed by the HCCH proposed to apply the Convention, *inter alia*, to IP judgments.[63] However, as a result of substantive disagreements between Member States on the matter, and after intensive discussions, the HCCH Diplomatic Session tasked with completing the work on the *2019 Convention* agreed to exclude IP judgments from the scope of the Convention altogether.[64]

Interestingly, this is not the first time such an occurrence has taken place in this forum. In the early 1990s, the HCCH Member States began to negotiate a convention on enforcement of foreign judgments and jurisdiction, only to have the negotiations collapse after a decade of work, due in large part to disagreements between Member States regarding if and how to include IP within the scope of the future convention.[65] Despite the general failure of these efforts, the work of the HCCH led, *inter alia*, to the conclusion of the *2005 Choice of Court Agreements Convention (2005 Convention)*, which refers partially and narrowly to disputes concerning IP.[66] The *2005 Convention* sets uniform rules on jurisdiction and enforcement of foreign judgments, but under very limited circumstances: it only applies if there is an exclusive choice of court agreement between the parties to the proceedings.[67] With regard to IP, the application of the *2005 Convention* is narrower still,

---

63   See *Judgments Section*, HCCH, https://www.hcch.net/en/instruments/conventions/ specialised-sections/judgments. For a general description of meetings leading to the adoption of the Convention and of its general structure, see Ronald A. Brand, "Jurisdiction and Judgments Recognition at the Hague Conference: Choices Made, Treaties Completed, and the Path Ahead" (2020) 67 Neth. Int'l L. Rev. 3, 14–15; Zhao, *supra* note 32 at 347–348, 362–363

64   See *2019 Convention, supra* note 38, at art. 2.1(m); HCCH Comm'n I, "Recognition and Enforcement of Foreign Judgments in Civil or Commercial Matters", 22d Sess., Minutes No. 7 (June 21, 2019); Zhao, *supra* note 32 at 362–363; David Goddard, "The Judgments Convention—The Current State of Play" (2019) 29 Duke J. Comp. & Int'l L. 473.

65   Intellectual property matters, together with electronic commerce matters, were the two main issues in dispute. See Brand, Intellectual Property, *supra* note 52, at 583–585; Graeme B. Dinwoodie, "Developing a Private International Intellectual Property Law: The Demise of Territoriality?" (2009) 51 Wm. & Mary L. Rev. 711 at 719; Michael Douglas et al, "The HCCH Judgments Convention in Australian Law" (2019) 47 Fed. L. Rev. 420, 421; see also Dreyfuss & Ginsburg, *supra* note 1 at 1065; Brand, *supra* note 63 at 7–14.

66   See *Convention of 30 June 2005 on Choice of Court Agreements*, at art. 2.2(n) and (o), June 30, 2005, 2005 O.J. (L 353) 5 [hereinafter *2005 Convention*]; Lydia Lundstedt, "The Newly Adopted Hague Judgments Convention: A Missed Opportunity for Intellectual Property" (2019) 50 Int'l Rev. Intell. Prop. & Competition L. 933 at 934; Brand, *supra* note 63 at 12–14; Asensio, *supra* note 1 at 473.

67   See *2005 Convention, supra* note 66 at art. 1; *id.* arts. 5–6, 8.

as the Convention applies only to very specific issues, namely, to disputes regarding the validity or infringement of copyright and related rights, and with regard to infringement proceedings concerning other IP rights—only insofar as they were brought, or could have been brought, for breach of contract between the parties (and, of course, subject to the existence of an exclusive choice of court agreement between them).[68]

The intersection between IP and PIL is thus mainly discussed, in the international level, under the auspices of PIL-specialized organizations.[69] Therefore, even if one of the goals of PIL is to provide flexibilities to accommodate the application of its rules to different fields of law and to the different national IP regimes, still the discussion on the intersection between IP and PIL as a whole, starts, takes place, and ends in the "home court" of PIL. Considering that in the last few decades, the international efforts to conclude an instrument on the matter both concerned enforcement of foreign judgments—which is the most problematic intersection of IP and PIL, and both failed after extensive (not to say heated) negotiations, a question regarding the compatibility of the matter to be discussed in PIL forums naturally arises.

It is worth noting in this regard that throughout the previous decades, numerous academic initiatives proposing mechanisms to systematically regulate the intersection between IP and PIL were published.[70] These initiatives, led mainly by scholars specializing in IP (if not

---

68   *id.* at arts. 2.2(n)-(o); Garcimartín & Saumier, *supra* note 32, para. 64–65; For a review of other multilateral private international law instruments on the matter, including instruments that were concluded by the HCCH and the European Union, see Brand, *supra* note 63, at 4–7.

69   Although this intersection was also discussed by the World Intellectual Property Organization (WIPO), the discussions there are of a more general nature, and concentrate on information sharing rather than policy or rule making. See, e.g., Eleonora Rosati, "The Localization of IP Infringements in the Online Environment: From Web 2.0 to Web 3.0 and the Metaverse" WIPO (Sep. 2023), online: WIPO https://www.wipo.int/export/sites/www/enforcement/en/pdf/case-study-the-localiaztion-of-ip-infringement.pdf; See *WIPO Forum on Private International Law and Intellectual Property*, WIPO (Jan. 30–31, 2001) online: https://www.wipo.int/meetings/en/details.jsp?meeting_id=4243; Annabelle Bennett & Sam Granata, *When Private International Law Meets Intellectual Property Law—A Guide for Judges* (Geneva: WIPO, 2019).

70   See, for example, Am. L. Inst., "Intellectual Property: Principles Governing Jurisdiction, Choice of Law and Judgments in Transnational Disputes" in Jürgen Basedow et al, eds, *Intellectual Property in the Global Arena* (Tübingen: Mohr Siebeck Tübingen, 2010) 347; Japanese Transparency Grp., "Transparency Proposal on Jurisdiction, Choice of Law, Recognition and Enforcement of Foreign Judgments in Intellectual Property" in Intellectual Property in the Global Arena, id. at 394; Priv. Int'l L. Ass'n of Kor. & Japan, "Joint Proposal" (2011) Q. Rev. Corp. L. & Soc'y

in both legal fields) have proposed wholesome instruments on the inter-section between IP and PIL, separated from general PIL instruments, tailoring them so as to better accommodate and protect IP notions and principles. This tendency seems to stand in direct contradiction to the discussions of the matter on the international level that take place in PIL forums. Once the discussion of the intersection takes place under general PIL instruments, IP is conceptually squeezed into these instruments and needs to be adjusted to them. That was the case in the *2019 Convention* negotiations, where numerous proposals were made to the plenary on how to try and adjust IP to the general PIL instrument that was being discussed.[71] Both the decision of the Diplomatic Session of the *2019 Convention* to eventually exclude IP from its scope, and the academic initiatives, indicate that despite the general international tendency to assume that PIL instruments are flexible enough to accommodate IP within them with no particular issues, they struggle and even fail to provide a solution comprehensive enough to genuinely accommodate and protect IP principles without necessitating significant adjustments.

It follows that at least on the international level, the natural envi-ronment, or "drawing board" where rules on this intersection are dis-cussed and drawn, is considered to be the PIL environment, rather than the IP one. The incorporation of references to IP rights into PIL instruments, which also refer to many other fields of law, formally seems to assume that PIL instruments are the ones "hosting" IP law notions, whereas the actual effect demonstrated in this chapter is reversed—at this intersection, IP principles are the ones being undermined by PIL

112; European Max Planck Group on Conflict of Laws in Intellectual Property, "Conflict of Laws in Intellectual Property: the CLIP Principles and Commentary) (Oxford : Oxford University Press, 2013). For a recent example see the Kyoto Guidelines, published after a decade of work by some 35 academics. Toshiyuki Kono et al., "annex, Guidelines on Intellectual Property and Private International Law ("Kyoto Guidelines")" (2021) 12 J. Intell. Prop. Info. Tech. & Elec. Com. L.; see also Rivoire, *supra* note 9 at 204.

71   See, e.g., HCCH Special Comm'n on the Recognition and Enforcement of Foreign Judgments (18 June–2 July 2019) Work. Doc. No 17E (Dist. May 17, 2019); HCCH Special Comm'n on the Recognition and Enforcement of Foreign Judgments (18 June–2 July 2019) Work. Doc. No 13 E (Dist. May 17, 2019); HCCH Special Comm'n on the Recognition and Enforcement of Foreign Judgments (18 June–2 July 2019) Work. Doc. No 9 E (Dist. May 17, 2019); HCCH Special Comm'n on the Recognition and Enforcement of Foreign Judgments (13–17 November 2017) Work. Doc. No 180 (Dist. Oct. 2017); HCCH Special Comm'n on the Recognition and Enforcement of Foreign Judgments (16–24 February 2017) Work. Doc. No 84 (Dist. February 14, 2017); HCCH Special Comm'n on the Recognition and Enforcement of Foreign Judgments (16–24 February 2017) Work. Doc. No 135 (Dist. February 20, 2017).

goals and notions. Doubts regarding the appropriateness of PIL as the drawing board to regulate the IP-PIL intersection come to mind considering the examples mentioned above, as well as the academic initiatives that propose to separate IP from general PIL instruments.

The analysis regarding the *prima facie* natural drawing board — or environment — in which the intersection between two legal regimes is discussed, and the actual effect of incorporating rules and notions from different legal sources into that environment, brings to mind the prism of legal transplants, and the criticism that developed in that regard. Coined in the 1970s under comparative law doctrine, the term "legal transplants" refers to situations in which a rule from one jurisdiction is being adopted or borrowed (transplanted) into the laws of another jurisdiction.[72] In general, a legal transplant is a rule, created and developed in a specific environment (jurisdiction), that is transplanted "as is" into another environment.[73] While some scholars view legal transplants as a natural and positive development of law, others maintain that they may create complications due to their incompatibility with the borrowing system.[74] Kahn-Freund noted that whoever requires to transplant (borrow) a rule from one jurisdiction to another should have knowledge not only of the foreign law they wish to borrow, but also of the social and political context of the transplanted rule.[75] Freedland noted that "[f]or Kahn-Freund, the 'problem of transplantation' was the inappropriateness of assuming that a legal norm or structure which had been seen

---

72   See Alan Watson, "Comparative Law and Legal Change" (1978) 37 Cambridge L.J. 313 [hereinafter Watson, Comparative Law & Legal Change]; Alan Watson, Legal Transplants: An Approach to Comparative Law 2d ed., (Athens: University of Georgia Press, 1993) [hereinafter Watson, Legal Transplants]; O. Kahn-Freund, "On Uses and Misuses of Comparative Law" (1974) 37 Mod. L. Rev. 1; Paul Edward Geller, "Legal Transplants in International Copyright: Some Problems of Method" (1994) 13 U.C.L.A. Pac. Basin L.J. 199 at 199; John W. Cairns, Watson, Walton, and the History of Legal Transplants (2013) 41 Ga. J. Int'l & Comp. L. 637 at 638; Toby Susan Goldbach, "Why Legal Transplants?" (2019) 15 Ann. Rev. L. & Soc. Sci. 583 at 583–597.

73   See, e.g., Watson, *Comparative Law & Legal Change, ibid.* at 313; Goldbach, *ibid.* at 584.

74   See WATSON, LEGAL TRANSPLANTS, *supra* note 72; Watson, *Comparative Law & Legal Change, supra* note 72 at 313; Kahn-Freund, *supra* note 72, at 5; Elkin-Koren & Netanel, *supra* note 23 at 1129.

75   See Kahn-Freund, *supra* note 72 at 6, 27 (maintaining that "in most cases one must ask what chances there are that the new law will be adjusted to the home environment and what are the risks that it will be rejected," as "any attempt to use a pattern of law outside the environment of its origin continues to entail the risk of rejection"); Cairns, *supra* note 72 at 644–645; Watson, *Comparative Law & Legal Change, supra* note 72 at 315–316.

to work well in one jurisdiction could be successfully introduced into another."[76] The basic question regarding legal transplants is whether a law originating in the society of one country may serve another country at all.[77] Scholars also argue that legal transplants raise questions that emerge from the different geographical, sociological, economic, cultural, and political nature and public policy considerations of the two jurisdictions—the donating jurisdiction and the borrowing jurisdiction, and their compatibility with each other.[78] These public policy considerations are similar to the ones incorporated by national IP laws.[79]

The next part applies an analysis based on the prism of legal transplants to the intersection between IP and PIL, particularly the pillar of enforcement of foreign judgments. On a case-by-case, *ad hoc* basis, the prism is applied directly; on the general scale of the intersection between the two fields of law, the prism is applied by analogy.

What's Legal Transplants Got to Do with It?

This analysis argues that the prism of legal transplants, and the criticism pertaining to it, may be used to better understand the intersection between IP and PIL on two significant levels. The first level is the case-by-case, *ad hoc* level, where the prism of legal transplants is applied directly and may be of use to understand the *de facto* results of applying PIL rules, such as enforcement of foreign judgments, to IP matters. The second level is a more general one, and on this level the prism of legal transplants is used by way of analogy to conceptualize the intersection between the two general fields of law—IP and PIL.

The Ad Hoc Level

On a case-by-case basis, the *de facto* result of applying PIL rules to IP matters can sometimes be equivalent to adopting a legal transplant by the enforcing country. Take, for example, the Renault v. Maxicar case, in which the CJEU ruled that Italy had no reason to refuse the

---

76   See Mark Freedland, Otto Kahn-Freund (1900–1979), in Jack Beatson & Reinhard Zimmermann, eds, *Jurists Uprooted: German Speaking Émigré Lawyers in Twentieth-Century Britain* (New York: Oxford University Press, 2004) at 299 311–312.
77   See Kahn-Freund, *supra* note 72 at 6–7; Cairns, *supra* note 72 at 644–645.
78   See Kahn-Freund, *supra* note 72 at 7–8, 12–13; R. B. Seidman, "Book Review: Legal Transplants: An Approach to Comparative Law" (1975) 55 B.U. L. Rev. 682 (referring to Watson, Legal Transplants, *supra* note 72).
79   See *supra* notes 10–11, and accompanying text.

enforcement of (or, in other words, is obligated to enforce) a French judgment that grants protection to spare car parts, even though Italian law did not grant such protection. [80] This case was discussed from the perspective of EU PIL instruments—the European Convention on the enforcement of foreign judgments—rather than IP instruments. [81] The court referred to the goals of the European Convention, stating that "[t]he court of the State in which enforcement is sought cannot, *without undermining the aim of the Convention*, refuse recognition of a decision emanating from another Contracting State solely on the ground that it considers that national or Community law was misapplied in that decision." [82] The CJEU therefore found that "a judgment of a court or tribunal of a Contracting State recognising the existence of an intellectual property right in body parts for cars, and conferring on the holder of that right protection by enabling him to prevent third parties trading in another Contracting State from manufacturing, selling, transporting, importing or exporting in that Contracting State such body parts, cannot be considered to be

---

80   See Renault v. Maxicar and Formento, *supra* note 39.

81   *Convention of 27 September 1968 on Jurisdiction and the Enforcement of Judgments in Civil and Commercial Matters* (OJ 1978 L 304, p. 36). The Court discussed the question of whether Italy was allowed to refuse enforcement of the French judgment on the ground that it was contrary to public policy. The public policy exception is often the main (if not only) substantive ground to refuse the enforcement of a foreign judgment, as opposed to refusal on procedural grounds, under private international law instruments. It was historically interpreted very narrowly. See, e.g., Asensio, *supra* note 1 at 490; Marketa Trimble Landova, "Public Policy Exception to Recognition and Enforcement of Judgments in Cases of Copyright Infringement" (2009) 40 Int'l Rev. Intell. Prop. & Competition L. 642; Daniel, *supra* note 51, at 125–127; the *2019 Convention, supra* note 38 at art. 7.1(c) and the *2005 Convention, supra* note 66 at art. 9(e); See, e.g., HCCH Special Commission on the Recognition and Enforcement of Foreign Judgments, Rep. Mtg. No. 5, para. 52–53 (2017); *S.A.R.L. Louis Feraud Int'l v. Viewfinder, Inc.*, 489 F.3d 474, 479 (2d Cir. 2007); Lydia Lundstedt, "Putting Right Holders in the Centre: 'Bolagsupplysningen and Ilsjan' (C-194/16): What Does It Mean for International Jurisdiction over Transborder Intellectual Property Infringement Disputes?" (2018) 49 Int'l Rev Intell. Prop. & Competition L. 1022 at 1038–1039; Yahoo!, Inc. v. La Ligue Contre Le Racisme et L'Antisemitisme, 433 F.3d 1199, 1252–1253 (9th Cir. 2006); De Fontbrune v. Wofsy, 39 F.4th 1214, 1227 n.11 (9th Cir. 2022). See also Ancel et al, *supra* note 9 at 68–69; Pedro de Miguel Asensio & Marketa Trimble, "International Law Association's Guidelines on Intellectual Property and Private International Law ("Kyoto Guidelines"): Recognition and Enforcement" (2021) 12 J. Intell. Prop. Info. Tech. & Elec. Com. L. 74 at 79–81; Karen E. Minehan, "The Public Policy Exception to the Enforcement of Foreign Judgments: Necessary or Nemesis" (1996) 18 Loy. L.A. Int'l & Comp. L.J. 795.

82   See Renault v. Maxicar and Formento, *supra* note 39 at para 33; emphasis added.

contrary to public policy." [83] As a result, enforcement of the foreign judgment cannot be refused. [84]

It should be noted that the French judgment in this case, which prompted the matter and for which enforcement was requested in Italy, was a monetary judgment for the sum of 100,000 Francs, i.e., no injunction was at issue in this case. However, the question that the Italian court referred to the CJEU was broader, namely, whether a judgment rendered by a court of an EU Member State is to be considered contrary to public policy according to EU laws (and therefore its enforcement may be refused) "if it recognises industrial or intellectual property rights over [spare parts], and affords protection to the holder of such purported exclusive rights by preventing third parties trading in another Member State from manufacturing, selling, transporting, importing or exporting in that Member State such [spare parts], or, in any event, by sanctioning such conduct?" This broader question is the one the CJEU answered. There is no indication in the CJEU's opinion that this answer would only apply to monetary judgments. [85]

Another example is the Trader Joe's Co. v. Hallatt case, where a US court ruled that the *US Trademark Act* applied to the acts done by the defendant who sold Trader Joe's products in Canada, although Trader Joe's owned no trademarks in Canada, nor did it operate there at the time. [86] *De facto*, the Court broadened the scope of protection of the territorial US trademark so as to apply it beyond the borders of the United States, to potentially prevent acts done in a country where the trademark was not registered and therefore (*prima facie*) not protected. [87]

Taking these cases as examples leads to the conclusion that PIL notions should be applied to IP extremely carefully, so they would not undermine the basic principle of IP territoriality. It can be inferred from the CJEU's decision in the Renault case, that if a French judgment would have ordered an injunction, the actual effect of the enforcement of the foreign French judgment by Italy, was that Italy was to prevent third parties trading in Italy from manufacturing and selling spare

---

83   Renault v. Maxicar and Formento, *ibid.*, at para 34.
84   Renault v. Maxicar and Formento, *ibid* at para 34.
85   Renault, E.C.R. I-2973.
86   Trader Joe's Co. v. Hallatt, 835 F.3d 960, 963 (9th Cir. 2016).
87   Trader Joe's Co. v. Hallatt, Ibid. at 975. It should be noted that in the recent case of Abitron Austria GMBH et al v Hetronic International, Inc., the US Supreme Court refused to apply the *US Trademark Act* (the *Lanham Act*) extraterritorially. Abitron Austria GMBH v. Hetronic International, Inc., 600 U.S. 412 (2023). See *infra*, notes 126–128 and accompanying text.

car parts in Italy, even though Italian law did not protect such objects by IP rights and left them in the possession of the public as public domain. According to the CJEU, *prima facie*, Italy had no ground to refuse such enforcement. The discrepancies between Italian and French laws on the matter are clearly based on differences in the internal public policy considerations that materialized in the different IP laws of the two countries. The Italian court, referring the matter to the CJEU, mentioned the principles of free movement of goods and freedom of competition—economic considerations—as standing to be affected by the possible enforcement of the foreign French judgment.[88] These economic considerations were obviously granted a different weight in the balance that constitutes the French IP regime. It could be that France granted more significance to other economic considerations, or to other types of national considerations altogether, for example, sociological considerations. In any case, France and Italy implement different national balances regarding the protection of spare car parts in their respective territories. Imposing an obligation on Italy to enforce a French judgment that protects subject matter that Italian law does not protect, interferes with the balances established by Italian IP laws.[89]

Moreover, in such a case, if France had granted an injunction that Italy was then obligated to enforce, the balances incorporated by the Italian legislature into Italian IP laws would have been *de facto* replaced by the balances incorporated by the French legislature into the French IP laws, as Italy would have been forced to forbid acts that its own legislation sought to allow. Marketa Trimble already noted in the context of enforcement of foreign IP judgments granting injunctions, that not only does the injunction limit the user's conduct in the enforcing country, in conflict with the laws of that country, but:

> [I]t also limits the [enforcing] country's public in their access to and enjoyment of the content, which the [enforcing] country's law is designed to provide. In this case the [user] is definitely not the only person affected negatively by the importation of the IP rights from another country; the importation diminishes the public domain and encroaches onto the rights of the public in the [enforcing] country.[90]

---

88   C-38/98, Renault v. Maxicar and Formento [2000] ECR I-2973 at para 31.
89   Regarding the problems arising from the enforcement of monetary IP judgments see *infra*, notes 96–97 and accompanying text.
90   Trimble, *supra* note 1 at 541–542.

This analysis seeks to expose such cases for what they are *de facto* — a legal transplant — and to view and analyze them as such. That the outcomes of such cases *prima facie* apply "only" in a certain case between specific parties should not matter, and indeed, this perception is even misleading, because the actual effect of such cases does not take place only between the parties.[91] The Italian public, to the benefit of which the Italian legislature sought to facilitate access to spare car parts as part of the balances incorporated into the Italian IP regime — is denied such access.[92] As Rochelle Dreyfuss describes, in the context of foreign IP judgments enforcement, "[I]ntellectual property suits are in some ways different from run-of-the-mill litigation: outcomes affect not only the parties to the suit, but also the health, safety, intellectual development, expressive capacity, and quality of life of the populace of the enforcing state."[93]

The enforcement of the French judgment here would thus have affected the Italian public, as well as Italian laws per se. In that case, French law would have been elusively transplanted into the Italian regime, undermining and overcoming the balances set by Italian laws. The same goes for the Trader Joe's case, and the possible enforcement of a US decision on the matter by courts in Canada.[94]

A further note should be made in this regard. This part focuses on foreign injunctions as more disruptive to national IP policies of the enforcing country, as it actually prohibits uses or acts. The enforcement of foreign monetary judgments has long been perceived as less intrusive regarding the enforcing country's laws.[95] However, enforcement of foreign monetary judgments may create a chilling effect deterring users in the enforcing country from making a use that is permitted according to the laws of the enforcing country.[96] In the Abitron case, the United States as *amicus curiae* argued that "[t]he court of appeals upheld a $90 million monetary award without analyzing whether 97% of petitioners' sales were likely to cause U.S. consumer confusion. That decision risks globalizing U.S. trademark law, allowing U.S. trademark

---

91   See Rochelle Cooper Dreyfuss, "An Alert to the Intellectual Property Bar: The Hague Judgments Convention" (2001) Univ. Ill. L. Rev. 421 at 436.

92   See *supra* sources cited in note 4 and accompanying text.

93   See Dreyfuss, *supra* note 91 at 436.

94   However, before such a judgment was granted, the defendant, Hallatt, decided to shut down said business in Canada due to the costs of legal proceedings. See Trader Joe's Co., *supra* note 43.

95   See e.g., *infra* notes 111-112 and accompanying text.

96   See Daniel, *supra* note 51 at 126–127.

protection to serve as a springboard for regulating foreign conduct that has no likelihood of affecting consumer perceptions in the United States."[97] It follows that the enforcement of foreign monetary IP judgments, while not as problematic as enforcement of foreign injunctions, may also interfere with national balances set forth by the IP laws of the enforcing country, and serve as a legal transplant.

The criticism pertaining to legal transplants, regarding the compatibility of a rule from one jurisdiction for transplantation into another, when the two jurisdictions developed under different sociological, economic, cultural, and political atmospheres and implement different such policies and considerations—is therefore extremely applicable to the enforcement of foreign IP judgments.[98] However, because such cases are often discussed from a PIL perspective and under PIL instruments, as opposed to IP ones, the outcomes of these cases are bound to favour PIL considerations over the balances incorporated into national IP laws.[99] For example, the starting point of international PIL instruments on enforcement of foreign judgments is, unsurprisingly, promoting the enforcement of foreign judgments. To refuse enforcement, the country where the enforcement is sought must find the appropriate ground for refusal, and discrepancies between the laws are not always (or not at all) considered to be a sufficient such ground. This was also the starting point of the *2019 Convention*. The explanatory report states that "[T]he court addressed cannot refuse recognition or enforcement on the ground that there is a discrepancy between the law applied by the court of origin and the law which would have been applied by the court addressed."[100] But, as shown above, when IP is concerned, in some cases it seems appropriate for this default to be reversed. If a country is being requested to enforce a judgment that contradicts its own IP policies, for example by enforcing an injunction prohibiting a use that is lawful in its territory, restricting the possibility of that country to refuse such enforcement is highly problematic. Looking at the matter

---

97   Brief for the United States as *amicus curiae*, Abitron Austria GMBH et al v Hetronic International, Inc., 600 U.S. 412 (2023) (No. 21–1043) at 19.

98   See Kahn-Freund, *supra* note 72 at 7–8, 12–13; Seidman, *supra* note 78.

99   In addition, international intellectual property instruments are undermined due to the diminishing of the territoriality principle and due to the fact that such enforcement *de facto* overpowers the freedom granted by these instruments to Member States, to design their intellectual property laws as they see fit, as long as they comply with the restrictions set by the international instruments. See *supra* notes 10, 11, and accompanying text.

100   Garcimartín & Saumier, *supra* note 32, ¶ 119 at 80–81.

from an IP perspective, no country should be forced to implement foreign IP laws in its own jurisdiction throughout the enforcement of foreign IP judgments.

On the *ad hoc* level, therefore, enforcement of foreign IP judgments can be described, analyzed, and criticized using the prism of legal transplants, which applies directly. However, in this case, the transplant is imposed upon the enforcing country externally, and, contrary to traditional legal transplants, with no intention of the enforcing country itself to adopt the transplant in question. This analysis leads to the second, more general level of the intersection between IP and PIL.

The General Level

On the general level, notions from the prism of legal transplants can be used, by way of analogy, to conceptualize the intersection between the two general fields of law—PIL and IP law. This level focuses on the implementation—or transplantation—of notions, principles, or rules from one general field of law into another, and it is derived from the *ad hoc* analysis. The *ad hoc* analysis above demonstrated that on a case-by-case basis, the enforcement of foreign IP judgments is equivalent to the external imposition of a legal transplant on the national IP laws of the enforcing country. This is a direct outcome of discussing the matter of enforcement of foreign IP judgments through the lens of PIL, rather than the lens of IP law. The *ad hoc* problem speaks volumes for the systematic problem. Because the instruments used to discuss the intersection between IP and PIL are almost exclusively PIL instruments, PIL considerations enjoy an inherent priority over IP considerations in this intersection and will always prevail. As shown above, when IP is concerned, in some cases it seems appropriate for the defaults provided by PIL instruments to be reversed. For example, when a country is being requested to enforce a judgment that contradicts its own IP laws allowing a specific use, countries should be sovereign to refuse such legal transplants not as an exception, but as the rule.

Similar to specific national laws, fields of law differ from one another in the goals they aim to achieve and in the public policy considerations they implement or prioritize, including in economic, sociological, political, and cultural notions and principles. Following Freedland and Kahn-Freund, this analysis considers the "inappropriateness of assuming" that a *general* legal norm, structure, principle, or rule that worked well in one field of law could be successfully introduced into another. [101] Taking inspiration from the field of legal transplants to examine the intersection between the two conceptual fields of IP law and PIL, we must first identify which is the recipient system ("home environment") and which is the donating system. [102] As shown above, on a case-by-case basis, IP law notions, considerations, as well as balances incorporated in national IP laws, are the ones standing to be affected in the intersection between PIL (enforcement of foreign judgments) and IP law, as it is applied today.

This chapter thus argues that despite the technique used by international forums, in which IP matters are formally incorporated into PIL instruments, the actual transplantation is reversed. IP matters are not "transplanted" into the field of PIL; rather, PIL notions are being "transplanted" into IP law regimes, and interfere with their principles and with the balances they incorporate. Reviewing the justifications on which the two fields are based may help in the understanding of this thesis. PIL goals are to facilitate mechanisms to minimize litigation and promote efficiency and global cooperation. [103] It is a system that presupposes a convergence of at least two national jurisdictions or cross-border elements and seeks to regulate it. IP law, on the other hand, is a system of national, territorial policies and balances, expressing a nation's public policy considerations in facilitating the goals of IP, namely, incentivizing and disseminating new inventions and creations to promote social welfare. IP is further deeply entwined with fundamental rights such as freedom of expression and freedom of information. [104]

Because IP is territorial and highly based on national policies, *inter alia* of fundamental rights, an act that is deemed an infringement of an IP right in one country may be deemed a permitted use in another. But applying PIL instruments to IP may interfere with this regime, thereby diminishing IP policies and principles such as the principle of territoriality, in the name of PIL policies such as efficiency. The critique

---

101   *Cf.* Freedland, *supra* note 76 at 311–312.

102   See Alan Watson, "Legal Transplants and Law Reform" (1976) 92 L.Q. Rev. 79. This identification is important not only from the perspective of critics, but from the perspective of advocates for legal transplants as well; it can be inferred that Watson, who is considered to be the conceptualizer of the term and a proponent of legal transplants, also recognized the importance of this identification, maintaining that the focus in transplanting a law should be on the borrowing (recipient) system. Watson, *Ibid.* at 79; Watson, Legal Transplants, *supra* note 72 at 316–318, 321; see Cairns, *supra* note 72 at 638–639, 646–647.

103   See, e.g., sources cited *supra* note 37; Garcimartín & Saumier, *supra* note 32 at para 12–19 at 48; Zhao, *supra* note 32 at 351.

104   See *supra* note 4 and accompanying text.

relating to legal transplants bears many similarities when analogized and applied in the intersection of PIL and the abundance of national IP laws, which incorporate national economic, cultural, political, and societal considerations. [105] Problems arise when we facilitate an approach viewing PIL as the drawing board where this intersection is regulated and therefore, to borrow the terms the prism of legal transplants uses, as the "home environment" of this intersection, and IP as the donating field, therefore naturally focusing on PIL goals and considerations and prioritizing them over IP ones, when the actual effect is reversed.

The analysis shows that the "home environment" being affected by an external transplant is thus IP law, and that the "donating" system is PIL. The misleading international technique used to regulate the intersection between IP and PIL under PIL instruments creates an elusive so-called transplant, which focuses the attention on the donating system—PIL—instead of on the real home environment, the recipient system—IP. And indeed, as mentioned, numerous academic initiatives offering mechanisms to deal with the intersection between IP and PIL, led mostly by IP scholars, have offered to regulate this intersection in an instrument separated from PIL instruments, re-focusing on the true home environment—IP—and seeking to use it as the drawing board to regulate this intersection. [106] Changing the drawing board to the IP one—indeed, acknowledging that the IP field is the home environment of this intersection—will naturally prioritize IP notions, principles, and goals over PIL ones, and will allow for their protection.

This part conceptualized the intersection between IP and PIL by using the prism of legal transplants. On the *ad hoc*, case-by-case level, the application of PIL to IP cases creates an outcome that is very close to (not to say, exactly the same as) an actual legal transplant. The critique pertaining to the risks of legal transplants therefore applies to this level directly. On the general level, PIL rules and norms are being elusively

---

105   See sources cited *supra* notes 10, 11, and accompanying text; Reichman & Okediji, *supra* note 4 at 1378–1380; Samuelson, *supra* note 10 at 12–59; Dreyfuss & Ginsburg, *supra* note 1 at 1066; Pamela Samuelson, "Implications of the Agreement on Trade Related Aspects of Intellectual Property Rights for Cultural Dimensions of National Copyright Laws" (1999) 23 J. Cultural Econ. 95 at 95–96, 102–103. Rochelle Dreyfuss notes that intellectual property law "is territorial precisely because its contours are importantly influenced by each society's cultural, social, and intellectual needs, technological capacity, and appetite for progress; [intellectual property law] is complex because it must provide adequate incentives to innovate while taking into account the cumulative nature of knowledge development. Countries take divergent approaches to resolving these tensions." Dreyfuss, *supra* note 91 at 441.

106   See *supra* note 70 and accompanying text.

transplanted into the IP regime. The critique used to illustrate the risks of legal transplants pertaining to national rules applies, *mutatis mutandis*, to criticize the implementation of PIL goals and notions into IP law. This part further demonstrated that these outcomes are enabled by viewing the drawing board to regulate the intersection between the two as a PIL board, rather than an IP board. Setting PIL as the drawing board for the discussions of both *ad hoc* and general intersections between IP and PIL, and discussing this intersection within the boundaries of the PIL board, allow PIL goals and principles to take precedence over IP goals and principles, to the extent that the latter are undermined, and even nullified. The next part looks to the future of the IP-PIL intersection and proposes solutions for its regulation.

Back to the Future

Building upon the analysis proposed in the previous part, this part looks to the future of the intersection between IP and PIL. This part demonstrates that applying PIL notions to IP while giving preference to PIL goals, creates problems that are especially severe in the global, digital age. This part further proposes solutions for a successful future discussion and regulation of the intersection.

The Global, Digital Age

Applying PIL rules to IP while giving preference to PIL goals and notions is especially problematic in the global, digital age. Both globalization and the digital age have led national courts to issue judgments granting remedies that reach well beyond their territorial borders in cases based on IP claims. For example, in the Google v. Equustek case, courts in Canada found that Datalink breached several Canadian judgments by continuing to unlawfully use the IP rights of Equustek in selling products on the Datalink website. [107] As a result, the Canadian courts enjoined Google from displaying any part of the Datalink website, on any of its search results, *worldwide*. [108] The case started in the Supreme Court of British Columbia, which gave the initial ruling, proceeded on appeal by Google to the British Columbia Court of Appeals that upheld the ruling, and went on to the Supreme Court of Canada which

---

107   [2017] 1 S.C.R. 824 at 826, 833–836.
108   *Ibid.* at 826, 841–846.

also upheld the ruling. [109] It is said to be the first time that a nation's highest court supported and upheld an injunction requiring a company—Google—to remove links to a website which allegedly infringe IP rights from its search results worldwide. [110] Subsequent to the ruling by the Supreme Court of Canada, Google initiated proceedings in the United States, seeking a preliminary injunction, followed by a permanent injunction, stating that the Canadian judgment will not be enforced in the United States. [111] The US District Court of the Northern District of California granted a preliminary injunction accordingly, holding that the Canadian judgment shall not be enforced in the United States as its enforcement would undermine policy goals of US legislation and threaten free speech on the global internet. [112] Following the preliminary injunction, the same court granted a default judgment and a permanent injunction, ruling that the Canadian judgment shall not be enforced in the United States. [113]

In addition, in the United States, the District Court for the Middle District of Florida issued, and the Eleventh Circuit affirmed, a global ("international") injunction in favour of the band The Commodores, prohibiting Thomas McClary, one of its original members, who left the

---

109 Equustek Sols. Inc. v. Jack, 2014 Can. LII 1063 (B.C.S.C.) at para 159, 161; Equustek Sols. Inc. v. Google Inc., 2015 B.C.C.A. 265, 113 at para 107; Google Inc. v. Equustek Solutions Inc., [2017] 1 S.C.R. 824.

110 Matthew Marinett, "The Race to the Bottom: Comity and Cooperation in Global Internet Takedown Orders" (2020) 53 U.B.C. L. Rev. 463 at 468; Robert Diab, "Search Engines and Global Takedown Orders: Google v Equustek and the Future of Free Speech Online" (2019) 56 Osgoode Hall L.J. 231 at 234. Recently, the Italian Supreme Court also recognized the possibility of the Italian Data Protection Authority to issue global delisting orders, in the context of the right to be forgotten. See Eleonora Rosati "Italian Supreme Court Admits Possibility of Global Delisting/ Removal Orders […] at Least Under Italian Law" IPKat (Nov. 26, 2022) online: https://ipkitten.blogspot.com/2022/11/italian-supreme-court-global-delisting.html.

111 Google LLC v. Equustek Sols. Inc., No. 5:17-cv-04207-EJD, 2017 WL 5000834 (N.D. Cal. Nov. 2, 2017) at 4; Google LLC v. Equustek Sols. Inc., No. 5:17-cv-04207-EJD, 2017 WL 11573727 (N.D. Cal. Dec. 14, 2017) at 2.

112 [2017] 1 S.C.R. at 828; 2017 WL 5000834 at 4.

113 2017 WL 11573727 at 2. Following the US district court decision, Google applied to the Supreme Court of British Columbia in Canada to have the global injunction set aside or varied. This application was dismissed. See Equustek v. Jack, 2014 Can. LII at para 159, 161; see also Marinett, *supra* note 110 at 469–475. This case was referred to as a "ping-pong match between the courts of two countries" – see Trimble, *supra* note 1 at 505. In Pro Swing Inc. v. Elta Golf Inc., the Supreme Court of Canada equally refused to enforce a foreign US judgment based on proceedings that stem from US trademark claims, due to the scope of the extraterritorial application of the US orders. See Pro Swing Inc. v. Elta Golf Inc., [2006] 2 R.C.S. 612; *infra*, notes 118–119 and accompanying text.

band, from using the name of the band in his performances around the world.[114] The injunction was granted on grounds of trademark infringement and unfair competition according to the *US Lanham Act*.[115]

The fact that IP national laws significantly differ from one another is the key threat to the balances they incorporate and to national policies in the context of enforcement of foreign judgments. The response of the US district court in granting an injunction to prevent the enforcement of the Canadian judgment on the Equustek case due to national balances incorporated in domestic legislation and freedom of expression considerations,[116] seems to exemplify the applicability of the critique derived from the prism of legal transplants to cases of enforcement of foreign IP judgments. This critique focuses on the compatibility of a rule from one jurisdiction to the geographical, sociological, economic, cultural, and political policies of another.[117] The Canadian Supreme Court referred to this issue in the Pro Swing case, when considering whether

---

114   After leaving the band, McClary continued performing under the band's name in different variations such as "The 2014 Commodores" and "The Commodores Featuring Thomas McClary." The District Court for the Middle District of Florida issued a preliminary global injunction prohibiting McClary from using the name of the band (the Eleventh Circuit affirmed), then issued a permanent global injunction (the Eleventh Circuit again affirmed), and later denied the motion of McClary to modify the permanent injunction to exclude from the injunctions a few countries (Mexico, New Zealand, and Switzerland; the Eleventh Circuit affirmed), and then denied a motion of McClary to have the injunction modified so as not to include the European Union, in light of McClary obtaining a registered trademark in his name for "The Commodores" there. See, e.g., Commodores Entm't Corp. v. McClary, 648 Fed. Appx. 771 (11th Cir. 2016) at 773, 777–778; Commodores Entm't Corp. v. McClary, 879 F.3d 1114, 1121–1122, 1139–1140, 1142 (11th Cir. 2018), *cert. denied*, 139 S. Ct. 225 (2018); Commodores Entm't Corp. v. McClary, 822 Fed. Appx. 904, 907, 910–911 (11th Cir. 2020); Commodores Ent. Corp. v. McClary, No. 22-10188, WL 5664170 (11th Cir. 2023).

115   See, e.g., Commodores Entm't Corp. v. McClary, 822 Fed. Appx. 904, 906–907 (11th Cir. 2020). On the fourth time this case was brought to the Eleventh Circuit on appeal by McClary, and in light of a US Supreme Court decision restricting the extraterritorial application of the *Lanham Act* that was granted in the meantime, the Eleventh Circuit vacated and remanded the case to the district court, to allow it to consider the extraterritorial application of the injunction in light of the said Supreme Court decision. See Commodores Ent. Corp. v. McClary, No. 22-10188, WL 5664170 (Sep. 1, 2023). The decision by the US Supreme Court is Abitron Austria GMBH et al v Hetronic International, Inc., 600 U.S. 412 (2023) (No. 21-1043).

116   See Google v. Equustek, [2017] 1 S.C.R. 824; Google LLC v. Equustek Sols. Inc., No. 5:17-cv-04207-EJD, 2017 WL 5000834 (N.D. Cal. Nov. 2, 2017); De Fontbrune v. Wofsy, 409 F. Supp. 3d 823 (N.D. Cal. 2019); De Fontbrune v. Wofsy, 39 F.4th 1214 (9th Cir. 2022).

117   See Google v. Equustek, [2017] 1 S.C.R. 824; Pro Swing Inc. v. Elta Golf Inc., [2006] 2 R.C.S. 612.

to enforce an injunction granted by a US court that stemmed from trade-mark infringement claims, and deciding to refuse such enforcement.[118] The Canadian Supreme Court, quoting Vaughan Black, stated that:

> A [foreign court] might issue an injunction which spells out in great detail what, when and how a defendant must do (or refrain from doing) something. If [a Canadian court] recognizes such an injunction then the courts in [the foreign country] have been per-mitted to reach deeply into the enforcement regime of [Canada]. It is the original [foreign order] [...] that will control what the defendant must and must not do in [Canada]. [W]hen [a Canadian court] agrees to enforce an injunction issued by a court in [a foreign country], then [the foreign country] is dictating and controlling the enforcement process in [Canada], something that does not occur when [the Canadian court] enforces a foreign money judgment.[119]

This is all but calling enforcement of foreign IP judgments "legal trans-plants," as this chapter proposes. The cases cited above, and others, indicate that national courts are more willing to adjudicate cases involv-ing transnational aspects of IP, and may try to apply their own laws, or aspects of them, globally, and even issue extraterritorial or global injunctions.[120] However, courts are reluctant to enforce IP judgments granted by foreign courts, especially when injunctions are concerned. Interesting to observe that the fact that courts in a given country assume jurisdiction over acts done outside their national borders, or grant

118 In this case, the Supreme Court of Canada discussed the enforcement of a US contempt of court judgment granting injunctions and orders based on the violation of a settlement agreement that was signed between the parties and endorsed by the Ohio Court. The underlying matter was based on US trademark infringement claims. Pro Swing Inc. v. Elta Golf Inc., [2006] 2 R.C.S. 612 at para 619–621.

119 Pro Swing Inc. v. Elta Golf Inc., [2006] 2 R.C.S. 612 at para 625 (quoting Vaughan Black, "Enforcement of Foreign Non-Money Judgments: Pro Swing v. Elta" (2005) 42 Can. Bus. L.J. 81 at 89. It should also be noted that while the Court found that "the time is ripe" to reconsider and revise the traditional common law rule that allows only for the enforcement of foreign money judgments, as opposed to injunctions, the Court also found that such a change must be made carefully and implement judicial discretion enabling Canadian courts to "ensure that the [foreign injunctions] do not disturb the structure and integrity of the Canadian legal system." *Ibid.* at 625–626.

120 See C-38/98, Renault v. Maxicar and Formento [2000] ECR I-2973; Trader Joe's Co. v. Hallatt, 835 F.3d 960 (9th Cir. 2016) at para 962–963; Daniel, *supra* note 51 at 135–140; Marinett, *supra* note 110 at 465, 475; Diab, *supra* note 110 at 255; Google Inc. v. Equustek Solutions Inc., [2017] 1 S.C.R. 824, para 44–49 at 846–848.

extraterritorial remedies including injunctions, does not compel courts
in the same country to enforce equivalent foreign judgments directed at
their territories. US courts assumed jurisdiction in the Trader Joe's case
and granted extraterritorial injunctions in The Commodores case, but
firmly refused to enforce the Canadian Equustek injunction. [121] Courts
in Canada issued a global injunction in the Equustek case, but refused
to enforce a US judgment in the Pro Swing case while criticizing the
idea of doing so. [122] This peculiarity is explained by going back to basics
again—as mentioned, IP and its limitations are mechanisms allowing
countries to realize their sovereign power and national policies by striking important balances pertaining, *inter alia*, to fundamental rights such
as freedom of expression and freedom of information, and to public
interests such as the development of their economies. Obligating a
country to enforce, with no review on the merits, a foreign judgment
that may well stand in direct contradiction to the enforcing country's
freedom of expression policies as implemented by its national IP laws,
is extremely problematic. Obligating a country to do so, again with no
review on the merits, when the judgment may negate the enforcing
country's economic policies designed to allow its citizens access to a
wide variety of goods and products, or to allow for the free movement
of goods, is also highly problematic. [123]

Taking the Equustek case as an example, the United States did
not adopt, within its national borders, the substantive rules that have
made such a judgment possible. The US court even viewed the Canadian
Equustek judgment as threatening free speech on the global internet,
fundamentally negating US policies. [124] The United States should not
be pushed to adopt a rule that it sees as extremely problematic, by way
of an elusive legal transplant resulting from PIL rules imposing such
obligation. [125] Obligating the United States to enforce such a judgment
interferes with the protection that the United States sought to grant

---

121   Trader Joe's Co. v. Hallatt, 835 F.3d 960, 962–963 (9th Cir. 2016); *supra* notes 114–115
       and accompanying text; *supra* notes 107–113.
122   *Ibid.*; Pro Swing Inc. v. Elta Golf Inc., [2006] 2 R.C.S. 612.
123   For comparison with the lack of enforcement of defamation and privacy judgments
       under the *2019 Convention*, see Daniel, *supra* note 51 at 149–154.
124   This is evident by the US court's reaction stating that the enforcement of the
       Canadian judgment would undermine policy goals of US legislation and threaten
       free speech on the global internet. See [2017] 1 S.C.R. at 828.
125   The possibility to refuse the enforcement on grounds of the judgment being
       manifestly repugnant to public policy was discussed above; see *supra* note 81 and
       accompanying text.

to fundamental rights such as freedom of expression through its IP laws (and related laws) within its territory. It is no wonder courts are reluctant to do so.

Therefore, future international instruments should be drafted carefully so as to avoid such outcomes, by ceasing to give preference to PIL principles and goals over IP ones. Moreover, this analysis demonstrates that in several cases, national courts refused to enforce foreign IP judgments as they viewed them as contradicting their internal, national IP laws. These refusals further indicate that the intersection between IP and PIL should be regulated within the drawing board of IP, rather than that of PIL.

This conclusion is further strengthened by a recent US case involving the European Union. In Abitron Austria GMBH et al v Hetronic International, Inc., a case pertaining to the applicability of national US IP laws abroad, and specifically to acts done in the European Union, the US Supreme Court refused to apply certain provisions of the *US Trademark Act* (the *Lanham Act*) extraterritorially. [126] The court ruled that the *Lanham Act* provisions prohibiting trademark infringement and unfair competition "are not extraterritorial and [...] they extend only to claims where the claimed infringing use in commerce is domestic." [127] While this may be seen as a pushback on the extraterritorial application of national laws and on the issuance of extraterritorial remedies, it is unclear how this standard will be interpreted, especially with regard to acts done over the internet. The judgment did not rule on this matter, which is at the heart of current IP litigation. [128] For the purposes of this

---

126   Abitron Austria GMBH v. Hetronic International, Inc., 600 U.S. (2023) 412 at 415. The *Lanham Act* provisions discussed in the judgment were 15 U. S. C. § 1114(1) (a) and § 1125(a)(1). *Ibid.*

127   *Ibid.*

128   See, e.g., Abitron Austria GMBH v. Hetronic International, Inc., 600 U.S. 412 (2023); See *ibid.*, Sotomayor J., concurring in judgment, n. 7, at 444 ("In today's increasingly global marketplace, where goods travel through different countries, multinational brands have an online presence, and trademarks are not protected uniformly around the world, limiting the *Lanham Act* to purely domestic activities leaves U.S. trademark owners without adequate protection"); Margaret Chon & Christine Haight Farley, Technology & Marketing Law Blog, "Trademark Extraterritoriality: Abitron v. Hetronic Doesn't Go the Distance" Guest Blog Post (17 July 2023) online: https://blog.ericgoldman.org/archives/2023/07/trademark-extraterritoriality-abitron-v-hetronic-doesnt-go-the-distance-guest-blog-post.htm; Linda J. Silberman & Rochelle C. Dreyfuss, "What is a 'Domestic Application' of the Lanham Act? The Supreme Court Creates More Questions than It Answers" TLB Transnational Litigation Blog (5 July 2023) online: https://tlblog.org/what-is-a-domestic-application-of-the-lanham-act/.

analysis, it is also interesting to note that the European Commission, on behalf of the European Union as *amicus curiae*, filed a brief to the US Supreme Court in this case, highlighting the problems in the extraterritorial application of foreign US laws to EU domestic activities, stating that:

> [e]xtraterritorial application of United States law to trademark use that occurs within the European Union threatens to interfere with the legal authority of the European Union and its member countries, in contravention of international law and principles of comity.[129]

In the brief, the European Commission further emphasized the importance of the territoriality principle in IP:

> The effect of the principle of territoriality in member countries of the [European] Union, as in all other nations, is that the very existence and exercise of an intellectual property right is closely related to the sovereignty of the State or regional authority granting recognition and protection of that right. Trademark rights end at the border of a national territory, so that, by definition, the infringement of a trademark right can only take place in the state that grants the right.[130]

The brief of the European Union in this multinational case again echoes the critique derived from the prism of legal transplants as applied to the intersection between IP and PIL, and the incompatibility of forcing the IP laws of a given country on another, especially via enforcement of extraterritorial injunctions, which may require the enforcing country to prohibit its own citizens from making a use that is permitted by the enforcing country, according to its national IP laws, which incorporate balances concerning fundamental rights and other public policy considerations. Following that, it is important to highlight that the judgments of which enforcement will be sought (setting aside purely monetary judgments), will in the vast majority of cases be judgments prohibiting acts, as opposed to judgments promoting permitted uses according to national IP laws. I expand on this point, stemming from what I refer to as "the ICE bias"

---

129   Brief for European Commission on Behalf of the European Union as *amicus curiae*, at 4, Abitron Austria GMBH et al v Hetronic International, Inc., 600 U.S. 412 (2023) (No. 21-1043). Also see Justice Alito's reference to the EU brief in Abitron Austria GMBH v. Hetronic Int'l Inc., 600 U.S. at 428.

130   *Ibid.*

of the IP regime combined with the PIL regime, elsewhere, and argue that this creates a risk of a race to the bottom where the most restrictive elements of each national law might be globally enforced. [131]

The digital era renders these problems even more complex, as determining the "place of infringement" of an IP right, when the act is done over the internet, is a complex matter. [132] The "localization" of the infringement of IP rights in the online environment is referred to differently by different countries, and has the potential of creating jurisdiction and applicable law clashes. [133] For example, courts in the United Kingdom recently decided on a case in which a certain trademark was owned by one entity in the UK (and the European Union), and by another entity in the United States. The defendant-appellant, Amazon, marketed and sold products of the US owner of the trademark on their US website. The plaintiff-respondent, Lifestyle Equities, who was the owner and exclusive licensee of the corresponding trademark in the UK and the European Union, sought and received in the UK Court of Appeal, *inter alia*, an injunction against Amazon, prohibiting the marketing of the products in the UK. The Supreme Court dismissed Amazon's appeal and affirmed that ruling. [134]

The age of globalization brings about similar issues. For instance, the German Supreme Court recently discussed a case in which a question arose regarding the possibility to order a defendant to cease and desist from possessing diving accessories in Spain for the purpose of offering or putting them on the market in Germany, where the trademark is protected. [135] The German Supreme Court referred the question to the CJEU, requesting a ruling on whether the possession of goods itself, outside of the country where the trademark is protected, constitutes trademark infringement if the goods are held for the purpose of offering them for sale in the country of protection. [136] The issue is thus pending before the CJEU.

131 Daniel, *supra* note 51 at 118–127.
132 Rosati, *supra* note 69.
133 *Ibid.*
134 Lifestyle Equities CV v. Amazon UK Services Ltd, [2024] UKSC 8 (appeal taken from Eng.) (U.K.). The Supreme Court noted that the dispute related entirely to events that occurred before the UK left the European Union, and that UK trademark law was at that time substantially governed by EU legislation and case law. *Id.*, at para 7.
135 Marcel Pemsel, "The global reach of trade mark law?" (04 March 2024) The IPKat online: https://ipkitten.blogspot.com/2024/03/the-global-reach-of-trade-mark-law.html?m=1
136 It seems the goods held in Spain were not even branded with the trademark. See *ibid.*

As judgments ruling on the multinational aspects of IP matters are bound to become more common, careful consideration should be given to maintaining IP balances and principles incorporated into national IP laws, and the sovereignty of countries on the matter. While the flexibilities of PIL may theoretically accommodate different national laws and regimes, discussing IP matters — territorial rights in a global, digital world where borders are often nonexistent — in PIL forums, sways the center of attention away from the internal balances incorporated by IP to the extent that it may render them null. This is reflected by the refusals of national courts to enforce foreign IP judgments. The next part looks to the future and proposes some solutions.

The Future of the Global IP-PIL System

The matter of applying PIL rules to IP matters is definitely not off the national and international agenda. From the national perspective, countries encounter *ad hoc* cases requiring them to decide on the optimal manner to reconcile IP and PIL issues. This is evident, *inter alia*, by the Canadian-American Equustek saga, the EU Italian-French Renault case, and the US Arbitron case that prompted a brief by the EU Commission. From the international perspective, international organizations continue to discuss the topic. [137] Moreover, numerous academic initiatives offering

---

137   For work done in international forums (HCCH, WIPO, and the United Nations Commission on International Trade Law (UNCITRAL)), see, e.g., HCCH Comm'n II General Affairs and Policy, 22d Sess., Min. No. 1 (21 October 2019); HCCH Comm'n II General Affairs and Policy, 22d Sess., Min. No. 2 at para 3 (21 October 2019); HCCH Comm'n II General Affairs and Policy, 22d Sess. of Jun. 18 June–Jul. 2, 2019, *Working Proposal No 1 REV from the Chair of the Commission on General Affairs and Policy* (dist. Jul. 1, 2019) ; HCCH CDAP Conclusions & Decisions at para 14 (adopted Mar. 3–6, 2020); HCCH CGAP C&D, at para 10 (Mar. 2022); Zhao, *supra* note 32 at 365–367; U.N. Comm'n on Inte'l Trade Law Work. Group II (Dispute Settlement) 75th Sess., *Draft Provisions for Technology-Related Dispute Resolution* U.N. Doc A/CN.9/WG.II/WP.224 (Jan. 31, 2022) https://documents-dds-ny.un.org/doc/UNDOC/LTD/V22/004/24/pdf/V2200424.pdf?OpenElement at 2–3, [https://perma.cc/LS7L-6BJD]; see also, HCCH & WIPO, *Identifying Actual and Practical Issues of Private International Law in Cross-Border Intellectual Property Dealings – Report* (Dec. 2022), online: https://www.wipo.int/export/sites/www/about-ip/en/judiciaries/docs/hcch-questionnaire-report-annex.pdf; Annabelle Bennett, Sam Granata, *When Private International Law Meets Intellectual Property Law – A Guide for Judges* (WIPO & the HCCH eds, 2019) online: <https://www.wipo.int/publications/en/details.jsp?id=446> [https://perma.cc/XFS5-HDTB] (last visited Nov. 7, 2023) (although this guide itself may be controversial).

mechanisms on the intersection between IP and PIL were published throughout the previous decades.[138]

This chapter uses the prism of legal transplants as a theoretical aid in any further discussion on the intersection between IP and PIL, both national and international. Based on the analysis in this chapter, countries and international organizations should acknowledge that the actual drawing board—the appropriate home environment to discuss the IP-PIL intersection—is IP. As IP principles and policies are the ones standing to be affected in the intersection between IP and PIL, the IP realm is the appropriate "drawing board," and rules on the matter should be drafted from the point of view of IP principles and notions. This is different from the point of view taken on this matter by international (and some national) entities thus far, as until now, it was viewed from the perspective of PIL, thereby downplaying IP principles, and exposing IP policies to unwanted so-called legal transplants that undermine them.

Therefore, national debates—whether in court regarding specific cases or in Government or Parliament regarding policymaking on the subject—should take notice of the possible outcomes of applying PIL rules to IP cases. For example, in some cases, the enforcement of foreign IP judgments in a given country is equivalent to the imposition of a legal transplant on that country, undermining its carefully crafted national IP policies and the balances they incorporate by *de facto* importing into its jurisdiction foreign IP rules, based on the balances set by the country that granted the judgment. Such enforcement further undermines the sovereign power of the enforcing country to express and protect fundamental rights and its national policies as it sees fit, within its borders. The critique associated with legal transplants is applicable here as it warns against the presumption that a rule that was designed by a certain country corresponding with its national economic, cultural, political, and social policies, features, and considerations, may serve another country that bears different such features and policies.[139]

These *ad hoc* or policy legal transplants equivalents are prompted by misconceptualizing the proper "home environment", i.e., by viewing the intersection between IP and PIL from the perspective of the latter, rather than the former, and discussing specific cases from the point of view of PIL rather than IP, thereby prioritizing PIL principles and notions over

138   See *supra* note 70.
139   See sources cited *supra* note 105.

IP ones. Countries should make sure to view any intersection between the fields from within the true "home environment" — IP laws — and should therefore design any future rule on the matter using the IP realm as the drawing board, with the view of protecting their own internal IP law policies. Following that, countries should carefully consider which PIL rules to adopt regarding IP, after analyzing all possible effects.[140] In addition, to avoid undermining their own national IP laws and the balances they incorporate, countries may choose to refrain from enforcement of foreign injunctions for the infringement of IP rights, at least insofar as they prohibit a use that is permitted within their borders, according to their national IP laws.[141] Viewing IP as the "home environment" or drawing board for setting such rules would allow countries to refuse such judgments as the rule, rather than as the exception (and rather still, a narrow one) that PIL would have allowed them.

From the international perspective, the prism of legal transplants is used by way of analogy, as PIL rules and norms are being elusively transplanted into the IP regime. This outcome is derived, in large part, from the mislocation of the international drawing board where international rules and regulations regarding the intersection between IP and PIL are being discussed and designed. This mislocation of the drawing board materialized as the international discussions on binding instruments regarding the intersection takes place, to this day, in PIL-specialized forums. Such forums are, of course, bound to prefer PIL principles and notions over IP ones, aggravating the problems exposed by this analysis. Following that, any further international discussion on the matter should take place in the natural habitat, or "home environment," of the intersection as exposed by this analysis — IP.[142] By discussing the matter in IP-specialized forums, IP notions, including

---

140   For example, countries may choose to adopt special and detailed rules on jurisdiction and applicable law when IP is concerned to preserve the principle of territoriality.

141   *Cf.* Dreyfuss & Ginsburg, *supra* note 1 at 1088, 1148–1149 (proposing to allow countries to refuse the enforcement of injunctions and accept damages in lieu of injunctions in certain cases if the original judgment "conflicts with fundamental cultural policies in the State where enforcement is sought"). This is no radical solution; as Dinwoodie noted, direct enforcement of injunctive relief is rarely acceptable. See Dinwoodie, *supra* note 65 at 762; *cf.* Dreyfuss, *supra* note 91 at 446–448. But see Asensio, *supra* note 1 at 479 (noting that traditionally, legal systems, especially common law jurisdictions, have been reluctant to enforce foreign non-monetary judgments, but in most jurisdictions, there is a current clear trend to now make such enforcement possible).

142   See, e.g., Dreyfuss & Ginsburg, *supra* note 1.

the balances implemented by national IP laws, and the principle of territoriality, will be upheld and protected.[143]

This part proposed a conceptual change in reversing the default of the "natural habitat" of discussions regarding the intersection between IP and PIL: no more discussing IP as yet another field of law that PIL applies to, and deciding whether to include or exclude IP matters under PIL instruments; but, rather, crafting the rules on the matter within the IP drawing board, therefore picking and choosing the appropriate PIL rules to apply to IP matters, in a manner that would comply and maintain IP principles and policies.

Conclusion

This chapter argues that any discussion on the future of IP will go amiss if it neglects to address the intersection between IP and PIL. The chapter emphasizes that IP rights are territorial, and that national IP laws are designed to accommodate internal, local balances based on the economic, cultural, political, and social features of the country where they are designed. In this regard, the principle of territoriality is, *inter alia*, a manifestation of the sovereign power of countries to express and protect fundamental rights and their national policies. Therefore, the importation of foreign IP rules into a country, as a result of PIL rules, and specifically by enforcement of foreign IP judgments, is problematic. The chapter uses the prism of legal transplants to analyze and conceptualize these problems, finding that on the *ad hoc*, case-by-case level, the application of PIL rules to IP cases creates the equivalent of legal transplants, whereas on the general level, PIL rules and norms are being elusively transplanted into the IP regime. The critique pertaining to the risks of legal transplants originating in a certain country, and their incompatibility to be transplanted into another jurisdiction as-is, therefore applies in both levels *mutatis mutandis* — whether directly or by analogy. Nevertheless, this chapter demonstrates that to this day, the intersection between IP and PIL is discussed, on the international level, as if PIL is its natural habitat, or "drawing board" — under PIL instruments. Because of the location of the discussions, IP goals and

---

143   I also propose elsewhere that any instrument regulating the intersection between intellectual property and private international law should be a wholesome one, pertaining to all aspects of the intersection, and paying special attention to national intellectual property policies and balances. See Daniel, *supra* note 51 at 143–147, 154–156.

principles are undermined and defeated by those of PIL. As the digital, global environment continues to develop, the risks posed to IP policies by the application of PIL rules become gradually more severe. This chapter argues that because the substantive outcomes of the intersection between the two fields of law actually take place in the IP realm, the correct location, natural habitat, or drawing board for any future discussion on this intersection should be the IP one. There, IP considerations would conceptually and effectively take precedence over PIL ones and would remain protected. This is supported by recent court rulings refusing to enforce foreign IP (or IP-based) judgments, as they are perceived as interfering with national balances incorporated into the national IP laws of the enforcing country. The analysis in this chapter thus seeks to give tools to legal professionals, judges, and policy makers, to better understand and resolve the problems arising at the intersection between IP and PIL in the future, and to maintain and protect national — and international — IP regimes. [144]

144   The author thanks Efrat Hakak, Guy Keinan, and the participants of the Future of the Global IP System Workshop at the University of British Columbia (June 2023) for insightful comments on early versions of this chapter.

CHAPTER 14

Artificial Intelligence and Challenges for the Patent System: An Economic Perspective

Luciano Póvoa and Andrea Cabello

Abstract

This chapter analyzes the impact of Artificial Intelligence (AI) on inventive activity, with particular attention to its implications for the patent system. We examine how AI's distinctive characteristics—its capacity to reduce the costs and uncertainties of discovery and innovation, its role as a general-purpose technology driving productivity across industries, and its potential to shift economic dynamics from exclusion to inclusion—challenge fundamental principles of the patent framework. Given the current scarcity of empirical data, this analysis adopts a theoretical approach to shed light on the complex relationship between innovation processes and intellectual property systems. The chapter also considers AI's application in drug development, discussing the broader implications for patents in the context of ongoing economic and societal transformations.

The potential of Artificial Intelligence (AI) has been widely acknowledged by experts since at least 2012 with the advancement of the technique known as deep learning.[1] In the past decade, significant advancements have been made, with applications spanning various fields. Particularly noteworthy is the application of these advancements to guide

---

[1]   Yann LeCun, Yoshua Bengio & Geoffrey Hinton, "Deep Learning" (2015) 521:7553 Nature 436–444.

and accelerate research and scientific discoveries. In 2020, DeepMind, an Artificial Intelligence lab, introduced AlphaFold. This AI system can predict the three-dimensional structure of proteins from their amino acid sequence with precision and at a reduced cost.[2] This task is recognized as one of the most challenging in biochemical research, as determining a protein's structure is crucial for understanding the nature of diseases and for the more effective development of vaccines and medications. AlphaFold transformed an activity that was traditionally experimental and could take months or even years to complete, allowing it to be done in minutes. In 2022, the AlphaFold code and the AlphaFold Protein Structure Database were made publicly available. This database includes the most complete human proteome to date, as well as that of over 20 other organisms, totaling more than 350,000 protein structures.

AI has been utilized not only to enhance Research and Development (R&D) activities but also an activity that was once considered intrinsically human: the ability to formulate hypotheses and invent.

The Organization for Economic Co-operation and Development (OECD) defines artificial intelligence as a technology that enables machines to make predictions, make decisions, automate tasks, and create, potentially influencing both the real and virtual worlds intelligently, based on objectives set by humans.

The emergence of these technologies immediately sparked debates on intellectual property issues, particularly regarding the authorship of AI-generated content and potential copyright infringements associated with the training of AI models.[3] Furthermore, AI has impacted an activity once considered inherently human: the capacity to invent.

This chapter aims to explore the impacts of employing AI tools on inventive activity, its economic aspects, and their repercussions on the patent system. In doing so, it seeks to contribute to the understanding of the complex interactions between technological innovation and intellectual property. Throughout the twentieth century, a series of technological innovations spurred the need to reinterpret or refine the framework of copyright laws to encompass new forms of intellectual

---

2   Andrew W Senior et al, "Improved Protein Structure Prediction Using Potentials from Deep Learning" (2020) 577:7792 Nature 706–710.

3   Michael M. Grynbaum & Ryan Mac, "The Times Sues OpenAI and Microsoft Over A.I. Use of Copyrighted Work" *The New York Times* (27 December 2023) https://www.nytimes.com/2023/12/27/business/media/new-york-times-open-ai-microsoft-lawsuit.html.

creations.[4] This need emerged with the advent of technologies such as xerography, software, and, later on, data transfer via the internet, which enabled the widespread dissemination of texts, images, and sounds to millions of users at nearly zero marginal cost.

These technological innovations induced significant transformations in the *process of reproducing* materials protected by copyright, leading to social and legal frictions. The historical response to these tensions often involved specific adjustments in the intellectual property regime, aiming to accommodate the new paradigms of content creation and distribution.

In contrast to the dynamism observed in the realm of copyright laws, patent legislations remained relatively stable and indifferent to innovations during the same period. While innovations may influence the pace and direction of patenting activities, they rarely provoke substantive changes in patent legislation.

However, this chapter proposes that the emergence and diffusion of AI represent a departure from previous trends, potentially triggering profound revisions in the foundations of patent law. We argue that AI, due to its distinctive characteristics, may challenge central premises of the patent system, including the extent of the conferred monopoly, the criteria for inventorship, and the requirements for patentability.

We highlight three distinctive features of AI. First, it is crucial to recognize that AI directly influences the *process of generating* discoveries, inventions, and intellectual creations, going beyond mere reproduction. AI contributes to a significant reduction in the costs associated with prediction and creation, thereby lowering Research and Development (R&D) expenses and affecting the demand and supply of inventions.

Second, from an economic perspective, AI stands out as a *general-purpose technology*, characterized as an enabling technology that can be employed across a wide range of sectors, enhancing productivity, and fostering new opportunities and complementary inventions.[5] It can lead to changes in the relative economic importance of sectors and to the overall significance attached to patents as a mechanism for recouping investments in innovation. In the past, similar technologies, such as electricity and the internal combustion engine, had profound impacts

---

4   David D Friedman, "Does Technology Require New Law?" (2001) 25 Harv.J.L.& Pub.Pol'y.

5   Manuel Trajtenberg, "AI as the Next GPT: a Political-Economy Perspective" in Ajay Agrawal, Joshua Gans & Avi Goldfarb eds, *The Economics of Artificial Intelligence: An Agenda* (Chicago: University of Chicago Press, 2019).

on various sectors, reshaping the urban structure of the twentieth century and labour relations.

Third, the configuration of the intellectual property system is shaped by economic and political factors. Intellectual property rights are often interpreted by economists as an incentive mechanism, where the state grants a temporary monopoly to stimulate the creation, development, and dissemination of inventions in society.[6] AI has the potential to alter this economic logic, favouring a model that privileges inclusion and access over exclusion and the appropriation of consumer surplus (the practice of charging the maximum price that consumers are willing to pay).

We note that our analysis is based on theoretical arguments, given the lack of empirical evidence on the concrete impacts of AI on the economy and society. We also dismiss the notion that an AI that completely replaces human reasoning is imminent. Therefore, this work aims to explore the *potential challenges* that AI poses to the current patent system. The remainder of this chapter is structured as follows: the second section discusses how AI can influence R&D activity and the innovation process. The following sections exemplify the application of AI in the development of new drugs, present some challenges of AI for the patent system, and then briefly examine how the current economic and social context, including the digital economy and demographic changes, might diminish the relevance of patents as a mechanism for appropriating the benefits of inventive activities, challenging patent legislation.

How AI Influences R&D Activities and the Innovation Process

Innovative activity is generally characterized as expensive, complex, and fraught with uncertainties. From an economic perspective, employing AI as a tool in R&D activities can lead to at least three effects on the innovation process: cost reduction, uncertainty reduction, and the improvement of firm's absorptive capacity. The combined effect results in greater efficiency of the resources used for R&D. This aspect also implies a decrease in opportunity cost, encouraging firms to invest in multiple invention projects simultaneously, without the fear of incurring significant losses for not exploring other opportunities.

---

6   Roberto Mazzoleni & Richard R Nelson, "The Benefits and Costs of Strong Patent Protection: A Contribution to the Current Debate" (1998) 27:3 Res Policy 273–284.

First, AI can substantially reduce the costs associated with the innovation process, from financial expenses and skilled labour to the time required to develop new inventions. One of the primary means of reducing these costs is through the automation of tasks at various stages of the innovation process, including model identification, conducting tests, and collecting and analyzing data. Moreover, AI enables the optimization of these processes and the improvement of decision making.

For example, the incorporation of new technologies associated with AI, such as machine learning and deep learning, began to revolutionize medical research. These technologies have shown tremendous promise in the development of new drugs and the discovery of vaccines.[7] Bagabir et al report that AI was employed to optimize mRNA sequences, significantly contributing to production efficiency. The integration of robotic automation and AI enabled Moderna to manufacture over 1,000 mRNA sequences per month, a notable increase from the previous manual production capacity of only 30 sequences.[8] In other words, what previously took a month could now be produced in a day.

The use of AI in medical research has accelerated stages that traditionally took months or years to conduct with conventional research methods. Even more remarkably, AI has enabled the acceleration *and* the discovery of new connections and outcomes previously unforeseen by scientific hypotheses and beyond human perception using traditional methods.[9]

In another example, AI was used to analyze over one hundred million chemical molecules in just a few days, identifying potential antibiotic candidates with innovative mechanisms of action, divergent from those used in existing drugs. This process resulted in the discovery of a new and potent antibiotic.[10]

Thus, AI has played a revolutionary role in inventive activities and innovation by providing greater efficiency to the R&D process, reducing

7   Sali Abubaker Bagabir et al, "COVID-19 and Artificial Intelligence: Genome Sequencing, Drug Development and Vaccine Discovery" (2022) 15:2 Journal of Infection and Public Health 289–296."

8   Ashwani Sharma et al, "Artificial Intelligence-Based Data-Driven Strategy to Accelerate Research, Development, and Clinical Trials of COVID Vaccine" (2022) 2022 BioMed Research International 7205241.

9   Jens Ludwig & Sendhil Mullainathan, *Algorithmic Behavioral Science: Machine Learning as a Tool for Scientific Discovery* (Rochester: NY, 2022).

10   "Artificial Intelligence Yields New Antibiotic," (20 February 2020), *MIT News Mass Inst Technol*, online: https://news.mit.edu/2020/artificial-intelligence-identifies-new-antibiotic-0220.

operational costs, and the time required for various research stages.

Ajay Agrawal et al highlight that the most significant aspect of this revolution is the drastic reduction in the *cost of prediction*.[11] In this context, prediction refers to the process of using a large set of available information (big data) to generate unknown information, such as filling gaps, anticipating future events, recognizing patterns, or generating insights. As the authors emphasize, we tend to utilize a resource (prediction) more when its costs are drastically reduced, often approaching zero, as happened with the spread of digital technology, which enabled the representation of information in bits. The transition to digital representation contributed to reducing the cost of searching for information, bringing various economic consequences, such as an increase in the diversity of available goods, the emergence of the sharing economy, and the development of platforms like Airbnb.[12]

Thus, recent advances in AI have facilitated the execution of automated and low-cost predictions, applied in task automation, image recognition, autonomous vehicles, and analysis of large datasets. This predictive capability of AI has significant implications for innovation. In this way, AI can be considered a *new method of invention*, characterizing itself as a general-purpose technology with the potential to fundamentally change the way R&D is conducted and innovation strategies.[13] According to Cockburn et al:

> One of the important insights to be gained from thinking about [the invention of a method of inventing], therefore, is that the economic impact of some types of research tools is not limited to their ability to reduce the costs of specific innovation activities – perhaps even more consequentially they enable a new approach to innovation itself, by altering the 'playbook' for innovation in the domains where the new tool is applied (p. 116).[14]

---

11   Ajay Agrawal, Joshua Gans & Avi Goldfarb, "Prediction, Judgment, and Complexity: A Theory of Decision-Making and Artificial Intelligence" in The Economics of Artificial Intelligence: An Agenda (Chicago: University of Chicago Press, 2019) 89.

12   *See* Avi Goldfarb & Catherine E. Tucker, "Digital Economics" (2019) 57:1 Journal of Economic Literature 3–43.

13   Iain M Cockburn, Rebecca Henderson & Scott Stern, "The Impact of Artificial Intelligence on Innovation: An Exploratory Analysis" in The Economics of Artificial Intelligence: An Agenda (Chicago: University of Chicago Press, 2019) 115; Stefano Bianchini, Moritz Müller & Pierre Pelletier, "Artificial Intelligence in Science: An Emerging General Method of Invention" (2022) 51:10 Res Policy 104604.

14   Cockburn, Henderson & Stern, *supra* note 1354.

AI as a general-purpose technology has the potential to influence various sectors of the economy. One way to verify the validity of this observation is through the analysis of how many inventions are currently related to AI, and how many technological fields are impacted. The US Patent and Trademark Office (USPTO) published the report "Inventing AI: Tracing the Diffusion of Artificial Intelligence with U.S. Patents" [15] in 2020, which shows that the volume and percentage of public patent applications related to AI grew 100 percent between 2002 and 2018. The study also shows that this technology is becoming increasingly important for invention and is rapidly diffusing across other sectors. The report highlights that "[i]n 1976, patents containing AI appeared in about 10% of the subclasses. By 2018, they had spread to more than 42% of all patent technology subclasses."

The predictive capability of AI also has implications for reduction of uncertainty, which is crucial for the decision-making process.

Firms engaged in innovation activities face *economic and technical uncertainties*. As highlighted by technology historian Nathan Rosenberg, the bulk of corporate R&D efforts are focused on development (D). [16] It is at this stage of the inventive activity that solutions are sought to reduce the costs arising from uncertainties.

Economic uncertainties can be mitigated through firms' enhanced ability to collect data and use AI to make better predictions about: consumer behaviour, supply and demand for products and services, anticipate changes in the supply chain, conduct consumer testing, obtain feedback, and make improvements before launching products or services.

Data-driven tools coupled with AI also contribute to the reduction of technical uncertainties through the improvement of the quality of predictions and the ability to identify patterns and envision new connections that were previously challenging for the human mind. Technical uncertainty is further reduced through AI-driven prototyping, which accelerates the stages of creation, and offers design options and uses in a more agile manner and at a lower cost than traditional methods. From prototypes, it is possible to conduct tests and obtain feedback to correct flaws and enhance the quality of products and services.

15   US Patent and Trademark Office, "Inventing AI: Tracing the Diffusion Of Artificial Intelligence with U.S. Patents" (October 2020) USPTO.GOV, online: https://www.uspto.gov/sites/default/files/documents/OCE-DH-AI.pdf

16   Nathan Rosenberg, *Schumpeter and the Endogeneity of Technology: Some American Perspectives*, The Graz Schumpeter lectures 3 (London; New York: Routledge, 2000).

Finally, AI is being employed in the innovation process to enhance the recognition of the value of external information by companies and individuals, as well as to expedite the trial-and-error cycle and foster knowledge accumulation. Cohen and Levinthal introduce the concept of absorptive capacity as crucial for innovation and organizational learning. [17] They argue that a firm's ability to recognize the value of new, external information, assimilate it, and apply it for commercial purposes is fundamental to its innovative capabilities. AI has been used for large-scale information gathering and transforming this information into knowledge. While "learning by doing" focuses on learning through continuous practice in activities in which the firm is already engaged and holds importance in generating internal information and knowledge, absorptive capacity enables an increase in the diversity of knowledge, especially when combining knowledge from other areas to generate innovative solutions. In our view, both processes are important for innovation and can be enhanced with the use of AI.

As previously mentioned, there is a limited body of research regarding the impact of AI applications on the innovation process. In particular, the most reliable data originates from extensive innovation surveys conducted by government agencies. However, these studies are typically carried out at intervals that have yet to encompass the most recent developments in AI and its application in the economy.

One of the studies that manages to derive some analysis of the influence of AI use on innovation is carried by Christian Rammer et al [18] when analyzing data from the German part of the Community Innovation Survey (CIS) 2018. The authors show that companies using AI are 8.5 percent more likely to introduce a new product to the market. Thus, AI plays a significant role in companies' ability to innovate and achieve economic gains.

It is important to note that firms that adopt artificial intelligence tend to be naturally more innovative. This is because they invest in R&D and skilled personnel, which enhances their capacity to absorb cutting-edge scientific and technological knowledge. Nevertheless, the main point of these results is to recognize that innovative companies are integrating AI into their innovation activities and, according to

---

17   Wesley M Cohen & Daniel A Levinthal, "Absorptive Capacity: A New Perspective on Learning and Innovation" (1990) 35:1 Administrative Science Quarterly 128–152.

18   Christian Rammer, Gastón P Fernández & Dirk Czarnitzki, "Artificial Intelligence and Industrial Innovation: Evidence from German Firm-Level Data" (2022) 51:7 Res Policy 104555.

the study by Christian Rammer et al, increasing its rate of innovation, particularly those most relevant innovations (new to the world). If this makes them more innovative than others, it is likely that other companies will follow suit.

In summary, the use of AI in the innovation process tends to reduce costs and uncertainties, as well as enhance the absorptive capacity of companies. Such factors result in improved efficiency in the inventive process, manifesting in an increase in the quantity and quality of inventions, or in both. In the following section, we will apply these insights to explore the use of AI in the development of new drugs.

AI and Drug Development

In this section, we detail the application of AI in the pharmaceutical sector, specifically in the development of new drugs. The particular interest in this sector stems from its traditional reliance on patents as a crucial mechanism to secure a return on investments in R&D. Based on national innovation surveys, Hall et al highlight that, generally, patents do not represent the primary method of intellectual property protection, being surpassed by the use of trade secrets and the advantage of lead time.[19] This trend applies to both product and process innovations. However, specifically for innovations in sectors focused on "discrete" products, such as pharmaceuticals and chemicals, patents remain the most valued strategy to safeguard the profits derived from IP. Thus, any eventual change in the dynamics of innovation and patent protection tends to affect these sectors more.

It has long been considered that research and development (R&D) in the pharmaceutical industry has become too expensive. From uncertain drug development to costly clinical trials that need patient participation rates to meet regulatory minimum standards, every step of the process has been criticized over time. This has driven the search for safe strategies aimed at cost reductions in the research of new drugs and processes.

Over the past few years, new technologies such as AI have brought new hopes to research in general and to pharmaceutical R&D in particular. The COVID-19 pandemic accelerated even more the excitement over the use of these techniques in the industry, due to its desperate and immediate nature.

---

19   Bronwyn Hall et al, "The Choice Between Formal and Informal Intellectual Property: A Review" (2014) 52:2 Journal of Economic Literature 375–423.

Much of the literature discussing the use of AI in the pharmaceutical field outlines how this technology can be applied across various steps, ranging from disease tracking and management to all phases of pharmaceutical R&D. Vora et al describe the use of machine learning in experimental design, pharmacokinetics prediction, and optimization of lead compounds, emphasizing how AI can reduce development costs and increase the likelihood of approval for new drugs.[20] In their study, a significant focus is given to drug discovery, where AI assists in the identification of therapeutic targets, virtual screening, structure-activity relationship modelling, design of new drugs, optimization of drug candidates, drug repurposing, and toxicity prediction. These processes benefit from AI's ability to rapidly analyze large volumes of individual and biological data to identify patterns and predict interactions between targets and drug candidates.

For example, during the COVID-19 pandemic, early on, simulation and prediction models were used to try to *track contamination patterns and disease development*. Models such as SIR (susceptible-infected-recovered) soon became very popular among health officials across the whole world.[21] As Wim Naudé points out, some of the uses of AI on disease management are early warnings and alerts, tracking and prediction, and data dashboards.[22] These are much more useful in a scenario like a pandemic, which possibly explains why these instruments became so popular back in 2020.

In the *pre-clinical stage*, the use of natural language processing on scientific literature, unstructured electronic medical records, and insurance claims is mentioned as a promising way to identify patterns and research targets. Much of the literature here focuses on protein structure prediction and drug repurposing.[23]

---

20   Lalitkumar K Vora et al, "Artificial Intelligence in Pharmaceutical Technology and Drug Delivery Design" (2023) 15:7 Pharmaceutics, online: https://www.ncbi.nlm.nih.gov/pmc/articles/PMC10385763/.

21   Nick H Ogden et al, "Modelling Scenarios of the Epidemic of COVID-19 in Canada" (2020) Can Commun Dis Rep 198–204.

22   Wim Naudé, "Artificial Intelligence Against COVID-19: An Early Review" (2020), IZA Discussion Papers No. 13110.

23   Arash Keshavarzi Arshadi et al, "Artificial Intelligence for COVID-19 Drug Discovery and Vaccine Development" (2020) 3 Frontiers in Artificial Intelligence 65; Sheela Kolluri et al, "Machine Learning and Artificial Intelligence in Pharmaceutical Research and Development: A Review" (2022) 24:1 The AAPS Journal 19; Sweta Mohanty et al, "Application of Artificial Intelligence in COVID-19 Drug Repurposing" (2020) 14:5 Diabetes & Metabolic Syndrome: Clinical Research & Reviews 1027–1031.

Especially in the early days of the pandemic, the focus of the literature was on *drug repurposing*. Drug repurposing leads to shorter development and research time and lower costs, including during clinical trial
phases, which are some of the most expensive stages of pharmaceutical
R&D.[24] The use of AI for drug repurposing predates the pandemic, but
it was certainly accelerated during it.[25] For a systematic review of drugs
considered during the COVID-19 pandemic, see Carla Pires.[26]

This ability to lower costs has to do with AI prediction capacities,
dealing with statistical issues that are complex without these tools.
According to Kolluri et al:

> [...] predictive modeling is used to predict protein structures and
> facilitate molecular compound design and optimization for enabling
> selection of drug candidates with a higher probability of success.
> The increasing volume of high-dimensional data from genomics,
> imaging, and the use of digital wearable devices, has led to rapid
> advancements in ML methods to handle the "Large p, Small n"
> problem where the number of variables ("p") is greater than the
> number of samples ("n").[27]

Other uses include developing predictive biomarkers and precision medicine to define target population and dose regimes; that is, to identify types
of patients who may benefit more from one group of treatment compared
to others, which also reduces development time and costs. Much of this is
based on evaluating and predicting success of different strategies and outcomes in automated ways beforehand without incurring costly trajectories.

Peter Henstock[28] argues that, although the use of AI in pre-clinical
phases and drug discovery predates the pandemic and has been going
on for years with "increasing sophistication," its use on later stages such
as clinical trials is recent.[29] The literature has emphasized the promises

---

24   Kumaraswamy Gandla et al, "A Review of Artificial Intelligence in Treatment of
      COVID-19" (2022) J Pharm Negat Results 254–264.
25   Kolluri et al, *supra* note 1364.
26   Carla Pires, "A Systematic Review on the Contribution of Artificial Intelligence in
      the Development of Medicines for COVID-2019" (2021) 11:9 Journal of Personalized
      Medicine 926.
27   Kolluri et al, *supra* note 1364.
28   Peter Henstock, "Artificial Intelligence in Pharma: Positive Trends but More
      Investment Needed to Drive a Transformation" (2021) Volume 2:Issue 2 Archives
      of Pharmacology and Therapeutics 24–28.
29   Kolluri et al, *supra* note 1364.

of clinical trial design and analysis using nonparametric Bayesian learning[30] and tools for clinical trial oversight.

During *clinical trial phases*, the use of AI tools includes patient selection, trial monitoring, and data collection and analysis, including the reports required by regulators, which can be very costly and time-consuming to produce. This is especially important, as some experts argue that a large number of clinical trials are unsuccessful due to problems with patient enrollment. Arash Keshavarzi et al suggest that artificial intelligence and machine learning tools can make patient selection smarter and lead to regulatory submission data packages, making the whole process easier.[31]

Several critical points regarding the use of AI in research have been raised in the literature. However, we note that the rapid advancement of AI techniques in the last three years has made such criticisms less relevant, and many obstacles are being overcome. Given that it is an ongoing revolution, many of these advancements have yet to be evaluated in terms of causality in academic studies, but they are being received with great enthusiasm by the academic community.[32]

One concerns is the fact that AI tools rely on data availability. This has implications that must be addressed. First, they can be limited by the lack of (public) data.[33] Much of the data here concerns health information that in most countries is protected by privacy laws to some extent. This is something that must be considered as either as a limitation of scope or something to be addressed. Second, even if all these data become available, there is a lot of data—and a lot of data does not always make decisions easier, as it may result in false leads, instead of shortcuts. Third, this means that not all is cost reduction when it comes to AI tools—investment to make these tools more efficient is also needed.[34] Last, this increased efficiency may not be enough (or may not act fast enough) to offset the diminishing returns that these tools probably present—that is, as they work on existing data, the more they are used, the harder it gets for them to bring back the expected results.

---

30   Subrat Kumar Bhattamisra et al., "Artificial Intelligence in Pharmaceutical and Healthcare Research" (2023) 7:1 Big Data and Cognitive Computing 10.

31   Arash Keshavarzi Arshadi et al, *supra* note 1364.

32   Ewen Callaway, "'A Pandora's Box': Map of Protein-Structure Families Delights Scientists" (2023) 621:7979 Nature 455–455; Artur M Schweidtmann, "Generative Artificial Intelligence in Chemical Engineering" (2024) 1:3 Nature Chemical Engineering 193–193.

33   Naudé, *supra* note 1364.

34   Henstock, *supra* note 1369.

It is still too early for rigorous academic studies to have sufficient data to test the actual effects of using AI on reducing the total cost for the pharmaceutical sector. However, as we have previously shown, various reports from academics and companies already indicate a significant reduction in the time required to complete many of the R&D stages. For example, the McKinsey Global Institute (MGI) estimates that AI could generate an annual economic value of $60 billion to $110 billion for the pharmaceutical and medical-product industries. This substantial economic impact is largely attributed to the technology's ability to enhance productivity. It accelerates the identification of compounds for potential new drugs, expedites their development and approval processes, and enhances marketing strategies.[35]

It is important to note that estimating changes and gains in the long run is a complex task, as not all R&D can be replaced by automated AI tools—there is still everyday R&D that needs to be done that is time consuming, prone to failure, and must meet regulatory standards.

However, drawing from our research and considering the available evidence on the current uses of AI in R&D activities, we are confident in the transformative potential of artificial intelligence. While the full extent of AI's impact remains to be seen, the trajectory is clear: AI is revolutionizing the way the pharmaceutical field discovers, develops, and delivers new medicines.

Some Challenges of AI for the Patent System

If AI can be used as a powerful research tool and as a method for inventing inventions, what will be its effect on the patent system?

In this chapter, the patent system refers to the set of institutions that ensure the effectiveness of patent protection. In this context, a country's patent legislation and courts constitute the fundamental elements of the patent system that enforce the rights of patent holders.

We highlight three main impacts that the use of AI may have on the patent system: inventorship, criteria for novelty and non-obviousness, and the increase in the number of inventions that "hide" AI as one of the authors, presented below.

---

35   McKinsey & Company, "The Economic Potential of Generative AI: The Next Productivity Frontier" (14 June 2023), McKinsey Digital, online: https://www.mckinsey.com/capabilities/mckinsey-digital/our-insights/the-economic-potential-of-generative-ai-the-next-productivity-frontier#introduction.

Inventorship

In 2021, the South African Patent Office granted the world's first patent that identified an artificial intelligence as the inventor, the Device for the Autonomous Bootstrapping of Unified Sentience (DABUS). Some authors argue that this decision aligns with South Africa's AI policy or suggest that the *Patent Act* can be amended to recognize AI as an inventor.[36] It's important to note that the South Africa patent law does not mandate a substantive examination of patent applications; it merely checks for compliance with application formalities. This procedural approach is why the patent was granted.

The decision of the South African Patent Office was in stark contrast to the approach of the US Patent and Trademark Office (USPTO), which had previously denied the patent application of Stephen Thaler, the developer of the DABUS system. The legal dispute escalated to the Court of Appeals for the Federal Circuit, where it was established that, under current law, an inventor must necessarily be *human*.

The UK Supreme Court also took a stance against the possibility of AI being recognized as an inventor in patent applications. In both legal scenarios, the courts emphasized that their decisions were based on the interpretation of current patent laws, which explicitly provide that the inventor must be a *natural person*. Therefore, for an AI to be recognized as an inventor, legislative reform would be essential, which in turn would bring complex legal challenges, including issues related to the transfer of ownership and the distribution of benefits derived from patents. To date, the possibility of amending patent legislation to accommodate AI as an inventor has not been a priority topic in debates on patent law reform. This situation reflects the complexity and ethical and legal implications involved in integrating AI into the field of intellectual property.

Ernest Fok, analyzing the case in the United States, presents arguments that the patent system could significantly benefit from recognizing inventing AI as inventors, shifting the global balance between economic incentives and societal costs.[37] Furthermore, this technology will continue to develop rapidly despite decisions not to recognize AI as an inventor in patents.

---

36   Caroline Ncube et al, *Artificial Intelligence and the Law in Africa* (Johannesburg, Cape Town, Durban: LexisNexis South Africa, 2023).

37   Ernest Fok, "Challenging the International Trend: The Case for Artificial Intelligence Inventorship in the United States" (2021) 19:1 St Clara J Int Law 51.

A similar argument is presented by Abbott, advocating that creative computers (AI) should be recognized as inventors under the Patent and Copyright clause of the US Constitution as a way to lead to scientific advances and stimulate innovation, reinforcing the patent system's goal of promoting the progress of science and useful arts.[38] To this end, the author suggests a dynamic interpretation of the existing patent legislation and the US Constitution to accommodate the concept of computers as inventors. This involves interpreting the term "inventor" in a way that includes non-human entities that perform creative acts resulting in patentable inventions, with the assignment of patent rights to the owners or operators of the creative computers.

Schuster[39] uses the Coase Theorem—which holds that aggregate wealth is maximized through transactions between firms when property rights are clearly allocated and transaction costs are zero—to propose that the efficiency of the patent system is best achieved by allocating AI property rights to the parties that value these rights the most, which would be the AI users (firms that purchase AI software and use it for invention).

In the debate on the patentability of inventions conceived by AI, Martin Kretschmer et al present a thoughtful analysis with a focus on the United Kingdom, advocating for the maintenance of the current legal framework without the need for reforms.[40] This position is based on the lack of compelling economic evidence or political rationale to justify the formal recognition of AI as an inventor, coupled with the perception that the debate around AI inventorship has been overly valorized, diverting attention from more pressing issues. The authors highlight the ability of the existing patent system to accommodate technological advancements, as demonstrated with biotechnology, and emphasize the importance of consistency and harmonization at the international level. Thus, in light of TRIPS, any changes to a national patent law would involve multilateral negotiations, which increases the transaction costs associated with potential legal changes. Moreover, the legal certainty provided by the current jurisprudence in the UK, which already establishes that AI

---

38   Ryan Abbott, "I Think, Therefore I Invent: Creative Computers and the Future of Patent Law" (2026) 57 B C L Rev 1079.

39   W Michael Schuster, "Artificial Intelligence and Patent Ownership" (2019) 75:4 Wash Lee Law Rev 1945.

40   Martin Kretschmer, Bartolomeo Meletti & Luis H Porangaba, "Artificial Intelligence and Intellectual Property: Copyright and Patents—A Response by the CREATe Centre to the UK Intellectual Property Office's Open Consultation" (2022) 17:3 J Intellect Prop Law Pract 321–326.

cannot be designated as an inventor, is underscored, and the viability
and necessity of a new form of protection for AI-generated inventions
are questioned, given the lack of evidence that AI systems can, in fact,
invent autonomously and effectively.

In our brief analysis, we observe that institutions responsible for
the patent system have adopted a conservative stance regarding the recognition of AI as an inventor (Supreme Court, Patent Offices, Congress).
However, we see young academics presenting interesting arguments
about the possibility, and necessity, of accommodating this remarkable
technological advance within the legal framework of patents.[41]

In this debate, we believe that a perspective to be considered is the
dual role of AI in technological innovation. On one hand, AI can perform
functions that replace human interventions, while on the other, it acts
as a catalyst that amplifies human inventive potential. We believe that
AI will have a greater impact as a research tool than as an autonomous
generator of inventions. As Iain Cockburn et al highlight, AI contributes
to the reduction of costs associated with prediction.[42] However, the
interpretation of results and the assessment of potential innovations
generated by AI remain inherently human competencies. This distinction underlines the importance of synergistic collaboration between
human and algorithmic capabilities in driving the innovation process.

To conclude, it is relevant to consider the analysis of Keith Pavitt,
which emphasizes that "major innovation decisions are a largely political
process, often involving professional groups advocating self-interested
outcomes under conditions of uncertainty (i.e., ignorance), rather than
balanced and careful estimates of costs, benefits and measurable risk"
(p. 108).[43]

AI and the Criteria of Novelty and Inventive Step

For an invention to be patentable, it must be new, involve an inventive
step (non-obvious), and have the capacity for industrial application
(article 27 TRIPS). The use of AI in the inventive process, as well as

---

41   Fok (n 1378); Lexi Heon, "Artificially Obvious but Genuinely New: How Artificial
      Intelligence Alters the Patent Obviousness Analysis" (2022) 53:1 Seton Hall Law
      Rev, online: https://scholarship.shu.edu/shlr/vol53/iss1/8; Lindsey Whitlow, "When
      the Invented Becomes the Inventor: Can, and Should AI Systems be Granted
      Inventorship Status for Patent Applications?" (2020) 2:2 Leg Issues Digit Age 3–23.
42   Cockburn, Henderson & Stern, *supra* note 1354.
43   Keith Pavitt, "Innovation Processes" in Jan Fagerberg & David C Mowery, eds,
      The Oxford Handbook of Innovation (Oxford University Press, 2006) 0.

in the process of evaluating patent applications, has the potential to affect the criteria of novelty and non-obviousness, imposing additional changes on the patent system.

Regarding the criterion of novelty, patent law requires that all claims made in a patent application be novel. The ability of AI to rapidly process large volumes of data and discern patterns or solutions may increase the possibility of a higher volume of inventions but also obscure the assessment of the inventiveness criterion necessary for patent grants due to a lack of transparency or difficulty in directly linking the process to human action. [44] Furthermore, there is evidence that the innovation process is primarily combinatorial, emphasizing the reuse and combination of existing technological capabilities to generate new inventions. [45] An implication is that the use of AI may accelerate this process.

For similar reasons, AI influences the assessment of the non-obviousness criterion. In the analysis of patent applications whose inventions were developed with the aid of AI tools, it now becomes necessary to consider that what may be classified as "non-obvious" to a skilled individual may be trivial for an AI system.

Thus, AI can challenge patent offices in three ways, all resulting in an increase in the number of patent applications: facilitating more discoveries; enabling well-founded patent applications for inventions with marginal novelties; and causing a flood of applications for properly grounded "imitations" (inventing around). [46]

Should there be an observed increase in inventions stemming from the process of inventing around existing patents, an increase in litigation is expected, and pressures will likely arise for the granting of broader patents.

A natural evolution will be the expansion and intensification of AI use by patent lawyers, patent offices, and even courts, aiming to assess the compliance of patent applications more objectively with patentability criteria, or to resolve legal disputes. One particular challenge for patent offices lies in keeping up with patent applicants in the effective use of AI to fulfill their institutional functions, thereby raising the standard of competence of the hypothetical "person having ordinary skill in

---

44   Cockburn, Henderson & Stern, *supra* note 1354.
45   See Deborah Strumsky & José Lobo, "Identifying the Sources of Technological Novelty in the Process of Invention" (2015) 44:8 Research Policy 1445–1461.
46   See Nancy T Gallini, "Patent Policy and Costly Imitation" (1992) 23:1 RAND Journal of Economics 52–63.

the art" (PHOSITA).[47] If patent offices and courts become proficient in identifying low-quality applications, it is possible that the phenomenon of a flood of applications may be mitigated.

AI, Demography, and the Relative Importance of Patents as Intellectual Property

In this section, we develop the argument that AI, in conjunction with the current context of the most relevant economic sectors in terms of size and political influence, has the potential to impact corporate choices between formal and informal intellectual property. This combination tends to lead to a diminishment in the relative importance of patents as a mechanism for intellectual property protection.

AI is rapidly integrating into the core business models of major global corporations, especially the so-called Big Tech companies (Apple, Microsoft, Alphabet, Amazon, and Meta/Facebook), which have significant resources to influence the regulation of this emerging technology. These corporations predominantly operate within the network economy paradigm — which is based on the principle that the value of a network grows proportionally to the increase in its users — promoting a *logic of inclusion*.

In this context, it is usual for such corporations to offer certain services for free to expand their user base. This approach contrasts sharply with the predominant commercial practices of the early 1990s, a period marked by the discussion and implementation of the Agreement on Trade-Related Aspects of Intellectual Property Rights (TRIPS). At that time, large companies tended to base their business models on temporary monopolies, especially companies in the pharmaceutical sector, seeking to maximize consumer surplus extraction, which highlighted a *logic of exclusion*.

In the last three decades, TRIPS represented the most significant revision of the patent system for the majority of developing countries, which were required to accept the patentability of all inventions, both products and processes, across all technological fields, with few exceptions. Particularly for the chemistry and pharmaceutical sectors, this agreement imposed limitations on the public health policy tools available to populous countries, such as India and Brazil, even with the

---

47   Fok, *supra* note 1378.

flexibilities provided by the agreement.[48] For instance, international pressures contributed to Brazil's decision not to adopt some of the flexibilities, which included the transition period for implementing patents in the pharmaceutical sector.[49]

In 1994, the year the *TRIPS Agreement* was signed, the pharmaceutical sector was represented by four companies (Merck, Johnson & Johnson, Bristol-Myers Squibb, and Pfizer) among the top 20 in terms of market capitalization in the Standard & Poor's index, whose combined capitalization exceeded that of Exxon Mobil, the largest company that year, by one and a half times. By 2024, Apple emerged as the highest market value corporation, with almost double the total capitalization of the listed pharmaceutical/healthcare companies (Eli Lilly, UnitedHealth, and Johnson & Johnson).

Big Tech companies distinguish themselves not only by their size superiority compared to other firms but also through unique strategic approaches to their intellectual assets. As observed, companies like Google prioritize the development of their AI platforms through significant investments in computational capacity, recruitment of highly specialized teams, and a focus on the advantages of being a first mover over the valuation of patents.

An example is Meta's decision to freely provide its Llama artificial intelligence code tools for research and commercial uses. The company's strategy is to increase its user base with the goal of becoming the leading AI platform. "Progress is faster when it is open [...] You have a more vibrant ecosystem where everyone can contribute," says Yann LeCun, Meta's chief AI scientist (*New York Times*, May 18, 2023).

This highlights the importance of the first-mover strategy for Big Tech. They understand that network economies depend on who takes the lead. In Meta's case, this strategy was considered even more important than industrial secrecy.

Given the highly dynamic nature of the sector, patent litigation is unappealing, as by the time disputes are resolved, the sector has already evolved technologically.

---

48   Hiroyuki Odagiri et al, eds, *Intellectual Property Rights, Development, And Catch-Up: An International Comparative Study* (New York: Oxford University Press, 2010).

49   Thiago Caliari, Roberto Mazzoleni & Luciano Martins Costa Póvoa, "Innovation in the Pharmaceutical Industry in Brazil Post-TRIPS" in Sunil Mani & Richard R Nelson, eds, TRIPS Compliance, National Patent Regimes and Innovation (Cheltenham: Edward Elgar Publishing, 2013) 16.

This suggests that patents as a strategy for reaping the benefits of innovations are losing importance. The world's largest companies are shifting their strategy toward a more intensive use of informal intellectual property.

On this aspect, Iain Cockburn et al offer pertinent insights on the impact of AI in the digital economy domain. [50] One consequence is the change in data accessibility and sharing. The potential for AI to reduce costs associated with the inventive process may widen opportunities for new market entrants, such as start-ups, intensifying competition. The offer of inventions increases. This could lead to a decreased need for strong intellectual property protections, particularly patents. Conversely, companies may be encouraged to resort to alternatives to gain from their innovations, such as intensifying the use of trade secrets and the exclusive control of vast datasets, limiting their sharing. The possession and accessibility of these data emerge as fundamental issues, as the monopolization of significant datasets can confer substantial competitive advantages, raising concerns about exclusivity and access in the context of R&D activities, and privacy.

If globalization was one of the key factors leading to the *TRIPS Agreement*, [51] we believe that any potential modification of the international patent system will be influenced by the impacts of AI on the innovation process and by demographic changes and their pressures on public health. Future amendments to patent laws or copyright law in the near future will undoubtedly be influenced by Big Tech, just as in 1994, when TRIPS was heavily influenced by the pharmaceutical sector. [52]

The pharmaceutical sector stands out for significantly valuing patents as a crucial instrument for the return of investments made in R&D, much more than other sectors. [53] It was one of the main beneficiaries of the harmonization of intellectual property rights rules promoted by TRIPS.

However, it is unlikely that the future will see an increase in patent durations similar to that facilitated by TRIPS. On the contrary,

---

50   Cockburn, Henderson & Stern, *supra* note 1354.

51   Suma Athreye, Lucia Piscitello & Kenneth C Shadlen, "Twenty-Five Years Since TRIPS: Patent Policy and International Business" (2020) 3:4 Journal of International Business Policy 315–328.

52   Charan Devereaux, Robert Z Lawrence & Michael Watkins, *Case studies in US trade negotiation* (Washington, DC: Institute for International Economics, 2006); Lori Wallach & Patrick Woodall, *Whose Trade Organization? A Comprehensive Guide to the WTO* (New York: New Press, 2004).

53   Hall et al, *supra* note 1394.

demographic pressures suggest a trend toward the reduction of patent terms and more flexibilities related to specific inventions. It is important to remember that the main flexibilities and exceptions of the *TRIPS Agreement* are related to public health and were incorporated into the agreement largely due to the pressure from developing countries, which face severe disease control problems. Now, the pressure for more flexibility and provisions on patents related to public health issues tends to emerge in wealthy countries.

According to the World Health Organization (WHO), the age profile of the global population is changing at an accelerated pace. By 2050, the population over 60 years of age will double.[54] The most recent censuses from the United States (2020),[55] China (2021),[56] and Canada (2021)[57] also confirm these data. On average, one in every six people is over 60 years old, with a tendency for this percentage to increase in the coming decades. In the European Union, the average was already one in 4.7 people in 2022. This shift imposes pressures on the health and social systems of countries. Public health spending as a proportion of GDP has been increasing over the past decades. Canada raised its spending from 5.01 percent to 7.64 percent between 1980 and 2019 (a relative increase of 52 percent). The United States saw a relative increase of 300 percent in the same period, going from 3.46 percent to 13.81 percent of GDP.[58] For the United States, the projection is that it will reach 19.6 percent in 2031.[59]

54   WHO, "Ageing and Health" (1 October 2022) WHO, online: https://www.who.int/news-room/fact-sheets/detail/ageing-and-health.

55   Zoe Caplan, "U.S. Older Population Grew from 2010 to 2020 at Fastest Rate Since 1880 to 1890" (25 May 2023) United States Census Bureau, online: https://www.census.gov/library/stories/2023/05/2020-census-united-states-older-population-grew.html.

56   Ning Jizhe, "Main Data of the Seventh National Population Census" (11 May 2021) National Bureau of Statistics, online: https://www.stats.gov.cn/english/PressRelease/202105/t20210510_1817185.html.

57   Statistics Canada. "In the Midst of High Job Vacancies and Historically Low Unemployment, Canada Faces Record Retirements from an Aging Labour Force: Number of Seniors Aged 65 and Older Grows Six Times Faster Than Children 0-14" (27 April 2022), online: https://www150.statcan.gc.ca/n1/daily-quotidien/220427/dq220427a-eng.htm.

58   Our World in Data, "Government Health Expenditure as A Share of GDP, 1980 to 2019" (22 August 2024), online: https://ourworldindata.org/grapher/public-health-expenditure-share-gdp?tab=table&time=1980.2019.

59   CMS.gov, "National Health Expenditure Projections 2023-2032 Forecast Summary" (22 August 2024), online: https://www.cms.gov/files/document/nhe-projections-forecast-summary.pdf.

Associated with this is the fact that a diffusion of the use of AI in medical research tends to reduce the costs of producing new drugs and treatments. Governments in more advanced countries have been pressured by the population in light of rising individual and public health expenditures. In this scenario, the usual justification provided by the pharmaceutical sector—that long durations are necessary to incentivize research and that a lengthy monopoly guarantees the continuity of pharmaceutical advances—is weakened, both politically and economically. Governments make decisions under pressure from voters. An electorate increasingly composed of senior individuals will support candidates sensitive to their budgetary concerns. A sign of this new reality is that, starting in 2024, Medicare in the United States will, for the first time, not accept drug pricing defined by the pharmaceutical industry for certain drugs.[60]

In this dispute, the interests of the pharmaceutical industry may not be aligned with the interests of Big Tech companies, which are focused on other business models.

These sectoral differences can drive the debate that is already happening among economists about the most efficient duration of patent terms to induce innovations. There are robust criticisms regarding the inefficiency of the current patent system. Michele Boldrin and David K. Levine, for example, argue that the patent system as a whole needs to be overhauled, arguing that the current system can, in fact, inhibit innovation rather than promote it, especially when long-duration patents create unnecessary monopolies in sectors where innovation costs are relatively low, and the product life cycle is fast.[61] The authors propose a significant overhaul of the patent system, including reducing the duration of patents and introducing more flexibility to accommodate the varied needs of different industries.

---

60   The White House, "FACT SHEET: Biden-⊕Harris Administration Announces First Ten Drugs Selected for Medicare Price Negotiation" (29 August 2023) online: https://www.whitehouse.gov/briefing-room/statements-releases/2023/08/29/fact-sheet-biden-harris-administration-announces-first-ten-drugs-selected-for-medicare-price-negotiation/.

61   Michele Boldrin & David K Levine, "The Case against Patents" (2013) 27:1 The Journal of Economic Perspectives 3–22.

Conclusion

This chapter explored the transformative influence of Artificial Intelligence (AI) on the landscape of innovation and its subsequent challenges to the patent system by analyzing the pivotal shifts engendered by the integration of AI into research and development (R&D) processes. At the heart of this investigation lies the realization that AI transcends mere technological advancement, positioning itself as a cornerstone in the redefinition of creativity, invention, and the mechanisms of intellectual property protection. The advent of AI technologies like AlphaFold signifies not just an acceleration in scientific discovery and inventive activities, but also poses profound questions on the nature of inventorship, the criteria of novelty, and the essence of non-obviousness in patent law. These questions underscore the complexity and dynamism introduced by AI into the domain of patent legislation, challenging traditional paradigms that have long governed the realm of intellectual creations.

The insights garnered from the analysis of the impact of AI on R&D efficiency, particularly within the pharmaceutical sector, serve as an indication of AI's capacity to drastically reduce the timelines and costs associated with the development of new drugs. This efficiency gain, however, extends beyond operational improvements, to the process of drug regulation and approval for new drugs.

Furthermore, we examined the extent to which socio-economic and demographic factors influence the relevance of patents in the evolving digital economy. The dominance of Big Tech and the shift toward a model of inclusion over exclusion of users illustrate a departure from traditional strategies of intellectual property protection. This shift, fuelled by the strategic imperatives of network economies and the first-mover advantage, suggests that the relative importance of patents can diminish.

In conclusion, the influence of AI on the innovation landscape and the patent system underscores a fundamental transformation in the ethos of invention and intellectual property. This chapter not only highlights the potential of AI in redefining the parameters of invention but also brings a critical argument on the challenges faced by the patent system.

CHAPTER 15

Owning Me, Owning You: How Private Companies Acquire Rights in Our Most Intimate Data

Andelka M. Phillips

Abstract

How many online contracts have you read? Are you considering buying a DNA test or signing up for online dating? The online world relies on the collection and use of a wide variety of our personal and most intimate data. This world is governed by contracts and privacy policies that most of us barely notice, let alone read. Yet, buried within these documents are terms that impact our rights even to our most intimate data. Furthermore, the licences acquired by businesses to our information pose privacy risks for us as individuals, as well as posing risks for wider groups whom we may belong to.

This chapter examines licence clauses from online contracts using case studies from three industries: personal genomics, wearable technology, and online dating. It discusses the issues that these clauses raise in relation to the rights of individuals in their personal data and concludes with some suggestions for reform. It highlights three areas of concern: (i) the collection of personal and specifically sensitive data by these industries and the broad scope of licences clauses, which allow broad powers to use such data; (ii) the uses (both present and future) of such information, which may pose risks to individuals and their families; and (iii) dangers that stem from the loss of this data. This includes the threat of discrimination based on such information, which could have impacts ranging from the ability to access health insurance or impact a person's employment to other risks to physical and cyber safety.

You can now learn about your genetic ancestry, track your fitness, and find love online. You can, in fact, do almost anything online, and likewise, businesses can track almost every aspect of your life. Increasingly people live in a manner that merges the cyber and physical worlds. What unites all these things is the use of contracts. Regardless of the nature of the product or service you are accessing, you will be doing this subject to a business's terms and conditions. These documents contain important information about how consumers' data can be used and reused. Regardless of the way something is sold or marketed to consumers online, it is often the case that companies will be doing additional things with users' data, which consumers may not anticipate, and these contracts together with privacy policies are the means that businesses often use as a legal basis for these activities.[1] This is extremely problematic, as it is very common for people not to read these documents.[2]

My previous work has considered the regulation of the direct-to-consumer genetic testing industry (also known as DTC or personal genomics),[3] as well as the Internet of Things (IoT),[4] specifically con-

---

1   M Haag, "FamilyTreeDNA Admits to Sharing Genetic Data with F.B.I.", *The New York Times* (4 February 2019), online: *The New York Times* https://www.nytimes.com/2019/02/04/business/family-tree-dna-fbi.html; RM Hendricks-Sturrup & CY Lu, "Direct-to-Consumer Genetic Testing Data Privacy: Key Concerns and Recommendations Based on Consumer Perspectives" (2019) 9:9:2 Journal of Personalized Medicine 25, DOI: 10.3390/jpm9020025.

2   S Becher, "Research Shows Most Online Consumer Contracts Are Incomprehensible, but Still Legally Binding" *The Conversation* (4 February 2019), online: The Conversation https://theconversation.com/research-shows-most-online-consumer-contracts-are-incomprehensible-but-still-legally-binding-110793; U Benoliel & SI Becher, "The Duty to Read the Unreadable" (2019) 60 B C L Rev 2255, online: SSRN https://ssrn.com/abstract=3313837; JA Obar and A Oeldorf-Hirsch, "The Biggest Lie on the Internet: Ignoring the Privacy Policies and Terms of Service Policies of Social Networking Services" (2020) 23:1 Information, Communication & Society 128–147.

3   *See generally* AM Phillips, *Buying Your Self on the Internet: Wrap Contracts and Personal Genomics* (Edinburgh: Edinburgh University Press, 2019) [Phillips, *Buying Your Self on the Internet*]; AM Phillips, "Reading the Fine Print When Buying Your Genetic Self Online: Direct-to-Consumer Genetic Testing Terms and Conditions" (2017) 36:3 New Genetics and Society 273–295; SI Becher and AM Phillips, "Data Rights and Consumer Contracts: The Case of Personal Genomic Services" in D Clifford, KH Lau & J Paterson, eds, *Data Rights and Private Law* (Oxford: Hart Publishing, 2023) [Phillips, *Data Rights*] 84–101.

4   AM Phillips, "All Your Data Will Be Held Against You: Secondary Use of Data from Personal Genomics and Wearable Tech" in S Sterett and LD Walker, eds, *Research Handbook on Law and Courts* (Cheltenham: Edward Elgar Publishing, 2019) 404-426; Andelka M Phillips, "Hacking your DNA? Some Things to Consider before Buying a DNA Test Online" *Health Law Blog Sweden* (2 March 2024), online: Health Law Sweden (blog) https://healthlawsweden.blogg.lu.se/2024/03/02/hacking-your-dna-some-things-to-consider-before-buying-a-dna-test-online/.

sidering the growth in popularity of one prong of IoT in the form of wearable technology, such as smart watches, wristbands, and now rings. IoT can be viewed as encompassing a diverse range of objects that have been equipped with the ability to connect to the internet.[5] This ranges from more traditional items such as kettles to the capacity for vehicles to record data about their drivers and occupants.[6] It should be noted that wearable technology now encompasses a range of clothing, (sometimes referred to as Fashion Technology[7]) which includes a variety of sensors, but the discussion in this chapter is limited to wearable fitness monitors, which take the form of devices worn on the wrist or finger. In consideration of the shared reliance that these industries have on sensitive data, this led me to query whether there are similarities in the intellectual property licences that these companies utilise. These licences appear in the online contracts of both industries and are being used in order to acquire rights in their customers' content and personal data in order for them to develop future products and services and use these data in secondary research.

While the DTC industry offers DNA tests as consumer services, wearable technology allows users to track a wide variety of their activity. Both industries collect and utilize a wide variety of personal data, some of which may be considered health or sensitive data. Genetic data is arguably one of the most intimate forms of personal data and is subject to special protection in some jurisdictions, with one example being the European Union's General Data Protection Regulation (GDPR). Specifically, article 9(1) includes genetic data as one example of Special Category data, which it prohibits from being processed and under the GDPR, such data can only be processed, if certain exceptions apply, as

---

5   Internet Society, *The Internet of Things (IoT): An Overview* (White Paper Oct. 2015) at 5, online: Internet Society https://www.internetsociety.org/resources/doc/2015/iot-overview/.

6   K Hill, "Automakers Are Sharing Consumers' Driving Behavior with Insurance Companies," *The New York Times* (11 March 2024), online: The New York Times https://www.nytimes.com/2024/03/11/technology/carmakers-driver-tracking-insurance.html.

7   R Willoughby, "Fashion Tech - Can Your Wardrobe Risk Your Privacy?" *Gerrish Legal* (first published on Tech Girl March 2020), online: Gerrish Legal (blog) https://www.gerrishlegal.com/blog/2020/03/05/2020-1-14-fashion-tech-can-your-wardrobe-risk-your-privacy; "Fashion Tech and Data Privacy: Legal Challenges in Wearable Technology and Smart Fashion" Fashion & Law Journal (18 September 2023), online: https://fashionlawjournal.com/fashion-tech-and-data-privacy-legal-challenges-in-wearable-technology-and-smart-fashion/> ; M Sawh, "The Best Smart Clothing: From Biometric Shirts to Contactless Payment Jackets" *WAREABLE* (16 April 2018), online: https://www.wareable.com/smart-clothing/best-smart-clothing.

set out in article 9(2) (a) to (j).[8] Canada also has legislation prohibiting discrimination on the basis of an individual's genetic information in the form of the *Genetic Non-Discrimination Act* 2017.[9]

This chapter focuses on these examples together with the online dating industry, because all three examples share a reliance on sensitive data, as well as data that could potentially be viewed as health data or health related. This chapter is framed more as a thought experiment, in the hope that it will represent the first step in a larger project. From impacting job prospects and insurance coverage[10] to the possibility of other forms of discrimination and exploitation, as well as the risk of a myriad of scams, the threat of violence, and identity theft, the need to consider how consumers' data derived from these three contexts is used is important.[11]

This chapter specifically explores the content of licence clauses contained in online contracts using case studies from three industries: direct-to-consumer genetic testing (DTC, also known as personal genomics); wearable technology which can be viewed as one example of the Internet of Things; and online dating. Examples are taken from each industry, and some shortened quotations highlight the content of these clauses. I then discuss the issues that these clauses raise in relation to

---

8   Council Regulation (EU) 2016/679 of 27 April 2016 on the Protection of Natural Persons with Regard to the Processing of Personal Data and on the Free Movement of Such Data, and Repealing Directive 95/46/EC (General Data Protection Regulation) [2016] OJ 2 119/1 online: *Eur-Lex* http://eur-lex.europa.eu/legalcontent/EN/TXT/?qid=1525272154893&uri=CELEX:32016R0679

9   *Genetic Non-Discrimination Act*, SC 2017, c 3, online: Justice Laws Website https://laws-lois.justice.gc.ca/eng/acts/G-2.5/page-1.html#h-3. This is also an interesting example, as section 3 prohibits individuals being required to undergo a genetic test, and the only exceptions set out in section 6(a) and (b) relate to genetic tests conducted in the context of healthcare or medical or scientific research if the person is a research participant; also see Office of the Privacy Commissioner of Canada (OPC), *Policy Statement on the Collection, Use and Disclosure of Genetic Test Results* (OPC, updated December 2017) online: Office of the Privacy Commissioner of Canada https://www.priv.gc.ca/en/privacy-topics/health-genetic-and-other-body-information/s-d_140710/.

10   See Phillips, *Buying Your Self on the Internet*, *supra* note 3 at 147–151, 154–157; M Griffith-Greene, "Home DNA Tests May Affect Insurance, Employment" *CBC News* (2 April 2015), online: *CBC News* https://www.cbc.ca/news/health/home-dna-tests-may-affect-insurance-employment-1.3018086.

11   As one example, NZ's CERT, which tracks cyber security attacks in its Cyber Security Insights Report, found a significant increase in online scams in just the first quarter of 2023. See CERT NZ, "Cyber Security Insights" (January to March 2023) 2, online: https://www.cert.govt.nz/assets/Uploads/Quarterly-report/2023-q1/Cyber-Security-Insight-Report-Q1-2023.pdf.

the rights of individuals in their personal data and conclude with some suggestions for reform. Examples are taken from the following companies: 23andMe; AncestryDNA; FamilyTreeDNA; Fitbit; Garmin; Oura; Match; Tinder; and eharmony. These companies were chosen as they are well-known market leaders, that operate internationally. An earlier version of this chapter was presented at the workshop "The Future of the Global IP System," and earlier versions of contracts were accessed for this purpose. However, with the goal of keeping the examples as up-to-date as possible, the contracts were accessed again in January and March 2024, from New Zealand; however some examples are instead from the Australian or American domain version of the site, as some sites do not have specific New Zealand–focused sites, despite targeting consumers based in New Zealand. Given the international nature of this collection and the pending litigation against 23andMe, it also seemed that accessing the American versions of these contracts might be more beneficial to readers. Given the international nature of these industries, the focus herein is to reflect on these clauses in relation to their effects on consumers' privacy.

This chapter builds upon previous work, that has considered the legislative framework applicable to the DTC industry in the context of United Kingdom (UK) and European Union (EU) consumer protection law and data protection law,[12] as well as joint work, which considered this in a New Zealand and Australian context and specifically considered how a consumer's data rights could be employed in the DTC context.[13] For the purposes of this chapter, in discussion, reference is made to the GDPR, given its global influence on data protection law. However, it should be noted that the *New Zealand Privacy Act* 2020 also has extraterritorial effect[14] and, consequently, businesses targeting

---

12   See Phillips, *Buying Your Self on the Internet*, *supra* note 3 at chs 4 and 5; and Council Directive 2011/83/EU of the European Parliament and of the Council of 25 October 2011 on consumer rights, amending Council Directive 93/13/EEC and Directive 1999/44/EC of the European Parliament and of the Council and repealing Council Directive 85/577/EEC and Directive 97/7/EC of the European Parliament and of the Council [2011] OJ; and L304/64Council Directive 93/13/EEC of 5 April 1993 on unfair terms in consumer contracts [1993] OJ L95/36/29; now also see the amending directive, Directive (EU) 2019/2161 of the European Parliament and of the Council of 27 November 2019 amending Council Directive 93/13/EEC and Directives 98/6/EC, 2005/29/EC and 2011/83/EU of the European Parliament and of the Council as regards the better enforcement and modernisation of Union consumer protection rule [2019] OJ L 328/7.

13   Becher and Phillips, *Data Rights*, *supra* note 3.

14   See *Privacy Act*, 2020 (NZ) s.4, online: https://www.legislation.govt.nz/act/public/2020/0031/latest/LMS23223.html.

New Zealand–based consumers should be complying with New Zealand privacy law.[15]

This chapter is divided into six parts. The first part provides an overview of the three industries considered herein and why they are being considered together. The next part then situates the discussion of these three industries in the context of the growth of data breaches, including examples of breaches that these industries have experienced. The following sections set out the three case studies of licence clauses and provide a discussion of the issues, which these clauses raise, followed by the conclusion.

Throughout this chapter, readers are encouraged to keep in mind three areas of concern: (i) the collection of personal and specifically sensitive data by these industries and the broad scope of licences clauses, which allow broad powers to use such data; (ii) the uses (both present and future) of such information, which may pose risks to individuals and their families; (iii) and dangers which stem from the loss of these data. This includes the threat of discrimination based on such information, which could have impacts ranging from the ability to access health insurance or affect a person's employment to other risks, including physical and cyber safety.

While the primary focus is on licence clauses, it is very common for companies to include other types of clauses, which may further limit opportunities for redress, such as indemnity or compulsory arbitration clauses.

Why Should We Consider These Three Industries Together?

Whether people want to learn about their genetic heritage, track aspects of their fitness, or find love in an increasingly cyber-physical world, they will be doing this subject to a company's contractual terms and privacy policies. Whether they choose to read them or not, these documents contain important information that may impact their rights and, specifically, their privacy. The examples considered here are used for the purposes of examining the extent to which companies in these three contexts seek to acquire intellectual property rights in the content posted or supplied by their consumers, which may be used in future products or services developed by these companies. This is intended to illuminate

---

15   In future work, I plan to conduct a larger review of contracts and privacy policies in these industries.

problems in this space. While it is understandable that companies will often seek to protect their intellectual property rights in the platforms, content, and services they create and provide, this becomes problematic, when through using a service or device a consumer is forced to agree to grant a licence to the company in future developments, that utilize user content, which may include sensitive personal information. The phrase "you are the product, not the consumer" is now well known in relation to free services. What is meant by this is that where a product appears free online, the user is paying with their personal data. This is exemplified by large social networks, such as Meta's Facebook. [16] Much has been written about the problems and privacy risks of such services. [17] However, what is argued herein is that where a service or product is offered in the consumer realm—that is, it requires the user to pay for it—but by its nature it relies on sharing and using a variety of personal data, the consumer is still the product. [18]

The three industries examined in this chapter all rely on collecting a wide range of data, some of which may be viewed as health or sensitive data. For example, while DTC companies such as 23andMe engage in medical research using consumers' genetic data, they also encourage users to share other forms of personal data in their online platforms and they may seek it out through surveys. DTC companies also often have social networking functions on their platforms, encouraging consumers to connect with unknown relatives, and while some may benefit from this experience, the nature of sharing on these platforms does create further privacy risks and makes it difficult for businesses to ensure data is deleted when a consumer requests account deletion, if they have shared widely. Meanwhile, wearable technology companies

---

16   O Solon, "You Are Facebook's Product, Not Customer" *Wired* (21 September 2009), online: https://www.wired.co.uk/article/doug-rushkoff-hello-etsy.

17   See, for example, EJ Sørensen, "The Post That Wasn't: Facebook Monitors Everything Users Type and Not Publish" (2016) 32:1 C L S Rev 146–151, https://doi.org/10.1016/j.clsr.2015.12.007; J King & A Stephan, "Regulating Privacy Dark Patterns in Practice-Drawing Inspiration from the California Privacy Rights Act" (2021) 5:2 Georgetown Law Technology Review 250–276; H Jones & JH Soltren, "Facebook: Threats to Privacy" (2005) 1:01 https://groups.csail.mit.edu/mac/classes/6.805/student-papers/fall05-papers/facebook.pdf; J Carrie Wong, "The Cambridge Analytica Scandal Changed the World – But It Didn't Change Facebook," *The Guardian* (18 March 2019), online: https://www.theguardian.com/technology/2019/mar/17/the-cambridge-analytica-scandal-changed-the-world-but-it-didnt-change-facebook.

18   A Jeffries, "Genes, Patents, and Big Business: At 23andMe, Are You the Customer or the Product?" *The Verge* (13 December 2012), online: https://www.theverge.com/2012/12/12/3759198/23andme-genetics-testing-50-million-data-mining.

also encourage and collect a wide range of deeply personal information (ranging from a user's heart rate, steps, weight, and height, to menstrual cycle, and geolocation) and also include social networking functions, which may be public by default.[19] A useful example to highlight the types of privacy risks involved in wearable technology was when it emerged in 2011 that Fitbit users who had inputted sexual activity data had these data appearing in public searches on Google.[20] Finally, online dating services collect information about their users, which ranges from sexual preferences, ethnicity, political views, and location, to COVID-19 vaccination status.[21] Online dating services also by their nature encourage sharing, and while their focus is not on health, since the advent of COVID-19 some online dating platforms have allowed users to share their vaccination status, and there have been examples of companies linking their services to their consumers' wearable devices.[22] They often now operate as applications on smartphones, meaning that they will often be able to track their users' locations. As the Internet of Things continues to blur the lines between our physical and online worlds, much more attention needs to be paid to the way these services operate and how they protect their users' data.

In considering the examples provided in this chapter, I wish to emphasize that these represent a very small sample of what consumers are confronted with in the online environment. While it is legitimate for companies to protect their interests, as one example, on some versions of DTC company websites, consumers may be confronted with 11 legal documents. There will often be a document entitled Terms and

19   Kaspersky Lab, "Do Fitness Trackers Put Your Privacy at Risk?" (2022) https://www.kaspersky.com/resource-center/preemptive-safety/fitness-tracker-privacy#.

20   L Rao, "Sexual Activity Tracked by Fitbit Shows Up in Google Search Results" *TechCrunch* (4 July 2011), online: https://techcrunch.com/2011/07/03/sexual-activity-tracked-by-fitbit-shows-up-in-google-search-results/; and see the original story Zee "Fitbit Users Are Unwittingly Sharing Details of their Sex Lives with the World" *The Next Web* (3 July 2011), online: https://thenextweb.com/news/fitbit-users-are-inadvertently-sharing-details-of-their-sex-lives-with-the-world.

21   See Becher and Phillips, *Data Rights, supra* note 3 at 85 citing R Amos et al, "Privacy Policies over Time: Curation and Analysis of a Million-Document Dataset" [2021] WWW '21: Proceedings of the Web Conference 2021 at 2165.

22   A Trozenski, "The Changing Spaces of Dating Apps since COVID-19" The Center for Digital Humanities, Vanderbilt University (2 March 2022) online:https://www.vanderbilt.edu/digitalhumanities/the-changing-spaces-of-dating-apps-since-COVID-19/; The company Once is one example of this. See S Shah, "Follow Your Fitbit Heart Rate to Find Love with This Dating App" *Digital Trends* (15 January 2016), online: https://www.digitaltrends.com/social-media/once-dating-app-fitbit-sync/.

Conditions, accompanied by a privacy statement and various other documents, ranging from a consent to participate in biobanking to legal disclaimers.[23] Unfortunately, even where companies do attempt to improve the clarity of their terms or compliance with the law, the sheer volume of contracts[24] that consumers encounter leads to a failure by consumers to engage with these documents.[25] A 2016 study by the Norwegian Consumer Council /Forbrukerrådet (NCC) estimated that the average smartphone contained 250,000 words of contracts and privacy policies.[26] However, given that study was conducted prior to the advent of the COVID-19 pandemic, the figure is likely to be higher now. The problem of volume is further exacerbated by three related issues. The first relates to readability, with many online contracts written at a reading level that equates with many academic journals.[27] The second is a trend toward increasing the length of such documents. As noted in previous work, another recent study, which examined a million privacy policies, has confirmed that these documents are generally getting longer.[28] The third is a problem with how contracts are presented and the designed environment of websites, which may influence consumers' behaviour, so that they are steered toward completing their purchase or creating their account without actually viewing these contracts. Such design practices can be referred to as dark patterns (or deceptive patterns), and in the context of services and products that rely on the collection of sensitive data they are extremely concerning. Much more

---

23   Becher and Phillips, *Data Rights, supra* note 3 at 22.

24   Obar and Oeldorf-Hirsch, *supra* n 2.

25   Becher, "Research," *supra* note 2; Benoliel and Becher, *supra* note 2; Yannis Bakos, Florencia Marotta-Wurgler & David R. Trossen, "Does Anyone Read the Fine Print? Consumer Attention to Standard-Form Contracts" (2014) 43:1 The Journal of Legal Studies 1–35, https://doi.org/10.1086/674424; K Conklin and R Hyde, "If Small Print 'Terms and Conditions' Require a PhD to Read, Should They be Legally Binding?" *The Conversation* (10 May 2018), online: https://theconversation. com/if-small-print-terms-and-conditions-require-a-phd-to-read-should-they-be-legally-binding-75101; B Frischmann and E Selinger, *Re-Engineering Humanity* (Cambridge, UK: Cambridge University Press, 2018) at chs 1, 2 and 5.

26   Norwegian Consumer Council, "250,000 Words of App Terms and Conditions" (24 May 2016), online: *Forbrukerradet* https://www.forbrukerradet.no/side/250000-words-of-app-terms-and-conditions/>; and Norwegian Consumer Council Forbrukerrådet (NCC), *APPFAIL Threats to Consumers in Mobile Apps* (March 2016) – available in the Internet Archive's Wayback Machine, online: https://storage.forbrukerradet.no/media/wp-content/uploads/2016/03/Appfail-Report-2016. pdf.

27   Benoliel and Becher, *The Duty to Read, supra* note 2.

28   Becher and Phillips, *Data Rights, supra* note 3.

work is needed to make companies engage in better practices and stop using these techniques.[29]

It also should be noted that these three industries can also be seen very much as part of the Big Tech ecosystem, which raises further issues in relation to how data are shared and reused. This brings in the possibility of companies sharing data with data brokers, which is an area of growing concern internationally.[30] Together with these three industries sharing a trend of partnerships and mergers with other businesses in those industries, there has also been significant investment by some of the largest technology companies in the world in these spaces. For example, Google has previously invested in 23andMe, and its cofounder Anne Wojcicki was formerly married to Google's cofounder Sergey Brin[31] — and Google has since acquired Fitbit, completing this acquisition

---

29   H Brignull et al, "Deceptive Design" (last updated 25 April 2023), online: https://www.deceptive.design/; Frischmann and Selinger, *supra* note 1427 at 35–42; and NCC, *Deceived By Design* (27 June 2018), online: https://storage02.forbrukerradet.no/media/2018/06/2018-06-27-deceived-by-design-final.pdf; and NCC, *You Can Log Out, But You Can Never Leave,* (14 January 2021), online: https://storage02.forbrukerradet.no/media/2021/01/2021-01-14-you-can-log-out-but-you-can-never-leave-final.pdf.

30   Australian Competition & Consumer Commission (ACCC), *Digital Platform Services Inquiry Interim Report 8: Data Products and Services – How Information Is Collected and Used by Data Firms in Australia* (March 2024), online: https://www.accc.gov.au/system/files/Digital-platform-services-inquiry-March-2024-interim-report.pdf; K Kemp, "Worried Your Address, Birth Date or Health Data Is Being Sold? You Should Be – And the Law Isn't Protecting You" *The Conversation* (22 May 2024), online: https://theconversation.com/worried-your-address-birth-date-or-health-data-is-being-sold-you-should-be-and-the-law-isnt-protecting-you-230540; NCC, *Out of Control: How Consumers Are Exploited by the Online Advertising Industry* (14 January 2020), online: https://storage02.forbrukerradet.no/media/2020/01/2020-01-14-out-of-control-final-version.pdf; BEUC, "Consumer Groups Launch Complaints Against Meta's Massive, Illegal Data Processing Behind Its Pay-Or-Consent Smokescreen" (29 February 2024) https://www.beuc.eu/press-releases/consumer-groups-launch-complaints-against-metas-massive-illegal-data-processing; a summary of the complaint is available here "How Meta Is Breaching Consumers' Fundamental Rights" (February 2024), online: https://www.beuc.eu/sites/default/files/publications/BEUC-X-2024-020_How_Meta_is_breaching_consumers_fundamental_rights.pdf; NCC, "The Norwegian Consumer Council Files Legal Complaint Against Meta for Numerous Violations of the GDPR," (29 February 2024), online: https://www.forbrukerradet.no/side/the-norwegian-consumer-council-files-legal-complaint-against-meta-for-numerous-violations-of-the-gdpr/.

31   A Hartmans et al, "Meet Anne Wojcicki: The Sister of Departing YouTube CEO, Susan Wojcicki, and A Self-Made Multimillionaire Who Founded the Genetic Testing Giant 23andMe" *Business Insider* (19 February 2023), online: https://www.businessinsider.com/23andme-ceo-anne-wojcicki-life-career-family-photos-2021-3?op=1.

in 2021.[32] 23andMe itself before merging with Virgin had acquired other entities, including CureTogether in 2012.[33] Meanwhile, in the context of online dating, Match.com now owns Tinder and Hinge, as well as the League.[34] Match itself was owned by InterActiveCorp, but separated its business from this parent company in 2020.[35] Furthermore, the dating company Once allows for its consumers to integrate their service with Fitbit or Android Wear in order to do things such as tracking heart rate, so there is already some overlap across these industries.[36] As well as the potential for sharing and reuse of data here, there are significant issues raised by all these mergers and acquisitions in antitrust and competition law, and future work will also explore these.

The hope herein is that this will encourage readers to question their own use of these technologies and to highlight the need for further work and improved governance in these three spaces. While this chapter is not primarily focused on cyber security, it will touch upon the importance of this in discussion of recent data breaches and the types of data, which these licences cover. In thinking about the protection of personal data, it should be noted that good cyber security practices and standards go hand in hand with this protection.

---

32   R Osterloh, "Google Completes Fitbit Acquisition" Google (14 January 2021), online: https://blog.google/products/devices-services/fitbit-acquisition/; Spirion, "Is Google's Purchase of Fitbit a Data Privacy Risk?" (2019) <https://www.spirion. com/blog/google-fitbit-acquisition-data-privacy-risk; PL Austin, "The Real Reason Google Is Buying Fitbit" *Time Magazine* (4 November 2019), online: https://time. com/5717726/google-fitbit/.

33   23andMe, "23andMe acquires CureTogether, Inc" (23andMe, Press Release, 10 July 2012), online: https://mediacenter.23andme.com/press-releases/23andmeacquires-curetogether-inc/.

34   A Malik, "Match Group Acquires Members-Only Dating App the League for ~$30M" *TechCrunch* (13 July 2022), online: https://techcrunch.com/2022/07/12/match-group-acquires-members-only-dating-app-the-league/.

35   IAC and Match Corp, "IAC and Match Group Complete Full Separation" Press Release (1 July 2020), online: https://www.prnewswire.com/news-releases/iac-and-match-group-complete-full-separation-301086627.html.

36   Once, "Homepage," https://www.getonce.com/; S Shah, "Follow your Fitbit Heart Rate To Find Love With This Dating App," *Digital Trends* (15 January 2016), online: https://www.digitaltrends.com/social-media/once-dating-app-fitbit-sync/; M Abrams, "The Dating App Based on a Fitness Tracker, a Wellness Festival Is Coming," *Observer* (12 October 2016), online: https://observer.com/2016/10/the-dating-app-based-on-a-fitness-tracker-a-wellness-festival-is-coming/.

Data Breaches Everywhere

All the industries discussed in this chapter share a reliance on personal and sensitive data, while they also share vulnerabilities. Likewise, while any organization is vulnerable to hacking today, all three industries have experienced significant data breaches. A few prominent examples will be considered below in order to demonstrate that data breaches have occurred and explore the risks to which those individuals have been exposed.

It should be emphasized that, globally, data protection and privacy law have encouraged a privacy or data protection by design and security by design approach. [37] While this is in fact something required by the GDPR under article 25, [38] it is unfortunately still not common practice, and for businesses that know from the outset of their operations that they will be collecting sensitive data, much more attention needs to be given to this concept along with the idea of security by design. These two approaches together with giving more thought to the principles of data minimization, purpose limitation, and transparency could help to significantly improve the protection of people's privacy rights. The recent complaint brought by BEUC and its members against Meta's Facebook in relation to their pay or consent model will hopefully lead to reform in this space. [39]

The first example of a data breach is from the DTC industry. It is the 23andMe data breach, [40] which occurred in 2023 and has led to

---

37   See for example, New Zealand's National Cyber Security Centre (NCSC), "Joint Guidance: Principles for Security-by-Design and -Default" (14 April 2023) https://www.ncsc.govt.nz/news/security-by-design/; this document was issued jointly with the respective agencies in Australia, the United States, Canada, the United Kingdom, Germany, the Netherlands, — see full guidance document here: NCSC et al, "Shifting the Balance of Cybersecurity Risk: Principles and Approaches for Security-by-Design and -Default" (13 April 2023) https://www.ncsc.govt.nz/assets/NCSC-Documents/Joint-Guidance-Security-by-Design-and-Default.pdf.

38   Council Regulation (EU) 2016/679 of 27 April 2016 on The Protection of Natural Persons with Regard to the Processing of Personal Data and on the Free Movement of Such Data, and repealing Directive 95/46/EC (General Data Protection Regulation) [2016] OJ 2 119/1, art 25.

39   BEUC, "Consumer Groups Launch Complaints Against Meta's Massive, Illegal Data Processing Behind Its Pay-or-Consent Smokescreen" (29 February 2024) https://www.beuc.eu/press-releases/consumer-groups-launch-complaints-against-metas-massive-illegal-data-processing; a summary of the complaint is available here "How Meta Is Breaching Consumers' Fundamental Rights" (February 2024) https://www.beuc.eu/sites/default/files/publications/BEUC-X-2024-020_How_Meta_is_breaching_consumers_fundamental_rights.pdf.

40   Phillips, *Hacking your DNA? supra* note 4.

around 40 class actions being filed against 23andMe in the United States,[41] with a further class action filed in San Francisco in March 2024.[42] A settlement has now received preliminary approval for US $30 million, but consumers will receive minimal relief, as they are only entitled to claim up to $10,000 even where they have suffered identity theft, or $100 if their "health information has been compromised."[43] At the time of writing, the one Canadian class action filed in the province of British Columbia is ongoing.[44] Due to the scale of the breach and this litigation, it seems a timely example to discuss in order to highlight the importance of having appropriate cyber security in the context of services that handle sensitive data. This breach was first made public in October of 2023 when 23andMe made an announcement that their systems had been compromised. However, it was not until December 2023 that it emerged that approximately half of 23andMe's customers could be impacted. This numbered almost seven million individuals.[45]

41   L Franceschi-Bicchierai, "23andMe Tells Victims It's Their Fault That Their Data Was Breached" *TechCrunch* (4 January 2024), online: https://techcrunch. com/2024/01/03/23andme-tells-victims-its-their-fault-that-their-data-was-breached/; J Bilyk, "Privacy Class Action Firms Jockey For Control of 23andme Data Breach Claims; Edelson Calls for New Approach" Northern California Record (19 April 2024) <https://norcalrecord.com/stories/657865535-privacy-class-action-firms-jockey-for-control-of-23andme-data-breach-claims-edelson-calls-for-new-approach.

42   J Dworetzky, "Hackers Target Jewish and Chinese 23andMe Customers; Class Action Lawsuit Filed Against South City DNA Data Company" *The Daily Journal* (13 March 2024), online: https://www.smdailyjournal.com/news/local/hackers-target-jewish-and-chinese-23andme-customers-class-action-lawsuit-filed-against-south-city-dna/article_22e9c192-e0e7-11ee-92c1-2bec18317904.html.

43   In re 23ANDME, Customer Data Sec. Breach Litig., 24-md-03098-EMC (N.D. Cal. Dec. 4, 2024) https://casetext.com/case/in-re-23andme-customer-data-sec-breach-litig-3/case-details; A Bronstad, "Judge Approves 23andMe's $30M Data Breach Settlement - With Conditions" *The Recorder* (6 December 2024), online: https:// www.law.com/therecorder/2024/12/06/judge-approves-23andmes-30m-data-breach-settlement-with-conditions/; S Alder, "23andMe Settles Data Breach Lawsuit for $30 Million" *The HIPAA Journal* (16 September 2024), online: https://www. hipaajournal.com/23andme-class-action-data-breach-settlement/.

44   Phillips, *Hacking your DNA? supra* note 4 citing KND Complex Litigation, "23andME Canadian Consumer Data Breach Class ACTION" CISION (20 December 2023) – case J. R. v 23andMe Holding Co et al, Vancouver Registry, S-237147 https:// www.newswire.ca/news-releases/23andme-canadian-consumer-data-breach-class-action-843706435.html; and D Xiong, "B.C. Class-Action Seeks Compensation Over Alleged 23andMe Breach" *BIV* (3 January 2024), online: https://www.biv.com/ news/economy-law-politics/bc-class-action-seeks-compensation-over-alleged-23andme-breach-8294786#:~:text=Canadian%20customers%20are%20suing%20 23andMe,by%20the%20alleged%20data%20breach.

45   M DeGuerin, "Hackers Got Nearly 7 Million People's Data From 23andMe. The Firm Blamed Users In 'Very Dumb' Move" *The Guardian* (15 February 2024),

It has also become clear in recent months that 23andMe should have known about the incident earlier, as it seems that their database was first breached in April 2023.[46] One of the most concerning aspects of this breach is that it has involved racial targeting of consumers who had Chinese or Ashkenazi Jewish heritage, and the information that was accessible to the hackers included genetic information, full names, home addresses, photographs, and family members.[47] Consequently, given the type of information that has been accessed, this does not merely create significant privacy risks, but also risks to physical safety for individuals and their families. This is exemplified by the fact that hackers have posted information on the Dark Web, seeking to sell this information to the Chinese government and also to those who may want to attack Jews.[48]

Another element that should be highlighted in relation to the 23andMe breach is that the attack was facilitated by credential stuffing, which meant that the system did not have to be hacked itself initially, but attackers were able to use usernames and passwords harvested from other sites in order to login as though they were users.[49] This was possible because 23andMe allowed users to create accounts linking them to their other accounts, such as Google, Facebook, and Apple. While many consumers may take advantage of the ease of creating an account by linking it to already existing accounts, this practice is problematic from a privacy perspective, and given the nature of this industry, it ought to be discontinued.

In June 2024, it was announced that the UK's Information Commissioner's Office (ICO) and the Privacy Commissioner of Canada (OPC) have launched a joint probe into the 23andMe breach.[50]

online: https://www.theguardian.com/technology/2024/feb/15/23andme-hack-data-genetic-data-selling-response; L Franceschi-Bicchierai, "23andme Confirms Hackers Stole Ancestry Data on 6.9 Million Users" *TechCrunch* (5 December 2023) https://techcrunch.com/2023/12/04/23andme-confirms-hackers-stole-ancestry-data-on-6-9-million-users/.

46   See Filing - Motion to Appoint Interim Leadership – *David Melvin and J.L v 23andMe Inc Case No.* 24-cv-00487-SK — hearing date set at 4 March 2024 https://fingfx.thomsonreuters.com/gfx/legaldocs/gkvlddmwnvb/frankel-23andMedatabreach–Edelsonleadcounsel.pdf.

47   *Ibid.*

48   *Ibid* at 4–10.

49   J McKeon, "What the 23andMe Data Breach Reveals About Credential Stuffing" *TechTarget* (7 December 2023), online: https://healthitsecurity.com/features/what-the-23andme-data-breach-reveals-about-credential-stuffing.

50   ICO, "ICO to Investigate 23andMe Data Breach with Canadian Counterpart" ICO Statement (10 June 2024), online: ICO (blog) https://ico.org.uk/about-the-ico/

The investigation will concentrate on three matters:[51]

- the scope of information that was exposed by the breach and potential harms to affected people;
- whether 23andMe had adequate safeguards to protect the highly sensitive information within its control; and
- whether the company provided adequate notification about the breach to the two regulators and affected people as required under Canadian and UK data protection laws.

This investigation is timely, and it is hoped that it will lead to better regulation of this industry and greater awareness of the risks it poses to consumers.

It should also be noted that this was not the first data breach to occur in the DTC industry, and another earlier significant example is the MyHeritage breach, which was disclosed in 2018. This impacted some 92 million consumers, but fortunately it did not involve the leaking of actual genetic data,[52] though this breach is also very problematic.

Meanwhile, in the context of wearable technology, two examples are useful to note. However, as will be mentioned later in this chapter, concerns have been raised over the security and reliability of several popular wearable fitness monitoring devices.[53] The incidents that I wish to highlight here, though, relate to Strava and GetHealth. In 2017, Strava, which is a fitness application that can be linked to a wearable device, such as a Fitbit wristband, published a Global Heat Map.[54] This heat map was based around the activity history of Strava's active users.[55] Unfortunately, after the map was released, it emerged that it

media-centre/news-and-blogs/2024/06/ico-to-investigate-23andme-data-breach-with-canadian-counterpart/.
51   *Ibid.*
52   S Ferguson, "MyHeritage Data Breach of 92M Accounts Raises Many Questions" *Dark Reading* (6 June 2018), online: https://www.darkreading.com/cloud-security/myheritage-data-breach-of-92m-accounts-raises-many-questions; Norton Security, "MyHeritage Data Breach Exposes Info of More Than 92 Million Users" *Norton Security* (8 August 2018), online: https://us.norton.com/blog/emerging-threats/myheritage-data-breach-exposes-info-of-more-than-92-million-user.
53   A Hilts, C Parsons & J Knockel, *Every Step You Fake: A Comparative Analysis of Fitness Tracker Privacy and Security* (Open Effect Report 2016), online: https://openeffect.ca/reports/Every_Step_You_Fake.pdf.
54   Phillips, *All Your Data Will Be Held Against You, supra* note 4 at 423.
55   *Ibid* at 423.

was possible to use it to locate military personnel and military bases, due to those in the military using the application.[56] This incident demonstrates that there are risks associated with using these devices and applications that can reach far beyond an individual and their family to impacting national security.

The second example of a data breach in the context of wearable technology involves GetHealth. GetHealth is a fitness company, and in 2021, researchers from Website Planet in collaboration with a security researcher located a "database that contained over 61 million records belonging to users around the world."[57] The database was not password protected, and while once the company was alerted, it remedied the situation very quickly, this is still a concerning example. The database included data from Apple and Fitbit users, and one of the most problematic aspects of this discovery was the nature of the data that was accessible. It included users' full names, dates of birth, and geolocations, together with other identifying information such as gender, display names, height, and weight.[58] Similar to the 23andMe breach, this example demonstrates the wide variety of personal and sensitive data that may be accessed by third parties and malicious actors and could cause problems for individuals impacted by the breach over the longer term.

There are two further examples from the online dating world that should be noted here. These relate to Tinder and Grindr. The Tinder problem stemmed from its location settings. There have actually been two different vulnerabilities that Tinder has experienced, which are rather unfortunately linked. The first, identified in 2013, stemmed from the application sharing location coordinates with matches on the iOS client.[59] According to research conducted by Veytsman, in fixing the earlier problem, another vulnerability was created. This permitted all Tinder users to see the location of all other Tinder users for a period of

---

56   *Ibid* [citing JE Dunn, "Secret Military Bases Revealed by Fitness App Strava" *Naked Security* (30 January 2018), online: https://nakedsecurity.sophos.com/2018/01/30/secret-military-bases-revealed-by-fitness-appstrava/]; and J Hsu, "The Strava Heat Map and the End of Secrets" *Wired* (29 January 2018), online: www.wired.com/story/strava-heat-map-military-bases-fitness-trackers-privacy/.

57   J Fowler, "Report: Fitness Tracker Data Breach Exposed 61 Million Records and User Data Online" *Website Planet* (blog) (September 2021), online: https://www.websiteplanet.com/blog/gethealth-leak-report/.

58   *Ibid.*

59   M Veytsman, "How I Was Able to Track the Location of Any Tinder User" *Include Security* (19 February 2014), online: https://blog.includesecurity.com/2014/02/how-i-was-able-to-track-the-location-of-any-tinder-user/.

time "with a very high degree of accuracy"; that is, within 100 feet.[60] While this has since been remedied, this last example also highlights that the risks in this context are not limited to concerns about informational privacy, but actual physical harm. Together, all the aforementioned breaches should highlight that even when industries do rely on collecting sensitive information, there is no guarantee that that information will be kept safe.

The last example is that of Grindr. This relates to the unauthorized sharing of consumers' data with data brokers. This led to a complaint by the NCC to the Norwegian Data Protection Authority, which has since fined the company €5.8 million.[61] The complaint emerged after the NCC's report *Out of Control*.[62] This report also detailed how Grindr shared a variety of data with data brokers for marketing and analytics purposes, including their GPS location, age, and gender, as well as HIV status.[63] While Grindr was not initially included in the case studies in this chapter, its "Terms of Service" were also accessed and are also mentioned briefly in Part (IV) (iii) given the significance of the NCC's complaint.

The following section of this chapter will consider some examples of licence clauses used in the online contracts of these three industries. It will use extracts from current contracts of these businesses to demonstrate potential privacy risks in these three contexts. It is likely that consumers may not always be aware of privacy risks in this space or may trust companies in handling their data. However, it is hoped that this discussion of the scope of these clauses will highlight the need for further research in this area and improved regulation along with improved business practice.

---

60   *Ibid.*; S Frizell, "Tinder Security Flaw Exposed Users' Locations," *Time* (19 February 2014), online: <https://time.com/8604/tinder-app-user-location-security-flaw/.

61   European Data Protection Board, "Norwegian DPA Imposes Fine Against Grindr LLC," *European Data Protection Board News* (19 December 2021), online: <https://www.edpb.europa.eu/news/national-news/2021/norwegian-dpa-imposes-fine-against-grindr-llc_en>; Norwegian Consumer Council, "€ 5,8 Million Fine for Grindr – the Norwegian Consumer Council's Complaint Fully Upheld by the Privacy Appeals Board," *Press Release* (29 September 2023), online: https://www.forbrukerradet.no/siste-nytt/e-58-million-fine-for-grindr-the-norwegian-consumer-councils-complaint-fully-upheld-by-the-privacy-board/; Norwegian Data Protection Authority, "The NO DPA Imposes Fine Against Grindr" (2021), online: https://www.datatilsynet.no/en/regulations-and-tools/regulations/avgjorelser-fra-datatilsynet/2021/gebyr-til-grindr/; LLC ACCC, *Digital platform services inquiry Interim report 8, supra* note 30.

62   NCC, *Out of Control, supra* note 30.

63   *Ibid* at 6 and 72.

Case Studies

Direct-to-Consumer Genetic Testing

The first case study is from the DTC industry. This industry has created a market for DNA tests as consumer services, taking them out of the clinic and into people's homes. The industry began in the late 1990s,[64] but it has only been in the last decade that there has been significant uptake of these tests by consumers. Purchase of the test is typically made via a website, and the consumer will then be sent a collection kit in the mail. The consumer then will collect a saliva sample or cheek swab and send it back to the company for processing. The industry is diverse and while ancestry and health testing have become relatively popular, especially in America, a wide range of more dubious types of tests are also available. These range from child talent and "peace of mind" paternity tests to infidelity (or surreptitious tests of other individuals).[65] A report from MIT's Technology Review estimated[66] that by 2019, 26 million people would have purchased a DNA test for ancestry. Meanwhile, according to YouGov in 2020, "one in twenty (5 percent)" of the UK's population have now had a commercial DNA test.[67] 23andMe's current database contains information of 14 million consumers.[68] Erlich et al's 2018 study suggested that a significant proportion of Americans with European ancestry could be linked to a "third cousin or closer using an open-access genetic genealogy database."[69]

---

64   S Hogarth & P Saukko, "A Market in the Making: The Past, Present and Future of Direct-to-Consumer Genomics" (2017) 36:3 New Genetics and Society 197–208, DOI: 10.1080/14636778.2017.1354692.

65   AM Phillips, "Only a Click Away – DTC Genetics for Ancestry, Health, Love… and More: A View of the Business and Regulatory Landscape" (2016) 8 Applied & Translational Genomics 16–22.

66   *Ibid* at 16–22; AM Phillips, "Buying Your Genetic Self Online: Pitfalls and Potential Reforms in DNA Testing" (May/June 2019) IEEE Security and Privacy 77–81, DOI: 10.1109/MSEC.2019.2904128; AM Phillips and S Becher, "At-Home DNA Tests Just Aren't That Reliable – And the Risks May Outweigh The Benefits" *The Conversation* (29 November 2022), online: https://theconversation.com/at-home-dna-tests-just-arent-that-reliable-and-the-risks-may-outweigh-the-benefits-194349.

67   C Ibbetson, "Should Police Have Access To Private DNA Data" *YouGov* (14 January 2020), online: https://yougov.co.uk/health/articles/25691-half-brits-say-police-should-have-access-private-d; J Kleeman, "These People Took DNA Tests. The Results Changed Their Lives" *BBC* (5 October 2023), online: BBC https://www.bbc.com/future/article/20231004-these-people-took-dna-tests-the-results-changed-their-lives.

68   23andMe, "Addressing Data Security Concerns" 6 October 2023, online: https://blog.23andme.com/articles/addressing-data-security-concerns

69   CY Johnson, "Even If You've Never Taken a DNA Test, a Distant Relative's Could Reveal Your Identity," *The Washington Post* (11 October 2018), online: https://www.

Suffice to say these tests are popular, and if only one member of a person's immediate family has had a test, this will pose privacy risks for a wider related group. Erlich's earlier work has also demonstrated that it is possible to identify individuals in quite large databases, and this has contributed to a general consensus that it is not really possible to anonymize genomic data[70] in a way that would completely prevent reidentification.[71] This means that in turn it is important to have good cyber security practices to afford sufficient protection to this data.

It is important to understand that the DTC industry is, by nature, an industry that is reliant on both data collection and secondary research based on that data.[72] Concerns have been raised about the standards, reliability, and clinical utility of testing,[73] and studies have shown that it is possible to obtain contradictory disease risk estimates from different companies for the same disease,[74] as well as conflicting ethnicity

---

washingtonpost.com/science/2018/10/11/even-if-youve-never-taken-dna-test-distant-relatives-could-reveal-your-identity/. – citing Yaniv Erlich et al, "Identity Inference of Genomic Data Using Long-Range Familial Searches" (2018) Science 362 at 690–694.

70   E Ayday et al, "Whole Genome Sequencing: Revolutionary Medicine or Privacy Nightmare?" (2015) 48:2 Computer 58–66; M Gymrek et al, "Identifying Personal Genomes by Surname Inference" (2013) 339:6117 Science 321–324; J Rahnasto, "Genetic Data Are Not Always Personal—Disaggregating the Identifiability and Sensitivity of Genetic Data" (July-December 2023) 10:2 J L B 1–45.

71   M Phillips, "GDPR Brief: Can Genomic Data Be Anonymised?" *Global Alliance for Genomics & Health* (10 October 2018), online: https://www.ga4gh.org/news_item/can-genomic-data-be-anonymised/; J Banda, "Inherently Identifiable: Is It Possible to Anonymize Health and Genetic Data?" *IAPP Privacy Perspectives* (13 November 2019), online: https://iapp.org/news/a/inherently-identifiable-is-it-possible-to-anonymize-health-and-genetic-data/.

72   C Seife, "23andMe Is Terrifying but Not for the Reasons the FDA Thinks," *Scientific American* (27 November 2013), online: https://www.scientificamerican.com/article/23andme-is-terrifying-but-not-for-the-reasons-the-fda-thinks/.

73   J Karow, "23andMe DTC Breast and Ovarian Cancer Risk Test Misses Almost 90 Percent of BRCA Mutation Carriers," *GenomeWeb* (5 April 2019), online: *Genome Web* https://www.genomeweb.com/molecular-diagnostics/23andme-dtc-breast-and-ovarian-cancer-risk-test-missesalmost-90-percent-brca#.XKfbrS1L1PU - citing E Esplin et al, "Limitations of Direct-to-Consumer Genetic Screening for HBOC: False Negatives, False Positives and Everything In Between" Abstract 27, Presented at the ACMG Annual Clinical Genetics Meeting, 4 April 2019, Washington State Convention Center, online: https://aacrjournals.org/cancerres/article/79/4_Supplement/P4-03-06/639589/Abstract-P4-03-06-Limitations-of-direct-to; R Collier, "Genetic Tests for Athletic Ability: Science or Snake Oil?" (2012) 184:1 Canadian Medical Association Journal E43–5.

74   US Government Accountability Office, (GAO) *Direct-To-Consumer Genetic Tests: Misleading Test Results Are Further Complicated by Deceptive Marketing and Other Questionable Practice* (GAO-10-847T, 2010) Testimony before the Subcommittee on

estimates from different companies. [75] It is important to note here that most tests offered by this industry are not standardized, and particularly for health tests, it remains unclear what benefit the consumer is actually getting from testing, if the test cannot be relied on. Despite these concerns, the industry has gained popularity, and it has been characterized by partnerships centred on secondary research and mergers. A few prominent examples of market leaders should suffice to demonstrate this. Firstly, 23andMe has had at least 15 partnerships with pharmaceutical companies [76] and merged with Virgin in 2021. [77] Meanwhile, Ancestry has also had partnerships, including with Google's Calico, [78] but also a rather unusual one with Spotify to create playlists based on a person's DNA, [79] and was acquired by Blackstone in 2020. [80] Meanwhile, an earlier market leader Navigenics was acquired by Life Technologies

Oversight and Investigations, Committee on Energy and Commerce, House of Representatives 1–8 http://www.gao.gov/assets/130/125079.pdf; Jessica Cussins, "Direct-to-Consumer Genetic Tests Should Come with a Health Warning" The Pharmaceutical Journal (15 January 2015), online: https://www.pharmaceutical-journal.com/opinion/comment/direct-to-consumer-genetic-tests-should-come-with-a-healthwarning/20067564.article?firstPass=false.

75   See Phillips, *Buying Your Self on the Internet*, *supra* note 3 at 105; and Kristen V Brown, "How DNA Testing Botched My Family's Heritage, and Probably Yours, Too," *GIZMODO* (16 January 2018), online: https://gizmodo.com/how-dna-testing-botchedmy-familys-heritage-and-probab-1820932637; R Letzter, "I Took 9 Different DNA Tests and Here's What I Found" *Live Science* (6 November 2018), online: Live Science https://www.livescience.com/63997-dna-ancestry-test-results-explained.html; WD Roth and B Ivemark, "Genetic Options: The Impact Of Genetic Ancestry Testing on Consumers' Racial and Ethnic Identities" (2018) 124:1 American Journal of Sociology 150–184.

76   Phillips, *All Your Data Will Be Held Against You*, *supra* note 4 at 404.

77   Virgin, "23andMe and Virgin Group's VG Acquisition Corp. Successfully Close Business Combination" (16 June 2021) https://www.virgin.com/about-virgin/virgin-group/news/23andme-and-virgin-groups-vg-acquisition-corp-successfully-close-business.

78   RNZ, "What Happens to Your DNA Information After an Ancestry Test?" (12 June 2018) https://www.rnz.co.nz/national/programmes/afternoons/audio/2018648929/what-happens-to-your-dna-information-after-an-ancestry-test; KM Palmer, "Another Personal Genetics Company Is Sharing Client Data," *Wired* (21 July 2015), online: https://www.wired.com/2015/07/another-personal-genetics-company-selling-client-data/.

79   R Arcand, "Please Don't Give Your Genetic Data to AncestryDNA as Part of Their Spotify Playlist Partnership," *SPIN* (23 September 2018), online: https://www.spin.com/2018/09/ancestry-dna-genetic-data-spotify-playlist-partnership/.

80   Blackstone, "Blackstone Completes Acquisition of Ancestry®, Leading Online Family History Business, for $4.7 Billion" Press Release (4 December 2020), online: https://www.blackstone.com/news/press/blackstone-completes-acquisition-of-ancestry-leading-online-family-history-business-for-4-7-billion/ last accessed 12 March 2024.

and ceased to offer DTC tests, but undoubtedly its database was used in ongoing research. [81]

It is also clear that much of the motivation behind these companies' research is fuelled by a desire to develop a range of products, including pharmaceutical drugs, and to patent these inventions. [82] In 23andMe's Annual Report for 2023, it states the following: "patent estate consists of 113 granted U.S. patents, which include 93 utility and 20 design patents that cover technologies that include graphical user interfaces, aspects of algorithms for processing genetic data, computer implemented inventions, bioinformatics, and genotyping." [83]

As well as secondary research by the companies themselves and their industry partners, the industry raises serious privacy risks, as it has also been used by law enforcement in criminal investigations. [84] The process used here is referred to as genetic genealogy or investigative genetic genealogy (or sometimes forensic investigative genetic

81   Phillips, *Buying Your Self on the Internet, supra* note 3 at 120.; *see also* Life Technologies Corporation, "Acquisition of Navigenics Expands Life Technologies' Capabilities in Diagnostics," PR *News Wire* (16 July 2012), online: https://www.prnewswire.com/news-releases/acquisition-of-navigenics-expands-life-technologies-capabilities-in-diagnostics-162631986.html.

82   M Allyse, "23 and Me, We and You: Direct-to-consumer Genetics, Intellectual Property and Informed Consent" (2013) 31(2) Trends in Biotechnology 68 https://www.ncbi.nlm.nih.gov/pmc/articles/PMC6309979/pdf/nihms-1000787.pdf; KV Brown, "All Those 23andMe Spit Tests Were Part of a Bigger Plan," *Bloomberg* (4 November 2021), online: https://www.bloomberg.com/news/features/2021-11-04/23andme-to-use-dna-tests-to-make-cancer-drugs; A Zalesky, "This Start-Up Is Betting Your Genes Will Yield the Next Wonder Drug," *CNBC* (22 June 2016), online: CNBC https://www.cnbc.com/2016/06/22/23andme-thinks-your-genes-are-the-key-to-blockbuster-drugs.html.

83   23andMe, *23ANDME HOLDING CO. ANNUAL REPORT FISCAL 2023* (25 May 2023) at 7, online: https://investors.23andme.com/static-files/aa2531b7-1142-4229-a4c1-ea23ff418aba; see also S Sterckx et al, "Trust Is Not Something You Can Reclaim Easily: Patenting in the Field of Direct-to-Consumer Genetic Testing" (2013) 15:5 Genetics in Medicine 382–387; and HC Howard et al, "The Convergence of Direct-to-Consumer Genetic Testing Companies and Biobanking Activities: The Example of 23andme" in M Wienroth and E Rodrigues, eds, *Knowing New Biotechnologies – Social Aspects of Technological Convergence,* 1st ed (London, UK: Routledge, 2015) at 59–74; In future work, the author plans to explore the patents acquired by the DTC industry.

84   Te Aka Matua o te Ture New Zealand Law Commission, *The Use of DNA in Criminal Investigations Q&A Summary* (November 2020) *at* 5 https://www.lawcom.govt.nz/assets/Publications/Reports/NZLC-R144-QA-summary.pdf; and Te Aka Matua o te Ture New Zealand Law Commission, *The Use of DNA in Criminal Investigations | Te Whakamahi i te Ira Tangata i ngā Mātai Taihara (NZLC R144)* chapter 15 <https://www.lawcom.govt.nz/our-work/the-use-of-dna-in-criminal-investigations/tab/report.

genealogy).[85] This became widely known after the use of GEDmatch to track down James DeAngelo in the Golden State Killer cold case,[86] but also through the publicity around FamilyTreeDNA's collaboration with the FBI.[87] There have also been instances of immigration authorities using ancestry tests to try to identify a person's origins, which has occurred in Canada.[88] This particular use of the DTC industry's databases is very problematic, as ethnicity estimates and even matches with distant relatives will not necessarily correlate with an individual's citizenship rights, and more work needs to be conducted in relation to this.

While privacy and data protection legislation as well as consumer protection legislation should be applicable and enforceable against the industry, it has to date remained largely unregulated.[89] In previous work, which included a review of the contracts of 71 companies marketing DNA tests for health purposes, it was argued that several terms commonly included in these contracts could be challenged on the basis of unfairness.[90] While this work focused on the UK legislative framework, these arguments can be made in several jurisdictions, including New Zealand, Australia, the Republic of Ireland, and the European Union, as all these jurisdictions have similar laws regulating unfair terms in consumer contracts.[91] This review included examination of

---

85   J Lynch, "Forensic Genetic Genealogy Searches: What Defense Attorneys & Policy Makers Need to Know" *Electronic Frontier Foundation* (26 July 2023) https://www.eff.org/wp/forensic-genetic-genealogy-searches-what-defense-attorneys-need-know; New South Wales Police, "Forensic Investigative Genetic Genealogy" https://www.police.nsw.gov.au/about_us/information_of_interest_to_the_community/forensic_investigative_genetic_genealogy#:~:text=FIGG%20combines%20new%20DNA%20analysis,built%20to%20identify%20potential%20candidates.

86   Haag, *supra* note 1.

87   P Aldhous, "Cops Forced a Company to Share a Customer's Identity for the Golden State Killer Investigation", *BuzzFeed News* (1 May 2018), online: https://www.buzzfeednews.com/article/peteraldhous/family-tree-dna-subpoena-golden-state-killer#.klPB3w6vpm.

88   E Campanella, "Government Using Ancestry Websites To Deport Immigrants: Lawyer, Court Documents," *Global News* (1 November 2018), online: Global News https://globalnews.ca/news/4616715/ancestry-dna-test-deportation-cbsa/; A Kassam, "Canada Uses DNA and Ancestry Sites to Check Migrants' Identity," *The Guardian* (30 July 2018), online: https://www.theguardian.com/world/2018/jul/30/canada-uses-dna-and-ancestry-sites-to-check-migrants-identity.

89   Phillips, *Buying Your Self on the Internet, supra* note 3 at chapters 1 and 6.

90   *Ibid* at chapter 5.

91   In the UK, see the *Consumer Rights Act* 2015 (c. 15); in New Zealand, see *Fair Trading Act* 1986 and *Fair Trading Amendment Act* 2021; in Australia, the relevant legislation can be found in the Australian Consumer Law, which is included in Schedule 2 to

several examples of licence clauses and intellectual property clauses,[92] and comparison will be made below between the previous study and the examples used in this chapter, where appropriate.

It is important to note that given the nature of the industry operating online, the contracts are subject to frequent changes, which are assisted by several companies giving themselves broad power to alter terms by including a variation clause that allows them to change their terms at any time. It should be noted too that throughout their online activities, consumers regularly encounter contracts and privacy policies that they disregard.[93]

Before examining the licence clauses from current versions of DTC contracts, it should be noted that the previous review of 71 DTC companies' contracts found it was common practice to include unilateral variation clauses, as well as indemnity clauses.[94] While there have been amendments to these contracts since this review was conducted, all three companies used in this case study still retain a broad power to alter their terms, and all contain an indemnity clause, which requires the consumer to indemnify the company against third party action. Unfortunately, in the examination conducted for this chapter, it was also found that all the wearable technology and online dating companies considered herein also included indemnity clauses. This is an area that really needs significant reform, and readers are encouraged to reflect on the possible harm that these clauses could cause consumers and the impact this has on their rights to redress.[95]

The first example comes from 23andMe's "Terms of Service," clause 3.[96] Note that the clause is the same whether you access the US version of the website or the international version, which is what consumers would likely access if purchasing from New Zealand or Australia. It is set out below in full, so as to give the reader a sense of

---

the *Competition and Consumer Act* 2010 (Cth) (CCA); and in the European Union see Council Directive 93/13/EEC of 5 April 1993 On Unfair Terms in Consumer Contracts [1993] OJ L95/36/29.

92   Phillips, *Buying Your Self on the Internet*, *supra* note 3 at 211–216; see also Becher and Phillips, *Data Rights*, *supra* note 3.

93   Becher and Phillips, *Data Rights*, *supra* note 3 at 86–91.

94   Phillips, *Buying Your Self on the Internet*, *supra* note 3 at chapter 5.

95   Future work will explore this in more detail.

96   23andMe, "Terms of Service" US Version (last updated 30 November 2023), online: https://www.23andme.com/legal/terms-of-service/#licensing-ip-rights; Please note that 23andMe, "Terms of Service" International Version (last updated 8 June 2022) contains the same clause <https://www.23andme.com/en-int/legal/terms-of-service/#licensing-ip-rights last accessed 18 June 2024.

the content covered within its scope and the extent of the licence clause itself. It reads as follows:

> "User Content" is all information, data, text, software, music, audio, photographs, graphics, video, messages, or other materials generated by users of the Services and transmitted, whether publicly or privately, to or through 23andMe. User Content does not include genetic or health information. To provide the Services to you, you must grant us a license to your User Content. We do not claim ownership of User Content, but you grant us a license to use it.

> You give 23andMe, its affiliated companies, sublicensees and successors and assignees a perpetual, irrevocable, worldwide, royalty-free, and non-exclusive license to host, reproduce, adapt, modify, translate, publish, publicly perform, store, publicly display, distribute, reproduce, edit, reformat, and create derivative works from any User Content that you submit, post, or display on or through the Services. This license is fully-paid and royalty free, meaning we do not owe you anything else in connection with our use of your User Content. You acknowledge and agree that this license includes a right for 23andMe to make such User Content available to other companies, organizations, or individuals with whom 23andMe has relationships, and to use such User Content in connection with the provision of those services.

There are several points that should be noted here. Firstly, the definition of what constitutes "User Content" does specifically exclude "genetic or health information." However, User Content does cover basically any other thing that a consumer might share, including their messages, photographs, information, text, and video, and furthermore, this applies to things that are shared both privately and publicly. Likewise, the exclusion of genetic and health data does not necessarily mean that such information will only be used in ways that consumers anticipate. I urge the reader to consider the scope of the licence itself. Specifically, it should be noted the licence is "irrevocable" and attaches not just to 23andMe, but its "successors" and "affiliated companies." Please consider what that means. It potentially includes all of 23andMe's partners—and remember that it has now merged with Virgin.

As 23andMe's licence clause was also examined in the previous review, it is possible to make some comparative comment. Referring to an earlier version of this clause, which was contained in clause 13 of the "Terms of Service," very little has changed.[97] The earlier clause did not define User Content and did mention that consumers retained their copyright in their content, but it still specified that "by submitting, posting, or displaying User Content," the consumer granted 23andMe and "its affiliated companies, sublicensees (including but not limited to sublicensees ...) and successors and assigns a perpetual, irrevocable, perpetual licence to use that content. What needs to be emphasized here is that this clause does seem to be framed in an overly broad manner given the nature of the service being sold.

The next example should demonstrate that 23andMe's contract is by no means unusual in terms of industry practice. This example is from AncestryDNA's "Terms and Conditions."[98] Here, the licence can also be found in clause 3. It reads as follows:

3.2 Use of Your Content

By submitting Your Content, you grant Ancestry a non-exclusive, sub-licensable, worldwide, royalty-free license to host, store, index, copy, publish, distribute, provide access to, create derivative works of, and otherwise use Your Content to provide, promote, or improve the Services, consistent with your privacy and sharing settings. You can terminate Ancestry's license by deleting Your Content, except to the extent you shared Your Content with others and they have used Your Content. You also agree that Ancestry owns any indexes and compilations that include Your Content and may use them after Your Content is deleted.

The final example from the DTC industry is that of clause 9 of FamilyTreeDNA's "Terms of Service." It reads as follows:[99]

(B) Personal Information and User Provided Content: You provide us with various types of information when you use the Services. For an explanation of Personal Information and a description of

---

97   Phillips, *Buying Your Self on the Internet*, *supra* note 3 at 215.
98   AncestryDNA, "Terms and Conditions" (effective date 17 Jan 2024), online: https://www.ancestry.com.au/c/legal/termsandconditions (last accessed 18 June 2024).
99   FamilyTreeDNA, "Terms of Service" (last updated 17 January 2022), online: https://www.familytreedna.com/legal/terms-of-service/04112024 (last accessed 18 June 2024).

the types of Personal Information you may provide to us, see our Privacy Statement. The steps to delete your Personal Information is explained in our Privacy Statement. In addition, you may provide us with information that is not treated as Personal Information. In these TOS, we refer to this type of information as "User Provided Content."

...

User Provided Content that you have shared or made public (e.g., by including such User Provided Content in a public FamilyTreeDNA family tree, as part of participating in a Group Project, as part of your public profile or a public posting in one of the Services) may be utilized by other users as part of, or in combination with, the Services. We will not be obligated to remove any information or User Provided Content that you have made public or has otherwise been shared from the public profiles, or Group Projects, or family trees of other users.

...

(D) Ownership of Personal Information, Self-Reported Information, and User Provided Content: You own your Personal Information, Self-Reported Information, and User Provided Content. Through use of the Services, you grant us the right to collect, process, analyze, store and communicate your Personal Information (including your Genetic Information) and Self-Reported Information for the purposes described in these TOS and our Privacy Statement and in order to (i) provide the Services to you and other users, (ii) to help our Users learn more about their ancestry, and (iii) for any other purpose you expressly agree to, such as sharing with others and joining Group Projects. Also, by submitting User Provided Content through any of the Services, you grant FamilyTreeDNA a sublicensable, worldwide, royalty-free license to host, store, copy, publish, distribute, provide access to, create derivative works of, and otherwise use such User Provided Content to the extent and in the form or context we consider suitable on or through any media or medium and with any technology or devices currently known or hereafter discovered or developed.

This last clause has been shortened, but note the similarity to 23andMe and AncestryDNA's clauses. Again, a very broad licence is acquired. Note that it allows the company to create works utilising such content "on any media or medium and with any technology or devices currently known or hereafter discovered or developed."

It should also be noted that the clause states that "Through use of the Services, you grant us the right to collect, process, analyze, store and communicate your Personal Information." This is deeming consent through use of the service. It cannot be viewed as true informed consent. Nor is this the type of consent required by the GDPR in articles 4(11), which defines consent, article 7, which sets out conditions for consent, and article 9(1), which prohibits the processing of genetic data unless certain exceptions apply. The most relevant exception, as set out in article 9(2)(a) is that the individual has given "explicit consent." This is unfortunately a common practice across the industry, and it is possible to purchase a test from multiple companies without ever viewing their terms and conditions.

The company has since updated its contract in April 2024 and does not contain the same wording. However, the current version of the contract does contain the following clause: [100]

> You hereby release FamilyTreeDNA from any and all claims, liens, demands, actions, or suits in connection with your DNA Sample, Genetic Results and/or Genetic Data, including, without limitation, errors, omissions, claims involving defamation, invasion of privacy, right of publicity, emotional distress or economic loss. This section will survive even if you stop using the Services. In addition, you acknowledge that by providing your DNA Sample and/or Genetic Results, you acquire no rights in any research or products that may be developed by FamilyTreeDNA that may relate to your DNA.

This clause is included here to give an example of a term that effectively limits a person's rights to legal redress.

---

100   FamilyTreeDNA, "Terms of Service" (last updated 11 April 2024), online: https://www.familytreedna.com/legal/terms-of-service.

Wearable Technology

The second case study is from the wearable technology industry, which can in turn be viewed as one prong in the growth of the Internet of Things (IoT). The market for wearable technology, especially smart watches and wristbands, has significantly grown in the last decade, and these devices have increased in popularity in recent years. According to the Tech Report, "From 2016 to 2019, connected wearable devices increased by 325 million to 722 million respectively."[101] An estimate from Grand View Research suggests that globally the "wearable technology market was valued at USD 61.30 billion in 2022 and is expected to expand at a compound annual growth rate (CAGR) of 14.6 percent from 2023 to 2030."[102]

These devices can also be viewed as an example of the Quantified Self Movement,[103] which can be broadly defined as referring to individuals tracking a wide variety of physical, biological, and environmental data about themselves. Smartwatches and wristbands, as well as some rings, are capable of tracking a wide variety of things including: steps, distance travelled, calories burnt, sleep, heart rate, menstrual cycle, and sexual activity.[104] Some of these data could be considered health data and could also be viewed as sensitive. While some consumers may benefit from engaging in health tracking, there are significant privacy risks from using these devices if companies do not afford adequate protection to their customers' privacy.

As noted above, this industry has experienced data breaches, and it collects information that has value for medical research as well as the insurance industry. In the UK, the Association of British Insurers(ABI) released a Code of Practice on the use of genetic tests by insurers in 2018 and a further guide for consumers in 2023.[105] The DTC industry

---

101   J Beckman, "15 Wearable Technology Statistics [2023 Edition]" *The Tech Report* (17 August 2023), online: https://techreport.com/statistics/wearable-technology-statistics/.

102   Grand View Research, "Wearable Technology Market Size, Share & Trends Analysis Report by Product (Eyewear & Headwear, Wristwear), by Application (Consumer Electronics, Healthcare), by Region, and Segment Forecasts, 2025 - 2030" Report ID: 978-1-68038-165-8, online: https://www.grandviewresearch.com/industry-analysis/wearable-technology-market.

103   M Swan, "The Quantified Self: Fundamental Disruption in Big Data Science and Biological Discovery" (2013) 1:2 Big Data 85–99.

104   Hilts et al, *supra* note 1455 at 52.

105   ABI, "ABI and Government Publish Updated Code on Genetic Testing & Insurance" (23 October 2018) https://www.abi.org.uk/news/news-articles/2018/10/abi-and-government-publish-updated-code-on-genetic-testing--insurance; ABI, *Consumer*

has also had problems with inaccuracy [106] and several devices have been found to be liable to spoofing or to possess security vulnerabilities. [107] If you wish to access an entertaining resource about the limitations of wearable fitness monitors and how they can be spoofed, the Unfit Bits website provides some guidance. [108] Several studies have highlighted security flaws in leading wearable technology devices, and three of these studies are considered briefly below.

Firstly, in their study of smartwatches aimed at children, the Norwegian Consumer Council identified security vulnerabilities, which would allow attackers to access a child's location in real time and also to contact the child directly. [109] They also found that it was possible for an attacker to make the watch transmit as though the child were in a very different location from where they actually were located. [110] Secondly, the study by Citizen Lab and Open Effect [111] examined eight wearable devices from leading brands and found a number of problems. This included the potential for an attacker to alter the fitness record and even delete data in that record. [112] Thirdly, another study by the Norwegian Consumer Council examined four popular wearable fitness devices from a consumer protection perspective. [113] This assessment included

---

Guide: Code on Genetic Testing & Insurance (July 2023), online: https://www.abi.org.uk/globalassets/files/publications/public/genetics/abi-consumer-guide-2023---code-on-genetic-testing-and-insurance.pdf>. ; E Worthington, "Government MP Julian Hill Joins Calls for Total Ban on Genetic Tests in Life Insurance Assessments," *ABC News* (1 June 2024), online: https://www.abc.net.au/news/2024-06-01/calls-for-genetic-testing-life-insurance-ban/103917632.

106   B Bent et al, "Investigating Sources of Inaccuracy in Wearable Optical Heart Rate Sensors" (2020) 3:18 NPJ Digital Medicine https://www.nature.com/articles/s41746-020-0226-6#citeas.

107   HP, "HP Study Reveals Smartwatches Vulnerable to Attack" *HP News Advisory* (22 July 2015) www8.hp.com/us/en/hp-news/press-release.html?id=2037386#.W3ahQS2ZPUo; HP, "HP Study Reveals 70 Percent of Internet of Things Devices Vulnerable to Attack" (29 July 2014) www8.hp.com/us/en/hp-news/press-release.html?id=1744676#.W3ag5i2ZPUo.

108   Unfit Bits, http://www.unfitbits.com/index.html (last accessed 18 June 2024).

109   Norwegian Consumer Council, *#WatchOut: Analysis of Smartwatches for Children* (October 2017) 3, online: https://storage02.forbrukerradet.no/media/2017/10/watchout-rapport-october-2017.pdf (last accessed 14 March 2024).

110   Norwegian Consumer Council, *#WatchOut: Analysis of smartwatches for children* – this includes a technical report provided by Mnemonic – Mnemonic, *Security Assessment Report GPS Watches for Children the Norwegian Consumer Council* at 4.3 which addresses location spoofing.

111   Hilts et al., *supra* note 53.

112   Hilts et al., *supra* note 53 at 31, para 2.7.1.

113   Norwegian Consumer Council, *Consumer Protection in Fitness Wearables* (November 2016) 3, online: https://storage02.forbrukerradet.no/media/2016/11/

consideration of the devices' contractual terms, as well as considering the level of control that these devices allowed consumers to exert over their data. [114] This work identified that some of the companies' practices violated European Union consumer protection and data protection law, which led them to initiate complaints with both the Norwegian Data Protection Authority and the Consumer Ombudsman. [115] It has also led to some improvements in the respective companies' terms, but as the Council highlight, there is still more work needed here. [116]

In light of this discussion, as I consider the clauses below from wearable technology contracts, the issue of data security and accuracy remains relevant. The first example is taken from Garmin's "Terms of Use." It is included under the heading "User Submissions" and reads as follows: [117]

> The Site may provide the opportunity for users to submit content ("User Submissions") for viewing by one or more Site users, such as a message board, chat or comment feature, or forum.
>
> By submitting User Submissions to the Site, you grant, or warrant that the owner of such material has expressly granted, Garmin the royalty-free, perpetual, irrevocable, non-exclusive right and license to use, reproduce, modify, adapt, publish, translate, and distribute such material (in whole or in part) worldwide and/or to incorporate it in other works in any form, media, or technology now known or hereafter developed for the full term of any copyright or other rights that may exist in such material. You will be solely liable for any damage resulting from any defamation, infringement of

---

2016-10-26-vedlegg-2-consumer-protection-in-fitness-wearables-forbrukerradet-final-version.pdf

114   *Ibid* at 4.

115   Norwegian Consumer Council, "Complaint Regarding Terms of Use and Privacy Policies for the Fitbit Charge HR, Garmin Vivosmart HR, Jawbone UP3 and Mio Fuse Activity Wristbands" (dated 3 November 2016), online: https://storage02. forbrukerradet.no/media/2016/11/2016-11-03-formal-complaint-wristbands-final1. pdf.

116   Norwegian Consumer Council, "Fitness Wristbands Violate European Law" (3 November 2016), online: https://www.forbrukerradet.no/side/ fitness-wristbands-violate-european-law/.

117   Garmin, "Terms of Use" US Version (effective date 17 February 2024) https://www. garmin.com/en-US/legal/terms-of-use/#section3-1. last accessed 18 June 2024; Note that the NZ Version includes the same clause. Garmin, "Terms of Use" NZ Version (effective date 17 February 2024), online: https://www.garmin.com/en-NZ/legal/ terms-of-use/#section3-1 (last accessed 18 June 2024).

copyrights, proprietary rights, or any other harm or claim resulting from a User Submission.

In considering the scope of this clause, note the similarity with the examples from the DTC industry. Again, it can be seen that the licence is irrevocable. It is also very broad and similar to the DTC contract clauses in that it covers a very broad range of potential formats, both now known and covering future technologies.

Our next example is taken from Fitbit's "Terms of Service" and is clause 5, which is entitled "Posting Your Content on the Fitbit Service." It reads as follows: [118]

> Fitbit may enable you to post, upload, store, share, send, or display photos, images, video, data, text, music, exercise regimens, food logs, recipes, comments, and other information and content ("Your Content") to and via the Fitbit Service. You retain all rights to Your Content that you post to the Fitbit Service. By making Your Content available on or through the Fitbit Service you hereby grant to Fitbit a non-exclusive, transferable, sublicensable, worldwide, royalty-free license to use, copy, modify, publicly display, publicly perform, reproduce, translate, create derivative works from, and distribute Your Content, in whole or in part, including your name and likeness, in any media. The rights you grant us in this Section 5 are only for the limited purpose of offering and improving the Fitbit Service.

Again, very similar language is used. The clause is framed broadly and seemingly covers almost anything that a consumer might put on their device or upload, including music and photographs. Note, it also allows for using the consumer's "name and likeness," which clearly seems to be at odds with the protection of privacy and the protection of consumers more generally.

The final example is from the Oura Ring's "Terms of Use." Oura differs from the other examples of wearable technology providers mentioned in this chapter in that it is a ring worn on the finger, but it tracks many of the same things that a Fitbit or Garmin product does. This clause differs from the others mentioned in that it does not explicitly say that it will acquire a licence to users' content. Its section on "Intellectual

---

118   Fitbit, "Terms of Service" (last updated 2 February 2024), online: https://www. fitbit.com/global/nz/legal/terms-of-service. last accessed 18 June 2024.

Property Rights" seems to be primarily concerned with protecting its own technology. However, the extract below provides as follows:[119]

> If you provide any communications or materials to Oura by mail, email, telephone, or otherwise, suggesting or recommending changes to the Services, including without limitation, new features or functionality relating thereto, or any comments, questions, suggestions, or the like ("Feedback"), Oura is free to use such Feedback irrespective of any other obligation or limitation between the Parties governing such Feedback. Oura is free to use, without any attribution or compensation to any party, any ideas, know-how, concepts, techniques, or other intellectual property rights contained in the Feedback, for any purpose whatsoever, although Oura is not required to use any Feedback.

While this clause does not seem to be quite as broad, as the others mentioned above, it is important to understand that Oura does allow itself broad discretion to alter the service. This is included in its Access and Use clause, which states that "Oura may modify, update, and otherwise change the Services at any time and in its sole discretion." It also has a very broad indemnity clause requiring the consumer to indemnify the company. It should be emphasized that indemnity clauses are very common in the online world, and in the previous review of DTC contracts, 44 percent of the companies' contracts examined included a clause of this type.[120] As was also highlighted in other work, such indemnity clauses are likely to conflict with what an ordinary consumer might expect to agree to, whether they are buying a genetic test or purchasing a wearable device or signing up for online dating.[121]

Similar to the examples from the DTC industry and the Garmin example above, this licence is framed in an exceptionally broad manner. A point to highlight here, though, is that unlike the other examples, the Fitbit clause does actually allow the company to make works that include the consumer's name and likeness. This seems to be overreach to a very significant extent.

---

119   OURA, "Terms of Use" NZ Version (last updated January 2024), online: https://ouraring.com/terms-and-conditions—there is now a more recently updated version, dated 2 April 2024, but it retains the same clause.

120   Phillips, *Buying Your Self on the Internet, supra* note 3 at 193.

121   Becher and Phillips, *Data Rights, supra* note 3 at 93.

Online Dating

The final case study is from the online dating industry. This encompasses websites that offer online dating services, as well as dating applications (apps),[122] which have experienced significant growth in the last decade. The industry has changed the way many people find partners, and it is an industry that is reliant on people connecting with others, which does necessitate sharing data. It should be noted that since the advent of the COVID-19 pandemic, there has been a significant increase in the popularity of online dating services.[123] This also saw a rise in new offerings from the industry in the realm of virtual dating and collaboration with public health authorities in relation to COVID-19 distancing measures, with one example being Tinder's addition of badges on users' profiles to indicate whether they had been vaccinated.[124] A recent report from PYMNTS also highlights the links between the online dating industry and social media,[125] and it had previously emerged that Facebook was able to collect sensitive information from dating apps including Tinder and Grindr, but also Femtech apps, such as Pregnancy+.[126] Facebook's own dating app Facebook Dating was unsuccessful.[127] Although joining an online dating platform or app can be free, services also offer subscriptions, and it is relatively common for consumers to opt for

122 M Stoicescu and C Rughiniş, "Perils of Digital Intimacy. A Classification Framework for Privacy, Security, and Safety Risks on Dating Apps" In 2021 23rd International Conference on Control Systems and Computer Science (CSCS) (pp. 457–462). IEEE https://www.researchgate.net/publication/353306998_Perils_of_digital_intimacy_A_classification_framework_for_privacy_security_and_safety_risks_on_dating_apps

123 Trozenski, *supra* note 22; BK Wiederhold, "How COVID Has Changed Online Dating – And What Lies Ahead" Editorial (2021) 24(7) Cyberpsychology, Behavior, and Social Networking http://doi.org/10.1089/cyber.2021.29219.editorial.

124 Trozenski, *supra* note 22.

125 EA Vogels and M Anderson, "Dating and Relationships in the Digital Age" Pew Research Center (8 May 2020), online: https://www.pewresearch.org/internet/2020/05/08/dating-and-relationships-in-the-digital-age/; PYMNTS, "Nearly 4 in 5 Consumers Screen Dating App Matches on Social Media" (21 April 2023), online: https://www.pymnts.com/connectedeconomy/2023/nearly-4-in-5-consumers-screen-dating-app-matches-on-social-media/.

126 A Al-Heeti, "Facebook Reportedly Gathering Personal Data from Tinder, Pregnancy+, Other Apps," *CNET* (19 December 2019), online: https://www.cnet.com/news/privacy/facebook-reportedly-gathering-personal-data-from-tinder-pregnancy-other-apps/.

127 T Yasseri, "Facebook Dating Was Set to Take Over the Market – Instead It Was Dead in the Water," (18 May 2022), online: The Conversation https://theconversation.com/facebook-dating-was-set-to-take-over-the-market-instead-it-was-dead-in-the-water-181375.

paid-for subscriptions. [128] Match and eharmony rely primarily on the paid membership model. [129]

The first example comes from Match.com's "Terms of Service." It should be noted that given the connection between Match and Tinder, their contracts are very similar, and as well as the licences mentioned below, they both contain clauses compelling the consumer to indemnify the company against third party actions, and reserve a broad power to alter their terms. Such variation clauses are very common, and in the previous review of DTC company contracts, it was found that 72 percent of the companies included in the review had some form of unilateral variation clause in their contract. [130]

Both Match.com and Tinder have their licence clauses contained in sections 7 and 3a of their contracts. The first example from Match.com's section 3a addresses users' content and is set out in its entirety below: [131]

> You are responsible for Your Content. Don't share anything that you wouldn't want others to see, that would violate this Agreement, or that may expose you or us to legal liability.
>
> You are solely responsible and liable for Your Content, and, therefore, you agree to indemnify, defend, release, and hold us harmless from any claims made in connection with Your Content.
>
> You represent and warrant to us that the information you provide to us or any other user is accurate, including any information submitted through Facebook or other third-party sources (if applicable), and that you will update your account information as necessary to ensure its accuracy.
>
> The content included on your individual profile should be relevant to the intended use of our Services. You may not display any personal contact or banking information, whether in relation to you or any other person (for example, names, home addresses

---

128   PYMNTS, "15% of Consumers with Dating Apps Opt for a Paid Subscription Service" (21 December 2023), online: https://www.pymnts.com/mobile-applications/2023/15-percent-of-consumers-with-dating-apps-opt-for-a-paid-subscription-service/.

129   Trozenski, *supra* note 22.

130   Phillips, *Buying Your Self on the Internet, supra* note 3 at 182–183.

131   Match.com, "Terms of Use," New Zealand Version (effective 28 February 2022), online: https://nz.match.com/masp/en-au/terms last accessed 14 March 2024.

or postcodes, telephone numbers, email addresses, URLs, credit/ debit card or other banking details). If you choose to reveal any personal information about yourself to other users, you do so at your own risk. We encourage you to use caution in disclosing any personal information online.

Your individual profile will be visible to other people around the world, so be sure that you are comfortable sharing Your Content before you post. You acknowledge and agree that Your Content may be viewed by other users, and, notwithstanding these Terms, other users may share Your Content with third parties. By uploading Your Content, you represent and warrant to us that you have all necessary rights and licenses to do so and automatically grant us a license to use Your Content as provided under Section 7 below.

A few points to note from this. First, this clause contains a requirement for the consumer to indemnify the company. This is potentially an example of an unfair term and is something that was identified as a problematic term in the previous review of DTC contracts. [132] There is also mention of users' Facebook accounts specifically, and the reference to the licence granted appears in the last sentence, which then references section 7 of the contract.

Section 7 is entitled Rights You Grant Match and is reproduced in abridged form below. This specifies that:

You own all of the content you provide to Match, but you also grant us the right to use Your Content as provided in this Agreement.

By creating an account, you grant to Match a worldwide, perpetual, transferable, sub-licensable, royalty-free right and license to host, store, use, copy, display, reproduce, adapt, edit, publish, translate, modify, reformat, incorporate into other works, advertise, distribute and otherwise make available to the general public Your Content, including any information you authorize us to access from Facebook or other third-party sources (if applicable), in whole or in part, and in any way and in any format or medium currently known or developed in the future. Match's license to Your Content shall be

---

132   Phillips, *Buying Your Self on the Internet, supra* note 3 at 193, 5.2 (d).

non-exclusive, except that Match's license shall be exclusive with
respect to derivative works created through use of our Services.
For example, Match would have an exclusive license to screenshots
of our Services that include Your Content…

As with the other clauses mentioned above from DTC and wearable
technology contracts, there is a lot of similarity in both the language
used and the scope of this term. Again, it contemplates a broad range
of uses capturing both known and future technology. Lastly, it also
includes a right to use screenshots of a user's content.

Tinder is owned by Match, and its "Terms of Use," when accessed
from New Zealand, purport to cover consumers in multiple jurisdictions.
In its first section, it mentions that depending on where the consumer
is based they may be dealing with a different branch of the company.
There is an office designated for those in the European Economic Area,
together with the UK and Switzerland, and a different office specified
for those based in Japan; and for all other customers, it specifies that
they are in fact making this agreement with Match Group, based in
Dallas, Texas. Consequently, it seems that consumers based in Australia,
New Zealand, or Canada would be making this agreement with the
American company.

Tinder's licence clauses are very similar to the Match examples
mentioned above and again included in sections 3a and 7. Due to this
close similarity, I have not set out section 3a, but it is worded in the
same way and also includes a requirement to indemnify the company.
The specific licence is included in section 7, Rights You Grant Tinder
and reads as follows: [133]

7. Rights you Grant Tinder.

**You own all of the content you provide to Tinder, but you also grant
us the right to use Your Content as provided in this Agreement.**

---

133   Tinder, "Terms of Use" NZ Version (effective 31 January 2024) https://policies.
tinder.com/terms/intl/en/?lang=en
Last accessed 18 June 2024 – note: the company has an NZ domain, www.
tinder.co.nz, and the previous version also included the same clause. The document has now been updated, effective 1 June 2024, but the contract still retains
this clause. Also the contract visible on the New Zealand website is the same as
the one on the American version of the website and seems to attempt to cover
all jurisdictions in the one document.

> By creating an account, you grant to Tinder a worldwide, perpetual, transferable, sub-licensable, royalty-free right and license to host, store, use, copy, display, reproduce, adapt, edit, publish, translate, modify, reformat, incorporate into other works, advertise, distribute and otherwise make available to the general public Your Content, including any information you authorize us to access from Facebook or other third-party sources (if applicable), in whole or in part, and in any way and in any format or medium currently known or developed in the future. Tinder's license to Your Content shall be non-exclusive, except that Tinder's license shall be exclusive with respect to derivative works created through use of our Services. For example, Tinder would have an exclusive license to screenshots of our Services that include Your Content.

Again, this clause is very similar to the other examples included above. Some points to note are that it does frame the licence as perpetual, and as with the Match example, it specifically mentions Facebook and also allows itself an exclusive licence to use screenshots of users' content. Furthermore, while the company updated its contract in June 2024, the current version retains this clause.

The final example is from eharmony's "Terms and Conditions of Service." It is contained in Clause 3, which is entitled "Proprietary Rights." It is set out below:[134]

> d. License to Posted or Accessed Content. By posting information or content to any profile pages or public area of the Services, or making it accessible to us by linking your eharmony account to any of your social network accounts (e.g. via Continue with Facebook) subject to applicable privacy laws as they relate to any personal information contained therein, you automatically grant, and you represent and warrant that you have the right to grant, to eharmony and its users,

---

134   Eharmony, "Terms and Conditions of Service" US Version (last updated 1 March 2024), online: <https://www.eharmony.com/wp-content/uploads/2024/03/eharmony_US_Terms_and_Conditions_2024_03_01.pdf> last accessed 14 March 2024 – note that this also has an Australian domain and the contracts appear the same. In section 2(f) 'Geographical Limitations' it also specifies that services are intended only for customers based in the United States, Canada, and Australia. However, as it is possible to view a page entitled "Navigating the NZ Dating Scene to Find Something Real" it does appear to be targeting New Zealanders. Note: this has now been updated, 20 March 2024, but the same clause is included.

an irrevocable, perpetual, non-exclusive, fully-paid, worldwide license to use, reproduce, perform, publicly display, modify and distribute such information and content, and to prepare derivative works of, or incorporate into other works, such information and content, and to grant and authorize sub-licenses of the foregoing. From time to time, we may create, test or implement new features or programs on the Services in which you may voluntarily choose to participate or may be a part of a test group with special access, in accordance with the additional terms and conditions of such features or programs. By your participation in such features or programs, you grant us the rights and waive certain other rights stated in this subsection in connection with the additional terms and conditions (if any) of such features or programs.

In the final example, again there is much similarity with the clauses previously discussed. It uses very similar language, is framed very broadly, and is "irrevocable." It also makes specific mention of Facebook and any other social media accounts. The contract as a whole also includes other problematic terms, specifically an indemnity clause.

While three examples have been used herein for each of these case studies, given the complaint against Grindr by the NCC mentioned earlier, Grindr's "Terms of Service" were also accessed. [135] It should be noted that the current version of this document exceeds 18,000 words in length and included a similarly framed licence in section 13, which addresses User Content. This licence is framed on an irrevocable basis. It also includes a waiver, "You agree to irrevocably waive (and cause to be waived) any claims and assertions of moral rights or attribution with respect to Your User Content." [136] Given the concerns that have been raised by the NCC about Grindr, it seems that its contractual terms still need further scrutiny and reform.

Discussion

What unites the three industry case studies considered above is that all three industries share a reliance on personal and sensitive data. While many free services online do rely on users sharing personal data, and there are significant privacy risks in using services such as Facebook

---

135   Grindr, "Terms of Service" (The earlier of April 30, 2023, or user acceptance), online: <https://www.grindr.com/terms-of-service> (last accessed 24 June 2024).

136   *Ibid.*

and Instagram, the products and services mentioned herein raise other questions, because they are not exclusively offered on a free basis. While some online dating platforms, such as Tinder, may offer a freemium option and then other services for additional fees, other online dating services, such as Match, do charge for their service, and DTC genetic test providers together with wearable technology providers do charge for their services and products.

In relation to the manner in which these licence clauses are framed, an important point is that companies are, at times, acquiring exclusive licences. [137] Such exclusive licences may in fact prevent a person whose data is licensed from exploiting or commercializing their own data. The import of such an exclusive licence is also likely to be something that a consumer may fail to appreciate or anticipate. Furthermore, purporting to acquire an exclusive licence in this way may also be potentially misleading to the consumer. This is because the examples given above seem to reserve ownership to the person who is providing their data, but by granting an exclusive licence, they have excluded themselves. [138] Non-exclusive licences framed very broadly may also have similar effects, given that some of these allow for the licence to be sub-licensed or transferred to another entity.

The problem with licences versus ownership can be exemplified by an earlier example where AncestryDNA changed its Terms and Conditions from including a section that said explicitly that they owned the consumer's genetic information, to giving them a perpetual licence to use it. Although they have now removed the word *perpetual*, it is still a very broad licence, which they can also sub-licence to others. [139] As has been shown, several other companies' contracts still frame these clauses on a perpetual or perpetual and irrevocable basis. This includes:

---

137   Corinne Tan, *Regulating Content on Social Media: Copyright, Terms of Service and Technological Features* (London: UCL Press, 2018) at 98–135.

138   A Tanner, "I Agreed to What? The Surprising Rights Companies Claim in Terms of Service" *Consumer Reports* (25 March 2022), online: https://www.consumerreports.org/electronics/digital-rights/surprising-rights-companies-claim-in-terms-of-service-a1175960373/.

139   H Kretchmer, "Ancestry.com Denies Exploiting Users' DNA," *BBC News* (25 May 2017), online: https://www.bbc.com/news/business-40045942; J Winston, "Ancestry. com Takes DNA Ownership Rights from Customers and Their Relatives," *Think Progress* (17 May 2017), online: https://archive.thinkprogress.org/ancestry-com-takes-dna-ownership-rights-from-customers-and-their-relatives-dbafeed02b9e/; also see J Schneider, "Ancestry.com's New Terms Allow It to Use Your Family Photos for Anything" (9 August 2021), online: https://petapixel.com/2021/08/09/ancestry-coms-new-terms-allow-it-to-use-your-family-photos-for-anything/.

23andMe, Garmin, and eharmony, Match, and Tinder. It is also important to recognize that even where a licence is not framed on an exclusive
basis it is also common practice for companies to frame the licence in a
manner that allows them to transfer it or to sub-license it, which could
mean that potentially a range of entities outside the original transaction
between consumer and company can acquire these rights.

Licences to user content were also highlighted as problematic in
Loos and Luzak's 2021 report addressing the need to further update
the European Union's Directive on Unfair Terms. [140] They specified that
where companies include a "gratuitous license for the exploitation of the
personal data," in some circumstances these may not be unfair, but they
note that "where the clause is not brought specifically to the consumer's
attention in an intelligible and easily accessible form, using clear and
plain language, as in such case the consumer's consent is not given in
accordance with Article 7(2) GDPR and, according to that provision, is
not binding." [141] Consequently, such terms are likely to be both unfair
and also in breach of the GDPR as they note both the GDPR and the
Directive on Unfair Terms would apply in "a complementary way." [142]

Given the nature of the products and services discussed herein
and the types of data they collect, it seems very likely that such licences
would be in breach of both EU consumer protection and data protection
law. Specifically, in the three case studies discussed, it is important to
understand that user content could encompass information ranging from
details about family history, personal health, and location, to sexual
orientation and HIV status. [143] Such information can easily be used in
ways that could lead to discrimination or risks to physical safety.

Furthermore, it is useful in examining these licence clauses to
reflect on the range of meanings and interpretations that consumers
may ascribe to particular terminology. For instance, the word *ownership*

---

140   M Loos and J Luzak, *Update the Unfair Contract Terms Directive for Digital Services*
(Policy Department for Citizens' Rights and Constitutional Affairs 2021) 2.11,
online: https://www.europarl.europa.eu/RegData/etudes/STUD/2021/676006/
IPOL_STU(2021)676006_EN.pdf.

141   *Ibid* at 2.11.2.

142   *Ibid* at 2.11.2.

143   J Brodkin, "Grindr Users Seek Payouts After Dating App Shared HIV Status
with Vendors," *Ars Technica* (24 April 2024), online: https://arstechnica.com/tech-
policy/2024/04/grindr-users-seek-payouts-after-dating-app-shared-hiv-status-
with-vendors/; J Florêncio, "Grindr's HIV Data Problem Began When It Asked
Users to Disclose their Status," *The Conversation* (7 April 2018), online: https://
theconversation.com/grindrs-hiv-data-problem-began-when-it-asked-users-to-
disclose-their-status-94337.

has different meanings to different people, and it is very likely that a company or a company's lawyers will have quite different understandings of what is meant by the phrase "you own your content" when this is placed together with a licence to use that content.[144]

In reflecting on the clauses discussed herein, it is important to consider the relative position of the contracting parties in these three contexts. In several jurisdictions, including New Zealand, the UK, and Australia, when assessing whether a term is likely to be deemed unfair, consideration will be given to whether the effect of the clause may result in detriment to the consumer. As one example, in the UK, the test for unfairness is set out in section 62 of the *Consumer Rights Act*[145] and specifies that "a term is unfair if, contrary to the requirement of good faith, it causes a significant imbalance in the parties' rights and obligations under the contract to the detriment of the consumer." Both Australia and New Zealand engage in similar tests, so there are possibilities here to challenge terms in several jurisdictions. In the UK, Australia, and New Zealand courts will also often be able to look at the surrounding circumstances in which the contract was made, together with the contract as a whole, and this could make it easier to challenge some of the terms included in the contracts used by these three industries.[146]

One unifying theme in the way these clauses are framed is that companies are in general not adhering to the principle of data minimization. As the GDPR has exerted a global influence on data protection law, it is helpful to refer to article 5(1)(c), which sets out this principle. All the clauses considered herein seem to go far beyond this principle, together with being at odds with the GDPR's purpose limitation set out in article 5(1)(b). While these clauses may purport to exclude some forms of information, and the contracts in full often incorporate other terms by reference, which may include a company's privacy statement, this is still problematic and needs reform, because the scope of these

---

144   Tanner, *supra* note 1540.

145   *Consumer Rights Act* 2015 (UK).

146   Phillips, *Buying Your Self on the Internet*, *supra* note 3 at 182–183; see Commerce Commission New Zealand, Unfair Contract Terms Guidelines (2022) 2, 20–22 https://comcom.govt.nz/__data/assets/pdf_file/0021/290190/Unfair-contract-terms-guidelines-August-2022.pdf; Australian Competition & Consumer Commission (ACCC), *Unfair Contract Terms: A Guide For Businesses and Legal Practitioners* (2016) 11–12, online: https://www.accc.gov.au/system/files/Unfair%20contract%20terms%20-%20A%20guide%20for%20businesses%20and%20legal%20practitioners.pdf

clauses in general covers such a broad range of uses and possibilities for sharing data that—given the nature of the services and products provided by all three industries—this cannot be justified.

It is also likely that given the length of all the contracts examined, they may fail to meet transparency requirements, such as those required by article 12(1) of the GDPR or those required under consumer law. [147] For example, as discussed in previous work, the UK's *Consumer Rights Act* in section 68 requires transparency for both contractual terms and consumer notices, and in section 68(2) requires that consumer notices are to be "expressed in plain and intelligible language and it is legible." [148] Furthermore, in line with the previous review of DTC contracts, it does appear that together with other problems raised by the scope of these licence clauses, several terms could also be challenged on the basis of unfairness. Indemnity clauses seem particularly likely to be challengeable, along with unilateral variation clauses. [149]

Given that in the contexts of all three of the industries discussed, companies will often be dealing with consumers with diverse needs and backgrounds, who may also be vulnerable in some way, there is likely to be a power imbalance in all three scenarios. It should also be kept in mind that consumers in these three contexts will have specific motivations and may be focusing on a particular aspect of a service or product, such as learning about their ancestry through a DTC test, or finding love through signing up to online dating. It is unlikely that they will simultaneously be paying sufficient attention to unknown future uses of their data and indeed, as has been previously mentioned, it is common for consumers to disregard privacy policies and contracts online. [150] While it is actually a reasonable decision for individuals not to read an online contract or privacy policy, given the amount they will encounter, the reality is that buried within these documents are

---

147   M Elshout et al, *Study on Consumers' Attitudes Towards Terms Conditions (T&Cs) Final Report* (Report for the European Commission, Consumer, Health and Food Executive Agency [CHAFEA] on behalf of Directorate-General for Justice and Consumers, 22 September 2016) https://ssrn.com/abstract=2847546 14 citing Which? study – R Parris, "Online T&Cs Longer than Shakespeare plays – Who Reads Them?" *The Conversation* (23 March 2012), online: https://www.muggaccinos.com/CreditCards/TheConversation/online_tcs_longer_than_shakespeare.htm.

148   AM Phillips, "Reading the Fine Print When Buying Your Genetic Self Online: Direct-To-Consumer Genetic Testing Terms and Conditions" (2017) 36:3 New Genetics and Society 273–295, 288.

149   Phillips, *Buying Your Self on the Internet, supra* note 3 at ch 5.

150   Frischmann & Selinger, *Re-Engineering Humanity supra* note 25 at chs 1, 2, and 5; Obar and Oeldorf-Hirsch, *supra* note 2.

important provisions that may impact not just their rights in relation to products and services, but also limit their rights under applicable consumer law. These may also limit their own data and content, and also limit their rights to redress if something goes wrong.

What is particularly problematic as well in these three industries are cyber security risks. As mentioned above, all three industries have experienced problems. The recent 23andMe data breach is a significant example, as it highlights the scale at which this can occur and the range of sensitive data that may be accessible, but this is not unique or likely to be the only incident on this scale. There is a real need for international cooperation to improve regulation of these industries and afford better protection to their consumers. The fact that the ICO and the OPC have begun an investigation into this breach is promising, but there is also a pressing need for more effort to be made to help people engaging with these services to understand the risks. The fact that the 23andMe breach was facilitated by credential stuffing is extremely problematic, and while linking accounts across platforms may seem an efficient thing for consumers, it is a practice that should be discontinued in relation to services and products that rely on sensitive data.

A final point to note is that all three industries have market leaders based in the United States, but operate internationally, and while there has been a relative lack of specific enforcement action of existing applicable law by American regulators, such as the Food and Drug Administration (FDA) and Federal Trade Commission (FTC), this may be starting to change. In late 2023, the FDA made an order against 1health requiring the company to improve its privacy practices.[151] Also in 2023, the FTC used a Penalty Offense Authority to warn several tax preparation companies that they could face penalties if they misuse their customers' data.[152] Interestingly, this notes practices that are illegal in relation to using such data, and for present purposes, this statement

---

151   FTC, "FTC Says Genetic Testing Company 1Health Failed to Protect Privacy and Security of DNA Data and Unfairly Changed Its Privacy Policy," *Press Release* (16 June 2023), online: https://www.ftc.gov/news-events/news/press-releases/2023/06/ftc-says-genetic-testing-company-1health-failed-protect-privacy-security-dna-data-unfairly-changed.

152   FTC, "FTC Warns Tax Preparation Companies About Misuse of Consumer Data," (18 September 2023), online: https://www.ftc.gov/news-events/news/press-releases/2023/09/ftc-warns-tax-preparation-companies-about-misuse-consumer-data and FTC, "List of September 2023 Recipients of the FTC's Notice of Penalty Offenses Concerning Misuse of Information Collected in Confidential Contexts," (updated 18 September 2023), online: https://www.ftc.gov/system/files/ftc_gov/pdf/NPO-Recipients-Misuse-Information-Collected-Confidential-Contexts.pdf.

seems significant: "It is an unfair or deceptive trade practice to use information collected in a context where an individual reasonably expects that such information will remain confidential ('Confidential Context') for any purpose not explicitly requested by the individual unless the individual first provides affirmative express consent for such use." [153] Seemingly, it could be argued in all three of the industries discussed herein that these contracts are being entered into in a confidential context. It is easier to argue this in relation to data that could be classed as health information, especially in the context of DTC and wearable technology providers, but it also seems plausible in the context of online dating.

It is hoped that the use of these three case studies will highlight the need for further work in this area.

Conclusion

This chapter has sought to shed light on what businesses are doing in the context of three specific industries that collect and utilize a variety of sensitive data. This is not a definitive review, and it is hoped that it will encourage further discussion of these issues. As mentioned in the introduction, there are three main concerns to highlight. These stem from: (i) the collection of personal and specifically sensitive data by these industries and the broad scope of licences clauses, which allow broad powers to use such data both using technologies now in existence and those that may be developed in the future; (ii) the uses (both present and future) of such information, which may pose risks to individuals and their families; and (iii) dangers that stem from the loss of this data. In our digital world many businesses rely on personal and sensitive data. The industries examined herein are not the only ones relying on harvesting a wide range of data, but given the nature of their services they all pose risks in relation to how data can be used. This is especially true where it is used in ways that people may not anticipate, or that may be against their interests. These industries pose significant risks to individuals and their families, where such data is lost or accessed by malicious actors.

As consumers access a diverse range of services online, where seemingly disparate industries may in fact collaborate and share data, the lack of oversight and standards is something that needs to be fixed. To some extent the clauses discussed herein can be viewed as examples

---

153   *Ibid.*

of a point at which intellectual property interests of businesses collide with the privacy and intellectual property rights of individuals. While it is legitimate to protect the intellectual property rights of companies in their own services and products, there is a real need for further oversight and appropriate limits in relation to data and content provided by consumers. Furthermore, the fact that such clauses are buried in generally lengthy contracts that consumers may fail to engage with or even notice makes the situation worse and means much more needs to be done in terms of regulatory oversight and public education.

All three industries pose future risks in relation to their consumers' data and content, not all of which can be anticipated at present. However, it is clear in relation to all three contexts, that there is the potential for use of data for secondary research purposes (including generative biology projects), which a consumer is unlikely to anticipate. There is also broad potential for marketing in unscrupulous ways that may ultimately allow for the manipulation of consumers and the potential to put them at risk of both online and physical harm. These risks mean that further regulatory action is needed. It is hoped that the probe by the OPC and ICO into the 23andMe breach, [154] together with the class actions filed against 23andMe, [155] the fine imposed upon Grindr, [156] and the complaint brought by BEUC and its members in the European Union against Meta, [157] will lead to reform.

---

154   ICO, *supra* note 51.
155   Bilyk, *supra* note 41; Phillips, *Hacking your DNA? supra* note 4.
156   European Data Protection Board, *supra* note 61.
157   N Lomas, "Meta's 'Consent or Pay' Data Grab in Europe Faces New Complaints," *TechCrunch* (29 February 2024), online: TechCrunch https://techcrunch. com/2024/02/28/meta-consent-or-pay-consumer-gdpr-complaints/; BEUC, "Consumer Groups Launch Complaints Against Meta's Massive, Illegal Data Processing Behind Its Pay-or-Consent Smokescreen" *supra* note 1432; and BEUC, *summary of complaint, supra* note 1432.

Part V
INTELLECTUAL PROPERTY, INEQUALITY, AND HUMAN RIGHTS

The Future of Geographical Indication Protection in Developing Countries— Is It the Answer to Rural Development, Food Security, and More?

David J. Watson

Abstract

Regional trade agreements negotiated, and technical assistance provided, by the European Union encourage partner countries to set up *sui generis* systems for the protection of geographical indications (GIs). The European Union has recently focused its efforts on Africa, which culminated in the Continental Strategy for Geographical Indications in Africa from 2018 to 2023. The European Union and a growing body of scholarship claim that *sui generis* systems with high levels of GI protection lead to a range of benefits including promoting rural development, preserving culture, and increasing food security and environmental sustainability. This chapter examines these claims and concludes that the adoption of *sui generis* systems by developing countries is unlikely to deliver such benefits. It is more likely to facilitate the inclusion of GI protection obligations in trade agreements between the European Union and such countries for the benefit of European Union producers, and enable the European Union to recruit support for its position in multilateral GI negotiations. There are better legal means for developing countries to protect their worthy GIs, with options including seeking trademark protection in key jurisdictions to which the product is exported and using a domestic trademark registration as the basis to obtain GI protection in the European Union.

The vision for the future is an improved enabling environment for successful GI development in Africa in order to foster sustainable rural development and increase food security.[1]

One feature of the global intellectual property (IP) system is the spread or transplant of particular IP rules from certain World Trade Organization (WTO) Members, often the European Union and United States, to other countries. The trading away of rights and flexibilities available under the *Agreement on Trade-Related Aspects of Intellectual Property Rights* in favour of stronger protection for IP rights,[2] through so-called TRIPS-plus bilateral or regional trade agreements (RTAs) involving developing countries, is one example that has been considered extensively.[3] The spread of IP rules as a result of the provision of technical assistance has received somewhat less attention.[4]

Certain RTAs, especially but not exclusively those of the European Union and United States,[5] and forms of technical assistance, aim to shape the domestic geographical indication (GI) systems of the parties or countries involved. GIs are indications that identify a good as originating in a territory, or a region or locality in that territory, where a given quality, reputation, or other characteristic of the good is essentially attributable to its geographical origin.[6] These RTAs and assistance build on WTO rules that accord Members significant

---

1   African Union Department of Rural Economy and Agriculture, *Continental Strategy for Geographical Indications in Africa 2018-2023* (2017) at 50 [African Continental Strategy].

2   *Agreement on Trade-Related Aspects of Intellectual Property Rights*, 15 April 1994, 1869 UNTS 299 (entered into force 1 January 1995) [*TRIPS Agreement*].

3   See, e.g., Peter Drahos, "BITs and BIPs: Bilateralism in Intellectual Property" (2001) 4:6 J World Intellect Prop 791; Henning Grosse Ruse-Khan, *The Protection of Intellectual Property in International Law* (Oxford: Oxford University Press, 2016) at 104–107.

4   But see, e.g., Peter Drahos, "Developing Countries and International Intellectual Property Standard-Setting" (2002) 5:5 J World Intellect Prop 765 and Daniel Acquah, "Technical Assistance as a Hedge to IP Exclusivity" in Jonathan Griffiths & Tuomas Mylly, eds, *Global Intellectual Property Protection and New Constitutionalism: Hedging Exclusive Rights* (Oxford: Oxford University Press, 2021) 197, who discuss the technical assistance provided by the World Intellectual Property Organization (WIPO).

5   See, e.g., *Comprehensive and Progressive Agreement for Trans-Pacific Partnership*, 8 March 2018, [2018] ATS 23 (entered into force on 30 December 2018) [*CPTPP*]. After the Trump Administration withdrew from the *Trans-Pacific Partnership Agreement*, 4 February 2016, most of its provisions (including chapter 18 section E on GIs) were incorporated by reference into the *CPTPP*. As a result, United States GI preferences, which are also shared by some other *CPTPP* parties like Australia, have been incorporated into modern mega-regional trade agreements.

6   *TRIPS Agreement*, *supra* note 2 at art 22.1.

flexibility in "provid[ing] the legal means for interested parties to prevent" the misuse of their GIs.[7]

While the European Union pushes trading partners to create a specific (*sui generis*) system for the protection of GIs along with strong protection for a list of product names that its producers can exclusively use in that partner country, the United States demands that RTA partners agree that GIs may be protected through either a trademark or *sui generis* system and to a series of procedural safeguards aimed at preventing the RTA partner from protecting GIs in certain circumstances. These positions reflect domestic concerns, with the European Union providing strong protection for GIs as a way to compensate for reduced subsidies and as part of a strategy to move away from commodity production to quality production and serving consumers, while the United States remains focused on competitive agriculture that uses its land and transportation advantages to export primary commodities.[8] The European Union combines very high levels of protection for GIs under a *sui generis* scheme, with public enforcement and coexistence with earlier registered trademarks in most circumstances. The United States instead protects GIs through its trademark system, with groups of producers often using certification or collective trademarks.[9] These differences have resulted in European Union RTAs obtaining protection for GIs in trading partner markets, including for terms that the United States perceives as being generic, which undermines United States market access and has caused animosity between the European Union and United States,[10] including a WTO dispute.[11]

---

7   See *TRIPS Agreement, supra* note 2 at arts 22.2, 23.1. On the flexibilities available in the *TRIPS Agreement* GI provisions, see Dev Gangjee, *Relocating the Law of Geographical Indications* (Cambridge: Cambridge University Press, 2012) at 183–264.

8   Tim Josling, "The War on Terroir: Geographical Indications as a Transatlantic Trade Conflict" (2006) 57:3 J Agric Econ 337 at 359.

9   Although wine appellations of origin are protected outside the US trademark system. See Alcohol and Tobacco Tax and Trade Bureau, US Department of the Treasury, "American Viticultural Area (AVA)," online: https://www.ttb.gov/wine/american-viticultural-area-ava.

10   GIs were blamed as one of the reasons for the failure of the Transatlantic Trade and Investment Partnership negotiations, which were abandoned in 2016. See, e.g., "Bernd Lange on the EU-US Trade Deal: 'a ship in troubled waters'," (21 January 2015), online: *European Parliament* https://www.europarl.europa.eu/RegData/presse/pr_post_story/2015/EN/03A-DV-PRESSE_STO(2015)01-20(11202)_EN.pdf.

11   *European Communities – Protection of Trademarks and Geographical Indications for Agricultural Products and Foodstuffs (United States and Australia v European Communities)* (2005) Panel Report, DS174 and DS290 [*EC – Trademarks and Geographical Indications*].

Some trading partners, possibly under the influence of technical assistance, adopt the justifications underlying the European Union or United States position on GI protection and form the view that an RTA or particular form of GI protection will benefit domestic producers.[12] Others simply decide that increased access to the European Union or US markets brought about by an RTA makes taking on additional GI commitments worthwhile.[13]

This chapter explores the future of the global spread of GI rules, with a focus on developing countries, particularly those located in Africa. A recent development has been a European Union drive to encourage African countries, through the use of technical assistance, to set up *sui generis* GI schemes. This chapter assesses whether this is a positive development for these countries. The European Union claims that such schemes deliver development benefits.[14] It is supported by a significant body of literature on the justifications for the protection of GIs as a distinct category of IP and a growing volume of scholarship on the potential benefits of the implementation of GI protection for developing countries. These benefits are described as being vast, with GIs proposed as the solution to a range of societal issues, including rural development, food security, environmental sustainability, biodiversity, and the preservation of local heritage and traditional knowledge.[15]

On the contrary, this chapter argues that the adoption of *sui generis* GI protection systems by developing countries is unlikely to deliver development benefits. A more likely future outcome of European Union technical assistance is the inclusion of GI obligations in RTAs between the European Union and such countries for the benefit of European Union producers, as well as enabling the European Union to recruit support for its position in multilateral GI negotiations. Uncritically following such assistance may lead to the formation of domestic IP regimes that disregard local conditions and exacerbate inequality. When considering substantive reforms to domestic GI systems, this

---

12   See section below titled "The European Union is Calling for the Development of Sui Generis GI Systems in Africa."

13   Josling, *supra* note 8 at 358. See section below titled "The Costs of Sui Generis GI Protection" and Xavier Carim, "South Africa, the EU, and the SADC Group Economic Partnership Agreement: Through the Negotiating Lens" in Annita Montoute & Kudrat Virk, eds, *The ACP Group and the EU Development Partnership: Beyond the North-South Debate* (Palgrave Macmillan, 2017) 161 at 175.

14   See section below titled "The European Union is Calling for the Development of Sui Generis GI Systems in Africa."

15   See African Continental Strategy, *supra* note 1 at 50–51.

future can potentially be avoided by being more selective in adopting international or other countries' IP norms.

The second section discusses the potential positive outcomes from the implementation of GI protection for developing countries, as espoused in the literature. While GI protection was originally justified using the communicative logic applicable to the protection of trademarks, higher levels of GI protection promoted by the European Union need to deliver other benefits in order to justify their drawbacks. The following section demonstrates, using theoretical arguments and empirical evidence, that the potential positive outcomes for developing countries from strong GI protection are likely overstated, with the rural development potential questionable and other claimed benefits, such as cultural preservation, unlikely to materialize.

In light of these conclusions, the following section critically assesses the positive reaction to recent developments relating to the protection of GIs in Africa. Contrary to the vast technical assistance provided by the European Union, which encourages countries to set up *sui generis* GI schemes and assume international treaty obligations, it is submitted that there are better legal means for developing countries to protect their worthy GIs. The future of GI protection should not be a one-size-fits-all adoption of the *sui generis* model.

The Potential Positive Outcomes for Developing Countries
Original Justification for GI Protection Based on the Theory of Trademark Protection

The original theoretical justification for protecting GIs is their dual ability to communicate geographical origin to consumers and to protect the reputation of producers. This justification also underlies IP protection for trademarks, which distinguish the origin of products, but from the perspective of commercial source rather than geographical location.

This justification is based on economic theory. There is asymmetric information between buyers and sellers in the market.[16] This is particularly the case for credence goods whose quality cannot be determined at the time of purchase or consumption.[17] The use of GIs can combat

---

16   Gangjee, *supra* note 7 at 164.
17   William A Kerr, "Product Differentiation, Geographical Indications and Trade" in David Blandford & Stefan Tangermann, eds, *Current Issues in Global Agricultural and Trade Policy: Essays in Honour of Timothy E Josling* (London: World Scientific, 2021) 181 at 183.

this problem by allowing consumers to identify the products they wish to purchase, thereby reducing search costs.[18]

Protection also allows producers to invest in maintaining quality, which avoids the market failure situation whereby lower-quality products push higher-quality goods out of the market.[19] In this way, a GI protects the valuable intangible of a collectively generated reputation,[20] an asset given value through a future price premium, justified as it allows consumers to predict quality.[21]

This justification underpins the standard level of protection for GIs as required by Article 22.2 of the *TRIPS Agreement*. This provision requires WTO Members to protect GIs against use that misleads the public as to geographical origin and has been implemented by Members through a range of different legal mechanisms, including trademarks, *sui generis* systems, unfair competition law and misleading labelling statutes. The original justification for GI protection relies on consumer confusion as to geographical origin—without the possibility of consumer confusion, there is no threat of misidentifying the product sought to be purchased, and as higher quality products can be identified, there is no threat to producer reputation or investment in quality.

Finally, there is no reason to think that these benefits do not hold in a developing country context. While it has been said that the majority of developing country populations may be "rather poor" and

---

18   Josling, *supra* note 8 at 338; Irene Calboli, "Geographical Indications between Trade, Development, Culture, and Marketing: Framing a Fair(er) System of Protection in the Global Economy?" in Irene Calboli & Wee Loon Ng-Loy, eds, *Geographical Indications at the Crossroads of Trade, Development, and Culture: Focus on Asia Pacific* (Cambridge: Cambridge University Press, 2017) 3 at 20.

19   Cerkia Bramley, Estelle Biénabe & Johann Kirsten, "The Economics of Geographical Indications: Towards a Conceptual Framework for Geographical Indication Research in Developing Countries" in WIPO, ed, *The Economics of Intellectual Property: Suggestions for Further Research in Developing Countries and Countries with Economies in Transition* (2009) at 115.

20   See Gangjee, *supra* note 7 at 30–41, who concludes that protection for indications of source, the country/region indicating the place of origin of a product, under the *Paris Convention for the Protection of Industrial Property*, 20 March 1883, 828 UNTS 305 (revised at Stockholm 14 July 1967; entered into force 26 April 1970) and *Madrid Agreement for the Repression of False or Deceptive Indications of Source on Goods*, 14 April 1891, 828 UNTS 163 (revised at Lisbon 31 October 1958; entered into force 1 June 1963) aimed to support the valuable intangible of a collectively generated reputation.

21   Bramley, Biénabe & Kirsten, *supra* note 19 at 151.

therefore not willing to pay the premium demanded by GI products, [22] it would still appear that many consumers in developing countries would lose the advantages set out above if consumer confusion was not prohibited. In any event, the key advantages of GI protection in a developing country context are likely to be preventing imitation in foreign markets and potentially increasing export revenue, so the protection for GIs required by Article 22.2 of the *TRIPS Agreement* remains important for producers.

The Second-Generation Justification of Rural Development

Of far greater controversy is the provision of higher levels of protection for GIs that exceed that required by Article 22.2 of the *TRIPS Agreement*. These are not contingent on any finding of consumer confusion. Article 23.1 requires additional protection for wine and spirit GIs, specifically the prevention of the use of a GI where the wine/spirit does not originate in the particular place, even where the true origin of the good is indicated, or the GI is translated or accompanied by a qualifying expression such as "style." European Union law imposes an even higher standard, for all agri-food products, with protection required against "any misuse, imitation or evocation." [23] The European Union exports this standard to its trading partners through RTAs. [24]

These higher levels of protection cannot be justified by relying on the communicative logic discussed above because protection is provided even in the absence of consumer confusion. [25] They cannot be explained by the conventional justification for trademark protection, even in its extended form, which may provide protection against dilution and misappropriation. [26] As a result, we need to look elsewhere for

---

22   *Ibid* at 130.
23   Regulation (EU) 2024/1143 of the European Parliament and of the Council of 11 April 2024 on geographical indications for wine, spirit drinks and agricultural products, as well as traditional specialities guaranteed and optional quality terms for agricultural products, amending Regulations (EU) No 1308/2013, (EU) 2019/787, and (EU) 2019/1753 and repealing Regulation (EU) No 1151/2012, OJ L 2024/1143 at art 26.1 [EU GI Regulation].
24   Hazel VJ Moir, "Understanding European Union Trade Policy on Geographical Indications" 51:6 J World Trade 1021 at 1030–1031.
25   Josling, *supra* note 8 at 351. The higher levels of GI protection, for example provided under *TRIPS Agreement, supra* note 2 at art 23.1 and European Union GI Regulation, *supra* note 23 at art 26.1, are referred to in this chapter also as strong GI protection.
26   Gangjee, *supra* note 7 at 172–177. Gangjee explains that all forms of trademark protection, including protection against dilution and misappropriation, take the

a justification for the high protection afforded to GIs. This is important because the protection of IP affects the activities people can do and the way they earn a living,[27] and restricts trade and the competitiveness of markets.[28]

Initially, enhanced protection for GIs was advocated for by claiming the existence of a unique link between the product's origin (climate and soil) and characteristics, known as *terroir*. The argument was that agricultural product names could not be used by outsiders in a descriptive sense without misleading consumers because such products could not be faithfully reproduced outside of their original growing conditions.[29] However, this has arguably faded as a justification over time with the recognition of the importance of human contribution to the quality of products, which is not geographically confined due to immigration.[30] Under the *TRIPS Agreement*, a GI does not even require a quality or characteristic attributable to geographical origin; a reputation is sufficient.[31] It was never a particularly convincing justification, with no proof required that the product possessed different characteristics due to the conditions prevailing at its origin, and some scholars questioning the rationale for affording higher protection to agricultural products than manufactured goods, which require "human ingenuity, craftsmanship, and entrepreneurship."[32]

As such, this section focuses on a key benefit that much of the literature claims will flow to developing countries from the protection of

consumer's perception of the sign into account in assessing infringement. As such, higher levels of GI protection that apply automatically in the absence of any attempt to take advantage of, or any impact on, the distinctiveness or repute of the GI, and even if the GI lacks any reputation or recognition, transcend the conventional justification applied in a trademark context.

27   *Ibid* at 8.

28   Sadulla Karjiker, "Geographical Indications: The Cuckoo in the IP Nest" (2020) 137:4 S Afr Law J 763 at 775–776.

29   Gangjee, *supra* note 7 at 69.

30   Karjiker, *supra* note 28 at 778–780.

31   *TRIPS Agreement, supra* note 2 at art 22.1 requires WTO Members to protect indications based on a reputation essentially attributable to geographical origin. Unlike under the *Lisbon Agreement for the Protection of Appellations of Origin and their International Registration*, 31 October 1958, 923 UNTS 189 (entered into force 25 September 1966) at art 2.1 [*Lisbon Agreement*], there is no requirement that the quality or characteristics of the good are due to its geographical origin, including both natural and human factors.

32   See, e.g., David M Higgins, *Brands, Geographical Origin, and the Global Economy: A History from the Nineteenth Century to the Present* (Cambridge: Cambridge University Press, 2018) at 183–184.

GIs, namely the development of impoverished rural regions. Depending on one's point of view, reliance on development arguments is either a pragmatic approach lacking a theoretical justification, [33] or an appropriate use of the IP system to support goals beyond purely enhancing innovation and correcting market information asymmetries, such as the provision of basic needs necessary for human development and the provision of public goods. [34]

The argument is that strong protection for GIs can increase the price that consumers are willing to pay for products, which improves producer incomes, leading to increased employment and sustainable rural development. [35] A number of steps are required to achieve this outcome – GI-labelled products need to actually earn a price premium, which must increase the income of producers, and the development needs to be sustainable in the sense of being distributed along the chain of production over a period of time.

Much of this claimed potential is based on theoretical arguments. For example, some scholars claim that the use of *sui generis* systems in developing countries that provide high levels of GI protection can deliver increased leverage in negotiations with intermediaries that process developing country commodities, [36] and can facilitate competitive trade of local products. [37] Some scholars also point to empirical studies conducted in the European Union, for example on increased willingness to pay for GI-labelled products, but also acknowledge that few studies have measured the impact of GI protection on rural development, such as through increased rural incomes and employment, and very few studies have examined products of developing countries. [38]

Finally, a theme of this body of literature is that certain structures need to be in place to deliver development benefits. Of course, GIs are not a "magic recipe" for success. [39] Many authors have emphasized the

---

33   Karjiker, *supra* note 28 at 787 argues that even though strong GI protection is theoretically problematic, advocates take a pragmatic approach when arguing that it serves economic development.

34   See Margaret Chon, "Intellectual Property and the Development Divide" (2006) 27:6 Cardozo L Rev 2821.

35   Gangjee, *supra* note 7 at 281.

36   Teshager W Dagne, *Intellectual Property and Traditional Knowledge in the Global Economy: Translating Geographical Indications for Development* (London: Routledge, 2014) at 95–97.

37   Titilayo Adebola, "Geographical Indications in the Era of the African Continental Free Trade Area (AfCFTA)" (2022) 17:9 J Intellect Prop Law & Pract 748 at 752.

38   See, e.g., Bramley, Biénabe & Kirsten, *supra* note 19 at 119–128.

39   Calboli, *supra* note 18 at 5.

need for the development of institutions and infrastructure in order for local producers to be able to benefit from GI protection. These include creating strong governance structures to organize stakeholders and agree on GI specifications (which set out the production requirements with which compliance is necessary in order to use the GI),[40] a framework to facilitate equitable and inclusive participation of stakeholders, national institutions such as GI committees, infrastructure for transporting and marketing the GI product, and mechanisms to monitor infringement and effectively enforce legal protection.[41]

However, the scale of this work does not prevent many authors from extolling the advantages of GI protection for rural development and claiming that there is a "strong justification for the protection of geographical indications in the developing world."[42]

Other Potential Positive Outcomes for Developing Countries

Some of the literature claims that GI protection can produce other positive outcomes for developing countries. These can be grouped into three main categories.

First, some authors claim that the requirement to use traditional production techniques as mandated by GI product specifications prevents the adoption of standardized production methods.[43] If this is correct, it could preserve traditional knowledge and cultural diversity in the face of globalization. Under a situation of open competition, traditional techniques might disappear without changing the final product, so GI product specifications could be mobilized to preserve historical methods of production and perhaps even the farm culture of production.[44]

---

40   *Sui generis* GI schemes require a GI product to meet certain conditions set out in a specification, such as the defined geographical area for production and the methods of obtaining the product, to guarantee the specific characteristics of the product: see, e.g., European Union GI Regulation, *supra* note 23 at art 49. Certification trademark systems (discussed below in section titled "Sui Generis GI Protection Overlooks Simpler Options") may also require production in accordance with particular requirements: see, e.g., *Trademarks Act*, RSC 1985, c T-13 at s 23(2), which allows a certification trademark owner to license others that meet the defined standard to use the mark.

41   See, e.g., Gangjee, *supra* note 7 at 285; Adebola, *supra* note 37 at 754–758; Bramley, Biénabe & Kirsten, *supra* note 19 at 113.

42   Bramley, Biénabe & Kirsten, *supra* note 19 at 136.

43   Dagne, *supra* note 36 at 160–161.

44   See Tomer Broude, "Taking 'Trade and Culture' Seriously: Geographical Indications

Second, some of the literature argues that the protection of GIs can increase food security.[45] This could occur if the price premium attached to GI products increases the ability of communities to obtain income, which can be spent on food.[46] Some scholars also analyze this issue from a food sovereignty perspective, which refers to the move away from large-scale farming to a localized system of food production.[47] For example, the use of traditional production methods may allow for better resource management than technology-driven agricultural practices, increasing local food production capacity and advancing the aim of feeding future generations.[48]

Finally, some scholars argue that GI protection has the potential to deliver biodiversity conservation and environmental sustainability.[49] The argument is that GI protection provides the economic incentive to use traditional production methods, which enhance biodiversity conservation.[50] One claimed reason for this is that GI protection encourages a move away from reliance on a small number of genetically modified crops, which also reduces the vulnerability of society to crop failure, and may therefore increase food security.[51]

The Potential for Positive Outcomes is Greatly Overstated
The Questions Surrounding the Rural Development Potential of GIs in Developing Countries

Rural development in developing countries is an unlikely future outcome of GI protection. Economic theory demonstrates that, because supply conditions primarily determine the return to labour, focusing on a strategy of delivering the constant increases to output prices required to increase farm income will rarely be feasible.

---

and Cultural Protection in WTO Law" (2014) 26:4 U Pa J Int'l Econ L 623 at 653–655, who outlines the theoretical case for GI protection as a means of preserving local cultures of production.

45   African Continental Strategy, *supra* note 1 at 50 states that its vision for the future is to develop GIs in Africa to "foster sustainable rural development and increase food security." See section below titled "The European Union is Calling for the Development of Sui Generis GI Systems in Africa."

46   Dagne, *supra* note 36 at 156–158.

47   See Richard Barichello, "The Challenge of Achieving Food Security" in David Blandford & Stefan Tangermann, eds, *Current Issues in Global Agricultural and Trade Policy: Essays in Honour of Timothy E. Josling* (London: World Scientific, 2021) 111 at 116.

48   Dagne, *supra* note 36 at 156–158.

49   See, e.g., Bramley, Biénabe & Kirsten, *supra* note 19 at 129, who note that developing countries may use GI protection to preserve their biodiversity.

50   Dagne, *supra* note 36 at 154–156.

51   *Ibid* at 78.

This theory was developed by D Gale Johnson in the context of the agricultural policies of industrialized countries, which aim to increase the income of the farming population, [52] by increasing the prices they receive for output or through providing subsidies. [53] While one might intuitively assume that increased output prices would increase producer income, this does not necessarily occur. Increasing output prices may increase wage prices in the short term, but this increase is partially offset by the increase in the level of farm employment. [54] Supply conditions primarily determine the return to labour, so following the output price increase, the same differential between the price of farm and non-farm labour will re-establish over time. [55] Instead, higher prices transfer income from consumers and taxpayers to farm landowners through higher rent (generally to higher-income families, not workers). [56] As such, the only way to sustainably increase farm income is to have migration of labour out of the agriculture sector because continuous output price increases are not possible. [57] In this way, agriculture is a declining industry in a growing economy. [58]

Applying this to the GI context, the question becomes whether protection is capable of delivering repeat increases in the price consumers are prepared to pay for GI products, in order to sustain an increase in farm wages. Alternatively, is GI protection capable of leading to other benefits in rural areas, such as infrastructure investment and opportunities for non-farm employment in sectors such as tourism?

These outcomes seem remote when considering the different position that the Global South occupies compared to the North. Developing country product names tend not to be used in other markets to describe product types. [59] While products like feta and champagne are well known around the world and are used to describe a class of products, [60] the

---

52   D Gale Johnson, *World Agriculture in Disarray* (London: Palgrave Macmillan, 1973) at 31–32.
53   See *ibid* at 34–39.
54   *Ibid* at 185–186.
55   *Ibid* at 196–198.
56   *Ibid* at 183–185.
57   *Ibid* at 199–203.
58   D Gale Johnson, "Role of Agriculture in Economic Development Revisited" in John Antle & Daniel Sumner, eds, *The Economics of Agriculture Volume 1: Selected Papers of D. Gale Johnson* (Chicago: University of Chicago Press, 1996) 319 at 326–328.
59   Karjiker, *supra* note 28 at 788.
60   Alternatively, they *were* used to describe a class of products prior to the European Union "clawing back" exclusivity for the names through protection in RTAs: see, e.g., *ibid* at 772.

same does not apply to, for example, Stellenbosch, which has a reputation for wine generally but does not designate a particular type of
wine. As a result, reputation needs to be developed through significant
marketing costs.[61]

This leads to an important point. GI protection alone does not
generate the reputation necessary to extract a price premium. As has
been observed in the context of the European Union scheme, a GI simply
certifies that a product has a characteristic or reputation attributable
to origin; it does not guarantee that the product aligns with consumer
perceptions of quality.[62] Many GIs are poorly positioned for global
markets, lacking name recognition even in their own country of origin.[63]

This is not to say that some developing country products do
not have significant reputations, including in international markets.
However, a number of caveats need to be noted. Firstly, to the extent
that such reputed products are in the nature of commodities, it has
been observed that commodities traded in bulk seem ill-suited to GI
protection.[64] This is presumably because there may be substitutes available for such products, giving them relatively elastic demand, except in
the case of commodities that are particularly distinct or subject to successful marketing. In contrast, for many consumers there is simply no
substitute for champagne, or certain other end-use products marketed
directly to consumers, particularly on special occasions.

Secondly, even if a price premium is obtained by a GI-labelled
product, it is difficult to determine how much of this premium is attributable to the GI because products are marketed with other cues, and
in any event, the real issue is the net contribution of the GI to profit,
with the additional costs of GI protection needing to be subtracted
from the difference in price.[65] Some of the literature arguably overlooks
the need to deduct the additional costs associated with producing GI
products, including for export, such as the costs of certifying products
as meeting the requirements of the GI product specification.[66] There is

---

61   Karjiker, *supra* note 28 at 789; William A Kerr, "Enjoying a Good Port with a Clear
      Conscience: Geographic Indicators, Rent Seeking and Development" (2006) 7:1
      Estey Centre Journal of International Law & Trade Policy 1 at 8.
62   *Higgins, supra* note 32 at 233–237.
63   Josling, *supra* note 8 at 360.
64   Bramley, Biénabe & Kirsten, *supra* note 19 at 136.
65   Kerr, *supra* note 17 at 193; Higgins, *supra* note 32 at 230.
66   See, e.g., Dagne, *supra* note 36 at 146–147, who calls for the use of quality control
      through non-codified protocols based on cooperation among traditional producers.
      This would not satisfy requirements for export to the European Union: see EU GI

an absence of empirical evidence that GI protection serves to increase profitability for farmers. [67]

Finally, the success of a GI-labelled product is likely to prompt a reaction from the market. [68] In addition to the costs of monitoring the market for infringement and seeking to enforce protection, there is nothing to prevent other producers from imitating product characteristics in order to satisfy market demand (including through the use of biotechnological means), engaging in marketing strategies to replicate the success, or even entering the relevant geographical area themselves for the purpose of producing the product and using the GI.

These factors lead some authors to the conclusion that the obstacles for developing countries are "almost insurmountable," even in terms of the prospect of securing a GI registration in the European Union, let alone that registration leading to market success. [69] Others urge developing countries and their businesses to instead focus resources on areas more likely to yield development outcomes. [70]

The Other Proposed Benefits Are Unlikely to Materialize

The other potential benefits identified above also seem unlikely to materialize. While traditional production methods certainly can be laid down in product specifications, [71] there is no legal requirement for traditional methods to be listed. [72] Furthermore, empirical studies demonstrate that GIs are ineffective in preventing cultural transformation due to the operation of market forces.

For example, a study conducted by Tomer Broude outlines the theoretical case for protecting culture through GIs by focusing on three dimensions of culture—the culture of production, consumption, and identity. [73] He explains that production methods are regulated by GI

Regulation, *supra* note 23 at art 39, which requires the verification of compliance with the specification to be completed by a competent authority designated by the country of origin or a product certification body.

67   Kerr, *supra* note 17 at 193.
68   Kerr, *supra* note 61 at 10–11.
69   Higgins, *supra* note 32 at 292.
70   Karjiker, *supra* note 28 at 790; Kerr, *supra* note 61 at 11.
71   Dagne, *supra* note 36 at 160–161.
72   EU GI Regulation, *supra* note 23 at art 49.1(e) allows, but does not require, traditional production methods to be contained in the product specification: "A product specification shall include at least: [...] a description of the method of obtaining the product and, where appropriate, the authentic and unvarying local methods."
73   Broude, *supra* note 44 at 645–662.

product specifications, that the local tradition of consumers preferring products from particular places relies on the informative function of GIs, and that food icons that construct national identity may be protected by GIs. Then, the author turns the analysis on its head by using empirical evidence in the form of case studies from the European wine industry to show that GIs cannot preserve culture. For example, even if traditional production methods are required by GI product specifications, the author's case studies demonstrate that specifications have been changed to no longer require their use, and production boundary delimitations are often altered, abandoning the link between quality and place.[74] Noting but one example, Broude shows that wine labelled with the Chianti GI, which gained modern protected status in 1932, required the addition of a high minimum content of white varieties in the red wine. After numerous changes to the specification, this practice was banned in wine labelled Chianti Classico to achieve "higher quality that conforms to internationally accepted tastes and standards."[75]

Such changes are not limited to wines in times gone by. Market changes brought about by the COVID-19 pandemic reinforce this conclusion that GIs are an ineffective means of preventing changes to production techniques. One example relates to the Italian hard sheep's milk cheese, pecorino. During the pandemic, reports indicate cheesemakers resorted to a tradition dating back hundreds of years of burying the cheese in caves, in order to prevent it from spoiling when it could not be sold due to public health restrictions.[76] At least one crafty producer of Pecorino di Picinisco, a GI protected under the European Union scheme that applies to a pecorino cheese made in the Comino valley of the Southern Lazio region, made bigger cheeses to allow for more to be preserved and took it to the wealthy northern region of Emilia-Romagna for burial.[77]

As a result of taking these actions designed to salvage his business, the producer deprived himself of the ability to use the Pecorino di Picinisco name on this product. This is because he failed to comply with the requirements of the product specification.[78] If the diameter

---

74   *Ibid* at 663–669.

75   *Ibid* at 667.

76   John Henderson, "Why Italian Cheesemakers Buried Their Pecorino," *BBC Travel* (26 January 2023), online: https://www.bbc.com/travel/article/20230124-why-italian-cheesemakers-buried-their-pecorino.

77   *Ibid.*

78   See Publication of an application pursuant to Article 50(2)(a) of Regulation (EU) No 1151/2012 of the European Parliament and of the Council on quality schemes

of the cheese exceeded 25 cm, the height 12 cm, or the weight 2 kg, the product no longer meets the description of Pecorino di Picinisco. The product specification also demands that the entirety of the production process, including the maturation phase, take place in the designated area of the Comino valley, preventing its maturation in Emilia-Romagna.

In summary, the presence of a GI product specification is not capable of enforcing compliance with the use of traditional production techniques. History shows that producers are prepared to walk away from the protection of a GI if required by business considerations based on the market. As such, GI protection is unlikely to be capable of preserving culture. The pecorino example shows that the techniques laid down in the product specification may not reflect traditional cultures of production in the first place. Despite the use of caves for cheese maturation purposes "dat[ing] back to the Middle Ages" and improving flavour and shelf life, [79] there is no requirement in the specification for underground pits to be used in modern times in order to use the GI. Given that practices evolve over time and culture is not static, [80] impractical or outdated methods should no longer be mandated. Some authors acknowledge that GI protection requires traditional practices to be "updated to meet quality control requirements or market informed demands." [81] GI specifications can be easily amended, [82] but *sui generis* GI systems do not contain mechanisms to ensure that production methods can only be updated in a manner that preserves tradition.

Secondly, the claim that GI protection can increase food security appears speculative. It is argued that food security can be increased, presumably for the society from which the relevant GI product emanates as a whole, "by ensuring that [GI protected] foods are maintained on local markets, and providing additional income by selling on international

---

for agricultural products and foodstuffs (Pecorino di Picinisco), 27 February 2013, OJ C 57/28. The EU GI Regulation, *supra* note 23 at art 36 allows any operator "marketing a product that complies with the corresponding product specification" to use the GI. Using the name without complying with the specification would constitute infringement under art 26.1(a).

79   Henderson, *supra* note 76.

80   Broude, *supra* note 44 at 692, explains that "[c]ulture is not static; it flows and changes as do the individuals who create and practice it. [...] Without international trade and interaction, global culture might simply dry up."

81   Adebola, *supra* note 37 at 756. For GI quality control requirements, see *supra* note 66.

82   See, e.g., the EU GI Regulation, *supra* note 23 at art 24, which provides that standard amendments to product specifications are assessed and approved by the relevant Member State.

differentiated markets," [83] and "provided that food GIs on local markets are accessible to the majority of consumers." [84]

Food security can be conceived of as consisting of four elements — food availability, accessibility, quality and safety, and sustainability to ensure long-run access. [85] A simple way to measure it is to examine the proportion of a household's budget spent on food. [86] A successful GI will extract a price premium, thereby increasing food prices and reducing accessibility. As a result, if the GI is having its intended effect, fewer consumers will be able to afford the product after it has received GI protection. The question thus becomes whether increased earnings for producers, including from export of the GI product, increase their ability to acquire food such that food security is increased overall for society after the detrimental impact on consumers is considered. Given the weak case for improved producer income and rural development from GI protection for most developing country products as outlined above, increased food security seems generally unlikely. Furthermore, given that the policies needed to create a local food economy would raise prices, arguments that GIs can increase food security by encouraging food sovereignty are unpersuasive. [87]

Finally, the argument that GI protection is likely to improve biodiversity and environmental outcomes is also questionable. There is no required correlation between a GI product specification and conservation or the use of sustainable production methods, [88] and given that the specification narrows production practices, including potentially limiting the varieties or species that can be used, GI protection may in fact

---

83   African Continental Strategy, *supra* note 1 at 12.
84   *Ibid* at 20.
85   Barichello, *supra* note 47 at 114.
86   *Ibid* at 117.
87   See *ibid* at 116, where Barichello concludes that the policies that would be needed to achieve the objectives of food sovereignty would "[a]lmost certainly [...] raise prices, thereby reducing food security."
88   Product specifications under the European Union scheme do not require the use of sustainable methods or even any environmental impact assessment. Recent modest amendments now allow, but do not require, producer groups to agree that sustainable practices are to be included in product specifications and to prepare sustainability reports published by the Commission: see EU GI Regulation, *supra* note 23 at arts 7, 8, 49.2. Despite this, the European Union claims that "Geographical Indications can also be considered to have a sustainability element as part of the system": see European Union Intellectual Property Office, "carIPI: Part 3: Sustainability of Geographical Indications", online: https://internationalipcooperation.eu/en/caripi/learning/2.2.3_GIs_sustainability.

result in a loss of biodiversity.[89] This is evident from the Tequila GI, for example, which reduced biodiversity by encouraging the production of only one agave variety, sending many other varieties into extinction.[90]

This analysis leads to the conclusion that strong GI protection is unlikely to lead to significant benefits for developing country products or societies.

Great Care Is Needed When Pursuing Higher Levels of GI Protection
Some Products May Benefit from Strong GI Protection

However, it is possible that strong protection for particular GIs of developing countries may be warranted. Empirical studies are needed on a product-by-product basis to determine whether GI protection is capable of delivering development benefits.

Such empirical studies should determine whether there is a correlation between the geographical origin and characteristics of the product, and whether the benefits to consumers through the provision of information and to producers through increased income outweigh the costs of enforcement and restrictions on competition.[91] As part of this, it would be necessary to determine whether at least part of the price premium increases producer income, rather than simply providing rent to those who own the land.[92]

If a particular developing country product passes these tests and has a genuine reputation or significant marketing potential (such as due to possessing a distinct quality) combined with resources to deliver on that potential, it cannot be ruled out that strong protection of the name through GI protection could result in rural development benefits. In such a case, the next question concerns the appropriate vehicle for legal protection.[93]

One option that has been touted is a domestic *sui generis* GI system, like that implemented in the European Union. This operates outside the registered trademark system and specifically protects GIs. Such systems normally consist of a number of features, including a register of protected GIs, an administrative process for verifying that the name has a

---

89   Gangjee, *supra* note 7 at 280.
90   Adebola, *supra* note 37 at 756; Karjiker, *supra* note 28 at 789.
91   Josling, *supra* note 8 at 341; Moir, *supra* note 24 at 1024.
92   See Johnson, *supra* note 52 at 183–185; Josling, *supra* note 8 at 339.
93   Bramley, Biénabe & Kirsten, *supra* note 19 at 131.

particular characteristic attributable to origin and is otherwise eligible for protection, and administrative enforcement by public authorities. [94] These do offer certain advantages to producers, such as the possibility of a high standard of protection for agri-food products beyond that required by Article 22.2 of the *TRIPS Agreement,* which obviates the need to prove consumer confusion to establish an infringement, as well as coexistence with earlier registered trademarks in most circumstances. [95] However, for the reasons explained below, caution is advised against such a system in developing countries.

The European Union Is Calling for the Development of Sui Generis GI Systems in Africa

In recent times, the European Union has ramped up its technical assistance in the field of GI protection in Africa, with the apparent objective of encouraging African countries to set up *sui generis* GI schemes.

In October 2017, the African Union released the Continental Strategy for Geographical Indications in Africa 2018–2023 (African Continental Strategy). [96] This document was prepared with support from international partners, including the European Uniion, the Food and Agriculture Organization, and WIPO. The significant input of the European Union is clear from the document itself, [97] with its support ranging from assistance registering pilot GI products as funded by the French Development Agency, to training organized by the European Union and African regional intellectual property organizations to develop facilitators, as well as training organized by the Africa-European Union partnership that produced the first draft outline of the African Continental Strategy.

This strategy develops a policy framework for GI development on the continent, with the aim of using GIs "to foster sustainable rural

---

94   See, e.g., Moir, *supra* note 24 at 1030.

95   EU GI Regulation, *supra* note 23 at art 30 allows GIs to be registered except where, in light of an earlier trademark's reputation and renown and the length of time it has been used, registration would be liable to mislead the consumer as to the true identity of the product. A WTO panel decided that a predecessor to the EU GI Regulation (which contained the same coexistence rule), while violating the exclusive right of trademark owners guaranteed by the *TRIPS Agreement, supra* note 2 at art 16, was a permissible limited exception under art 17. See *EC – Trademarks and Geographical Indications, supra* note 11 at DS174: paras 7.644–7.688.

96   African Continental Strategy, *supra* note 1.

97   See *ibid* at 2–5.

development and increase food security."[98] It also records as other objectives the promotion of traditional knowledge, preservation of natural resources, and promotion of local identity.

While the strategy is light on detail about the means to be used to achieve these objectives, it lays down six strategic outcomes.[99] These include creating national and regional institutional and legal frameworks for protecting GIs, developing and registering pilot GI products, developing markets for GI products through regional and international trade, and conducting research, training, and communication programs. While stating that each country is free to choose whichever system suits its interests, the document clearly favours the *sui generis* approach, highlighting perceived advantages including lower costs for producers (including through enforcement by public authorities), higher levels of protection, and coexistence with earlier registered trademarks.[100]

Implementation of the strategy is supported by a manual developed by the Intellectual Property Rights & Innovation in Africa (AfrIPI) project (AfrIPI Manual).[101] AfrIPI is funded by the European Union and implemented by the European Union Intellectual Property Office, and candidly says that it supports African countries approximate to European Union IP standards.[102]

The AfrIPI Manual catalogues the variety of technical assistance provided by international partners, including the French Ministry of Agriculture, the European Union and international organizations.[103] The authors conclude that these participants have caused significant progress to be made in Africa, in terms of modernizing legal and institutional frameworks, identifying GI-worthy products, codifying product specifications, and obtaining GI registrations. The creation of *sui generis*

98   *Ibid* at 50.
99   *Ibid* at 53.
100   *Ibid* at 25–38. For example, the African Continental Strategy only awards countries the top (green) rating of "complete legal framework" if they have both trademark legislation that allows for the protection of geographical names as well as a specific system for the protection of GIs: see *ibid* at 29–30.
101   Intellectual Property Rights & Innovation in Africa (AfrIPI), *Manual for Geographical Indications in Africa* (2022) [AfrIPI Manual].
102   European Union Intellectual Property Office, "AFRIPI," online: https://internationalipcooperation.eu/en/afripi (when viewed in February 2023). As of May 2024, the webpage states that the project "specifically aims to create, protect, utilise, administer and enforce Intellectual Property Rights across Africa, in line with international and European best practices": see European Union Intellectual Property Office, "What is AfrIPI?", online: https://afripi.org/about-afripi.
103   AfrIPI Manual, *supra* note 101 at 19–28.

systems for GI protection is again applauded as the way to strengthen legal frameworks in a way that recognizes "an enhanced awareness that African GIs need to enjoy additional protection." [104]

The next section of the AfrIPI Manual considers areas in which more limited progress has been made. It identifies the importance of having effective and representative producer organizations underpinned by internal governance processes, in order to fulfill functions including drafting the product specifications, marketing the product, monitoring the market for infringing products, and resolving issues among stakeholders. [105] It also suggests the development of independent control mechanisms to enforce the requirements laid down in the GI product specifications. [106] The manual concludes by making a number of specific recommendations on these matters, [107] including allocating additional resources to raise awareness of the purpose of GIs and encouraging countries to ratify the *Geneva Act of the Lisbon Agreement on Appellations of Origin and Geographical Indications* to obtain protection for their GIs in regional and international markets. [108]

In addition to technical assistance, a more direct means through which the European Union encourages African countries to set up *sui generis* GI schemes is through its program of RTAs. The use of trade agreements to obtain protection for specific GIs in other countries can be viewed as a contractual approach to GI protection, with each party agreeing to protect a list of the other's GIs to a high standard due to the expectation of mutual benefits. [109]

For example, under the *European Union – Southern African Development Community Economic Partnership Agreement*, [110] the European Union and South Africa agreed to protect a list of each other's GIs. The agreement requires the listed GIs to be protected to a high standard equivalent to that required by European Union law, provides for coexistence with earlier registered trademarks, and mandates enforcement by administrative action of public authorities, including at the request

---

104   *Ibid* at 29.
105   *Ibid* at 46–49, 59–73.
106   *Ibid* at 49–50, 73–87.
107   *Ibid* at 87–89.
108   *Geneva Act of the Lisbon Agreement on Appellations of Origin and Geographical Indications*, 20 May 2015, OJ L 271/15 (entered into force 26 February 2020) [*Geneva Act*].
109   Gangjee, *supra* note 7 at 176–177.
110   *Economic Partnership Agreement between the European Union and its Member States and the Southern African Development Community Economic Partnership Agreement States*, 10 June 2016, OJ L 250/3 (entered into force 10 October 2016) [*EU-SADC EPA*].

of interested parties.[111] South Africa implemented these obligations by making a regulation that creates a specific register for protected GIs.[112]

The Costs of Sui Generis GI Protection

While it is understandable that African countries would want a higher level of protection for food and handicraft GIs, to match that required to be given to wine and spirit GIs under the *TRIPS Agreement*,[113] this does not necessarily mean that transplanting European Union-style *sui generis* GI systems into their domestic legal systems will be to their advantage. The more likely future outcome of this approach is simply conferring benefits on European Union producers.

Firstly, much of the literature examined above understates the challenges and expenses involved in setting up *sui generis* GI schemes, for developing country governments, producers, consumers, and taxpayers. While the African Continental Strategy and AfrIPI Manual tout the advantages of *sui generis* schemes, such as lower producer enforcement costs,[114] they neglect to mention who has to pick up the tab, namely consumers through higher food prices and taxpayers through funding enforcement by public authorities.

These two documents give a good idea of the types of infrastructure that need to be put in place to create functional *sui generis* systems, such as setting up the legal scheme, creating national GI committees, fostering producer cooperation through the development of organizations (for activities including agreeing product specifications), and devising control and certification systems.[115] This attributes a very significant role to governments, in circumstances where it is far from clear that they are in the best position to achieve beneficial outcomes through market intervention. Query whether governments are well placed, for example, to select "champion GIs" to receive protection.[116]

---

111   *Ibid* at protocol 3 arts 5.1, 6.4, 8.1.

112   Regulations Relating to the Protection of Geographical Indications used on Agricultural Products Intended for Sale in the Republic of South Africa, 22 March 2019, No R 447.

113   See, e.g., Kenya on behalf of the African Group, *Preparations for the 1999 Ministerial Conference: The TRIPS Agreement*, 6 August 1999, WT/GC/W/302 at paras 26–27.

114   AfrIPI Manual, *supra* note 101 at 10.

115   See *ibid* at 28–50, 59–87.

116   *Ibid* at 33. This is reminiscent of one of the criticisms of infant industry protection, namely the inability of governments to pick the right winners. See, e.g., David M Trubek & Patrick Cottrell, "Robert Hudec and the Theory of International Economic Law: The Law of Global Space" in Joel P Trachtman & Chantal Thomas, eds,

Given the weak case for positive outcomes from the implementation of GI protection in developing countries, as discussed above, would it not be a better use of resources to directly target rural development through infrastructure development and agricultural research? [117]

Secondly, adopting a *sui generis* system could harm the competitiveness of developing country markets due to the strong possibility of European Union producers protecting their GIs by making administrative applications to these countries' schemes. European Union producers are likely to benefit disproportionately, particularly in the short term. [118] Much of the literature, including the Continental Strategy and AfrIPI Manual, overlooks the issue that European Union producers benefit when developing countries create *sui generis* schemes, preventing local producers from even evoking European Union GI names. [119] The literature that does consider it is optimistic. Some authors consider that it is an open, empirical question as to whether the benefits to local GI producers outweigh the costs associated with the restrictions relating to the use of European Union names. [120] Another acknowledges the "attendant advantage" to the European Union of African countries having functioning GI systems, but considers that creating inclusive, sustainable, and effective GI regimes will benefit African producers. [121] Given that the European Union is home to many more reputed GI products than developing countries, it is difficult to envisage a scenario in which the benefits outweigh the costs.

Thirdly, it is a reasonable hypothesis that the European Union's technical assistance relating to GI protection in Africa, at the very least, has multiple motives including an element of self-interest. If African countries set up *sui generis* GI schemes, this may allow for the protection of European Union GIs as referred to above, but it may also facilitate the inclusion of GI obligations in RTAs between the European Union and such countries, as well as enable the

---

Developing Countries in the WTO Legal System (Oxford: Oxford University Press, 2009) 129 at 145.

117   See Johnson, *supra* note 58 at 327–328.

118   Kerr, *supra* note 17 at 192.

119   EU GI Regulation, *supra* note 23 at art 26.1 requires protection against evocation, a standard that the European Union transplants elsewhere via RTAs. Protection against evocation has been interpreted very broadly in the European Union, as preventing the use of a term if the image triggered directly in the consumer's mind is that of the GI-protected product: see *Scotch Whisky Association v Klotz*, Case C-44/17 [2018] ECR I-415 at para 51.

120   See, e.g., Bramley, Biénabe & Kirsten, *supra* note 19 at 129–130.

121   Adebola, *supra* note 37 at 754.

European Union to recruit support for its position in multilateral GI negotiations. [122]

Being obliged to create a *sui generis* system under an international agreement with the European Union brings additional risks for developing countries. As with other areas of IP, there is a risk that developing countries agree to particular outcomes, including TRIPS-plus standards, in order to avoid a loss of preferential market access. As one South African official explained in the context of negotiations for the *EU-SADC EPA*, the requirement to create a *sui generis* scheme to protect a list of European Union GIs was "payment" for South Africa's access to the European Union market. [123] Given the possibility of preference erosion, it is debatable whether such a trade-off is in the interests of developing countries. [124]

Such RTAs may have serious consequences for local producers. They may require developing countries to trade away the flexibility provided by Article 24.6 of the *TRIPS Agreement* not to protect names that are generic in their territories. The clawback of generic terms by protecting European Union GIs in RTAs prevents direct competition, with non-European Union producers incurring the additional costs associated with educating consumers that their products are equivalent. [125] An example is the requirement in an earlier European Union-South Africa agreement to phase out the use of port and sherry as names for fortified wines produced in South Africa. [126] Despite use of these names since the nineteenth century, [127] South Africa was required to cease

---

122   *TRIPS Agreement, supra* note 2 at arts 23.4, 24.1 require negotiations concerning the establishment of a multilateral system for notification and registration of wine GIs and negotiations aimed at increasing the protection of individual GIs under art 23. See generally Getachew Mengistie & Michael Blakeney, "Geographical Indications and the Scramble for Africa" (2017) 25:2 Afr J Int'l & Comp L 199. For more detail on the various negotiating positions, see, e.g., Michael Blakeney, "Geographical Indications and TRIPS" in Michael Blakeney, Thierry Coulet, Getachew Mengistie & Marcelin Tonye Mahop, *Extending the Protection of Geographical Indications: Case Studies of Agricultural Products in Africa* (London: Routledge, 2012) 7 at 15–24.

123   Carim, *supra* note 13 at 175.

124   See Henning Grosse Ruse-Khan, "Effects of Combined Hedging: Overlapping and Accumulating Protection for Intellectual Property Assets on a Global Scale" in Jonathan Griffiths & Tuomas Mylly, eds, *Global Intellectual Property Protection and New Constitutionalism: Hedging Exclusive Rights* (Oxford: Oxford University Press, 2021) 23 at 37–38.

125   Karjiker, *supra* note 28 at 775. This is at the heart of the European Union and the United States' battle on GIs, as referred to in the introduction to this chapter.

126   *Agreement on Trade, Development and Cooperation between the European Community and its Member States, and the Republic of South Africa*, 11 October 1999, OJ L 311/3 (entered into force 1 May 2004), annex X.

127   See Tim James, *Wines of the New South Africa: Tradition and Revolution* (Berkeley:

exporting these products to the European Union in 1999, phase out the use of the names on other export markets within five years, and cease marketing the products domestically using the names after 12 years.

As such, it is best to attempt to avoid GI protection obligations in trade agreement negotiations with the European Union. It is noteworthy in this regard that the European Union appears to have a practice of not requiring less developed developing countries from taking on GI protection obligations in RTAs. [128]

Finally, it is submitted that an even worse option for developing countries is acceding to the *Geneva Act* as recommended by the AfrIPI Manual. [129] This agreement updates the existing international registration system for the protection of appellations of origin created by the *Lisbon Agreement*, allowing for the protection of GIs that satisfy the *TRIPS Agreement* definition. [130] It requires the parties to protect GIs that have been registered by other parties on an international register, to a high standard, unless they have grounds to refuse protection and do so within a time limit. [131]

Deciding to accede to the *Geneva Act* would likely represent an "uncritical ratification" of an international agreement in response to European Union technical assistance. [132] While accession would protect the country's GIs to a high standard in its limited number of parties, [133] it would also require the protection of a large number of European Union GIs domestically. [134] Avoiding accession to the *Geneva Act* also preserves leverage that countries may choose to deploy in future trade negotiations with the European Union, should they at some stage, like South Africa,

University of California Press, 2013) at 78, 80.

128   See e.g., *EU-SADC EPA, supra* note 110, protocol 3 applies to South Africa only, not the other SADC EPA States (Botswana, eSwatini, Lesotho, Namibia, and Mozambique).

129   AfrIPI Manual, *supra* note 101 at 88.

130   *Geneva Act, supra* note 108 at art 2.1(ii).

131   *Ibid* at arts 9, 11, 15.

132   See Acquah, *supra* note 4 at 215.

133   As of May 2024, the only parties to the *Geneva Act* are the African Intellectual Property Organization (OAPI) and some of its Member States, Albania, Cabo Verde, Cambodia, Djibouti, the European Union and some of its Member States, Ghana, Laos, North Korea, Oman, Peru, Russia, Samoa, Sao Tome and Principe, Switzerland, and Tunisia: see WIPO, "WIPO-Administered Treaties – Contracting Parties Lisbon Agreement Geneva Act [2015]," online: https://www.wipo.int/wipolex/en/treaties/ShowResults?search_what=A&act_id=50.

134   See WIPO, "Lisbon Express Structured Search: Appellations of Origin and Geographical Indications", online: https://lisbon-express.wipo.int/struct-search?lang=en.

need to make GI protection concessions in exchange for preferential market access. There are also easier ways for developing countries to protect key GIs in export markets.

Sui Generis *GI Protection Overlooks Simpler Options*

In light of the likely limited benefits of GI protection for developing countries and the significant costs of setting up *sui generis* schemes, it is worthwhile to consider alternate options for protecting developing country GIs that would benefit from strong GI protection.

One option is seeking trademark protection in key jurisdictions to which the product is exported, with a view to reducing the gap between producer earnings and the product's retail price. In 2005, the Ethiopian Intellectual Property Office (EIPO) followed this route by applying for trademark registrations for three of the country's reputed geographical coffee designations, Harar, Sidamo, and Yirgacheffe, in 36 countries.[135]

In the United States, the National Coffee Association objected to two of the applications, contending that they were generic descriptions for coffee. Starbucks offered to help to create a system of certification marks, but the EIPO declined on the basis that this would be impractical.[136] As WIPO said:

> Specialty coffee in Ethiopia is grown on over four million small plots of land by an estimated 600,000 independent farmers spread throughout the country in remote areas. Although Ethiopian coffees such as Sidamo and Harrar are named after specific regions, all of it is not produced in the same region under the same circumstances. Distribution is also a problem, as it is predominately done informally by hauling bags of coffee on foot for many kilometers. Government oversight of coffee producers is therefore nearly impossible. Farmers would be required to pay a surcharge for government oversight, and this would only be an additional burden on them, many of who [sic] are already living below the subsistence level.[137]

The EIPO proceeded to sign voluntary, royalty-free, trademark licensing agreements with importers, roasters, and distributors. Starbucks even

---

135   Mengistie & Blakeney, *supra* note 122 at 219.
136   *Ibid.*
137   WIPO, "The Coffee War: Ethiopia and the Starbucks Story", online: https://www.wipo.int/web/ip-advantage/w/stories/the-coffee-war-ethiopia-and-the-starbucks-story.

relented, signing a distribution, marketing, and licensing agreement in 2007, and the trademarks were eventually registered in the United States after the EIPO proved acquired distinctiveness.[138] The idea behind the royalty-free licensing agreements was to require the licensees to use the trademarks and promote Ethiopian coffee in the market.[139] Prices of the trademarked Ethiopian coffee increased by 10 percent relative to non-trademarked coffee.[140]

This example demonstrates that it is possible to protect distinct products with a reputation using alternate means that do not incur the significant costs involved in setting up a *sui generis* GI scheme. It is not necessarily simple, with barriers potentially including the need to negotiate with those that consider the name generic or have preexisting rights to the name in the relevant market, and the potential need to establish infringement, which may not be possible where use of the name is accompanied by "style," "type," etc. However, it has many advantages for developing countries including avoiding having to set up a *sui generis* GI scheme and engage in enforcement, including of European Union GIs. Using regular rather than certification trademarks, as in the Ethiopia example, also saves producers from wasting money on control and certification costs.[141]

In addition, securing a trademark registration can act as an entry point into *sui generis* GI systems in foreign markets. For example, it is possible to register a product name domestically as a trademark and then use this as the basis to seek protection via a direct, administrative application to the European Union GI scheme. This allows protection to be gained in the European Union without having to agree to protect European Union GIs under a similar domestic *sui generis* scheme. One example is the registration of Ceylon Cinnamon,[142] which is based on a Sri Lankan certification trademark registration.[143]

---

138   Mengistie & Blakeney, *supra* note 122 at 219.
139   WIPO, *supra* note 137.
140   Aslihan Arslan & Christopher P Reicher, "The Effects of the Coffee Trademarking Initiative and Starbucks Publicity on Export Prices of Ethiopian Coffee" (2011) 20:5 J Afr Econ 704.
141   Although this does create a potential risk of inferior product being able to be marketed under the trademark, which would potentially undermine the marketing efforts under the licensing agreements. In the Ethiopia case, there is a consortium of cooperatives, exporters, and government bodies, the Ethiopian Fine Coffee Stakeholder Committee, which may be able to informally manage quality control of the product.
142   Commission Implementing Regulation (EU) No 2022/144 of 2 February 2022 entering a name in the register of protected designations of origin and protected geographical indications (Ceylon cinnamon (PGI)), OJ L 24/3.
143   See Sri Lanka Export Development Board, "Specification for 'Ceylon Cinnamon'," online: https://ec.europa.eu/geographical-indications-register/eambrosia-public-api/

While the *TRIPS Agreement* does not require WTO Members to protect GIs that are not protected in their country of origin,[144] a WTO Member cannot decline to protect another's GI on the basis that it is not protected through a particular legal means.[145] In other words, a WTO Member with a *sui generis* system cannot decline to protect a GI on the basis that it is protected in its country of origin through a trademark. The European Union now follows this approach, simply requiring the GI to be protected in its country of origin.[146] As a result, developing countries have the legal means to protect their GIs in the European Union, without needing to create a domestic *sui generis* system, agree to GI obligations in an RTA with the European Union, or accede to the *Geneva Act*.

Concluding Remarks

The African Continental Strategy envisages a future in which GI protection following a European Union model fosters sustainable rural development and increased food security in Africa. This chapter paints a less rosy picture of the spread of GI rules from the Global North to the South.

This chapter has critically assessed the justifications for protecting GIs in developing countries. A growing volume of scholarship claims that strong GI protection will lead to benefits including rural development, cultural preservation, increased food security, and biodiversity conservation. However, it is submitted that the likely benefits to developing countries are overstated. This chapter also reviewed the recent developments in technical assistance provided by the European Union to African countries in the area of GI protection. It is argued that this assistance focuses on encouraging countries to create *sui generis* systems of GI protection, when it may not be in their interests to do so.

---

api/v1/attachments/64212.

144   *TRIPS Agreement, supra* note 2 at art 24.9.

145   A WTO panel decided that a predecessor to the EU GI Regulation, *supra* note 23, violated the national treatment obligation in the *TRIPS Agreement, supra* note 2 at art 3. This was for reasons including that registration of a GI from a non-European Union country was contingent upon the country of origin adopting a system of GI protection equivalent to the European Union's system and offering reciprocal protection to European Union GIs. See *EC – Trademarks and Geographical Indications, supra* note 11 at DS174: paras 7.52–7.103, 7.123–7.213.

146   EU GI Regulation, *supra* note 23 at art 13.2(d) requires that applications from non-European Union countries include legal proof that the name is protected in the country of origin.

Great care needs to be taken in choosing the legal mechanism through which to protect worthy GIs, i.e., those that empirical evidence demonstrates might derive rural development benefits through high levels of GI protection, by delivering increased prices leading to higher producer incomes. Developing countries are likely to be better off by protecting their GIs through trademarks in key export jurisdictions or by using a domestic trademark registration as the basis for an application to the European Union's GI scheme. This avoids the costs of setting up *sui generis* schemes, including reduced market competitiveness as a result of the need to protect European Union GIs. Protecting European Union GIs through an RTA or the *Geneva Act* brings heightened risks, with the latter in particular to be avoided to preserve negotiating capital for potential use in future trade negotiations.[147]

147   Email: dwat8318@student.ubc.ca. I am grateful to Dr Ljiljana Biuković, Dr Graham Reynolds, and Dr Richard Barichello for comments on an earlier draft, and also to the anonymous reviewer. All errors are my own. This chapter draws on research supported by the Social Sciences and Humanities Research Council and the Peter A. Allard School of Law.

CHAPTER 17

Public Interest, Human Rights, and Copyright: The Road Less Travelled?

Lisa Macklem

Abstract

Recent copyright cases at both the US Supreme Court and the Canadian Supreme Court have emphasized the public interest goals underlying copyright. These cases lean into the educational public interest role of copyright. Creators are users, and users are creators. Media conglomerates and corporate owners of Intellectual Property are able to leverage their economic power to influence legislation worldwide, and those deep pockets are also able to litigate effectively and often, thus throwing copyright out of balance. Developing countries often have much more restrictive copyright regimes than developed countries such as Canada with fair dealing or the United States with fair use. This in turn problematizes access to the materials necessary for research, education, and innovation: the very tools necessary to move from developing to developed economies. If users' rights are understood as a positive right and even more properly as a human right, this may be a more fruitful avenue to pursue. Economic interests, such as the large media conglomerates, as well as legislators who may be focused simply on the concerns of trade and lobbying interests, need to be actively shown that public interest can serve their agenda and should be a part of that agenda. The road ahead should see activism in support of human rights and where necessary law reform that provides access to information and education that can benefit all: users, creators, distributors, and owners.

There is a basic tension that exists in copyright between the public interest goals to further creation and innovation and the economic goals of all intellectual property to garner profit for creators and owners. Recent copyright cases at both the US Supreme Court and the Canadian Supreme Court have emphasized the public interest goals underlying copyright. In the *Society of Composers, Authors and Music Publishers of Canada v. Entertainment Software Association*,[1] Rowe, J. states that the *Copyright Act*'s "overarching purpose is to balance authors' and users' rights by securing just rewards for authors while facilitating public access to works."[2] Both *Google v Oracle*[3] in the United States and *York v Access Copyright*[4] in Canada emphasize the educational public interest role of copyright in their decisions. Media conglomerates and corporate owners of intellectual property are able to leverage their economic power to influence legislation worldwide, and those deep pockets are also able to litigate effectively and often, thus throwing copyright out of balance. Developing countries often have much more restrictive copyright regimes than developed countries such as Canada with fair dealing or the United States with fair use. Brazil, for instance, only allows for short quotations of other works in publications and only allows for excerpts to be reproduced for research purposes.[5] This in turn problematizes access to the materials necessary for research, education, and innovation: the very tools necessary to move from developing to developed economies. If users' rights are understood as a positive right and even more properly as a human right, this may be a more fruitful avenue to pursue, and there are international agreements in place, such as the International Covenant on Civil and Political Rights,[6] the International Covenant on Economic, Social, and

---

1   2022 SCC 30 [Socan v ESA].

2   Socan v ESA, *ibid* at para 5.

3   *Google LLC v. Oracle Am., Inc.* 141 S. Ct. 1163 (2021). [Google]

4   *York University v. Canadian Copyright Licensing Agency (Access Copyright)*, 2021 SCC 32. [*York*]

5   Sean Flynn, Luca Schirru, Michael Palmedo, and Andrés Izquierdo, "Research Exceptions in Comparative Copyright," (2022) PIJIP/TLS Research Paper Series no. 75, online: https://digitalcommons.wcl.american.edu/research/75

6   United Nations, *International Covenant on Civil and Political Rights*. [ICCPR] General Assembly resolution 2200A (XXI) (16 December 1966), online: https://www.ohchr.org/en/instruments-mechanisms/instruments/international-covenant-civil-and-political-rights. Ratified by Canada on May 19, 1976, and June 8, 1996 by the United States. Article 1(1) states, "All peoples have the right of self-determination. By virtue of that right they freely determine their political status and freely pursue their economic, social and cultural development."

Cultural Rights,[7] and the Marrakesh Treaty.[8] However, the question remains as to whether these agreements have enough enforcement power. The United Nations Sustainable Development Goals,[9] which focus on Education (Goal 4); Industry, Innovation, and Infrastructure (Goal 9); and Good Health and Well-Being (Goal 3), may provide an additional avenue through which to influence more restrictive Intellectual Property regimes. Finally, the United Nations Declaration on the Rights of Indigenous Peoples[10] also provides important guidance in safeguarding human rights.

In order to follow a clear path toward thinking of users' rights in terms of human rights, a good starting point is the history of copyright's public interest roots. As one travels the road of copyright's development, it is clear that economic interests, through corporate ownership and trade deals, are often steering the direction of legislation and jurisprudence. However, recent jurisprudence has steered the conversation toward the less trodden road of the public interest, thus reaffirming the inherent balance of copyright. Human rights create an international duty that may be more universally persuasive and thus help to outweigh corporate voices. Jessica Litman points out that "what was billed as a conflict between authors and users was never about that at all. Instead, what seems to have been happening is a fight to the death among intermediaries."[11] This chapter explores whether pursuing an approach on human rights that follows the path of copyright discussions that focus on the public interest can help to rebalance the discussion. By reflecting more carefully on the core purposes of fair dealing and fair use, such as research and education, a more human rights–centric focus may elicit more progressive change.

---

7   United Nations, *International Covenant on Civil and Political Rights*. General Assembly resolution 2200A (XXI) (16 December 1966), online: https://www.ohchr.org/en/instruments-mechanisms/instruments/international-covenant-economic-social-and-cultural-rights. [ICESCR]

8   WIPO, *Marrakesh Treaty to Facilitate Access to Published Works for Persons Who Are Blind, Visually Impaired or Otherwise Print Disabled* (30 September 2016), online: https://www.wipo.int/treaties/en/ip/marrakesh/

9   United Nations, *Department of Economic and Social Affairs: Sustainable Development: The 17 Goals* (nd) https://sdgs.un.org/goals.

10   United Nations, *United Nations Declaration on the Rights of Indigenous Peoples* [UNDRIP] (13 September 2007), online: https://www.ohchr.org/en/indigenous-peoples/un-declaration-rights-indigenous-peoples

11   Jessica Litman, "What We Don't See When We See Copyright as Property." (Nov 2018) 77:3 C L J 536–558 at 537.

A Brief History of Copyright's Public Interest Roots

The history of the development of copyright helps to illustrate the role that the public interest has traditionally played. Copyright systems that trace their roots back to Britain begin with the Stationers' Monopoly of 1557. The main purpose of the Stationers' Monopoly was to vest the control of printed works in the hands of the distributors: the Stationers. This suited the Crown, who granted the Monopoly, as a way of preventing seditious works from being propagated. [12] Today's efforts to shut down or at least tightly oversee social media to combat fake news can be seen in much the same light: monopolies controlling the flow of information. The return on investment for the owners of copyright still relies on minimizing competition and tightly controlling access. Scraping the internet for data to "teach" AI systems and an increased concern with privacy have only encouraged more restrictions on access to information.

With the advent of the Enlightenment, traditional views that God breathed creation through authors, who thus had a very minimal role in the process, were changing to recognize the central role of the creator. Scientific studies, debating societies, and an increased demand for books, which were becoming less expensive to produce, also marked the Enlightenment. The Stationers' Monopoly was replaced by *The Statute of Anne* in 1710 to respond to the increased demand for accessible knowledge. Rather than restricting public discourse, this first *Copyright Act* would enable it. The full title of the Act is "An Act for the Encouragement of Learning, by Vesting the Copies of Printed Books in the Authors or Purchasers of such Copies, during the Times therein mentioned." The term was 14 years, after which another 14 years could be applied for *if* the author was still alive: the intention was to benefit the author during their lifetime and to make works available for the inspiration and further innovation and creation of other authors. Oren Bracha points out that "the Statute recognized a reversionary interest of authors, possibly intended to mitigate cases of inequitable treatment by publishers." [13] Canada has such a reversionary right, but it engages 25 years after the author's death, hardly enabling them to benefit during

---

12   See Laura J Murray and Samuel E Trosow, *Canadian Copyright: A Citizen's Guide*, 2nd ed (Toronto: Between the Lines, 2013) at 17; see also Lyman Ray Patterson, "The Statute of Anne: Copyright Misconstrued" (1966) 3 Harv J on Legis at 229.

13   Oren Bracha, "The Adventures of the Statute of Anne in the Land of Unlimited Possibilities: The Life of a Legal Transplant" (2010) 25:3 Berkeley Tech LJ at 1438.

their lifetime. Bryan Adams lobbied to have the right attach 25 years after first assignment during the Copyright review in 2018.[14] The reversionary right might also bring works back into print that publishers weren't utilizing because they were not lucrative enough to publish. In addition, Canada's recent extension of duration to life of the author plus 70 years is tipping the scale away from users: users who may also be authors and creators in their own right or aspiring to be so.

The *Statute of Anne* also provided for one copy of every work to be sent to nine copyright libraries throughout Great Britain; this commitment to learning is reflected in the same requirement for copies to be sent to the Library of Congress. In addition, the Act required that books be available at a reasonable price. Jaszi et al explain that "U.S. copyright law has been conceived as an instrument of national cultural policy, rather than a mere scheme of private rights. From its inception, it has been the vehicle for the balancing of private proprietary claims and the public interest in access to information resources."[15] Bracha addresses the question of why the United States would adopt a British standard after having just broken away from the country's control:

> The Statue of Anne arguably represented a moment of universalization. Its main innovation was exactly in detaching the copyright regime from its entanglement with the guild institutional context and the censorship apparatus, thereby creating a general template for the protection of authors' rights. Such a general template, being free from the specifics of a particular society and culture, was highly transportable. That is to say, it was particularly suited for being borrowed and implemented in other societies, even those with very different social and cultural conditions.[16]

There are several important points here that resonate with copyright today. Arguably, entertainment conglomerates can be seen as monopolistic bodies exerting a type of censorship and control over access to

14   Kathleen Harris. "Bryan Adams to MPs: Give Artists More Control over Their Work" *CBC News*. (18 September 2018), online: https://www.cbc.ca/news/politics/bryan-adams-copyright-act-heritage-committee-1.4828097#:~:text=Canadian%20singer%2Dsongwriter%20Bryan%20Adams,been%20sold%20to%20a%20company.
15   Peter Jaszi, Craig Joyce, Marshall Leaffer, and Tyler Ochoa, "Epilogue: The Statute of Anne: Today and Tomorrow," *SSRN* (1 December 2011), online: https://houstonlawreview.org/article/4179-epilogue-the-statute-of-anne-today-and-tomorrow.
16   Bracha, *supra* note 1721 at 1456.

works. The Writers Guild of America (WGA) and the Screen Actors Guild (SAG-AFTRA) both held historic strikes in the spring and summer of 2023 to demand concessions over AI use. The Writers Guild of Canada overwhelmingly voted in favour of a strike (if necessary) to secure the same protections[17] but were ultimately able to reach a deal with similar protections against the use of AI.[18] However, Bracha's comments also underscore the universality of the *Statute of Anne* and its basic transportability. International instruments today can perhaps serve a similar function.

Access to information sources is important to satisfy numerous public interest goals. An educated populace is integral to a functioning democracy. Indeed, this belief in the importance of an educated populace to support democracy was the driving force behind the United States Federal Communications Commission (FCC) mandating that basic television should be available for free for all citizens. The FCC's mandate according to 47 U.S. Code § 151 is "to make available, so far as possible, to all the people of the United States, without discrimination on the basis of race, color, religion, national origin, or sex, a rapid, efficient, Nation-wide, and world-wide wire and radio communication service with adequate facilities at reasonable charges." The Canadian Radio-television and Telecommunications Commission (CRTC) in Canada has a similar mandate to provide access to news, particularly in both official languages, to all citizens.[19]

Artists must learn their craft from those who came before. Nothing is created in a vacuum and few geniuses spring fully formed from their mothers. Marc Greenberg points out that

> the history of human society is, in many regards, a history of creativity. It was through the creative process that civilizing inventions like the use of fire for cooking, diversion of water for irrigation and bathing, [...] and related items were discovered and became key

---

17   Etan Vlessing, "Writers Guild of Canada Overwhelmingly Votes to Authorize Strike Over AI, Fair Pay," *The Hollywood Reporter* (25 April 2024), online: https://www.hollywoodreporter.com/business-news/writers-guild-of-canada-votes-to-authorize-strike-1235881245/.

18   Jesse Whittock. "Writers Guild of Canada Members Ratify New Contract With Producers – Update," *Deadline* (22 May 2024), online: https://deadline.com/2024/05/writers-guild-canada-cmpa-reach-production-agreement-1235906997/.

19   CRTC. "Our Mandate, Mission and What We Do." *Canadian Radio-television and Telecommunications Commission.* (18 May 2023) https://crtc.gc.ca/eng/acrtc/acrtc.htm.

elements in improving our lives. Those same creative processes yielded the arts of storytelling, painting, and the beginnings of what became human cultures.[20]

Having access to culture and education through which to learn a craft are crucial and valuable parts of the process. It is also in the public interest to maintain and foster cultural heritage as well as make cultural heritage accessible. Drassinower points out that the author is both a creator and a user and that "the author is not isolated from the world in which she lives and from which she draws her intellectual nourishment."[21] Thus, the history of copyright maps out two paths, which may not have been intended to become divergent, but in practice, the economic interests have become dominant.

The Economic Landscape and Tipping the Scales in Favour of Economic Interests

To understand the dynamics influencing both legislation and jurisprudence affecting copyright, it is important to understand the economic landscape. Economic interests are maximalist, wanting the most control over copyrighted works in order to maximize profit. In order for works to be made available to libraries and users of all kinds, the fixation requirement means that an author must first produce the work in a tangible medium and then find a way to get the work into the users' hands.[22] Creators are the first owners, but in order to disseminate their work, they license that work to distributors, and distributors monetize through controlled access. Economies of scale require that distribution industries (publishing, music, television, film) make far more money than individual authors. These industries have the deep pockets to finance lobbying for legislation that benefits them, both nationally and internationally. They can afford to prosecute even minor infringements and subsequently go to court frequently, which benefits their lawyers who know the system and know how to win. In point of fact, many cases

---

20   Marc H Greenberg, *Comic Art, Creativity and the Law*. (Cheltenham, UK: Edward Elgar, 2014) at 7.

21   Abraham Drassinower. "Taking User Rights Seriously" in *In the Public Interest: The Future of Canadian Copyright Law*, Michael Geist, ed, Irwin Law, 2005 https://papers.ssrn.com/sol3/papers.cfm?abstract_id=839988 at 466.

22   The issue of requiring works to be in a tangible medium to procure copyright protection is problematized by oral cultures as well as cultures that do not adhere to the same ideas of property and ownership.

that are filed (or threatened) never come to fruition because defendants simply settle: no one wins against Disney or Marvel or Universal Music Group. At least, that is the prevalent assumption. A single, new creator is unlikely to have the legal knowledge to know the strength of their case nor are they likely to have the money necessary to mount a defence. If the case is settled quickly, it may not even come to the attention of a public interest group such as the Electronic Frontier Foundation who might be able to help. Courts have noticed that the public interests of copyright are in danger of not being served, and a number of recent cases address this central issue.[23]

Copyright is based on balancing a public interest goal of furthering the useful arts and sciences with economic incentives. This is enshrined in the United States Constitution,[24] but is the underpinning of many countries, including Canada, through the *Statute of Anne*'s goal of a limited monopoly "for the encouragement of learning." Michelle Wu points out that copyright has been essentially hijacked by large corporate interests that value profit over public interest and asserts that "when profit undermines that public purpose, Congress has the right and obligation to revoke the grant or take remedial steps to restore the public good."[25] Legislation, however, is interpreted by the courts, and recent copyright cases in both the US and Canadian Supreme Courts have seen the courts step in to support the public interest of copyright. Both *Google v Oracle*[26] in the United States and *York v Access Copyright*[27] in Canada emphasize the educational public interest role of copyright in their decisions, and both include a rebalancing, or at least a re-examination, of the relevant fairness factors. The recent decision in *Andy Warhol Foundation for the Visual Arts, Inc. v. Goldsmith et al*[28] takes a disappointing turn by focusing on the economic goals of copyright in the majority's analysis of the four-factor test. However, even this decision may be helpful in protecting creators in the AI space as the decision emphasizes the purpose of the

---

23   See for example *Google* (n 1711) and *York* (n 1712), both discussed at length below.

24   The oft-cited Article 1, Section 8, Clause 8: "To promote the Progress of Science and useful Arts, by securing for limited Times to Authors and Inventors the exclusive Right to their respective Writings and Discoveries." https://constitution.congress. gov/browse/article-1/section-8/clause-8/.

25   Michelle Wu. "The Corruption of Copyright and Returning It to Its Original Purposes" (24 August 2012) Legal Ref Serv Q DOI: 10.1080/0270319X.2021.1966238 at 43.

26   Google, *supra* note 1711.

27   York, *supra* note 1712.

28   598 U.S. 2023, docket no. 21-869 [Warhol v Goldsmith].

use. Goldsmith wins the case primarily on the basis that the purpose of both works was a magazine cover. [29]

Copyright ensures that owners of copyrightable material can economically benefit from the reproduction of their work, as well as derivatives of that work. This economic advantage is then supposed to spur further creation and innovation as creators can afford to further create. In addition, new creators can benefit from exposure to works that inspire and educate them. Gustafsson and Lazzaro highlight "the importance of culture, cultural heritage and creative industries (CCI) in making a significant contribution to Europe's economy" in 2021. [30] While they stress the economic advantages to the GDP, they also stress that "CCI can foster societal values of identity, belonging, democracy and participation in innovative ways." [31] However, owners of copyrighted works, who are often large media conglomerates, generally want to maximize their economic advantage by maintaining strict control over the property and ideally maximizing scarcity and limiting access to the work; here again, refer back to the Stationers' Monopoly, which was used by publishers of the time to achieve much the same goals.

Large media companies, such as Disney or Universal Music Group, control huge catalogues of copyrighted works. The profits from these holdings allow them to hire the best lawyers and to litigate frequently. This allows these lawyers to know the system and know how to win. Another effect of the deep pockets of media conglomerates is their ability to influence the law itself through lobbying. As if the huge media conglomerates weren't enough in and of themselves, in the lobby-sphere, it is the industry bodies, such as the Motion Picture Association of America (MPAA) and the Recording Industry of America (RIAA), that combine these media conglomerates into an even more effective wedge. Corporations with deep pockets and especially industries with organizations with deep pockets and common goals can afford to pay for the best lobbyists to influence the policy that feeds into both trade

---

29   Whether a work is transformative or not, if they are competing for the same pur-
      pose, it might be seen as infringing. Therefore, if an artist's work is used in the
      training material for an AI, it might not be necessary to prove that the work is a
      direct copy if the work is preventing the artist from benefitting from their own
      work.

30   Christer Gustafsson and Elisabetta Lazzaro. "The Innovative Response of Cultural
      and Creative Industries to Major European Societal Challenges: Toward a
      Knowledge and Competence Base" (November 2012) 13:23 *Sustainability* 13267.
      DOI: 10.3390/su132313267.

31   Gustafsson and Lazzaro, *ibid.* note 1738.

negotiations and legislation. This phenomenon was first identified in the Hargreaves Report from 2011: "Much of the data needed to develop empirical evidence on copyright and designs is privately held. It enters the public domain chiefly in the form of 'evidence' supporting the arguments of lobbyists ('lobbynomics') rather than as independently verified research conclusions."[32] The phenomenon of lobbynomics has far-reaching implications. David Vaver posits that "[i]nternational corporate power has effectively curbed national sovereignty in the field of [Intellectual Property] policy," and he attributes this trend to globalization.[33] Furthermore, Peter Drahos states that "[b]ilateral intellectual property and investment agreements are part of a ratcheting process that is seeing intellectual property norms globalize at a remarkable rate."[34] Lobbyists are skilled at presenting evidence in easily consumable portions. Lobbyists are also able to provide those glossy, pithy nuggets in a timely manner. Jeremy de Beer points out that:

> governments have short time frames that are not always amenable to rigorous scholarly standards. Commissioning research favours professional consultancies over academic investigators; therefore, there are likely to be biases in the data and evidence presented to policy makers. Organized and well-financed industry lobbyists are advantaged over small business or consumers.[35]

Benjamin Mitra-Kahn, in responding to the Hargreaves Report's negative comments on the evidence used for policymaking, defends the government economists who are instructed to "[p]rovide the *best* advice you can, given what you know at this point. That does not mean providing the *right* advice after 12 months of research."[36] The recent *US CASE Act (Copyright Alternative in Small-Claims Enforcement Act* of 2019)

---

32   Ian Hargreaves, *Digital Opportunity: A Review of Intellectual Property and Growth.* (May 2011), online: https://www.gov.uk/government/publications/digital-opportunity-review-of-intellectual-property-and-growth at 18.

33   David Vaver, *Intellectual Property Law: Copyright, Patents, Trade-marks.* (Toronto: Irwin Law, 2011) at 5.

34   Peter Drahos, "BITS and BIPS: Bilateralism in Intellectual Property" (November 2001) 4.6 The Journal of World Intellectual Property, 791–808 at 798.

35   Jeremy de Beer, "Evidence-Based Intellectual Property Policymaking: An Integrated Review of Methods and Conclusions" (2016) 19.5-6 The Journal of World Intellectual Property 150–177 at 153.

36   Benjamin H Mitra-Kahn. "Copyright, Evidence and Lobbynomics: The World After the UK's Hargreaves Review" (2011) 8.2 *Review of Economic Research on Copyright Issues* 65–100 at 83.

is a good example of legislation that was lobbied for by the big media concerns. The Bill had previously failed to pass but was slipped into an omnibus bill on COVID-19 spending. This creates a Small Claims Board within the Copyright Office that can decide on any copyright claim and award damages up to $30,000. Numerous organizations have criticized the initiative for being outside the judicial system and therefore unconstitutional. There is no evidence that such a system will adhere to current judicial precedence or protect small copyright owners as is its stated purpose.[37]

Media in the United States have not been shy about intruding into other countries' attempts to balance their copyright legislation in order to make it serve the public interests of access to both education and culture. A recent example of this is the US Trade Representative's influence through the President of the Republic of South Africa to veto the Copyright Amendment Bill, sending it back to Parliament with an 11-page letter detailing concerns.[38] The USTR's concerns stemmed from a number of American media organizations: the Association of American Publishers (AAP), the Entertainment Software Association (ESA), the Independent Film & Television Alliance (IFTA), the Motion Picture Association of America (MPAA), and the Recording Industry Association of America (RIAA). As of this writing, after the Bill was sent back to Parliament on a technicality, it has once again passed and now only awaits the President's signature.[39] In fact, intruding into other

37   See for example Jason Kelley, "The CASE Act Is Just the Beginning of the Next Copyright Battle," *Electronic Frontier Foundation* (22 December 2020) https://www.eff.org/deeplinks/2020/12/case-act-hidden-coronavirus-relief-bill-just-beginning-next-copyright-battle; Katherine Trendacosta, "This Disastrous Copyright Proposal Goes Straight to Our Naughty List," *Electronic Frontier Foundation.* (22 December 2020) https://www.eff.org/deeplinks/2020/12/disas-trous-copyright-proposal-goes-straight-our-naughty-list; Meredith Whipple, "Public Knowledge Condemns Passage of CASE Act in Funding Bill," *Public Knowledge.* (21 December 2020) https://www.publicknowledge.org/press-release/public-knowledge-condemns-passage-of-case-act-in-funding-bill/.

38   See for example, Jonathan Klaaren, "What Role Can Regulations Play? A South African Public Law Perspective on the Potential Response Through Regulations to Perspective on the Potential Response Through Regulations to Constitutional Reservations about the Copyright Amendment Bill, B-13B of 2017" (June 2020) *Digital Commons @ American University Washington College of Law.* https://digitalc-ommons.wcl.american.edu/cgi/viewcontent.cgi?article=1056&context=research; Thiru, "2020: USTR Takes Aim at South Africa Over Copyright Limitations and Exceptions." *Knowledge Ecology International* (22 April 2020) https://www.keionline.org/32804.

39   "Welcome Progress, But One Key Step Remains in Updating South Africa's Copyright Law." *International Federation of Library Associations and Institutions.*

countries is a regular occurrence in trade negotiations. These lobbyists are able to push their agenda, and the trade negotiators on all sides of the negotiation table are unlikely to be experts in intellectual property, let alone the process of creation and innovation. The negotiators are skilled at negotiating and will try to find the best deal they can based on how lobbyists have portrayed the value of their interests. Do creators/ authors truly have a voice at this table?

Traditionally, creators/authors have relied on the owners (buyers) of their intellectual property rights and collective societies to look after their interests, collect royalties, and be their advocates. It is clear, however, that popular artists receive the most support—monetary and otherwise. Many countries have incentives and programs for emerging artists, but the bar to obtain these funds is often high. The criteria and paperwork to obtain the funds is often very complicated, particularly for new and emerging artists. Canada has always been concerned with protecting its own culture from being drowned out by the very loud voice to the south—a land border does nothing to stop radio or television signals, let alone internet and satellite communications. However, geo-blocking is yet another way that the big media conglomerates ensure they maintain the scarcity of their content. The more markets that they can delineate and sell into, the more money they make. Canada is referred to as part of the "domestic" market by US media, yet content is distributed as a separate market. Canada has long instituted Canadian content rules for radio and traditional television. The government supports publicly funded television in the Canadian Broadcasting Corporation (CBC), and the Canadian Media Fund and other funding opportunities provide money to Canadian projects to ensure a robust Canadian culture. However, Canada has always had an issue with determining what makes a work "Canadian." The CRTC through its mandate from the *Broadcasting Act*[40] is charged with overseeing the Canadian Content rules, which decide on a points system whether a work qualifies as Canadian.[41] However, the efficacy of the points system has to be questioned by the fact that Bryan Adams' internationally successful song "(Everything I Do) I Do It For You" failed to qualify

---

(4 March 2024) https://www.ifla.org/news/welcome-progress-but-one-key-step-remains-in-updating-south-africas-copyright-law/.

40   S.C. 1991, c. 11.

41   CRTC, "So What Makes It Canadian?" *CRTC* (13 October 2016) https://crtc.gc.ca/eng/cancon/c_cdn.htm.

as Canadian in 1991.[42] Adams maintains that with the exception of his hometown, Canada did nothing to really help his career, and further maintained that the CanCon system bred mediocrity.

Particularly in a country that prides itself on multiculturalism, it is difficult to pinpoint which voices are distinctly Canadian and what is meant by "culture." Raymond Williams points out that "Culture is one of the two or three most complicated words in the English language. This is so partly because of its intricate historical development [...] but mainly because it has now come to be used for important concepts in several distinct intellectual disciplines and in several distinct and incompatible systems of thought."[43] Indigenous voices, while having dedicated television and radio channels, have still been underserved. Traditional copyright does not mesh well with Indigenous ways of sharing and curating knowledge. Meanwhile, Canadian content rules determine that if certain key positions and percentages are filled by Canadians, regardless of subject matter, the work is deemed Canadian. Given that the digital environment has challenged access to and availability of cultural materials, Adams' remarks in 1991 that music is "international" seem particularly relevant today.[44] Further examples of artistic endeavors deemed not Canadian enough include the television series based on Margaret Atwood's novel *The Handmaid's Tale*, the adaptation of which was also filmed in Canada, and Justin Bieber's "Despacito."[45]

The *Online Streaming Act*[46] is the Canadian government's attempt to bring streaming services under the control of the *Broadcasting Act* in addition to "tweaking" the CanCon rules. The CRTC is still working through implementing the new Act. Streaming services will now be treated like broadcast services, and the Act requires foreign streaming services like Netflix, YouTube, and Spotify to extensively promote Canadian content in Canada, and pay into a fund that supports the creation of Canadian content. The federal government has said that they could see these online streaming services forking over $740 million to

---

42   "When the Music of Bryan Adams Wasn't Canadian Enough" *CBC Archives* (accessed 14 January 2022) https://www.cbc.ca/archives/when-the-music-of-bryan-adams-wasn-t-canadian-enough-1.4974779.

43   Raymond Williams, *Keywords: A Vocabulary of Culture and Society* (Oxford: Oxford University Press, 1985) at 87.

44   *CBC Archives, supra* note 1750.

45   Lawrence Zhang. "Still Buffering: Why Canada's Online Streaming Act Isn't a Blockbuster Hit" ITIF (22 March 2024) https://itif.org/publications/2024/03/22/still-buffering-why-canadas-online-streaming-act-wont-be-a-blockbuster-hit/.

46   *Online Streaming Act*, SC 2023, c 8, https://canlii.ca/t/5610g.

a media fund, or over 22 percent of the total online streaming market in Canada. These costs will be passed on directly to consumers, with Spotify already doing just that in France after the French government implemented a streaming tax to support its music sector. [47]

In 2017, Netflix pledged to spend $500 million on Canadian projects over five years to avoid just such an eventuality. They honored this pledge within three years. The question arises as to whether Netflix or other streamers will still be interested in spending even more money and whether increased prices to consumers, in fact, reduce access to Canadian culture. In addition, the CRTC is also busy implementing the *Online News Act*, [48] and it has already seen effects to the availability of Canadian news on Google and Facebook. The Act requires platforms to pay for the privilege of supplying links to Canadian news outlets. [49] Google has since come to an agreement to pay $100 million annually to Canadian news publishers, indexed to inflation, [50] but Facebook refuses to pay for the privilege, leaving many Canadians out of the loop if Facebook was a major way for them to consume news. A recent study by Kaiser & Partners reveals that "Many Millennials (66 percent) and most Gen Z respondents (85 percent) report seeking Canadian news on social media channels versus traditional news platforms." [51] Furthermore, "Recent policy changes and barriers to consuming news online and via social media have impacted Canadians' trust levels, with 26 per cent of those surveyed indicating Canada's *Online News Act* (Bill C-18) and the ban of media outlets by Meta have eroded their trust in the media." [52] Clearly, recent regulatory and legislative changes in Canada

---

47   Klaaren, (n 1746). See also Reuters. "Spotify to Increase Prices in France Over New Tax" *Reuters* (7 March 2024) https://www.reuters.com/technology/spotify-increase-prices-france-over-new-tax-2024-03-07/.

48   *Online News Act*, SC 2023, c 23, https://canlii.ca/t/562f6.

49   *Online News Act*, (n 1756) sec. 4: "The purpose of this Act is to regulate digital news intermediaries with a view to enhancing fairness in the Canadian digital news marketplace and contributing to its sustainability, including the sustainability of news businesses in Canada, in both the non-profit and for-profits sectors, including independent local ones."

50   Mickey Djuric, "Google Signs Deal with Organization to Distribute $100M to Canadian News Companies," *Global News* (7 June 2024) https://globalnews.ca/news/10553090/google-compensation-canada-online-news-act/#:~:text=Google%20agreed%20to%20pay%20Canadian,into%20agreements%20with%20news%20publishers.>

51   Kaiser & Partners, "Young Canadians Are Increasingly Trusting News Broadly Shared on Social Media," *kaiser & partners* (15 November 2023) https://kaiserpartners.com/young-canadians-are-increasingly-trusting-news-broadly-shared-on-social-media.

52   Djuric, *supra* note 1758.

have not increased Canadians' access to culture and information, one of the primary public interest goals of copyright.

Trade Deals Favour Economic Interests

International bilateral and multinational trade deals are another way that copyright has been moved away from public interest goals to favour economic interests. Trade deals have seen the increasing prevalence of TRIPS-plus standards, such as Canada's recent increase of duration to the US standard of life of the author plus 70 years, which was negotiated during the United States-Mexico-Canada Agreement (referred to as CUSMA in Canada).[53] The longer duration went into effect on December 30, 2022. Christophe Geiger points out that "investment induced by these bilateral treaties reflects a more fundamental change and is the sign of a broader reconceptualization through international law of IP from a mechanism to incentivize innovation to a commodity and finally to an asset [...] protecting IP as an 'investment' under international investment law, leads to a change in the rationale of the IP system and thus to a major risk of an enforcement of IP rights beyond their limits and their *raison d'etre*."[54] Geiger goes on to state that "IP rights have the purpose of encouraging creativity to enable access to science and culture while protecting 'material and moral interests of creators', as international human rights treaties have put it."[55] Helfer sees one "approach to the intersection of human rights and intellectual property [as seeing] both areas of law as concerned with the same fundamental question: defining the appropriate scope of private monopoly power that gives authors and inventors a sufficient incentive to create and innovate, while ensuring that the consuming public has adequate access

---

53   Agreement on Trade-Related Aspects of Intellectual Property Rights, Apr. 15, 1994, Marrakesh Agreement Establishing the World Trade Organization, Annex 1C, 1869 U.N.T.S. 299, 33 I.L.M. 1197 (1994) [hereinafter *TRIPS Agreement*]. TRIPS established the duration of copyright as life of the author plus 50 years. See article 9 which cites the Berne Convention for the Protection of Literary and Artistic Works, 828 U.N.T.S. 221, Article 7. Life of the author plus 50 years was considered to be the lower threshold, leaving countries free to increase the duration. Such increases are referred to as TRIPS-plus.

54   Geiger, Christophe, "Excluding Intellectual Property from Bilateral Trade and Investment Agreements: A Lesson from the Global Health Crisis" (March 31, 2023) in S Frankel, M Chon, G Dinwoodie, J Schovsbo & B Lauriat, eds, *Improving Intellectual Property: A Global Project* (Cheltenham, UK/ Northampton, MA, Edward Elgar 2023) Available at SSRN DOI: http://dx.doi.org/10.2139/ssrn.4405880 at 426.

55   Geiger, *ibid.* at 9.

to the fruits of their efforts." [56] Helfer also acknowledges the growing privileging of economic over other concerns, beginning most prominently with TRIPS as "unlike earlier intellectual property agreements, TRIPS has teeth. Non-compliance with the treaty can be challenged through the WTO's hard-edged dispute settlement system [which is] backed up by the threat of trade sanctions." [57] Peter Yu comments on the impact of bilateral and multilateral trade agreements using TRIPS, especially on developing countries, as "the standards of intellectual property protection vary according to a country's economic strength, not to mention the additional impact of resource constraints on its overall ability to enforce intellectual property rights." [58] There is no question that western developed countries have the greater share of power in such negotiations. Yu points to some of the inherent problems with such negotiations: "Because these agreements are being negotiated in nontransparent processes that aimed to establish club-based memberships, they have raised serious concerns about both human rights protections and the promotion of the rule of law." [59] Trade treaties should focus on trade but not at the expense of human rights. Trade treaties can also be renegotiated and should be. The USMCA for example has a clause to revisit the agreement every six years with a 16-year sunset clause. It's clear, however, that the inherent biases of the negotiation process toward "intellectual property regimes [that] primarily protect business and corporate interests and investments" [60] need to be offset by an equally compelling force for the public interest and human rights goals of intellectual property.

While international instruments lack enforcement mechanisms with the "teeth" of TRIPS, it is still possible for them to gain momentum, such as was seen with the Marrakesh Treaty. Yu points out that the Marrakesh Treaty "has become the first WIPO agreement to explicitly state the interrelationship between the intellectual property system and international human rights instruments." [61] New limitations and exceptions were granted for those with visual disabilities. Though its outcome was more circumspect and narrower than many would wish,

---

56   Laurence R Helfer, "Human Rights and Intellectual Property: Conflict or Coexistence?" (2003) 5:1 Minn Intell Prop Rev at 48.

57   Helfer (n 1764) 54-55.

58   Peter Yu, "Intellectual Property and Human Rights 2.0" 53 U. Rich. L. Rev. (2019) at 1419.

59   Yu, *ibid* at 1396.

60   Laurence R Helfer, "Towards a Human Rights Framework for Intellectual Property." 40 U.C. Davis L. Rev. (2007).

61   Yu, *supra* note 1766 at 1445.

as it initially included "persons with other disabilities," [62] it still garnered significant support. Once again, the motion picture industry was one of the most vocal opponents. [63]

Okediji points out the deficiencies of the Berne Convention and TRIPs when it comes to limitations and exceptions, particularly in the educational space: "There are neither specific L&Es for educational institutions nor for making copies for students or for distributing protected works." [64] In developing countries, which rarely have fair use or fair dealing exceptions, lack of support in the educational area is most acutely felt. Michael Palmedo found a statistical link between access to knowledge and research output: "Overall the econometric tests support the hypothesis that copyright exceptions for researchers are associated with greater publishing of scholarly works, that the effect is stronger when copyright protection is stronger, and that the exceptions matter more to researchers in less wealthy countries." [65] Furthermore, Palmedo found that "scientists residing in countries which have implemented more robust copyright exceptions for research published approximately 17–22% more papers and books in subsequent years." [66] Such statistical evidence is important to demonstrate the value of public interest goals and to support that aspect of copyright. Another important source for statistical support is the Sustainable Development Goals. While the SDGs are unfortunately unlikely to meet their goals for 2030, participating countries do submit detailed statistical reports annually. [67] Furthermore, the United Nations Global Compact's "Action Platform" focuses on helping businesses with reporting on and incorporating the SDGs in

62   Harsh Mahaseth, "The Marrakesh Treaty and the Approach Towards Social Inclusion" (Dec. 2018) 1:2 Stockholm Intellectual Property Law Review at 55.

63   See EBU, "Questions and Answers on the Marrakesh Treaty" (nd) *European Blind Union*. https://www.euroblind.org/newsletter/2022/july-september/en/ questions-and-answers-marrakesh-treaty#:~:text=The%20EU%20and%20 the%20US,%E2%80%9Csoft%20law%E2%80%9D%20or%20recommendations; "International publishers and other lobbies such as the Motion Picture Industry opposed the treaty for years almost down to the final days of negotiations in Marrakesh. The EU and the US were also against a legally binding treaty for many years as they preferred a voluntary agreement, 'soft law' or recommendations."

64   Ruth Okediji, "The Limits of International Copyright Exceptions for Developing Countries" (Spring 2019) 21.3 Vand J Ent & Tech L at 727.

65   Michael Palmedo, "The Impact of Copyright Exceptions for Researchers on Scholarly Output" (2021) 2.6 Efil Journal at 130.

66   Palmedo, *supra* note 1773 at 135.

67   United Nations: Department of Economic and Social Affairs. "Implementation." https://sdgs.un.org/goals.

their businesses. [68] The economic interests are powered by their own profit figures, and those profits are utilized for further litigation and lobbying. Both litigation and influencing trade deals are out of reach for most users to pursue individually. Economically motivated owners need to be motivated to accept changes that can help to create a more robust copyright ecosystem for everyone. Increased access to and more robust limitations and exceptions can help to benefit both economic and public interest goals.

Human Rights, the Public Interest, and Users' Rights

Human rights' abuses certainly garner international attention, but they shouldn't have to rise to the level of war crimes before attention is garnered or action is taken. The pandemic certainly helped to highlight many of the disparities between developed and developing countries when it came to vaccine access. Yu points out that "the arrival of trade discussions has created an unhealthy gloss that disturbs law and policy analysis in the intellectual property area [...] [However,] the distortion largely originates from a narrow emphasis on profit maximalization – an emphasis that privileges trade over the social function of intellectual property rights." [69] Citing numerous U.N. resolutions, Yu underscores the Sub-Commission's emphasis on not privileging economic agreements over human rights obligations. [70] Human rights and intellectual property instruments have largely developed separately despite having overlapping concerns. Helfer points out that "no references to human rights appear in the major intellectual property treaties such as the Paris and Berne Conventions," but of course, those treaties are very much concerned with "the protections granted to authors and inventors as 'rights.'" [71] While human rights have been separated into categories (cultural, social, and economic), there has been a growth in the protection of Intellectual Property. [72] Helfer goes on to point out that "A human rights approach to intellectual property [...] grants [...] users a status conceptually equal to owners and producers." [73] One need only look

---

68   United Nations: Global Compact, "Action Platform," *United Nations: Global Compact.* https://unglobalcompact.org/take-action/action-platforms/sdg-reporting.

69   Yu, *supra* note 1766 at 1444.

70   Yu, *ibid.* at 385; see also footnote 7 at 1377.

71   Helfer, *supra* note 1764 at 50.

72   Helfer, *ibid.* at 51.

73   Helfer, *ibid.* at 58.

to Canadian jurisprudence to see a similar support for users' rights. In *CCH Canadian Ltd. v. Law Society of Upper Canada*, McLachlin, C.J. stated that "The fair dealing exception, like other exceptions in the Copyright Act, is a user's right. In order to maintain the proper balance between the rights of a copyright owner and users' interests, it must not be interpreted restrictively." [74] Current jurisprudence in both Canada and the United States emphasizes the public interest goals of copyright, and while this is encouraging, it is only part of the equation.

The York and Google Decisions Focus on the Public Interest

Courts are able to refocus on users' and authors/creators' rights as human rights by listening to the details of those cases before them, through a more nuanced approach to purpose, and what the use of a work is really about. Focusing on users' goals and how they may serve the public interest is a great starting point for any court analysis. In *CCH*, McLachlin C.J. emphasized that "As discussed, these allowable purposes should not be given a restrictive interpretation or this could result in the undue restriction of users' rights." [75] In *Google v Oracle* in the United States, the Supreme Court clearly understood the basics of the history of open software. Breyer J. references the National Commission on New Technological Uses of Copyrighted Works that concluded that "copyright's existing doctrines (e.g., fair use) applied by courts on a case-by-case basis, could prevent holders from using copyright to stifle innovation." [76] Justice Breyer links public interest goals to the nuances afforded through a careful attention to context: fair use "can carry out its basic purpose of providing a context-based check that can help to keep a copyright monopoly within its lawful bounds." [77] In declaring so much of the code as fair use, the Court underscored the amount of education needed to create code and honored it. By allowing coders to skip re-inventing the wheel, they allowed them to concentrate on new modes of transportation. Michael Carroll and Peter Jaszi point out the importance of this decision as precedence for lower courts going forward: "The invitation to broaden the inquiry by taking public value added into account along with private monetary losses." [78]

---

74   2004 SCC 13 (CanLII), [2004] 1 SCR 339 at para 48. [*CCH*]
75   *CCH, ibid.* at para 54.
76   Google, *ibid.* at 16.
77   Google, *ibid.* at 17.
78   Michael W Carroll & Peter Jaszi, "The Triumph of Three Big Ideas in Fair

In *York v Access Copyright*, the court determined that copyright tariffs are not mandatory and that institutions are free to enter into contracts, licensing agreements, and database subscription agreements with whomever they please. Access Copyright tried to shout down the real facts by claiming that the university — and all post-secondary institutions not simply acquiescing to their demands — were essentially stealing from the authors in their catalogue. This completely negates the fact that Access Copyright does not hold exclusive licenses in these works and that authors are free to monetize their works elsewhere, so these institutions were simply paying royalties somewhere else: hundreds of millions of dollars worth of other licenses.[79] Abella points out that "Nothing in the *Act* is designed to prop-up collectives that have become less valuable to users and/or rights-holders."[80] In 2010, Access Copyright applied to the Board to raise its tariff from $3.38 per FTE (full-time equivalent) student to $45 per FTE — plus additional royalties for course packs. Abella states that "Instead of operating as part of a scheme designed to control collective societies' potentially unfair market power, Access Copyright's interpretation would turn tariffs into a plainly anti-competitive tool, boosting collective societies' power to the detriment of users."[81] Once again, just like the Stationer's Monopoly, anti-competitive monopolies have their own interests at heart, and are not speaking to the best interests of authors/creators. While the Supreme Court of Canada declined to provide a ruling on the fair dealing claims of York because without an exclusive license to the works Access Copyright had no standing in the case, the Court nevertheless made some very important statements.

In *York*, Abella, J stresses that "Copyright law has public interest goals"[82] and a careful balance needs to be maintained between incentivizing creation and ensuring that "owners' rights and the public interest should not conflict with one another."[83] Abella echoes and cites the

---

Use Jurisprudence" (March 29, 2024) 99:2 Tul L Rev, online: https://ssrn.com/abstract=4778293.

79   Canadian Association of Research Libraries, "CARL Statistics | Statistiques de l'ABRC 2018-2019" (May 2022) https://www.carl-abrc.ca/measuring-impact/statistics/. For the 2019–2020 period, CARL lists expenditures for university library collections as $362,913,423 at 9. This amount will only have gone up in the last four years.

80   York, *supra* note 1712 at para 64.

81   York, *ibid* at para 71.

82   York, *ibid* at para 91.

83   York, *ibid* at para 94.

decision in *Théberge v. Galerie d'Art du Petit Champlain Inc.*, in stating that "increasing public access to and dissemination of artistic and intellectual works, which enrich society and often provide users with the tools and inspiration to generate works of their own, is a primary goal of copyright."[84] Education and research do not only happen in a classroom.

Abella acknowledges the importance of "institutionalized guidelines [to] help overcome [the] impediment" caused by users' (professors' and students') lack of knowledge of Copyright law.[85] Abella's criticism of the lower courts' analyses focus on users' rights and the public interest goals of copyright law:

> The main problem with their analysis was that they approached the fairness analysis exclusively from the institutional perspective. This error tainted their analysis of several fairness factors. By anchoring the analysis in the institutional nature of the copying and York's purported commercial purpose, the nature of fair dealing as a user's right was overlooked and the fairness assessment was over before it began.[86]

Abella focuses attention on the enumerated purposes within fair dealing of research and education, and the decision echoes Breyer's analysis of the amount and substantiality factor. The end user is the student, not the institution. The court does not dismiss the rights of creators but does stress that "owner's rights and the public interest should not conflict with one another."[87] It's also important to remember that creators had to learn their craft and were once students too.

Working through the fair dealing analysis, Abella points out that the first step is satisfied in that "it was common ground in this case that York's teachers make copies for their students for the allowable purpose of education."[88] It was appropriate to move to the second step of the analysis, whether the dealing was fair. Here Abella criticized the lower courts for approaching "the analysis from an institutional perspective only, leaving out the perspective of the students who use the materials."[89] The students and teachers are the actual users here.

---

84   York, *ibid* at para 92 and citing [2002] 2 S.C.R. 336, at para 32, per Binnie J.
85   York, *ibid* at para 85.
86   York, *ibid* at para 89.
87   York, *ibid* at para 94.
88   York, *ibid* at para 97.
89   York, *ibid* at para 98.

The university's purpose in refusing the tariff was to obtain the same licenses in a more cost-effective manner, not to get something for nothing. Abella points out that "funds 'saved' by proper exercise of the fair dealing right go to the University's core objective of education, not to some ulterior commercial purpose."[90] Indeed, as the cost of the tariff was included in student fees, the real savings was for the students—the end users—themselves. It is important to stress that creators/authors were receiving royalties through licensing agreements, and that creators/authors also benefit from education—about their craft and about the law and their rights.

Jurisprudence provides important signposts to help interpret legislation. In both *Google* and *York*, the courts provide important insights. The public interest goals of copyright that underpin the fair use and fair dealing purpose of education are key aspects of both cases. Creators are also users who need access to educational materials. Education is also an important aspect of the Sustainable Development Goals.

Sustainable Development Goals and Balancing Copyright

The United Nations Sustainable Development Goals could help to combat maximalist copyright owners by utilizing the existing exceptions and limitations and championing less developed and developing countries. Goal four seeks to "ensure inclusive and equitable quality education and promote lifelong learning opportunities for all."[91] Having an education fair dealing exception is key to helping secure access. Goal 3 seeks to "ensure healthy lives and promote well-being for all ages."[92] Well-being and a healthy life are tied to one's community and cultural heritage. Goal 9 seeks to "build resilient infrastructure, promote inclusive and sustainable industrialization and foster innovation."[93] The United Nations Human Rights Office of the High Commissioner specifically links the SDGs to specific human rights. SDG 4 is linked to the "Right to education [UDHR art. 26; ICESCR art. 13], particularly in relation to children [CRC arts. 28, 29]; persons with disabilities [CRC art. 23(3), CRPD art. 24]; and Indigenous peoples [UNDRIP art. 14]."[94]

---

90   York, *ibid* at para 103.
91   SDG 4 https://sdgs.un.org/goals/goal4.
92   SDG 3 https://sdgs.un.org/goals/goal3.
93   SDG 9 https://sdgs.un.org/goals/goal9.
94   United Nations Human Rights Office of the High Commissioner. "SDG Human Rights Table" https://www.ohchr.org/Documents/Issues/MDGs/Post2015/

SDG 9 is linked to the "Right to enjoy the benefits of scientific progress and its application [UDHR art. 27; ICESCR art. 15(1)(b)] [and the] Right to access to information [UDHR art. 19; ICCPR art. 19(2)]." [95] SDG 11, which concerns sustainable cities and communities, also encompasses the "Right to participate in cultural life [UDHR art. 27(1); ICESCR art. 15; ICERD arts. 5, 7; CRPD art. 30; CRC art. 31]." [96] At COP28, "UN Secretary-General António Guterres and SDG Advocate Dia Mirza call[ed] for urgent climate action, global cooperation and youth empowerment." [97] For all these goals to be a reality, researchers need access to research and youth need to be empowered through education. All the 17 goals are focused with regular updates and initiatives. It is quite an active network, which provides an infrastructure to afford change as well as providing quantitative evidence. [98] The global participation in the SDGs is another avenue to provide more consistent and human rights–centred approaches through which to pursue limitations and exceptions to owners' rights that benefit both creators and users.

People Are at the Heart of Human Rights

Finally, it is important to centre the debate as a human right. The right to education and a right to research are *human* rights. Review and criticism are ways by which users take advantage of their human rights to freedom of expression and the right to participate in culture. Concerns over text and data mining that are essential to many research endeavors have arisen due to Artificial Intelligence's use of data scraping to

---

SDG_HR_Table.pdf UDHR is the Universal Declaration of Human Rights; CRPD is Convention on the Rights of Persons with Disabilities; CRC is the Convention on the Rights of the Child.

95   United Nations Human Rights Office of the High Commissioner, *supra* note 1802.

96   United Nations Human Rights Office of the High Commissioner, *supra* note 1802. ICERD is the International Convention on the Elimination of All Forms of Racial Discrimination.

97   UNSDGs News, "UN Secretary-General António Guterres and SDG Advocate Dia Mirza Call for Urgent Climate Action, Global Cooperation and Youth Empowerment" (4 December 2023), online: https://unpartnerships.un.org/news/2023/un-secretary-general-antonio-guterres-and-sdg.

98   See for instance: UN. "4 Quality Education." Sustainable Development Goals. https://www.un.org/sustainabledevelopment/education/. This update highlights the struggles of Sub-Saharan Africa in particular that has little or no access to internet and other resources. It also highlights that women and girls have the least access to education. Even so, "the percentage of students attaining basic reading skills by the end of primary school is projected to rise from 51 per cent in 2015 to 67 per cent by 2030."

supply the data needed to train the necessary large language models (LLMs).[99] By stressing *human* rights, concerns over use by AI can be sidestepped.[100] Creating and using large datasets is an important tool in research, but that is a different use than AI scraping the same data and creating arguably infringing uses, such as the Drake and Weeknd song that went viral. The US Copyright office has categorically stated that Artificial Intelligence has no claim to copyright because it is not human. According to the Federal Register, "[w]hen an AI technology determines the expressive elements of its output, the generated material is not the product of human authorship. As a result, that material is not protected by copyright and must be disclaimed in a registration application."[101]

By focusing on the purpose of the use—education and research— once again, the human element can provide guidance. The concern with equating AI data scraping with research-focused text and data mining is that restrictions on AI might also limit text and data mining. In this instance, the decision in *Warhol v Goldsmith*[102] can be helpful in that the output of AI might be a direct competitor for the inputted data whereas text and data mining's explicit purpose is research, which falls squarely under the allowable purposes of fair use and fair dealing.

Human rights concerns are perhaps more universal than has been considered in relation to Indigenous people in particular. Yu points out that "countries in the developed West have ... privileged civil and political rights over economic, social, and cultural rights,"[103] which have been identified as the least developed in the context of human rights. Helfer suggests that "when Indigenous culture is analyzed from a human rights perspective, intellectual property rules are seen as one of the problems facing Indigenous communities and—only perhaps—as part of a solution to those problems."[104]

---

99   The scope of this piece will not permit an extended discussion of these issues.

100   An in-depth discussion of the potential concerns created by AI especially in the cultural space and intellectual property is not within the scope of this writing.

101   Copyright Office: Library of Congress, "Copyright Registration Guidance: Works Containing Material Generated by Artificial Intelligence" (16 March 2023) *Federal Register: The Daily Journal of the United States Government* <https://www.federal-register.gov/documents/2023/03/16/2023-05321/copyright-registration-guidance-works-containing-material-generated-by-artificial-intelligence#:~:text=When%20an%20AI%20technology%20determines,disclaimed%20in%20a%20registration%20application>.

102   Warhol v Goldsmith, *supra* note 1736.

103   Yu, *supra* note 1766 at 1434. See also Helfer, *supra* note 1764 at 51.

104   Helfer, *ibid.* at 54.

Western approaches to intellectual property do not necessarily serve Indigenous cultures even within western countries. Traditionally, Indigenous people have not had "the right to recognition of and control over their culture [and] much of this knowledge was treated as part of the public domain, either because it did not meet established subject matter criteria for protection, or because the Indigenous communities who created it did not endorse private ownership rules." [105] Article 31 of the United Nations Declaration on the Rights of Indigenous Peoples [106] states:

> Indigenous peoples have the right to maintain, control, protect and develop their cultural heritage, traditional knowledge and traditional cultural expressions, as well as the manifestations of their sciences, technologies and cultures, including human and genetic resources, seeds, medicines, knowledge of the properties of fauna and flora, oral traditions, literatures, designs, sports and traditional games and visual and performing arts. They also have the right to maintain, control, protect and develop their intellectual property over such cultural heritage, traditional knowledge, and traditional cultural expressions.

Numerous articles in UNDRIP reference the right of Indigenous people to control their culture, but Article 31 specifically mentions intellectual property. [107] Article 14 specifically addresses education and "cultural methods of teaching and learning." Article 16(1) addresses the issue of access to cultural materials. Canada finally ratified UNDRIP on June 21, 2021, but initially, the United States, Australia, New Zealand, and Canada were the only nations to vote against UNDRIP (144 voted for and there were 11 abstentions). These four nations have well-developed intellectual property regimes and a long history of oppressive (at best) treatment of the Indigenous populations. Strong corporate voices have been heard over Indigenous voices. The ratification of UNDRIP has not seen major changes to Canada's *Copyright Act*, which is still in the process of review. To date little appears to change the direction of copyright in relation to Indigenous people and differing theories of ownership and fixation. Changes that would benefit Indigenous

---

105   Helfer, *ibid.* at 52.
106   UNDRIP, *supra* note 1718.
107   See also Articles 5, 8(1)(2), 11(1)(2), 12(1)(2), 13(1)(2), 15, 16(1), and 24(1), all of which concern culture.

peoples should, however, be done through consultation with those stakeholders to take into account how they wish to protect their own culture, including oral artifacts.

All users, creators, and owners should be taken into consideration in finding the best road forward to maximize creation and innovation. In designing a path forward to achieve this goal, it is important to remember that budding creators are also users who require access to materials with which to be educated. It is also important to remember that these issues are ongoing, with new issues such as AI and an increased awareness of the disparities between countries and people that must be accommodated.

Conclusion

From its beginnings with the *Statute of Anne*, copyright law has been concerned with striking a balance between purely economic concerns and public interest goals. The two are not mutually exclusive and in fact should support each other when in balance. Equity, which is at the heart of this balancing act, is reflected in the terms *fair* use and *fair* dealing—fair to all parties. By emphasizing the public interest goals of copyright, using support from the courts, and remembering that according to McLachlin, C.J. users' rights are rights, it should be possible to argue against copyright maximalists who would continue to restrict fair access to works. Sean Flynn points out that there is a difference between a copyright exception that is a users' right and human rights that create a duty for the state to act. The fair dealing and fair use purposes, such as research and education, are human rights, and there is an affirmative duty attached to a right while an exception may be seen as merely a freedom to do something within the narrower parameters of a privilege. Canadian jurisprudence has made a clearer distinction. Drassinower points out that "Fair dealing is ... not about a wrong that must be excused but about the exercise of a right to respond to another's original expression through one's own."[108] Limitations and exceptions are important users' rights, but it is often the case that these are absent from developing countries where they might be most helpful, particularly in the areas of research and education. In addition, even developed countries often fall short in finding ways to support Indigenous peoples' culture. The SDGs would not carry the weight of

---

108   Drassinower, *supra* note 1729 at 475-476.

an international agreement like the Marrakesh Treaty or UNDRIP for countries to ratify an agreement by changing national laws to comply, but the SDGs can create a positive influence and provide data that can then build evidence-based support for international instruments to address the inequalities that allow corporate interests to exploit Indigenous peoples as well as less developed and less economically robust countries.

Litman points out that in order to encourage cooperation, it is important that all stakeholders are at least travelling in the same direction:

> Twenty-first-century copyright law is a complex system with a bunch of interlocking and sometimes inconsistent purposes, but [she believes] that the most important purposes are these: first, copyright law should encourage authors to create and widely disseminate works of authorship; second, it should give them meaningful opportunities to earn money from doing so; and third, copyright law should encourage readers, listeners, viewers, and other users to encounter, enjoy and learn from those works of authorship. [109]

Creators are users, and users are creators. This seems like a simple two-way street, but as Litman points out this is a messy, multi-dimensional road. By emphasizing the balance inherent in the roots of copyright to serve both public interest and economic interests, a better understanding of the intersecting interests can be sought. Economic interests, such as the large media conglomerates, as well as legislators who may be focused simply on the concerns of trade and lobbying interests, need to be actively shown that public interest can serve their agenda and should be a part of that agenda. The road ahead should see activism in support of human rights and where necessary law reform that provides access to information and education that can benefit all: users, creators, distributors, and owners.

---

109   Litman, *supra* note 1719 at 539.

CHAPTER 18

Unseen Hands, Invisible Rights: Unmasking Digital Workers in the Shadows of AI Innovation and Implications for the Future of Copyright Law

Teshager W. Dagne

Abstract

This chapter examines the often invisible contributions of digital workers—frequently located in low-income regions—who perform vital tasks in training and refining AI systems. It argues that while AI development is widely perceived as highly automated, much "ghostwork" underpins modern innovations in machine learning and generative AI models. Drawing parallels to other creative industries, such as screenwriters and performing artists, the chapter reveals how systemic power imbalances in copyright law contribute to the exploitation of digital workers' labour, by consolidating creative outputs under corporate control.

Focusing on the intersection of AI and copyright, the chapter explores whether datasets and AI-assisted outputs meet the criteria for copyright protection and how ownership is allocated in light of digital workers' roles in collecting, annotating, and curating data essential for training AI models. It then investigates how existing private ordering mechanisms typically assign rights and economic advantages to AI designers or corporate proprietors rather than those performing the underlying tasks, exacerbating the invisibility and marginalization of digital workers' contributions.

The chapter concludes by highlighting the need for reconfiguring copyright law to recognize collaborative authorship and calling for solutions to address ongoing fairness concerns, including contractual reforms and broader labour protections. As AI technology advances and the role of digital workers becomes increasingly significant, this chapter underscores the importance of ensuring that copyright frameworks in an AI-driven world equitably reflect all contributors' creative input.

Artificial Intelligence (AI) systems often give the impression that they operate through automated processes, minimizing or completely excluding human involvement. However, this perception obscures a significant amount of labour essential for training these systems and is reflected in their outcomes. Behind every Artificial Intelligence model created by companies in countries like the United States, Germany, and Canada, individuals in places such as Venezuela, Kenya, and the Philippines contribute to this technology despite facing unfavourable economic, social, and legal conditions. These individuals, often called "ghost workers," drive many recent AI advancements yet remain invisible, underpaid, and unrecognized.[1] What is often described as the "paradox of automation's last mile" explains the phenomenon that while AI has made significant strides, the demand for human intelligence to manage a wide range of tasks and maintain the seamless operation of automated or "artificially intelligent" systems is steadily increasing and shows no signs of diminishing.[2]

This chapter explores the role of copyright law in consolidating the contributions of digital workers to data works and AI-assisted outputs, placing these under the exclusive control of corporations that reap economic benefits. Most discussions about the relationship between copyright and AI technology have focused on the implications of using protected works in machine learning and whether copyright exists in AI outputs.[3] Little attention has been paid to how copyright enables the proactive exploitation of digital workers' contributions as inputs to AI training as data works or, in some cases, AI-assisted outputs, usually entailing copyright protection.[4]

---

1   See Mary L Gray and Siddharth Suri, *Ghost Work: How to Stop Silicon Valley from Building a New Global Underclass* (Boston: Houghton Mifflin, 2019).

2   *Ibid.*

3   See the implications of copyright in the training of machine learning systems in AI, Mark A Lemley & Bryan Casey, "Fair Learning" (2021) 99:4 Tex L Rev 743; on copyright implications of AI outputs, see Michael D Murray, "Generative and AI Authored Artworks and Copyright Law" (2023) 45 Hastings Comm. & Ent. L.J. 27

4   The words "exploit" and "exploitation" are used in two different senses in this chapter; "exploit," when used in the context of works of authorship, refers to the utilization of the economic rights by owners of copyright that are recognized under s. 3 (1) of Canada's *Copyright Act. Copyright Act* (R.S.C., 1985, c. C-42). "Exploitation" when used in the context of the position of data workers and their

This chapter, first, sets up the background for the issue under consideration by exploring the various ways machine learning occurs in AI systems, in which the preparation of datasets is a significant component. The following sections further elaborate on the role of digital workers and other parties in the AI pipeline in the collaborative dataset creation process. With this background, the subsequent section outlines the interface between AI and copyright, focusing on when copyright over datasets might subsist in the form of data works and closely examining the nature of tasks often assigned to digital workers. The final section emphasizes that even when copyright may not subsist over training datasets, there are circumstances established in other scholarship in which AI-assisted outputs might attract copyright.

Sections five and six shed light on the trend in relation to data work and other works, such as works by screenwriters and performing artists in which copyright law has enabled proprietors of rights to establish exploitation rights to the disadvantage of authors. It demonstrates that digital workers in the AI pipeline are often denied authorial rights through private ordering mechanisms enabled by the shift in the focus of modern copyright law and jurisprudence toward proprietors of rights. The last section poses questions about the future of copyright law in attempting to return the focus of copyright to collaborative authors in a way that will respond to the fair allocation of rights between digital workers as authors, or joint authors in some cases, and AI designers as exploiters of digital works.

Approaches to Machine Learning in AI: Supervised and Un (Self) Supervised Learning

There are two major machine learning (ML) approaches by which algorithmic systems learn from training datasets. [5] The first, "supervised

---

"clients," most of whom are AI designers, AI owners, and in some cases, AI users, takes a broader meaning of the extraction of surplus labour in relation to power imbalances reinforced by social, economic, and legal factors that empower the exploiter. See Jakob Rigi, "The Demise of the Marxian Law of Value? A Critique of Michael Hardt and Antonio Negri" in Eran Fisher & Christian Fuchs, *Reconsidering Value and Labour in the Digital Age* (London: Palgrave Macmillan, 2015) at 202.

5   ML is a subfield of Artificial Intelligence (AI) that involves various techniques of learning that can broadly be categorized into "supervised" and "unsupervised" learning. The third type of learning, called reinforcement learning, is outside the scope of discussion in this article. See discussion of the types of ML in Richard

learning," is a process in which the algorithm system learns from a training set of prepared data provided by a knowledgeable human supervisor, for the system to extrapolate or generalize its responses so that it acts correctly in situations that are not present in the training sets.[6] The technique is overwhelmingly used to train commercial AI systems; in this system, machine learning coupled with human expertise assists the AI in correcting errors or faulty correlations.[7] This type of learning is often created for a specific task. It resembles a classroom setting in which a teacher guides students on a large amount of manually prepared data that can be divided into three categories: training data, testing data, and validation data.[8]

"Unsupervised learning" (also called "self-supervised learning"), on the other hand, involves teaching the AI algorithm to operate on unprepared data and allowing the algorithm to act on it without supervision.[9] A method predominantly used in such popular large language models as ChatGPT and generative art AIs, having its origin in the natural language processing domain of machine learning, unsupervised learning requires large amounts of data and little human oversight.[10] Here, for example, a data scientist merely gives photos in the dataset, and it is up to the system to examine the data and determine whether they are cat images, to find patterns in the dataset and rate the data points according to those patterns.[11]

Although often categorized as unsupervised learning, there is also a learning method called r"reinforcement learning" and other forms of learning.[12] Even the distinction between supervised and unsupervised learning is not tight, as categories exist within them that range from weakly supervised learning to semi-weak supervised learning and semi-supervised learning.[13]

S Sutton & Andrew G Barto, *Reinforcement Learning: An Introduction* (Mountain View: MIT Press, 2018) at 1–4.

6   *Ibid.*
7   See generally H B Barlow, "Unsupervised Learning" in Geoffrey Hinton & Terrence J Sejnowski, eds, *Unsupervised Learning: Foundations of Neural Computation* (Cambridge: The MIT Press, 1999).
8   Veenu Rani et al, "Self-Supervised Learning: A Succinct Review" (2023) 30, Archives of Computational Methods in Engineering, 2761 at 2763.
9   *Ibid.*
10   See *ibid.* at 2762.
11   Samreen Naeem, "An Unsupervised Machine Learning Algorithms: Comprehensive Review" (2023) 13: 1 Int J Com Dig Sys at 912–913.
12   See generally Rani et al. *supra* note 8 at 2763–2767.
13   Padmanabha Reddy Y C A, "Semi-Supervised Learning: A Brief Review" (2018)

Despite the technical distinctions among the algorithmic learning methods described above, the pertinent issue in this chapter relates to the contribution of human labour and ingenuity in the methods ranging from supervised learning to semi-supervised learning. It is noted that "[AI] doesn't run on magic pixie dust [...] [AI training] is a job that actually takes quite a bit of creativity and insight and judgment."[14] In the range of supervised learning activities, digital workers and AI designers engage in activities that might constitute "authorship" of data works and, in some cases, AI-assisted outputs. The preparation of AI training datasets and the resulting AI-assisted outputs is often a process in which an "ecosystem" of actors makes data valuable and meaningful for AI training iteratively and collaboratively. The following section describes how such a process unfolds in the context of existing arrangements between actors and the preparation steps of data works that often result in AI-assisted outputs.

Collaborative Authorship of Data Works: Actors and Steps

"Data works" refer to data and datasets considered "works" under copyright law. Data works could be copyright protected in two ways: original data works that are transformed through a data-value chain as processed data or as compilations.[15] Data production is increasingly fragmented and distributed in an *increasingly precarious globalized workforce of underpaid digital workers.*[16]

Preparing data works for the datasets used to train and build AI technologies involves a number of decisions as to the kind of data to collect, curate, clean, label, abstract, index, etc. The process of dataset development starts with formulating the problem, which is the conceptualization and construction of the machine learning task by making the problems "into questions that data science can answer."[17] The problem

7 International Journal of Engineering & Technology at 81–85.

14   Karen Hao, "The AI Gig Economy Is Coming for You" (May 31, 2019), online: https://www.technologyreview.com/2019/05/31/103015/the-ai-gig-economy-is-coming-for-you/.

15   An example would be what is described as "processed data" that attracts copyright in Geophysical Service Incorporated v EnCana Corporation, 2016 ABQB 230. See also the discussion in section 4.1 below.

16   See Clément Le Ludec, Maxime Cornet & Antonio A Casilli, "The Problem with Annotation. Human Labour and Outsourcing Between France and Madagascar" (2023) 10:2 Big Data & Society at 3.

17   Samir Passi & Solon Barocas, "Problem Formulation and Fairness" FAT* '19: Proceedings of the Conference on Fairness, Accountability, and Transparency

formulation stage implicates all forthcoming steps in developing the training dataset. Defining the task through problem formulation is the role of the AI designer, which seems straightforward but is often "complicated and shifting as the understanding of the problem and the available data and features change in the machine learning development lifecycle." [18]

An AI designer who formulates the problem may be an AI-specific company or a technology platform company that incorporates and develops AI systems in its business operations. Examples of the former type can be such AI companies as OpenAI, Anthropic, Inflection AI, You.com, Primer AI, Substack, etc. Companies in the latter category are Google, Microsoft, X, formerly Twitter, Amazon, Meta, Apple, etc.

Once a problem is formulated, the next step is the data collection stage, which is "the iterative process of collecting data instances (for example, individual images, video stills, and/or accompanying metadata or captions, textual documents, code repositories)". [19] Often addressed in the literature about data mining, data collection is the process of gathering and measuring information by automatic or semiautomatic means. [20]

The collected data is usually in raw data form as unstructured data and, hence, needs to be processed for AI training. Data processing involves a series of steps, such as data cleaning, annotating, abstracting, and indexing, and it may involve algorithmic verification. [21] In addition, the dataset development stage of data processing includes model training and model evaluation, which are described respectively as "the act of modifying a machine learning model by being exposed to data instances within the dataset" and "the act of assessing the accuracy or performance of a machine learning model." [22] In short, according to Tubaro et al, the contribution of digital workers to the

---

January 2019 cited in Mehtab Khan & Alex Hanna, "The Subjects and Stages of AI Dataset Development: A Framework for Dataset Accountability" (2023) 19 Ohio St. Tech. L.J. at 55.

18   *Ibid.* at 24.

19   *Ibid.*

20   Although data mining and data collection are used somewhat interchangeably in the literature, technically, "data mining" is the process "to filter out relevant data from a database of data collections using various techniques and algorithms such as associations, clustering and classics." Mayank Pareek & Purushottam Bhari, "A Review Report on Knowledge Discovery in Databases and Various Techniques of Data Mining" (2020) 5:12 Open Access International Journal of Science and Engineering at 79.

21   See Khan and Hanna *supra* note 17 at 59 ff.

22   *Ibid.* at 25.

training process of AI systems can involve three steps: generating and annotating data (AI preparation), verifying model output (AI verification), and directly mimicking model behaviour to produce a service (AI impersonation).[23]

In the data works marketplace, the AI designer who formulates the problem serves as "the requester or client seeking services," whereas many start-ups and businesses that often call themselves "business insights" or "intelligence and analytics" serve as intermediaries or platforms for data work.[24] The intermediaries or data platforms often serve as outsourcing companies for AI companies and rely on digital workers for the above-described data processing activities. Examples of intermediaries that usually work with AI companies include Appen Ltd., Accenture Plc., Clickworker, Tellus, Remotasks, Scale AI, Surge AI, etc. There are also crowd-work platforms, such as Hive, Microworkers, Mechanical Turk, gethybrid.io, and dataannotation.tech, taskup.ai, etc., that provide direct and open recruitment of data workers through their platforms.

Digital workers range "from higher-skilled, 'macro-task' [...] workers [who] offer their services as graphic designers, computer programmers, statisticians, translators, and other professional services, to [those engaged in] 'micro-task' [work] which typically involve clerical tasks that can be completed quickly and require less specialized skills."[25] The latter describes a situation in which "complex projects are broken down into smaller, easily accomplished tasks, which can then be distributed to a large number of workers."[26] Micro-task activities mainly involve the AI preparation aspect of AI training processes but can also include AI verification and AI impersonation steps in AI training.

AI and Copyright Interface

There are many intersections between copyright and AI technologies.[27] The most pertinent aspect of copyright's intersection with AI relates

---

23   See P Tubaro, AA Casilli and M Coville, "The Trainer, The Verifier, The Imitator: Three Ways in Which Human Platform Workers Support Artificial Intelligence" (2020) 7:1 Big Data & Society.

24   See Janine Berg, Miriam Cherry & Uma Rani, "Digital Labour Platforms: A Need for International Regulation?" (2019) 16 Revista de Economía Laboral 104, at 108.

25   *Ibid.* at 109.

26   See Casilli et al, *supra* note 16 at 2.

27   For discussion topics that address the intersection of IP and AI broadly as well as focusing on issues associated with specific types of IP, copyright, trademark,

to the data used in input and its outputs. Much of the scholarship on copyright and AI has focused on whether using the underlying work of which inputs are constituted (images, texts, musical works, and other subject matter) for unsupervised learning constitutes copyright infringement. [28] In supervised learning, the AI input is prepared as a "training dataset," from which the AI machine learns in training, modelling (testing), and benchmarking (validation) before the deployment stages of AI development. [29]

The first question is whether the "training datasets" so developed are copyright protected. There are two ways the training datasets could be considered copyright protected: on their own, irrespective of the underlying work of which they are constituted (images, texts, musical works, and other subject matter), or as original data works in the form of created data, compilations, or collective works.

Copyright over Training Datasets as Data Works

With respect to when data may be protected as original data work, the guiding principle accepted across many jurisdictions is that copyright protection only extends to the expression of ideas rather than the underlying ideas or facts. [30] To the extent that data equates with facts, as Justice Brandeis of the US Supreme Court famously stated in his dissent in *International News Service*, "[T]he general rule of law is, that the noblest of human productions—knowledge, truths ascertained, conceptions and ideas—after voluntary communication to others, are free as the air to common use." [31] The US Supreme Court in *Feist Publications v. Rural Telephone Service* (*Feist*) further elaborates on the nature of facts based on

---

design, patent, and trade secret law, see generally Ryan Abbott, *Research Handbook on Intellectual Property and Artificial Intelligence* (Cheltenham and Northampton: Edward Elgar, 2022).

28   See Carys Craig, "AI and Copyright" in Florian Martin-Bariteau & Teresa Scassa, eds, *Artificial Intelligence and the Law in Canada* (Toronto: LexisNexis Canada, 2021); Daniel Gervais, "Exploring the Interfaces between Big Data and Intellectual Property Law" (2019) 10 J. Intell. Prop. Info. Tech. & Elec. Com. L. 3 at 6.

29   See discussion of "stages of dataset development" in Khan & Hanna, *supra* note 17.

30   See CCH Canadian Ltd. v. L. Soc'y Upper Can., [2004] 1 S.C.R. 339, para. 25 (Can.) (noting that facts are in the public domain as "trite law"); Feist Publ'ns, Inc. v. Rural Tel. Serv. Co., 499 U.S. 340, 348 (1991) (noting that "[a]ll facts—scientific, historical, biographical, and news of the day" may not be copyrighted and are part of the public domain available to every person).

31   Int'l News Serv. v. Associated Press, 248 U.S. 215, 250 (1918) (Brandeis, J., dissenting).

the idea-and fact-expression dichotomy, stating, "The fact/expression dichotomy limits severely the scope of protection in fact-based works [...] copyright is limited to those aspects of the work—termed 'expression'—that display the stamp of the author's originality."[32]

In a simple case of data annotation and labelling, copyright may not protect such datasets as labelling a picture of a cat as a "cat" and similar categorizations and labelling because they may fall in the realm of facts. However, it is less clear whether data is always indistinguishable from facts and whether copyright protection sometimes extends to data.[33]

Courts in the United States and Canada have attempted to distinguish between facts and data, leaving the possibility that data can be a subject of copyright protection in some cases. In *New York Mercantile Exchange, Inc. (NYMEX) v. IntercontinentalExchange, Inc.* (*IntercontinentalExchange*), the US Court of Appeals for the Second Circuit considered whether copyright protection exists in the individual price values that NYMEX sets as settlement prices for its own futures contracts and hybrid commodity instruments.[34] The court considered whether NYMEX could receive copyright protection in its settlement prices, relying on the issue of whether settlement prices were figures that merely existed within the marketplace and were subsequently discovered by NYMEX or whether NYMEX created its settlement prices.[35] The court ultimately determined not to provide copyright protection, arguing that the merger doctrine must apply.[36] The merger doctrine, broadly recognized in the United States and Canada, upholds that when a work of authorship is incapable of being expressed as a practical matter in more than one or a small number of ways, such work is "merged" with the idea that is expressed.[37] However, it noted that the matter of whether

---

32   *Feist*, 499 U.S. at 349.
33   For the conceptual distinction between facts and data, Teresa Scassa, "Ownership and Control over Publicly Accessible Platform Data" (2019) 43 Online Info. Rev. 986 at 3–4 (noting the distinction between representative data from implied and derived data and observing that implied and derived data may be treated differently in both Canada and the United States). *See also* Justin Hughes, "Created Facts and the Flawed Ontology of Copyright Law" 83 Notre Dame L Rev 43 (2007) (arguing that original expressions that generate facts once adopted by social convention should be protected to incentivize the creation of the expression and the generated facts).
34   N.Y. Mercantile Exch., Inc v. Intercont'l, Inc., 497 F.3d 109, 110 (2d Cir. 2007).
35   *Ibid.* at 114.
36   *Ibid.* at 118.
37   *See* Pamela Samuelson, "Reconceptualizing Copyright's Merger Doctrine" (2016)

settlement prices are "discovered" or "created" was a "close question"; it would not "decide whether settlement prices are unoriginal" and was "particularly reluctant to hold, as a matter of law, that [NYMEX] [...] discover[ed] the settlement prices." [38]

Similarly, the court in *BanxCorp v. Costco Wholesale Corp.* seemed open to the possibility that copyright could extend to "raw data that have been converted into a final value through the use of an original formula," depending on the "degree of consensus and objectivity that attaches to the formula." [39] In considering the originality of—and thus the possibility of extending copyright protection to—calculated percentages, the court explained that "the more acceptance a financial measure obtains (i.e., the more successful it is), the more 'fact-like' it becomes." [40]

In both *BanxCorp* and *IntercontinentalExchange*, the ultimate decision relied on applying the merger doctrine. [41] The data cannot be protected by copyright law. [42] Notably, the data under consideration in both cases constituted an authored work of expression; therefore, it could be covered by copyright as an authored work. [43] However, considering that these data represented the idea behind the analytics that led to their creation, extending copyright protection would have been equivalent to granting a monopoly over the idea. [44] Thus, copyright can protect data if the process through which it is created fulfills the legal requirements of creation as an original expression.

Jurisprudence in the United States on the copyrightability of raw and processed data is consistent with the decision in *Geophysical Service, Inc. v. Encana Corp.* in Canada. [45] In this case, the Alberta Court of Queen's Bench categorized seismic data about the ocean floor into field and processed data. [46] The field data were described as "[t]he original recorded geophysical data, sometimes referred to as basic or raw data,

---

63 J. Copyright Soc'y U.S.A. 417 at 417; Red Label Vacations, Inc. v. 411 Travel Buys Ltd., [2015] 18 F.C.R. 473, para 98 ("[W]hen an idea can be expressed in only a limited number of ways, then its expression is not protected as the threshold of originality is not met."). For Canada, see Delrina Corp. v. Triolet Systems Inc., 2002 CanLII 11389 (ON CA).

38   *N.Y. Mercantile*, 497 F.3d at 116.

39   BanxCorp v. Costco Wholesale Corp., 978 F. Supp. 2d 280, 300 (S.D.N.Y. 2013).

40   *Ibid.* at 303.

41   *Ibid.* at 311; *N.Y. Mercantile*, 497 F.3d at 118.

42   *N.Y. Mercantile*, 497 F.3d at 118.

43   See Scassa, *supra* note 33, at 8.

44   See *id.* at 8–9.

45   Geophysical Serv. Inc. v. EnCana Corp., 2016 ABQB 230, para 115.

46   *Ibid.*

together with the description of the complete recording parameters."[47] Justice Eidsvik decided that field data constitutes a literary work as a "compilation" and meets the "skill and judgment" test of originality that the Canadian Supreme Court laid out in *CCH Canadian Ltd.* ("*CCH Canada*").[48] Given that originality in a compilation lies in the "selection or arrangement of data," copyright does not exist in the raw data itself when it comes to field data.[49] Here, the judge defined "processed data" as "any product derived, generated or created from the data, including, but not limited to any and all processed and reprocessed data, interpretations, maps or analyses, regardless of the form or medium on which it is displayed or stored."[50] She wrote:

> [A]s for the processed data, the processors exercise skill and judgment in the decisions they make to create a usable product from the [raw] data [...] [t]he evidence is clear that the processed product can be quite different depending on the skill of the processor and that exploration companies have their favourite processors who create the best quality product for their purposes.[51]

Making a distinction between raw and processed data as to the type of "skills and judgment" exercised—with raw data, the skill and judgment concerning "the collection, arrangement, distillation, and compilation," and with processed data, "the decisions [made] to create a usable product from the field data"—Justice Eidsvik recognized copyright in the processed data itself but excluded raw data from copyrightability.[52] Therefore, as applied in US and Canadian jurisprudence, data that merely represents objective facts does not have copyright protection; instead, copyright subsists only in compilations of such data. Moreover, data processed from raw data can attract copyright, depending on the

---

47   *Ibid.* at para 47.
48   *Ibid.* at paras 74, 77–78; CCH Canadian Ltd. v. L. Soc'y Upper Can., [2004] 1 S.C.R. 339, para 16.
49   Geophysical Serv. Inc. v. EnCana Corp., 2016 ABQB 230, para 77 ("[D]ata becomes a 'work' when it is compiled. One ping from a hydrophone would not suffice; it is the collection, arrangement, distillation and compilation that creates the work."); *Copyright Act*, R.S.C. 1985, c C-42, s 2 (Can.) (defining "compilation" as "a work resulting from the selection or arrangement of literary, dramatic, musical or artistic works or parts thereof, or . . . a work resulting from the selection or arrangement of data").
50   *Geophysical*, 2016 ABQB 230 at para 58.
51   *Ibid.* at para 83.
52   *See* Scassa, *supra* note 33, at 10.

process of its creation. In this respect, it is worth asking: given that compilations and processed data are theoretically copyrightable, why can these works be denied protection based on how they are created?

As discussed above, most data used in unsupervised (self-supervised) learning are collected by AI-enabled sensors and processed by AI-based data analytics.[53] For the results of data collection and data processing to enjoy copyright as a "work" distinguishable from facts, it must be authored by a human.[54] If a fully automated process has generated the data without human involvement, which is the case in the case of unsupervised learning, such data will not be covered by copyright.[55]

There is an extensive debate about the fate of AI-generated works, where fully-generative AI, through interaction with a human, generates works that are otherwise copyrightable but lack human authorship.[56] Nevertheless, AI being involved in creation will not necessarily result in a denial of copyright to the resulting work.[57] In the above-mentioned US and Canadian cases, the data under consideration were generated by either non-AI algorithms in settlement prices and calculated percentages or by complex processes, such as those used to collect underwater seismic data.[58]

If copyright subsists over data, as was laid out in the US and Canadian cases, the question that arises then is whether digital workers' activities that sometimes but not always involve interacting with

---

53   See discussion in section 2 above.

54   See Urantia Found. v. Maaherra, 114 F.3d 955, 958 (9th Cir. 1997) ("[S]ome element of human creativity must have occurred in order for the book to be copyrightable."). The United States Copyright Office will refuse to register a claim that lacks human authorship. See U.S. Copyright Off., *Compendium of U.S. Copyright Office Practices* § 608 (3d ed. 2021), https://www.copyright.gov/comp3/docs/compendium.pdf [https://perma.cc/4M2L-VHYE] [hereinafter Compendium of U.S. Copyright Office Practices]; *see also* Pamela Samuelson, "Allocating Ownership Rights in Computer-Generated Works" (1986) 47 Pitt L Rev 1186, 1224 ("[I]f there is no human author of such a work [computer-generated works], how can any human be motivated to create it? The copyright system assumes that society awards a set of exclusive rights to authors for limited times in order to motivate them to be creative.").

55   See *Telstra Corp. Ltd. v. Phone Directories Co. Pty. Ltd.* [2010] FCA 44 (8 February 2010) (Austl.). The High Court of Australia denied copyright protection for telephone directories that were created by automated process, on the ground that such process lacks human authorship. *See ibid.*

56   Jared Vasconcellos Grubow, "O.K. Computer: The Devolution of Human Creativity and Granting Musical Copyrights to Artificially Intelligent Joint Authors" (2018) 40 Cardozo L Rev 387, 420. (arguing that the "promotion of progress is best served by giving AIs rights and regulating them").

57   See Scassa, *supra* note 33, at 9–10.

58   See *Urantia Found.*, 114 F.3d at 956–959; Scassa, *supra* note 33, at 9–10.

AI-generated data in the preparation of training datasets in the AI pipeline constitute copyright-protected works. This question can be answered by examining the nature of digital workers' contribution to the tasks assigned to them and the ownership of copyright under the contractual agreements that digital workers sign with platforms.

The Nature of Tasks Assigned to Digital Workers

In a typical arrangement between a client (often the AI designer) and the digital workers, either mediated through an intermediary or directly under a crowdsourcing platform, the digital workers are expected to perform activities described as "tasks." Tubaro et al propose a framework to differentiate the tasks by defining three moments in the AI production chain: "artificial intelligence preparation," "artificial intelligence verification," and "artificial intelligence impersonation."[59]

The AI preparation stage is the first stage of the AI production chain that satisfies the unmet data needs of collecting raw data and its annotation.[60] Digital workers engage not only in collecting raw data but also in annotations that add extra meaning by associating each data point, such as an image, with relevant attribute tags.[61] Despite the claim from some that data generation and annotation tasks are mundane acts that will ultimately be fully automated, Tubaro et al argue that some essential tasks will always be directed to humans as indispensable though hidden providers for the foreseeable future because of what they describe as the "heteromation" paradigm, precisely because humans have the (biologically-based) capacity to recognize and classify data.[62]

It is important to note that providing services like captioning a translation or cleaning training data for training algorithms in the data annotation process is often written off as mundane drudgery.[63] However, with computers now good at such tasks as "distinguishing" a dog from another animal, human capacity is now in demand to recognize details and nuances, indispensable to increase the precision

---

59   Tubaro et al *supra* note 23.
60   *Ibid.* at 4.
61   *Ibid.*
62   The "heteromation" paradigm describes a situation in which *"critical tasks are pushed to end users as indispensable* [human] mediators," in contrast to a paradigm oriented to the actions of machines. See Hamid Ekbia and Bonnie Nardi, "Heteromation and Its (Dis)Contents: The Invisible Division of Labor Between Humans and Machines" 19:6 First Monday (2014) at 2.
63   Hao, *supra* note 14.

of computer vision software for sensitive applications such as autonomous vehicles and medical image analysis. [64] In medical image analysis,
for example, a skilled radiologist who might be employed as a digital
worker would always be needed to describe different features of an
image and add professional annotations using a distinct vocabulary,
manifesting a complex skill that is taught through a mix of scientific
theory and apprenticeship, and such annotations along with the images
might be used to train AIs. [65] In her interview with digital workers, Mary
L. Gray notes that her subjects understand their job as one that "takes
quite a bit of creativity, insight and judgment." [66]

Digital workers' activities can be categorized into those offered to
"macro-task" and "micro-task" platforms. The former involves "platforms
where workers offer their services as graphic designers, computer programmers, statisticians, translators, and other professional services." [67]
Meanwhile, micro-task activities typically involve clerical tasks that can
be completed quickly and often require less specialized skills. [68] These
activities range from "filling out surveys, captioning, transcribing and
translating work as well as anything one can think of as knowledge work,
such as content creation, writing editorial, doing design." [69]

In particular, the "artificial intelligence verification" and "artificial intelligence impersonation" aspects of tasks increasingly require
sophisticated and specialized knowledge and skillsets. [70] In an article
published in June 2023, the New York Magazine reports that "[l]ately,

---

64   Tubaro, et al *supra* note 23 at 5.
65   See Giuseppina D'Agostino, David, Vaver, Chris Hinds, & Marina Jirotka,
      "Ownership of Intellectual Property Rights in Medical Data in Collaborative
      Computing Environments" (2005) All Papers 103.
66   Hao, *supra* note 14. Gregory Hagen, Associate Professor at the University of
      Calgary Faculty of Law, notes that in such situations, "the human role is indis-
      pensable because humans can perceive and engage in perceptual judgments,
      whereas the network can't. Instead of the AI agent perceiving the input, a human
      does so, allowing the network to simulate the perception of other data. It is the
      human perception that is the source of the value of the AI agent simulation."
      Personal Note, October 21, 2023.
67   Berg et al, *supra* note 24 at 109.
68   *Ibid.*
69   Angela Chen, "How Silicon Valley's Successes are Fueled by an Underclass of
      'Ghost Workers': The Invisible Labor that Makes our Technology Run" (May 13,
      2019), *The Verge*, online: https://www.theverge.com/2019/5/13/18563284/mary-gray-
      ghost-work-microwork-labor-silicon-valley-automation-employment-interview.
70   See examples of tasks performed in these categories in Milagros Miceli and Julian
      Posada, "The Data-Production Dispositif" Proc. ACM Hum.-Comput. Interact. 6,
      CSCW2, Article 460 (November 2022) at 14.

the best-paying work [in AI] is in the U.S. In May, Scale [AI] started listing annotation jobs on its own website, soliciting people with experience in practically every field AI is predicted to conquer." [71]

From a copyright law perspective, the question that requires consideration is whether these categories of tasks, when performed by digital workers, meet the threshold of originality under Canadian Law as described in *CCH Canadian et al v Law Society of Upper Canada*: [72]

> an exercise of skill and judgment: "[...] By skill, I mean the use of one's knowledge, developed aptitude or practiced ability in producing the work. By judgment, I mean the use of one's capacity for discernment or ability to form an opinion or evaluation by comparing different possible options in producing the work. This exercise of skill and judgment will necessarily involve intellectual effort.

Whether the contribution of digital workers meets the threshold of originality may be necessary in addressing the inequity and invisibility such workers are subjected to in a working condition commonly described as "precarious." Based on the standard of originality developed in the *CCH Canadian* case, and as demonstrated in the previous section, copyright may subsist over the products of tasks that digital workers are assigned, as such tasks involve—at the very least—the curation, annotation, selection, and arrangement of data. [73]

The question that arises then is: what is the significance of recognizing copyright over the data works resulting from the tasks assigned to digital workers? Authorship in copyright does not always translate to ownership of the rights resulting from it. Ownership of the rights, whether arising from the statutory allocation of authorship (where the work meets the threshold of originality) or as stipulated in the contractual relationship between digital workers and intermediaries

---

71   The Magazine reports that "[t]here were listings for AI trainers with expertise in health coaching, human resources, finance, economics, data science, programming, computer science, chemistry, biology, accounting, taxes, nutrition, physics, travel, K-12 education, sports journalism, and self-help [...] There were also listings for people with security clearance, presumably to help train military AI." https://nymag.com/intelligencer/article/ai-artificial-intelligence-humans-technology-business-factory.html.

72   CCH Canadian et al v Law Society of Upper Canada, 2004 SCC 13.

73   See also how the standards of originality developed in the CCH Canadian case were applied in the context of copyright claims over databases. Toronto Real Estate Board v. Canada (Commissioner of Competition), 2017 FCA 236 (CanLII), [2018] 3 FCR 563.

(even when the threshold of originality is not met), determines the value attached to digital worker's contribution. In collaborative authorship of datasets for training in supervised learning, even though the resulting dataset and associated AI output may attract copyright, the allocation of ownership among the actors who interact with AI systems is determined through contractual agreement.[74] With a significant power imbalance in the exploitation of work at different stages of the AI pipeline, such allocation is bound to tilt the balance in favour of data intermediaries and AI designers.[75] This exacerbates a problem in copyright law that is already common in other realms of works covered under copyright, not just data works: the lopsided balance between authors and proprietors of copyright.

Contracting Authorship

Data workers usually sign contractual agreements that transfer ownership of the works to AI designers (referred to as "clients") through copyright transfers.[76] In most cases, these workers are not classified as employees.[77] Therefore, upon initial allocation, they might be considered the first copyright owners, potentially on a joint authorship basis.[78] When disputes arise over first copyright ownership, courts tend to favour the hiring party, citing the economic efficiency of awarding copyright to the better exploiter and traditional notions of sole

---

74   See scenarios where copyright may subsist over AI outputs in Jane C Ginsburg & Luke A. Budiardjo, "Authors and Machines" (2019) 34 Berkeley Tech. L. J. 343; Also see US Copyright Office (USCO) Guidance (2023); Daniel J Gervais, "The Human Cause" in *Research Handbooks on Intellectual Property and Artificial Intelligence* (Cheltenham: Edward Elgar Publishing, 2022).

75   See Kate Crawford, *The Atlas of AI: Power, Politics, and the Planetary Costs of Artificial Intelligence* (Yale University Press, 2021) at 63.

76   Such contracting around the statutory allocation of first copyright ownership is provided for under Art 13 (4) of the *Canadian Copyright Act*.

77   Most contracts that digital workers sign with data platforms explicitly provide that there are no employment relationships. See, for example Clickworker, one of the data platforms, provide that "As a Clickworker, You are performing Services as an individual independent contractor of the Company and not as an employee of the Company or of any Service Requester." S. 4.4, General Terms and Conditions (Clickworkers), online: https://workplace.clickworker.com/en/agreements/5908.

78   Joint authorship arises based on statutory allocation where certain requirements set by courts are met. Canada's *Copyright Act* defines joint work as "a work produced by the collaboration of two or more authors in which the contribution of one author is not distinct from that of the other author or authors." *Copyright Act*, R.S.C. 1952, c. C-42.

"authorship." [79]

The prevailing economic perspective within the Anglo-Canadian legal system becomes problematic when copyright and labour contract issues intersect, especially in AI development. Copyright law empowers AI designers to benefit exclusively from data works. The exploitation of copyright-protected works by employers is accepted in ordinary employment relationships in which corporations usually become the first copyright owners. [80] However, the "precarious" condition of digital workers' labour relations in a scattered global environment makes the situation a matter requiring special consideration, as this facilitates the exploitation of copyright's financial benefits in data works on terms that are more favourable to the hiring corporation than would be possible under an ordinary employment situation. [81]

In circumstances where digital workers' contribution attracts copyright, they are required to either grant the proprietors (such as data companies, AI intermediaries, AI designers, and AI developers) an exclusive license or assign the rights. [82] The proprietors' terms of service agreement, which workers must accept to begin working, often set the rules regarding ownership and control of data works involving stakeholder collaboration. These terms, set by the proprietors, form contractual agreements on copyright,

79   See generally, discussion of economic justification for the works-for-hire doctrine in the United States in I. Trotter Hardy, "An Economic Understanding of Copyright Law's Work-Made-for-Hire Doctrine" (1988). Faculty Publications. 1087. https://scholarship.law.wm.edu/facpubs/1087; for discussion of the conception of sole authorship, see Peter Jaszi, "Toward a Theory of Copyright: Metamorphosis of 'Authorship'" (1991) Duke L.J. 455, 488.

80   Corporate ownership of IP rights at the expense of individual creators, though barely justified under foundational principles of IP, is generally accepted as "it is important for the legal system to recognize that corporate IP owners mediate between the creative interests of the professional creators they employ and the business objectives of their managers." See Robert P Merges, *Justifying Intellectual Property* (Cambridge: Harvard University Press, 2011) at 22.

81   Precarious employment is a non-standard employment relationship that lacks protections found in the standard employment relationship and is, according to Rodgers, identified with four characteristics: uncertainty of continuing work, receiving little income, lack of control over work, and having few regulatory protections. See G Rodgers, (1989). "Precarious Work in Western Europe: The State of the Debate" in J Rodgers & G Rodgers, eds., *Precarious Jobs in Labour Market Regulation: The Growth of Atypical Employment in Western Europe* (Geneva: International Institute for Labour Studies, 1989).

82   Sangeet Paul Choudary, "The Architecture of Digital Labour Platforms: Policy Recommendations on Platform Design for Worker Well-Being," (2018) ILO Future of Work Working Paper Series, online: https://socialprotection-human-rights.org/wp-content/uploads/2018/07/wcms_630603.pdf

according to which the economic benefits of data works are exploited. [83]

It is widely recognized that copyright structured as an exclusive property right gives authors something to sell to a third party for exploitation, typically assigning or licensing the copyright to a publisher or producer. [84] Despite making the rights fully assignable to a "proprietor" (printers, publishers, or producers), the 1710 *Statute of Anne* marked a threshold by recognizing these author's rights for the first time and reducing the powers enjoyed by proprietors. [85] However, as Patterson and Birch argue, a never-ending campaign of "strategic copyright litigation" in courts across the Anglosphere (most recently in the United States) has returned to copyright proprietors' powers last enjoyed before the *Statute of Anne* in 1710. [86] As D'Agostino also argues, nineteenth-century United Kingdom case law favoured authors. [87] Yet the introduction of new media and the prevalence of complete freedom of contract at present have restricted such pro-author rules. [88] This has allowed the proprietors to "usurp equity from creators [and] use private law to control access." [89]

For example, Clickworker—an intermediary platform—requires, in a typical term of service agreement, that digital workers agree to vest all ownership rights in "the applicable Service Requester immediately upon your submission of such Work Product to the Company." [90]

83   ILO, "Policy Responses to New Forms of Work: International Governance of Digital Labour Platforms" (Paper prepared for the 2nd Meeting of the G20 Employment Working Group under Japan's Presidency 2019, 22–24 April, Tokyo) at 2.

84   See Martin Kretschmer, "Copyright and Contract Law: Regulating Creator Contracts: The State of the Art and a Research Agenda" (2010) 18:1 J Intell Prop L 141.

85   Nevertheless, the passage of the *Statute of Anne* in 1710 is seen by some as furthering the interest of publishers in making the rights fully assignable to a "proprietor." See, e.g., Mark Rose, *Authors and Owners: The Invention of Copyright* (Cambridge: Harvard University Press, 1993).

86   See L Ray Patterson & S. F. Birch, Jr., "A Unified Theory of Copyright" (2009) 46 Houston Law Review 215 at 224.

87   See generally. Giuseppina D'Agostino, *Copyright, Contracts, Creators: New Media, New Rules* (Cheltenham: Edward Elgar, 2010).

88   *Ibid.*

89   Harry Hillman Chartrand, "The 2010 *Copyright Modernization Act* & the *Licensing Act* of 1662" Canadian Copyright Reform Policy Research Note #3 (Compiler Press, August 31, 2010).

90   See Section 4.5, which provides, "You hereby agree that all right, title and interest and ownership rights, including, without limitation, worldwide intellectual property rights in the related Work Product, will vest in the applicable Service Requester immediately upon your submission of such Work Product to the Company...You hereby grant the Company and its affiliates a nonexclusive, royalty-free, perpetual, transferrable, irrevocable and fully sublicensable right to use, reproduce, modify,

It also provides that digital workers agree to "forever waive" their moral rights, and those who might be determined to retain any moral rights agree not to "require that any personally identifying information be used in connection with the Work Product."[91] Additionally, in the United States context, where most AI companies are located, the work-for-hire doctrine that is incorporated in the contract of digital workers creates a legal fiction of authorship on behalf of AI designers and data intermediaries, despite the factual authorship of some works by digital workers.

Considering these scenarios, the need for a shift toward authors' rights in jurisprudence governing copyright-protected works created through contractual labour relations is apparent. Such a need, though especially relevant in the unique context of the scattered AI pipeline, is something that has become apparent in other contexts of contributions to collective works in general.[92] Although copyright law often favours AI designers with significant resources and market influence, acknowledging the collaborative nature of creativity within the AI pipeline brings the need to address copyright's long-standing problem in recognizing contributors to collective authorship, as the following examples demonstrate.

---

adapt, translate, distribute, publish, create derivative works from and publicly display and perform such Work Product throughout the world in any media, now or hereafter devised." General Terms and Conditions (Clickworkers) (Effective Date August 26, 2011), online: https://workplace.clickworker.com/en/agreements/5908

91   See *ibid.* "If it is determined that You retain any moral rights (including rights of attribution or integrity) in any Work Product, You hereby declare that (a) You do not require that any personally identifying information be used in connection with the Work Product, or any derivative works thereof, (b) You have no objection to the publication, use, modification, deletion and exploitation of the Work Product by the Service Requester for whom such Work Product was produced or by the Company or its licensees, successors and assigns, (c) You forever waive and agree not to claim or assert any entitlement to any and all moral rights of an author in any of the Work Product, and (d) You forever release the Service Requester for whom such Work Product was produced and the Company, its licensees, successors and assigns, from any and all claims that You could otherwise assert against such parties by virtue of any such moral rights."

92   "The AI pipeline" refers to the different stages in the development of AI, from the input stage to the end use, in which data is processed in different ways in order to create the desired output. See discussion in section 3 below.

Performing Artists, Screenwriters, and Contributions in Copyright

The situation that digital workers find themselves in resembles that of screenwriters and musical performers, not only in terms of work conditions but also in the lack of recognition for their contributions to "works" that end up generating income for proprietors. Indeed, the term "gig," as in the "gig economy" that characterizes digital work in modern times, comes out of contexts of musical performance as a slang term for a short engagement.[93] Like today's AI platforms, data brokers, and data intermediaries with respect to digital workers in remote developing countries, recording industry firms have historically exploited rural artists and have used exploitative tactics with multiple generations of African American artists.[94]

A similar situation also arises regarding writers' status grievances in the conflict between writers and directors over film authorship. Often, writers, like digital workers, sign away the copyrights in their work and their legal rights as authors as a condition of hire.[95] Despite the lack of a legal enforcement system for the royalty terms in collectively or individually bargained agreements, where such agreements for royalty exist, "private intellectual property rights" and other forms of "soft" law that shape behaviour have emerged through a "credit system" that operates irrespective of authorship entitlement.[96] "Credit determinations" by the Writers' Guild of America (WGA) dictate whether and what writers get paid, whether they will be hired in the future, and future uses and interpretations that could be made of a work to which writers contributed, even when authorship of such works resides with directors.[97] The "fair and accurate determination" of credits ensures the allocation of the stream of revenues associated with copyright ownership through forms of compensation called separated rights, residuals, and bonuses.[98]

---

93   See James Bau Graves, "The Original Gig Economy, Many Futures of Work: Possibilities and Perils 2018 Conference" cited in Matt Stahl & Olufunmilayo B Arewa, "Accounting for Injustice: AFTRA, Work & Singers' Royalties" in Seán O'Connor, ed, *The Oxford Handbook of Music Law and Policy* (New York: Oxford University Press, 2021) at 4.

94   *Ibid.*

95   Catherine L Fisk, *Writing for Hire: Unions, Hollywood, and Madison Avenue* (Cambridge: Harvard University Press, 2016).

96   Catherine L Fisk, "The Role of Private Intellectual Property Rights in Markets for Labor and Ideas: Screen Credit and the Writers Guild of America, 1938-2000" (2011) 32 Berkeley J Emp & Lab L at 2.

97   *Ibid.*

98   *Ibid.* at 29.

"Separated rights" are rights the WGA negotiated for to be separated out and held by writers as a "bundle of rights encompassed in a copyright."[99] These rights may not be negotiated in a writer's individual contract and allow the writer of an "original story (or an original story and screenplay)" to retain some rights to exploit the story elements other than through the film or TV show.[100] Residuals are payments made to a credited writer's work for the reuse of the work and not for the original use.[101] And thirdly, a credit bonus system exists in which a writer receives a bonus if the writer is determined to get screen credit, in essence, if the script is not substantially rewritten during the production process.[102]

The case of digital workers manifests similar structural asymmetries of power that characterize musical performers and screenwriters' situations. The credit system that recognizes the contribution of writers has been developed to account for deficiencies in the copyright system in allocating ownership to proprietors, instead of those involved in the creativity of works. Similarly, the American Federation of Television and Radio Artists ("AFTRA") Health and Retirement Funds ("AFTRA H&R Funds") exists to monitor and enforce contractually mandated earnings through an accounting system.[103] The systems rely on the strength of the organized labour unions of the writers and performing artists as bargaining units. However, digital workers face unique challenges that do not bring success in securing collective representation in the form of collective bargaining.[104] It has been suggested that the *Status of the Artist Act* (SOA) in Canada can serve as a model for digital workers' access to collective bargaining on a sectoral basis that is better adapted to the needs of these workers.[105]

Addressing the situation of digital workers, therefore, might involve reforms in other areas of law. From a copyright perspective, the circumstance underscores the trend of categorical expansion of proprietors' rights in private ordering mechanisms, with relatively little corresponding

---

99   Writers Guild of America West, "Understanding Separated Rights" (2000), online: https://www.wga.org/contracts/know-your-rights/understanding-separated-rights

100   Fisk, *supra* note 96 at 37.

101   Writer's Guild of America West, "Residuals Survival Guide" (2022), online: https://www.wga.org/members/finances/residuals/residuals-survival-guide#:~:text=Residuals%20are%20compensation%20paid%20for,and%20not%20the%20original%20use.

102   Fisk, *supra* note 96.

103   Stahl and Arewa, *supra n* 1910.

104   See Sara J Slinn, "Exploring Sectoral Solutions for Digital Workers: The Status of the Artist Act Approach" (2021) 65:1 St Louis U L J 2816.

105   *Supra* note 93.

effort that ensures actual benefits flow to authors.[106] As a result of the successful lobbying of rightsholders, the modern copyright regime is geared more toward protecting the corporations involved in producing and distributing creative works than it is toward rewarding and incentivizing authors.[107] This has contributed to the perception among scholars that copyright law appears to be suffering from a crisis of legitimacy.[108] Responding to the crisis of copyright legitimacy in the context of valuing and recognizing the contribution of digital workers in the age of AI requires addressing several questions concerning the future of copyright law. In the concluding section, I explore questions about the subsistence of copyright and authorship in the context of data works.

Questions in the Future of Canadian Copyright Law

The discussion in this chapter addressed an emerging landscape in AI development that concerns the role of digital workers in contributing to training datasets that are essential for the training, testing, benchmarking, and deployment of foundational AI systems in AI development. In supervised learning, an area of AI development that has a specific task of solving a particular problem (also referred to as narrow AI), such as in healthcare, agriculture, education, banking, etc., digital workers play a crucial role in collaborating with AI designers/developers to create data works. These data works can exist either in the form of training

---

106 See Robert Shepard, "Copyright's Vicious Triangle: Returning Author Protections to Their Rational Roots" (2014) 47 Loy L A L Rev 731; B. Khan, "An Economic History of Copyright in Europe and the United States" in Robert Whaples, ed, EH.Net Encyclopedia (March 16, 2008), online: http://eh.net/encyclopedia/an-economic-history-of-copyright-in-europe-and-the-united-states/.

107 It is a general trend across all industries of copyright works that creators who are dependent on intermediaries to fund/disseminate their work, often make little money from their creations, and any control that they might exercise over them is likely to be short-lived. It has been noted by scholars that despite the enormous value that copyright industries add to the economy, most creators cannot earn a living from their creative work. See J Litman, "Real Copyright Reform" (2010) 96:1 Iowa LRev 1; J Ginsburg, "How Copyright Got a Bad Name For Itself" (2002) 26:1 Columbia J of L and the Arts 61; R Giblin and K Weatherall, "A Collection of Impossible Ideas" in R Giblin and K Weatherall, eds, "What if We Could Reimagine Copyright?" (Canberra: ANU Press, 2017) at 316.

108 See Daniela Simone, *Copyright and Collective Authorship: Locating the Authors of Collaborative Work* (Cambridge: University Printing House, 2019) at 3, citing S Dusollier, "Open Source and Copyleft: Authorship Reconsidered?" (2003) 26 Columbia J of L and Arts 281: "The Institution of Copyright is in Ill Repute These Days."; N Elkin-Koren, "Tailoring Copyright to Social Production" (2011) 12:1 Theoretical Inquiries in L 309 at 310.

dataset development or, in cases where significant human involvement is found, they may exist in AI-assisted outputs as well.[109]

Currently, the apportionment of copyright ownership between AI designers and digital workers is conducted via a private ordering mechanism of contracts. In recognition of the inherent power imbalances in such contractual agreements, there have been calls for changes in the protection of labour standards for works in the digital sphere.[110] Similarly, in the past, the interface between copyright law and technology has filtered through into active changes to substantive law at both national and international levels.[111] It is likely that copyright law is called upon to increase legal certainty by resolving the many intricate interfaces with AI.[112]

As countries grapple with AI governance mechanisms under the guidance of fundamental principles, Canadian Copyright is likely to be confronted with a significant issue of primary importance to achieving AI fairness in which copyright is implicated:[113] ensuring economic fairness in the exploitation of works of authorship in the AI pipeline. As discussed above, there are scenarios in which copyright might exist in applying established approaches to determining originality in the context of training datasets and AI outputs, where the "human cause" is found. Ownership rights are allocated to governance under lopsided private ordering mechanisms in such cases.

Assessing AI fairness through the lens of economic exploitation suggests that extracting and using data works and AI-assisted outputs under default copyright and contract rules might be inherently unfair. Taking AI fairness as a policy goal in AI governance would mean that legislative, regulatory, and interpretive guidelines that favour authors

---

109   See Gervais, *supra* note 74; also, Ginsburg & Budiardjo, *supra* note 74.

110   See Tammy Katsabian, "The Rule of Technology: How Technology Is Used to Disturb Basic Labor Law Protections" (2021) 25 Lewis & Clark Law Review 895.

111   See Ben Depoorter, "Technology and Uncertainty: The Shaping Effect on Copyright Law" (2008) 157 University of Pennsylvania Law Review 1831; Graeme B Dinwoodie, "New Copyright Order: Why National Courts Should Create Global Norms" (2000) 149 University of Pennsylvania Law Review 469.

112   See such interfaces between copyright and AI in Ryan Abbott (ed), *Research Handbook on Intellectual Property and Artificial Intelligence* (Cheltenham: Edward Elgar Publishing, 2022).

113   The principle of AI fairness is often understood in the context of preventing discrimination and mitigating bias in AI systems. In its broader understanding, it also refers to fairness in economic equity and exploitation through AI systems. See Weinberg, Lindsay. "Rethinking Fairness: An Interdisciplinary Survey of Critiques of Hegemonic ML Fairness Approaches." (2022) 74 Journal of Artificial Intelligence Research 75–109.

should be developed in contracting and exploiting data works and, in some cases, AI-assisted outputs by rightsholders.

The inequality in the exploitation of data works in AI bears upon copyright the challenge of restructuring the relationship between authors and proprietors of works. There are long-standing doctrinal options that may hold the solution. The doctrinal option arises from the trend mentioned above that shifted the focus of copyrights from authors to proprietors. In this respect, rebalancing the focus of copyright might involve recognizing the contribution of digital authors in the collaborative (collective) authorship of data works. Mary Gray, an anthropologist who wrote a book titled *Ghost Work*, a term she coined for the invisible labour that powers AI technology platforms, notes the long-felt need to value everybody's contribution in the AI pipeline:[114]

> The first step [in addressing the problem of "ghost work"] is being able to identify the people who have contributed. In Bangladesh, it made a huge difference in textiles when companies selling products had to tell us who was involved in making the shirt on my back. There should be a clear record [of] thanking anybody who contributes labour to an output or service. The consumer should always be able to trace back the supply chain of people who have had a hand in helping them achieve their goals.

Canadian copyright law recognizes the contribution of individuals in collaborative authorship under the doctrine of joint authorship.[115] One approach to recognizing digital workers in circumstances where proprietors exploit economic interests, in a way responding to the "legitimacy crisis" in the allocation of rights, according to Jane Ginsburg, who argued for "[restoring] a proper perspective," is by "refocusing on authors [and] the task of creating."[116] Recognizing the centrality of digital workers to the work of authorship (data work) entails, at least, recognizing "the moral claims" of authors that "neither corporate intermediaries nor consumer end-users can (straightfacedly) assert" as

---

114   Chen, *supra* note 69.
115   Canadian copyright law defines joint work as "[a] work produced by the collaboration of two or more authors in which the contribution of one author is not distinct from that of the other author or authors." *Copyright Act*, R.S.C. 1952, c. C-42.
116   Jane Ginsburg, "The Concept of Authorship in Comparative Copyright Law" (2003) 52 De Paul L Rev 1063 at 1083.

these claims arise out of the "act of creating a work."[117]

The key to whether digital workers could be treated as joint authors in collaborative authorship of data works is, in copyright's traditional criteria of joint authorship, whether the very "acts of creating a work" demonstrate creative contributions from them that are inseparable in the data work.[118] Though outside the scope of the chapter, in some cases, when originality subsists in the preparation of AI training datasets and AI-assisted outputs, creative contributions could be established.[119]

As to AI-assisted outputs, it has been demonstrated in the scholarship as well as in the US court that AI outputs autonomously generated by an AI machine are not copyright protected.[120] However, it is unclear whether copyright does not subsist in all circumstances where AI is used as a mere instrument of human ingenuity. In such cases, whether copyright exists in the AI outputs would be based on the "human cause" in the training datasets as inputs.[121] This is the case in situations where the AI input has undergone specific human-based processes that dictate the form of the output. In their co-authored article, Professor Ginsburg and Budiardjo distinguish between fully generative AI and partially generative AIs in which a human interacts with the AI to assess whether copyright subsists in the output.[122] In such cases, it is argued that the question is not whether copyright exists but how to allocate authorship among the human creators who interact with AI machines.[123] Similarly, the US Copyright Office issued a Guidance in which it said whether "work containing AI-generated material will also contain sufficient

---

117   *Ibid.* at 1068 "Moral claims" in this context does not refer to moral rights in the sense they are understood in Copyright law, but authorial rights that are necessitated by moral exigencies.

118   See the discussion regarding the contributions of digital workers in section 4.2 above.

119   See discussion in Section 4.1 above.

120   See Stephen Thaler v. Shira Perlmutter and The United States Copyright Office (1:22-cv-01564) (June 2, 2022) (ruling that AI cannot be an author of a copyright under the U.S. *Copyright Act*, because "United States copyright law protects only works of human creation."); also see Carys Craig & Ian Kerr, "The Death of the AI Author" (2021) 52:1 Ottawa L Rev 31; James Grimmelmann, "There's No Such Thing as a Computer-Authored Work—And It's a Good Thing, Too" (2016) 39:3 Colum J L & Arts 403; Daniel J Gervais, "The Machine as Author" (2020) 105:5 Iowa L Rev 2053.

121   See when a "human cause" may result in the subsistence of copyright in AI outputs in Daniel J Gervais, "The Human Cause" in *supra* note 74.

122   See Ginsburg & Budiardjo, *supra* note 74 at 404–426.

123   *Ibid.*

human authorship to support a copyright claim" is determined based on a "case-by-case inquiry." [124]

It is more challenging to the future of copyright law, however, whether it recognizes the contribution of digital workers when these contributions do not attract copyright in themselves but are incorporated in a data work on which copyright subsists and is under the owner- ship of an AI designer. In this respect, copyright's complicity with the systematic invisibility of digital workers and the devaluing of their contribution is encapsulated in Woodmansee's writing in 1997 about the conceptions of authorship that legal institutions bring to bear in decid- ing copyright-related disputes, in which she concluded: "As creative production becomes more corporate, collective and collaborative, the law invokes the Romantic author all the more insistently." [125] In an area where the act of creating is inherently collaborative, such as in the case of data works, copyright law is said to be caught into two conflicting ideologies: "one the false vision of a solitary Romantic author, the other an instinctively familiar but unnamed collaborator." [126]

One way of recognizing these unnamed collaborators, such as digital workers, could be by recognizing their contributions to the data work in cases where these contributions are not expressive but incorporated in an expressive and, hence, copyright-protected data work. Aspects of training datasets, whether in themselves or as pos- sibly manifested in AI-assisted outputs, could be considered complex, detailed, and developed ideas, which in some cases could be copyright protected. [127] When contributing to data work and AI-assisted outputs that result from a collaborative effort by AI designers and digital work- ers, would these ideas entitle digital workers to be, at least, joint authors? David Vaver supports recognizing complex and specific ideas in the collaborative authorship context, saying that ignoring the contributor

---

124   U.S. Copyright Office, Library of Congress, *Copyright Registration Guidance: Works Containing Material Generated by Artificial Intelligence* (03/16/2023) 37 CFR 202 88 FR 16190.

125   Martha Woodmansee, "On the 'Author Effect': Recovering Collectivity," in Woodmansee and Jaszi, eds, *The Construction of Authorship: Textual Appropriation in Law and Literature* (Durham and London: Duke UP, 1994) at 28.

126   Shaheed Fatima, "A Legal Philosophy for Technological Informatics?" (15th BILETA Conference: "Electronic Datasets and Access to Legal Information") 14th April 2000, online: https://www.bileta.org.uk/wp-content/uploads/A-Legal-Philosophy- for-Technological-Informatics.pdf.

127   According to Canada's Supreme Court decision in *Cinar Corporation v. Robinson*, ideas expressed in detail could themselves be considered expressions. See *Cinar Corporation v. Robinson*, 2013 SCC 73, [2013] 3 S.C.R. 1168.

of the idea may prevent future collaborations.[128]

Copyright law faces multifaceted challenges in an era of AI. Many of these challenges are recognized in the scholarly literature, some dealing with whether and when copyright subsists in AI outputs and others with whether the use of copyright-protected materials to train AIs infringes copyright. However, there is not much consideration of the implications of collaborative authorship of data works, either copyright-protected in themselves, or possibly resulting in copyright-protected AI-assisted outputs. Distributional injustices to digital workers occur under the complicity of the current copyright law, which is recognized as ill-equipped to meet the challenges of determining the authorship of highly collaborative works. Whether and how copyright law embraces forms of creativity that flourish in the AI pipeline has implications for addressing distributional fairness questions that AI technology brings.[129]

---

128   See David Vaver, *Intellectual Property Law: Copyright, Patent, Trade-Marks* (2d ed., Toronto: Irwin Law, 2011) at 121 ("This collaboration [between A and B] has sometimes not counted as joint authorship unless A's ideas were independently copyrightable—a result that promotes certainty but seems harsh. There would have been no play at all without A's input. To elevate B's contribution and entirely discount A's may discourage some fruitful collaborations...Any substantial intellectual contribution to a work's composition pursuant to a common design... should, in principle, count as joint authorship.")

129   The author extends sincere thanks to participants who provided feedback on an earlier presentation of this paper at the Future of IP conference at the University of British Columbia in June 2023. Special thanks to Gregory R. Hagen, Margaret Chon, and an anonymous referee for helpful comments.

Author Biographies

Bassem Awad

Bassem Awad is an Assistant Professor and Director of the Area of Concentration in Intellectual Property, Information and Technology law in the Faculty of Law at the University of Western Ontario. He is also a Professor at the Academy of the World Intellectual Property Organization (WIPO) in Geneva. Prior to joining Western Law, Bassem was the Deputy Director for Intellectual Property Law and Innovation at the Centre for International Governance Innovation in Canada.

Sara Bannerman

Sara Bannerman, Canada Research Chair in Communication Policy and Governance and Professor of Communication Studies at McMaster University, is the author of *International Copyright and Access to Knowledge* (2016) and *The Struggle for Canadian Copyright: Imperialism to Internationalism, 1842-1971* (2013). She has published various articles and book chapters on international copyright and copyright history.

Mauro Barelli

Mauro Barelli is Professor of International Law at City St George's, University of London. His research looks at the rights of ethno-cultural groups, especially Indigenous Peoples, the law on the use of force and Chinese perspectives on international law. He has also written about the intersection of Indigenous Peoples' rights and intellectual property rights.

Enrico Bonadio

Enrico Bonadio is Professor of Intellectual Property Law at City St George's University of London. His research agenda is wide ranging, having recently focused on international trade aspects of IP and the intersection between IP and new technologies, including artificial intelligence. He is the author of numerous publications on several aspects of IP law, including books, academic articles, book chapters, and journalistic pieces.

Andrea Cabello

Andrea Cabello is an Associate professor at the Department of Economics at the University of Brasilia and has published more than 50 papers, on various topics such as education, innovation, digital transformation, industrial and sectoral policies, energy transition, and the history of economic thought, among others. She has been involved in several projects sponsored by international organizations such as UNDP and OAS. She was a visiting professor at the University of Antwerp, the University of Cantabria, and the Prague Economic School.

Teshager W. Dagne

Professor Dagne is an associate professor at York University and holds the Ontario Research Chair position. He teaches at the School of Public Policy and Administration and Osgoode Hall Law School. With expertise in innovation and knowledge governance, Professor Dagne's current research examines the instrumentality of intellectual property, privacy, and data governance rules and norms in influencing societal outcomes.

Naama Daniel

Naama Daniel is a Research Fellow at the Federmann Cyber Security Research Center – Cyber Law Program, Hebrew University of Jerusalem. She is also the Deputy Legal Adviser to the Economic Affairs Committee at the Israeli Parliament (on sabbatical). Prior to her work in the Israeli Parliament, she served as a legal adviser at the Intellectual Property Law Department, Office of Legal Counsel and Legislative Affairs, Israeli Ministry of Justice.

Cheryl Dine

Cheryl Dine is a PhD candidate at City St George's University of London. She undertakes research on trade and trade-related issues, particularly on intellectual (IP) law. Her recent interests in the field of IP law include the nuances of national security issues, access and benefit sharing of genetic resources, and the impact of AI on IP protection and regulation.

Mistrale Goudreau

Mistrale Goudreau is a full professor at the Civil Law Section of the University of Ottawa. She has also been a visiting professor and lecturer in many other universities, as well as a visiting researcher at the Max-Planck-Institut Für Ausländisches Und Internationales Patent-, Urheber- Und Wettbewerbsrecht (Munich, Germany) and consultant for the Government of Canada.

Gregory R. Hagen

Gregory R. Hagen is an Associate Professor of Law at the University of Calgary. His research interests lie primarily in technology law, intellectual property law, and legal theory. He earned an LL.B. at Dalhousie University and an LL.M. at the University of Ottawa. Prior to pursuing law, he completed a PhD in the Philosophy of Science at Western University.

Johnny Mack

Johnny Mack (Haynahmeek, Toquaht Nation) is an Associate Professor at the Allard School of Law and Co-Director of Indigenous Legal Studies. A Trudeau Scholar and Killam Teaching Prize recipient, his research explores Indigenous legal traditions, constitutionalism, and settler relations. He resides on the unceded lands of the Musqueam people.

Lisa Macklem

Lisa Macklem is a legal scholar specializing in copyright, entertainment, and media law. Access to information and human rights, especially in the digital environment, are central to her research interests. AI and its intersections with the creative industries has been a recent focus. She was cited by the Supreme Court of Canada in *York University v. Canadian Copyright Licensing Agency.*

Faith O. Majekolagbe

Faith O. Majekolagbe is an Assistant Professor at the Faculty of Law, University of Alberta, and a Faculty Associate at Harvard University's Berkman Klein Center for Internet and Society. Her primary specialization is international intellectual property (IP) law. Her research delves into the role of IP frameworks and institutions in knowledge governance, innovation policy, and development.

Alexandra Mogyoros

Alexandra Mogyoros, JD, BCL (Oxon), DPhil (Oxon) is an Assistant Professor at the Lincoln Alexander School of Law, at Toronto Metropolitan University. She is a trademark law scholar with a speciality in certification marks and sustainability logos. Her current research explores issues arising at the intersection of brands, trust, intellectual property, and expression.

Richard Overstall

Richard Overstall is a former mining geologist who drifted into research for public-interest and Indigenous groups, including coordinating expert opinion evidence for the Gitxsan and Wet'suwet'en plaintiffs in the *Delgamuukw* aboriginal title trial. He is now a semi-retired lawyer who has also published and presented on Indigenous law and history, global warming, criminal evidence, human rights, and monitoring trusts.

Anmol Patel

Anmol Patel is a PhD candidate at the University of Ottawa and a Research Assistant with OpenAIR and ABS-Canada. He holds an LLM from the University of Toronto and a BBA-LLB from India. He previously served as Assistant Professor and Assistant Dean at IFIM Law School, India, as Research Fellow at Unitedworld School of Law, India, and worked with LSAC-USA.

Andelka M. Phillips

Andelka M. Phillips is an Associate Professor in the School of Law at the University of Leicester in the UK. She is also an Academic Affiliate at HeLEX Centre, University of Oxford and an Affiliate at the Bioethics Institute Ghent, Ghent University. She is the author of *Buying Your Self on the Internet: Wrap Contracts and Personal Genomics* and is an Associate Editor for the Journal of the Royal Society of New Zealand.

Luciano Póvoa

Luciano Póvoa is a Legislative Advisor for microeconomic policy at the Brazilian Federal Senate. He has worked on the legislative process of several laws, including the legal framework for Science, Technology, and Innovation. Before joining the Senate, he was a faculty member in the economics departments at two Brazilian Federal Universities. His current research focuses on innovation for the public purpose.

Cody Rei-Anderson

Cody Rei-Anderson is Lecturer in Law and Technology at Edinburgh Napier University. He received his JD and LLM from the University of British Columbia, and his PhD from Victoria University of Wellington. His research interests include copyright law, digital media, and technology as a mode of regulation or governance.

Graham J. Reynolds

Graham J. Reynolds is an Associate Professor at the Peter A. Allard School of Law, University of British Columbia, where his work focuses on the relationship between intellectual property and human rights. Graham received his BCL, MPhil, and DPhil degrees from the University of Oxford, where he studied as a Rhodes Scholar and a Trudeau Scholar. The recipient of several teaching prizes, Graham has held visiting positions at the National University of Singapore and the University of Bern, Switzerland.

Anthony D. Rosborough

Anthony D. Rosborough is an Assistant Professor of Law & Computer Science at Dalhousie University. Anthony's research explores intersections between intellectual property, embedded computer systems, market competition, and personal property rights. The Right to Repair is a core focus of Anthony's scholarly and policy advocacy work. Anthony is the President and Co-founder of the Canadian Repair Coalition.

Myra Tawfik

Myra Tawfik is Distinguished University Professor Emerita, Faculty of Law, University of Windsor. She held the inaugural Don Rodzik Family Chair in Law and Entrepreneurship at the Faculty. Her research interests lie in intellectual property law, especially copyright law and copyright history. Her publications include the recent monograph *For the Encouragement of Learning: The Origins of Canadian Copyright Law* (2023).

David J. Watson

David J. Watson is a candidate for the PhD in Law at the Peter A. Allard School of Law, at the University of British Columbia. He specializes in the fields of international trade and intellectual property law and his research focuses on the protection of geographical indications in trade agreements.

Peter K. Yu

Peter K. Yu is University Distinguished Professor, Regents Professor of Law and Communication, and Director of the Center for Law and Intellectual Property at Texas A&M University. He is Vice-President of the American Branch of the International Law Association and has served as the general editor of *The WIPO Journal* published by the World Intellectual Property Organization.

Law, Technology, and Media

Series editor: Michael Geist

The *Law, Technology, and Media* series explores emerging technology law issues with an emphasis on a Canadian perspective. It is the first University of Ottawa Press series to be fully published under an open access licence.

Previous titles in the *Law, Technology, and Media* Series

Yan Campagnolo, ed, *Artificial Intelligence's Impact on Legal: Challenges and Opportunities for the Ottawa Law Review*, 2025.

Pamela Robinson and Teresa Scassa, eds, *The Future of Open Data*, 2022.

Elizabeth Dubois and Florian Martin-Bariteau, eds., *Citizenship in a Connected Canada: A Research and Policy Agenda*, 2020.

Alana Maurushat, *Ethical Hacking*, 2019.

Derek McKee, Finn Makela, & Teresa Scassa, eds, *Law and the "Sharing Economy": Regulating Online Market Platforms*, 2018.

Karim Benyekhlef, Jane Bailey, Jacquelyn Burkell, and Fabie Gélinas, eds, *eAccess to Justice*, 2016.

Michael Geist, *Law, Privacy and Surveillance in Canada in the Post-Snowden Era*, 2015.

Jane Bailey and Valerie Steeves, *eGirls, eCitizens*, 2015.

Lucie Thibault and Jean Harvey, *Sport Policy in Canada*, 2013.

For a complete list of the University of Ottawa Press titles, please visit:

www.Press.uOttawa.ca

www.ingramcontent.com/pod-product-compliance
Lightning Source LLC
Chambersburg PA
CBHW070931050326
40689CB00014B/3153